The Rome Statute as Evidence of Customary International Law

International Criminal Law Series

Founding Editor
M. Cherif Bassiouni

Editor-in-Chief
William Schabas, Professor of International Law, Department of Law, Middlesex University;
Professor of International Criminal Law and Human Rights, Leiden University; Honorary Chairman,
Irish Centre for Human Rights, National University of Ireland, Galway; Canada/Ireland

Editorial Board

Kai Ambos, Judge at the Kosovo Specialist Chambers (KSC), The Hague; Professor of Law and Head, Department for Foreign and International Criminal Law, Georg August Universität; Gottingen, Germany

Mahnoush Arsanjani, Member, Institut de Droit International; former Director, Codification Division, United Nations Office of Legal Affairs, Iran

M. Cherif Bassiouni, Distinguished Research Professor of Law Emeritus, President Emeritus, International Human Rights Law Institute, DePaul University College of Law; Honorary President, International Institute of Higher Studies in Criminal Sciences; Honorary President, Association Internationale de Droit Pénal; Chicago, USA/Egypt

Mohamed Chande Othman, Chief Justice, Court of Appeal of Tanzania; Dodoma, Tanzania

Eric David, Professor of Law, Free University of Brussels, Faculty of Law, Brussels, Belgium

Mireille Delmas-Marty, Professor of Comparative Legal Studies and Internationalisation of Law, Collège de France; former Professor of Criminal Law, University of Paris; Paris, France

Adama Dieng, UN Secretary-General's Special Adviser on the Prevention of Genocide; former Registrar, International Criminal Tribunal for Rwanda; former Secretary General, International Commission of Jurists, Senegal

Mark Drumbl, Class of 1975 Alumni Professor of Law, Director, Transnational Law Institute, Washington and Lee University School of Law, USA

Chile Eboe-Osuji, Judge, Trial Division, International Criminal Court; former Legal Adviser to the High Commissioner for Human Rights, Office of the High Commissioner for Human Rights, Nigeria

Geoff Gilbert, Professor of Law and Head of the School of Law, University of Essex, Colchester UK

Philippe Kirsch, Ad hoc Judge, International Court of Justice; former President, International Criminal Court; Ambassador (Ret.) and former Legal Advisor, Ministry of Foreign Affairs of Canada; Sallèles d'Aude, Belgium/Canada

André Klip, Professor of Law, Department of Criminal Law and Criminology, Faculty of Law, Maastricht University; Maastricht, The Netherlands

Errki Kourula, Former Judge and President of the Appeals Division, International Criminal Court; The Hague, Finland

Motoo Noguchi, Chair of the Board of Directors, ICC Trust Fund for Victims; Ambassador for International Judicial Cooperation, MOFA; Former UN International Judge, ECCC, Japan

Diane Orentlicher, Professor of International Law, Co-Director, Center for Human Rights and Humanitarian Law, Washington College of Law, American University; Washington, USA

Fausto Pocar, Judge and former President, International Criminal Tribunal for the Former Yugoslavia; President, International Institute of Humanitarian Law; Professor of International Law Emeritus, University of Milan; Italy

Leila Nadya Sadat, Henry H. Oberschelp Professor of Law, Director, Whitney R. Harris World Law Institute, Washington University School of Law; Alexis de Tocqueville Distinguished Fulbright Chair, University of Cergy-Pontoise; St. Louis, France/USA

Michael Scharf, Dean and John Deaver Drinko-Baker & Hostetlier Professor of Law, Director, Frederick K. Cox International Law Center, Case Western Reserve University School of Law; Cleveland, USA

Ulrich Sieber, Professor of Criminal Law, Director, Max Plank Institute for Foreign and International Criminal Law, University of Freiburg; Freiburg, Germany

Goran Sluiter, Professor of Law, Department of Criminal Law and Criminal Procedure, Faculty of Law, University of Amsterdam; Amsterdam, The Netherlands

Françoise Tulkens, Former Vice-President, European Court of Human Rights; Strasbourg, France

Xuimei Wang, Professor of International Criminal Law, College for Criminal Law Science, Beijing Normal University; Executive Director, ICC Project Office; Beijing, China

Christine van den Wyngaert, Judge, International Criminal Court; former Judge, International Criminal Tribunal for the Former Yugoslavia; former Ad hoc Judge, International Court of Justice, Belgium

Gert Vermeulen, Professor of Criminal Law, Director, Research Group Drug Policy, Criminal Policy and International Crime, Ghent University; Extraordinary Professor of Evidence Law, Maastricht University; Ghent, Belgium

Giuliana Ziccardi Capaldo, Professor of International Law, Faculty of Law, University of Salerno; Salerno, Italy

VOLUME 16

The titles published in this series are listed at *brill.com/icls*

The Rome Statute as Evidence of Customary International Law

By

Yudan Tan

BRILL
NIJHOFF

LEIDEN | BOSTON

Library of Congress Cataloging-in-Publication Data

Names: Tan, Yudan, 1988-author.
Title: The Rome statute as evidence of customary international law /
   by Yudan Tan.
Description: Leiden; Boston : Brill Nijhoff [2021] | Series: International
   criminal law series, 2213-2724 ; volume 16 | Based on author's thesis
   (doctoral - Universiteit Leiden, 2019). | Includes bibliographical references
   and index. | Summary: "In this book, Yudan Tan offers a detailed analysis
   of topical issues concerning the Rome Statute of the International Criminal
   Court as evidence of customary international law"– Provided by publisher.
Identifiers: LCCN 2021026893 (print) | LCCN 2021026894 (ebook) |
   ISBN 9789004439405 (hardback) | ISBN 9789004439412 (ebook)
Subjects: LCSH: Customary law, International. | International criminal law. |
   Rome Statute of the International Criminal Court (1998 July 17)–Influence.
Classification: LCC KZ1277 .T36 2021 (print) | LCC KZ1277 (ebook) |
   DDC 341–dc23
LC record available at https://lccn.loc.gov/2021026893
LC ebook record available at https://lccn.loc.gov/2021026894

Typeface for the Latin, Greek, and Cyrillic scripts: "Brill". See and download: brill.com/brill-typeface.

ISSN 2213-2724
ISBN 978-90-04-43940-5 (hardback)
ISBN 978-90-04-43941-2 (e-book)

Copyright 2021 by Yudan Tan. Published by Koninklijke Brill NV, Leiden, The Netherlands.
Koninklijke Brill NV incorporates the imprints Brill, Brill Nijhoff, Brill Hotei, Brill Schöningh, Brill Fink, Brill mentis, Vandenhoeck & Ruprecht, Böhlau Verlag and V&R Unipress.
Koninklijke Brill NV reserves the right to protect this publication against unauthorized use. Requests for re-use and/or translations must be addressed to Koninklijke Brill NV via brill.com or copyright.com.

This book is printed on acid-free paper and produced in a sustainable manner.

Contents

Acknowledgements IX
Abbreviations X
Table of Legislation XIV
Table of Cases XXXVII
United Nations Documents LXI

1 **Introduction** 1
   1.1 The Role of Customary International Law in the International Criminal Court 2
   1.2 Aim, Questions and Scope of This Book 8
   1.3 Method and Terms of This Book 17
   1.4 Structure of This Book 20
   1.5 Merits and Limits of This Book 23

2 **Methodological Framework of This Book** 28
   2.1 Introductory Remarks 28
   2.2 Interpreting Provisions of the Rome Statute 28
   2.3 Method: The Two-Element Approach to Identifying Customary Rules 33
   2.4 Terms: A Treaty Was or Is of a 'Declaratory' Nature of Custom 51
   2.5 Preconditions for This Study 60
   2.6 Concluding Remarks 64

3 **War Crimes in Non-international Armed Conflict**
Article 8 of the Rome Statute and Custom 66
   3.1 Introductory Remarks 66
   3.2 Provisions on War Crimes in Non-international Armed Conflict in the Rome Statute 67
   3.3 War Crimes in Armed Conflict 70
   3.4 War Crimes in Non-international Armed Conflict: Were Articles 8(2)(c) and (e) Declaratory of Custom? 104
   3.5 Further Recognition of War Crimes in Non-international Armed Conflict: Are Articles 8(2)(c) and (e) Declaratory of Custom? 124
   3.6 Concluding Remarks 132

4 Crimes against Humanity
  Article 7 of the Rome Statute and Custom 134
  4.1   Introductory Remarks   134
  4.2   Provisions on Crimes against Humanity in the Rome Statute   136
  4.3   Crimes against Humanity as International Crimes under Customary Law   138
  4.4   No Nexus with an Armed Conflict: Was and Is Article 7(1) Declaratory of Custom?   149
  4.5   The Policy Element: Was and Is Article 7(2)(a) Declaratory of Custom?   166
  4.6   Concluding Remarks   187

5 The Crime of Aggression
  Articles 8bis and 25(3bis) of the Rome Statute and Custom   189
  5.1   Introductory Remarks   189
  5.2   The Crime of Aggression in International Law   192
  5.3   Provisions on the Crime of Aggression in the Rome Statute   195
  5.4   The Leadership Element for the Crime of Aggression: Were Articles 8*bis* and 25(3*bis*) Declaratory of Custom?   202
  5.5   The Leadership Element for the Crime of Aggression: Are Articles 8*bis* and 25(3*bis*) Declaratory of Custom?   239
  5.6   Concluding Remarks   246

6 Indirect Co-perpetration
  Article 25(3)(a) of the Rome Statute and Custom   247
  6.1   Introductory Remarks   247
  6.2   The Attribution of Liability to Individuals at the Leadership Level   249
  6.3   Is Indirect Co-perpetration Encompassed in Article 25(3)(a) of the Rome Statute?   253
  6.4   Non-acceptance of Indirect Co-perpetration in Post-World War II Trials   265
  6.5   Indirect Co-perpetration: Is Article 25(3)(a) Declaratory of Custom?   272
  6.6   Concluding Remarks   311

7 An Exception to Personal Immunity for International Crimes
  Article 27(2) of the Rome Statute and Custom   312
  7.1   Introductory Remarks   312
  7.2   Immunity under International Law   314

7.3 Personal Immunity: Article 27(2) of the Rome Statute   324
7.4 Non-availability of Personal Immunity for International Crimes: Was Article 27(2) Declaratory of Custom?   335
7.5 Non-availability of Personal Immunity for Committing International Crimes: Is Article 27(2) Declaratory of Custom?   343
7.6 Concluding Remarks   377

8 **Conclusions**   378
   8.1 Synthesis   379
   8.2 Discussions and Concluding Remarks   383

Bibliography   389
Index   413

Acknowledgements

This book is a revised and updated version of my doctoral dissertation that I completed in October 2018 and defended in April 2019 at Leiden University. I could not have completed this book without the assistance and encouragement of many people. I am much obliged to my supervisors, William Schabas and Robert Heinsch, at Leiden University. I was fortunate enough to work with William Schabas, a leading authority in international criminal law. I would like to express my great appreciation to him for his wide insight and encouraging supervision. I am also thankful to Robert Heinsch, for his patient guidance during the planning and development of my work and his careful reading of all drafts of my doctoral dissertation. The earlier drafts of the book would not have been completed without their critical, constructive and swift feedback.

I am grateful to André Klip, Carsten Stahn, Claus Kreß, Emma Irving, Jens Iverson, Larrisa van den Herik and Rod Rastan, for their invaluable reviews of the doctoral dissertation as well as the anonymous reviewers for their thoughtful comments on my book proposal. I also wish to express gratitude to many people whom I met at conferences, workshops and symposia, in particular, Judge LIU Daqun, for the countless inspiring discussions. Thanks also due to my lovely former colleagues at Leiden University, who constantly challenged me to articulate my positions more clearly and stimulated discussions on matters of international (criminal) law. The book benefits from their views and comments, although many of them may disagree with a few or many points. None of them can be blamed for any errors or omissions in the text.

I owe my sincere gratitude to the China Scholarship Council, the Grotius Centre for International Legal Studies and the European Society of International Law for their financial support throughout the years in Leiden and The Hague. My thanks are extended to our secretariats and the staff of the Leiden Law Library, the Peace Palace Library, Max Planck Institute for Foreign and International Criminal Law in Freiburg and Soochow University (Suzhou) for all tangible and intangible resources. I am also grateful to Lindy Melman and Bea Timmer of Brill for their trust and patience. I am also thankful to Brill for permitting me to include part of my journal article that has been published in the Asian Yearbook of International Law, Volume 24 (2018) into chapter 4 of the book.

Last but not least, I am particularly indebted to my family, parents and grandma for their endless support to me and my academic endeavours. Weichun, thanks for your encouragement and patience. Leika, I am blessed to have you. Special thanks are owed to my grandma for her unconditional love. To her, I dedicate this book.

Yudan Tan

Abbreviations

AATA	Administrative Appeals Tribunal of Australia
AC	Appeal Cases (the UK cases)
A Ch	Appeals Chamber
AI	Amnesty International
AJCL	American Journal of Comparative Law
AJIL	American Journal of International Law
Am U Intl L Rev	American University International Law Review
Am U L Rev	American University Law Review
ARIEL	Austrian Review of International and European Law
art(s)	Article(s)
ASP	Assembly of States Parties
Australian J HR	Australian Journal of Human Rights
Australian Ybk Intl L	Australian Yearbook of International Law
British Ybk Intl L	British Yearbook of International Law
Cal L Rev	California Law Review
Canadian Ybk Intl L	Canadian Yearbook of International Law
Cardozo L Rev	Cardozo Law Review
Case W Res J Intl L	Case Western Reserve Journal of International Law
Chicago J Intl L	Chicago Journal of International Law
Chinese J Intl L	Chinese Journal of International Law
Cir	Circuit (the US cases)
CLB	Commonwealth Law Bulletin
CLF	Criminal Law Forum
Columbia L Rev	Columbia Law Review
Cornell Intl LJ	Cornell International Law Journal
Crim Law & Philos	Criminal Law & Philosophy
CUP	Cambridge University Press
Dalhousie LJ	Dalhousie Law Journal
Denver J Intl L& P	Denver Journal of International Law and Policy
DePaul L Rev	DePaul Law Review
DLR	Dominion Law Reports
Doc	Document
Duke LJ	Duke Law Journal
ECCC	Extraordinary Chambers in the Courts of Cambodia
ECtHR	European Court of Human Rights
ed(s)	editor(s)
edn	edition

ABBREVIATIONS

EJCCLCJ	European Journal of Crime, Criminal Law and Criminal Justice
EJIL	European Journal of International Law
Emory Intl L Rev	Emory International Law Review
et al	Et alii (and others)
EWCA Crim	Court of Appeal Criminal Division (the UK)
F 3d	Federal Reporter, Third Series (the US Circuit Court of Appeals)
FC	Federal Court (Canada)
FCA	Federal Court of Appeal (Canada)
FCAFC	Federal Court of Australia – Full Court
Finnish Ybk Intl L	Finnish Yearbook of International Law
fn	Footnote
Fordham Intl LJ	Fordham International Law Journal
GA	General Assembly
GAOR	General Assembly Official Records
Georgetown LJ	Georgetown Law Journal
GSU L Rev	Georgia State University Law Review
Harvard Intl LJ	Harvard International Law Journal
Harvard J on Legis	Harvard Journal on Legislation
HCA	High Court of Australia
HMSO	Her Majesty's Stationery Office
Houston J Intl L	Houston Journal of International Law
ICC	International Criminal Court
ICJ	International Court of Justice
ICJ Rep	ICJ Report
ICLQ	International and Comparative Law Quarterly
ICLR	International Criminal Law Review
ICRC	International Committee of the Red Cross
ICT	International Crimes Tribunal (Bangladesh)
ICTR	International Criminal Tribunal for Rwanda
ICTY	International Criminal Tribunal for the former Yugoslavia
ILA	International Law Association
ILC	International Law Commission
ILDC	International Law in Domestic Courts
ILM	International Legal Materials
ILR	International Law Reports
Intl Community LR	International Community Law Review
Intl J HR	International Journal of Human Rights
IOLR	International Organizations Law Review
IRRC	International Review of the Red Cross
Israel Ybk HR	Israel Yearbook on Human Rights

J Armed Conflict L	Journal of Armed Conflict Law
J Conflict & Security L	Journal of Conflict and Security Law
J Crim L & Criminology	Journal of Criminal Law and Criminology
Jewish Ybk Intl L	Jewish Yearbook of International Law
JICJ	Journal of International Criminal Justice
LJIL	Leiden Journal of International Law
LJN	Landelijk Jurisprudentie Nummer (country case number) (the Netherlands)
LPICT	Law and Practice of International Courts and Tribunals
LQR	Law Quarterly Review
LRTWC	Law Reports of Trials of the War Criminals
MJECL	Maastricht Journal of European and Comparative Law
Melbourne J Intl L	Melbourne Journal of International Law
Melbourne U L Rev	Melbourne University Law Review
Michigan J Intl L	Michigan Journal of International Law
Military L & L War Rev	Military Law and the Law of War Review
Military L Rev	Military Law Review
MPEPIL	Max Planck Encyclopedia of Public International Law
MPUNYB	Max Plank Yearbook of United National Law
Netherland Intl L Rev	Netherland International Law Review
No.	Number
n	note
Nordic J Intl L	Nordic Journal of International Law
OUP	Oxford University Press
Pace Intl L Rev	Pace International Law Review
para(s)	Paragraph(s)
PTC	Pre-Trial Chamber
Recueil des cours	Recueil des cours de l'Académie du droit international de la Haye (Collected Courses of The Hague Academy of International Law)
Res	Resolution
RIDP	Revue Internationale de Droit Pénal (International Review of Penal Law)
SC	Security Council
SCSL	Special Court for Sierra Leone
SPSC	Special Panels for Serious Crimes
Stanford J Intl L	Stanford Journal of International Law
STL	Special Tribunal for Lebanon
St. John's L Rev	St. John's Law Review
Supp	Supplement

SWGCA	Special Working Group on the Crime of Aggression
TC	Trial Chamber
Tex Intl L J	Texas International Law Journal
TOAEP	Torkel Opsahl Academic EPublisher
Tilburg L Rev	Tilburg Law Review
TMWC	Trial of the Major War Criminals before the International Military Tribunals: Nuremberg
TWC	Trials of the War Criminals before the Nuremberg Military Tribunals Under Control Council Law No. 10
U Pa L Rev	University of Pennsylvania Law Review
U.S.	United States Reports (United States Supreme Court)
UJIEL	Utrecht Journal of International and European Law
UK	United Kingdom
UKHL (now SC)	United Kingdom House Lord (now Supreme Court)
UKTS	United Kingdom Treaty Series
UN	United Nations
UNTS	United Nations Treaty Series
UNWCC	United Nations War Crimes Commission
US	United States
USC	Unites States Code
USGPO	Unites States Government Printing Office
v	Versus (against)
Vand J Transnatl L	Vanderbilt Journal of Transnational Law
Vand L Rev	Vanderbilt Law Review
Va J Intl L	Virginia Journal of International Law
Vol (s)	Volume (s)
Wis Intl LJ	Wisconsin International Law Journal
WLR	Weekly Law Reports (the UK)
YIHL	Yearbook of International Humanitarian Law
ZAGPPHC	South Africa North Gauteng High Court, Pretoria
ZASCA	South Africa Supreme Court of Appeal
ZIS	Zeitschrift für Internationale Strafrechtsdogmatik (Journal for International Doctrine in Criminal Law)
§(§)	section(s)

Table of Legislation

Treaties

Treaty of Peace with Germany (signed 28 June 1919, entered into force 10 January 1920) 2 Bevans 43 [Treaty of Versailles]

Treaty of Peace between the Allied and Associated Powers and the Ottoman Empire (signed 10 August 1920) (1920) UKTS 11 [Treaty of Sèvres]

Treaty of Peace with Turkey (signed 24 July 1923, entered into force 6 August 1924) 28 LNTS 11 [Treaty of Lausanne]

General Treaty for Renunciation of War (signed 27 August 1928) 94 LNTS 57 [Kellogg–Briand Pact]

Agreement for the Prosecution and Punishment of the Major War Criminals of the European Axis (singed 8 August 1945) 82 UNTS 280 [London Agreement]

Charter of the International Military Tribunal–Annex to the Agreement for the Prosecution and Punishment of the Major War Criminals of the European Axis (signed 8 August 1945) 82 UNTS 284 [Nuremberg Charter]

Charter of the International Military Tribunal for the Far East (signed 19 January 1946, as amended 26 April 1946) TIAS 1589 [Tokyo Charter]

Statute of the International Court of Justice (adopted 26 June 1945, entered into force 24 October 1945) 33 UNTS 993

Geneva Convention (I) for the Amelioration of the Condition of Wounded and Sick in Armed Forces in the Field (adopted 12 August 1949, entered into force 21 October 1950) 75 UNTS 31 [Geneva Convention I]

Geneva Convention (II) for the Amelioration of the Condition of Wounded, Sick and Shipwrecked Members of Armed Forces at Sea (adopted 12 August 1949, entered into force 21 October 1950) 75 UNTS 85 [Geneva Convention II]

Geneva Convention (III) Relative to the Treatment of Prisoners of War (adopted 12 August 1949, entered into force 21 October 1950) 75 UNTS 135 [Geneva Convention III]

Geneva Convention (IV) Relative to the Protection of Civilian Persons in Time of War (adopted 12 August 1949, entered into force 21 October 1950) 75 UNTS 287 [Geneva Convention IV]

Convention for the Prevention and Punishment of the Crime of Genocide (adopted 9 December 1948, entered into force 12 January 1951) 78 UNTS 277 [Genocide Convention]

Convention for the Protection of Human Rights and Fundamental Freedoms (European Convention on Human Rights, as amended) [ECHR]

Convention on the Protection of Cultural Property in the Event of Armed Conflict (adopted 14 May 1954, entered into force 7 August 1956) 249 UNTS 215

Geneva Convention on the Continental Shelf (adopted 29 April 1958, entered into force 10 June 1964) 499 UNTS 312

Vienna Convention on Diplomatic Relations (adopted 18 April 1961, entered into force 24 April 1964) 500 UNTS 95

Convention on the Non-Applicability of Statutory Limitations to War Crimes and Crimes Against Humanity (adopted 26 November 1968, entered into force 11 November 1970) 754 UNTS 73

Vienna Convention on the Law of Treaties (adopted 23 May 1969, entered into force 27 January 1980) 1155 UNTS 331

Convention on Special Missions (adopted 8 December 1969, entered into force 21 June 1985) 1400 UNTS 231

Protocol Additional to the Geneva Conventions of 12 August 1949 and Relating to the Protection of Victims of International Armed Conflicts (adopted 8 June 1977, entered into force 7 December 1978) 1125 UNTS 3 [the 1977 Additional Protocol I]

Protocol Additional to the Geneva Conventions of 12 August 1949 and Relating to the Protection of Victims of Non-international Armed Conflicts (adopted 8 June 1977, entered into force 7 December 1978) 1125 UNTS 609 [the 1977 Additional Protocol II]

Convention against Torture and Other Cruel, Inhuman or Degrading Treatment or Punishment (adopted 10 December 1984, entered into force 26 June 1987) 1465 UNTS 85

Rome Statute of the International Criminal Court (adopted 17 July 1998, entered into force 1 July 2002) 2187 UNTS 90 [1998 Rome Statute]

Agreement between the United Nations and the Government of Sierra Leone on the Establishment of a Special Court for Sierra Leone (with Statute) (Sierra Leone–United Nations) (16 January 2002) 2178 UNTS 137

Agreement between the United Nations and the Royal Government of Cambodia concerning the Prosecution under Cambodian Law of Crimes Committed during the Period of Democratic Kampuchea (Cambodia–United Nations) (6 June 2003) 2329 UNTS 117

United Nations Convention against Transnational Organized Crime (adopted 15 November 2000, entered into force 29 September 2003) 2225 UNTS 209

United Nations Convention on Jurisdictional Immunities of States and Their Property (adopted 2 December 2004)

Amendment to article 8 of the Rome Statute of the International Criminal Court (adopted 10 June 2010, entered into force 26 September 2012) 2868 UNTS 195

Statute of the Extraordinary African Chambers within the Courts of Senegal Created to Prosecute International Crimes Committed in Chad between 7 June 1982 and 1 December 1990 (African Union–Senegal) (2013) 52 ILM 1028 [Statute of the Extraordinary African Chambers within the Senegalese Judicial System]

Protocol on Amendments to the Protocol on the Statute of the African Court of Justice and Human Rights (adopted 27 June 2014, not entered into force) STC/Legal/Min/7 (I) Rev 1

National Legislation

Afghanistan
Penal Code 1976
    art 38(1)
    art 39(2)
    art 49
Law on Combat against Terrorist Offences 2008
    art 18

Albania
Criminal Code 1995, amended 2013
    arts 27-28
    arts 211-212

Andorra
Penal Code 2005, amended 2008
    art 21

Angola
Constitution of the Republic of Angola 2010
    art 61

Argentina
Criminal Code 1984, amended 2016
    art 215
Act Implementing the Rome Statute of the International Criminal Court 2001
    arts 40-41

Armenia
Criminal Code 2003, amended 2013
    art 38(3)
    art 41(2)
    arts 41(4)-(5)
    arts 384-385
    art 390

Austria
Cooperation with the International Criminal Court 2002
§ 9.1.3
Criminal Code 1974, amended 2015
§ 12
Law of Armed Conflicts Manual 2006
§ 13.39
Australia
ICC (Consequential Amendments) Act 2002
§ 12(4)
§§ 268.69-268.94
Criminal Code 1995
§ 11.2A
Azerbaijan
Criminal Code 1999, amended 2020
arts 32.2, 33.2
arts 34.5-34.6
arts 100-101
arts 105-113
art 116
Bangladesh
International Crimes (Tribunals) Act 1973, amended 2013
§ 3(2)(a)
§ 3(2)(b)
§§ 3(2)(g)-(h)
§ 4(1)
Penal Code 1860, amended 1973
arts 34-35, 37
Law of Armed Conflicts Manual 1999
§ 2
Law of Armed Conflicts Manual 2001
§§1602-1603, 1610
Bahamas
Penal Code 1924, amended 2014
arts 14(1)-(2), 14(4)
Belarus
Penal Code 1999, amended 2012
arts16(1), 17
arts 18(2), 19(4)
art 122

arts 134-136
arts 137-138
Belgium
Judicial Power Organisation Act 1985, amended 1999
    art 23.4
Organisation Act No 1/2009
    art 1
Code of Criminal Procedure 1878, amended 2007
    art 1*bis*
Act of 16 June 1993 concerning the punishment of Grave Breaches of the Geneva Conventions of 12 August 1949 and their Additional Protocols I and II of 18 June 1977
    art 7
Act of 10 February 1999, amending Act of 16 June 1993
    art 5(3)
Act of 23 April 2003, amending Act of 16 June 1993
    art 2
    art 5
Act of 5 August 2003, amending Act of 16 June 1993
    art 7
    art 13
Belize
Criminal Code 2000
    § 11(4)
    § 24(1)
Bolivia
Criminal Code and Criminal Procedural Code 1997, amended 2010
    art 20
Bosnia and Herzegovina
Criminal Code 2003, amended 2018
    art 31
    art 157
    art 172
    arts 173-175, 177-179
    art 342(3)
Botswana
Penal Code 1964, amended 2005
    § 22
    § 38

Brunei Darussalam
Penal Code 1951, amended 2001
 §§ 34-35, 37
Bulgaria
Criminal Code 1968, amended 2017
 arts 407-409
Burkina Faso
Act on the determination of competence and procedures for application of the Rome Statute of the International Criminal Court 2009
 arts 7 and 15.1
Burundi
Regulations on International Humanitarian Law 2007
 Part I*bis*
Law on Genocide, Crimes against Humanity and War Crimes 2003
 art 4
 art 5
Penal Code 2009
 art 37(1)
 art 20
Cabo Verde
Penal Code 2003
 art 25
 art 267(2)
Cameroon
Instructor's Manual 2006
 § 551
Penal Code 1967, amended 2016
 art 96
Cambodia
Provisions relating to the Judiciary and Criminal Law and Procedure Applicable in Cambodia during the Transitional Period 1991
 art 27
Law on the Establishment of the ECCC, amended 2004
 art 1
Canada
Extradition Act 1999
 § 6.1
Crimes against Humanity and War Crimes Act 2000, amended 2019
 § 4 (4)
 § 6 (4)

LOAC at the Operational and Tactical Levels 2001
   § 1610
   § 1725
Criminal Code 1985, amended 2020
   § 21(2)
   §§ 467.1, 467.13
Central African Republic
Penal Code 2010
   arts 156-157
Chile
Criminal Code 2011
   art 15(3)
China
Law Governing the Trial of War Criminals of the Republic of China 1946
   art 3
Criminal Law of the People's Republic of China 1997, amended 2017
   art 25
   art 26(3)
Colombia
Penal Code 2000
   art 29(1)
   art 29(2)
Comoros
Act concerning the application of the Rome Statute 2011
   art 7.2
Congo
Genocide, War Crimes and Crimes against Humanity Act 1998
   arts 4(c)-(d)
Cook Islands
Criminal Act 1969
   § 68(2)
Costa Rica
Criminal Prosecution to Punish War Crimes and Crimes against Humanity 2002
   art 2
Penal Code 1970, amended 2002
   art 45
Côte d'Ivoire
Penal Code 1981, amended 1995
   art 25
   arts 26, 29

Croatia
Law on the Implementation of the Statute of the ICC and the Prosecution of Crimes against International Law of War and Humanitarian Law 2003
    art 6.4
Criminal Code 1998, amended 2011
    art 36(1)
    art 36(2)
    art 39
    arts 89(1)-(3)
    art 90
    art 91

Cuba
Penal Code 1987, amended 1997
    art 18(2)(d)
    art 18(2)(ch)

Cyprus
Criminal Code 1959
    § 21

Czech Republic
Criminal Code 2009, amended 2011
    § 22(2)
    § 23

Democratic Republic of the Congo
Criminal Code 1940, amended 2004
    art 21(1)
    art 21(3)

Djibouti
Penal Code 1995
    art 23(3)

East Timor
Regulation for Special Panels for Serious Crimes 2000
    § 5
    § 6
    § 14.3
    § 15.2

Ecuador
Penal Code 1997, amended 2013
    art 42

El Salvador
Penal Code 1997, amended 2010

art 33
art 34
Eritrea
Penal Code 2015
   art 37(1)(c)
   art 37(3)
Estonia
Criminal Code 2002, amended 2017
   § 21(1)
   § 21(2)
   § 89
   § 91
   § 94
Ethiopia
Criminal Code 2005
   art 32(1)(c)
   art 38
   art 246
   arts 269-280
Fiji
Crimes Decree 2009
   § 46
Finland
Criminal Code 1889, amended 2015
   chapter 1, §§ 7(3)-(4)
   chapter 1, § 15
   chapter 5, §§ 3-4
   chapter 11, § 3
   chapter 11, § 5(1)
   chapter 12, § 2
France
Law of Armed Conflicts Manual 2001
   §§ 44-46
Penal Code 1994, amended 2016
   § 121-7
   § 461-1
Code of Criminal Procedure 2002
   art 627.8
Georgia

Constitutional Law 1995
   art 6(2)
Criminal Code 1999, amended 2016
   arts 22, 25(2), 27(2)
   art 27(4)
   arts 404-405
   art 408
   arts 411-412

Germany
Humanitarian Law in Armed Conflicts Manual 1992
Soldiers' Manual 2006
   R113
Code of Crimes against International Law 2002, amended 2016
   §§ 1(7), 8(1)-(2), 9(1), 10(1)-(2), 11(1)-(2),12
Law on Cooperation with the International Criminal Court 2002
   § 70
Criminal Code 1998, amended 2016
   § 25(1)
   § 80a

Ghana
Criminal Code 1960
   art 13(1)
   art 13(2)

Greece
Law on the adaptation of internal law to the provisions of the ICC Statute 2002, amended 2011
   art 8
Penal Code 1950, amended 2003
   art 45

Grenada
Criminal Code 1987, amended 1993
   § 14(2)

Guatemala
Penal Code 1973
   art 36

Guinea
Criminal Code 1998
   art 52
   art 80

Haiti
Penal Code 1995
    art 44
Honduras
Penal Code 1983, amended 2008
    art 32
    art 34(1)
Hungary
Criminal Code 1978, amended 2012
    § 4(5)
    §§ 13(2)-(3)
    § 153
Indonesia
Penal Code 1999
    art 111
Iran
The Islamic Penal Code 2013
    art 125
    art 128
    art 130
Iraq
Iraqi High Criminal Court Law 2005
    art 1(a)
    art 12
    art 14(2)
    art 15(2)(a)
    art 15(2)(d)
Penal Code 1969
    § 47(2)
Israel
Penal Code 1977, amended 1990
    § 29(b)
    § 29(c)
Italy
Criminal Code 1930, amended 2017
    art 112
    art 113
India
Penal Code 1860, amended 2013
    §§ 34-35, 37
    §§ 121-121A, 122

TABLE OF LEGISLATION

Ireland
Criminal Code 1997
   art 2(2)
International Criminal Court Act 2006
   § 6(1)
   § 61(1)
Geneva Conventions Act 1962, amended 1998
   § 4
Japan
Criminal Code 1907, amended 2006
   art 60
Jordan
Military Penal Code 2000
   art 41
Kazakhstan
Criminal Code 1997, amended 2014
   art 2
   art 29(2)
   art 31(3)
   art 31(4)
   arts 160-161
Kenya
International Crimes Act 2008
   § 6(1)
   § 6(4)
   § 27(1)(a)
Criminal Code 1930, amended 2010
   § 21
   § 44
Kiribati
Geneva Conventions (Amendment) Act 2010
   § 5
Criminal Code 1965, amended 1977
   art 22
Kosovo
Law on Specialist Chambers and Specialist Prosecutor's Office 2015
   arts 3(2)(d), 3(3), 12-14
Kyrgyzstan
Criminal Code 1997, amended 2006
   art 30(3)
   arts 29(3), 34(1)

Latvia
Criminal Law 1998, amended 2013
  § 2(2)
  § 17
  § 19
  § 21(2)
  § 71(2)
  §§ 72, 77
  § 78
Lebanon
Statute for the Special Tribunal for Lebanon
  art 3(1)
Lebanese Criminal Code 1943
  art 197
Lesotho
Penal Code 2010, amended 2012
  § 94(2)
  §§ 95(1)(c)-(d)
  §26
Liberia
Criminal Code 1976
  § 3.1(a)
Liechtenstein
Act on Cooperation with the International Criminal Court and other International Tribunals 2004
  art 3
  arts 10.1(c), 10.3
Criminal Code 1988, amended 2013
  § 12
Lithuania
Criminal Code 2000, amended 2015
  art 4(4)
  art 24(3)
  art 26(4)
  art 100
  art 110
  arts 333-344
Luxembourg
Criminal Code 1879, amended 2016
  art 66(1)
  art 66(3)

Malawi
Penal Code 1930
   § 22
   § 40
Malaysia
Penal Code 1936, amended 2014
   §§ 34-35, 37
Maldives
Penal Code 1968, amended 2004
   § 10
   § 14
Malta
Extradition Act 1982, amended 2010
   art 26S
Criminal Code 1854, amended 2016
   § 45
   § 47(b)
   § 54C(2)(a)
   § 54D
   § 82C(2)
Macedonia
Criminal Code 1996, amended 2009
   art 22
   art 415
Mauritius
International Criminal Court Act 2011
   § 2
   § 4
   § 4(2)(b)
Criminal Code
   § 51
Mexico
International Humanitarian Law Guidelines 2009
   § 5
Criminal Code 1931, amended 2013
   art 13(3)
   art 13(4)
   art 149
Moldova
Criminal Code 2002, amended 2009
   art 42(2)

art 44
arts 47(2), 47(4)
art 139
art 391

Mongolia
Constitutional Law 1992
art 10
Criminal Code 2002
art 2(1)
art 36.2
art 37.2
arts 297-298

Montenegro
Criminal Code 2003, amended 2012
arts 23(1)-(2)
art 427
art 442

Morocco
Penal Code 1962, amended 2016
art 128

Myanmar
Penal Code 1861, amended 2016
§§ 34-35, 37

Nauru
Criminal Code 1899, amended 2011
§ 8

Netherlands
Criminal Law in Wartime Act 1958, amended 1990
Preamble and § 1(3)
Humanitarian Law of War Manual 2005
§§ 1131-1132, 1134
§§ 1147-1148
Act of 19 June 2003 containing rules concerning serious violations of international humanitarian law (International Crimes Act 2003)
§ 4(2)
§ 6
§ 16(a)
Criminal Code 1881, amended 2012
§ 47(1)(1)

New Zealand
Interim Law of Armed Conflict Manual 1992
International Crimes and International Criminal Court Act 2000
   § 10 (2)
   § 11
   § 31(1)
Criminal Code 1961, amended 2013
   § 66(2)
Nicaragua
Penal Code 1974, amended 1998
  art 24.2
  art 24.3
  art 551
Niger
Penal Code 1961, amended 2003
  art 72
  art 208.8
Nigeria
Criminal Code 1916, amended 1990
   § 8
The Laws of War States (undated)
   § 6
Norway
Act of 15 June 2001 relating to the Implementation of the Statute of the International Criminal Court of 17 July 1998 (Rome Statute) in Norwegian law (Implementation Act 2001)
   § 2
Penal Code 1902, amended 2008
   §§ 83-84
   § 107
   §§ 101-110
Pakistan
Penal Code 1860, amended 2017
   §§ 34-35
   §§ 121-121A, 122
Panama
Penal Code 2007
  art 43
  art 44

Paraguay
Penal Code 1997
 art 29(1)
 art 29(2)
Peru
Presidential Decree on the National Human Rights Plan 2005
 § 3.1.3 A1
Penal Code 1991, amended 2010
 art 23
International Humanitarian Law Manual 2004
 § 31a
International Humanitarian Law and Human Rights Manual 2010
 § 32(a)
Philippines
Act on Crimes against International Humanitarian Law, Genocide, and Other Crimes against Humanity 2009
 § 6
 § 8(a)(3)
 § 9(b)
Penal Code 1930, amended 2012
 art 17(3)
Poland
Criminal Code 1997, amended 2016
 art 18 § 1
 art 117
 arts 118-120
Portugal
Adaptation of Criminal Legislation to ICC Statute 2004
 art 9
Criminal Code 2006, amended 2015
 art 26
Papua New Guinea
Criminal Code 1974
 § 8
Republic of Korea
Criminal Act 1953, amended 2005
 art 30
Act on the Punishment of Crimes within the Jurisdiction of the International Criminal Court 2007
 art 9

Romania
Criminal Code 2009, amended 2012
    art 46
    art 439
Rwanda
Law Setting up Gacaca Jurisdictions 2001
    art 1
    art 51
Law on Repressing the Crime of Genocide, Crimes against Humanity and War Crimes 2003
    art 17
Penal Code 1977, amended 2012
    art 90
Russian Federation
Criminal Code 1996, amended 2012
    arts 33(2), 34(2)
    art 35(5)
    arts 353-354
    art 356
Sao Tome and Principe
Penal Code 2012
    arts 26(a), 26 (c)
Samoa
International Criminal Court Act 2007
    § 6
    § 7
    § 32(1)
Crimes Act 2013
    § 33(2)
Senegal
Extraordinary African Chambers within the Senegalese Judicial System 2013
    art 4(b)
    art 6
    art 7(2)
Penal Code 1965, amended 2007
    art 66
    arts 431-433(d)
Serbia
Criminal Code 2006, amended 2012
    art 10(3)

art 33
art 376
art 386
Seychelles
Penal Code 1955, amended 2014
§ 23
Sierra Leone
The Law of Armed Conflict Instructor Manual 2007 (Instructor Manual 2007)
at 65
Singapore
Penal Code 1871, amended 2015
§§ 34-35
§ 37
Slovakia
Criminal Code 2005, amended 2009
§ 20
§ 417(1)
§ 425
Slovenia
Criminal Code 2008, amended 2009
art 20(1)
art 20(2)
art 41(3)
art 101
arts 102(3)-(4)
art 103
Solomon Islands
Penal Code 1996, amended 2016
§ 22
Somalia
Constitution of Somalia 1960
§ 3.5.4.1
Penal Code 1963
art 72
art 73
South Africa
Implementation of the Rome Statute of the International Criminal Court Act 2002 (Implementation Act 2002)
§ 1
§ 2

§ 4(1)
§§ 4(2)(a)(i), 4(3)(c)
Spain
Criminal Code 1995, amended 2015
   art 28
   arts 607-614
   art 607*bis*
   art 614
Organic Act 2015
   art 22
Sri Lanka
Penal Code 1883, amended 2006
   §§ 32-33, 35
Geneva Conventions Act 2006
   § 2(1)
   §§ 2-3
Sudan
Criminal Act 1991
   § 21
Sweden
Penal Code 1962, amended 1998
   § 6
Switzerland
Federal Law on Cooperation with the International Criminal Court 2001
   art 6
Military Criminal Code 1927, amended 2011
   arts 111-112d
Criminal Code 1937, amended 2017
   art 264a(1)(E)
   art 264b
   art 264(j)
   art 266(2)
Regulation on Legal Bases for Conduct during an Engagement 2005
   §152
Tajikistan
Criminal Code 1998
   art 1(2)
   arts 36(2), 37(2)
   art 39(5)
   art 39(6)

art 43
arts 395-396
art 404
Tanzania
Code of Criminal Law 1945, amended 2007
§ 23
§ 43
Thailand
Penal Code 1956, amended April 2016
§ 83
Prisoners of War Act 1955
§§ 12-19
Timor-Leste
Constitutional Law 2002
§ 9(1)
Penal Code 2009
art 30(1)
art 30(2)
art 124
Togo
Criminal Code 1992, amended 2012
art 247
Trinidad and Tobago
International Criminal Court Act 2006
§ 10
§ 31(1)(a)
Turkmenistan
Penal Code 1997, amended 2013
art 33(2)
Turkey
Penal Code 2016
art 37(1)
art 37(2)
art 77(1)
art 300
Tuvalu
Penal Code 2008
§ 22
Uganda
International Criminal Court Act 2010
§ 8

Penal Code 1950, amended 1998
  § 20
UK
Geneva Convention Act 1957, amended 1995
  § 1(1)
International Criminal Court Act 2001
  §§ 23(1)-(2)
  § 23(5)
  § 50
International Criminal Court Act (Isle of Man) Oder 2004
  Explanatory Note
Penal Code 1990, amended 2014
  § 20
The Manual of the Law of Armed Conflict 2004
  §§ 15.32, 15.32.1
  §16.26
  §16.35
Ukraine
Criminal Code 2001, amended 2010
  art 27(2)
  art 28(1)-(2)
  art 30(1)
  art 437
  arts 438, 441, 444
International Humanitarian Law Manual 2004
  § 1.8.4
Uruguay
Criminal Code 1933, amended 2010
  art 61
  art 60(2)
Uzbekistan
Criminal Code 1994, amended 2012
  art 27
  art 28(2)
  art 29
  art 30
  art 151
  art 152
US
Manual for Military Commissions of 2010
  § 950v (29)

Military Commissions Act of 2006
  10 USC 948a §6(b)(1)(A)
Criminal Justice Code 1967
  § 46.3207
War Crimes Act of 1996
  18 USC 2441(c)(3)
The Law of Land Warfare (Field Manual 2004)
  § 500

Vanuatu
Penal Code 1981, amended 2016
  § 31

Venezuela
Code of Military Justice 1998
  art 474
Penal Procedure Code 2009
  art 124

Vietnam
Penal Code 1999
  art 20(3)
  art 342
  arts 313-314, 336-340
  art 341
  art 343

Yemen
Republican Decree for Law No 12 for the Year 1994 Concerning Crimes and Penalties
  art 21

The Socialist Federal Republic of Yugoslavia
Penal Code 1976, amended 2001
  art 142

Zambia
Geneva Conventions Act 1998, amended 1996
Penal Code 1931, amended 2011
  art 22

Table of Cases

International Court of Justice

Reservations to the Convention on the Prevention and Punishment of the Crimes of Genocide, Advisory Opinion, [1951] ICJ Rep 15

North Sea Continental Shelf cases (Germany v Denmark; Germany v Netherlands), Judgment, [1969] ICJ Rep 3

Barcelona Traction, Light and Power Company, Limited (Belgium v Spain), Judgment, [1970] ICJ Rep 3

Continental Shelf (Libyan Arab Jarnahiriya/Malta), Judgment, [1985] ICJ Rep 13

Military and Paramilitary Activities in and against Nicaragua (Nicaragua v USA), Merits, [1986] ICJ Rep 14

Legality of the Threat or Use of Nuclear Weapons, Advisory Opinion, [1996] ICJ Rep 226

Maritime Delimitation and Territorial Questions between Qatar and Bahrain, Merits, Judgment, [2001] ICJ Rep 40

Arrest Warrant of 11 April 2000 (Democratic Republic of the Congo v Belgium), Judgment, [2002] ICJ Rep 3

Legal Consequences of the Construction of a Wall in the Occupied Palestinian Territory, Advisory Opinion, [2004] ICJ Rep 136

Case concerning Certain Questions of Mutual Assistance in Criminal Matters (Djibouti v France), Judgment, [2008] ICJ Rep 177

Armed Activities on the Territory of the Congo (Democratic Republic of the Congo v Rwanda), Jurisdiction and Admissibility, Judgment, [2006] ICJ Rep 6

Jurisdictional Immunities of the State (Germany v Italy: Greece Intervening), Judgment, [2012] ICJ Rep 99

Questions relating to the Obligation to Prosecute or Extradite (Belgium v Senegal), Judgment, [2012] ICJ Rep 422

Nuremberg and Tokyo International Military Tribunals

France et al v Göring et al, Judgment and Sentence of the Nuremberg International Military Tribunals, in *Trial of the Major War Criminals before the International Military Tribunals: Nuremberg, 14 November 1945–1 October 1946*

France et al v Göring et al, Preliminary Hearing (14–15, 17 November 1945), (1948) 2 TMWC 1

France et al v Göring et al, Attorney General Sir Hartley Shawcross's Opening Speech (4 December 1945), (1948) 3 TMWC 91

France et al v Göring et al, Sir Hartley Shawcross Makes Final Speech on behalf of Prosecution (26 July 1946), (1948) 19 TMWC 433

US et al v Araki et al, Judgment, 1 November 1948, in United Nations War Crimes Commission (ed), *Transcripts of Proceedings and Documents of the International Military Tribunals for the Far East (Tokyo Trials)*: Judgment

US et al v Araki et al, Dissenting Opinion of Judge Röling, 12 November 1948

US et al v Araki et al, Indictment (English), in Annex No A-6

UN International Criminal Tribunal for the Former Yugoslavia

Prosecutor v Tadić (Decision on the Defence Motion on Jurisdiction) ICTY-94-1-T (10 August 1995)

Prosecutor v Tadić (Interlocutory Appeal Decision on Jurisdiction) ICTY-94-1-AR72 (2 October 1995)

Prosecutor v Tadić (Interlocutory Appeal Decision on Jurisdiction) ICTY-94-1-AR72 (2 October 1995) (Separate Opinion of Judge Li on the Defence Motion for Interlocutory Appeal on Jurisdiction)

Prosecutor v Tadić (Interlocutory Appeal Decision on Jurisdiction) ICTY-94-1-AR72 (2 October 1995) (Separate Opinion of Judge Abi-Saab on the Defence Motion for Interlocutory Appeal on Jurisdiction)

Prosecutor v Tadić (Opinion and Judgement) ICTY-94-1-T (7 May 1997)

Prosecutor v Tadić (Sentencing Judgement) ICTY-94-1-T (14 July 1997)

Prosecutor v Tadić (Judgement) ICTY-94-1-A (15 July 1999)

Prosecutor v Karadžić (Decision on prosecution's motion appealing trial chamber's decision on JCE III foreseeability) ICTY-95-5/18-AR72.4 (25 June 2009)

Prosecutor v Karadžić (Judgement) ICTY-95-5/18-AR98*BIS*.1 (11 July 2013)

Prosecutor v Karadžić (Judgement) MICT-13-55-A (20 March 2019)

Prosecutor v Simić et al (Judgement) ICTY-95-9-T (17 October 2003)

Prosecutor v Simić et al (Judgement) ICTY-95-9-T (17 October 2003) (Separate and Partly Opinion of Judge Per-Johan Lindholm)

Prosecutor v Simić et al (Judgement) ICTY-95-9-A (28 November 2006)

Prosecutor v Simić et al (Judgement) ICTY-95-9-A (28 November 2006) (Dissenting Opinion of Judge Schomburg)

Prosecutor v Simić et al (Judgement) ICTY-95-9-A (28 November 2006) (Dissenting Opinion of Judge Shahabuddeen)

Prosecutor v Martić (Decision on the Issuance of an International Arrest Warrant) Transcript of Oral Proceedings (8 March 1996)

Prosecutor v Martić (Judgement) ICTY-95-11-T (12 June 2007)

Prosecutor v Martić (Judgement) ICTY-95-11-A (8 October 2008)

TABLE OF CASES   XXXIX

Prosecutor v Blaškić (Decision on the Objection of the Republic of Croatia to the Issue of *subpoena duces tecum*) ICTY-95-14-PT (18 July 1997)

Prosecutor v Blaškić (Decision on the Admissibility of the Request for Review by the Republic of Croatia of an Interlocutory Decision of a Trial Chamber (Issuance of Subpoenae Duces Tecum) and Scheduling Order) ICTY-95-14-AR108BIS (29 July 1997)

Prosecutor v Blaškić (Judgement on the request of the Republic of Croatia for review of the Decision of Trial Chamber II of 18 July 1997) ICTY-95-14-AR108BIS (29 October 1997)

Prosecutor v Blaškić (Judgement) ICTY-95-14-T (3 March 2000)

Prosecutor v Blaškić (Judgement) ICTY-95-14-A (29 July 2004)

Prosecutor v Aleksovski (Judgement) ICTY-95-14/1-T (25 June 1999)

Prosecutor v Kordić & Čerkez (Judgment) ICTY-95-14/2-T (26 February 2001)

Prosecutor v Kordić & Čerkez (Judgment) ICTY-95-14/2-A (17 December 2004)

Prosecutor v Kupreškić et al (Judgement) ICTY-95-16-T (14 January 2000)

Prosecutor v Furundžija (Judgement) ICTY-95-17/1-T (10 December 1998)

Prosecutor v Furundžija (Judgement) ICTY-95-17/1-A (12 July 2000)

Prosecutor v Furundžija (Judgement) ICTY-95-17/1-A (12 July 2000) (Declaration of Judge Patrick Robinson)

Prosecutor v Mucić et al (Judgement) ICTY-96-21-T (16 November 1998)

Prosecutor v Mucić et al (Judgement) ICTY-96-21-A (20 February 2001)

Prosecutor v Kunarać et al (Judgement) ICTY-96-23-T and ICTY-96-23/1-T (22 February 2001)

Prosecutor v Kunarać et al (Judgement) ICTY-96-23 and ICTY-96-23/1-A (12 June 2002)

Prosecutor v Erdemović (Joint Separate Opinion of Judge McDonald and Judge Vohrah) ICTY-96-22-A (7 October 1997)

Prosecutor v Stakić (Judgement) ICTY-97-24-T (31 July 2003)

Prosecutor v Stakić (Judgement) ICTY-97-24-A (22 March 2006)

Prosecutor v Krnojelac (Judgement) ICTY-97-25-T (15 March 2002)

Prosecutor v Krnojelac (Judgement) ICTY-97-25-A (17 September 2003)

Prosecutor v Milošević et al (Decision on Review of Indictment and Application for Consequential Orders) ICTY-99-37-PT (24 May 1999)

Prosecutor v Milošević (Preliminary Protective Motion) ICTY-99-37-PT (9 August 2001)

Prosecutor v Milošević (Decision on Preliminary Motions) ICTY-02-54-PT (8 November 2001)

Prosecutor v Milošević (Decision on Motion for Judgement of Acquittal) ICTY-02-54-T (16 June 2004)

Prosecutor v Galić (Judgement) ICTY-98-29-T (5 December 2003)

Prosecutor v Galić (Judgement) ICTY-98-29-T (5 December 2003) (Separate and Partially Dissenting Opinion of Judge Rafael Nieto-Navia)
Prosecutor v Kvočka et al (Judgement) ICTY-98-30/1-T (2 November 2001)
Prosecutor v Kvočka et al (Judgement) ICTY-98-30/1-A (28 February 2005)
Prosecutor v Vasiljević (Judgement) ICTY-98-32-T (29 November 2002)
Prosecutor v Vasiljević (Judgement) ICTY-98-32-A (25 February 2004)
Prosecutor v Krstić (Judgement) ICTY-98-33-T (2 August 2001)
Prosecutor v Krstić (Judgement) ICTY-98-33-A (1 July 2003)
Prosecutor v Krstić (Judgement) ICTY-98-33-A (1 July 2003) (Dissenting Opinion of Judge Shahabuddeen)
Prosecutor v Naletilić & Martinović (Judgement) ICTY-98-34-T (31 March 2003)
Prosecutor v Brđanin & Talin (Decision on Form of Further Amended Indictment and Prosecution Application to Amend) ICTY-99-36-PT (26 June 2001)
Prosecutor v Brđanin (Judgement) ICTY-99-36-T (1 September 2004)
Prosecutor v Brđanin (Judgement) ICTY-99-36-A (1 April 2007)
Prosecutor v Brđanin (Judgement) ICTY-99-36-A (1 April 2007) (Declaration of Judge Van den Wyngaert)
Prosecutor v Brđanin (Judgement) ICTY-99-36-A (1 April 2007) (Partly dissenting Opinion of Judge Shahabuddeen)
Prosecutor v Brđanin (Judgement) ICTY-99-36-A (1 April 2007) (Separate Opinion of Judge Meron)
Prosecutor v Šainović et al (Decision on *Dragoljub* Ojdanić's Preliminary Motion to Dismiss for Lack of Jurisdiction: Joint Criminal Enterprise) ICTY-99-37-PT (13 February 2003)
Prosecutor v Šainović et al (Appeal Judgment) ICTY-05-87-A (23 January 2014)
Prosecutor v Milutinović et al (Decision on Dragoljub Ojdanić's Motion Challenging Jurisdiction: Joint Criminal Enterprise) ICTY-99-37-AR72 (21 May 2003)
Prosecutor v Milutinović et al (Decision on Dragoljub Ojdanić's Motion Challenging Jurisdiction: Joint Criminal Enterprise) ICTY-99-37-AR72 (21 May 2003) (Separate Opinion of Judge David Hunt on Challenge by Ojdanić to Jurisdiction Joint Criminal Enterprise)
Prosecutor v Milutinović et al (Prosecution's Notice of Filing Amended Joinder Indictment and Motion to Amend the Indictment with Annexes) ICTY-05-87-PT (16 August 2005)
Prosecutor v Milutinović et al (Decision on Dragoljub Ojdanić's Motion Challenging Jurisdiction: Indirect Co-perpetration) ICTY-05-87-PT (22 March 2006)
Prosecutor v Milutinović et al (Decision on Dragoljub Ojdanić's Motion Challenging Jurisdiction: Indirect Co-perpetration) ICTY-05-87-PT (22 March 2006) (Separate Opinion of Judge Iain Bonomy)
Prosecutor v Milutinović et al (Judgement) ICTY-05-87-T (26 February 2009)

TABLE OF CASES

Prosecutor v Krajišnik (Judgement and Sentence) ICTY-00-39-T (27 September 2006)
Prosecutor v Krajišnik (Judgement) ICTY-00-39-A (17 March 2009)
Prosecutor v Strugar et al (Judgement) ICTY-01-42-T (31 January 2005)
Prosecutor v Hadžihasanović et al (Decision on Interlocutory Appeal Challenging Jurisdiction in Relation to Command Responsibility) ICTY-01-47-AR72 (16 July 2003)
Prosecutor v Hadžihasanović et al (Decision on Interlocutory Appeal Challenging Jurisdiction in Relation to Command Responsibility) ICTY-01-47-AR72 (16 July 2003) (Partial Dissenting Opinion of Judge Shahabuddeen)
Prosecutor v Hadžihasanović et al (Decision on Interlocutory Appeal Challenging Jurisdiction in Relation to Command Responsibility) ICTY-01-47-AR72 (16 July 2003) (Separate and Partially Dissenting Opinion of Judge David Hunt)
Prosecutor v Hadžihasanović & Kubura (Judgement) ICTY-01-47-T (15 March 2006)
Prosecutor v Halilović (Judgement) ICTY-01-48-T (16 November 2005)
Prosecutor v Blagojević & Jokić (Judgement) ICTY-02-60-T (17 January 2005)
Prosecutor v Deronjić (Judgement) ICTY-02-61-A (20 July 2005)
Prosecutor v Orić (Judgement) ICTY-03-68-T (30 June 2006)
Prosecutor v Orić (Judgement) ICTY-03-68-A (3 July 2008) (Separate and Partially Dissenting Opinion of Judge Schomburg)
Prosecutor v Limaj et al (Judgement) ICTY-03-66-T (30 November 2005)
Prosecutor v Limaj et al (Judgement) ICTY-03-66-A (27 September 2007)
Prosecutor v Šešelj (Decision on Motion by Vojislav Šešelj Challenging Jurisdiction and Form of Indictment) ICTY-03-67/PT (26 May 2004)
Prosecutor v Šešelj (Decision on the Interlocutory Appeal Concerning Jurisdiction) ICTY-03-67-AR72.1 (31 August 2004)
Prosecutor v Šešelj (Decision on Motion for Reconsideration of the 'Decision on the Interlocutory Appeal Concerning Jurisdiction' Dated 31 August 2004) ICTY-03-67-AR72.1 (15 June 2006)
Prosecutor v Stanišić & Simatović (Judgement) ICYT-03-69-T (30 May 2013
Prosecutor v Stanišić & Simatović (Judgement) ICTY-03-91-A (9 December 2015)
Prosecutor v Babić (Sentencing Judgement) ICYT-03-72-S (29 June 2004)
Prosecutor v Prlić et al (Decision to Dismiss the Preliminary Objections against the Tribunal's Jurisdiction, Trial Chamber) ICTY-04-74-PT (26 September 2005)
Prosecutor v Prlić et al (Decision on Petković's Appeal on Jurisdiction) ICTY-04-74-AR72.3 (23 April 2008)
Prosecutor v Prlić et al (Second Amended Indictment) ICTY-04-74-T (11 June 2008)

Prosecutor v Prlić et al (Judgement) ICTY-04-74-T (29 May 2013)
Prosecutor v Prlić et al (Judgement) ICTY-04-74-A (29 November 2017)
Prosecutor v Perišić (Judgement) ICTY-04-81-T (6 September 2011)
Prosecutor v Boškoski and Tarčulovski (Judgement) ICTY-04-82-T (10 July 2008)
Prosecutor v Delić (Judgement) ICTY-04-83-T (15 September 2008)
Prosecutor v Haradinaj et al (Amended Indictment) ICTY-04-84-PT (25 October 2006)
Prosecutor v Haradinaj et al (Revised Second Amended Indictment) ICTY-04-84-PT (11 Jan 2007)
Prosecutor v Haradinaj et al (Third Amended Indictment) ICTY-04-84-PT (7 September 2007)
Prosecutor v Haradinaj et al (Judgement) ICTY-04-84-T (3 April 2008)
Prosecutor v Haradinaj et al (Retrial Judgement) ICTY-04-84BIS-T (29 November 2012)
Prosecutor v Đorđević (Vlastimir Đorđević's Appeal Brief) ICTY-05-87/1-A (15 August 2011)
Prosecutor v Đorđević (Judgement) ICTY-05-87/1-A (27 January 2014)
Prosecutor v Tolimir (Decision on preliminary motions on the indictment pursuant to Rule 72 of the Rules) ICTY-05-88/2-PT (14 December 2007)
Prosecutor v Tolimir (Judgement) ICTY-05-88/2-T (12 December 2012)
Prosecutor v Tolimir (Judgement) ICTY-05-88/2-A (8 April 2015)
Prosecutor v Popović et al (Decision on Motions Challenging the Indictment pursuant to Rule 72 of the Rules) ICTY-05-88-PT (31 May 2006)
Prosecutor v Popović et al (Judgement and Sentence) ICTY-05-88-T (10 June 2010)
Prosecutor v Popović et al (Judgement) ICTY-05-88-A (30 January 2015)
Prosecutor v Gotovina et al (Decision on Prosecution's Consolidated Motion to Amend the Indictment and Joinder) ICTY-03-73-PT, ICTY-01-45-PT (14 July 2006)
Prosecutor v Gotovina & Markač (Judgement) ICTY-06-90-A (16 November 2012)
Prosecutor v Stanišić & Župljanin (Judgement) ICTY-08-91-T (27 March 2013)
Prosecutor v Stanišić & Župljanin (Judgement) ICTY-08-91-A (30 June 2016)
Prosecutor v Mladić (Judgment) ICTY-09-92-T (22 November 2017)

UN International Criminal Tribunal for Rwanda

The Prosecutor v Kayishema & Ruzindana (Judgment) ICTR-95-1-T (21 May 1999)
The Prosecutor v Bagilishema (Judgement) ICTR-95-1A-T (7 June 2001)
The Prosecutor v Muhimana (Judgement) ICTR-95-1B-T (28 April 2005)

The Prosecutor v Rutaganda (Judgement and Sentence) ICTR-96-3-T (6 December 1999)
The Prosecutor v Akayesu (Judgement) ICTR-96-4-T (2 September 1998)
The Prosecutor v Akayesu (Judgment) ICTR-96-4-A (1 June 2001)
The Prosecutor v Musema (Judgement and Sentence) ICTR-96-13-T (27 January 2000)
The Prosecutor v Semanza (Judgement and Sentence) ICTR-97-20-T (15 May 2003)
Semanza v The Prosecutor (Judgement) ICTR-97-20-A (20 May 2005)
The Prosecutor v Ruggiu (Judgement and Sentence) ICTR-97-32-T (1 June 2000)
The Prosecutor v Munyakazi (Appeals Judgement) ICTR-97-36A-A (28 September 2011)
The Prosecutor v Karemera et al (Decision on the Preliminary Motions by the Defence of Edouard Karamera *et al*, Challenging Jurisdiction in Relation to Joint Criminal Enterprise) ICTR-98-44-T (11 May 2004)
The Prosecutor v Karemera et al (Decision on Defence Motion Challenging the Jurisdiction of the Tribunal – Joint Criminal Enterprise Rules 72 and 73 of the Rules of Procedure and Evidence) ICTR-98-44-R72 (5 August 2005)
The Prosecutor v Karemera et al (Appeal of Decision Denying Preliminary Motion on Joint Criminal Enterprise) ICTR-98-44-AR72.5 (19 August 2005)
Karemera et al v The Prosecutor (Decision on Jurisdictional Appeals: Joint Criminal Enterprise) ICTR-98-44-AR72.5, ICTR-98-44-AR72.6 (12 April 2006)
Karemera et al v The Prosecutor (Decision on Interlocutory Appeal of Edouard Karemera *et al* against Oral Decision of 23 August 2010) ICTR-98-44-AR50 (24 September 2010)
Karemera & Ngirumptse v The Prosecutor (Judgment) ICTR-98-44-A (29 September 2014)
Karemera & Ngirumptse v The Prosecutor (Judgment) ICTR-98-44-A (29 September 2014) (Partially Dissenting Opinion of Judge Tuzmukhamedov)
The Prosecutor v Kajelijeli (Judgment and Sentence) ICTR-98-44A-T (1 December 2003)
Kajelijeli v The Prosecutor (Judgment) ICTR-98-44A-A (23 May 2005)
Rwamakuba v The Prosecutor (Decision on Interlocutory Appeal on Joint Criminal Enterprise to the Crimes of Genocide) ICTR-98-44-AR72.4 (22 October 2004)
Nahimana et al v The Prosecutor (Judgement) ICTR-99-52-A (28 November 2007)
Nahimana et al v The Prosecutor (Judgement) ICTR-99-52-A (28 November 2007) (partly dissenting opinion of Judge Shahabuddeen)
The Prosecutor v Ntagerura et al (Judgement and Sentence) ICTR-99-46-T (25 February 2004)

The Prosecutor v Kamuhanda (Judgement) ICTR-99-54A-T (22 January 2004)
Mugenzi & Mugiraneza v The Prosecutor (Judgement) ICTR-99-50-A (4 February 2013)
The Prosecutor v Muvunyi (Judgement and Sentence) ICTR-00-55A-T (12 September 2006)
Nizeyimana v The Prosecutor (Judgement) ICTR-00-55C-A (29 September 2014)
The Prosecutor v Gacumbitsi (Judgement) ICTR-01-64-T (17 June 2004)
Gacumbitsi v The Prosecutor (Judgement) ICTR-01-64-A (7 July 2006)
Gacumbitsi v The Prosecutor (Judgement) ICTR-01-64-A (7 July 2006) (Separate Opinion of Judge Shahabuddeen)
Gacumbitsi v The Prosecutor (Judgement) ICTR-01-64-A (7 July 2006) (Separate Opinion of Judge Schomburg on the Criminal Responsibility of the Appellant for Committing Genocide)
Gacumbitsi v The Prosecutor (Judgement) ICTR-01-64-A (7 July 2006) (Partially Dissenting Opinion of Judge Güney)
The Prosecutor v Seromba (Judgement) ICTR-01-66-T (13 December 2006)
The Prosecutor v Seromba (Judgement) ICTR-01-66-A (12 March 2008)
The Prosecutor v Seromba (Judgement) ICTR-01-66-A (12 March 2008) (Dissenting Opinion of Judge Liu)
Rukundo v The Prosecutor (Judgement) ICTR-2001-70-A (20 October 2010)
The Prosecutor v Uwinkindi (Decision on Defence Appeal against the Decision Denying Motion Alleging Defects in the Indictment) ICTR-01-75-AR72 (C) (16 November 2011)
Kalimanzira v The Prosecutor (Judgement) ICTR-05-88-A (20 October 2010)
Ngirabatware v The Prosecutor (Judgement) MICT-12-29-A (18 December 2014)

International Criminal Court

ICC (Report of the Registry on information received regarding Omar Al Bashir's travels to States Parties and Non-States Parties from 5 October 2016 to 6 April 2017 and other efforts conducted by the Registry regarding purported visits, Registry) ICC-02/05-01/09-296 (11 April 2017)
ICC, 'Twenty-Eighty Report of the Prosecutor of the International Criminal Court to the UN Security Council Pursuant to UNSCR 1593 (2005)' (14 December 2018)
ICC, 'Twenty-Ninth Report of the Prosecutor of the International Criminal Court to the UN Security Council Pursuant to UNSCR 1593 (2005)' (19 June 2019)

ICC, 'Thirty-Second Report of the Prosecutor of the International Criminal Court to the UN Security Council Pursuant to UNSCR 1593 (2005)' (10 December 2020)

Bangladesh/Myanmar Situation
ICC (Decision on the "Prosecution's Request for a Ruling on Jurisdiction on Article 19(3) of Statute", PTC I) ICC-ROC46(3)-01/18-37 (6 September 2018)

DRC Situation
Lubanga case
The Prosecutor v Lubanga (Judgment on the Prosecutor's Application for Extraordinary Review of the Pre-Trial Chamber I's 31 March 2006 Decision Denying Leave to Appeal, A Ch) ICC-01/04-168 (13 July 2006)

The Prosecutor v Lubanga (Decision on the Practices of Witness Familiarisation and Witness Proofing, PTC I) ICC-01/04-01/06-679 (8 November 2006)

The Prosecutor v Lubanga (Judgment on the Appeal of Mr. Thomas Lubanga Dyilo against the Decision on the Defence Challenge to the Jurisdiction of the Court pursuant to article 19(2)(a) of the Statute of 3 October 2006, A Ch) ICC-01/04-01/06-772 (21 December 2006)

The Prosecutor v Lubanga (Decision on the Confirmation of Charges, PTC I) ICC-01/04-01/06-803-tEN (29 January 2007)

The Prosecutor v Lubanga (Judgment pursuant to Article 74 of the Statute, TC I) ICC-01/04-01/06-2842 (14 March 2012)

The Prosecutor v Lubanga (Dissenting Opinion of Judge Odio Benito) ICC-01/04-01/06-2842 (14 March 2012)

The Prosecutor v Lubanga (Separate opinion of Judge Fulford) ICC-01/04-01/06-2842 (14 March 2012)

The Prosecutor v Lubanga (Judgment on the Appeal of Thomas Lubanga Dyilo against his Conviction, A Ch) ICC-01/04-01/06-3121-Red (1 December 2014)

Ntaganda case
The Prosecutor v Ntaganda (Decision Pursuant to Article 61(7)(a) and (b) of the Rome Statute on the Charges of the Prosecutor against Bosco Ntaganda, PTC II) ICC-01/04-02/06-309 (9 June 2014)

The Prosecutor v Ntaganda (Judgment on the appeal of Mr Ntaganda against the 'Second decision on the Defence's challenge to the jurisdiction of the Court in respect of Counts 6 and 9', A Ch) ICC-01/04-02/06-1962 (15 June 2017)

The Prosecutor v Ntaganda (Judgment, TC VI) ICC-01/04-02/06-2359 (08 July 2019)

Katanga & Ngudjolo case

The Prosecutor v Katanga & Ngudjolo (Defence Written Observations Addressing Matters that Were Discussed at the Confirmation Hearing, Defence) ICC-01/04-01/07-698 (28 July 2008)

The Prosecutor v Katanga & Ngudjolo (Decision on the confirmation of charges, PTC I) ICC-01/04-01/07-717 (30 September 2008)

The Prosecutor v Katanga & Ngudjolo (Defence for Germain Katanga's Pre-Trial Brief on the Interpretation of Article 25(3)(a) of the Rome Statute, Defence) ICC-01/04-01/07-1578-Corr (30 October 2009)

The Prosecutor v Katanga (Judgment pursuant to article 74 of the Statute, TC II) ICC-01/04-01/07-3436-tENG (27 March 2014)

The Prosecutor v Katanga (Judgment pursuant to article 74 of the Statute–Minority Opinion of Judge Christine Van den Wyngaert, TC II) ICC-01/04-01/07-3436-AnxI (7 March 2014)

The Prosecutor v Ngudjolo (Judgment pursuant to article 74 of the Statute, TC II) ICC-01/04-02/12-3-tENG (18 December 2012)

The Prosecutor v Ngudjolo (Judgment pursuant to Article 74 of the Statute–Concurring Opinion of Judge Christine Van den Wyngaert) ICC-01/04-02/12-4 (18 December 2012)

Mbarushimana case

The Prosecutor v Mbarushimana (Decision on the confirmation of charges, PTC I) ICC-01/04-01/10-465-Red (16 December 2011)

The Prosecutor v Mbarushimana (Judgment on the appeal of the Prosecutor against the decision of Pre-Trial Chamber I of 16 December 2011 entitled Decision on the confirmation of charges, A Ch) ICC-01/04-01/10-514 (30 May 2012)

Uganda Situation

Ongwen case

The Prosecutor v Ongwen (Decision on the confirmation of charges, PTC II) ICC-02/04-01/15-422-Red (23 March 2016)

The Prosecutor v Ongwen (Decision on Defence Motions Alleging Defects in the Confirmation Decision, TC IX) ICC-02/04-01/15-1476 (7 March 2019)

CAR Situation

Bemba case

The Prosecutor v Bemba (Decision Pursuant to Article 61(7)(a) and (b) of the Rome Statute on the Charges, PTC II) ICC-01/05-01/08-424 (15 June 2009)

The Prosecutor v Bemba (Judgment pursuant to Article 74 of the Statute, TC III) ICC-01/05-01/08-3343 (21 March 2016)

The Prosecutor v Bemba (Judgment pursuant to Article 74 of the Statute, TC III) (Separate Opinion of Judge Kuniko Ozaki) ICC-01/05-01/08-3343-AnxII (21 March 2016)

The Prosecutor v Bemba (Judgment on the appeal of Mr Jean-Pierre Bemba Gombo against Trial Chamber III's "Judgment pursuant to Article 74 of the Statute") (Separate opinion of Judge Christine Van den Wyngaert and Judge Howard Morrison) ICC-01/05-01/08-3636-Anx2 (8 June 2018)

Darfur, Sudan Situation
Harun & Kushayb case

The Prosecutor v Ahmad Harun & Ali Kushayb (Decision on the Prosecution Application under Article 58(7) of the Statute (2), PTC I) ICC-02/05-01/07-1-Corr (29 April 2007)

Al Bashir case

The Prosecutor v Al Bashir (Public Redacted Version of the Prosecution's Application under Article 58, Office of the Prosecutor) ICC-02/05-157-AnxA (12 September 2008)

The Prosecutor v Al Bashir (Warrant of Arrest for Omar Hassan Ahmad Al Bashir, PTC I) ICC-02/05-01/09-1 (4 March 2009)

The Prosecutor v Al Bashir (Decision on the Prosecution's Application for a Warrant of Arrest against Omar Hassan Ahmad Al Bashir, PTC I) ICC-02/05-01/09-3 (4 March 2009)

The Prosecutor v Al Bashir (Corrigendum to the Decision Pursuant to Article 87(7) of the Rome Statute on the Failure by the Republic of Malawi to Comply with the Cooperation Requests Issued by the Court with Respect to the Arrest and Surrender of Omar Hassan Ahmad Al Bashir, PTC I) ICC-02/05-01/09-139-Corr (13 December 2011)

The Prosecutor v Al Bashir (Decision Pursuant to Article 87 (7) of the Rome Statute on the Refusal of the Republic of Chad to Comply with the Cooperation Requests Issued by the Court with Respect to the Arrest and Surrender of Omar Hassan Ahmad Al Bashir, PTC I) ICC-02/05-01/09-140-tENG (13 December 2011)

The Prosecutor v Al Bashir (Decision on the Non-compliance of the Republic of Chad with the Cooperation Requests Issued by the Court Regarding the Arrest and Surrender of Omar Hassan Ahmad Al-Bashir, PTC II) ICC-02/05-01/09-151 (26 March 2013)

The Prosecutor v Al Bashir (Decision on the Cooperation of the Democratic Republic of the Congo Regarding Omar Al Bashir's Arrest and Surrender to the Court, PTC II) ICC-02/05-01/09-195 (9 April 2014)

The Prosecutor v Al Bashir (Decision under article 87(7) of the Rome Statute on the non-compliance by South Africa with the request by the Court for the arrest and surrender of Omar Al-Bashir, PTC II) ICC-02/05-01/09-302 (6 July 2017)

The Prosecutor v Al Bashir (Decision under article 87(7) of the Rome Statute on the non-compliance by South Africa with the request by the Court for the arrest and surrender of Omar Al-Bashir, PTC II) ICC-02/05-01/09-302-Anx (6 July 2017) (Minority Opinion of Judge Marc Perrin De Brichambaut)

The Prosecutor v Al Bashir (Decision under article 87(7) of the Rome Statute on the non-compliance by Jordan with the request by the Court for the arrest and surrender of Omar Al-Bashir, PTC II) ICC-02/05-01/09-309 (11 December 2017)

The Prosecutor v Al Bashir (Decision under article 87(7) of the Rome Statute on the non-compliance by Jordan with the request by the Court for the arrest and surrender of Omar Al-Bashir– Minority Opinion of Judge Marc Perrin De Brichambaut, PTC II) ICC-02/05-01/09-309-9-Anx-tENG (11 December 2017)

The Prosecutor v Al Bashir (The Hashemite Kingdom of Jordan's appeal against the "Decision under article 87(7) of the Rome Statute on the non-compliance by Jordan with the request by the Court for the arrest and surrender [of] Omar Al-Bashir") ICC-02/05-01/09-326 (12 March 2018)

The Prosecutor v Al Bashir (Order inviting expressions of interest as *amici curiae* in judicial proceedings (pursuant to Rule 103 of the Rules of Procedure and Evidence), AC) ICC-02/05-01/09-330 (29 March 2018)

The Prosecutor v Al Bashir (Request by Professors Robinson, Cryer, deGuzman, Lafontaine, Oosterveld, Stahn and Vasiliev for Leave to Submit Observations) ICC-02/05-01/09-337 (26 April 2018)

The Prosecutor v Al Bashir (Request by Max du Plessis, Sarah Nouwen and Elizabeth Wilmshurst for leave to submit observations on the legal questions presented in 'The Hashemite Kingdom of Jordan's appeal against the "Decision under article 87(7) of the Rome Statute on the non-compliance by Jordan with the request by the Court for the arrest and surrender [of] Omar Al-Bashir"') ICC-02/05-01/09-338 (27 April 2018)

The Prosecutor v Al Bashir (Request by Professor Paola Gaeta for leave to submit observations on the merits of the legal questions presented in the Hashemite Kingdom of Jordan's appeal against the "Decision under Article 87 (7) of the Rome Statute on the non-compliance by Jordan with the request by the Court for the arrest and surrender [of] Omar Al-Bashir" of 12 March 2018) ICC-02/05-01/09-349 (30 April 2018)

The Prosecutor v Al Bashir (Request by Prof. Flavia Lattanzi for leave to submit observations on the merits of the legal questions presented in "The Hashemite Kingdom of Jordan's appeal against the 'Decision under article 87(7) of the Rome Statute on the non-compliance by Jordan with the request by the Court for the arrest and surrender" [of] Omar Al-Bashir) ICC-02/05-01/09-341 (30 April 2018)

The Prosecutor v Al Bashir (Request by Professor Claus Kreß with the assistance of Erin Pobjie for leave to submit observations on the merits of the legal questions presented in 'The Hashemite Kingdom of Jordan's appeal against the "Decision under article 87(7) of the Rome Statute"') ICC-02/05-01/09-346 (30 April 2018)

The Prosecutor v Al Bashir (The League of Arab States' Observations on the Hashemite Kingdom of Jordan's appeal against the "Decision under article 87(7) of the Rome Statute on the non-compliance by Jordan with the request by the Court for the arrest and surrender [of] Omar Al-Bashir") ICC-02/05-01/09-367 (16 July 2018)

The Prosecutor v Al Bashir (The African Union's Submission in the "Hashemite Kingdom of Jordan's Appeal against the 'Decision under Article 87(7) of the Rome Statute on the Non-Compliance by Jordan with the Request by the Court for the Arrest and Surrender [of] Omar Al-Bashir"') ICC-02/05-01/09-370 (16 July 2018)

The Prosecutor v Al Bashir (Transcript, A Ch) ICC-02/05-01/09-T-4-ENG, ICC-02/05-01/09-T-5-ENG, ICC-02/05-01/09-T-6-ENG (10-12 September 2018)

The Prosecutor v Al Bashir (Final Submissions of the Prosecution following the Appeal Hearing, A Ch) ICC-02/05-01/ 09-392 (28 September 2018)

The Prosecutor v Al Bashir (Judgment in the Jordan Referral re Al-Bashir Appeal, A Ch) ICC-02/05-01/09-397-Corr (6 May 2019)

The Prosecutor v Al Bashir (Judgment in the Jordan Referral re Al-Bashir Appeal, A Ch) ICC-02/05-01/09-397-Anx1-Corr (17 May 2019) (Joint Concurring Opinion of Judges Eboe-Osuji, Morrison, Hofmański and Bossa)

Abu Garda case

The Prosecutor v Abu Garda (Decision on the Confirmation of Charges, PTC I) ICC-02/05-02/09-243-Red (8 February 2010)

Kenya Situation

Situation in the Republic of Kenya (Decision Pursuant to Article 15 of the Rome Statute on the Authorization of an Investigation into the Situation in the Republic of Kenya, PTC II) ICC-01/09-19-Corr (31 March 2010)

Situation in the Republic of Kenya (Dissenting Opinion by Judge Hans-Peter Kaul to Pre-Trial Chamber II's "Decision Pursuant to Article 15 of the Rome Statute on the Authorization of an Investigation into the Situation in the Republic of Kenya")

Ruto, Kosgey and Sang (Ruto et al) case

The Prosecutor v Ruto et al (Dissenting Opinion by Judge Hans-Peter Kaul to Pre-Trial Chamber II's "Decision on the Prosecutor's Application for Summons to Appear for William Samoei Ruto, Henry Kiprono Kosgey and Joshua Arap Sang") ICC-01/09-01/11-2 (15 March 2011)

The Prosecutor v Ruto et al (Decision on the Confirmation of Charges Pursuant to Article 61(7)(a) and (b) of the Rome Statute, PTC II) ICC-01/09-01/11-373 (23 January 2012)

The Prosecutor v Ruto et al (Decision on the Confirmation of Charges Pursuant to Article 61(7)(a) and (b) of the Rome Statute, PTC II) ICC-01/09-01/11-373 (23 January 2012) (Dissenting Opinion by Judge Hans-Peter Kaul)

The Prosecutor v Ruto & Sang (Prosecution's Submissions on the law of indirect co-perpetration under Article 25(3)(a) of the Statute and application for notice to be given under Regulation 55(2) with respect to William Samoei Ruto's individual criminal responsibility, OTP) ICC-01/09-01/11-433 (3 July 2012)

The Prosecutor v Ruto & Sang (Decision on Defence Applications for Judgments of Acquittal, Trial Chamber V(A)) ICC-01/09-01/11-2027-Red-Corr (5 April 2016)

The Prosecutor v Ruto & Sang (Decision on Defence Applications for Judgments of Acquittal, Trial Chamber V(A)) ICC-01/09-01/11-2027-Red-Corr (5 April 2016) (Reasons of Judge Eboe-Osuji)

Muthaura, Kenyatta and Ali (Muthaura et al) case

The Prosecutor v Muthaura et al (Dissenting Opinion by Judge Hans-Peter Kaul to Pre-Trial Chamber II's "Decision on the Prosecutor's Application for Summonses to Appear for Francis Kirimi Muthaura, Uhuru Muigai Kenyatta and Mohammed Hussein Ali") ICC-01/09-02/11-3 (15 March 2011)

The Prosecutor v Muthaura et al (Decision on the Confirmation of Charges Pursuant to Article 61(7)(a) and (b) of the Rome Statute, PTC II) ICC-01/09-02/11-382-Red (23 January 2012)

The Prosecutor v Muthaura et al (Decision on the Confirmation of Charges Pursuant to Article 61(7)(a) and (b) of the Rome Statute–Dissenting Opinion by Judge Hans-Peter Kaul, PTC II) ICC-01/09-02/11-382-Red (26 January 2012)

The Prosecutor v Muthaura & Kenyatta (Prosecutions Submissions on the Law of Indirect co-perpetration under Article 25(3)(a) of the Statute and Application for Notice to be Given under Regulation 55 (2) with respect to the Individual's Individual Criminal Responsibility, OTP) ICC-01/09-01/11-433 (3 July 2012)

The Prosecutor v Kenyatta (Transcript, TC V) ICC-01/09-02/11-T-22-ENG (14 February 2013)

The Prosecutor v Kenyatta (Decision on Defence Request for Conditional Excusal from Continuous Presence at Trial, TC V(b)) ICC-01/09-02/11-830 (18 October 2013)

Libya Situation
Abuminyar Gaddafi, Saif Al-Islam Gaddafi and Abdullah Al-Senussi (Gaddafi et al) case

The Prosecutor v Gaddafi et al (Decision on the "Prosecutor's Application Pursuant to Article 58 as to Muammar Mohammed Abuminyar Gaddafi, Saif Al-Islam Gaddafi, and Abdullah Al Senussi", PTC I) ICC-01/11-01/11-1 (30 June 2011)

Côte d'Ivoire Situation
Situation in the Republic of Côte d'Ivoire (Decision Pursuant to Article 15 of the Rome Statute on the Authorisation of an Investigation into the Situation in the Republic of Côte d'Ivoire, PTC III) ICC-02/11-140-Corr (15 November 2011)

Gbagbo & Blé Goudé case
The Prosecutor v Gbagbo (Decision adjourning the hearing on the confirmation of charges pursuant to Article 61(7)(c)(i) of the Rome Statute, PTC I) ICC-02/11-01/11-432 (3 June 2013)

The Prosecutor v Gbagbo (Judgment on the appeal of the Prosecutor against the decision of Pre-Trial Chamber I of 3 June 2013 entitled "Decision adjourning the hearing on the confirmation of charges pursuant to article 61(7)(c)(i) of the Rome Statute", A Ch) ICC-02/11-01/11-572 (16 December 2013)

The Prosecutor v Gbagbo (Decision on the confirmation of charges against Laurent Gbagbo, PTC I) ICC-02/11-01/11-656-Red (12 June 2014)

The Prosecutor v Blé Goudé (Decision on the confirmation of charges against Charles Blé Goudé, PTC I) ICC-02/11-02/11-186 (11 December 2014)

The Prosecutor v Gbagbo & Blé Goudé (Public Redacted Version of Reasons of Judge Geoffrey Henderson, TC I) ICC-02/11-02/15-1263-AnXB-Red (16 July 2019)

Egypt Situation
Situation in the Arab Republic of Egypt (Decision on the 'Declaration under Article 12(3) and Complaint regarding International Crimes Committed in Egypt', OTP) OTP-CR-460/13 (23 April 2014)

Mali Situation
Al Mahdi case
The Prosecutor v Al Mahdi (Public Redacted Decision on the confirmation of charges against Ahmad Al Faqi Al Mahdi, PTC I) ICC-01/12-01/15-84-Red (24 March 2016)

Special Court for Sierra Leone

Prosecutor v Norman (Decision on Preliminary Motion Based on Lack of Jurisdiction (Child Recruitment), A Ch) SCSL-2004-14-AR72 (E) (31 May 2004)
Prosecutor v Brima et al (Judgment) SCSL-04-16-T (20 June 2007)
Prosecutor v Fofana & Kondewa (Judgment) SCSL-2004-14-T (2 August 2007)
Prosecutor v Fofana & Kondewa (Judgment) SCSL-2004-14-A (28 May 2008)
Prosecutor v Sesay et al (Judgment) SCSL-04-15-T (2 March 2009)
Prosecutor v Sesay et al (Judgment) SCSL-04-15-A (26 October 2009)
Prosecutor v Charles Taylor (Decision on Immunity from Jurisdiction, A Ch) SCSL-2003-L-AR72 (E) (31 May 2004)

Extraordinary Chambers in the Courts of Cambodia

Co-Prosecutors v Ieng Sary (Decision on Appeals by Nuon Chea and Ieng Thirith against the Closing Order) 002/19-09-2007-ECCC/OCIJ (PTC 145 &146) (15 February 2011)
KAING Guek Eav alias Duch (Trial Chamber Judgment) 001/18-07-2007/ECCC/TC (26 July 2010)

European Court of Human Rights

Al-Adsani v UK (Judgment) ECtHR Application No. 35763/97 (21 November 2001)
Kolk and Kislyiy v Estonia (Decision, Fourth Section Court) ECtHR Application No. 23052/04 (17 January 2006)

Kononov v Latvia (Judgment, Merits and Just Satisfaction, Third Section) ECtHR Application No. 36376/04 (24 July 2008)

Korbely v Hungary (Merits and Just Satisfaction, Grand Chamber) ECtHR Application No. 9174/02 (19 September 2008)

Streletz, Kessler and Krenz v Germany (Merits) ECtHR Application No. 34044/96, 35532/97 and 44801/98 (22 March 2001)

Van Anraat v the Netherlands (Decision on admissibility, Third Section) ECtHR Application No. 65389/09 (6 July 2010)

Vasiliauskas v Lithuania (Judgment, Grand Chamber) ECtHR Application No. 35343/05 (10 October 2015)

National Courts and Tribunals

Argentina

Jorge Rafaél Videla case (Motion submitted by the defence of Jorge Rafaél Videla, Incident of *res judicata* and lack of jurisdiction, Supreme Court, Argentina) Record v.34.XXXVI (21 August 2003)

René Jesús Derecho case (Decision about incidental proceeding on the extinguishment of a criminal complaint, Supreme Court, Argentina) Case No. 24079 (11 July 2007)

René Jesús Derecho case (Judgment, Argentina) Case No. 24079 (29 November 2011)

Victorio Derganz and Carlos Jose Fateche case (Juan Demetrio Luna, accused) (Judgment, Supreme Court, Argentina) Case No. 2203

Australia

AXOIB v Australia (Minister for Immigration and Multicultural and Indigenous Affairs) [2002] AATA 365 (17 May 2002)

Polyukhovich v The Commonwealth of Australia and Another (Order, High Court) [1991] HCA 32 (14 August 1991)

SAH v Australia (Minister for Immigration and Multicultural and Indigenous Affairs) [2002] AATA 263 (18 April 2002)

SAL v Australia (Minister for Immigration and Multicultural and Indigenous Affairs) [2002] AATA 1164 (2 November 2002)

SHCB v Australia (Minister for Immigration and Multicultural and Indigenous Affairs) [2003] FCAFC 308 (22 December 2003)

SRNN v Australia (Minister for Immigration and Multicultural and Indigenous Affairs) [2000] AATA 983 (10 November 2000)

SRYYY v Australia (Minister for Immigration and Multicultural and Indigenous Affairs) [2005] FCAFC 42 (25 March 2005)
SZCWP v Australia (Minister for Immigration and Multicultural and Indigenous Affairs) [2006] FCAFC 9 (20 February 2006)
VAG v Australia (Minister for Immigration and Multicultural and Indigenous Affairs) [2002] AATA 1332 (23 December 2002)
WBR v Australia (Minister for Immigration and Multicultural Affairs) [2006] AATA 754 (5 September 2006)

Bangladesh: International Crimes Tribunal
Chief Prosecutor v Salauddin Quader Chowdhury (Judgment, International Crimes Tribunal-1) ICT-BD 02 of 2011 (1 October 2013)
Chief Prosecutor v Delowar Hossain Sayeedi (Judgment, International Crimes Tribunal-1) ICT-BD 01 of 2011 (28 February 2013)

Belgium
H.A.S. et al v Ariel Sharon, Amos Yaron et al (Decision Related to the Indictment of Ariel Sharon, Amos Yaron and others, Court of Cassation, Belgium) Case No. P.02.1139.F/1 (12 February 2003), (2003) 42 ILM 596
José J. Basulto et al v Fidel Castro Ruz et al (Court of Cassation, Belgium) (29 July 2003)

Bosnia and Herzegovina
Prosecutor's Office v Anić (Preliminary Hearing Decision, Court of Bosnia and Herzegovina) S11 K 005596 11 Kro (31 May 2011)
Prosecutor's Office v Bundalo et al (Second Instance Verdict, Court of Bosnia and Herzegovina) X-KRŽ-07/419 (28 Jan 2011)
Prosecutor's v Rašević and Todović (First Instance Verdict, Court of Bosnia and Herzegovina) (28 February 2008)

Canada
Bukumba v Canada (Minister of Citizenship and Immigration), [2004] FC 93
Ezokola v Canada (Minister of Citizenship and Immigration), [2013] 2 SCR 678
R v Finta (Judgment, Supreme Court), [1994] 1 SCR 70
Moreno v Canada (Minister of Employment and Immigration), [1994] 1 FC 298
Mugesera v Canada (Minister of Citizenship and Immigration), [2003] FCA 325
Mugesera v Canada (Minister of Citizenship and Immigration), [2005] 2 SCR 100
Peters v Canada (Minister of Citizenship and Immigration) (Record of an Admissibility Hearing under the Immigration and Refugee Protection Act, Immigration and Refugee Protection Board) 0003-B2-02557 (29 January 2013)

R v Munyaneza (Judgment, Supreme Court of Quebec, Canada) 2009 ACCS 2201 (22 May 2009)
Naredo and Arduengo v Canada (Minister of Employment and Immigration), (1990) 37 FTR 161
Ramirez v Canada (Minister of Employment and Immigration), [1992] 2 FC 306
Rudolph v Canada (Minister of Employment and Immigration), [1992] 2 FC 653
Sapkota v Canada (Minister of Citizenship and Immigration), [2013] FC 790
Sivakumar v Canada (Minister of Citizenship and Immigration), [1994] 1 FC 433

China
China v Takashi Sakai (1949) 14 LRTWC 1

Democratic Republic of the Congo
Garrison Military Auditor, Public Prosecutor's Office and civil parties v Kyungu Mutanga (Judgment, Military Garrison Court of Haut-Katanga, DRC) (5 March 2009)
Garrison Military Auditor, Public Prosecutor's Office and civil parties v Barnaba Yonga Tshopena (Judgment, Military Garrison Court of Ituri-Bunia, DRC) RP No 071/09, 009/010 and 074/010, RMP No 885/EAM/08, RMP No 1141/LZA/010, RMP No 1219/LZA/010 and RMP No 1238/LZA/010 (9 July 2010)

East Timor: Special Panels for Serious Crimes
Prosecutor v Jose Cardoso (Judgment, District Court of Dili) SPSC-4C/2001 (5 April 2003)
Prosecutor v de Carvalho (Judgment, District Court of Dili) SPSC-10/2001 (18 March 2004)
Prosecutor v João Sarmento (Judgment, District Court of Dili) SPSC-18A/2001 (12 August 2003)
Prosecutor v Anastacio Martins and Domingos Gonçalves (Judgment, District Court of Dili) SPSC-11/2001 (13 November 2003)
Prosecutor v Domingos Mendonca (Judgment and Dissenting Opinion, District Court of Dili) SPSC-18B/2001 (12 October 2003)
Prosecutor v Salvador Soares (Judgment, District Court of Dili) SPSC-7A/2002 (9 December 2003) [*Salvador Soares* Judgment]
Prosecutor v Agostinho Cloe et al (Judgment, District Court of Dili) SPSC-4/2003 (16 November 2004)
Prosecutor v Anton Lelan Sufa (Judgment, District Court of Dili) SPSC-4A/2003 (25 November 2004)
Prosecutor v Lino Beno (Judgment, District Court of Dili) SPSC-4B/2003 (16 November 2004)

Prosecutor v Domingos Metan (Judgment, District Court of Dili) SPSC-4C/2003(16 November 2004)

Prosecutor v Lino Beno (Judgment, District Court of Dili) SPSC-4B/2003 (16 November 2004)

Prosecutor v Alarico Mesquita et al (Judgment, District Court of Dili) SPSC-10/2003 (6 December 2004)

Prosecutor v Marcelino Soares (Judgment, District Court of Dili) SPSC-11/2003 (11 December 2003)

Prosecutor v Sisto Barros and Cesar Mendonca (Judgment, District Court of Dili) SPSC-1/2004 (12 May 2005)

Prosecutor v Domingos de Deus (Judgment, District Court of Dili) SPSC-2A/2004 (12 April 2005)

France

Advocate General v Gaddafi (Appeal Judgment, Court of Cassation, France) 00-87215 (13 March 2001), ILDC 774 (FR 2001)

Advocate General v Klaus Barbie (Judgement, Court of Cassation, France) 86-92714 (25 November 1986)

Advocate General v Klaus Barbie (Judgement, Court of Cassation, France) 85-95166 (20 December 1985), (1985) 78 ILR 124

Advocate General v Touvier (Judgment, Court of Cassation, France), (1995) 100 ILR 337

French v Roechling et al, in Trials of the War Criminals before the Nuremberg Military Tribunals Under Control Council Law No. 10 [TWC] (USGPO 1953)

Germany

Chechen Refugee case (Judgment, Federal Supreme Administrative Court, Germany) 10.C.7.09 (16 February 2010)

Prosecutor v Abdelkarim El. B. (Judgment, Higher Regional Court, Frankfurt am Main, Germany) 3 StE 4/16 (8 November 2016)

Prosecutor v Klein and *Wilhem* (Termination of proceedings pursuant to Penal Procedure Code, Federal Public Prosecutor General, Germany) 3 BJs 6/10-4 (16 April 2010)

Prosecutor v Aria Ladjedvardi (Decision, Federal Supreme Court, Germany) 3 StR 57/17 (27 July 2017)

Prosecutor v Ignace Murwanashyaka and *Straton Musoni* (Decision, Federal Supreme Court, Germany) AK/13 (17 June 2010)

Prosecutor v Ignace Murwanashyaka and *Straton Musoni* (Judgment, Higher Regional Court, Stuttgart, Germany) 3 StE 6/10 (28 September 2015)

Iraq (The Iraqi High Tribunal)

The Public Prosecutor in the High Iraqi Court et al v Saddam Hussein Al Majeed et al (Opinion, Appeals Commission, IHT) 29/c/2006 (26 December 2006)

The Public Prosecutor in the High Iraqi Court et al v Saddam Hussein Al Majeed et al (Verdict, Second Criminal Court, IHT)1/(C) Second/2006 (24 June 2007)

Israel

Attorney General v Eichmann (Judgment, District Court of Jerusalem, Israel) (11 November 1961), (1968) 36 ILR 5

Attorney General v Eichmann (Appeal Judgment, Supreme Court, Israel) (29 May 1962), (1968) 36 ILR 277

Poland

Poland v Goeth (1948) 7 LRTWC 1
Poland v Hoess Commandant of the Auschwitz Camp (1948) 7 LRTWC 11
Poland v Artur Greiser (1949) 13 LRTWC 70

Spain

Augusto Pinochet case (Order, Central Criminal Court, Spain) No 1998/22605 (5 November 1998) and No 1999/28720 (24 September 1999)

The Foundation for Human Rights v Fidel Castro (Order, Central Criminal Court, Spain) No 1999/2723 (4 March 1999)

Sweden

Public Prosecutor v Mouhannad Droubi (Judgment, Svea Court of Appeal, Sweden) B 4770-16 (5 August 2016)

Public Prosecutor v Haisam Omar Sakhanh (Judgment, District Court of Stockholm, Sweden) B 378716 (16 February 2017)

South Africa

The Southern Africa Litigation Centre v The Minister of Justice and Constitutional Development (27740/2015) [2015] ZAGPPHC 402

The Minister of Justice and Constitutional Development v The Southern African Litigation Centre (867/15) [2016] ZASCA 17

The Netherlands

Public Prosecutor v Kouwenhoven (Judgment, District Court of The Hague, the Netherlands) LJN: AX7098 (7 June 2006)

Public Prosecutor v Menten (Judgment, Supreme Court, the Netherlands), (1981) 75 ILR 331

Public Prosecutor v Ramalingam/Liberation Tigers of Tamil Eelam (LTTE) (Judgment, District Court of The Hague, the Netherlands) LJN: BU9716, 09/748802-09 (21 October 2011)

Public Prosecutor v Van Anraat (Judgment, District Court of The Hague, the Netherlands) LJN: AX6406 (23 December 2005)

Public Prosecutor v Van Anraat (Judgment, Court of Appeal of The Hague, the Netherlands) LJN: BA6734 (9 May 2007)

Public Prosecutor v Van Anraat (Judgment, Supreme Court, the Netherlands) LJN: BG4822 (30 June 2009)

United Kingdom

UK v Erich Heyer and Six Others (1945) 1 UNWCC 88

UK v Otto Sandrock and Three Others (1947) 1 LRTWC 35

UK v Josef Kramer et al (1947) 2 LRTWC 1

UK v Bruno Tesch et al (1947) 1 LRTWC 93

R v Bow Street Metropolitan Stipendiary Magistrate, Ex Parte Pinochet Ugarte (Opinions of the Lords of Appeal for Judgement in the Cause) (25 November 1998) [1998] 3 WLR 1456, [1998] UKHL 41

R v Bartle, Evans and Another and the Commissioner of Police for the Metropolis and Other, Ex Parte Pinochet (Judgment) (24 March 1999) [2000] 1 AC 147, [1999] UKHL 17, (1999) 38 *ILM* 581

R v Chan Wing-siu (21 June 1984) [1985] 1 AC 168, [1984] UKPC 27

Jogee and Ruddock v R (Jamaica) (Judgment) (18 February 2016) [2016] UKSC 8, [2016] UKPC 7

R v Jones et al (29 March 2006) [2006] UKHL 16

Jones v Ministry of Interior for the Kingdom of Saudi Arabia et al (Opinions of the Lords of Appeal for Judgement in the Cause) (14 June 2006) [2006] UKHL 26, [2006] 2 WLR 1424, [2007] 1 AC 270

R v Sawoniuk (Judgment) [2000] EWCA Crim 9 (10 February 2000)

Application for a Warrant for the Arrest of Robert Mugabe (First instance) (14 January 2004), ILDC 96 (UK 2004)

United States of America

US v Brandt et al [The *Medical* case], (1949) 1TWC 1, (1950) 2 TWC1

US v Milch [The *Milch* case], (1950) 2 TWC 353

US v Altstötter et al [The *Justice* case], (1951) 3 TWC 1, (1947) 6 LRTWC 1

US v Ohlendorf et al [The *Einsatzgruppen* case], (1950) 4 TWC 1

US v Greifelt et al [The *RuSHA* case], (1950) 4 TWC 597, (1950) 5 TWC 1

US v Pohl et al [The *Pohl* case], (1950) 5 TWC 195

TABLE OF CASES

US v Flick et al [The *Flick* case], (1952) 6 TWC 1
US v Krauch et al [The *I.G. Farben* case], (1953) 7 TWC 1, (1952) 8 TWC 1
US v Krupp et al [The *Krupp* case], (1950) 9 TWC 1
US v von Leeb et al [The *High Command* case], (1951) 10 TWC 1, (1950) 11 TWC 1
US v List et al [The *Hostage* case], (1950) 11 TWC 757
US v von Weizaecker et al [The *Ministries* case], (1952) 12 TWC 1, (1952) 13 TWC 1, (1953) 14 TWC 1
US v Greifelt et al (1947) 13 LRTWC 1
Prosecutor v Eisentrager et al (Judgment, Military Commission, the US), (1949) 14 LRTWC 8
Yamashita v United States of America, [1946] USSC 27, (1948) 4 LRTWC 1
Schooner Exchange v McFaddon, 11 U.S. 116 (1812)
The Paquete Habana, 175 U.S. 677 (1900)
Belhas et al v Ya'alon (Appeal from the US District Court for the District of Columbia) (15 February 2008) [2008] USCADC 15
US v Harman (Judgment, US Army Court of Criminal Appeals) Army 20050597 (30 June 2008)
Re Hilao and ors v Estate of Ferdinand Marcos (Interlocutory Appeal Decision), 25F3d 1467 (9th Cir 1994)
Yousuf and ors v Samantar, 699 F 3d 763 (4th Cir 2012)

Other International and National Courts and Tribunals

Public Prosecutor v Momcillo Trajković (Opinions on Appeals of Conviction of Momcillo Trajković, Office of the Public Prosecutor of Kosovo) 68/2000 (30 November 2001)
Prosecution v Abílio Soares (Judgment, Indonesian *Ad Hoc* Human Rights Court for East Timor, Central Jakarta District Court) 01/PID.HAM/AD. Hoc/2002/ph.JKT.PST (14 August 2002)
Recao case (Judgment, Supreme Tribunal of Justice, Venezuela) 27 July 2004
Clandestine Detention Centres of DINA case (Application for revocation of immunity of Augusto Pinochet Ugarte, Supreme Court, Chile) 21 April 2006
Cruz Mojica Flores Case (Appeal motion, Supreme Court, Panama) 26 January 2007
Víctor Raúl Pinto v Tomás Rojas (Supreme Court, Chile) 3125-04, ILDC 1093 (CL 2007)
Almonacid Arellano et al v Chile (Judgment, Preliminary Objections, Merits, Reparations and Costs, Inter-American CtHR), Series C No 154 (26 September 2006)
Mario Luiz Lozano v General Prosecutor (Sentence, Supreme Court of Cassation, Italy) 31171/2008, ILDC 1085 (IT 2008)

Prosecutor v Alberto Fujimori (Judgment, Supreme Court of Justice, Special Criminal Chamber, Peru) A.V 19-2001 (7 April 2009)

Repak case (Judgment, Court of Appeal, Norway) 12 April 2010

Interlocutory Decision on the Applicable Law: Terrorism, Conspiracy, Homicide, Perpetration, Cumulative Charging, STL-11/01/1 (16 February 2011)

José Rubén Peña Tobón et al case (Ruling and motion for comprehensive reparations, Colombia) 1 December 2011

A v Public Ministry of the Confederation, B and C (Decision, Federal Criminal Court, Switzerland) BB. 2011.140 (25 July 2012)

United Nations Documents

United Nations Resolutions (Security Council and General Assembly)

'Resolution 794 (1992), Adopted by the Security Council at its 3145th meeting, on 3 December 1992', SC Res 794 (1992), UN Doc S/RES/794 (1992)

'Resolution 814 (1993), Adopted by the Security Council at its 3188th meeting, on 26 March 1993', SC Res 794 (1992), UN Doc S/RES/814 (1993)

'Resolution 827 (1993), Adopted by the Security Council at its 3217th meeting, on 25 May 1993', SC Res 827(1993), UN Doc S/RES/827 (1993)

'Resolution 935 (1994), Adopted by the Security Council at its 3400th meeting, on 1 July 1994', SC Res 935 (1994), UN Doc S/RES/935 (1994)

'Resolution 955 (1994), Adopted by the Security Council at its 3453rd meeting, on 8 November 1994', SC Res 955 (1994), UN Doc S/RES/955 (1994)

'Resolution 1087 (1996), Adopted by the Security Council at its 3722nd meeting, on 11 December 1996', SC Res 1087 (1996), UN Doc S/RES/1087 (1996)

'Resolution 1593 (2005), Adopted by the Security Council at its 5158th meeting, on 31 March 2005', SC Res 1593 (2005), UN Doc S/RES/1593 (2005)

'Affirmation of the Principles of International Law Recognized by the Charter of the Nuremberg Tribunal', GA Res 95 (I) (1946), UN Doc A/RES/95 (I)

'Establishment of an International Law Commission', GA Res 174 (II) (1947), UN Doc A/RES/174 (II)

'Formulation of the principles recognized in the Charter of the Nuremberg Tribunal and in the judgment of the Tribunal', GA Res 177(II) (1947), UN Doc A/RES/177(II)

'Universal Declaration of Human Rights', GA Res 217 (III) (1948), UN Doc A/RES/217 (III) A

'Prevention and Punishment of the Crime of Genocide, Study by the International Law Commission of the question of an International Criminal Jurisdiction', GA Res 260 B (III) (1948), UN Doc A/Res/260 B (III)

'Formulation of the Nuremberg Principles', GA Res 488 (V) (1950), UN Doc A/RES/488 (V)

'International Criminal Jurisdiction', GA Res 687 (VII) (1952), UN Doc A/RES/687 (VII)

'Question of definition aggression', GA Res 688 (VII) (1952), UN Doc A/RES/688 (VII)

'International Criminal Jurisdiction', GA Res 898 (IX) (1954), UN Doc A/RES/898 (IX)

'Draft Code of Offences against the Peace and Security of Mankind', GA Res 897 (IX) (1954), UN Doc A/RES/897 (IX)
'International Criminal Jurisdiction', GA Res 1187 (XII) (1957), UN Doc A/RES/1187 (XII)
'Declaration on Principles of International Law Concerning Friendly Relations and Co-operation Among States in Accordance with the Charter of the United Nations', GA Res 2625 (XXV) (1970), UN Doc A/RES/2625 (XXV)
'Definition of Aggression', GA Res 3314 (XXIX) (1974), UN Doc A/RES/3314 (XXIX) (1974)
'Draft Code of Offences against the Peace and Security of Mankind', GA Res 36/106 (1981), UN Doc A/RES/36/106
'Draft Code of Offences against the Peace and Security of Mankind', GA Res 37/102 (1982), UN Doc A/RES/37/102
'International Criminal Responsibility of Individuals and Entities Engaged in Illicit Trafficking of Narcotic Drugs Across National Frontiers and Other Transnational Criminal Activities: Establishment of an International Criminal Court with Jurisdiction over Such Crimes', GA Res 44/39 (1989), UN Doc A/RES/44/39
'Establishment of an international criminal court', GA Res 49/53 (1994), UN Doc A/RES/49/53
'Establishment of an international criminal court', GA Res 50/46 (1995), UN Doc A/RES/50/46
'Establishment of an international Criminal Court', GA Res 51/207 (1997), UN Doc A/RES/51/207
'Israeli settlements in the Occupied Palestinian Territory, including East Jerusalem, and the occupied Syrian Golan', GA Res 67/120 (2013), UN Doc A/RES/67/120
'Resolution adopted by the General Assembly on 23 December 2015: Report of the International Law Commission on the work of its sixty-seventh session', GA Res 70/236 (2015), UN Doc A/RES/70/236

United Nations Meeting Records

GAOR 52nd session, 23rd plenary meeting, UN Doc A/52/PV.23 (3 October 1997)
GAOR 53rd session, 10th plenary meeting, UN Doc A/53/PV.10 (22 September 1998)
GAOR 53rd session, 22nd plenary meeting, UN Doc A/53/PV.22 (30 September 1998)

GAOR 58th session, 95th plenary meeting, UN Doc A/58/PV.95 (13 September 2004)
GAOR 67th session, 31st plenary meeting, UN Doc A/67/PV.31 (6 November 2012)
GAOR 69th session, 35th plenary meeting, UN Doc A/69/PV.35 (31 October 2014)
GAOR 70th session, 48th plenary meeting, UN Doc A/70/PV.48 (5 November 2015)
'Summary record of the 44th meeting [of the ILC]', UN Doc A/CN.4/SR.44 (1950)
'Summary record of the 49th meeting', UN Doc A/CN.4/SR.49 (1950)
'Summary record of the 1958th meeting', UN Doc A/CN.4/SR.1958 (1986)
'Summary record of the 1960th meeting', UN Doc A/CN.4/SR.1960 (1986)
'Summary record of the 1961st meeting', UN Doc A/CN.4/SR.1961 (1986)
'Summary record of the 1962nd meeting', UN Doc A/CN.4/SR.1962 (1986)
'Summary record of the 1963rd meeting', UN Doc A/CN.4/SR.1963 (1986)
'Summary record of the 1965th meeting', UN Doc A/CN.4/SR.1965 (1986)
'Summary record of the 2101st meeting', UN Doc A/CN.4/SR.2101 (1989)
'Summary record of the 2096th meeting', UN Doc A/CN.4/SR.2096 (1989)
'Summary record of the 2097th meeting', UN Doc A/CN.4/SR.2097 (1989)
'Summary record of the 2240th meeting', UN Doc A/CN.4/SR.2240 (1991)
'Summary record of the 2330th meeting', UN Doc A/CN.4/SR.2330 (1994)
'Summary record of the 2331st meeting', UN Doc A/CN.4/SR.2331 (1994)
'Summary record of the 2384th meeting', UN Doc A/CN.4/SR.2384 (1995)
'Summary record of the 2437th meeting', UN Doc A/CN.4/SR.2437 (1996)
'Summary record of the 3132nd meeting', UN Doc A/CN.4/SR.3132 (2012)
'Summary record of the 3280th meeting', UN Doc A/CN.4/SR.3280 (2015)
'Summary record of the 3301st meeting', UN Doc A/CN.4/SR.3301 (2016)
'Summary records of the 26th-30th meetings [of the Sixth Committee]', UN Doc A/C.6/50/R.26-30 and 48-50 (1995)
'Summary record of the 11th meeting', UN Doc A/C.6/52/SR.11 (1997)
'Summary record of the 13th meeting', UN Doc A/C.6/52/SR.13 (1997)
'Summary record of the 14th meeting', UN Doc A/C.6/52/SR.14 (1997)
'Summary record of the 15th meeting', UN Doc A/C.6/52/SR.15 (1997)
'Summary record of the 9th meeting', UN Doc A/C.6/53/SR.9 (1998)
'Summary record of the 10th meeting', UN Doc A/C.6/53/SR.10 (1998)
'Summary record of the 11th meeting', UN Doc A/C.6/53/SR.11 (1998)
'Summary record of the 12th meeting', UN Doc A/C.6/53/SR.12 (1998)
'Summary record of the 11th meeting', UN Doc A/C.6/54/SR.11 (1999)
'Summary record of the 14th meeting', UN Doc A/C.6/54/SR.14 (1999)
'Summary record of the 9th meeting', UN Doc A/C.6/55/SR.9 (2000)
'Summary record of the 11th meeting', UN Doc A/C.6/55/SR.11 (2000)
'Summary record of the 12th meeting', UN Doc A/C.6/55/SR.12 (2000)
'Summary record of the 13th meeting', UN Doc A/C.6/55/SR.13 (2000)

United Nations Reports and Other Documents

ILC, 'Report of the International Law Commission', GAOR 4th Session Supp No 10, UN Doc A/925 (1949)
ILC, 'Report of the ILC', GAOR 5th Session Supp No 12, UN Doc A/1316 (1950)
ILC, 'Report of the ILC', GAOR 6th Session Supp No 9, UN Doc A/1858 (1951)
ILC, 'Report of the ILC', GAOR 8th Session Supp No 9, UN Doc A/2456 (1953)
ILC, 'Report of the ILC', GAOR 9th Session Supp No 10, UN Doc A/2693 (1954)
ILC, 'Reports of the ILC', GAOR 37th-38th Sessions Supp No 10, UN Doc A/37-38/10 (1982–1983)
ILC, 'Reports of the ILC', GAOR 41st-44th Sessions Supp No 10, UN Doc A/41-44/10 (1986–1989)
ILC, 'Reports of the ILC', GAOR 48th-49th Sessions Supp No 10, UN Doc A/48-49/10 (1993–1994)
ILC, 'Report of the ILC', GAOR 51st Session Supp No 10, UN Doc A/51/10 (1996)
ILC, 'Reports of the ILC', GAOR 61st-63rd Sessions Supp No 10, UN Doc A/61-63/10 (2006–2008)
ILC, 'Reports of the ILC', GAOR 65th -67th Sessions Supp No 10, UN Doc A/65-67/10 (2010–2012)
ILC, 'Reports of the ILC', GAOR 69th-70th Sessions Supp No 10, UN Doc A/69-70/10 (2014–2015)
ILC, 'Reports of the ILC', GAOR 72nd-74th Sessions Supp No 10, UN Doc A/72-74/10 (2017–2019)
'Revised Report of the Working Group on a draft statute for an international criminal court', UN Doc A/CN.4/L.490 and Add.1(1993)
'Report of the Working Group on the question of a Draft Statute for an International Criminal Court-Revision', UN Doc A/CN.4/L.491/Rev.2, UN Doc A/CN.4/L.491/Rev.2/Corr.1, and UN Doc A/CN.4/L.491/Rev.2/Add.1-3 (1994)
'Summary of the Proceedings of the *Ad Hoc* Committee During the Period 3 – 13 April 1995', UN Doc A/AC.244/2 (1995)
'Report of the *Ad Hoc* Committee on the Establishment of an International Criminal Court', GAOR 50th Session Supp No 22, UN Doc A/50/22 (1995)
'Summary of the Proceedings of the Preparatory Committee during the Period 25 March – 12 April 1996', UN Doc A/AC.249/1 (1996)
'Report of the Preparatory Committee on the Establishment of an International Criminal Court', GAOR 51st Session Supp No 22, UN Doc A/51/22 (1996)
'Report of the Preparatory Committee on the Establishment of an International Criminal Court' (14 April 1998), UN Doc A/CONF.183/2
'Report of the Working Group on General Principles of Criminal Law' (18 June 1998), UN Doc A/CONF.183/C.1/WGGP/L.4 and Corr.1

'Discussion Paper prepared by the Bureau' (6 July 1998), UN Doc A/CONF.183/C.1/L.53

'Proposal prepared by the Bureau' (11 July 1998), UN Doc A/CONF.183/C.1/L.59 and Corr.1

'Report of the Drafting Committee, Draft Statute for the International Criminal Court' (14 July 1998), UN Doc A/CONF.183/C.1/L.65/Rev.1

'Report of the Committee of the Whole, Draft Statute for the International Criminal Court' (17 July 1998), UN Doc A/CONF.183/8

'Official Records of the United Nations Diplomatic Conference of Plenipotentiaries on the Establishment of an International Criminal Court' (Rome, 15 June – 17 July 1998), UN Doc A/CONF.183

'Summary records of the 1st – 9th Plenary Meetings of the Rome Conference', UN Doc A/CONF.183/SR.1-9

'Summary records of 1st – 36th meetings of the Committee of the Whole', UN Doc A/CONF.183/C.1/SR.1-36

UN Press Release, 'Eight Speakers Comment on Draft Code of Crimes against Peace and Security' (16 October 1995), UN Doc GA/L/2865

UN Press Release, 'Sixth Committee Hears Differing Views on Code of Crimes against International Peace and Security' (16 October 1995), UN Doc GA/L/2866

UN Press Release, 'Committee is Told Aggression Should be Within Jurisdiction of Proposed International Criminal Court' (31 October 1995), UN Doc GA/L/2877

UN Press Release, 'Preparatory Committee on Establishment of International Criminal Court First Session' (25 March 1996), UN Doc GA/L/2761

UN Press Release, 'Preparatory Committee for Establishment of International Criminal Court, Discussed Definitions of "Genocide", "Crimes against Humanity"' (25 March 1996), UN Doc GA/L/2762

UN Press Release, '"Crimes against Humanity" Must be Precisely Defined Say Speakers in Preparatory Committee for International Court' (26 March 1996), UN Doc GA/L/2763

UN Press Release, 'Preparatory Committee on International Criminal Court Concludes First Session' (12 April 1996), UN Doc GA/L/2787

'Topical summary of the discussion held in the Sixth Committee of the General Assembly during its 47th session' [French], UN Doc A/CN.4/446 (1992), prepared by Secretariat

'Comments of Governments on the report of the Working Group on the question of an international criminal jurisdiction', UN Doc A/CN.4/452 and Add.1-3 (1993)

'Comments and observations received from Governments', UN Doc A/CN.4/448 and Add.1(1994)

'Topical summary of the discussion held in the Sixth Committee of the General Assembly during its 48th session', UN Doc A/CN.4/457 (1994)

'Observations of Governments on the report of the Working Group on a draft statute for an international criminal court', UN Doc A/CN.4/458 and Add.1-8 (1994)

'Topical summary of the discussion held in the Sixth Committee of the General Assembly during its 49th session', UN Doc A/CN.4/464/Add.1 (1995)

'Topical summary of the discussion held in the Sixth Committee of the General Assembly during its 50th session', UN Doc A/CN.4/472 (1996)

'Secretary-General Report on the establishment of the Commission of Experts submitted to the Security Council' (14 October 1992), UN Doc S/24657 (1992)

'Report of the Secretary-General Pursuant to Paragraph 2 of Security Council Resolution 808 (1993)' (3 May 1993), UN Doc S/25704 (1993)

'Letter dated 24 May 1994 from the Secretary-General to the President of the Security Council' (27 May 1994), UN Doc S/1994/674

'The Final Report of the Commission of Experts established pursuant to Security Council Resolution 780 (1992)' (27 May 1994), UN Doc S/1994/674, annex

'Report of the Secretary-General Pursuant to Paragraph 5 of the Security Council Resolution 955 (1994)' (13 February 1995), UN Doc S/1995/134

'Report of the Security Council Mission to Djibouti (on Somalia), the Sudan, Chad, the Democratic Republic of the Congo and Côte d'Ivoire, 31 May to 10 June 2008', UN Doc S/2008/460

'Reports of the Secretary-General on the Sudan and South Sudan', UN SCOR, 7963rd meeting, UN Doc S/PV.7963 (8 June 2017)

'Reports of the Secretary-General on the Sudan and South Sudan', UN SCOR, 8554th meeting, UN Doc S/PV.8554 (19 June 2019)

'The Charter and Judgment of the Nuremberg Tribunal – History and Analysis: Memorandum submitted by the Secretary-General', UN Doc A/CN.4/5 (1949)

'Formulation of Nuremberg Principles, Report by Jean Spiropoulos, Special Rapporteur', UN Doc A/CN.4/22 (1950)

'Formulation of the Nuremberg Principles', UN Doc A/CN.4/34 (1950)

The first, second, fourth, fifth, seventh, eleventh and thirteenth reports on Draft Code of Crimes (Offences) against the Peace and Security of Mankind to the ILC, by Special Rapporteur Mr J. Spiropoulos, UN Doc A/CN.4/25 (1950), UN Doc A/CN.4/44 (1951), UN Doc A/CN.4/398 and Corr.1-3 (1986), UN Doc A/CN.4/404 (1987), UN Doc A/CN.4/419 and Add.1 (1989), UN Doc A/CN.4/449 and Corr.1 (1993), UN Doc A/CN.4/466 (1995)

'Draft Code of Offences against the Peace and Security of Mankind' in 'Report of the International Law Commission', UN Doc A/37/10 (1982), Vol II (2)

'Articles of the draft Code of Crimes against the Peace and Security of Mankind' in 'Report of the International Law Commission', UN Doc A/51/10 (1996), Vol II (2)

'Fragmentation of International Law: Difficulties Arising from the Diversification and Expansion of International Law', Report of the Study Group of the International Law Commission, UN Doc A/CN.4/L.702 (2006)

The preliminary and second reports on Immunity of State Officials from Foreign Criminal Jurisdiction to the ILC, by Special Rapporteur Roman Anatolevich Kolodkin, UN Doc A/CN.4/601 (2008), UN Doc A/CN.4/631 (2011)

'Peremptory norms of general international law (jus cogens)' in 'Report of the International Law Commission', UN Doc A/74/10 (2019)

'Guide to Practice on Reservations to Treaties' in 'Report of the International Law Commission', UN Doc A/66/10/Add.1 (2011)

The second, fourth, fifth, sixth, seventh reports on Immunity of State Officials from Foreign Criminal Jurisdiction, by Special Rapporteur Concepción Escobar Hernández, UN Doc A/CN.4/661 (2013); UN Doc A/CN.4/686 (2015); UN Doc A/CN.4/701 (2016); UN Doc A/CN.4/722 (2017); UN Doc A/CN.4/729 (2018)

'Memorandum by the Secretariat', UN Doc A/CN.4/691 (2016)

The first and third reports on Crimes against Humanity to the ILC, by Special Rapporteur Sean D. Murphy, UN Doc A/CN.4/680 (2015), UN Doc A/CN.4/704 (2017)

The Note, first, second, third, fourth, and fifth reports and its addendum on Identification of Customary International Law to the ILC, by Michael Wood, Special Rapporteur, UN Doc A/CN.4/653 (2012), UN Doc A/CN.4/663 (2013), UN Doc A/CN.4/672 (2014), UN Doc A/CN.4/682 (2015), UN Doc A/CN.4/695 and Add.1 (2016), UN Doc A/CN.4/717 (2018), UN Doc A/CN.4/717/Add.1 (2018)

'Topical summary of the discussion held in the Sixth Committee of the General Assembly during its seventy-second session, prepared by the Secretariat', UN Doc A/CN.4/713 (2018)

'Identification of customary international law: Comments and observations received from Governments' (14 February 2018), UN Doc A/CN.4/716 (2018)

'Text of the draft conclusions as adopted by the Drafting Committee on second reading', UN Doc A/CN.4/L.908 (2018)

'Text of the draft articles on prevention and punishment of crimes against humanity', UN Doc A/74/10 (2019)

'General principle of law', UN Doc A/74/10 (2019)

CHAPTER 1

Introduction

The relationship between treaties and customary international law remains a highly debated topic in international law.[1] Treaties and customary international law may co-exist on the same subject matter.[2] The rules of the two sources may overlap or conflict with each other or may have identical content. The International Court of Justice (ICJ) in *Nicaragua* upheld that the two sources do not supplant with each other for their separate methods of application and interpretation.[3] As opposed to a treaty rule, a customary international rule is usually unwritten and less detailed. A treaty rule covering the same subject matter could be an important starting point in identifying the (possible) content of a customary international rule.[4] According to the ICJ, a multilateral treaty rule which is clearly articulated may play a role in 'recording

---

1   See R.R. Baxter, 'Multilateral Treaties as Evidence of Customary International Law' (1965) 41 *British Ybk Intl L* 275; R.R. Baxter, 'Treaties and Custom' (1970) 129 *Recueil des cours* 27; M. Akehurst, 'Custom as a Source of International Law' (1976) 47 *British Ybk Intl L* 1, 42–52; M. Villiger, *Customary International Law and Treaties: A Study of Their Interactions and Interrelations, with Special Consideration of the 1969 Vienna Convention on the Law of Treaties* (Martinus Nijhoff Publishers 1985) 156–67; O. Schachter, 'Entangled Treaty and Custom' in Y. Dinstein and M. Tabory (eds), *International Law at a Time of Perplexity: Essays in Honour of Shabtai Rosenne* (Martinus Nijhoff Publishers 1989) 732; M. Villiger, *Customary International Law and Treaties: A Manual on the Theory and Practice of the Interrelation of Sources* (Fully revised 2nd edn, Kluwer Law International 1997); Y. Dinstein, 'The Interaction Between Customary Law and Treaty' (2006) 322 *Recueil des cours* 243; M. Mendelson, 'The International Court of Justice and the Sources of International Law' in V. Lowe and M. Fitzmaurice (eds), *Fifty Years of the International Court of Justice: Essays in Honour of Sir Robert Jennings* (CUP 2009) 72–79; B.B. Jia, 'The Relations between Treaties and Custom' (2010) 9 *Chinese J Intl L* 81.
2   R. Jennings and A. Watts (eds), *Oppenheim's International Law*, Vol 1 (9th edn, Longmans 1996) §§ 24–32.
3   *Military and Paramilitary Activities in and against Nicaragua (Nicaragua v USA)*, Merits, [1986] ICJ Rep 14, 93-96, paras 175-79. For further discussion on their differences, H.E. Chodosh, 'An Interpretive Theory of International Law: The Distinction between Treaty and Customary Law' (1995) 28 *Vand J Transnatl L* 973.
4   K. Gastorn, Secretary-General of the Asian-African Legal Consultative Organisation (AALCO), Address in regard to the theme 'Identification of Customary International Law: Legal and Policy Implications' on 2 November 2016 at the UN Trusteeship Council Chambers, 10. For discussions on the advantages and disadvantages of deriving the content of customary law from a treaty formulation, see D. Bethlehem, 'The Methodological Framework of the Study' in E. Wilmshurst and S. Breau (eds), *Perspectives on the ICRC Study on Customary International Humanitarian Law* (CUP 2007) 1–14.

and defining rules deriving from customary international law'.[5] For example, in the *North Sea Continental Shelf* cases of the ICJ, States invoked a treaty rule as evidence of the existence of a customary rule binding upon all States.[6] The ICJ analysed whether a principle set out in article 6(2) of the 1958 Geneva Convention on the Continental Shelf had passed into customary international law.[7] International and national criminal tribunals have also contemplated similar issues of a customary rule paralleling a treaty rule with the same matter in the field of international criminal law.[8] This book studies the status of the 1998 Rome Statute of the International Criminal Court (Rome Statute)[9] as evidence of customary rules in international (criminal) law.

1.1 The Role of Customary International Law in the International Criminal Court

Customary international law is either a source of international law[10] or an aid to interpreting written rules.[11] Parallel with the development of international criminal law since the middle of the 20th century,[12] customary international law also plays a significant role as a source or an interpretive aid in this field.[13]

---

5   *Continental Shelf (Libyan Arab Jamahiriya/Malta)*, Judgment, [1985] ICJ Rep 13, 29-30, para 27; Baxter (1965) (n 1) 275–300; *North Sea Continental Shelf* cases (*Germany v Denmark; Germany v Netherlands*), Judgment, [1969] ICJ Rep 3, 39, 41, paras 63, 69; *Military and Paramilitary Activities* Judgment (n 3), 97, para 183; Villiger (1985) (n 1) 227, 238; 'Text of the draft conclusions on identification of customary international law' in 'Report of the International Law Commission', UN Doc A/73/10 (2018), para 65, Conclusions 11.1–11.2.

6   *North Sea Continental Shelf* cases (n 5), 41, para 70.

7   ibid 39, 41, paras 63, 71; Geneva Convention on the Continental Shelf, 29 April 1958, 10 June 1964, 499 UNTS 312.

8   *Prosecutor v Mucić et al* (Judgement) ICTY-96-21-T (16 November 1998), para 302. For a detailed analysis, see Baxter (1965) (n 1); Baxter (1970) (n 1) 58–61.

9   Rome Statute of the International Criminal Court, 17 July 1998, 1 July 2002, 2187 UNTS 90 [1998 Rome Statute].

10 Jennings and Watts (eds) (n 2) § 10, at 26 and fn 1; J. Crawford, *Brownlie's Principles of Public International Law* (8th edn, OUP 2012) 23–27; A. Clapham, *Brierly's the Law of Nations* (7th edn, OUP 2012) 57–63; M. Shaw, *International Law* (8th edn, CUP 2017) 286–88; H. Thirlway, *The Sources of International Law* (2nd edn, OUP 2019) 60–105; Statute of the International Court of Justice, 26 June 1945, 24 October 1945, 33 UNTS 993, art 38.

11 Jennings and Watts (eds) (n 2) § 10, at 26 and fn 1; Thirlway, ibid.

12 C. Kreß, 'International Criminal Law' in R. Wolfrum (ed) (2009) *MPEPIL*, paras 22–29.

13 *Prosecutor v Furundžija* (Judgement) ICTY-95-17/1-A (12 July 2000) (Declaration of Judge Patrick Robinson), paras 275–81; J. Powderly, 'The Rome Statute and the Attempted Corseting of the Interpretative Judicial Function: Reflections on Sources of Law and Interpretative Technique' in C. Stahn (ed), *The Law and Practice of the International*

The idea of customary international law as a source of international criminal law has been contested.[14] Rules derived from customary international law are unwritten and some of them are quite vague. Its attributes of ambiguous and unwritten seem to be incompatible with the principle of legality requiring specificity and certainty, particularly in civil law systems.[15] However, the difference between treaties and customary international law in legal certainty is a matter of degree. As Kenneth Gallant noted, the uncertainty enshrined in the language of law (either national law or international law) defining crimes, liabilities and defences is unavoidable.[16] If the ambiguity attribute of customary international law were to deny its source status, treaties would also be excluded as a source in this field, which would be unacceptable.[17] Only if the customary rule was reasonably foreseeable (and accessible) to individuals concerned at the time to act, with certain limitations, the core of the principle of legality will be harmonised.[18] The principle of legality itself serves to restrict the interpretation of applicable rules, including customary international law, instead of excluding custom as a source of international criminal law.[19] The UN

Criminal Court (OUP 2015) 444–98; A. Bufalini, 'The Principle of Legality and the Role of Customary International Law in the Interpretation of the ICC Statute' (2015) 14 *LPICL* 233.

[14] For discussions, see A. Pellet, 'Applicable Law' in A. Cassese *et al* (eds), *The Rome Statute of the International Criminal Court: A Commentary* (OUP 2002) 1070–72; L. May, *Aggression and Crimes Against Peace* (CUP 2008) 160–61; B. Van Schaack, '*Crimen Sine Lege*: Judicial Lawmaking at the Intersection of Law and Morals' (2008) 97 *Georgetown LJ* 119, 138; H. Van der Wilt, 'State Practice as Element of Customary International Law: A White Knight in International Criminal Law?' (2019) 20 *ICLR* 784, 784–86.

[15] K.S. Gallant, *The Principle of Legality in International and Comparative Law* (CUP 2008) 352–78; S. Dana, 'Beyond Retroactivity to Realizing Justice: A Theory on the Principle of Legality in International Criminal Law Sentencing' (2009) 99 *J Crim L & Criminology* 857; Bufalini (n 13), 233–37.

[16] Gallant (n 15) 359–60.

[17] P.G. Staubach, *The Rule of Unwritten International Law: Customary Law, General Principles, and World Order* (Routledge 2018) 78–81.

[18] Gallant (n 15) 359–66; May (n 14) 156–57.

[19] *The Prosecutor v Ntaganda* (Judgment on the appeal of Mr Ntaganda against the 'Second decision on the Defence's challenge to the jurisdiction of the Court in respect of Counts 6 and 9', A Ch) ICC-01/04-02/06-1962 (15 June 2017), paras 1, 54-55; *Prosecutor v Milutinović et al* (Decision on Dragoljub Ojdanić's Motion Challenging Jurisdiction: Joint Criminal Enterprise) ICTY-99-37-AR72 (21 May 2003), paras 37-38; *Prosecutor v Mucić et al* (Judgement) ICTY-96-21-A (20 February 2001), para 173; *Nahimana et al v The Prosecutor* (Judgement) ICTR-99-52-A (28 November 2007) (partly dissenting opinion of Judge Shahabuddeen), para 19; M. Shahabuddeen, 'Does the Principle of Legality Stand in the Way of the Progressive Development of the Law?' (2004) 2 *JICJ* 1013, 1017; R. Cryer *et al, An Introduction to International Criminal Law and Procedure* (3rd edn, CUP 2014) 17–19; L.J. van den Herik, *The Contribution of the Rwanda Tribunal to the Development of International Law* (Brill | Nijhoff 2005) 213–14; Powderly (n 13); P. Merkouris, *Article 31(3)*

Secretary-General's report, which was approved by the UN Security Council,[20] also noted that the International Criminal Tribunal for the former Yugoslavia (ICTY) should only apply 'rules of international humanitarian law that are beyond any doubt part of customary law'.[21] The drafters of the ICTY Statute aimed to limit the ICTY's jurisdiction over crimes existent under customary international law so as to avoid violating the principle of legality prohibiting retroactive application of law.[22] In short, customary international law remains a source of international criminal law.[23] Jurisprudence of international and national criminal tribunals also support that view.[24]

This study of the nature of the Rome Statute as evidence of customary international law could not have been done two decades ago. In 1998, a United Nations Diplomatic Conference of Plenipotentiaries on the Establishment of an International Criminal Court was held in Rome (Rome Conference).[25] After a month of negotiations at the Rome Conference, the Rome Statute

---

(c) *VCLT and the Principle of Systemic Integration: Normative Shadows in Plato's Cave* (Brill | Nijhoff 2015) 231–300; Gallant (n 15) 19–30.

[20] SC Res 827 (1993) on establishment of the ICTY and adoption of the Statute of the Tribunal, UN Doc S/RES/827 (1993), para 1.

[21] 'Report of the Secretary-General pursuant to Paragraph 2 of Security Council Resolution 808 (1993)' (3 May 1993), UN Doc S/25704, para 34.

[22] *Prosecutor v Tadić* (Interlocutory Appeal Decision on Jurisdiction) ICTY-94-1-AR72 (2 October 1995), para 94.

[23] A. Cassese et al (eds), *Cassese's International Criminal Law* (3rd edn, OUP 2013) 13–14; A. Pellet (n 14) 1072; Y. Tan, 'The Identification of Customary Rules in International Criminal Law' (2018) 34 UJIEJ 92. For supporting the use of customary law in international criminal proceedings, see T. Meron, 'Editorial Comment: Revival of Customary Humanitarian Law' (2005) 99 AJIL 817.

[24] *Prosecutor v Blaškić* (Judgement on the Request of the Republic of Croatia for Review of the Decision of Trial Chamber II of 18 July 1997) ICTY-95-14-AR108BIS (29 October 1997), para 64; *Kajelijeli v Prosecutor* (Judgment) ICTR-98-44A-A (23 May 2005), para 209; *Chief Prosecutor v Delwar Hossain Sayeedi* (Judgment, International Crimes Tribunal-1) ICT-BD 01 of 2011 (28 February 2013), para 30(4); *Chief Prosecutor v Salauddin Quader Chowdhury* (Judgment, International Crimes Tribunal-1) ICT-BD 02 of 2011 (1 October 2013), para 36(4); *Prosecutor v Lino Beno* (Judgment, District Court of Dili) SPSC-4b/2003 (16 November 2004), paras 13-14; W.A. Schabas, 'Customary Law or Judge-Made Law: Judicial Creativity at the UN Criminal Tribunals' in J. Doria et al (eds), *The Legal Regime of the International Criminal Court: Essays in Honour of Professor Igor Blishchenko (1930–2000)* (Brill | Nijhoff 2009) 75–101; B. Schlütter, *Developments in Customary International Law: Theory and the Practice of the International Court of Justice and the International ad hoc Criminal Tribunals for Rwanda and Yugoslavia* (Brill | Nijhoff 2010).

[25] 'Official Records of the United Nations Diplomatic Conference of Plenipotentiaries on the Establishment of an International Criminal Court' (Rome, 15 June-17 July 1998) (17 July 1998), UN Doc A/CONF.183.

was adopted with 120 States voting for, 21 States abstaining and 7 States voting against, and it entered into force on 1 July 2002.[26] By virtue of the Statute, the International Criminal Court (ICC) was established to deal with individual criminal responsibility for the most serious crimes of concern to the international community as a whole.[27]

It seems that customary international law is of less importance at the ICC after the adoption of the Rome Statute.[28] Pursuant to articles 21(1)(a) and (b) of the Statute, customary international law is not the primary but secondary source of applicable law for the ICC.[29] Significantly, article 22(1) of the Statute reads: '[a] person shall not be criminally responsible under this Statute unless the conduct in question constitutes, at the time it takes place, a crime within the jurisdiction of the Court'. The reference to 'a crime within the jurisdiction of the Court' prevents the ICC from prosecuting crimes that are not defined in the Statute but merely based on customary law.[30] Article 22(1) also implies that the ICC will not automatically apply existing rules and new developments in customary international law regarding crimes.[31] Aside from articles 21 and 22, article 25(2) reads: '[a] person who commits a crime within the jurisdiction of the Court shall be individually responsible and liable for punishment in accordance with this Statute.' The emphasis on 'in accordance with this Statute' also demonstrates that the ICC is prevented from employing a mode of liability that is recognised under customary law but goes beyond the scope of the Statute.

---

26 There were 185 UN member States in 1998. 'Summary record of the 9th Plenary Meetings of the Conference' (17 July 1998), UN Doc A/CONF.183/SR.9, para 10. Voting against see UN Doc A/CONF.183/SR.9, paras 17 (India), 28 (US), 33 (Israel), 40 (China); for further explanations, see 'Summary record of the 9th meeting', UN Doc A/C.6/53/SR.9 (1998), paras 30-43 (China), 52–63 (US).
27 1998 Rome Statute, Preamble, arts 1 and 5(1).
28 L.J. van den Herik, 'The Decline of Customary International Law as a Source of International Criminal Law' in C.A. Bradley (ed), *Custom's Future: International Law in a Changing World* (CUP 2016) 231, 239–41, 251–52. Cf. Kreß (n 12) para 12; id, 'Preliminary Observations on the ICC Appeals Chamber's Judgment of 6 May 2019 in the Jordan Referral re Al-Bashir Appeal' (2019) Occasional Paper Series No. 8; *Prosecutor v Galić* (Judgement) ICTY-98-29-T (5 December 2003) (Separate and Partially Dissenting Opinion of Judge Rafael Nieto-Navia), paras 108-113 and fn 389.
29 1998 Rome Statute, art 21; Powderly (n 13) 453.
30 1998 Rome Statute, art 22(1); W.A. Schabas, *The International Criminal Court: A Commentary on the Rome Statute* (2nd edn, OUP 2016) 543.
31 L.N. Sadat, 'Custom, Codification and Some Thoughts about the Relationship between the Two: Article 10 of the ICC Statute' (1999) 49 *DePaul L Rev* 909, 910–12; K. Kittichaisaree, *International Criminal Law* (OUP 2001) 52.

Yet, customary international law is not merely a theoretical issue at the ICC.[32] Articles 11(2), 13(b) and 24(1) of the Rome Statute allow the ICC to try individuals for an offence committed after the entry into force of the Statute (1 July 2002), but prior to a State's ratification of it. According to the Rome Statute, the ICC may retroactively apply the Statute to exercise jurisdiction over situations in two contexts.[33] Firstly, article 12(3) of the Statute permits non-party States' acceptance of the ICC's jurisdiction by lodging a declaration with the Registrar.[34] For example, Ukraine has accepted the jurisdiction of the ICC over alleged crimes committed in its territory from November 2013 onwards through declarations in 2014 and 2015.[35] Secondly, article 13(b) of the Statute empowers the UN Security Council to refer a situation concerning a non-party State to the Rome Statute. The Situation in Darfur, Sudan referred to the ICC by the UN Security Council is a good example.[36] Due to non-party States' acceptance and the Security Council's referral, the ICC may exercise jurisdiction over crimes committed by nationals of a non-party State in the territory of non-party States. In the two circumstances, the ICC cannot 'retroactively' apply the Rome Statute to prosecute alleged crimes that were committed prior to the 'consent' of that non-party State. But how can the ICC exercise jurisdiction over these situations without violating the principle of legality prohibiting retroactive application of law? As Bruce Broomhall wrote: '[t]he only legitimate basis for establishing the criminal responsibility of individuals [at the ICC] would presumably – in the absence of relevant national criminal prohibitions at the time of the alleged conduct – be that of customary international law.'[37] Therefore, in the two contexts, a good choice for the ICC is to establish whether these offences in the Statute are reflections of customary

---

32 Powderly (n 13) 453; Kreß (2019) (n 28) 24.
33 A. Cassese, 'When May Senior State Officials be Tried for International Crimes? Some Comments on the *Congo v Belgium* Case' (2002) 13 *EJIL* 853, 875; M. Milanović, 'Is the Rome Statute Binding on Individuals? (And Why We Should Care)' (2011) 9 *JICJ* 25, 51–52; M. Milanović, 'Aggression and Legality: Custom in Kampala' (2012) 10 *JICJ* 165.
34 For discussions on article 12(3) and the ICC's temporal jurisdiction to crimes, see C. Stahn *et al*, 'The International Criminal Court's *Ad Hoc* Jurisdiction Revisited' (2005) 99 *AJIL* 421, 429–31.
35 'Declaration by Ukraine lodged under Article 12(3) of the Rome Statute' (9 April 2014); 'Declaration by Ukraine lodged under Article 12(3) of the Rome Statute' (8 September 2015).
36 SC Res 1593 (2005) on violations of international humanitarian law and human rights law in Darfur, Sudan, UN Doc S/RES/1593 (2005).
37 B. Broomhall, 'Article 22' in O. Triffterer (ed), *Commentary on the Rome Statute of the International Criminal Court: Observers' Notes, Article by Article* (2nd edn, Hart/Beck 2008) 720.

law at the material time.[38] Other commentators share the view and argue for the necessity to study the status of the Rome Statute as evidence of customary international law.[39]

In addition, the ICC may rely on customary international law to clarify the content of unclearly written texts of the Rome Statute, in particular, if that treaty rule is a restatement of a customary rule.[40] When nationals of non-party States are involved, the definitions of core crimes in the Statute should be interpreted strictly to adhere to existent customary rules. In the spirit of equal application and enforcement of law, rules on crimes and liabilities ultimately must also be read down to customary international law.[41]

Last, the ICC can resort to customary international law as a secondary source to fill applicable gaps in the Rome Statute.[42] Pre-Trial Chambers of the

---

38 For discussions on other solutions, see T.d.S. Dias, 'The Retroactive Application of the Rome Statute in Cases of Security Council Referrals and Ad hoc Declarations: An Appraisal of the Existing Solutions to an Under-discussed Problem' (2018) 16 *JICJ* 65; Kreß (2019) (n 28) 22–25.

39 G.M. Danilenko, 'The Statute of the International Criminal Court and Third States' (2000) 21 *Michigan J Intl L* 445, 468; L. Grover, 'A Call to Arms: Fundamental Dilemmas Confronting the Interpretation of Crimes in the Rome Statute of the International Criminal Court' (2010) 21 *EJIL* 543, 567; L.N. Sadat and J.M. Jolly, 'Seven Canons of ICC Interpretation: Making Sense of Article 25's Rorschach Blot' (2014) 27 *LJIL* 755, 786; L. Grover, *Interpreting Crimes in the Rome Statute of the International Criminal Court* (CUP 2014) 244–45, 257–58; C. Lind, 'Article 22' in M. Klamberg (ed), *The Commentary on the Law of the International Criminal Court* (TOAEP 2017) 257; C. McDougall, 'The Crimes Against Peace Precedent' in C. Kreß and S. Barriga (eds), *The Crime of Aggression: A Commentary* (CUP 2017) 105; F. Pocar, 'Transformation of Customary Law Through ICC Practice' (2018) 112 *AJIL Unbound* 182, 184–85.

40 *The Prosecutor v Al Bashir* (Judgment in the Jordan Referral re Al-Bashir Appeal, A Ch) ICC-02/05-01/09-397-Corr (6 May 2019), para 98; *The Prosecutor v Ntaganda* (Judgment on the appeal of Mr Ntaganda against the 'Second decision on the Defence's challenge to the jurisdiction of the Court in respect of Counts 6 and 9', A Ch) ICC-01/04-02/06-1962 (15 June 2017), para 1; 'Report of the International Law Commission', UN Doc A/61/10 (2006), para 251; D. Akande, 'Sources of International Criminal Law' in A. Cassese (ed), *Oxford Companion on International Criminal Justice* (OUP 2009) 50–51; Cassese *et al* (eds) (n 23) 13–14; Powderly (n 13) 478; Grover (2014) (n 39) 228–30; Schabas (n 30) 335; Bufalini (n 13).

41 Kreß (n 12) para 12 and (n 28) 24. Cf. *The Prosecutor v Al Bashir* (Final Submissions of the Prosecution following the Appeal Hearing, A Ch) ICC-02/05-01/ 09-392 (28 September 2018), para 6.

42 *The Prosecutor v Lubanga* (Judgment on the Appeal of Mr Thomas Lubanga Dyilo against the Decision on the Defence Challenge to the Jurisdiction of the Court pursuant to Article 19(2)(a) of the Statute of 3 October 2006, A Ch) ICC-01/04-01/06-772 (21 December 2006), para 34; Schabas (n 30) 383–85; V.-D. Degan, 'On the Sources of International Criminal Law' (2005) 4 *Chinese J Intl L* 45, 52; M.M. DeGuzman, 'Article 21' in O. Triffterer and K. Ambos (eds), *Commentary on the Rome Statute of the International Criminal*

ICC once held that 'the question as to whether customary law admits or discards the "joint commission through another person" is not relevant for this Court', because 'the Rome Statute expressly provides for this specific mode of liability'.[43] This statement indirectly affirms the gap-filling role of custom at the ICC. In all of these circumstances, the ICC needs to consider the existence and the content of customary rules in international criminal law.[44] Customary international law continues to play a role within the framework of the ICC.

1.2   Aim, Questions and Scope of This Book

This book aims to examine the nature of selected rules of the Rome Statute as evidence of customary international law. The central question is whether and to what extent a rule of the Rome Statute was or is declaratory of a customary rule on the same subject matter. This book mainly addresses three sub-questions: (1) whether a provision of the Rome Statute reflected a pre-existing customary rule at its adoption or crystallised itself into custom upon its inclusion in the Statute; (2) whether a provision of the Statute that was of a declaratory nature continues to be declaratory of a customary rule; and (3) whether a provision of the Statute that was not of a declaratory nature has subsequently become so. The first decisive date is the critical moment when the provision of the (updated) Rome Statute was adopted. The second is late December 2020, when this book was completed.

It is debatable whether the Rome Statute is either a mirror of customary international law or creates new rules. In the drafting process of the Rome Statute, some State delegations explicitly addressed whether the aim of the Rome Statute was to codify or crystallise crimes under customary international law rather than to create new crimes.[45] Some delegations considered that the

---

Court: Observers' Notes, Article by Article (3rd edn, Hart/Beck 2016) 939. Cf. Bufalini (n 13), 238–52.

43   *Prosecutor v Ruto et al* (Decision on the Confirmation of Charges Pursuant to Article 61(7)(a) and (b) of the Rome Statute, PTC II) ICC-01/09-01/11-373 (23 January 2012), para 289; *The Prosecutor v Katanga & Ngudjolo* (Decision on the confirmation of charges, PTC I) ICC-01/04-01/07-717 (30 September 2008), paras 508; *The Prosecutor v Al Bashir* (Decision on the Prosecution's Application for a Warrant of Arrest against Omar Hassan Ahmad Al Bashir, PTC I) ICC-02/05-01/09-3 (4 March 2009), para 44.

44   *First Warrant of Arrest* Decision for *Al Bashir*, ibid, para 126.

45   'Second Informal Inter-Sessional Workshop for experts from Member States of the Atlantic Alliance with regard to the issue of War Crimes', UD/A/AC-249/1997/WG-1/IP, UK; 'Summary Records of the Plenary meetings', UN Doc A/CONF.183/SR.2, para 44 (Japan); UN Doc A/CONF.183/SR.5, para 77 (Israel); UN Doc A/CONF.183/SR.9, para 38

INTRODUCTION

task was to transpose the accumulated body of customary law into a treaty text.[46] The Preparatory Committee on the establishment of an international criminal court, established by the UN General Assembly,[47] also upheld this opinion so as to attract wide acceptance.[48] States at the Rome Conference relied on custom to argue for or against the inclusion or exclusion of specific underlying offences in the Statute, for instance, war crimes committed in non-international armed conflict.[49] A Chilean court openly stated that '[t]he Rome Statute became the expression of existing international law at the time of its creation'.[50] The Federal Court of Australia also noted:

> [T]he Rome Statute was drawn up to provide for the crimes it defined and purported to define those crimes as crimes that had crystallised into crimes in international law as at the date of the Statute, notwithstanding that the Statute was to come into force, and the ICC was to be established, at a later date.[51]

(China); 'Summary Records of meetings of the Committee of the Whole', UN Doc A/CONF.183/C.1/SR.4, paras 49-54 (USA), 55 (Germany), 68 (Spain); UN Doc A/CONF.183/C.1/SR.5, paras 24 (Thailand), 30 (Egypt); UN Doc A/CONF.183/C.1/SR.9, para 20 (Italy); UN Doc A/CONF.183/C.1/SR.26, paras 93 (USA), 37 (the Dominican Republic); UN Doc A/CONF.183/C.1/SR.29, para 75 (China); 'Summary record of the 11th meeting', UN Doc A/C.6/52/SR.11(1997), para 96 (China). Also see HU. Scupin, 'History of International Law, 1815 to World War I' in R. Wolfrum (ed) (2011) *MPEPIL*, para 36; C. McDougall, *The Crime of Aggression under the Rome Statute of the International Criminal Court* (OUP 2013)137–38.

46 Scupin, ibid; S. Sivakumaran, *The Law of Non-International Armed Conflict* (OUP 2012) 107; UN Doc A/CONF.183/SR.3, para 21 (Czech Republic); UN Doc A/CONF.183/SR.3, para 4 (Singapore).

47 'Establishment of an international criminal court', GA Res 50/46 (1995), UN Doc A/RES/50/46.

48 'Summary of the Proceedings of the Preparatory Committee during the Period 25 March-12 April 1996', UN Doc A/AC.249/1 (1996), para 38; 'Report of the Preparatory Committee on the Establishment of an International Criminal Court', UN Doc A/51/22 (1996), Vol I, para 78.

49 P. Kirsch and J.T. Holmes, 'The Rome Conference on an International Criminal Court: The Negotiating Process' (1999) 93 *AJIL* 2, 6; P. Kirsch and D. Robinson, 'Reaching Agreement at the Rome Conference' in Cassese *et al* (eds) (n 14) 79–80. Some delegations argued that only weapons prohibited under customary international law could be included, see UN Doc A/CONF.183/C.1/SR.4, paras 52-53 (US); UN Doc A/CONF.183/C.1/SR.5, paras 28 (France), 77 (Israel); UN Doc A/CONF.183/C.1/SR.26, para 55 (Korea); UN Doc A/CONF.183/C.1/SR.5, para 87 (India); UN Doc A/CONF.183/C.1/SR.27, para 33 (Israel), 43 (Bosnia and Herzegovina).

50 *Víctor Raúl Pinto v Tomás Rojas* (Supreme Court, Chile) 3125-04, ILDC 1093 (CL 2007), para 29.

51 *SRYYY v Australia* [2005] FCAFC 42 (25 March 2005), para 75, confirmed in *SZCWP v Australia* [2006] FCAFC 9 (20 February 2006), para 107. Cf. *SRNN v Australia* [2000]

Different views exist.[52] Some States argued that the list of offences should consider the development of law, in particular, the law of weapons.[53] The Indian delegation, however, commented that the Rome Conference 'is an institution-setting conference and not one meant to progressively develop and codify substantive parts of international law'.[54] The employment of chemical and bacteriological weapons as a war crime was generally supported at the Conference, but the use of them was not listed as a war crime due to disagreements on the use of nuclear weapons.[55] Article 10 of the Statute provides that '[n]othing in this Part [about jurisdiction, admissibility and applicable law] shall be interpreted as limiting or prejudicing in any way existing or developing rules of international law for purposes other than this Statute'. This provision indicates that the crimes outlined in the Statute are not exhaustive restatements of the entire corpus of international criminal law.[56]

The International Law Commission (ILC) and States rarely determine whether a treaty is a restatement (the transformation of a pre-existing customary rule into written form) or is a progressive development (the drafting of newly written rules) of customary law. The ILC, established by the UN General Assembly to promote the codification of international law and its progressive development,[57] usually refrains from categorising clearly or exclusively that treaty provisions are either a codification or a progressive development of international law.[58] The Commission never clarified to what extent the Draft text for the Establishment of an International Criminal Court (1994 Draft Statute)[59]

AATA 983 (10 November 2000), para 63; *AXOIB v Australia* [2002] AATA 365 (17 May 2002), para 32.

52 'Summary record of the 14th meeting', UN Doc A/C.6/52/SR.14 (1997), para 52 (Georgia).
53 UN Doc A/CONF.183/C.1/SR.27, para 4 (Algeria); UN Doc A/CONF.183/C.1/SR.28, para 25 (Namibia); UN Doc A/CONF.183/SR.5, par 62 (New Zealand).
54 UN Doc A/CONF.183/SR.4, para 52 (India).
55 Schabas (n 30) 277–82.
56 *Situation in the Republic of Kenya* (Dissenting Opinion by Judge Hans-Peter Kaul to Pre-Trial Chamber II's "Decision Pursuant to Article 15 of the Rome Statute on the Authorization of an Investigation into the Situation in the Republic of Kenya") ICC-01/09-19-Corr (31 March 2010), para 32; T. McCormack and S. Robertson, 'Jurisdictional Aspects of the Rome Statute for the New Industrial Criminal Court' (1999) 23 *Melbourne U L Rev* 635, 653; Grover (2014) (n 39) 266–67; O. Triffterer and A. Heinze, 'Article 10' in Triffterer and Ambos (eds) (n 42) 645–49; Schabas (n 30) 335–36.
57 Statute of the International Law Commission, as amended by GA Res 36/39 (1981), arts 1(1) and 15; 'Establishment of an International Law Commission', GA Res 174 (II) (1947), UN Doc A/RES/174 (II).
58 'Report of the International Law Commission', UN Doc A/51/10 (1996), Vol II, 84, 86–87, paras 147 (a), 156–59.
59 'Report of the International Law Commission', UN Doc A/49/10 (1994), 20–73.

was a codification or progressive development of international criminal law. In addition, the 2000 Crimes against Humanity and War Crimes Act of Canada stipulates that '[f]or greater certainty, crimes described in articles 6 and 7 and paragraph 2 of article 8 of the Rome Statute are, as of July 17, 1998, crimes according to customary international law, and may be crimes according to customary international law before that date'.[60] The Philippines also stated that 'basic tenets of the Court [ICC] were consistent with customary international law'.[61] Fourteen member States of the Caribbean Community have also repeatedly held that some 'provisions of the Rome Statute' had attained 'the status of or represent customary international law'.[62] The US legal adviser remarked at the 2010 Kampala Review Conference that '[u]nlike genocide, war crimes, and crimes against humanity – which plainly violated customary international law when the Rome Statute was adopted – as yet, no authoritative definition of aggression exists under customary international law'.[63] The ILC and States did not clarify to what extent provisions of the Statute are codifications of pre-existing customary law, or are crystallisations of emerging customary law through the adoption of the Statute.

Commentators argued that the result of the Rome Statute with 'uneasy technical solutions, awkward formulations, [and] difficult compromises' was aimed to attract as much ratification as possible.[64] Roy Lee, executive

---

[60] Canada, Crimes against Humanity and War Crimes Act 2000, amended 2019, § 4(4); *Sapkota v Canada*, [2013] FC 790, para 28.

[61] 'Summary record of the 12th meeting', UN Doc A/C.6/55/SR.12 (2000), para 20 (Philippines).

[62] UN Doc A/C.6/52/SR.11 (1997), para 46 (Trinidad and Tobago, speaking on behalf of the 14 member States of the Caribbean Community); GAOR 67th session, 31st plenary meeting, UN Doc A/67/PV.31 (6 November 2012), and in GAOR 70th session, 48th plenary meeting, UN Doc A/70/PV.48 (5 November 2015), Statement of Trinidad and Tobago on behalf of 14 member States of the Caribbean Community. See also Switzerland, 'Report by the Federal Council on Private Security and Military Companies' (Report to the Parliament in response to the Stähelin Postulate 04. 3267 of 1 June 2004, Private Security Companies), 2 December 2005, 5.5.2.1: 'The crimes against international law named in the Rome Statute of the International Criminal Court reflect customary international law, as is broadly recognised'.

[63] H.H. Koh, Legal Adviser, US Department of State, 'Statement at the Review Conference of the International Criminal Court' (Kampala, Uganda, 4 June 2010).

[64] 'Summary record of the 9th meeting', UN Doc A/C.6/55/SR.9 (2000), para 4 (Mr Kirsch, Chairman of the Preparatory Commission for the International Criminal Court); P. Kirsch, 'Customary International Humanitarian Law, its Enforcement, and the Role of the International Criminal Court' in L. Maybee and B. Chakka (eds), *Custom as a Source of International Humanitarian Law: Proceedings of the Conference to Mark the Publication of the ICRC Study 'Customary International Humanitarian Law'* (ICRC 2006) 79–80; L.N.

secretary to the Preparatory Committee and the Rome Conference, stated that 'the definition of crimes contained in the Statute reflects existing practices and affirms current developments in international law'.[65] Theodor Meron asserted that:

> Articles 6 to 8 [...] will take a life of their own as an authoritative and largely customary statement of international humanitarian and criminal law [...]. [T]he Statute is largely reflective of customary law. Largely, but not completely.[66]

Provisions of the Rome Statute to some degree are clearly codifications of customary law.[67] As noted by William Schabas, the Statute also progressively develops international criminal law, for instance, its article 8 includes a new rule concerning enlisting child soldiers under the age of 15 years as a war crime.[68] The majority of the Special Court for Sierra Leone (SCSL),[69] however, disagreed with this view. In its opinion, enlisting child soldiers as a war crime was recognised in custom before November 1996.[70] Whether a provision of the Rome Statute was a reflection of a pre-existing customary rule or was a

---

Sadat, 'Custom, Codification and Some Thoughts about the Relationship between the Two: Article 10 of the ICC Statute' (1999) 49 *De Paul L Rev* 910.

[65] R.S. Lee, 'The Rome Conference and Its Contributions to International Law' in R.S. Lee (ed), *The International Criminal Court: The Making of the Rome Statute: Issues, Negotiations and Results* (Kluwer Law International 1999) 1, 38; P. Kirsch, 'The Development of the Rome Statute' in id 458.

[66] T. Meron, 'Crimes under the Jurisdiction of the International Criminal Court' in H. von Hebel *et al* (eds), *Reflection on the International Criminal Court: Essays in Honour of Adriaan Bos* (TMC Asser Press 1999) 48.

[67] L.N. Sadat and R. Carden, 'The New International Criminal Court: An Uneasy Revolution' (1999) 88 *Georgetown LJ* 381, 423; P. Kirsch, 'Foreword' in K. Dörmann (ed), *Elements of War Crimes under the Rome Statute of the International Criminal Court: Sources and Commentary* (CUP 2003) xiii; H.-P. Kaul, 'Ten Years International Criminal Court', at the Experts' Discussion '10 years International Criminal Court and the Role of the United States in International Justice' (Berlin, 2 October 2012).

[68] Schabas (n 30) 221; H. von Hebel and D. Robinson, 'Crimes within the Jurisdiction of the Court' in Lee (ed) (n 65) 104, 126; *Gacumbitsi v The Prosecutor* (Judgement) ICTR-01-64-A (7 July 2006), paras 49-52; *The Prosecutor v Seromba* (Judgement) ICTR-01-66-A (12 March 2008) (Dissenting Opinion of Judge Liu), paras 9-10, 15.

[69] Statute of the Special Court for Sierra Leone, annexed to the Agreement between the United Nations and the Government of Sierra Leone on the Establishment of a Special Court for Sierra Leone (16 January 2002) 2178 UNTS 137 [Statute of the SCSL], art 1.

[70] *Prosecutor v Norman* (Decision on Preliminary Motion Based on Lack of Jurisdiction (Child Recruitment), A Ch) SCSL-2004-14-AR72 (E) (31 May 2004), para 51.

INTRODUCTION

crystallisation of an emerging customary rule at the 1998 Rome Conference is still controversial.[71]

As Mark Villiger wrote: 'customary law is dynamic and the customary rule underlying a treaty text may change; the treaty rule may generate new customary law'.[72] The Rome Statute reserves the possibility of a treaty rule developing into custom after its adoption. In its Part II, article 10 implies the possible impact of the Rome Statute on the 'existing or developing rules of international law' as an aid to interpreting other treaties.[73] Other international tribunals also referred to the Statute to interpret and clarify the definition of crimes.[74] Commentators have argued that the provisions of the Rome Statute and their interpretations will 'influence the evolution of international law' and subsequent State practice.[75] It remains unclear whether treaty rules that were of a declaratory nature continue to be declaratory of customary law and whether newly drafted rules of the Rome Statute have passed into the corpus of customary international law.[76]

A number of studies have examined and commented on rules of the Rome Statute and the practice of the ICC.[77] Several academics have published relevant books on specific issues of the Rome Statute and international criminal law.[78] A considerable amount of research has also been carried out on

---

71   UN Doc A/CONF.183/SR.2, paras 40-8 (Japan); UN Doc A/CONF.183/C.1/SR.3, paras 89, 91 (UK), 109 (Slovenia); UN Doc A/CONF.183/C.1/SR.4, paras 2-3 (Canada), 24-5 (Israel); UN Doc A/CONF.183/C.1/SR.26, paras 40 (Switzerland), 51 (Brazil), 95-7 (US); UN Doc A/CONF.183/SR.9, para 38 (China).

72   Villiger (1985) (n 1) 227, 238; Baxter (1965) (n 1) 275–300; *North Sea Continental Shelf* cases (n 5), 41, para 71; *Libya-Malta Continental Shelf* Judgment (n 5), 29–30, para 27; *Military and Paramilitary Activities* Judgment (n 3), 95, para 177; UN Doc A/73/10 (2018), para 65, Conclusion 11; UN Doc A/71/10 (2016), para 62, Conclusion 11.

73   Schabas (n 30) 335–36.

74   For a detailed analysis, ibid.

75   Grover (2010) (n 39) 571 with further reference in fn 183; Triffterer and Heinze (n 56) 654.

76   M.C. Bassiouni, *Introduction to International Criminal Law* (2nd edn, Brill 2012) 144.

77   Lee (ed) (n 65); Cassese et al (eds) (n 14); C. Stahn and G. Sluiter (eds), *The Emerging Practice of the International Criminal Court* (Brill | Nijhoff 2009); Triffterer and Ambos (eds) (n 42); Schabas (n 30); Klamberg (ed) (n 39); C. Stahn, *A Critical Introduction to International Criminal Law* (CUP 2018).

78   For crimes, see E. La Haye, *War Crimes in Internal Armed Conflicts* (CUP 2008); W.A. Schabas, *Genocide in International Law, The Crime of Crimes* (2nd edn, CUP 2009); M.C. Bassiouni, *Crimes Against Humanity* (CUP 2011); L.N. Sadat (ed), *Forging a Convention for Crimes Against Humanity* (CUP 2011); McDougall (n 45); K. Ambos, *Treatise on International Criminal Law, Vol II: The Crimes and Sentencing* (OUP 2014); G., Kemp, *Individual Criminal Liability for the International Crime of Aggression* (2nd edn, Intersentia 2016); C. Kreß and S. Barriga (eds), *The Crime of Aggression: A Commentary* (CUP 2017); R. Dubler and M. Kalyk, *Crimes Against Humanity in the 21st Century: Law, Practice, and*

customary international law, in particular on the nature of customary international law.[79] The ILC in 2018 adopted a set of 16 draft conclusions guiding the identification of customary international law.[80] Some recent works observing customary international law have either assessed the approach on how to identify a rule of customary international law[81] or analysed specific issues, in particular, the role of non-State actors in the formation of customary

---

Threats to International Peace and Security (Brill | Nijhoff 2018); G. Mettraux, *International Crimes and Practice Volume I: Genocide* (OUP 2019). For modes of liability, see G. Boas et al, *International Criminal Law Practitioner Library: Vol 1, Forms of Responsibility in International Criminal Law* (CUP 2007); G. Mettraux, *The Law of Command Responsibility* (OUP 2009); H. Olásolo, *The Criminal Responsibility of Senior Political and Military Leaders as Principals to International Crimes* (Hart Publishing 2009); C. Meloni, *Command Responsibility in International Criminal Law* (TMC Asser Press 2010); E. van Sliedregt, *Individual Criminal Responsibility in International Law* (OUP 2012); K. Ambos, *Treatise on International Criminal Law, Vol I: Foundations and General Part* (OUP 2013), chapters 4–6; L.D. Yanev, *Theories of Co-perpetration in International Criminal Law* (Brill | Nijhoff 2018). For defences and personal immunities, see Y. Dinstein, *The Defence of 'Obedience of Superior Orders' in International Law* (OUP 2012); R. Pedretti, *Immunity of Heads of State and State Officials for International Crimes* (Brill | Nijhoff 2015).

79 For a bibliography on customary international law, see 'Fifth report on identification of customary international law', by Michael Wood, Special Rapporteur, Addendum, UN Doc A/CN.4/717/Add.1 (2018). For recent books, see Maurice Mendelson, 'The Formation of Customary International Law' (1998) 272 *Recueil des cours* 155; M. Byers, *Custom, Power and the Power of Rules: International Relations and Customary International Law* (CUP 1999); B. Chigara, *Legitimacy Deficit in Custom: A Deconstructionist Critique* (Ashgate | Dartmouth 2001); A. Perreau-Saussine and J.B. Murphy (eds), *The Nature of Customary Law* (CUP 2009); B. Lepard, *Customary International Law: A New Theory with Practical Applications* (CUP 2010); D. Bederman, *Custom as a Source of Law* (CUP 2010); Y. Hassabe, *International Custom as a Source of International Criminal Law: in Light of the Principle of Legality The Status of International Custom to Create* (VDM 2011); M. Scharf, *Customary International Law in Times of Fundamental Change: Recognizing Grotian Moments* (CUP 2013); Thirlway (n 10) 60–105; L.R. Helfer and I.B. Wuerth, 'Custom in the Age of Soft Law' (working paper) < https://www.iilj.org/wp-content/uploads/2016/07/WuerthIILJColloq2014.pdf > accessed 30 December 2020; H. Taki, *State Recognition and Opinio Juris in Customary International Law* (Chuo University Press 2016); Bradley (ed) (n 28); B. Lepard (ed), *Reexamining Customary International Law* (CUP 2016); M.P. Beham, *State Interest and the Sources of International Law: Doctrine, Morality, and Non-Treaty Law* (Routledge 2018); Staubach (n 17); B.S. Chimni, 'Customary International Law: A Third World Perspective' (2018) 112 *AJIL* 1; G. Nolte, 'How to Identify Customary International Law? – On the Outcome of the Work of the International Law Commission (2018)' (2019) 62 *Japanese Ybk Intl L* 251.

80 'Report of the International Law Commission', UN Doc A/73/10 (2018), paras 58, 60, 65.

81 Bradley (ed) (n 28); Lepard (ed) (n 79); L.J. van den Herik, 'Using Custom to Reconceptualize Crimes Against Humanity' in S. Darcy and J. Powderly (eds), *Judicial Creativity at the International Criminal Tribunals* (OUP 2010) 80–105.

international law.[82] Meron, Schabas and the International Committee of the Red Cross (ICRC) have dealt with substantive aspects of customary law in the field of human rights law and international humanitarian law.[83] Recent literature on customary law in international criminal law has drawn attention to the approaches to developing, interpreting or identifying customary rules in international criminal tribunals.[84]

The majority of these efforts, however, have not fully accommodated the interaction between substantive provisions of the Rome Statute and customary international law. Apart from a few writings analysing a rule of the Statute as a reflection of or departure from a pre-existing customary rule,[85] there has been little research dealing with rules of the Rome Statute as evidence of parallel customary rules and as evidence of the progressive development of custom. Robert Dubler and Matthew Kalyk's book concerns crimes against humanity in this regard,[86] but leaving other specific topics untouched. Leena Grover's work concluded that the crimes in articles 6-8 and 8*bis* of the Statute are 'in

---

[82] L. Lijnzaad (ed), *The Judge and International Custom* (Brill | Nijhoff 2016); N. Blokker, 'International Organisations and Customary International Law' (2017) 14 *IOLR* 1; S. Droubi, 'The Role of the United Nations in the Formation of Customary International Law in the Field of Human Rights Law' (2017) 19 *Intl Community LR* 68; N. Carrillo-Santarelli, 'The Possibilities and Legitimacy of Non-State Participation in the Formation of Customary Law' (2017) 19 *Intl Community LR* 98; G. Fox *et al*, 'The Contributions of United Nations Security Council Resolutions to the Law of Non-International Armed Conflict: New Evidence of Customary International Law' 2017 (67) *Am U L Rev* 649; P. Merkouris, 'Interpreting the Customary Rules on Interpretation' (2017) 19 *Intl Community LR* 126.

[83] T. Meron, *Human Rights and Humanitarian Norms as Customary Law* (Clarendon Press 1989); JM. Henckaerts and L. Doswald-beck (eds), *Customary International Humanitarian Law*, Vols I and II (CUP 2005); W.A. Schabas, *The Customary International Law of Human Rights* (forthcoming OUP 2021).

[84] Schlütter (n 24); Tan (n 23); J. d'Aspremont, 'An Autonomous Regime of Identification of Customary International Humanitarian Law: Do Not Say What You Do or Do Not Do What You Say?' in R. van Steenberghe (eds), *Droit International Humanitaire: un Régime Spécial de Droit International?* (Bruylant 2013); N. Arajärvi, *The Changing Nature of Customary International Law: Methods of Interpreting the Concept of Custom in International Criminal Tribunals* (Routledge 2014); T. Rauter, *Judicial Practice, Customary International Criminal Law and Nullum Crimen Sine Lege* (Springer 2017); H. Van der Wilt, 'State Practice as Element of Customary International Law: A White Knight in International Criminal Law?' (2019) 20 *ICLR* 784.

[85] Cassese *et al* (eds) (n 23) 101–08, 129–30; M. Bothe, 'War Crimes' in Cassese *et al* (eds) (n 14); P.V. Sainz-Pardo, 'Is Child Recruitment as a War Crime Part of Customary International Law?' (2008) 12 *Intl J H R* 555; P. Gaeta, 'Does President Al Bashir Enjoy Immunity from Arrest?' (2009) 7 *JICJ* 315, 315–32; McDougall (n 45) 137–55; O.A. Hathaway *et al*, 'Aiding and Abetting in International Criminal Law' (2019) 104 *Cornell L Rev* 1593.

[86] Dubler and Kalyk (n 78) chapters 9–10.

general' codifications of custom.[87] Her book focused on the role of custom as an aid to interpreting 'crimes' especially 'codified' in the Rome Statute; therefore, the question is unanswered as to whether a specific element of crimes or other substantive provisions of the Statute codified custom or generated new custom.

This book aims to explore whether the Rome Statute is reflective of customary international law through a historical-legal analysis. The terms 'custom', 'customary law' and 'customary international law' are used interchangeably in this book.[88] The Rome Statute as a whole is impossible to be a codification of existing international law. Definitions of crimes in its articles 6-8 and 8*bis*, liabilities in articles 25, 28 and 30 and defences in articles 27, 29, 31-33 are related to customary law. This book does not aim to look into all these articles and subparagraphs, but utilises case-studies and concentrates on selected provisions. The provisions selected are articles 8(2)(c) and (e) about war crimes in non-international armed conflict, article 7 regarding crimes against humanity, articles 8*bis* and 25(3*bis*) about the crime of aggression, article 25(3)(a) concerning indirect co-perpetration, and article 27(2) concerning personal immunity. These provisions were either disputable when the Rome Statute was adopted or have been significant in the ICC's present practice.[89] Article 6 of the Rome Statute is not considered, as the definition of genocide under this provision is a replication of that under article II of the Genocide Convention and the corresponding customary law.[90]

Besides, a provision on a matter that was included in the Rome Statute is the starting point. Customary rules on subjects that are not covered by the Statute go beyond the scope of this research.[91] This book concerns general customary law and does not examine regional customary law. International criminal tribunals also resort to general principles of criminal law in the absence of customary law and treaty law.[92] This book does not discuss such questions as

---

87   Grover (2014) (n 39) 220–344.
88   A. Perreau-Saussine and J.B. Murphy (eds), *The Nature of Customary Law* (CUP 2009).
89   For further clarifications of the importance of these provisions, see each chapter.
90   For a comparison, see Cassese *et al* (eds) (n 14) 129–30. For discussions on genocide, see Schabas (n 78); Mettraux (2019) (n 78); Ambos (2014) (n 78) 1–44. Cf. B. Van Schaack, 'The Crime of Political Genocide: Repairing the Genocide Convention's Blind Spot' (1997) 106 *Yale LJ* 2259.
91   Vienna Convention on the Law of Treaties, 1155 UNTS 331, Preamble.
92   *Prosecutor v Hadžihasanović et al* (Decision on Interlocutory Appeal Challenging Jurisdiction in Relation to Command Responsibility) ICTY-01-47-AR72 (Partial Dissenting Opinion of Judge Shahabuddeen), para 9; *Prosecutor v Furundžija* (Judgement) ICTY-95-17/1-T (10 December 1998), para 177.

the source of general principles of law[93] and the application of customary law by national criminal courts.[94]

1.3 Method and Terms of This Book

This section outlines the methodological framework for this book, which is analysed in detail in chapter 2. Four steps have to be followed to decide whether a treaty rule was or is declaratory of customary law.

The first step is to show that a rule/practice on a subject is found in a treaty rule. This step relates to the reading of the Rome Statute. This research generally applies the principles of interpretation embedded in articles 31-33 of the Vienna Convention on the Law of Treaties,[95] which are confirmed by the ICC.[96] In addition, article 21(3) of the Rome Statute, requiring the interpretation be consistent with 'internationally recognised human rights', is taken into account.[97] According to Grover, article 21(3) is a 'background' interpretive principle, which is applicable to interpreting crimes and other parts of the Rome

---

[93] ibid; W.A. Schabas, 'General Principles of Criminal Law in the International Criminal Court Statute (Part III)' (1998) 6 *EJCCLCJ* 400; K. Ambos, 'General Principles of Criminal Law in the Rome Statute' (1999) 10 *CLF* 1; F. Raimondo, *General Principles of Law in the Decisions of International Criminal Courts and Tribunals* (Brill | Nijhoff 2008) 73-164. See also 'General principle of law' in 'Report of the International Law Commission', UN Doc A/74/10 (2019), chapter IX; B. Simma and P. Alston, 'The Sources of Human Rights Law: Custom, Jus Cogens, and General Principles' (1988–1989) *Australian Ybk Intl L* 82, 90–107.

[94] For a general discussion, see M. Mendelson, 'The Effect of Customary International Law on Domestic Law: An Overview' (2004) 4 *Non-State Actors and International Law* 75; D. Shelton (ed), *International Law and Domestic Legal Systems: Incorporation, Transformation, and Persuasion* (OUP 2011); W.N. Ferdinandusse, *Direct Application of International Criminal Law in National Courts* (TMC Asser Press 2006).

[95] Vienna Convention on the Law of Treaties, 1155 UNTS 331.

[96] See *The Prosecutor v Lubanga* (Judgment on the Prosecutor's Application for Extraordinary Review of the Pre-Trial Chamber I's 31 March 2006 Decision Denying Leave to Appeal, A Ch) ICC-01/04-168 (13 July 2006), paras 33-42; *Prosecutor v Lubanga* (Decision on the Practices of Witness Familiarisation and Witness Proofing, PTC I) ICC-01/04-01/06-679 (8 November 2006), para 8; *The Prosecutor v Lubanga* (Decision on the Confirmation of Charges, PTC I) ICC-01/04-01/06-803-tEN (29 January 2007), para 283; *Situation in the Republic of Kenya* (Decision Pursuant to Article 15 of the Rome Statute on the Authorization of an Investigation into the Situation in the Republic of Kenya, PTC II) ICC-01/09-19-Corr (31 March 2010) (Dissenting Opinion by Judge Hans-Peter Kaul), paras 33-35.

[97] 1998 Rome Statute, art 21(3).

Statute.[98] Furthermore, in interpreting core crimes in the jurisdiction of the ICC, article 22(2) of the Statute requires faithful compliance with the principle of strict construction.[99] The principle of legality is the 'guiding interpretive principle' for the interpretation of crimes.[100]

The second step is to confirm whether a treaty rule articulates itself as declaratory of pre-existing customary law.[101] An affirmative answer to this question illustrates a preliminary but not decisive conclusion about the status of a customary rule. For this purpose, this research looks into the text of the treaty rule and the preamble of the treaty, the structure and context of the treaty rule and the *travaux préparatoires* of that treaty rule. If there is no claim in the treaty or its preparatory works, this does not exclude a conclusion that the treaty rule is declaratory of custom.[102]

The third step is to prove the existence or non-existence of a customary rule. This step pertains to the method of ascertaining the status of a customary rule. In the identification of customary international rules, there is little possibility that one academic theory can perfectly deal with every controversial issue.[103] From a legal positivist perspective, subjective and objective elements, i.e., State practice and *opinio juris*, constitute the elements of customary law.[104] The classic approach to identifying the state of a customary rule, therefore, is to seek sufficient evidence of the two distinctive elements (the two-element approach).[105] In 2018, the ILC also adopted that an accepted guideline for the identification of customary law is to ascertain the two-element, namely, a general practice and accepted as law (*opinio juris*).[106] An identification approach

---

98   Grover (2014) (n 39) 122–23.
99   1998 Rome Statute, art 22(2).
100 Grover (2014) (n 39) 102–33.
101 *North Sea Continental Shelf* cases (n 5), 41, paras 63, 71; *Military and Paramilitary Activities* Judgment (n 3), 95, para 177; UN Doc A/73/10 (2018), para 65, Conclusion 11.
102 Dinstein (n 1).
103 Rauter (n 84) 87–116.
104 ibid 87–92.
105 UN Doc A/CN.4/682; Henckaerts and Doswald-beck (eds) (n 83) 33; The American Law Institute, 'Restatement of the Law of Foreign Relations Law of the United States' (Third), 1986, para 102, Comment b; S. Donaghue, 'Normative Habits, Genuine Beliefs and Evolving Law: Nicaragua and the Theory of Customary International Law' (1995) 16 *Australian Ybk Intl L* 327; O. Schachter, 'International Law in Theory and Practice: General Course in Public International Law' (1982) 178 *Recueil des cours* 32; *North Sea Continental Shelf* cases (n 5), 43–44, paras 74, 77; *Jurisdictional Immunities of the State (Germany v Italy: Greece Intervening)*, Judgment, [2012] ICJ Rep 99, 122, para 55.
106 'Identification of Customary International Law' in 'Report of the International Law Commission', UN Doc A/73/10 (2018), para 65, Conclusion 2.

that departs from the two-element method has not been reached in the field of international criminal law.[107] This book also employs the two-element identification approach.

In this book, practice refers to physical behaviour and verbal acts (statements) between or among States. The practice also includes actions of international organisations. *Opinio juris* refers to the unilateral acceptance of what practice reflects customary law. Given the prohibitive feature of substantive rules in international criminal law and the scarcity of hard evidence of national prosecution, this book adopts a flexible two-element approach focusing more on *opinio juris*. Several scholars and the recent ILC work both support a flexible application of the two-element approach in a particular context.[108] Chapter 2 further observes the identification method, and the forms and evidence of the two elements in detail.

The fourth and last step is to demonstrate that a treaty rule was or is evidence of the status of customary law. This step concerns how to illustrate the relationship between custom and treaty rules. This book employs the notion of 'declaratory' in a general sense to illustrate the relationship between custom and provisions of the Rome Statute. A treaty rule 'was declaratory' of custom if it incorporated a pre-existing customary rule during the process of its formation, or crystallised an emerging customary rule when the treaty was adopted. Accordingly, an historical overview of the development of a 'rule' or practice is required. Additionally, the phrase 'is declaratory' is employed to illustrate the nature of a treaty rule as a reflection of custom at present. This phrase covers two circumstances. First, if a treaty rule that was declaratory feature continues to be a reflection of a given customary rule to date, such a treaty

---

107   M. Wood, 'Foreword' in Lepard (ed) (n 79); Schlütter (n 24). Cf. Arajärvi (n 84); G. Mettraux, *International Crimes and the Ad hoc Tribunals* (OUP 2006) 18.

108   F. Kirgis, 'Custom on a Sliding Scale' (1987) 81 *AJIL* 146; A.E. Roberts, 'Traditional and Modern Approaches to Customary International Law: A Reconciliation' (2001) 95 *AJIL* 757, 764; J. Wouters and C. Ryngaert, 'Impact on the Process of the Formation of Customary International Law' in M.T. Kamminga and M. Scheinin (eds), *The Impact of Human Rights Law on General International Law* (OUP 2009) 111–12; R. Kolb, 'Selected Problems in the Theory of Customary International Law' (2003) 50 *Netherlands Intl L Rev* 119, 128; 'Second report on Identification of Customary International Law to the Sixty-sixth Session of the ILC', by Michael Wood, Special Rapporteur, UN Doc A/CN.4/672 (2014), para 3; UN Doc A/73/10 (2018), para 65, Conclusion 3.1 and its commentary (2)-(6); 'Preliminary summary record of the 3301st meeting', UN Doc A/CN.4/SR.3301 (2016), 16 (Mr Murase). For a different view, see M. Mendelson, 'The Formation of Customary International Law' (1998) 272 *Recueil des cours* 155; M. Mendelson, 'The Subjective Element in Customary International Law' (1995) 66 *British Ybk Intl L* 177; R. Müllerson, 'On the Nature and Scope of Customary International Law' (1997) 2 *ARIL* 341.

rule 'is declaratory' of custom. Second, if a treaty rule that was not declaratory in nature but its substantial content has progressively passed into the corpus of customary law at the time of assessment, this treaty rule 'is declaratory' of custom.

1.4 Structure of This Book

This book consists of eight chapters. Chapter 1 introduces the importance of customary law, the aim of the research, the questions raised as well as the book's general methodology and merits. Chapter 2 outlines the methodological framework of this book in more detail: (1) the interpretation of the Rome Statute; (2) the method of identifying the existence of a customary rule; (3) the role of treaty law in the identification of custom and the term 'declaratory' used to clarify the relationship between treaty and custom; and (4) preconditions for a provision of the Rome Statute to be declaratory of custom.

Chapter 3 examines the relationship between article 8 of the Rome Statute and customary law concerning war crimes in non-international armed conflict. The chapter briefly reviews the historical development of war crimes trials and analyses the negotiations on article 8 of the Rome Statute, and then considers the practice of prosecuting war crimes in non-international armed conflict after the adoption of the Statute. The chapter concludes that war crimes for violations of Common Article 3 of the 1949 Geneva Conventions in non-international armed conflict were codified in article 8(2)(c) of the Rome Statute. However, war crimes for other serious violations in non-international armed conflict were crystallised in article 8(2)(e) at the Rome Conference. Articles 8(2)(c) and (e) of the Rome Statute in general were and are declaratory of custom concerning war crimes in non-international armed conflict.

Chapter 4 focuses on the relationship between article 7 of the Rome Statute and customary law concerning crimes against humanity. Since World War II, there have been several formulations of crimes against humanity in international instruments. The chapter argues that multiple definitions do not affect the customary state of crimes against humanity in general but indicate different understandings of elements of the crimes. The contextual requirements and some underlying prohibited acts of crimes against humanity remain controversial. This chapter critically analyses two contextual elements concerning the issue of the removal of a nexus with an armed conflict and the issue of policy requirement. The armed conflict nexus requirement was a substantive element for the notion of crimes against humanity in the Nuremberg Charter. Later on, as a departure from pre-existing customary law, the link to the armed conflict requirement disassociated itself within the notion of crimes against humanity. It remains unclear when this nexus disappeared under customary law before the adoption of the Statute of the International Criminal Tribunal for Rwanda (ICTR Statute).[109] By excluding the armed conflict nexus, article 7 codified or, at the very least, crystallised this development of crimes against humanity under customary law. The chapter concludes that article 7(1) of the Statute was and is declaratory of custom on the nexus issue.

In addition, 'the policy to commit such an attack' is deemed a requisite legal element of crimes against humanity at the ICC. After the ICTY's *Kunarać et al* Appeals Chamber judgment, the policy was considered an evidentiary consideration to establish an attack in the jurisprudence of the ICTY and the ICTR. However, the fact that subsequent jurisprudence of the ICTY repeatedly subscribed to the view in the *Kunarać et al* Appeals Chamber judgment does not mean that the policy issue was settled under customary law. This chapter argues that article 7(2)(a) was and is declaratory of custom with regard to the policy element.

Chapter 5 explores the relationship between articles 8*bis* and 25(3*bis*) of the Rome Statute and customary law concerning the crime of aggression. Articles 8*bis* and 25 (3*bis*) of the Rome Statute were adopted at the 2010 Kampala Review Conference, and the ICC's jurisdiction over the crime of aggression became effective in December 2018. It is generally accepted that the crime of aggression was part of customary international law. However, debates exist as to the appropriate definition of this crime and its elements. Unlike the concept of crimes against peace defined in the Nuremberg and Tokyo Charters, articles 8*bis* and 25(3*bis*) restrict the scope of potential perpetrators and participators prosecuted for the crime of aggression to persons 'in a position effectively to exercise control over or to direct the political or military action of a State'. This leadership clause raises the question of whether the leadership element of 'control or direct' was and is declaratory of customary law. The chapter covers the Nuremberg and Tokyo trials, several trials in Subsequent Proceedings, the work of the International Law Commission, the negotiating and drafting history of the crime of aggression, in particular, discussions about proposals at the Rome Conference, and in the Preparatory Commission and the Special Working Group on the Crime of Aggression. States' attitude towards the definition of the crime of aggression on the restriction of potential persons will be analysed. The chapter argues that a consensus has been reached that the crime

---

109   SC Res 955 (1994) on establishment of the ICTR and adoption of the Statute of the Tribunal, UN Doc S/RES/955 (1994).

of aggression requires a leadership element. However, the specific 'control or direct' leadership clause in articles 8*bis* and 25(3*bis*) of the Rome Statute has not been accepted as a substantial element of the crime of aggression in customary law. The chapter concludes that articles 8*bis* and 25(3*bis*) neither were nor are declaratory of customary international law concerning the leadership requirement.

Chapter 6 discusses the relationship between article 25(3)(a) of the Rome Statute and customary law concerning indirect co-perpetration. The notion of indirect co-perpetration defined by the ICC aims to attribute liability to an individual at the leadership level, regardless of whether the crimes committed are within the scope of the common plan among the accused. However, an examination of the text and the drafting history of article 25(3)(a) indicates that article 25(3)(a) does not contain a form of indirect co-perpetration. Since this rule does not deal with indirect co-perpetration, it seems that it is not necessary to examine the relationship between article 25(3)(a) and custom on the issue of indirect co-perpetration. Nevertheless, assuming it is well accepted that indirect co-perpetration liability is embedded in article 25(3)(a), it is required to examine its customary status to date. The chapter observes the necessity of attributing liability to individuals at the leadership level, post-World War II practice, the jurisprudence of other international criminal tribunals and implementation legislation to assess the customary status of indirect co-perpetration liability. The chapter concludes that apart from the case law of the ICC and a few cases of the ICTY, there is little evidence of the acceptance of indirect co-perpetration as a customary rule. Indirect co-perpetration has not been sufficiently supported by practice and *opinio juris* to constitute a customary rule to date. Therefore, even assuming this provision covers indirect co-perpetration liability, article 25(3)(a) is not declaratory of a customary rule about indirect co-perpetration.

Chapter 7 examines the relationship between article 27(2) of the Rome Statute and customary international law. Article 27(2) provides that international immunities and special procedural rules cannot bar the exercise of jurisdiction by the ICC. After analysing the text and the structure of the Statute, as well as the preparatory works of article 27(2), the chapter argues that article 27(2) does not derogate from the pre-existing traditional customary law respecting personal immunity. After examining international jurisprudence, national cases, the attitude of the UN Security Council and the work of the ILC, chapter 7 concludes that article 27(2) neither was declaratory nor is declaratory of a modified customary rule.

In closing, chapter 8 highlights the general conclusions of this book.

1.5 Merits and Limits of This Book

The study of the nature of the Rome Statute as evidence of custom is of substantial practical significance. The analysis of the interrelation between treaty and custom is relevant to the task of interpretation and application of law within and outside the ICC.

As illustrated above, customary law continues to play a role at the ICC. The questions of the validity and applicability of a provision of the Rome Statute and its customary status have emerged in the *Al Bashir* case of the Darfur Situation, which was referred by the UN Security Council to the ICC.[110] Further issues may also arise in potential cases of the Afghanistan, Bangladesh/Myanmar, Côte d'Ivoire, Georgia, Libya, Palestine and Ukraine Situations as to whether the crimes charged with and the liability attributed to the defendants were recognised under customary law.

Similar questions about the applicability of the Rome Statute and the validity of customary law may also arise outside the framework of the ICC. Firstly, as of December 2020, 123 States are parties to the Rome Statute,[111] and another 30 countries have signed but not ratified it.[112] Russia, Sudan, Israel and the US have declared their will no longer sign the treaty. More than 60 States are not parties to the Rome Statute.[113] States are not bound by a rule of a treaty to which they have not explicitly consented.[114] Their non-party State status to the Rome

---

110 *The Prosecutor v Al Bashir* (Decision on the Failure by the Republic of Malawi to Comply with the Cooperation Requests Issued by the Court with Respect to the Arrest and Surrender of Omar Hassan Ahmad Al Bashir, PTC I) ICC-02/05-01/09-139-Corr (13 December 2011); id, (Decision Pursuant to Article 87(7) of the Rome Statute on the Refusal of the Republic of Chad to Comply with the Cooperation Requests Issued by the Court with Respect to the Arrest and Surrender of Omar Hassan Ahmad Al Bashir, PTC I) ICC-02/05-01/09-140-tENG (13 December 2011).

111 Burundi and Philippines submitted their official withdrawal notifications to the UN Secretary-General. Burundi's withdrawal became effective on 27 October 2017, and the Philippines' withdrawal became effective on 17 March 2019, see C.N.805.2016.TREATIES-XVIII.10 and C.N.138.2018.TREATIES-XVIII.10. In 2016, South Africa and Gambia also submitted their withdrawal notifications to the Secretary-General, but later they rescinded their notifications of withdrawal, see C.N.786.2016.TREATIES-XVIII.10, C.N.62.2017.TREATIES-XVIII.10, C.N.862.2016.TREATIES-XVIII.10 and C.N.121.2017.TREATIES-XVIII.10.

112 Depository of Status of Treaties, TREATIES-XVIII.10.

113 The US, Russian Federation and China have actively participated in the 1998 Rome Conference. The US and Russia both signed but expressly rejected to ratify the Statute. China, Egypt, Libya, India, Iraq, Pakistan, Somalia, South Sudan, Syria, and Yemen are neither States Parties to the Statute nor have they expressed the intention to ratify the treaty in the future.

114 R. Cryer, 'The ICC and its Relationship to Non-States Parties' in Stahn and Sluiter (eds) (n 77) 261–62.

Statute does not mean that international crimes committed by their nationals in their territory would be subject to impunity. Aside from their respective national law, general principles of law and customary law play a vital role at the national level. If rules of the Rome Statute concerning an offence, a mode of liability, or personal immunity are generally recognised under customary law, these rules will apply to crimes committed everywhere, irrespective of whether the crimes were committed by citizens of States that have not ratified a treaty.[115] In interpreting and applying law, as well as filling gaps in the law, the findings of this book might be of relevance in courts of these non-party States.

Secondly, debates about the customary status of the provisions of the Rome Statute might arise in domestic courts of States (including non-party States and States Parties) in analysing issues concerning civil compensation and the exclusion of refugee protection for committing international crimes, as well as with regard to exercising universal jurisdiction to prosecute international crimes. Despite that the concept and requirements of universal jurisdiction are controversial,[116] and that States rarely exercise universal jurisdiction for political pressure or lack of resources and evidence,[117] many States are active in prosecuting international crimes based on universal jurisdiction.[118] Many States Parties to the Rome Statute have also incorporated or transformed the crimes falling within the ICC's jurisdiction into their national laws. Some States can rely on customary law, directly or indirectly depending on their national

---

115 Von Hebel and Robinson (n 68) 79, 122.
116 T. Meron, 'Is International Law Moving towards Criminalization?' (1998) 9 *EJIL* 18–31.
117 S. van der Oije and S. Freeland, 'Universal Jurisdiction in the Netherlands-the right approach but the wrong case? *Bouterse* and the *'December Murders"'* (2001) 7 *Australian J HR* 89; A. Klip, 'Universal Jurisdiction: Regional Report for Europe' (2008) 79 *RIDP* 173; N. Arajärvi, 'Looking Back from Nowhere: Is There a Future for Universal Jurisdiction over International Crimes?' (2011) 16 *Tilburg L Rev* 5–29.
118 See ICRC, 'Table of National Case Law on International Crimes and Universal Jurisdiction' in *Report of the Third Universal Meeting of National Committees on International Humanitarian Law*, 'Preventing and Repressing International Crimes: Towards an "Integrated" Approach Based on Domestic Practice', Vol II, Annexes, prepared by AM. La Rosa (2014) 123–32; Amnesty International, 'Universal Jurisdiction: Belgian prosecutors can investigate crimes under international law committed abroad', 1 February 2003, IOR 53/001/2003; International Federation for Human Rights, 'Universal Jurisdiction Developments: January 2006-May 2009', 2 June 2009; Trial, ECCHR, FIDH, 'Make Way for Justice: Universal Jurisdiction Annual Review 2015', April 2015; Trial, ECCHR, FIDH, FIBGAR, 'Make Way for Justice #2: Universal Jurisdiction Annual Review 2016', February 2016; FIDH, ECCHR, REDRESS, FIBGAR, 'Make Way for Justice #3: Universal Jurisdiction Annual Review 2017', March 2017; Human Rights Watch, 'Report on "These are the Crimes we are Fleeing" Justice for Syria in Swedish and German Courts and Annex', 3 October 2017.

INTRODUCTION   25

legal systems, to prosecute international crimes.[119] Findings of this book might be helpful for national courts when they try to analyse issues about customary law and the applicability of the Rome Statute as a reflection of customary law in these circumstances.

Thirdly, when the law applies to prosecuting crimes committed before the law was adopted or approved (*ex post facto* law), an observation on the customary status of a rule as promulgated in the Rome Statute before and after its adoption is valuable.[120] In fact, after the commission of international crimes, special tribunals were designed to prosecute international crimes, for example, the Extraordinary Chambers in the Courts of Cambodia (ECCC),[121] the SCSL and the Special Panels for Serious Crimes in East Timor. The applicable law for the 2015 Kosovo Specialist Chambers and Specialist Prosecutor's Office includes customary international law that was in force in Kosovo from January 1998 to December 2000.[122] It is undesirable but possible that similar international or national tribunals would be established in the future. In these post-ICC tribunals, customary law continues to play a role.[123] In this regard,

---

119   Canada, Crimes against Humanity and War Crimes Act 2000, amended 2019, § 4; Denmark, Military Penal Code 2005, art 36(1); Finland, Penal Code 1889, amended 2015, chapter 1, § 15; Georgia, Constitutional Law 1995, art 6(2); Hungary, Fundamental Law 2011, art XXVIII (5); Kenya, International Crimes Act 2008, § 6(1); Mongolia, Constitutional Law 1992, art 10; Mongolia, Criminal Code 2002, art 2(1); Samoa, ICC Act 2007, § 7; Serbia, Criminal Code 2006, amended 2012, art 10 (3); South Africa, Implementation Act 2002, § 2; Switzerland, Criminal Code 1937, amended 2017, art 264(j); Tajikistan, Criminal Code 1998, art 1(2); Timor-Leste, Constitutional Law 2002, § 9(1).

120   *Vasiliauskas v Lithuania* (Judgment, Grand Chamber) ECtHR Application No. 35343/05 (10 October 2015), Dissenting opinion of Judge Ziemele, paras 1-10, Dissenting opinion of Judge Power-Forde; UN Doc A/CONF.183/C.1/SR.3, para 100; *Streletz, Kessler and Krenz v Germany* (Merits, Concurring Opinion of Judge Loucaides) ECtHR Application No. 34044/96, 35532/97 and 44801/98(22 March 2001); UN Doc S/25704 (1993), para 34; *The Prosecutor v Rutaganda* (Judgement and Sentence) ICTR-96-3-T (6 December 1999), para 86.

121   Law on the Establishment of the ECCC, amended 2004, art 1.

122   Kosovo, Law on Specialist Chambers and Specialist Prosecutor's Office 2015, arts 3(2)(d), 3(3), 12-14.

123   For example, *Prosecutor v Anastacio Martins and Domingos Gonçalves* (Judgment, District Court of Dili) SPSC-11/2001 (13 November 2003), 10; *Prosecutor v Marcelino Soares* (Judgment, District Court of Dili) SPSC-11/2003 (11 December 2003), paras 16-17; *Prosecutor v Domingos Metan* (Judgment, District Court of Dili) SPSC-4c/2003(16 November 2004), paras 12-14; *Prosecutor v Lino Beno* (Judgment, District Court of Dili) SPSC-4b/2003 (16 November 2004), paras 12-14; *Prosecutor v Agostinho Cloe et al* (Judgment, District Court of Dili) SPSC-4/2003 (16 November 2004), paras 13-14; *Prosecutor v Anton Lelan Sufa* (Judgment, District Court of Dili) SPSC-4a/2003 (25 November 2004), paras 24-25; *Prosecutor v Alarico Mesquita et al* (Judgment, District

findings of this book about the existence of a customary rule at the material time are of importance.¹²⁴

There are mainly three limits of this book. Firstly, this research does not examine all international crimes, liabilities and defences in the Rome Statute. It does not provide a survey of all underlying acts or all contextual elements of war crimes, crimes against humanity and the crime of aggression. The findings in this research about the selected crimes are of restricted value as to the issues of other underlying acts and other contextual elements. Secondly, there were certain barriers to collecting all the evidence required to assess whether a customary rule exists, including the availability of the evidence, and certain language barriers involved in its collection. The 1943 United Nations War Crimes Commission selectively reported on post-World War II trials by Australian, British, Canadian, French, German, Norwegian, Polish, and the US tribunals.¹²⁵ Conclusive findings, however, cannot be directly drawn from these under-reported records because many of these records are brief summaries of arguments and findings, leaving their relevance uncertain for the custom-identification. The judgments of post-World War II trials conducted in mainland China are also far from well-substantiated. Lastly, even with all available and accessible resources, identifying the state of a customary rule is not a task free from subjectivity. The assessment deals with evidence of objective and subjective aspects of States. This study cannot be value-free in the evaluation of evidence to reach conclusions.

Despite these limits, this book adds to the ongoing exploration of the relationship between the sources of international law and the perplexing question of how and why custom matters at the ICC. In addition, through the historical-legal analysis, this book seeks to substantiate whether certain provisions of the Rome Statute possess a customary status, which should be of interest to international lawyers with a theoretical focus, as well as legal practitioners who work in the fields of international criminal law and public international law. Lastly, adopting the flexible two-element approach and the four-step

---

Court of Dili) SPSC-10/2003 (6 December 2004), paras 62-68, concerning crimes against humanity under customary law.

124 *Prosecutor v Norman* (Decision on Preliminary Motion Based on Lack of Jurisdiction (Child Recruitment) SCSL-2004-14-AR72 (E) (31 May 2004), para 17; *Co-Prosecutors v Ieng Sary* (Decision on Appeals by Nuon Chea and Ieng Thirith against the Closing Order) 002/19-09-2007-ECCC/OCIJ (PTC 145 &146) (15 February 2011), para 144.

125 *Law Reports of Trial of War Criminals: Selected and Prepared by the United Nations War Crimes Commission* (London: HMSO 1947–1949).

guidelines, this book will hopefully provide lawyers and non-lawyers working for international and non-international organisations with novel arguments and materials that can be used to assess whether a customary rule exists or whether the Rome Statute is applicable to specific issues.

CHAPTER 2

Methodological Framework of This Book

2.1   Introductory Remarks

As mentioned in chapter 1, chapter 2 outlines the methodological framework adopted in this research in detail. For this purpose, section 2.2 first sets out the guidelines for interpreting a provision of the Rome Statute and other treaty rules. Section 2.3 endeavours to set up the method for the identification of customary rules. Section 2.4 clarifies the terms employed to qualify the relationship between a treaty rule and custom. The means of identifying the preliminary declaratory nature of a treaty rule is also analysed in this section because it is a layer of analysis of this book. Finally, section 2.5 briefly examines whether obstacles exist for the study of the declaratory nature of the Rome Statute provisions as evidence of custom.

2.2   Interpreting Provisions of the Rome Statute

The relationship between treaties and custom remains a highly debated topic in international law.[1] Treaty rules may be broader or narrower than customary law by removing a contextual requirement or including more underlying offences,[2] or adding a new restrictive element[3] or excluding underlying acts.[4]

---

1   R.R. Baxter, 'Multilateral Treaties as Evidence of Customary International Law' (1965) 41 *British Ybk Intl L* 275; R.R. Baxter, 'Treaties and Custom' (1970) 129 *Recueil des cours* 27; M. Akehurst, 'Custom as a Source of International Law' (1976) 47 *British Ybk Intl L* 1, 42–52; M. Villiger, *Customary International Law and Treaties: A Study of Their Interactions and Interrelations, with Special Consideration of the 1969 Vienna Convention on the Law of Treaties* (Brill | Nijhoff 1985) 156–67; M. Villiger, *Customary International Law and Treaties: A Manual on the Theory and Practice of the Interrelation of Sources* (Fully revised 2nd edn, Kluwer Law International 1997); Y. Dinstein, 'The Interaction Between Customary Law and Treaty' (2006) 322 *Recueil des cours* 243.
2   'Report of the Secretary-General Pursuant to Paragraph 5 of the Security Council Resolution 955 (1994)' (13 February 1995), UN Doc S/1995/134, para 12.
3   *Prosecutor v Tadić* (Interlocutory Appeal Decision on Jurisdiction) ICTY-94-1-AR72 (2 October 1995), paras 139–40; *The Prosecutor v Akayesu* (Judgement) ICTR-96-4-A (1 June 2001), paras 465; *The Prosecutor v Muvunyi* (Judgement and Sentence) ICTR-00-55A-T (12 September 2006), para 514.
4   *Prosecutor v Orić* (Judgement, Separate and Partially Dissenting Opinion of Judge Schomburg) ICTY-03-68-A (3 July 2008), para 20; *Prosecutor v Hadžihasanović et al* (Decision

In this book, the text of the Rome Statute is the starting point for determining its provisions as declaratory of customary law. The first step is to construe the meaning of selected provisions of the Statute.[5] For this purpose, this section mainly aims to set out the guidelines in interpreting the provisions of the Rome Statute.

Article 22 of the Rome Statute is the first guidance for interpretation. Article 22 explicitly stipulates the principle of legality. The fundamental principle of legality requires that prosecution and punishment be based on clear provisions of international law at the time the crime was committed.[6] The strict principle of legality contains four derivatives: specificity and certainty; non-retroactivity (*lex praevia*); the ban on analogy (*lex stricta*); and favouring the accused (*in dubio pro reo*).[7] The rule of specificity and certainty requires the definition of crimes to be sufficiently clear and precise. The rule of non-retroactivity prohibits prosecuting an individual for acts committed before the conduct was criminalised. The first two sub-rules are provided in articles 22(1) and 24 (non-retroactivity *ratione personae*). The rule of the ban on analogy and the rule of favouring the accused are enshrined in article 22(2) of the Statute. It provides:

> The definition of a crime shall be strictly construed and shall not be extended by analogy. In case of ambiguity, the definition shall be interpreted in favour of the person being investigated, prosecuted or convicted.

Article 22(2) requires faithful compliance with the principle of strict construction in interpreting the definition of a core crime in the ICC's jurisdiction.[8] An interpretation should be in favour of the accused, when in doubt. Despite the reference to 'the definition of a crime', there is support for the view that strict

---

on Interlocutory Appeal Challenging Jurisdiction in Relation to Command Responsibility) ICTY-01-47-AR72 (16 July 2003), Partial Dissenting Opinion of Judge Shahabuddeen, Separate and Partially Dissenting Opinion of Judge David Hunt; *Vasiliauskas v Lithuania* (Judgment, Grand Chamber) ECtHR Application No. 35343/05 (10 October 2015), Dissenting Opinion of Judge Ziemele, paras 1-10, Dissenting Opinion of Judge Power-Forde; UN Doc A/CONF.183/C.1/SR.3, para 100.

5   Baxter (1965) (n 1) 290.
6   JM. Henckaerts and L. Doswald-beck (eds), *Customary International Humanitarian Law*, Vol I (CUP 2005), Rule 101. For an analysis of this principle at the ICC, see L. Grover, *Interpreting Crimes in the Rome Statute of the International Criminal Court* (CUP 2014) 186–218.
7   A. Cassese *et al* (eds), *Cassese's International Criminal Law* (3rd end, OUP 2013) 27–36.
8   For a recent analysis of this provision, see W.A. Schabas, *The International Criminal Court: A Commentary on the Rome Statute* (2nd edn, OUP 2016) 546–48.

construction applies to the interpretation of modes of liability and defences.[9] And, the principle of legality overrides a teleological interpretative method by referring to the purpose of the Rome Statute to end impunity.[10]

Article 21(3) of the Statute also requires the interpretation be consistent with 'internationally recognised human rights'.[11] Leena Grover argued that this article is a 'background' interpretive principle, which is applicable in interpreting crimes and other parts of the Rome Statute.[12] This article does not aim to expand the scope of crimes to a maximum protection of victims.[13] All these interpretative limitations should be kept in mind in interpreting provisions of the Rome Statute concerning crimes, liabilities and defences.[14]

In addition to the two interpretive principles mentioned above, this book also follows the principles of interpretation embedded in articles 31-33 of the 1969 Vienna Convention on the Law of Treaties. The ICC in its jurisprudence accepted the applicability of these principles of interpretation.[15] We first have

9 ibid 547; *The Prosecutor v Ngudjolo* (Judgment pursuant to Article 74 of the Statute – Concurring Opinion of Judge Christine Van den Wyngaert) ICC-01/04-02/12-4 (18 December 2012), para 18, fn 28; *Prosecutor v Milutinović et al* (Decision on Dragoljub Ojdanić's Motion Challenging Jurisdiction: Joint Criminal Enterprise) ICTY-99-37-AR72 (21 May 2003), para 37.

10 P. Robinson, 'Legality and Discretion in the Distribution of Criminal Sanctions' (1988) 25 *Harvard J on Legis* 393, 426–27; Grover (n 6) 167–69, 184; C. Davidson, 'How to Read International Criminal Law: Strict Construction and the Rome Statute of the International Criminal Court' (2017) 91 *St. John's Law Review* 37, 92–95; W.A. Schabas, 'Strict Construction and the Rome Statute' in S. Dewulf (ed), *La (CVDW): Liber Amicorum Chris Van den Wyngaert* (Maklu 2018) 423–38; *Ngudjolo* Trial Chamber Judgment (Concurring Opinion of Judge Christine Van den Wyngaert) (n 9), para 18; *The Prosecutor v Bemba* (Judgment on the appeal of Mr Jean-Pierre Bemba Gombo against Trial Chamber III's "Judgment pursuant to Article 74 of the Statute", Separate opinion of Judge Christine Van den Wyngaert and Judge Howard Morrison) ICC-01/05-01/08-3636-Anx2 (8 June 2018) para 5. Cf. *The Prosecutor v Ruto & Sang* (Decision on Defence Applications for Judgments of Acquittal, TC V(A)) ICC-01/09-01/11-2027-Red-Corr (4 April 2016), para 437.

11 1998 Rome Statute, art 21(3).

12 Grover (n 6) 122–23.

13 ibid 122.

14 For seven cannons of ICC interpretation, see L.N. Sadat and J.M. Jolly, 'Seven Canons of ICC Interpretation: Making Sense of Article 25's Rorschach Blot' (2014) 27 *LJIL* 755.

15 See *The Prosecutor v Lubanga* (Judgment on the Prosecutor's Application for Extraordinary Review of the Pre-Trial Chamber I's 31 March 2006 Decision Denying Leave to Appeal, A Ch) ICC-01/04-168 (13 July 2006), paras 33-42; *Prosecutor v Lubanga* (Decision on the Practices of Witness Familiarisation and Witness Proofing, PTC I) ICC-01/04-01/06-679 (8 November 2006), para 8; *The Prosecutor v Lubanga* (Decision on the Confirmation of Charges, PTC I) ICC-01/04-01/06-803-tEN (29 January 2007), para 283; *Situation in the Republic of Kenya* (Decision Pursuant to Article 15 of the Rome Statute on the Authorization of an Investigation into the Situation in the Republic of Kenya, PTC II) ICC-01/09-19-Corr (31 March 2010), paras 33-35.

to study and analyse the terms, in accordance with article 31 of the Vienna Convention, to identify the meaning of the text in a treaty provision. A textual reading of the words, the context, and the object and purpose of the provision are examined. A special meaning can also be given if the parties so intended.[16] Second, by virtue of article 32 of the Vienna Convention, the preparatory works and the circumstances are considered as supplementary means either to determine the meaning of the terms if the meaning is still ambiguous or manifestly unreasonable after the application of article 31, or to confirm the meaning as interpreted under article 31.[17] Third, article 33 stresses the equally authentic effect of the text in different languages. These principles of interpretation apply to understanding the provisions of the Rome Statute and other treaty rules.

The portrayal of the work on the Rome Statute illustrated here provides the framework for the analysis of the preparatory works. The drafting history of the Rome Statute is mainly divided into four stages.[18] Firstly, the International Law Commission (ILC), established by the UN General Assembly to promote the codification of international law and its progressive development,[19] resumed the work it had begun in 1949 on the issue of establishing an international criminal court or an international criminal trial mechanism.[20] In 1994, the ILC prepared a draft text for the Establishment of an International Criminal Court (the ILC 1994 Draft).[21] Secondly, an *Ad Hoc* Committee on the establishment of an international criminal court, established by the General Assembly,[22] reviewed issues arising out of the ILC 1994 Draft and prepared the

---

16 P. Merkouris, *Article 31(3)(c) VCLT and the Principle of Systemic Integration: Normative Shadows in Plato's Cave* (Brill | Nijhoff 2015); H. Fox, 'Article 31(3)(a) and (b) of the Vienna Convention and the *Kasikili/Sedudu Island* Case' in M. Fitzmaurice *et al* (eds), *Treaty Interpretation and the Vienna Convention on the Law of Treaties: 30 Years on* (Martinus Nijhoff Publishers 2010) 59–74.
17 *Legal Consequences of the Construction of a Wall in the Occupied Palestinian Territory*, Advisory Opinion, [2004] ICJ Rep 136, 174, para 94.
18 M.C. Bassiouni and W.A. Schabas (eds), *The Legislative History of the International Criminal Court*, Vol 2 (2nd Revised and Expanded edn, Brill 2016) 3–5.
19 Statute of the International Law Commission, arts 1(1) and 15; UN Doc A/RES/174 (II) (1947).
20 'International Criminal Responsibility of Individuals and Entities Engaged in Illicit Trafficking of Narcotic Drugs Across National Frontiers and Other Transnational Criminal Activities: Establishment of an International Criminal Court with Jurisdiction over Such Crimes', GA Res 44/39 (1989), UN Doc A/RES/44/39, para 1; 'Report of the International Law Commission', UN Doc A/925 (1949), paras 32-34.
21 UN Doc A/49/10 (1994), 20–73.
22 'Establishment of an international criminal court', GA Res 49/53 (1994), UN Doc A/RES/49/53.

text of a convention for an international criminal court.[23] Thirdly, relying on the work of the *Ad Hoc* Committee, the Preparatory Committee on the establishment of an international criminal court, also established by the General Assembly,[24] prepared its Draft Statute of an international criminal court and transmitted it to the Rome Conference for discussion.[25] Fourthly, at the 1998 Rome Conference, the Committee of the Whole with a series of working groups considered the Draft Statute prepared by the Preparatory Committee. The Drafting Committee of the Rome Conference was entrusted with coordinating and refining the drafting of all texts, formulating drafts, as well as giving advice on drafting. Delegations at the Plenary Meeting gave several statements at the beginning of the conference and finally voted for the adoption of the package of the Rome Statute prepared by the Committee of the Whole on 17 July 1998. Besides, as for the 2010 Amendments on the crime of aggression, a series of meetings in Princeton, New York, Montreux and The Hague lead the road from Rome to Kampala.

The interpretation of substantive provisions of the Rome Statute interacts with the interpretation of provisions of international humanitarian law and international human rights law, as many rules of international criminal law derive from prohibitions in the two regimes.[26] Darryl Robinson notes that it is required to bear different interpretive assumptions and fundamental principles in mind among the three branches of international law.[27] International criminal law mainly focuses on the responsibilities of individuals (individuals shall refrain from certain conducts), while international humanitarian law and international human rights law concern the obligations of collective entities (parties to the conflicts or States shall restrain or engage in certain acts to protect the benefits of individuals). Furthermore, international criminal law addresses a narrow scope of serious crimes, while the other two branches of law focus on a system to promote the protection of identified beneficiaries. Moreover, due to the severity of punishment, international criminal law

---

23   'Report of the *Ad Hoc* Committee on the Establishment of an International Criminal Court', UN Doc A/50/22 (1995).

24   'Establishment of an international criminal court', GA Res 50/46 (1995), UN Doc A/RES/50/46.

25   'Reports and other Documents (United Nations publication)', UN Doc A/CONF.183/2/Add.1; 'Report of the Preparatory Committee on the Establishment of an International Criminal Court', UN Doc A/CONF.183/2 (1998), 13–82.

26   *The Prosecutor v Katanga & Ngudjolo* (Decision on the confirmation of charges, PTC I) ICC-01/04-01/07-717 (30 September 2008), para 448.

27   D. Robinson, 'The Identity Crisis of International Criminal Law' (2008) 21 *LJIL* 925.

contains several restraining principles, such as the principle of legality as illustrated above.[28]

These differences among the three regimes also indicate that construction of a rule in international criminal law may be inconsistent with the purposes of the other two regimes. In light of the diversification and expansion of international law, there are some discussions about substantive, institutional and methodological fragmentation of international law.[29] The ILC recommended four techniques of interpretation to address the fragmentation of international law. These techniques are to: (1) view international law as a legal system so that each norm relates to others; (2) determine the precise relationship between them either as normative fulfilment or conflicts; (3) apply the general rules of treaty interpretation reflected in articles 31-33 of the 1969 Vienna Convention; and (4) interpret in accordance with the principle of harmonisation.[30] These techniques are also guidelines for the systematic interpretation of treaty provisions.

2.3 Method: The Two-Element Approach to Identifying Customary Rules

The determination of whether a treaty rule was or is declaratory of custom cannot be undertaken without identifying the state of a customary rule. The main challenge of this book concerns the method of ascertaining the existence of customary law. This section aims to set out the approach to identifying customary rules in international (criminal) law. When we ask how to identify customary rules, we refer to a method to ascertain the existence and the content of a customary rule. The 'identification' exercise deals with the process of determining whether a customary rule has been formed at a critical moment.[31]

---

28 ibid Grover (n 6) 126–27.
29 M. Andenas and E. Bjorge, 'Introduction' in M. Andenas and E. Bjorge (eds), *A Farewell to Fragmentation: Reassertion and Convergence in International Law* (CUP 2015) 4–11; 'Fragmentation of International Law: Difficulties Arising from the Diversification and Expansion of International Law' in 'Report of the Study Group of the International Law Commission, finalised by Martti Koskenniemi', UN Doc A/CN.4/L.682 and Corr.1-3 (2006), para 192.
30 'Fragmentation of International Law: Difficulties Arising from the Diversification and Expansion of International Law' in 'Report of the Study Group of the International Law Commission', UN Doc A/CN.4/L.702 (2006), para 14.
31 M.H. Mendelson, 'The Formation of Customary International Law' (1998) 272 *Recueil des cours* 155, 284; C. Tams, 'Meta-Custom and the Court: A Study in Judicial Law-making' (2015) 14 *LPICT* 51.

The word 'identification' refers to a pre-application exercise, which is a preliminary exercise for the interpretation and application of a customary rule.[32] This section first briefly reviews the peculiarities of international criminal law and outlines a flexible two-element approach for the identification of a customary rule. Then, this section assesses the requirements of the two elements, the forms of their evidence and other indicators.

2.3.1   *A Flexible Formula for Identifying the Existence of a Customary Rule*

In determining how a certain practice becomes a customary rule, the prevailing view is the presence of two elements, namely, a subjective element (*opinio juris* or *opinio juris sive necessitatis*) and an objective element (State practice).[33] This two-element theory for the formation of customary law is widely accepted and acknowledged by a large number of international scholars and international bodies.[34] Article 38(1)(b) of the ICJ Statute also reads that custom derives from a 'general practice, accepted as law'.[35] Hence, the classic approach

---

32   For a definition of the 'identification', see 'Report of the International Law Commission', UN Doc A/73/10 (2018), para 78, commentaries (2)-(3) to Guideline 9 (1).

33   T. Treves, 'Customary International Law' in R. Wolfrum (ed) (2006) *MPEPIL*, paras 7-8. For discussions on other theories, see B. Schlütter, *Developments in Customary International Law: Theory and the Practice of the International Court of Justice and the International ad hoc Criminal Tribunals for Rwanda and Yugoslavia* (Brill | Nijhoff 2010) 1–68; T. Rauter, *Judicial Practice, Customary International Criminal Law and Nullum Crimen Sine Lege* (Springer 2017) 87–92. Cf. M.H. Mendelson, 'The Subjective Element in Customary International Law' (1995) 66 *British Ybk Intl L* 177.

34   S. Donaghue, 'Normative Habits, Genuine Beliefs and Evolving Law: Nicaragua and the Theory of Customary International Law' (1995) 16 *Australian Ybk Intl L* 327; O. Schachter, 'International Law in Theory and Practice: General Course in Public International Law' (1982) 178 *Recueil des cours* 32; *North Sea Continental Shelf* cases (*Germany v Denmark; Germany v Netherlands*), Judgment, [1969] ICJ Rep 3, 43–44, paras 74, 77; *Jurisdictional Immunities of the State (Germany v Italy: Greece Intervening)*, Judgment, [2012] ICJ Rep 99, 122, para 55; Henckaerts and Doswald-beck (eds) (n 6) 33; The American Law Institute, 'Restatement of the Law of Foreign Relations Law of the United States' (Third), 1986, para 102, Comment b. Cf. R. Ago, 'Legal Science and International Law' (1956) 90 *Recueil des Cours* 85, 758; Akehurst (n 1); Mendelson (n 31); Mendelson (n 33); R. Müllerson, 'On the Nature and Scope of Customary International Law' (1997) 2 *ARIL* 341; ILA, Committee on Formation of Customary (General) International Law, 'Final Report, by Chairman Professor M.H. Mendelson, Rapporteur Professor Rein Müllerson' in International Law Association Report of the 65th Conference (London 2000) (ILA, London 2000) 712, 718, § 1; B.S. Chimni, 'Customary International Law: A Third World Perspective' (2018) 112 *AJIL* 1, 27–30; G. Nolte, 'How to Identify Customary International Law? – On the Outcome of the Work of the International Law Commission (2018)' (2019) 62 *Japanese Ybk Intl L* 251.

35   Statute of the International Court of Justice, 26 June 1945, 24 October 1945, 33 UNTS 993. For interpretations of this paragraph, see R. Jennings and A. Watts (eds), *Oppenheim's International Law*, Vol 1 (9th edn, Longmans 1996), § 10, at 26. For critics of this paragraph,

to identifying the existence of a customary rule is to seek sufficient evidence of these two elements; this is known as the two-element approach.

The ILC in its recent work supported this two-element approach. In 2012, the ILC included the topic 'Formation and Evidence of Customary International Law' on its agenda and appointed Michael Wood as Special Rapporteur for this topic.[36] The title of this topic was later changed to 'Identification of Customary International Law'. Wood submitted five reports with proposed conclusions to the ILC.[37] In 2018, the ILC adopted a set of 16 draft conclusions on 'Identification of Customary International Law'.[38] Its conclusion 2 under the title of 'two constituent elements' reads that: '[t]o determine the existence and content of a rule of customary international law, it is necessary to ascertain whether there is a general practice that is accepted as law (*opinio juris*)'.[39]

Proposals for a different identification approach exist as to customary rules of international criminal law. Recent researchers observed that customary law remains the object of numerous controversies.[40] There existed different views with regard to the theories of custom-formation and the method of custom-identification.[41] Considering the high moral character of certain rules deriving from value-oriented norms, Theodor Meron proposed a 'core right' theory in the formation of customary law in international humanitarian law and international human rights law.[42] In his view, the content of customary law can be inferred from the 'core values' of the international community.[43] As Birgit Schlütter observed, some authors in international criminal law, for example, Fausto Pocar and Antonio Cassese, support this 'core right' theory if the rules

---

see M.H. Mendelson, 'The International Court of Justice and the Sources of International Law' in V. Lowe and M. Fitzmaurice (eds), *Fifty Years of the International Court of Justice: Essays in Honour of Sir Robert Jennings* (CUP 2009) 63, 67.

36   'Summary record of the 3132nd meeting', UN Doc A/CN.4/SR.3132 (2012), 16; UN Doc A/67/10 (2012), para 167.

37   See the Note, the first, second, third, fourth, and fifth reports to the ILC, by Michael Wood, Special Rapporteur, UN Doc A/CN.4/653 (2012), UN Doc A/CN.4/663 (2013), UN Doc A/CN.4/672 (2014), UN Doc A/CN.4/682 (2015), UN Doc A/CN.4/695 and Add.1 (2016), UN Doc A/CN.4/717 (2018).

38   UN Doc A/73/10 (2018), paras 58, 60, 65; 'Text of the draft conclusions as adopted by the Drafting Committee on second reading', UN Doc A/CN.4/L.908 (2018).

39   UN Doc A/73/10 (2018), para 65, Conclusion 2.

40   See C.A. Bradley (ed), *Custom's Future: International Law in a Changing World* (CUP 2016); B. Lepard (ed), *Reexamining Customary International Law* (CUP 2016).

41   Ago (n 34).

42   T. Meron, 'International Law in the Age of Human Rights' (2003) 301 *Recueil des cours* 9, 378, 384–86; Schlütter (n 33) 42 and fn 211.

43   Meron, ibid 377–78; C. Tomuschat, 'International Law: Ensuring the Survival of Mankind on the Eve of a New Century' (1999) 281 *Recueil des cours* 9, 334.

belong to the 'canon of norms which can be held to represent the "core values" of the international community'.[44] Meron's 'core right' idea is similar to that of Christian Tomuschat, who suggested that the content of customary rules in the two fields of international law can be inferred 'from the basic values cherished by the international community'.[45] Despite Tomuschat adopted a deductive method for the custom-formation, his view did not deviate from the two-element approach in the custom-identification.[46] In contrast to Tomuschat's position on the method of custom-identification, Meron's 'core right' theory indicates that evidence of one element, *opinio juris* alone, is sufficient in the two fields.[47] He wrote that: '[i]t is, of course, to be expected that those rights which are most crucial to the protection of human dignity and of universally accepted values of humanity, and whose violation triggers broad condemnation by the international community, will require a lesser amount of confirmatory evidence'.[48]

In the identification of customary law, international criminal law presents some peculiarities when compared to other branches of international law. Its objects are individuals and it is a regime inspired by both civil and common law criminal systems.[49] Hard evidence of national practice is also not readily available in this field.[50] One reason is that international criminal law introduces a multitude of punishable acts.[51] Simply put, the customary status of a rule criminalising underlying acts contemplates no obligation on States but obligations on individuals, who are prohibited from and responsible for committing international crimes. States affected and third States rarely prosecute underlying acts of international crimes, for various political or legal reasons, for example, because of the lack of evidence or sources, or the lack of motivation, or scarcity of support in national law. Another significant reason is that

---

44 Schlütter (n 33) 44.
45 C. Tomuschat, 'Obligations arising for states without or against their will' (1993) 241 *Recueil des cours* 195, 291. Cf. Schlütter (n 33) 37–38.
46 Tomuschat, ibid.
47 Schlütter (n 33) 42–43; T. Meron, *Human Rights and Humanitarian Norms as Customary Law* (Clarendon Press 1989) 9, 94.
48 Meron, ibid 94.
49 Y. Kirakosyan, 'Finding Custom: The ICJ and the International Criminal Courts and Tribunals Compared' in C. Stahn and L.J. van den Herik (eds), *The Diversification and Fragmentation of International Criminal Law* (Brill | Nijhoff 2012) 149–61.
50 For more discussions on State practice, see Y. Tan, 'The Identification of Customary Rules in International Criminal Law' (2018) 34 UJIEL 92; H. Van der Wilt, 'State Practice as Element of Customary International Law: A White Knight in International Criminal Law?' (2019) 20 ICLR 784, 787, 799–804.
51 Kirakosyan (n 49) 149–61.

those accused of international crimes are generally tried by international criminal tribunals, rather than national courts. Therefore, the record of national investigation and prosecution of international crimes is not very substantial. Compared to evidence of *opinio juris*, evidence of State practice is more rarely obtainable.

Nevertheless, it would be going too far to adopt the one-element 'core right' theory, since it leaves much room for powerful States to manipulate the law.[52] The deductive method embedded in the 'core right' theory might also conflict with the strict principle of legality prohibiting analogy.[53] Given these features mentioned above, the two UN *ad hoc* tribunals for the former Yugoslavia and Rwanda, in their statements, have not departed from the two-element approach.[54] Commentators have also concluded that in theory a different method, deviating from the two-element approach, has not been found to identify customary rules of international criminal law.[55] The Appeals Chamber of the ICC in its 2019 *Jordan* decision confirms the two-element approach.[56] In short, the two-element approach remains applicable to the identification of customary rules of international criminal law.[57]

This book adopts a flexible approach in the identification of the two elements by focusing more on *opinio juris*. Wood mentioned that the two elements might sometimes be 'closely entangled' and evidence of them may be given different weight depending on the 'contexts'.[58] The ILC's draft conclusion 3 also addressed that in assessing evidence of each element, the 'overall context', 'the nature of the rule' and 'the particular circumstances' had to

---

52 For more discussions, see Schlütter (n 33).
53 C. Tomuschat, 'The Legacy of Nuremberg' (2006) 4 *JICJ* 835.
54 W.A. Schabas, 'Customary Law or "Judge-Made" Law: Judicial Creativity at the UN Criminal Tribunals' in J. Doria *et al* (eds), *The Legal Regime of the International Criminal Court: Essays in Honour of Professor Igor Blishchenko (1930–2000)* (Brill | Nijhoff 2009) 75–101; Rauter (n 33) 127–70, 234; Tan (n 50).
55 M. Wood, 'Foreword' in Lepard (ed) (n 40); Schlütter (n 33); N. Arajärvi, *The Changing Nature of Customary International Law: Methods of Interpreting the Concept of Custom in International Criminal Tribunals* (Routledge 2014).
56 *The Prosecutor v Al Bashir* (Judgment in the Jordan Referral re Al-Bashir Appeal, A Ch) ICC-02/05-01/09-397-Corr (6 May 2019), paras 113, 116. See also id, (Decision on the Failure by the Republic of Malawi to Comply with the Cooperation Requests Issued by the Court with Respect to the Arrest and Surrender of Omar Hassan Ahmad Al Bashir, PTC I) ICC-02/05-01/09-139-Corr (13 December 2011), paras 39-42.
57 Tan (n 50).
58 'Second report on Identification of Customary International Law to the Sixty-sixth Session of the ILC', by Michael Wood, Special Rapporteur, UN Doc A/CN.4/672 (2014), para 3; R. Kolb, 'Selected Problems in the Theory of Customary International Law' (2003) 50 *Netherlands Intl L Rev* 119, 128.

be considered.[59] Other legal writers have also suggested a flexible application of the two-element approach.[60] For instance, Frederic Kirgis wrote that the identification of a customary rule should be analysed on a case-by-case basis depending on different rules and acts.[61] According to his idea of a sliding scale, more attention should be paid to evidence of *opinio juris* than State practice for a moral-oriented rule, such as the prohibition of the use of nuclear weapons.[62] Also, Anthea Roberts distinguished facilitative rules from moral rules in customary international law. In her view, the former tends to regulate the coexistence of States without taking into account the content of the rules, while the latter are rules with moral content. State practice is becoming less important for the latter rules.[63] The regime of international criminal law shares this value-oriented characteristic. Max Sørensen provided a practical suggestion that 'in cases where a consistent practice can be proven, a certain presumption may arise in favour of the existence of *opinio juris*'.[64] The converse of the 'presumed acceptance' idea is also true in the context of international crimes. If a general acknowledgment of a rule (*opinio juris*) can be proven, less practice is presumed sufficient. Once there is enough confirmatory *opinio juris* for a rule, less practice is sufficient for the identification of a customary rule. In this book, more attention is paid to States' statements or recognition as opposed to their physical acts.

---

59   UN Doc A/73/10 (2018), para 66, Conclusion 3.1 and its commentaries (2)-(6).
60   Kolb (n 58); M. Scharf, *Customary International Law in Times of Fundamental Change: Recognizing Grotian Moments* (CUP 2013) 139–56; B. Lepard, *Customary International Law: A New Theory with Practical Applications* (CUP 2010); B. Lepard, 'Toward a New Theory of Customary International Human Rights Law' in Lepard (ed) (n 40) 233, 259–61; ILA, Committee on Formation of Customary (General) International Law (n 34) 751, § 19; 'Summary record of the 3301st meeting', UN Doc A/CN.4/SR.3301 (2016), 16 (Mr Murase).
61   F. Kirgis, 'Custom on a Sliding Scale' (1987) 81 *AJIL* 146.
62   ibid 149; A.E. Roberts, 'Traditional and Modern Approaches to Customary International Law: A Reconciliation' (2001) 95 *AJIL* 757, 764; J. Wouters and C. Ryngaert, 'Impact on the Process of the Formation of Customary International Law' in M. Kamminga and M. Scheinin (eds), *The Impact of Human Rights Law on General International Law* (OUP 2009) 111–12; *Legality of the Threat or Use of Nuclear Weapons*, Advisory Opinion, [1996] ICJ Rep 226, 253, 256, paras 64, 75; *Prosecutor v Kupreškić et al* (Judgement) ICTY-95-16-T (14 January 2000), para 527.
63   Roberts, ibid 764.
64   H. Waldock, 'General Course on Public International Law' (1962) 106 *Recueil des cours* 41, 49. For further discussions on different approaches in human rights law, see B. Simma and P. Alston, 'The Sources of Human Rights Law: Custom, Jus Cogens, and General Principles' (1988–1989) 12 *Australian Ybk Intl L* 82, 90–107.

A lack of evidence of instances of investigation and prosecution by States does not mean that a customary rule cannot be formed and identified based on sufficient *opinio juris*, although it may affect the enforcement and the development of international criminal law gradually and negatively.[65] Torture as a crime against humanity is a good example. States throughout the world have tolerated or sometimes even authorised torture. But torture is generally recognised as an international crime under customary law.[66] In addition, as the ICJ held, '[i]f a State acts in a way *prima facie* incomptabile with a recognised rule, but defends its conduct by appealing to exceptions or justifications contained within the rule itself [...] the significance of that attitude is to confirm rather than to weaken the rule'.[67]

One may concern that such a custom-identification approach will affect the certainty of the content of a customary law and the respect for strict principle of legality under article 22 of the Rome Statute.[68] With a conservative approach to custom, Meron has strongly supported customary law in international criminal proceedings.[69] As Larry May summarised, Meron's conservative approach to custom cover three elements:

> 1. look only to those rules 'which are beyond any doubt part of customary law' (epistemological element); 2. use only those methods for establishing customary norms that are traditional (methodological element); and 3. resolve any doubts about custom in favor of the defendant (outcome element).[70]

In practice, the foreseeability requirement and the maxim of *in dubio pro reo* should be strictly applied in international criminal proceedings. I believe that the three tests would guarantee the respect for the principle of legality if we are committed seriously to them.[71] A flexible two-element identification approach

---

65 For data emerges from the post-World War II conflicts, see M.C. Bassiouni, *Crimes Against Humanity: Historical Evolution and Contemporary Application* (CUP 2011) 650.

66 1998 Rome Statute, art 7; *Questions relating to the Obligation to Prosecute or Extradite (Belgium v Senegal)*, Judgment, [2012] ICJ Rep 422, 457, para 99.

67 *Military and Paramilitary Activities in and against Nicaragua (Nicaragua v USA)*, Merits, [1986] ICJ Rep 14, 98, para 186. See also UN Doc A/73/10 (2018), para 66, commentary (8) to Conclusion 8.

68 A. Bufalini, 'The Principle of Legality and the Role of Customary International Law in the Interpretation of the ICC Statute' (2015) 14 *LPICL* 233, 234.

69 T. Meron, 'Editorial Comment: Revival of Customary Humanitarian Law' (2005) 99 *AJIL* 817.

70 L. May, *Aggression and Crimes Against Peace* (CUP 2008) 156 (citations omitted).

71 Cf. ibid 158.

is better than a loose or modern one-element approach. *Opinio juris* is raised to a higher rank, as opposed to practice (in particular, physical acts) of States, which will also be carefully examined in this book.[72] In a nutshell, this book sets out a flexible formula of the two-element approach in the identification of customary rules.

2.3.2 The Two Elements

Issues about the two elements are controversial. This subsection does not aim to deal with all matters about the two elements but to highlight their requirements and forms of evidence anchoring this book.

2.3.2.1 Practice and *Opinio Juris*: Quantity and Quality

Requiring a practice observed by every State is not feasible and has never been a requirement for the formation of customary law.[73] The relevant practice 'must be general', which means that 'it must be sufficiently widespread and representative, as well as consistent'.[74] Michael Akehurst noted that 'the number of States taking part in the practice is more important than the number of acts of which the practice is composed'.[75] Also, as correctly noted by Brian Lepard, the precise degree of consensus among States is unclear to establish a customary rule: a simple majority or supermajority.[76] The 2005 ICRC *Study on Customary International Humanitarian Law* (2005 ICRC *Study*) even showed that practice of a few States is sufficient to create a customary rule, as long as these States play a great role in the formation of a rule.[77]

The definitions of *opinio juris* are also quite controversial among international scholars.[78] Lepard proposed a new notion of *opinio juris*: 'states

---

72   A. Cassese, 'The Martens Clause: Half a Loaf or Simply Pie in the Sky?' (2000) 11 *EJIL* 187, 188–89; *Tadić* Appeals Chamber Decision on Jurisdiction (n 3), para 99. Cf. Simma and Alston (n 64), 102–06.

73   Jennings and Watts (eds) (n 35) § 10, at 29; *Prosecutor v Furundžija* (Judgement) ICTY-95-17/1-A (12 July 2000) (Declaration of Judge Patrick Robinson), para 281; The ICJ Statute, art 38(1)(b); K. Wolfke, *Custom in Present International Law* (Springer 1993) 87.

74   UN Doc A/73/10 (2018), para 65, Conclusion 8.1; UN Doc A/71/10 (2016), para 62, Conclusion 8.1; art 38(1)(b) of the ICJ Statute; *Maritime Delimitation and Territorial Questions between Qatar and Bahrain*, Merits, Judgment, [2001] ICJ Rep 40, 101–02, para 205.

75   Akehurst (n 1) 16, 18–19.

76   ibid 16–18; for 'considerable majority', 'overwhelming majority', 'large majority' requirements of practice, see Lepard (2010) (n 60) 26 and fn 85, 151–52.

77   For comments on the custom-identification approach in the ICRC *Study*, see E. Wilmshurst and S. Breau (eds), *Perspectives on the ICRC Study on Customary International Humanitarian Law* (CUP 2007) 3–49. Cf. *North Sea Continental Shelf* cases (n 34), 43, para 73.

78   For discussions on the meaning of *opinio juris*, see Lepard (2010) (n 60) 20–29, 112, 118–21.

generally believe that it is desirable now or in the near future to have an authoritative legal principle or rule prescribing, permitting, or prohibiting certain state conduct'.[79] The idea of the desirability of what practice should be law might be covered by the phrase *opinio necessitatis*. This definition, however, is not compatible with the principle of legality in international criminal law. In this research, *opinio juris* still refers to the acceptance of a practice that reflects international law. Unlike State practice with general requirements, no criterion exists in identifying the quantity and quality of *opinio juris* of States for the formation of customary law.[80]

It is presumed that all States are potentially affected by international law. But not every State has the opportunity or capacity to participate in a practice, to do or to say; even so, not every State is interested in a specific practice. Some States may lack the motivation to engage in or to address their legal views for different reasons.[81] The practice and *opinio juris* may be different among States for a specific rule.[82] Then, whose practice and *opinio juris* do matter? The ICJ proposed a test of 'States whose interests are specially affected'.[83] This position has been criticised for its inconsistency with the principle of equality of States.[84] Sørensen and Alfred Verdross proposed a better test to cover 'all those States who have the opportunity to engage in practice', including practice in the UN framework and based on treaties.[85] It is noteworthy that the 'specially affected States' and the 'most engaged States' tests do not mean that sufficient consistent practice of these States with their *opinio juris* would lead to the formation of a new customary rule.[86] The most engaged States test is by no means a constitutive element

---

79 ibid 121.
80 For criticism of customary law, see J.P. Kelly, 'The Twilight of Customary International Law' (2000) 40 *Va J Intl L* 449, 518–19.
81 See comments by Government, Information submitted by Botswana to the 66th Session of the ILC (2014).
82 'Report of the International Law Commission', UN Doc A/69/10 (2014), para 181; Baxter (1970) (n 1) 66; Villiger (1985) (n 1) 30–33. For further debate and references, see Lepard (2010) (n 60) 27–28, 153–54; J. Charney, 'The Persistent Objector Rule and the Development of Customary International Law' (1986) 56 *British Ybk Intl L* 1, 19.
83 *North Sea Continental Shelf* cases (n 34), 43, para 74. For a discussion on this issue, see UN Doc A/73/10 (2018), para 66, commentary (4) to Conclusion 8.
84 A. Cassese and J. Weiler (eds), *Change and Stability in International Law-Making* (Walter de Gruyter 1988) 2; Villiger (1985) (n 1) 30–33; Jennings and Watts (eds) (n 35) § 10, at 29.
85 Villiger (1985) (n 1) 32.
86 *North Sea Continental Shelf* cases (n 34), 42–43, paras 73-74. For an analysis of this test, see K.J. Heller, 'Specially-Affected States and the Formation of Custom' (2018) 112 *AJIL* 191.

of customary law, instead it provides a way to qualify relevant evidence of the two elements.[87]

This study admits that all States are relevant to the issue of international crimes, but relative weight is given to the practice and *opinio juris* of the most engaged States. All participating States had the opportunity to discuss and vote at the Rome Conference, despite their lack of capacity or motivation. The most engaged States generally include those who actively participated in the drafting of the 1998 Rome Statute and the 2010 Kampala Amendments, in the debates of the UN organs and in the ICC's Assembly of States Parties (ASP) meetings, and the States who were involved in the specific practice of a rule.[88] Additionally, recognition of international crimes through the establishment and exercise of universal jurisdiction also evidences the practice and *opinio juris* of these most engaged States.

These States most engaged in a particular rule should be analysed on a case-by-case basis. As to international crimes, States affected may be less reluctant to prosecute international crimes at the national level for political reasons; their submissions and calls for intervention by international tribunals indicate their acknowledgement of the crimes. As for non-international armed conflicts, the interests of other States are not affected in most cases. States involved in non-international armed conflicts in some areas, such as Rwanda and the former Yugoslavia, would be more affected States than other States for the war crime issue. With regard to modes of liability, the selection of the most engaged States pertains to investigating national legislation and decisions in representative major legal systems. The personal immunity issue at international criminal tribunals requires an inquiry of these States involved and other States' responses, claims and reactions in various contexts. States, that exercised universal jurisdiction and to which suspected senior acting officials have visited, are the most engaged States.

2.3.2.2 Practice: Forms of Evidence

According to the ILC's draft conclusions on 'Identification of Customary International Law', the form of evidence of practice includes but is not limited to:

---

87 Cf. 'Identification of customary international law: Comments and observations received from Governments', UN Doc A/CN.4/716 (2018), 31 (China), 32 (Israel), 33 (Netherlands), 35 (US).

88 An exhaustive examination can be done with a group of researchers with translated documents of different languages, including English, Chinese, Arabic, Russia, Spanish, French, Germany, Greek, Danish and some other languages. In this book, the author focuses on available and accessible resources to reach her conclusions.

diplomatic acts and correspondence; conduct in connection with resolutions adopted by an international organisation or at an intergovernmental conference; conduct in connection with treaties; executive conduct, including operational conduct "on the ground"; legislative and administrative acts;[89] and decisions of national courts.[90]

The ILC adopted the view of verbal acts as State practice.[91] In fact, a statement as evidence of practice is an academic debate.[92] Anthony D'Amato distinguished between statements as evidence of *opinio juris* and actions as evidence of State practice.[93] By contrast, Akehurst argued that any behaviour or abstract statements of a State may constitute evidence of State practice, including 'any instance of State behaviour – including acts, omissions, statements, silence, treaty ratifications, negotiation positions reflected in preparatory works and votes of resolutions and declarations'.[94] Akehurst qualified verbal acts of a State by requiring acts of 'organs' that 'are competent to make treaties in the nature of the State'.[95] Also, Tullio Treves noted that the expression of views concerning whether a rule of customary law exists might be in the form of acts and real expressions of belief.[96] He argued that governmental statements in the national framework (for instance, declarations in Parliament) and international contexts (for example, notes, protests or claims, or reactions to other States' claims) are manifestations of practice.[97]

This book qualifies a State's (written or verbal) statements that have an impact outside its territory as relevant evidence of State practice. The idea of verbal acts is important for States that have no capacity, or are unable, to act

---

89   Arajärvi (n 55); N. Arajärvi, 'Looking Back from Nowhere: Is There a Future for Universal Jurisdiction over International Crimes?' (2011) 16 *Tilburg L Rev* 5, 16–17 and fn 65.
90   UN Doc A/73/10 (2018), para 65, Conclusion 6.2; UN Doc A/71/10 (2016), para 62, Conclusion 6.2. See also J. Crawford, *Brownlie's Principles of Public International Law* (8th edn, OUP 2012) 6–7.
91   UN Doc A/73/10 (2018), para 65, Conclusion 4.1, 4.3, 6.1; UN Doc A/71/10 (2016), paras 62-63, Conclusion 4.3, Conclusion 6.1 and its commentary (2).
92   M. Byers, *Custom, Power and the Power of Rules: International Relations and Customary International Law* (CUP 1999) 133–36; A. da Rocha Ferreira *et al*, 'Formation and Evidence of Customary Law' (2013)1 *UFRGSMUN* 182, 188.
93   A. D'Amato, *The Concept of Custom in International Law* (Cornell University Press 1971) 73–102.
94   Akehurst (n 1) 2, 10, 53.
95   ibid 8.
96   Treves (n 33) para 9.
97   ibid para 26.

perfectly, but they contribute to the formation of custom through their verbal acts. Bilateral or multilateral statements count as verbal acts if they are justified elsewhere and are not contradicted by what States do.[98] Positions of representatives of States in international organisations and conferences form part of State practice individually or collectively.[99] States' positions in drafting a treaty, their voting and accession to a treaty, namely, the Rome Statute in this book, are valuable verbal acts.[100] Debates, statements and voting of States in the UN General Assembly, and comments of representatives in the Sixth Committee, as well as their attitude towards specific provisions in other international fora are also part of their verbal acts.[101] These verbal acts addressed in connection with particular and concrete cases are given much weight for the identification of custom.[102]

In addition, the practice of the executive, legislative and judicial organs of a State is deemed State practice.[103] National laws and cases are not *per se* sources of international law because most of them do not deal with international law issues.[104] They also rarely deal with the issue of whether a customary international rule exists.[105] However, as Lassa Oppenheim noted, national cases, in 'cumulative effect', may afford evidence for the identification of customary law.[106] National laws and cases addressing international law issues are relevant.[107] In the case of practice that varies among executive, legislative and judicial branches of a State, Sienhe Yee commented that:

---

98 *Military and Paramilitary Activities* Judgment (n 67), 98, para 186.
99 *Barcelona Traction, Light and Power Company, Limited (Belgium v Spain)*, Judgment, [1970] ICJ Rep 3, Separate Opinion of Judge Ammoun, 302-03, para 11.
100 *Military and Paramilitary Activities* Judgment (n 67), 100, para 18; ILA (n 34) 725, § 4.
101 Treves (n 33) paras 47-49. Cf. ibid 99–100, paras 188-89, considering these statements as evidence of *opinio juris*, rather than State practice.
102 Villiger (1997) (n 1) 19; Treves (n 33) paras 44-46.
103 UN Doc A/73/10 (2018), para 65, Conclusion 5. See also UN Doc A/71/10 (2016), para 62, Conclusion 5; ILA (n 34) 728, § 9.
104 *Prosecution v Abílio Soares* (Judgment, Indonesian *Ad Hoc* Human Rights Court for East Timor, Central Jakarta District Court) 01/PID.HAM/AD. Hoc/2002/ph.JKT.PST (14 August 2002) 70.
105 Jennings and Watts (eds) (n 35) § 13, at 41.
106 ibid § 13, at 41–42 and fn 6, 8, giving examples of collections of municipal decisions dealing with matters of international law. See also Memorandum by the Secretariat, UN Doc A/CN.4/691 (2016), paras 40-49; UN Doc A/73/10 (2018), para 65, Conclusion 13.2; UN Doc A/71/10 (2016), para 62, Conclusion 13.2; *Prosecutor v Đorđević* (Judgement) ICTY-05-87/1-A (27 January 2014), para 44.
107 C. Emanuelli, 'Comments on the ICRC Study on Customary International Humanitarian Law' (2007) 44 *Canadian Ybk Intl L* 437, 445.

If a 'variation' appears in the practice of different organs at the same highest level of a State, such a 'variation' is *usually* also a false one because *usually* the executive branch has the charge of managing international affairs and it is the practice of this branch that counts in the formation of international law. [...] [I]t is important for a decision-maker in the identification process to identify the conduct of the organ (whether executive, legislative or judicial) of a particular State that speaks finally for a particular State internationally and give effect to that conduct only.[108]

By contrast, the ILC's work provides that 'the weight to be given to that practice may, depending on the circumstances, be reduced'.[109] In general, foreign ministries with greater expertise address self-seeking and abstract statements, and courts with impartiality deal with specific issues. A better view is that 'differences between the practice followed by different organs of a State tend to disappear in time, as the views of one organ prevail over the views of others'. Before the disappearance of conflicting practice, the practice of a State is inconsistent and is less capable of contributing to the formation of international law.[110] In this book, almost all national laws and cases are drawn from the ICC's 'National Implementing Legislation Database (NILD)',[111] the ICRC's 'Customary IHL Database',[112] the Asser Institute's 'International Crimes Database (ICD)',[113] and collections of the 'Legal Tools Database'.[114]

Furthermore, in this book, practice is not limited to practice of States but also includes practice of international organisations acting as independent entities.[115] Practice of international organisations in their own right, in

---

108 S. Yee, 'Report on the ILC Project on "Identification of Customary International Law"' (2015) 14 *Chinese J Intl L* 375, para 44 (emphasis in original).

109 UN Doc A/73/10 (2018), para 65, Conclusion 7.2. See also M. Wood, 'The Present Position within the ILC on the Topic "Identification of Customary International Law": in Partial Response to Sienho Yee's Report on the ILC Project on "Identification of Customary International Law"' (2016) 15 *Chinese J Intl L* 3. Cf. L.J. van den Herik, 'The Decline of Customary International Law as a Source of International Criminal Law' in Bradley (ed) (n 40) 250–51.

110 Akehurst (n 1) 21–22.

111 ICC, National Implementing Legislation Database <https://iccdb.hrlc.net/data/> accessed 30 December 2020.

112 ICRC, Customary IHL Database <https://ihl-databases.icrc.org/customary-ihl/eng/docs/Home> accessed 30 December 2020.

113 Asser Institute, International Crimes Database (ICD) <http://www.internationalcrimes-database.org/> accessed 18 December 2020.

114 Legal Tools Database <https://www.legal-tools.org> accessed 30 December 2020.

115 'Identification of customary international law, Statement of the Chair of the Drafting Committee, by Mr Charles C. Jalloh', 25 May 2018, 3; J. Odermatt, 'The Development of

particular the UN organs, should be considered in the identification of custom. The ILC supports that, 'in certain cases', 'general practice' also includes practice of international organisations for the formation of customary law.[116] The International Law Association (ILA) has also proposed that 'the practice of intergovernmental organisations in their own right is a form of "State practice"'.[117] Alternatively, Treves employs the phrase 'international practice' rather than 'State practice' to illustrate what international organisations do and say.[118] The ICJ has also referred to 'international practice' to show that the prohibition of torture is part of customary law.[119] Commentators have argued that the UN Security Council played a significant role 'in generating evidence of custom related to non-international armed conflicts'.[120] Resolutions of the General Assembly are also rich sources of evidence of the development of customary law.[121]

The traditional position is left behind that only States are subject to international law.[122] Individuals and international organisations are also bound by international (criminal) law. The practice of international organisations as an autonomous actor as opposed to States, such as the UN Security Council, its General Assembly and its Secretary-General, are involved in the creation of

Customary International Law by International Organisations' (2017) 66 *ICLQ* 491; Treves (n 33) paras 50-52. For discussions on whether resolutions of international organisations can generate law for States as opposed to institutions, see Mendelson (n 35) 85–88.

116   UN Doc A/73/10 (2018), para 65, Conclusions 4.1–4.2; UN Doc A/71/10 (2016), para 62, Conclusions 4.1–4.2; M. Wood, 'International Organisations and Customary International Law' (2015) 48 *Vand J Transnatl L* 609. For an analysis of this conclusion, see N. Blokker, 'International Organisations and Customary International Law' (2017) 14 *IOLR* 1.
117   ILA (n 34) 730, § 11. Cf. Yee (n 108) para 42.
118   Treves (n 33) paras 10, 50–52, 77, 80.
119   *Obligation to Prosecute or Extradite* Judgment (n 66), 457, paras 99-100.
120   G. Fox *et al*, 'The Contributions of United Nations Security Council Resolutions to the Law of Non-International Armed Conflict: New Evidence of Customary International Law' (2017) 67 *Am U L R* 649; UN Doc A/73/10 (2018), para 66, Conclusion 12 and its commentary.
121   Treves (n 33) paras 44-46; R. Higgins, *The Development of International Law Through the Political Organs of the United Nations* (OUP 1963) 5; UN Doc A/73/10 (2018), para 65, Conclusion 12. Cf. Scharf (n 60) 51–53 (political show-off); Jennings and Watts (eds) (n 35) § 16, at 49 (expressions of a political view); *Legality of the Threat or Use of Nuclear Weapons* Advisory Opinion (n 62), 254–55, para 70 (evidence of *opinio juris*).
122   A. Peters, *Beyond Human Rights: The Legal Status of the Individual in International Law* (OUP 2016); C. Greenwood, 'Sovereignty: A View from the International Bench' in R. Rawlings *et al* (eds), *Sovereignty and the Law: Domestic, European and International Perspectives* (OUP 2013) 255; Jennings and Watts (eds) (n 35) § 16, at 45–50.

a customary rule.[123] In addition to UN organs, jurisprudence of international and internationalised tribunals manifests the practice of international judicial organs. Jurisprudence of international criminal tribunals is not evidence of State practice for its attribute in nature[124] and for the tribunals' jurisdictional limitations,[125] but it is a subsidiary means, from which the content of a customary rule can be identified.[126] Decisions of international bodies, such as the IMT and IMTFE, the ICTY, the ICTR and the ICC, as well as other international and internationalised tribunals, constitute persuasive evidence in ascertaining the state of customary rules.[127] Principles and rules identified by pre/post-ICC tribunals and the ICC are useful to determine the existence and the content of a customary rule.[128] It should be noted that findings in these decisions are not conclusive evidence for the existence of customary law because custom is not static and may evolve after the delivery date of a decision.[129] In the two UN *ad hoc* tribunals, decisions of their Appeals Chamber would be given more weight than the findings of Trial Chambers, in particular, the latter were subsequently overturned on appeal.[130]

2.3.2.3 *Opinio Juris*: Forms of Evidence

According to the ILC, the form of evidence of *opinio juris* includes but is not limited to

---

123   Jennings and Watts (eds) (n 35) § 16, at 48–49; ILA (n 34) 731, 751, §§ 12, 19; UN Doc A/67/10 (2012), 8; UN Doc A/71/10 (2016), para 62, Conclusion 4.2; UN Doc A/73/10 (2018), para 65, Conclusion 4.2; Akehurst (n 1) 11. For discussions on the role of international organisations practice, see Lepard (2010) (n 60) 41–42.
124   ILA (n 34) 729, § 10.
125   *The Prosecutor v Kayishema & Ruzindana* (Judgment) ICTR-95-1-T (21 May 1999), para 138.
126   Jennings and Watts (eds) (n 35) § 13, at 41; Mendelson (n 35) 81–83; UN Doc A/73/10 (2018), para 65, Conclusion 13.2; UN Doc A/71/10 (2016), para 62, Conclusion 13.2.
127   T. Ginsburg, 'Bounded Discretion in International Judicial Lawmaking' (2004) 45 *Va J Intl L* 631, 639; J. Powderly, 'The Rome Statute and the Attempted Corseting of the Interpretative Judicial Function: Reflections on Sources of Law and Interpretative Technique' in C. Stahn (ed), *The Law and Practice of the International Criminal Court* (OUP 2015) 483; Henckaerts and Doswald-beck (eds) (n 6) xxxiv; UN Doc A/73/10 (2018), para 65, Conclusion 13. For International Case Law Database, see World Courts, <http://www.worldcourts.com/> accessed 4 December 2020.
128   V. Nerlich, 'The Status of ICTY and ICTR Precedent in Proceedings before the ICC' in C. Stahn and G. Sluiter (eds), *The Emerging Practice of the International Criminal Court* (Brill | Nijhoff 2009) 313 and fn 36, 316–24.
129   UN Doc A/71/10 (2016), paras 62-63, Conclusion 13.1 and its commentary (3).
130   Nerlich (n 128) 314.

[...] public statements made on behalf of States; official publications; government legal opinions; diplomatic correspondence; decisions of national courts; treaty provisions; and conduct in connection with resolutions adopted by an international organisation or at an intergovernmental conference. [...] [F]ailure to react over time to a practice may serve as evidence of acceptance as law.[131]

At first glance, forms of evidence of the two elements overlap in the ILC's draft conclusions.[132] For instance, diplomatic correspondence, decisions of national courts and conduct in connection with resolutions are forms of evidence of both practice and *opinio juris*. International and internationalised criminal tribunals have attempted to distinguish between evidence of the two elements, but most of them failed.[133] As the ICRC claimed in its 2005 *Study*, the separation of practice and *opinio juris* is 'very difficult and largely theoretical'.[134]

Although a strict separation is hard, this book counts bilateral and multilateral (verbal and written) statements as forms of practice. Unilateral statements are considered as forms of *opinio juris*.[135] The drafting and voting for resolutions count as forms of practice, while subsequent action in accordance with resolutions indicating commitments is deemed evidence of *opinio juris*. Whether decisions of national courts count as State practice or *opinio juris* depends on the subject matter of these decisions. National decisions exercising universal jurisdiction over international crimes are mostly considered as practice of States. Other national decisions, dealing with defences of domestic crimes, civil liabilities, refugee status and immigration issues related to international crimes, might also address judicial organs' positions on customary law. One has to admit that, as for national decisions, 'more often than not, one and the same act reflects practice and legal conviction'.[136] If these national decisions are expressed in a general and abstract way, or they are inconsistent with government legal opinions simultaneously, they may be of less or no value as forms of *opinio juris*.

---

131 UN Doc A/73/10 (2018), para 65, Conclusions 6.2–6.3.
132 For criticism of double counting, see Mendelson (n 35) 68, 87. Cf. UN Doc A/73/10 (2018), para 66, commentary (8) to Conclusion 3(2).
133 Schabas (n 54) 77–101; Schlütter (n 33); Rauter (n 33) 234.
134 See also N.J. Arajärvi, 'The Requisite Rigour in the Identification of Customary International Law' (2017) 19 *I Community LR* 9, 32–36; 'Summary record of the 3280th meeting', UN Doc A/CN.4/SR.3280 (2015).
135 Yee (n 108) paras 39-42.
136 Henckaerts and Doswald-beck (eds) (n 6) § 4942.

Treaties as a form of evidence of *opinio juris* deserve two comments. Firstly, tribunals and scholars differ on the role of a treaty rule as evidence of State practice or *opinio juris*.[137] The ICTY resorted to the 1998 Rome Statute to confirm its findings on the existence and content of a customary rule.[138] In the ILC's draft conclusions, the conduct and position in connection with treaties (voting and accession) count as evidence of practice, while the attitude towards material terms of the treaty rule is regarded as evidence of *opinio juris*.[139] Indeed, verbal statements of States and their corresponding legal views may not be present at the same time in the drafting of a rule of a treaty. For example, States may support the inclusion of war crimes in non-international armed conflict for different reasons: either serious violations 'are' or 'should be' legally criminalised as an international crime in international law, or only in the spirit of compromise. Therefore, acts and statements related to a treaty rule may either indicate State practice or illustrate *opinio juris*, depending on how States have articulated their views and explained their voting. These forms of evidence include States' comments, proposals and debates at the conference on the text of a treaty rule, the voting, adoption and ratification of the treaty, as well as explanations of voting. Besides, subsequent practice, interpretation, application and modification of a treaty, if going beyond the meaning of treaty rules, would be considered as practice of States giving rise a new customary rule.[140]

Secondly, a clarification of three phrases: 'treaty as evidence of *opinio juris*/State practice of custom', 'the nature of treaty as evidence of custom', and 'treaty as evidence of the state of custom' is needed. The first phrase is used to

---

137 For the Rome Statute as evidence of *opinio juris* of States, see *Prosecutor v Furundžija* (Judgement) ICTY-95-17/1-T (10 December 1998), para 227; R. Pisillo-Mazzeschi, 'Treaty and Custom: Reflections on the Codification of International Law' (1997) 23 *CLB* 549, 559; *Tadić* Appeals Chamber Judgment, para 223; *Kupreškić et al* Trial Chamber Judgment (n 62), paras 579-81; Lepard (2010) (n 60) 191–207. For the Rome Statute as evidence of State practice, see *Prosecutor v Krnojelac* (Judgement) ICTY-97-25-A (17 September 2003), para 221; A. D'Amato, 'Treaty-Based Rules of Custom' in A. D'Amato (ed), *International Law Anthology* (Anderson Publishing Company 1994) 94–101; Treves (n 33) para 47. For discussions on a treaty as evidence of State practice, see Lepard (2010) (n 60) 34, 191–207.
138 *Furundžija* Trial Chamber Judgment, ibid; *Tadić* Appeals Chamber Judgment, ibid; *Krnojelac* Appeals Chamber Judgment, ibid. For other cases, see Schabas (n 8) 336 and fn 16.
139 UN Doc A/73/10 (2018), para 66, commentary (5) to Conclusion 6, commentary (5) to Conclusion 11; Schlütter (n 33) 337–40.
140 Treves (n 33) para 86. Cf. P. Sands and J. Commission, 'Treaty, Custom and Time: Interpretation/Application' in M. Fitzmaurice *et al* (eds), *Treaty Interpretation and the Vienna Convention on the Law of Treaties: 30 Years on* (Martinus Nijhoff Publishers 2010) 39–58, discussing art 31(3)(c) of the VCLT.

elaborate on materials/manifestations relating to treaties as forms of evidence of the two elements of custom. Its essence is what States say and do. The second phrase is the main question of this book and provides a clear exposition on whether a treaty rule constitutes a declaration of a pre-existing customary rule on the same subject matter. Its essence is the formulation of the treaty rule and the existence of a customary rule. The third phrase 'treaty as evidence of the state of custom' concerns the role of a treaty in the identification of a customary rule. The meaning of this phrase is further clarified in section 2.4.

2.3.3 *Other Indicators for the Identification of Customary Law*

There are other subsidiary means for the determination of the rules in customary law. For instance, the ICRC's official statements, the work of the ILC and teachings of the most highly qualified publicists.[141] These indicators are not evidence of practice of States or international organisations, but they do play an essential role in shaping the content of customary law.

The work of the ILC on international law is an important indicator, in particular, if it was adopted by the UN General Assembly, even if it was not formed as a treaty, such as the 1996 Draft Code of Crimes. The ICTY Trial Chamber remarked that:

> [...] the Draft Code is an authoritative international instrument which, depending upon the specific question at issue, may (i) constitute evidence of customary law, or (ii) shed light on customary rules which are of uncertain contents or are in the process of formation, or, at the very least, (iii) be indicative of the legal views of eminently qualified publicists representing the major legal systems of the world.[142]

The Institut de Droit International (Institute of International Law) and the ILA are two examples of collective communities in academia. Their output may provide important sources. However, 'the value of each output needs to be carefully assessed in the light of the mandate and expertise of the body concerned, the care and objectivity with which it works on a particular issue,

---

141 UN Doc A/71/10 (2016), paras 62-63, Conclusion 4 and its commentary (10), Conclusions 13.1 and 14.

142 *Furundžija* Trial Chamber Judgment (n 137), para 227. See also T. McCormack and G. Simpson, 'The International Law Commission's Draft Code of Crimes against the Peace and Security of Mankind: An Appraisal of the Substantive Provisions' (1994) 5 CLF 1; J. Allain and J. Jones, 'A Patchwork of Norms: A Commentary on the 1996 Draft Code of Crimes against the Peace and Security of Mankind' (1997) 8 EJIL 100.

the support a particular output enjoys within the body and the reception of the output by States.'[143]

2.3.4 *Summary*

The above observation shows that the two-element approach continues to apply in the identification of customary rules of international criminal law. Scarce or limited physical practice by States does not hinder the formation of customary law. A flexible formula of the two elements is also acceptable in certain contexts. This book adopts a flexible two-element approach in the identification of customary law by focusing more on *opinio juris*. Practice refers to physical behaviour and verbal acts (statements) between or among States. In some contexts, practice also includes acts of international organisations.[144] *Opinio juris* refers to the acceptance of practice that reflects international law. The weight of evidence of the two elements among States should be analysed on a case-by-case basis as to a specific rule. Apart from the evidence of the two elements, other indicators are also helpful for the identification of the state of customary law.

2.4 Terms: A Treaty Was or Is of a 'Declaratory' Nature of Custom

This section aims to clarify the role of a treaty as evidence of the state of customary law and the terms employed to illustrate the finding on the relationship between a treaty rule and a customary rule on a same subject matter. To this end, this section first discusses Richard Baxter's view concerning the role of a treaty rule as evidence of custom, and then analyses the meaning of the term 'declaratory' employed in this book.

2.4.1 *The Role of Treaties as Evidence of the State of Customary Law*

In 1965, Baxter described the role of treaties as evidence of the state of customary law in a journal article about multilateral treaties as evidence of custom.[145] He argued that a treaty rule might be a reflection, crystallisation, or the origin of adoption of customary international law.[146] The ICJ in the 1969 *North Sea*

---

143 UN Doc A/71/10 (2016), paras 62-63, Conclusion 14 and its commentary (5).
144 Cf. Asian-African Legal Consultative Organisation Informal Expert Group (AALCOIEG), 'Comments on the ILC Project on Identification of Customary International Law', Comment G '(1) only State conduct in relation to an international question be counted as practice'.
145 Baxter (1965) (n 1) 275.
146 ibid 287.

Continental Shelf cases later adopted Baxter's idea on this point.[147] The 1969 Vienna Convention also recognises that a customary rule continues to exist in parallel with a treaty provision about an identical subject and that a treaty rule can pass into a customary law.[148] In 1970, Baxter gave a lecture on 'treaties and custom' in The Hague Academy of International Law.[149] He further addressed the distinction between a treaty of 'declaratory' nature of custom and a treaty of 'constitutive' nature of custom. This distinction was later endorsed by the ICJ in the 1986 *Military and Paramilitary Activities* case, which stated: 'those cases turned on the question whether a rule enshrined in a treaty also existed as a customary rule, either because the treaty had merely codified the custom, or caused it to "crystallise", or because it had influenced its subsequent adoption'.[150] Many scholars have confirmed such a role for treaties, including D'Amato, Villiger and Yoram Dinstein.[151] The ILC specifically endorsed a treaty rule of declaratory function and a treaty rule of an innovative character in its draft conclusions on 'Identification of Customary International Law'.[152]

2.4.1.1   Baxter's Concept of 'Declaratory' Nature of Custom

According to Baxter, if a contemporary treaty rule has codified or crystallised custom, the treaty rule is declaratory of custom. He adopted two means to establish a treaty rule as declaratory of custom.[153] The first one is to check the textual language of the treaty rule or other treaty provisions, such as the preamble of the treaty.[154] Baxter also concerned that 'the draftsmen of treaties will attempt to disguise a change in the law as a mere expression of existing law'.[155] The second alternative is to examine the preparatory works of the

---

147   *North Sea Continental Shelf* cases (n 34), 39, 41, 45, paras 63, 71, 81; *Continental Shelf (Libyan Arab Jarnahiriya/Malta)*, Judgment, [1985] ICJ Rep 13, 29-30, para 27.
148   Vienna Convention on the Law of Treaties, 1155 UNTS 331, Preamble, arts 38, 43.
149   Baxter (1970) (n 1) 42.
150   *Military and Paramilitary Activities* Judgment (n 67), 95, para 177; *Maritime Delimitation and Territorial (Qatar v Bahrain)* (n 74), 100, para 201.
151   I.F.I. Shihata, 'The Treaty as a Law-Declaring and Custom-Making Instrument' (1966) *Revue Egyptienne de Droit International* 51, cited in A. D'Amato, 'Manifest Intent and the Generation by Treaty of Customary Rules of International Law' (1970) 64 AJIL 892, 899 and fn 37; Villiger (1997) (n 1); Dinstein (n 1). Cf. Pisillo-Mazzeschi (n 137) 552. For a summary of the role of the treaty in the identification of *opinio juris*, see Lepard (2010) (n 60) 30–32. For an analysis of the treaty interpretation rule, see Merkouris (n 16) 120–67.
152   UN Doc A/73/10 (2018), para 65, Conclusion 11.
153   Baxter (1965) (n 1) 275–300; Baxter (1970) (n 1) 42.
154   Baxter (1970), ibid.
155   Baxter (1965) (n 1) 290.

specific treaty rule or 'the instrument under the authority of which the treaty was drawn up'. Dinstein confirmed the two methods.[156]

D'Amato criticised the two methods for subjectivity.[157] In his view, the text of a treaty may be abused, as Baxter admitted. The statements of negotiators in the preparatory works may be 'self-serving words of declaration'. Some negotiators may also use the term 'declaratory' as a strategy to persuade the other side to accept its position by arguing that these rules accurately reflect existing law.[158] D'Amato argued that it is sufficient to decide whether a treaty rule is law-declaring through analysis of the treaty text and the treaty structure. But other scholars argued that the preamble of the treaty and the preparatory works of a treaty rule should also be examined.[159]

2.4.1.2 Baxter's Concept of 'Constitutive' Nature of Custom

As noted by Baxter, a treaty rule that does not purport to be declaratory at the time when the treaty was adopted may formulate the substantial content of a rule to develop or change a customary rule on the same subject matter.[160] If such a treaty rule has passed into a customary rule at present, the treaty rule is 'constitutive' of custom.[161] The treaty rule is a starting point for a new or modified customary rule, and it becomes a mirror of an existing customary rule by post-treaty progress or State practice.[162] If a customary rule is not established when the assessment is made, the treaty is not of a constitutive nature. In addition, article 38 of the 1969 Vienna Convention confirms the interaction between a treaty rule and a customary rule by providing that 'nothing [...] precludes a rule set forth in a treaty from becoming binding upon a third State as a customary rule of international law, recognised as such'.[163] The result of this process is that the same obligations and rights of international law bind all States, including non-party States to the treaty. Roberts also suggested that

---

156   Dinstein (n 1) 363.
157   D'Amato (n 151) 895–902.
158   ibid 900.
159   For debates about the hierarchy of the evidential value of internal indicia (a treaty text) and the external indicia (the preparatory works of the treaty text and concrete conducts of States), see Dinstein (n 1) 363; Villiger, (1985) (n 1) 244, 247; Pisillo-Mazzeschi (n 137) 556–57, 559.
160   Baxter (1970) (n 1) 57.
161   Baxter (1965) (n 1) 278, 291, 299–300.
162   ibid.
163   For a commentary on art 38, see A. Proelss, 'Article 38' in O. Dörr and K. Schmalenbach (eds), *Vienna Convention on the Law of Treaties: A Commentary* (2nd edn, Springer 2018) 743–54.

substantive moral customs adopted by a representative majority of States in treaties are to prescribe future action based on 'normative evaluation of ideal practice'.[164]

In his 1965 journal article, Baxter did not discuss the test used to determine the constitutive nature of a treaty rule.[165] The ICJ in the *North Sea Continental Shelf* cases analysed whether a treaty rule had passed into customary law binding on all States. The ICJ set forth three conditions for a treaty rule to be transformed into a customary rule.[166] The first requirement is the 'norm-creating character' of that rule (a treaty rule was intended to generate a rule of law). The other two conditions, 'accepted by other State practice with the sense of legal obligation', in effect, are the two elements required for the formation of customary law.[167]

Accordingly, for a treaty rule to be constitutive of custom, the first step is to determine whether a treaty provision was of a norm-making character. The second step is to check whether such a provision passed into a customary rule later on.[168] The custom-identification method applies to decide whether a norm-creating treaty rule is of a constitutive nature at the present time.[169] The ICJ in the *North Sea Continental Shelf* cases set up an objective test. In its view, the treaty rule concerned 'should, at all events potentially, be of a fundamentally norm-creating character such as could be regarded as forming the basis of a general rule of law'.[170] The ICJ further clarified this test with references to the particular form of a treaty rule and the structure of that treaty.[171] The ICJ did not suggest whether the preparatory works of that treaty rule are relevant to the determination of the norm-making nature. Different from a treaty rule of a declaratory nature, the actual intent of the drafters seems to be irrelevant. D'Amato supported the ICJ's approach and called it the 'manifest intent' test.[172] It seems that Baxter also agreed with the general approach of the ICJ on this point.[173] A treaty rule of a 'norm-creating' character manifests a presumed *opinio juris* of States Parties to that practice.

---

164   Roberts (n 62) 764.
165   Baxter (1965) (n 1) 290.
166   *North Sea Continental Shelf* cases (n 34), 42–43, paras 71-72.
167   ibid; Baxter (1970) (n 1) 73.
168   *North Sea Continental Shelf* cases (n 34), 43, para 73.
169   Baxter (1970) (n 1).
170   *North Sea Continental Shelf* cases (n 34), 42–43, para 72.
171   ibid.
172   D'Amato (n 151) 895–902.
173   Baxter (1970) (n 1) 62–64.

2.4.1.3 Assessment and Conclusions

The concepts of 'declaratory' and 'constitutive' as defined by Baxter need to be clarified. First of all, if there is no claim in the treaty or preparatory works of the treaty, it does not preclude the treaty from having a declaratory attribute.[174] Also, a treaty rule of norm-making nature may have never passed into a customary rule. It means that States Parties wanted to establish a rule and pushed the content of the rule in such a direction. Practice, however, develops in different ways, and a new customary rule may be established. Despite attitudes expressed by States in the treaty, if there is no general practice among States, no new customary rule is formed from that treaty rule. The new customary rule and the treaty rule diverge in this circumstance.[175]

In addition, it seems that apart from State practice and *opinio juris*, the ICJ might not have intended to add a third element for a treaty rule passing into custom. A treaty rule not of a norm-making nature may also be transformed into customary law. The ICJ had borne in mind rules in the 1958 Geneva Convention on the Continental Shelf that entered into force in 1964. The 'norm-making' requirement provides a shortcut for further analysis of the attitude and positions of States Parties and signatory States. The norm-making character is not a necessity for a treaty rule to pass into custom but can simplify proof of evidence of the two elements. Akehurst notes that 'whether a rule laid down in a treaty is subsequently accepted as a rule of customary law is a question of fact'.[176] The norm-making character has never been a requirement for a treaty rule developing into custom.

Furthermore, it should also be stressed that the declaratory or constitutive nature of a treaty rule as defined by Baxter provides preliminary rather than conclusive evidence as to the state of customary law. The ICJ has observed that:

> It is of course axiomatic that the material of customary international law is to be looked for primarily in the actual practice and *opinio juris* of States, even though multilateral conventions may have an important role to play in recording and defining rules deriving from custom, or indeed in developing them.[177]

As Villiger stated, 'the conventional text has only a stimulating function'.[178]

---

174 Dinstein (n 1).
175 Baxter (1970) (n 1).
176 Akehurst (n 1) 50.
177 *Libya-Malta Continental Shelf* Judgment (n 147), 29–30, para 27.
178 Villiger (1997) (n 1) 193.

Finally, Baxter's idea of a treaty rule either of declaratory or constitutive nature does not deal with the issue of 'whether there are any law-creating consequences', as pointed out by D'Amato.[179] A pre-existing customary rule as a parallel to a treaty rule of declaratory nature may be modified by subsequent practice after the adoption of a treaty; and a treaty rule might be neither declaratory nor constitutive. For example, according to the ICTY, '[d]epending on the matter at issue, the Rome Statute may be taken to restate, reflect or clarify customary rules or crystallise them, whereas in some areas it creates new law or modified existing law.' Although States Parties did not 'intend' to alter an existing customary rule or to formulate a new customary rule, practice, later on, develops in the same direction as the text of that rule and forms a customary rule.[180] The construction of the concept 'constitutive' is, thus, of limited utility to describe the current relationship between custom and a treaty rule that was neither law-declaring nor norm-creating.

Despite its inconclusive nature, a preliminary observation of whether a treaty rule was of a 'declaratory' or 'norm-making' nature is valuable for this research. As analysed by many commentators, a treaty rule articulating itself as a codification of customary law provides substantial evidence of the *opinio juris* of States to a particular rule.[181] Also, in general, statements and conducts of non-party States to a treaty, in general, are evidence of State practice.[182]

Since States Parties to a treaty may invoke a treaty rule rather than custom, it is hard to ascertain whether a State Party behaved with the general acceptance of practice as custom.[183] The ICJ in the *North Sea Continental Shelf* cases held that only practice of non-parties to a treaty counts as evidence to analyse whether a treaty rule has passed into customary law.[184] Nevertheless, if the practice of States Parties to a treaty is not deemed valuable for the development of custom, it is difficult to find State practice.[185] Baxter argued that a successful treaty with a substantial number of States Parties might lead to a paradox in the identification of customary law (the 'Baxter Paradox').[186] Due

---

179　D'Amato (n 151) 901.
180　*Furundžija* Trial Chamber Judgment (n 137), para 227. Confirmed by *Tadić* Appeals Chamber Judgment (n 137), para 223; *Kupreškić et al* Trial Chamber Judgment (n 62), para 580.
181　Lepard (2010) (n 60) 204–05.
182　*North Sea Continental Shelf* cases (n 34), 43, para 76.
183　Baxter (1970) (n 1) 64; M. Villiger, 'The 1969 Vienna Convention on the Law of Treaties: 40 Years After' (2009) 344 *Recueil des cours* 9, 67–69.
184　*North Sea Continental Shelf* cases (n 34), 43, para 76.
185　D'Amato (n 151) 900–01.
186　Baxter (1970) (n 1) 64, 73.

to the requirement of general (the widespread and representative consistent) practice, the greater the number of States Parties and correspondingly the smaller the number of non-party States, the more difficult it becomes to demonstrate what is the state of customary international law outside the treaty is.[187] D'Amato also noted that the idea of relying only on the practice of non-party States would render the treaty itself valueless.[188] If a treaty rule in itself recognised its law-declaring or norm-creating nature of custom, the practice of States Parties in accordance with that rule also counts as valuable evidence of State practice.

Other commentators have also proposed that if the content of an emerging customary rule is identical to the treaty formulation, a conclusion might be reached with less practice of non-party States but more *opinio juris* reflected in a multilateral treaty as to the customary status of a treaty rule.[189] A better view might be that both practice of States Parties under a treaty and practice of non-party States count as evidence of practice for a treaty rule developing into custom.[190] The value of practice of States Parties is strengthened if a treaty rule is of a norm-making nature, whereas the value is weakened if a denial exists in the treaty that acts of States Parties are not informed by *opinio juris*.[191] Accordingly, the preliminary law-declaring or norm-creating nature of a treaty rule adds another layer of analysis in this book.

Baxter's idea of declaratory nature merely revealed the state of customary rules at the adoption of an ideal 'contemporary' treaty, rather than a treaty in the past.[192] Indeed, the difference between past and contemporary is relative for observers. The 1998 Rome Statute, as a past treaty for observers at present, was deemed a 'contemporary' treaty for observers in 1998. The term 'declaratory' applies to describe the preliminary finding on a rule of the Rome Statute as declaratory of custom in 1998 (2010). The concepts of law-declaring and norm-making, therefore, are used as an analytical tool to illustrate the 'preliminary findings' on the relationship between the Rome Statute and custom in 1998 (2010). The law-declaring nature is identified through expressive statements in

---

187   ibid.
188   D'Amato (n 151) 901; Lepard (2010) (n 60) 196–99.
189   P. Weil, 'Towards Relative Normativity in International Law?' (1983) 77 *AJIL* 413, 435; G. Scott and C. Carr, 'Multilateral Treaties and the Formation of Customary International Law' (1996) 25 *Denver J Intl L& P* 71, 78.
190   Lepard (2010) (n 60) 196–99; Treves (n 33) para 86.
191   A.M. Weisburd, 'Customary International Law: The Problem of Treaties' (1988) 21 *Vand J Transnatl L* 1, 23–29. For further clarification, see chapter 2.5.2.
192   Baxter (1970) (n 1) 37.

the treaty and the drafting history to that effect.[193] The norm-making nature is analysed with reference to the form of a treaty rule, the structure of the treaty and its preparatory works.

In conclusion, a treaty rule plays a role as evidence of the state of customary law. An observation of the law-declaring nature or norm-making character of a treaty rule assists in identifying a customary rule but is not conclusive. After interpreting the treaty rule, a layer of analysis is followed to answer the question whether a treaty rule is preliminary evidence as declaratory of customary law. Bearing in mind that the actual intent of the drafters might be ambiguous, this layer of analysis examines the text of the treaty rule and the preamble of the treaty, the structure and context of the treaty rule and the preparatory works of that treaty rule to show whether a treaty rule articulated itself as declaratory of customary law.

2.4.2 *Terminology: Declaratory*

This book employs the term 'declaratory' in determining the nature of selected provisions of the (updated) Rome Statute as evidence of customary law on the same subject in the past and at present. Baxter's notion of 'declaratory' focuses on the role of a treaty rule in the identification of customary law, but the term 'declaratory' in this book aims to qualify the relationship between a treaty text and a (potential) customary rule. Additionally, in the context of customary law, Hiram Chodosh considered 'declarative law' as a source of international law that was 'not accepted as law by a generality of States'.[194] In his view, the absence of either State practice or *opinio juris* distinguished declarative law from customary law.[195] The notion of 'declarative law' as a source is not closely relevant to the term 'declaratory' used in this book.

As observed above, Baxter's term 'constitutive' illustrates the preliminary finding that before the adoption of a norm-making treaty rule, a customary rule with the same content did not exist but come into being afterwards. This term is of limited utility to cover a situation where a treaty rule was not of a norm-making nature but also passed into custom. This book does not employ the notion of 'constitutive' to describe the nature of treaty at

---

193   ibid 37, 54, 56.
194   H.E. Chodosh, 'Neither Treaty nor Custom: The Emergence of Declarative International Law' (1991) 26 *Tex Intl LJ* 87, 89.
195   ibid 91, 119–24. For further discussions on the relationship between custom and soft (declarative) law, see L.R. Helfer and I.B. Wuerth, 'Custom in the Age of Soft Law' (working paper) <https://www.iilj.org/wp-content/uploads/2016/07/WuerthIILJColloq2014.pdf> accessed 30 December 2020.

present. The paragraphs that follow attempt to clarify the main meaning of 'declaratory'.

In this book, a treaty rule 'was declaratory' of custom at the time when the (updated) Rome Statute was adopted if: (1) it was a reflection of a pre-existing customary rule governing a particular matter, or (2) it was a crystallisation of an emerging customary rule during the process of formation and adoption of that treaty rule on a particular matter. In addition, a treaty rule 'is declaratory' of custom if: (1) the rule that was declaratory continues to be declaratory of custom, or (2) the rule that was not declaratory has become declaratory of custom. If a treaty rule was of a declaratory nature, the two elements should be satisfied to determine whether a treaty rule continues to be declaratory of contemporary custom; in the case of a treaty rule that was not declaratory, the two-element approach also applies in ascertaining whether the treaty rule has passed into a customary rule.

The phrases 'was declaratory' and 'is declaratory' simply describe the factual nature of a treaty rule as evidence of custom in the past or at present. The former phrase does not disclose the current nature of the treaty rule as evidence of custom at present, while the latter expression does not attempt to indicate the nature of a treaty rule as evidence of custom in the past. Simply put, a treaty rule that 'is or is not declaratory' of custom does not mean that this treaty rule 'was or was not declaratory' of custom in the past. The converse is also true. Besides, the finding of a treaty rule 'is not declaratory' does not disclose the existence or non-existence of customary rule on the same subject matter.

Lastly, this book defines three categories of distinction. Firstly, a distinction is made between a rule of 'reflection' and a rule of 'crystallisation'. Secondly, a difference exists between the declaratory nature in the past (was declaratory) and the declaratory nature at present (is declaratory). Thirdly, the last distinction is between the positive finding of a treaty rule 'was/is' declaratory of custom and the negative finding of 'was not/is not' declaratory of custom. The first distinction indicates that the time when a customary rule of international criminal law came into existence may be slightly different. The second differentiation reveals the existence of a customary rule at the time when the Rome Statute was adopted and subsequently. This requires an historical overview of the development of practice. The third distinction relates to the central question of whether a rule of the Rome Statute was/is declaratory of custom.

These three distinctions are of central importance in the context of sources and in the context of custom as an interpretative aid.[196] The difference between codification of existing customary rules, crystallisation of a rule into custom

---

196   Villiger (1997) (n 1) 126.

during the process of adoption of a treaty,[197] and the progressive development of international law, is 'a matter of degree',[198] 'between minor and major changes of the law'.[199] D'Amato also criticised that 'insofar as most treaties at present purport to declare existing law rather than to signal their departure from it, the distinction suggested by Baxter might diminish in objective importance'.[200] The first category of distinction remains crucial to tribunals that rely on customary law to punish international crimes at present. States can and indeed do prosecute crimes that occurred decades ago, for instance, Cambodia, Kosovo and Bangladesh. In the future, the distinction between reflection and crystallisation may fade into irrelevance as many suspects in advanced age die. Yet, the second and third categories of distinction continue to provide a perspective to understand the customary status of a treaty rule along with the development of international law and new amendments to the Rome Statute. In short, ascertaining the customary status of a provision of the Statute before and after its adoption is valuable, whether or not a treaty rule is applicable and a given customary rule exists concerning a specific criminal matter.

2.5 Preconditions for This Study

This section analyses the preconditions for the study in this book. The question here is whether the Rome Statute itself deny an analysis of its rule as declaratory of custom.

2.5.1 A Treaty Rule of a Declaratory Nature: Any Obstacles in the Rome Statute?

This subsection mainly focuses on the legal impact of reservation and the ICC jurisdictional mechanisms to analyse whether there are obstacles to determining the declaratory nature of a rule of the (updated) Rome Statute at the time when the treaty or its amendment was adopted.

The first issue is whether articles 10 and 124 of the Rome Statute are obstacles to the examination of provisions of the Rome Statute as being declaratory

---

197 Pisillo-Mazzeschi (n 137) 552; C. Kreß, 'War Crimes Committed in Non-International Armed Conflict and the Emerging System of International Criminal Justice' (2001) 30 *Israel Ybk HR* 103, 175.
198 Jennings and Watts (eds) (n 35) § 31, at 110. For discussions on the differences between codification and progressive development of law, see Grover (n 6) 231–42.
199 Villiger (1997) (n 1) 126.
200 D'Amato (n 151) 899–901.

of custom. Article 10 provides that '[n]othing in this Part [about jurisdiction, admissibility and applicable law] shall be interpreted as limiting or prejudicing in any way existing or developing rules of international law for purposes other than this Statute'. Some commentators have considered article 10 to be a kind of 'reservation clause'.[201] Article 124 allows States to enter a declaration suspending the ICC's jurisdiction for up to seven years concerning war crimes. It seems that the two provisions do not exclude the possibility that a rule of the Rome Statute was of a declaratory nature.

Articles 10 and 124 were not inserted as substantive reservation provisions.[202] Article 10 as a 'without prejudice clause' reserves the status of custom as an independent source outside the Statute, which is similar to the function of article 43 of the Vienna Convention providing that a State may 'be subject [to obligations] under international law independently of the treaty'.[203] Other provisions related to the Statute endorse the view that article 10 is not a true reservation clause. For instance, footnotes for the Elements for articles 8(2)(b)(xviii) and 8(2)(e)(xiv) mentioned that '[n]othing in this element shall be interpreted as limiting or prejudicing in any way existing or developing rules of international law with respect to the development, production, stockpiling and use of chemical weapons'.[204] Additionally, Understanding 4 in Annex III to the resolution on the crime of aggression provides that 'the definition of the act of aggression and the crime of aggression do so for the purpose of this Statute only', whereas Understanding 4 further adds a similar wording to article 10.[205] Both the footnotes and Understanding 4 confirm that article 10 is not a valid reservation clause.

In addition, article 124 of the Statute is a transitional provision providing an exception to the prohibition on reservation in article 120. To date, only two States have invoked article 124 to lodge declarations. France withdrew its declaration, and Colombia's declaration has expired. It is said that Burundi aimed to invoke article 124 but finally ratified the Statute without making a declaration.[206] In 2015, the ASP adopted an amendment to delete this transitional

---

201   For discussions, see Grover (n 6) 264–65; O. Triffterer and A. Heinze, 'Article 10' in O. Triffterer and K. Ambos (eds), *Commentary on the Rome Statute of the International Criminal Court: Observers' Notes, Article by Article* (3rd edn, Hart/Beck 2016) 648.
202   For discussions on art 120 of the Rome Statute, see UN Doc A/C.6/55/SR.9 (2000), para 34 (Canada). Cf. S. Tabak, 'Article 124, War Crimes, and the Development of the Rome Statute' (2009) 40 *Georgetown J Intl L* 1069, 1076–77.
203   Vienna Convention on the Law of Treaties, art 43.
204   Elements of Crimes, art 8(2)(e)(xiv), element 2.
205   'Understandings regarding the amendments to the Rome Statute of the International Criminal Court on the crime of aggression', Resolution RC/Res.6 of 11 June 2010, Annex III.
206   Tabak (n 202) 1094–95 and fn 150.

provision.[207] It is clear that article 124 is a temporal jurisdiction limitation rather a substantive reservation or modification to the definition of war crimes.[208]

Even if articles 10 and 124 were deemed reservation clauses, they have no direct legal impact on the analysis of whether the definition of crimes in the ICC's jurisdiction was declaratory of custom. The ICJ in the *North Sea Continental Shelf* cases examined whether a treaty allowing reservation excludes its declaratory nature of custom. The ICJ held that reservations of a treaty rule of a declaratory nature are incompatible with customary law.[209] However, the ICJ in the *Nicaragua* case held that the legal effect of reservation has no direct impact on existing customary law.[210] Baxter and Villiger both shared the latter view that a treaty rule permitting a reservation does not indicate it cannot be of a declaratory nature. In determining if a treaty rule was declaratory of custom, whether the provision is permitted to be reserved is not relevant.[211] The ILC in its 2011 'Guide to Practice on Reservations to Treaties' also endorsed the ICJ's view in *Nicaragua*.[212] The ICJ's view in the *North Sea Continental Shelf* cases thus might be less persuasive on this point.

Another issue here is whether other specific obstacles exist for the discussions on crimes being of a declaratory nature. Rules of the Rome Statute concerning the ICC jurisdictional mechanisms might be relevant. Articles 11 and 24 (temporal jurisdiction) and articles 12-13 (personal jurisdiction) design the

---

207 Amendment to Article 124 of the Rome Statute of the International Criminal Court, ICC-ASP/14/Res.2, 26 November 2015.

208 For debates about the legal effect of a temporal jurisdiction restriction, see Schabas (n 8) 1519–20; Grover (n 6) 258–59. For discussions on the expiry of the transitional period, see E. Wilmshurst, 'Jurisdiction of the Court' in R.S. Lee (ed), *The International Criminal Court: The Making of the Rome Statute: Issues, Negotiations and Results* (Kluwer Law International 1999) 127–41; Tabak (n 202) 1082–83.

209 *North Sea Continental Shelf* cases (n 34), 38–39, para 63. See also *Reservations to the Convention on the Prevention and Punishment of the Crimes of Genocide*, Advisory Opinion, [1951] ICJ Rep 15; Human Rights Committee (HRC), CCPR 'General Comment No 24: Issues Relating to Reservations Made upon Ratification or Accession to the Covenant or the Optional Protocols thereto, or in Relation to Declarations under Article 41 of the Covenant' (4 November 1994), UN Doc CCPR/C/21/Rev.1/Add.6, para 8. However, see *North Sea Continental Shelf* cases (n 34) (Dissenting Opinion of Judge Morelli), 198–99.

210 *Military and Paramilitary Activities* Judgment (n 67), 38, 93, paras 56, 174.

211 Baxter (1907) (n 1) 47–51; Villiger (n 183) 67–69. See also Meron (n 47) 7–8, 10–25; 'Guide to Practice on Reservations to Treaties' in 'Report of the International Law Commission', UN Doc A/65/10 (2010), para 106, commentary to Guideline 4.4.2; Lepard (2010) (n 60) 199–200.

212 'Guide to Practice on Reservations to Treaties' in 'Report of the International Law Commission', UN Doc A/66/10/Add.1 (2011), para 75, Guideline 3.1.5.3.

jurisdictional mechanisms of the ICC. And the Rome Statute does not adopt universal jurisdiction for the ICC. It seems that these rules are not hard evidence to conclude that crimes defined in the Rome Statute are not the subject for the analysis of a rule as declaratory of custom.[213] Should the Statute have adopted universal jurisdiction, the recognition of universal jurisdiction would indirectly suggest that crimes in the Statute are declaratory of custom.[214] But the absence of universal jurisdiction is also not relevant to the analysis in this book because it can neither affirm nor deny that the offences are international crimes in custom. Thus, rules concerning the limited jurisdictional mechanisms of the ICC as opposed to universal jurisdiction are not obstacles to the discussion of whether crimes are declaratory of custom.[215] The phrase 'under this Statute' in article 22(1) of the Rome Statute concerning the principle of legality also indicates that the crimes outlined in the Statute may be retrogressive than custom, which is not an obstacle to an analysis of their declaratory nature. In short, provisions of the Rome Statute do not impede the analysis of crimes being declaratory of custom.

2.5.2 *A Treaty Rule Develops into Custom: Any Obstacles on the Passage?*

As noted above, the ICJ in the 1969 *North Sea Continental Shelf* cases required that a treaty rule be of a fundamentally 'norm-making' character, forming 'the basis of a general rule of law', to be transformed into customary law.[216] The ICJ also implicitly concluded that a treaty rule subject to reservation would affect its norm-making character.[217] It is necessary to stress again that the norm-making character is not a legal requirement for a treaty rule passing into custom. This subsection discusses the issues of reservation clauses and restrictions on the passage in the Rome Statute to evaluate whether the Statute itself impedes its rules developing into custom.

As Baxter observed, a treaty rule of 'norm-making' nature can be subject to reservation. In his view, in determining the nature of a treaty rule after its adoption, the fact that States avail themselves of their rights to reservation demonstrates the acceptance of the rule by States Parties.[218] Therefore, even if the Rome Statute contains reservation clauses in its articles 10 and 124, both

---

213   Grover (n 6) 250–53.
214   UN Doc A/C.6/52/SR.15 (1997), para 15 (ICRC); 'Summary record of the 11th meeting', UN Doc A/C.6/55/SR.11 (2000), para 47 (ICRC).
215   Grover (n 6) 250–53.
216   *North Sea Continental Shelf* cases (n 34), 42–43, paras 71-72.
217   ibid 41–42, 50.
218   Baxter (1970) (n 1) 63–64.

articles would not affect the norm-making nature of the treaty rule or hinder the passage of a treaty rule into custom.

With regard to the legal impact of a treaty rule with restrictions on its passage into custom, William Butler admitted that drafters of a treaty and States Parties can 'expressly restrict the passage of a treaty rule into custom'.[219] It is the rights of the parties, whether expressly or implicitly, to deny that 'their practice is informed by *opinio juris* and can contribute little to establishing a rule of customary international law'.[220] In this circumstance, a treaty rule plays a lesser role as evidence of the customary status of a rule. These denials, however, do not indicate that a customary rule would not emerge outside the treaty on the subject. They suggest that the treaty provisions and practice of States Parties concerning treaty obligations should be given reduced weight.

In general, the Rome Statute provides no obstacles to a treaty provision passing into customary law after its adoption. The Rome Statute contains an express disclaimer in article 80 that provisions on penalties in articles 77–79 do not affect national practice of States.[221] These provisions on penalty, thus, are of limited value in an assessment of whether they have developed into custom at present. Parts II and III of the Rome Statute do not contain a disclaimer such as article 80. As noted in chapter 1 of this book, article 10 in Part II implies the potential impact of the Rome Statute on the 'existing or developing rules of international law' as an aid to interpreting other treaties. This finding applies to Understanding 4 in Annex III to the resolution on the crime of aggression. Drafters of the Rome Statute did not deny that the selected provisions in this book may affect the development of law outside the instrument. States Parties also do not send such a message. Subsequent practice of States Parties to the Statute will significantly contribute to the development of customary law. The Rome Statute itself does not provide a hindrance to its provisions being declaratory of customary law.

2.6 Concluding Remarks

In this book, a treaty rule is the starting point for determining whether the rule is declaratory of custom. As shown above, the Rome Statute and the 1969

---

219   W. Butler, 'Custom, Treaty, State Practice and the 1982 Convention' (1988) 12 *Marine Policy* 182, 184–85.
220   Weisburd (n 191) 23–29.
221   ILA (n 34) 745, § 17; 1998 Rome Statute, art 80 reads: 'Nothing in this Part [Part 7 penalties] affects the application by States of penalties prescribed by their national law, nor the law of States which do not provide for penalties prescribed in this Part.'

Vienna Convention qualify the interpretation of provisions in the Statute. The two-element approach serves as a general guideline for the identification of customary law. This approach, however, should not be too rigid for specific rules. This book adopts a flexible two-element approach focusing more on *opinio juris* to identify the existence of customary law. Before ascertaining the status of custom, another layer of analysis is added as to whether a treaty rule articulates itself as a reflection of a pre-existing customary rule or is of a norm-making nature. This layer of analysis provides a preliminary but inconclusive finding for the status of a customary rule. It is the evidence of the two elements that assists in identifying the existence or non-existence of a customary rule. A treaty rule of 'declaratory' nature illustrates the relationship between a treaty rule and custom on the same subject matter at the adoption of that provision and at present. The following chapters examine the nature of selected provisions of the Rome Statute based on this methodological framework.

CHAPTER 3

War Crimes in Non-international Armed Conflict

Article 8 of the Rome Statute and Custom

3.1 Introductory Remarks

This chapter examines the relationship between articles 8(2)(c) and (e) of the Rome Statute and customary law with regard to the definition of war crimes committed in non-international armed conflict.[1] War crimes in the strict sense are violations of international humanitarian law that are criminalised under international law.[2] Although only a few conventions of international humanitarian law expressly identify violations of their rules as war crimes,[3] the definition of war crimes under international law was well developed after World War II. Up to the early 1990s, the customary nature of war crimes in non-international armed conflict (also referred to as internal armed conflict) was controversial. In 1995, the Appeals Chamber of the ICTY in the *Tadić* Interlocutory Appeal Decision on jurisdiction upheld that war crimes can also be committed in non-international armed conflict, and that this reflects customary international law.[4] In 1998, war crime was explicitly provided in article 8 of the Rome Statute. Articles 8(2)(c) and 8(2)(e) of the Rome Statute list serious violations of Common Article 3 of the 1949 Geneva Conventions and other serious violations of the laws and customs committed in the context of non-international armed conflict.[5] At the present time, commentators agree that the rule of war crimes in non-international armed conflict is a part of

---

1 1998 Rome Statute, art 8.
2 The concept of war crimes is different from crimes occurred in or of war, see G. Abi-Saab, 'The Concept of War Crimes' in S. Yee and T. Wang (eds), *International Law in the Post-Cold War World: Essays in Memory of Li Haopei* (Routledge 2001) 112–13; M. Cottier, 'Article 8' in O. Triffterer and K. Ambos (eds), *Commentary on the Rome Statute of the International Criminal Court: Observers' Notes, Article by Article* (3rd edn, Hart/Beck 2016) 304–05 and fn 1; T. McCormack, 'Crimes against Humanity' in D. McGoldrick *et al* (eds), *The Permanent International Criminal Court: Legal and Policy Issues* (Hart Publishing 2004) 204–05.
3 Geneva Convention II, art 49; Geneva Convention II, art 51; Geneva Convention III, art 130; Geneva Convention IV, art 147; the 1977 Additional Protocol I, arts 11 and 85.
4 *Prosecutor v Tadić* (Interlocutory Appeal Decision on Jurisdiction) ICTY-94-1-AR72 (2 October 1995), paras 130-34.
5 1998 Rome Statute, arts 8(2)(c) and (e).

customary law.[6] For example, Rule 156 of the 2005 ICRC *Study* provides that 'serious violations of international humanitarian law constitute war crimes, applicable in both international and non-international armed conflicts'.[7] The central question here is whether articles 8(2)(c) and (e) were and are declaratory (reflection or crystallisation) of customary law in 1998 and at present with respect to war crimes in non-international armed conflict.

For this purpose, section 3.2 interprets the texts of the Rome Statute to show whether articles 8(2)(c) and (e) were articulated as being declaratory of custom concerning war crimes in non-international armed conflict. Section 3.3 explores the development of war crimes trials and the concept of war crimes in armed conflict before and after World War II to show whether the definition of war crimes in non-international armed conflict under international law developed before the 1998 Rome Conference. The 1949 Geneva Conventions, the 1977 Additional Protocol II, the two *Tadić* decisions on jurisdiction and the work of the International Law Commission (ILC) on the Draft Code of Crimes are mainly discussed in section 3.3. Section 3.4 observes the drafting of the Rome Statute on the issue of war crimes in non-international armed conflict, in which positions of States and their statements at the Rome Conference are carefully explored. Further developments of war crimes in this context after the adoption of the Rome Statute are examined in section 3.5. Section 3.6 concludes with closing remarks.

3.2 Provisions on War Crimes in Non-international Armed Conflict in the Rome Statute

Article 8 of the Rome Statute includes war crimes committed in both international and non-international armed conflicts.[8] The text of article 8 does not expressly address whether article 8 is declaratory of custom with respect to war crimes in non-international armed conflict. A further assessment of the Rome Statute helps to answer whether other provisions indicate a preliminary affirmation for article 8 as declaratory of custom. First, the Preamble of the Rome Statute provides that crimes in the jurisdiction of the International

---

6 JM. Henckaerts and L. Doswald-beck (eds), *Customary International Humanitarian Law*, Vols I and II (CUP 2005), Rule 156 and accompanying commentary; R. Heinsch, 'Commentary on Rule 84 "Individual Criminal Responsibility for War Crimes"' in M.N. Schmitt (ed), *Tallinn Manual 2.0 on the International Law Applicable to Cyber Warfare* (2nd edn, CUP 2017) 392.
7 Henckaerts and Doswald-beck (eds), ibid, Rule 156.
8 1998 Rome Statute, art 8.

Criminal Court (ICC) are 'grave crimes [that] threaten the peace, security and well-being of the world'.[9] These crimes are 'the most serious crimes of concern to the international community as a whole' and 'must not go unpunished'.[10] The notion of seriousness is also reiterated in articles 8(2)(c) and (e) of the Rome Statute.[11] The wording of grave and serious crimes in the Preamble does not suggest that these crimes are in nature crimes under customary law rather than that these offences are widespread and heinous.[12]

In addition, the statement that 'it is the duty of every State to exercise its criminal jurisdiction over those responsible for international crimes'[13] suggests that States are obliged to prosecute international crimes, including war crimes. The ICJ once held that some international crimes give rise to the *erga omnes* nature of an obligation.[14] However, the '*erga omnes*' status of an obligation may derive from crimes embedded in either treaty or custom.[15] Thus, the *erga omnes* obligation to prosecute crimes in the Preamble of the Rome Statute does not indicate whether these crimes are exclusively crimes under customary law. Leena Grover also supports this view.[16] The Preamble, therefore, does not assist in assessing whether articles 8(2)(c) and (e) were declaratory rules of custom concerning war crimes.

According to Grover, article 5 of the Statute (material jurisdiction) and the *jus cogens* nature of these crimes suggest that crimes in the Rome Statute may well be reflective of customary law.[17] Indeed, if the prohibition of war crimes is a rule of *jus cogens*, all individuals under customary law are prohibited from committing war crimes, and States cannot derogate from this rule by reserving the right to permit impugned conducts of war crimes. However, the nature of *jus cogens* does not imply an inherent obligation upon all States to prosecute war

---

9   ibid, Preamble, para 3.
10   ibid, para 4.
11   Elements of Crimes, UN Doc PCNICC/2000/1/Add.2, in 'Official Records of the Assembly of States Parties to the Rome Statute of the International Criminal Court', ICC-ASP/1/3 and Corr.1, 108.
12   M.M. deGuzman, 'Gravity and Legitimacy of the International Criminal Court' (2008) 32 *Fordham Intl LJ* 1400.
13   1998 Rome Statute, Preamble, para 6.
14   *Barcelona Traction, Light and Power Company, Limited (Belgium v Spain)*, Judgment, [1970] ICJ Rep 3, 32, para 33.
15   Institut de Droit International, 'Obligations and rights *erga omnes* in international law', Resolution of the Fifth Commission (2005) (Rapporteur Giorgio Gaja), art 1; L. Grover, *Interpreting Crimes in the Rome Statute of the International Criminal Court* (CUP 2014) 250.
16   Grover, ibid 249–50.
17   ibid 220–344.

crimes.[18] The gravity threshold, article 5 of the Rome Statute and the *jus cogens* nature of war crimes are evidence but not conclusive as to whether war crimes in non-international armed conflict and its underlying offences in the Statute were declaratory of custom. Other provisions of the Statute do not clarify whether these war crimes are declaratory of custom.[19] These findings also apply to crimes against humanity and the crime of aggression, discussed in the following chapters.

The text of article 8 and other rules of the Rome Statute only draw a frame for the picture of war crimes in non-international armed conflict as a mirror of custom in general. Detailed issues about the inclusion of war crimes in non-international armed conflict beg the question whether war crimes in non-international armed conflict were a restatement (codification) or crystallisation of custom at the Rome Conference. During the preparatory works for the 1998 Rome Statute, representatives of States expressed their claims and acceptable options for the inclusion of war crimes in the ICC's jurisdiction.[20] One issue fiercely debated was whether the concept of war crimes covers violations in non-international armed conflict. The majority of State representatives supported the inclusion of war crimes in non-international armed conflict;[21] arguments to the contrary existed among a small group of States.[22] Some States continued to challenge the customary status of war crimes in non-international armed conflict.[23] These debates indicate that the answer is unclear.

---

18   Cf. 'Fragmentation of International Law: Difficulties Arising from the Diversification and Expansion of International Law, Report of the Study Group of the International Law Commission, finalised by Martti Koskenniemi', UN Doc A/CN.4/L.682 and Corr.1 (2006), paras 188-89; L.N. Sadat and R. Carden, 'The New International Criminal Court: An Uneasy Revolution' (1999) 88 *Geo LJ* 381, 409–10; Grover (n 15) 250.
19   For a detailed analysis, see Grover, ibid 246–70.
20   UN Doc A/CONF.183/2/Add.1 and Corr.1, UN Doc A/CONF.183/2/Add.1 and Corr.1, UN Doc A/CONF.183/C.1/L.1 and Corr.1, and UN Doc A/CONF.183/C.1/L.4; M. Arsanjani, 'The Rome Statute of the International Criminal Court' (1999) 93 *AJIL* 22, 32.
21   UN Doc A/CONF.183/SR.7, 4–5 (Bangladesh); US, 'Statement by the US delegation to the Preparatory Committee on the Establishment of an International Criminal Court' (23 March 1998).
22   UN Doc A/CONF.183/C.1/SR.33, paras 33 (Syrian Arab Republic), 37 (India); UN Doc A/CONF.183/C.1/SR.34, para 48 (Turkey); UN Doc A/CONF.183/C.1/SR.35, paras 2, 4 (Egypt), 54 (Pakistan), 64 (Iraq); UN Doc A/CONF.183/C.1/SR.36, para 6 (Libya).
23   For example, China, see UN Doc A/CONF.183/C.1/SR.5, para 120; A/CONF.183/C.1/SR.25, para 36, UN Doc A/CONF.183/SR.9, para 38.

3.3 War Crimes in Armed Conflict

This section provides an historical overview of the concept of war crimes. This section covers three periods, first from 1919 to 1945, then from 1945 to 1949, and last from 1949 to the early 1990s. During the first two periods, war crimes in non-international armed conflict were not discussed. A short overview of war crimes trials in the first two periods intends to provide a background for understanding some arguments in the following sections of this chapter and the following chapters.

3.3.1 *Stocktaking of War Crimes and War Crimes Trials: 1919–1945*

War crimes trials have been conducted by national authorities for a long time,[24] but the idea of prosecuting war crimes through international tribunals against large-scale atrocities has emerged mainly only after World War I.[25] After World War I, the Preliminary Peace Conference of Paris established the Commission on Responsibilities of the Authors of the War and on Enforcement of Penalties (1919 Commission on Responsibilities) to inquire into 'the responsibilities relating to the war'.[26] The 1919 Commission on Responsibilities elaborated a list of 32 offences criminalising violations of the laws and customs of law.[27] The list was not a text invention but reflected main facts at that time.[28] The idea of prosecuting individuals for war crimes was included under article 228 of the 1919 Treaty of Versailles.[29] There were trials of Germans accused of war crimes by the Allied national tribunals, but there was no extradition

---

24 W.A. Schabas, 'Atrocity Crimes (Genocide, Crimes against Humanity and War Crimes)' in W.A. Schabas (ed), *The Cambridge Companion to International Criminal Law* (CUP 2016) 208; M.C. Bassiouni, *Introduction to International Criminal Law: 2nd Revised Edition* (Brill | Nijhoff 2013) 540–48; A. Cullen, 'War Crimes' in N. Bernaz and W.A. Schabas (eds), *Routledge Handbook of International Criminal Law* (Routledge 2011); T. McCormack, 'From Sun Tzu to the Sixth Committee: The Evolution of an International Criminal Law Regime' in T. McCormack and G.J. Simpson (eds), *The Law of War Crimes: National and International Approaches* (Kluwer Law International 1997).

25 Y. Dinstein and M. Tabory (eds), *War Crimes in International Law* (Martinus Nijhoff Publishers 1996) 51; S. Darcy, *Judges, Law and War: The Judicial Development of International Humanitarian Law* (CUP 2014) 266–68.

26 See G.A. Finch, 'The Peace Conference of Paris, 1919' (1919) 13 *AJIL* 159, 168–71; United Nations War Crimes Commission (ed), *History of the United Nations War Crimes Commission and the Development of the Laws of War* (HMSO 1948) 34.

27 Commission on Responsibilities, 'Report on the Commission on the Responsibility of the Authors of the War and on Enforcement of Penalties Presented to the Preliminary Peace Conference' reprinted in (1920) 14 *AJIL* 95, 114–15.

28 Y. Sandoz, 'The History of the Grave Breaches Regime' (2009) 7 *JICJ* 657, 667–69.

29 Treaty of Peace with Germany [Treaty of Versailles], in 2 Bevans 43, 137, art 228(1).

after the armistice. Also, few of the accused were tried for mistreating prisoners of war and murdering survivors of shipwrecks by the German Supreme Court in Leipzig.[30] The Report of the Commission on Responsibilities and article 228 indicate that the Allies States attempted to prosecute individuals for war crimes at an international level. Nevertheless, it is uncertain whether they intended to pursue justice or only to achieve political ends by using justice.

From World War I to World War II, except for the effort of the International Law Association (ILA) to include war crimes as an international crime, not much constructive contribution to the definition of war crimes existed.[31] In 1926, the ILA adopted a Draft Statute for a Permanent International Criminal Court, which suggested including 'violations of treaties, conventions or declarations regulating the methods of conduct of warfare and violations of the laws and customs of war' into the jurisdiction of that proposed court.[32] That definition of war crimes is quite open.

During the period from 1919 to 1945, the notion of war crimes was mostly defined as 'violations of the laws and customs of war'. The phrase 'war crimes' referred to the non-fulfilment of obligations under the law or violations of law, which was used in a general sense rather than in a technical legal sense.[33] This general definition constitutes the main substantive part of war crimes now. The notion of international prosecution of war crimes in non-international armed conflict was not considered in that period.

3.3.2 *War Crimes Trials after World War II: 1945–1949*

The outcome of World War I practice was unsatisfactory, but it began a trend of trying individuals for violations of international law during a war. The first actual international prosecution of war crimes before international tribunals began after World War II.[34] The work of the United Nations War Crimes Commission (UN War Crimes Commission) paved the way for this.[35] In 1943,

---

30   UNWCC (ed) (n 26) 45–51; Bassiouni (n 24) 547–48.
31   UNWCC (ed), ibid; W.A. Schabas, 'The United Nations War Crimes Commission's Proposal for an International Criminal Court' (2014) 25 *CLF* 171.
32   Committee on Permanent International Criminal Court, 'Statute of the Court (as amended by the Conference)' in International Law Association Report of the 34th Conference (Vienna 1926) (ILA, London 1926) 118, art 21.
33   'Articles of the draft Code of Crimes against the Peace and Security of Mankind' in 'Report of the International Law Commission', UN Doc A/51/10 (1996), Vol II (2), para 50, commentary to art 20.
34   W.A. Schabas, *The UN International Criminal Tribunals: The Former Yugoslavia, Rwanda and Sierra Leone* (CUP 2006) 226–27.
35   Schabas (n 31); Bassiouni (n 24) 549–51.

the Allied Powers established the UN War Crimes Commission to investigate and collect evidence of war crimes for further prosecutions at national courts.[36] The UN War Crimes Commission adopted a 'draft convention of a permanent United Nations War Crimes Court' (Draft Convention), relying on a draft statute prepared by Lawrence Preuss (Preuss Draft).[37] Article 1 of the Preuss Draft provided a list of offences constituting war crimes with 15 offences.[38] By contrast, the UN War Crimes Commission dropped the list so as to 'give the [UN War Crimes] Court the necessary latitude of action to carry out the intention of the Allied governments' to prosecute Germans.[39] It seems that this Commission did not aim to provide a detailed enumeration of war crimes.

Aiming to prosecute and punish German major war criminals of the European Axis in World War II,[40] governments of the UK, the US, France and the Union of Soviet Socialist Republics (USSR) adopted the London Agreement, to which they annexed the Nuremberg Charter, on 8 August 1945.[41] In accordance with the London Agreement, the Nuremberg International Military Tribunal (IMT) was established, and the Nuremberg Charter set out the IMT's constitution, jurisdiction and function.[42]

---

36   It was established by the meeting of the Allied and Dominions representatives held in London on 20 October 1943. The 'United Nations' in this Commission was unrelated to the present world body founded in 1945. The evidence collected by the United Nations War Crimes Commission was not relied upon by the later international tribunals, but by national prosecutions. See Bassiouni, *Introduction to International Criminal Law* 549–51.

37   'Draft Convention on the Trial and Punishment of War Criminals', 11/11 (14 April 1944); Schabas (n 31) 175–76; 'Minutes of Thirty-third Meeting' (26 September 1944), M. 33 (corrected text), 6; 'Draft Convention for the Establishment of a United Nations War Crimes Court' (30 September 1944), C. 50(1).

38   These offences were murder or massacre, rape, enforced prosecution, terrorisation, wanton devastation, other serious acts, which by reason of their atrocious character, their ruthless disregard of the sanctity of human life and personality or their wanton interference with rights of property, are unrelated to reasonably conceived requirements of military necessity.

39   'Explanatory Memorandum to Accompany the Draft Convention for the Establishment of a United Nations War Crimes Court' (6 October 1944), C.58.

40   'The Moscow Declaration on General Security, Joint Four-Nation Declaration' (30 October 1943).

41   'Agreement for the prosecution and punishment of the major war criminals of the European Axis' (8 August 1945) [London Agreement], 82 UNTS 280; 'Charter of the International Military Tribunal-Annex to the Agreement for the prosecution and punishment of the major war criminals of the European Axis' (8 August 1945) [Nuremberg Charter], 82 UNTS 284.

42   London Agreement, art 2; Nuremberg Charter; *France et al v Göring et al*, Preliminary Hearing (14–15, 17 November 1945), (1948) 2 TMWC 1, 1–27.

According to article 6(b) of the Nuremberg Charter, the IMT had jurisdiction over:

> War crimes: namely, violations of the laws or customs of war. Such violations shall include, but not be limited to, murder, ill-treatment or deportation to slave labour or for any other purpose of civilian population of or in occupied territory, murder or ill-treatment of prisoners of war or persons on the seas, killing of hostages, plunder of public or private property, wanton destruction of cities, towns or villages, or devastation not justified by military necessity.[43]

Article 6(b) defined war crimes with a non-exhaustive catalogue and from a general aspect of actions that violate 'the laws or customs of war'. The IMT held that '[t]his law [of war] is not static, but by continual adaptation follows the needs of a changing world.'[44] The UN Secretary-General commented that '[a]ny enumeration or exemplification of particular war crimes [...] seems to be [...] of rather limited value for the future. Such a catalogue may be an adequate expression of the present situation'.[45] The Nuremberg Charter thus left the door open for further development of war crimes. In the IMT, 18 of 24 individuals were indicted for war crimes, and 16 of the 18 indicted were convicted of war crimes.[46]

Based on the Tokyo Charter, the Tokyo International Military Tribunal for the Far East (IMTFE) was established to try Japanese officials.[47] Article 5(b) of the Tokyo Charter stipulated that the IMTFE had jurisdiction over 'conventional war crimes: namely, violations of the laws or customs of war'.[48] Article 5(b) did not specify what and the extent to which acts constituted violations of laws of war leading to criminalisation.[49] In addition, the IMTFE was required to establish a connection between war crimes and crimes against peace in exercising jurisdiction over war crimes. This jurisdictional requirement limited

---

43 Nuremberg Charter, art 6(b).
44 *France et al v Göring et al*, Judgment and Sentence of the Nuremberg International Military Tribunals, (1948) 1 TMWC 171, 221.
45 'The Charter and Judgment of the Nuremberg Tribunal – History and Analysis: Memorandum submitted by the Secretary-General', UN Doc A/CN.4/5 (1949), 62–63.
46 *France et al v Göring et al* (n 44); M.C. Bassiouni, *Crimes Against Humanity* (CUP 2011) 154.
47 'Charter of the International Military Tribunal for the Far East' (19 January 1946, as amended on 26 April 1946) [Tokyo Charter], TIAS 1589.
48 Tokyo Charter, art 5.
49 *France et al v Göring et al* (n 44) 221; UN Doc A/CN.4/5 (1949), 51.

the suspects prosecuted in the Tribunal to major war criminals. The IMTFE found seven of 28 Japanese individuals guilty of conventional war crimes.[50]

A number of national trials also took place.[51] From 1946 to 1949, the Nuremberg Military Tribunals (NMTs) held 12 trials (Subsequent Proceedings)[52] in Germany in accordance with Control Council Law No. 10.[53] The definition of war crimes in Control Council Law No. 10 is substantively consistent with that in the Nuremberg Charter.[54] In addition, some other States also prosecuted suspects of war crimes committed during World War II.[55] Australia, China, the US, the USSR, the UK, the Philippines and the Netherlands (Indonesia) were all involved in war crimes trials.[56] There were proceedings in the Asia Pacific region, including war crimes trials at Yokohama.[57] Many suspected war

---

50   *US et al v Araki et al*, Judgment, 1 November 1948, in United Nations War Crimes Commission (ed), *Transcripts of Proceedings and Documents of the International Military Tribunals for the Far East (Tokyo Trials)*: Judgment, 1145–211 and Dissenting Opinion of Judge Röling, 12 November 1948, 178–249.

51   UNWCC (ed) (n 26) 522–24; US et al, 'Report of the Deputy Judge Advocate for War Crimes, European Command June 1944 to July 1948' (War Crimes Division, Office of the Judge Advocate General, 1948) concerning German and other Axis individuals, there were practices of charging, prosecuting or trying at separate locations, in and outside German.

52   *US v Brandt et al* [The *Medical* case], *US v Milch* [The *Milch* case], *US v Altstötter et al* [The *Justice* case], *US v Ohlendorf et al* [The *Einsatzgruppen* case], *US v Greifelt et al* [The *RuSHA* case], *US v Pohl et al* [The *Pohl* case], *US v Flick et al* [The *Flick* case], *US v Krauch et al* [The *I.G. Farben* case], *US v Krupp et al* [The *Krupp* case], *US v von Leeb et al* [The *High Command* case], *US v List et al* [The *Hostage* case], *US v von Weizaecker et al* [The *Ministries* case], in *Trials of the War Criminals before the Nuremberg Military Tribunals Under Control Council Law No. 10* [TWC] (USGPO 1949–1953).

53   Control Council Law No. 10, 'Punishment of Persons Guilty of War Crimes, Crimes against Peace and against Humanity', enacted by the Allied Control Council of German, in T. Taylor, *Final Report to the Secretary of the Army on the Nuremberg War Crimes Trials under Control Council Law No. 10* (USGPO 1949) 6. For a detailed analysis of these trials, see K.J. Heller, *The Nuremberg Military Tribunals and the Origins of International Criminal Law* (OUP 2011).

54   Control Council Law No. 10, art II.

55   UNWCC (ed) (n 26); *R v Finta* (Judgment, Supreme Court), [1994] 1 SCR 701; *Advocate General v Klaus Barbie* (Judgment, Court of Cassation, France), (1985) 78 ILR 124; *Polyukhovich v Commonwealth* (Order, High Court) [1991] HCA 32 (14 August 1991); *Public Prosecutor v Menten* (Judgment, Supreme Court), (1981) 75 ILR 331; *R v Sawoniuk* (Judgment) [2000] EWCA Crim 9 (10 February 2000).

56   See S. Linton (ed), *Hong Kong's War Crimes Trials* (OUP 2013); K. Sellars, *Trials for International Crimes in Asia* (CUP 2016); G. Fitzpatrick, T. McCormack and N. Morris (eds), *Australia's War Crimes Trials 1945–51* (Brill | Nijhoff 2016); F.L. Borch, *Military Trials of War Criminals in the Netherlands East Indies 1946–1949* (OUP 2017).

57   *Yamashita v United States of America*, [1946] USSC 27, (1948) 4 LRTWC 1; *Prosecutor v Eisentrager et al* (Judgment, Military Commission, the US), (1949) 14 LRTWC 8. For a table

criminals were accused of or found guilty of ordering or perpetrating 'conventional war crimes' in these tribunals.[58] These post-World War II trials leave much legacy for the latter UN ad hoc tribunals and the ICC,[59] despite criticism of their procedures.[60]

Despite debates about retroactive prosecution over other crimes, war crimes as international crimes in the jurisdiction of the IMT was well supported.[61] It is accepted that the Nuremberg Charter contributed to the formation of customary international law and it forms part of contemporary customary law.[62] The following international instruments and subsequent case law also confirmed that the Nuremberg Charter was an established part of international law.[63]

---

of war crimes trials in the Far East, see P. Post et al (eds), *The Encyclopedia of Indonesia in the Pacific War* (Brill 2010) 409.

[58] UNWCC (ed) (n 26); P. Piccigallo, *The Japanese on Trial: Allied War Crimes Operations in the East, 1945–1951* (University of Texas Press 2013).

[59] D. Luban, 'The Legacies of Nuremberg' (1987) 54 *Social Research* 779; G. Ginsburgs and V.N. Kudriavtsev, *The Nuremberg Trial and International Law* (Martinus Nijhoff Publishers 1990); C. Tomuschat, 'The Legacy of Nuremberg' (2006) 4 *JICJ* 830; A. Cassese, 'Introductory Note to Affirmation of the Principles of International Law recognized by the Charter of the Nürnberg Tribunal General Assembly resolution 95 (I)' (June 2009), UN Audiovisual Library of International Law, Historical Archives < https://legal.un.org/avl/ha/ga_95-I/ga_95-I.html > accessed 12 December 2020.

[60] Bassiouni (n 24) 556; Ginsburgs and Kudriavtsev, ibid; T. Taylor, 'The Nuremberg Trials' (1955) 55 *Columbia L Rev* 488; H. Ehard, 'The Nuremberg Trial Against the Major War Criminals and International Law' (1949) 43 *AJIL* 223.

[61] For debates, see *France et al v Göring et al* (n 44) 218–20; 'Summary record of the 44th meeting', UN Doc A/CN.4/SR.44 (1950), paras 71, 72, 77, 79; J.L. Kunz, 'The Nature of Customary International Law' (1953) 47 *AJIL* 662, 669; Heller (n 53) 123–24. For support, see L. Wright, 'War Crimes under International Law' (1946) 62 *LQR* 40, 41; 'Minutes of Conference Session of July 19, 1945' and 'Minutes of Conference Session of July 23, 1945' in *Report of Robert H. Jackson, United States Representative to the International Conference on Military Trials: London, 1945* (USGPO 1949) [296] (Professor André Gros), [331] (Justice Robert H. Jackson).

[62] 'Universal Declaration of Human Rights', UN Doc A/RES/217 (III) A (1948); Convention for the Protection of Human Rights and Fundamental Freedoms (as amended) [ECHR], art 7(2); UN Doc S/25704 (1993), para 35; *Tadić* Appeals Chamber Decision on Jurisdiction (n 4), para 141.

[63] The *Justice* case, (1951) 3 TWC 1, 966; *Attorney General v Eichmann* (Appeal Judgment, Supreme Court, Israel) (29 May 1962), (1968) 36 ILR 277, para 11; *Prosecutor v Erdemović* (Joint Separate Opinion of Judge McDonald and Judge Vohrah) ICTY-96-22-A (7 October 1997), para 51; *Prosecutor v Tadić* ((Judgement) ICTY-94-1-A (15 July 1999), para 289; 'Summary record of the 54th Meeting', UN Doc E/CN.4/SR.54 (1948), 13; *Kononov v Latvia* (Judgment, Merits and Just Satisfaction, Third Section) ECtHR Application No. 36376/04 (24 July 2008), para 115(b); W.A. Schabas, 'Synergy or Fragmentation? International Criminal Law and the European Convention on Human Rights' (2011) 9 *JICJ* 609, 609–10; W.A. Schabas, *The European Convention on Human Rights: A Commentary* (OUP 2015).

A unanimously adopted General Assembly resolution, 'Affirmation of the Principles of International Law Recognised by the Charter of the Nuremberg Tribunal' (1946 GA Resolution) explicitly confirmed that a war crime is an international crime.[64] William Schabas argued that by referring to 'international law' in article 11 of the 1948 Universal Declaration of Human Rights,[65] debates about the rule against non-retroactivity in article 11 indicate States' recognition of the legitimacy of the IMT judgment and the Subsequent Proceedings.[66] War crimes embedded in the 1950 Nuremberg Principles, which was adopted by the ILC,[67] are part of the corpus of customary law now.[68]

In a nutshell, the notion of war crimes has been well recognised in international law. Nevertheless, similar to the period after World War I, issues about war crimes in non-international armed conflict were not raised during the discussions in the IMT and IMTFE judgments, and on these subsequent international instruments, including the 1950 Nuremberg Principles.[69]

3.3.3 Common Article 3 of the 1949 Geneva Conventions and Additional Protocol II of 1977: 1949–Early 1990s

During the timeframe from 1949 to the early 1990s, the four 1949 Geneva Conventions and their two 1977 Additional Protocols further developed the definition of war crimes.[70] The 1960 ICRC Commentary wrote that '[t]he Geneva Conventions form part of what are generally known as the laws and customs of war, violations of which are commonly called "war crimes".'[71] Common Article 3 of the 1949 Geneva Conventions and Additional Protocol

---

64 'Affirmation of the Principles of International Law Recognized by the Charter of the Nuremberg Tribunal', UN Doc A/RES/95 (I) (1946).
65 UN Doc A/RES/217 (III) A (1948).
66 'Summary record of the 115th Meeting' (28 October 1948), UN Doc A/C.3/SR.115; 'Summary record of the 116th Meeting' (29 October 1948), UN Doc A/C.3/SR.116; 'Summary record of the 54th Meeting' (10 June 1948), UN Doc E/CN.4/SR.54, 13. See W.A. Schabas (ed), *The Universal Declaration of Human Rights: The Travaux Préparatoires* (CUP 2013) 2369–78, 2380–90.
67 'Report of the Committee on the plans for the formulation of the principles of the Nuremberg Charter and judgment' (17 June 1947), UN Doc A/AC.10/52, para 2; UN Doc A/RES/94 (I) (1946).
68 Cassese (n 59).
69 For discussions on war crimes, see 'Summary record of the 49th meeting', UN Doc A/CN.4/SR.49 (1950), paras 2, 15.
70 Geneva Convention I, arts 49 and 50; Geneva Convention II, arts 51 and 52; Geneva Convention III, arts 130 and 131; and Geneva Convention IV, arts 147 and 148. See Cullen (n 24); Darcy (n 25).
71 J. Pictet, *Commentary on the Geneva Conventions of 12 August 1949*, Vol II (ICRC 1960) 261.

II of 1977 are the primary rules applicable to non-international armed conflict. This subsection first briefly examines Common Article 3 and then introduces article 6 of Additional Protocol II.

3.3.3.1   Common Article 3 of the Geneva Conventions

Common Article 3 of the 1949 Geneva Conventions concerns the application of principles of the Geneva Conventions to non-international armed conflicts. Common Article 3 prohibits acts against protected persons,[72] which was the only provision in the Geneva Conventions that dealt with the protection of persons as human beings rather than as combatants in non-international armed conflict.[73] This provision applies to both kinds of armed conflicts because this 'minimum requirement of humanitarian guarantees in the case of a non-international armed conflict is a *fortiori* applicable in international conflicts'.[74]

However, Common Article 3 does not include an enforcement mechanism by prosecuting violations of it as war crimes in international law.[75] At the 1949 Geneva Conference, there was no discussion on violations of Common Article 3 as war crimes.[76] Common Article 3 was finally adopted with the compromise that:

> It makes it absolutely clear that the object of the Convention is a purely humanitarian one, that it is in no way concerned with the internal affairs of States, and that it merely ensures respect for the few essential rules of humanity [...]. Consequently, the fact of applying Article 3 does not in itself constitute any recognition by the *de jure* Government that the adverse Party has authority of any kind; [...]; it does not in any way affect its [the Government's] right to prosecute, try and sentence its adversaries for their crimes, according to its own laws.[77]

The parties to a non-international armed conflict are neither obliged nor entitled by Common Article 3 to punish violations of Common Article 3 as 'war

---

72   1949 Geneva Conventions, common article 3.
73   J. Pictet, *Commentary on the Geneva Conventions of 12 August 1949*, Vol I (ICRC 1952) 48.
74   *Military and Paramilitary Activities in and against Nicaragua (Nicaragua v USA)*, Merits, [1986] ICJ Rep 14, 114, para 218; J. de Preux, *Commentary on the Geneva Conventions of 12 August 1949*, Vol III (ICRC 1960) 16.
75   L. Cameron et al, 'Article 3' in ICRC (ed), *Commentary on the First Geneva Convention: Convention (I) for the Amelioration of the Condition of the Wounded and Sick in Armed Forces in the Field* (CUP 2016), para 520.
76   Final Record of the Diplomatic Conference of Geneva of 1949, Vol II-B.
77   Pictet (n 73) 60–61.

crimes' at the international level at that time. Rather, Common Article 3 recognises the competency of a State Party to punish rebels and soldiers' violations as crimes at the national level 'according to its own laws'.[78]

At that time, the grave breaches regime of the Geneva Conventions was the only category of war crimes recognised at the international level, which is one of the four categories of war crimes now.[79] In addition, the idea of extending the grave breaches regime to non-international armed conflict was not envisaged by States at the 1949 Conference.[80] As Sandesh Sivakumaran observed, although the majority of States favoured the extension of regulation to non-international armed conflict, 'a number of States took the view that civil wars should not be regulated through international law'.[81] It is inconclusive to argue that those States supporting regulation of civil wars had considered the criminalisation of violations of Common Article 3 as war crimes.[82]

To sum up, at the 1949 Geneva Conference, States Parties had not recognised such violations in non-international armed conflict as war crimes. The 1968 Convention on the Non-Applicability of Statutory Limitations to War Crimes and Crimes against Humanity simply referred to the definition of war crimes committed in international armed conflict in the Nuremberg Charter.[83] There was no further development about war crimes in non-international armed conflict in international law in that period, despite many conflicts at that time.

3.3.3.2   Additional Protocol II of 1977

The 1977 Additional Protocol II, according to its article 1(1), covers the applicable humanitarian law in non-international armed conflict. The following paragraphs discuss whether the notion of war crimes in non-international armed conflict was recognised in Protocol II. Article 6 of Additional Protocol II deals with 'penal prosecution'. Article 6(1) provides the scope of the

---

78   Henckaerts and Doswald-beck (eds) (n 6) Rule 157; Cameron *et al* (n 75) para 528.
79   JM. Henckaerts and H. Niebergall-Lackner, 'Introduction' in ICRC (ed) (n 75) paras 1, 11.
80   'Fourth Report drawn up by the Special Committee of the Joint Committee' in *Final Record of the Diplomatic Conference of Geneva of 1949*, Vol II-B, 114–18; *Tadić* Appeals Chamber Decision on Jurisdiction (n 4), paras 79-81, 84. Cf. 'Submission of the Government of the United States of America Concerning Certain Arguments Made by Counsel for the Accused in the Case of *The Prosecutor of the Tribunal v Tadić*, 17 July 1995 (Case No. IT-94-1-T)', 35; *Tadić* Appeals Chamber Decision on Jurisdiction (n 4), para 83.
81   S. Sivakumaran, *The Law of Non-International Armed Conflict* (OUP 2012) 40–41.
82   'Prosecutor's Response to the Defence's Motions filed on 23 June 1995' (7 July 1995), 44–47. Cameron *et al* (n 75), confirming this interpretation.
83   Convention on the Non-Applicability of Statutory Limitations to War Crimes and Crimes against Humanity, 754 UNTS 73.

application of article 6 to the trial of 'criminal offences related to the armed conflict'. Article 6(5) concerning amnesty reads that: '[a]t the end of hostilities, the authorities in power shall endeavour to grant the broadest possible amnesty to persons who have participated in the armed conflict, or those deprived of their liberty for reasons related to the armed conflict, whether they are interned or detained.' By contrast, according to Rule 159 of the 2005 ICRC *Study*,

> At the end of hostilities, the authorities in power must endeavour to grant the broadest possible amnesty to persons who have participated in a non-international armed conflict, or those deprived of their liberty for reasons related to the armed conflict, with the exception of persons suspected of, accused of or sentenced for war crimes.[84]

By referring to article 6(5) to support Rule 159, the ICRC *Study* appears to interpret article 6(5) in such a way that amnesty does not apply to persons who committed war crimes in non-international armed conflict.[85] This interpretation is contestable.[86] If States Parties had not recognised serious violations in non-international armed conflict as war crimes in the text of Additional Protocol II, how could they consider war crimes in this context as an exception to amnesty?

The text of article 6 does not stipulate war crimes. It seems that drafters of Additional Protocol II also did not aim to include war crimes in non-international armed conflict in international law.[87] Article 6(2)(c) of Additional Protocol II confirms the non-retroactivity principle under 'the law' that 'no one shall be held guilty of any criminal offence [...] which did not constitute a criminal offence, under the law, at the time when it was committed'. The French text of the phrase 'the law' in article 6(2)(c) refers to 'national or international law'.[88] What criminal offences in international law were in the mind of the drafters? The commentary to article 6(2)(c) explained that

---

84 Henckaerts and Doswald-beck (eds) (n 6) Rule 159.
85 ibid.
86 C. Kreß, 'War Crimes Committed in Non-International Armed Conflict and the Emerging System of International Criminal Justice' (2001) 30 *Israel Ybk HR* 103, 133–34.
87 W.A. Schabas, *Unimaginable Atrocities Unimaginable Atrocities: Justice, Politics, and Rights at the War Crimes Tribunals* (OUP 2012) 180.
88 See also 'Amendment to article10(1)(d), Belgium, Netherlands, New Zealand' (24 March 1975), CDDH/I/262, in 'Official Records of the Diplomatic Conference in Geneva' (1974–1977), Vol IV, 35; C. Pilloud *et al* (eds), *Commentary on the Additional Protocols of 8 June 1977 to the Geneva Conventions of 12 August 1949* (Martinus Nijhoff Publishers 1987) § 4606.

'the reference to international law is mainly intended to cover crimes against humanity'.[89] There was no mention of war crimes. The drafters did not address whether the notion of war crimes in non-international armed conflict is recognised in international law. They did not recognise or deny the authorisation of amnesty to war crimes in non-international armed conflict.[90] In fact, during the 1974–1977 negotiations, war crimes for violations of Protocol II were discussed but never recognised. States intended to avoid interference in their sovereign right to punish individuals' taking part in hostilities.[91] Article 6(2), thus, was irrelevant to the issue of war crimes in non-international armed conflict at that time.[92]

As cited above, article 6(5) of Additional Protocol II concerns the granting of amnesty. According to articles 6(1) and 6(5), State authorities should grant an amnesty to persons who have 'participated in the armed conflict', been 'deprived of liberty for reasons related to the armed conflict', or committed other offences related to non-international armed conflict. Some States considered the amnesty provision as interference and limitation of their sovereignty.[93] They gave further explanations and considered article 6(5) as a recommendation.[94] Article 6(5) thus aimed to promote the peace and development of a State rather than justice through prosecution of national offences or war crimes.[95] As Canadian military manual (2001) notes,

---

89   Pilloud *et al* (eds), ibid § 4607; 'Summary Record of Committee I, Second Session, 33rd meeting' (20 March 1975), CDDH/I/SR.33, in 'Official Records of the Diplomatic Conference in Geneva' (1974–1977), Vol VIII, para 26.

90   'Amendment to article 10, Bulgaria, Byelorussian Soviet Socialist Republic, Cuba, Czechoslovakia, Democratic Republic of Viet Nam, German Democratic Republic, Hungary, Mongolia, Poland, Ukrainian Soviet Socialist Republic, Union of Soviet Socialist Republics' (24 March 1975), CDDH/I/260, in 'Official Records of the Diplomatic Conference in Geneva' (1974–1977), Vol IV, 34.

91   'Summary Record of Committee I, Second Session, 34th meeting' (20 March 1975), CDDH/I/SR.34, paras 7 (ICRC), 13 (India), 15 (Sweden), 17 (Pakistan), 34 (Mongolia); 'Amendment to article 10, Sweden' (24 March 1975), CDDH/I/261, 35. There was no discussion on this issue in the plenary meeting, see 'Summary record of the 50th plenary meeting', and 'Annex-Explanations of vote', CDDH/SR.50, paras 56-102.

92   T. Meron, 'War Crimes in Yugoslavia and the Development of International Law' (1994) 88 *AJIL* 78, 80; 'The Final Report of the Commission of Experts established pursuant to Security Council Resolution 780 (1992)' (27 May 1994), UN Doc S/1994/674, annex, para 42.

93   'Summary record of the 50th plenary meeting', and 'Annex-Explanations of vote', CDDH/SR.50, Nigeria, Spain. See also CDDH/I/SR.34, para 21 (Nigeria).

94   CDDH/SR.50, ibid, paras 70 (Nigeria), 73 (Syria), 78 (Saudi Arabia), 79 (Canada), Explanations of Saudi Arabia, Spain, Zaire.

95   Pilloud *et al* (eds) (n 88) § 4618.

When AP II [the 1977 Additional Protocol II] was adopted, states refused to make violations of its provisions regarding criminal offences. Certain nations were reluctant to allow other states to interfere in their internal affairs by way of trials for war crimes alleged to have taken place in their national territory.[96]

Given the reluctance of States Parties to recognise rebels as combatants, individuals participating in civil wars against the government, regardless of whether they comply with international humanitarian law, may be prosecuted for national offences in national law, for instance, crimes of rebellion, rather than war crimes in international law. Therefore, the idea of war crimes in non-international armed conflict was not covered under article 6(5) at that time.

In short, article 6 of Additional Protocol II did not envisage the notion of war crimes in non-international armed conflict. Article 6(5) does not reveal the idea that war crimes committed in this context was accepted in international law at that time.

3.3.3.3 Summary

The above observation reveals that States did not recognise war crimes in non-international armed conflict in Common Article 3 of 1949 Geneva Conventions or the 1977 Additional Protocol II. Common Article 3 did not criminalise violations of the law of war in non-international armed conflict as war crimes. The concept of war crimes in non-international armed conflict was not well developed in 1977. During this period, States did not contemplate treating serious violations in non-international armed conflict as war crimes, and they seldom prosecuted serious violations of Common Article 3 at the national level.[97] Even in the early 1990s, a legal adviser to the ICRC pointed out that 'international humanitarian law applicable to non-international armed conflict does not provide for international penal responsibility of persons guilty of violations'.[98] In international law, no sign indicated a shift to criminalise offences committed

---

96 Canada, Law of Armed Conflict at the Operational and Tactical Levels 2001, § 1725.1 'Breaches of Protocol II'. See also R. Wolfrum, 'Enforcement of International Humanitarian Law' in D. Fleck (ed), *The Handbook of Humanitarian Law in Armed Conflicts* (OUP 1995) 524.
97 L. Perna, *The Formation of the Treaty Law Applicable in Non-International Armed Conflicts* (Brill | Nijhoff 2006) 139–43.
98 D. Planner, 'The Penal Repression of Violations of International Humanitarian Law Applicable in Non-International Armed Conflicts' (1990) 30 *IRRC* 409, 414.

in non-international armed conflict as war crimes until the establishment of the two UN *ad hoc* tribunals.

3.3.4 Shifts since the Establishment of the Two UN Ad Hoc Tribunals: 1993–1996

Concerning the two UN *ad hoc* tribunals, this subsection first examines the Statutes of the two tribunals and then considers the *Tadić* Appeals Chamber Decision on jurisdiction and certain shifts subsequent to this decision.

3.3.4.1 Statutes of the Two UN *Ad Hoc* Tribunals

The preparatory process of the two UN *ad hoc* tribunals' Statutes appears to show that no consensus existed among States concerning war crimes in non-international armed conflict. However, the court of Bosnia and Herzegovina held that 'the customary status of criminal liability for [...] war crimes against civilians and individual responsibility for war crimes committed in 1992 was confirmed by UN Secretary-General, International Law Commission and jurisprudence of the ICTY and the International Criminal Tribunal for Rwanda (ICTR).'[99] As will be seen below, this statement is not persuasive.

The ICTY Statute does not use the term 'war crimes'. Its article 2 refers to 'grave breaches' of the four Geneva Conventions, and its article 3 provides for 'violations of the laws or customs of war'.[100] Drafters for the ICTY Statute in the UN Secretariat did not distinguish war crimes in international armed conflict from offences committed in non-international armed conflict.[101] The UN Secretary-General commented that 'the laws or customs of war' included the 1907 Hague Convention (IV) and its Annex and the Hague Regulations.[102]

However, some States expressed a different view about the term 'the laws or customs of war' in article 3 of the ICTY Statute at the UN Security Council debate. France, the US and the UK gave an interpretative clarification of this term to cover all applicable international conventions.[103] Representatives of the US commented to the Security Council:

---

99 *Prosecutor's Office v Anić* (Preliminary Hearing Decision, Court of Bosnia and Herzegovina) S11 K 005596 11 Kro (31 May 2011), para 35.
100 1993 ICTY Statute, art 3.
101 UN Doc S/25704 (1993), para 62.
102 ibid, paras 41-43, 62.
103 Security Council, 'Provisional Verbatim Record of the 3217th meeting', UN Doc S/PV. 3217 (25 May 1993), 11 (France), 15 (US), 19 (UK).

[...] it is understood that the 'laws or customs of war' referred to in Article 3 [of the ICTY Statute] include all obligations under humanitarian law agreements in force in the territory of the former Yugoslavia at the time the acts were committed, including common article 3 of the 1949 Geneva Conventions, and the 1977 Additional Protocols to those Conventions.[104]

The US delegation noted that 'other members of the [Security] Council share our view regarding the [...] clarifications related to the Statute'.[105] This interpretative statement indicates that some member States of the Security Council intended to include all applicable 'humanitarian law agreements', including Common Article 3 and the Additional Protocols.

The absence of protest by other States also showed the implicit willingness of the Security Council to criminalise serious violations in non-international armed conflict. The Security Council continually asserted that individuals would be held responsible for serious violations of international humanitarian law in non-international armed conflict, such as on the occasions of armed conflicts in Afghanistan, Somalia, Burundi and Rwanda.[106] The call for the creation of the Commission of Inquiry further confirmed the Security Council's aim to criminalise serious violations in non-international armed conflict.[107]

A Commission of Experts made a distinction between international and non-international armed conflict. The Commission of Experts, chaired by Frits Kalshoven and later by Cherif Bassiouni,[108] was set up in 1992 by the Security Council to investigate violations of international humanitarian law in the former Yugoslavia.[109] In its 1994 Report, the Commission of Experts stated that:

[...] unless the parties to an internal armed conflict agree otherwise, the only offences committed in internal armed conflict for which universal

---

104   ibid, 15 (US).
105   ibid.
106   UN Doc S/PRST/1994/12; UN Doc S/RES/794 (1992), para 5; UN Doc S/RES/814 (1993), para 13; UN Doc S/RES/935 (1994). For other resolutions in the Security Council and the General Assembly, see Henckaerts and Doswald-beck (eds) (n 6) Vol I: Rules, Rule 151, 554 and fn 15.
107   For a detailed analysis, see *Tadić* Appeals Chamber Decision on Jurisdiction (n 4), paras 72–78; D. Momtaz, 'War Crimes in Non-International Armed Conflicts under the Statute of the International Criminal Court' (1999) 2 *YIHL* 177.
108   'Letter dated 24 May 1994 from the Secretary-General to the President of the Security Council' (27 May 1994), UN Doc S/1994/674, para 2.
109   UN Doc S/RES/780 (1992), para 2; 'Secretary-General Report on the establishment of the Commission of Experts submitted to the Security Council' (14 October 1992), UN Doc S/24657 (1992).

jurisdiction exists are 'crimes against humanity' and genocide, which apply irrespective of the conflicts' classification. [...] It is probable that common article 3 would be viewed as a statement of customary international law, but unlikely that the other instruments would be so viewed. In particular, there does not appear to be a customary international law applicable to internal armed conflicts which includes the concept of war crimes.[110]

In addition, '[i]t must be observed that the violations of the laws or customs of war referred to in article 3 of the statute of the International Tribunal [the ICTY] are offences when committed in international, but not in internal [,] armed conflicts.'[111] The statements show that according to the Commission of Experts, war crimes in non-international armed conflict may be a treaty-based crime, and article 3 of the ICTY Statute is confined to violations committed in international armed conflict. This Report shared the view of Theodor Meron, who wrote in 1993 that:

> Were any part of the former Yugoslav conflict deemed internal rather than international, the perpetrators of even the worst atrocities could not be prosecuted for grave breaches or war crimes but only for the crime of genocide, which is much more difficult to establish, and for crimes against humanity.[112]

Article 4 of the ICTR Statute is the first provision that expressly criminalised violations of the 1977 Additional Protocol II and Common Article 3 in non-international armed conflict.[113] The UN Secretary-General commented that the UN Security Council incorporated article 4 into the Statute because the Rwanda conflict was in nature a non-international armed conflict.[114] The Secretary-General also admitted the progressive innovation of article 4

---

110 'The Final Report of the Commission of Experts established pursuant to Security Council Resolution 780 (1992)' (27 May 1994), UN Doc S/1994/674, annex, paras 42, 52.
111 ibid, para 54.
112 T. Meron, 'The Case for War Crimes Trials in Yugoslavia' (1993) 72 *Foreign Affairs* 122, 128; repeated in Meron (n 92) 80.
113 'Report of the Secretary-General Pursuant to Paragraph 5 of the Security Council Resolution 955 (1994)' (13 February 1995), UN Doc S/1995/134, para 12; L.J. van den Herik, *The Contribution of the Rwanda Tribunal to the Development of International Law* (Brill | Nijhoff 2005) 205.
114 UN Doc S/1995/134, para 11.

criminalising serious violations in non-international armed conflict as war crimes. He noted that as opposed to the ICTY Statute, 'the Security Council took a more expansive approach to include the applicable law and international instruments [namely, Additional Protocol II and Common Article 3 to the Geneva Conventions] [...] regardless of whether they customarily entailed the individual criminal responsibility of the perpetrator of the crime'.[115] The Secretary-General, thus, acknowledged that the Security Council adopted an 'expansive approach' by including violations of Additional Protocol II and Common Article 3.

The observation indicates that the Security Council and States at the Council supported prosecuting individuals for violations in non-international armed conflict. The US in its interpretative statement, however, did not clarify whether serious violations in non-international armed conflict constitute war crimes or crimes against humanity. It is also unclear whether other States considered 'war crimes in non-international armed conflict' when they in Security Council meetings or other fora addressed individual responsibility for violations of international humanitarian law in non-international armed conflict.[116] These practices, therefore, do not demonstrate the strong acceptance of a customary rule criminalising these violations as war crimes at that time. Also, the establishment of the two UN *ad hoc* tribunals by the Security Council is not an explicit articulation of concession of the sovereignty of the community of nations about war crimes.[117] The Secretary-General was doubtful whether violations of Common Article 3 in non-international armed conflict entail individual criminal responsibility for war crimes.[118] In light of these divergent positions, it is less convincing to conclude that the UN Security Council and the Secretary-General intended to confirm a pre-existing customary rule of war crimes in non-international armed conflict.

---

115   ibid, para 12.
116   France, 'Minister of State and Minister of Foreign Affairs, Letter dated 16 January 1993 to the Procurator-General of the Court of Cassation and Chairman of the Committee of French Jurists, annexed to Letter dated 10 February 1993 to the UN Secretary-General', UN Doc S/25266 (10 February 1993), 52; Statement before the UN Security Council, UN Doc S/PV.3217 (1993), 20 (Hungary), 25(France); UN Doc S/PV.3400 (1994), 8 (UK); UN Doc S/PV.3692 (1996), 12 (South Africa), 21(Indonesia); Ethiopia, 'Transitional Government, Statement by the Chief Special Prosecutor before the UN Commission on Human Rights' (17 February 1994), UN Doc E/CN.4/1994/SR.28, para 2.
117   Bassiouni (n 46) 535–36.
118   UN Doc S/1995/134, para 12 and fn 8.

3.3.4.2 *Tadić* Appeals Chamber Decision on Jurisdiction

Article 4 of the ICTR Statute first criminalised serious violations in non-international armed conflict,[119] whereas it is generally argued that the ICTY in the 1995 *Tadić* jurisdiction decision addressed firstly war crimes in non-international armed conflict. Similar to the idea of expanding article 3 of the ICTY Statute advanced by the US, the ICTY progressively departed from the restrictive idea of the Commission of Experts by applying article 3 to offences committed in non-international armed conflict. The ICTY appears to follow the Security Council's approach concerning article 4 of the ICTR Statute.

The ICTY indeed extended article 3 of its Statute to cover violations in non-international armed conflicts. The most frequently referred case is the 1995 *Tadić* Interlocutory Appeal Decision on jurisdiction, the reasoning of which was subscribed to in subsequent cases.[120] In this case, the prosecution charged Dusko Tadić with a list of crimes allegedly committed in a region of Bosnia-Herzegovina in 1992. Some of the charges were cruel treatment and murder under article 3 of the ICTY Statute. Tadić challenged the subject-matter jurisdiction of the ICTY. One reason was that article 3 of the ICTY Statute only conferred jurisdiction over violations of the laws or customs of war in international armed conflict because war crimes were confined to conflicts of that character. And the acts charged happened in a non-international armed conflict.[121]

The prosecution replied that these crimes were committed in the context of international armed conflict.[122] Alternatively, even if the conflict was non-international, the ICTY also had jurisdiction, because 'violations of law or customs of war' in article 3 were not confined to violations committed in international armed conflict.[123] The US also addressed the same view in its *amicus curiae* that article 3 of the ICTY Statute 'is only an exemplary and not an exhaustive list, and the language of Article 3 is otherwise broad enough to cover all relevant violations of the laws or customs of war, whether applicable in international or non-international armed conflict'.[124] The Trial Chamber supported the prosecutor's alternative argument about the interpretation of

---

119   ibid, para 12.
120   *Tadić* Appeals Chamber Decision on Jurisdiction (n 4), para 94.
121   ibid, para 65; Brief to Support the Motion on the Jurisdiction of the Tribunal (23 June 1995), Section 3.
122   'Prosecutor's Response to the Defence's Motions filed on 23 June 1995' (7 July 1995), paras 36-45.
123   ibid.
124   US, '*Amicus Curiae* brief presented to the ICTY, *Tadić* case, Motion Hearing' (25 July 1995), 35–37.

'violations of law or customs of war' without further explanation,[125] and dismissed Tadić's jurisdictional challenge.

The defendant appealed on this issue. The Appeals Chamber also rejected the challenge to its jurisdiction.[126] After examining the 'intent of the Security Council and the logical and systematic interpretation of article 3 as well as customary international law', the Appeals Chamber held that 'violations of the laws or customs of war' under article 3 of the ICTY Statute included violations of international humanitarian law applicable in non-international armed conflict.[127] The Appeals Chamber explained firstly that article 3 aimed to prosecute all serious violations of international humanitarian law, including Common Article 3 applicable to non-international armed conflict.[128] Violations of laws or customs of war as war crimes go beyond grave breaches regime in the Geneva Conventions to include 'serious' violations in non-international armed conflict.[129]

Secondly, the Appeals Chamber provided four cumulative requirements for violations to be subject to being charged under article 3. The four requirements are:

> (i) the violation must constitute an infringement of a rule of international humanitarian law; (ii) the rule must be customary in nature, or, if it belongs to treaty law, the required conditions must be met; (iii) the violation must be 'serious', that is to say, it must constitute a breach of a rule protecting important values, and the breach must involve grave consequences for the victim; and (iv) the violation of the rule must entail, under customary or conventional law, the individual criminal responsibility of the person breaching the rule.[130]

In the view of the Appeals Chamber, only if the four requirements are satisfied, 'the tribunal has jurisdiction over **any** serious violations of laws or customs of

---

125 *Prosecutor v Tadić* (Decision on the Defence Motion on Jurisdiction) ICTY-94-1-T (10 August 1995), para 53.
126 *Tadić* Appeals Chamber Decision on Jurisdiction (n 4), paras 71-137.
127 ibid, para 86.
128 ibid, paras 87-93, 94–127; *Prosecutor v Mucić et al* (Judgement) ICTY-96-21-A (20 February 2001), para 136.
129 The ICTY Statute does not mention whether 'serious' is necessary for the assessment of a war crime of 'violations of laws or customs of war'.
130 *Tadić* Appeals Chamber Decision on Jurisdiction (n 4), para 94; J. Trahan, *Genocide, War Crimes, and Crimes Against Humanity: A Topical Digest of the Case Law of the International Criminal Tribunal for the Former Yugoslavia* (Human Rights Watch 2006) 55–76.

war, regardless of whether they occurred within an internal or international armed conflict'.[131] The Appeals Chamber carefully analysed the last requirement.[132] The Chamber held that an express treaty rule criminalising violation in non-international armed conflict and entailing individual criminal responsibility is not necessary for the prosecution of international crimes.[133] The absence of penalising provisions in a treaty does not mean that serious violations of them cannot be prosecuted as international crimes. The Appeals Chamber then resorted to customary international law.

The Chamber stressed that prohibitions in international humanitarian law entails individual criminal responsibility under customary law, if the two criteria of 'the clear and unequivocal recognition of the rules of warfare in international law' and 'States practice indicating an intention to criminalise the norm' were satisfied.[134] According to the Appeals Chamber, '[n]o one can doubt the gravity of the acts at issue, nor the interest of the international community in their prohibition' and 'many elements of international practice show that States intend to criminalise serious breaches' in non-international armed conflict.[135] Thus, the two criteria were fulfilled, and an individual who seriously violated law applicable in non-international armed conflict could incur individual responsibility under customary law.[136] In addition to this, after analysing the prosecution in Nigeria, military manuals of four States, national legislation of two States (Belgium and the former Yugoslavia) and a Security Council resolution on Somalia, the Appeals Chamber concluded that 'customary international law imposes criminal liability for serious violations of Common Article 3' in non-international armed conflict.[137]

In discussing the individual responsibility, the Appeals Chamber might have considered the idea proposed by Meron. In his paper published in 1995, months before the delivery of the *Tadić* Appeals Chamber Decision, Meron argued that 'the concept of international criminality' should be extended 'to violations of Common Article 3 and Protocol II' because serious violations of them are of universal concern and subject to universal condemnation.[138] He

---

131 *Tadić* Appeals Chamber Decision on Jurisdiction (n 4), paras 91, 94, 137 (emphasis in original).
132 ibid, paras 128-36.
133 ibid, para 128.
134 ibid.
135 ibid.
136 ibid, paras 128-37.
137 ibid, paras 130-34, Germany, Humanitarian Law in Armed Conflicts Manual 1992; New Zealand, Interim Law of Armed Conflict Manual 1992; US, Manual of the United States 1956; UK, LOAC Manual 1958.
138 T. Meron, 'International Criminalization of Internal Atrocities' (1995) 89 *AJIL* 554, 576.

wrote that: 'whether the prohibition is unequivocal in character, the gravity of the act and the interests of the international community are all relevant factors in determining the criminality of various acts.'[139] This statement is very similar to the sentences in the *Tadić* Appeals Chamber Decision cited above.[140] Nevertheless, Meron did not claim that violations of Common Article 3 and Additional Protocol II incur individual criminal responsibility for 'war crimes'.[141] As cited above in his journal article in 1993, Meron might have preferred to criminalise some violations in non-international armed conflict as crimes against humanity or genocide, rather than war crimes.[142] Meron also referred to the US Joint Chiefs of Staff's proposal defining 'other inhumane acts' in article 5 of the ICTY Statute (crimes against humanity) to cover violations of Common Article 3.[143] Even the *Tadić* Appeals Chamber did not expressly declare that those guilty under article 3 of the ICTY Statute were responsible for 'war crimes'. Instead, the Appeals Chamber interpreted article 3 as a 'residual clause' that covers violations of international humanitarian law not falling under the definitions of other crimes (crimes against humanity, genocide and grave breaches of Geneva Conventions).[144]

Judge Li in his separate opinion took a different position on the issue of war crimes in non-international armed conflict. Judge Li agreed with the US's interpretations of article 3 of the ICTY Statute proposed covering violations of Additional Protocol II and Common Article 3.[145] He also referred to the reports of the Commission of Experts and Meron's work published in 1994.[146] He considered that 'the notion of war crimes is limited to situations in international armed conflicts.'[147] In light of these observations, Judge Li might also share Meron's view that violations of Common Article 3 and Additional Protocol II in non-international armed conflict incur individual criminal responsibility for crimes against humanity or genocide, rather than war crimes.

---

139   ibid 562.
140   *Tadić* Appeals Chamber Decision on Jurisdiction (n 4), paras 128-29.
141   Meron (1993) (n 112) 128.
142   ibid.
143   Meron (n 138) 560-61.
144   *Tadić* Appeals Chamber Decision on Jurisdiction (n 4), paras 87, 89, and 91.
145   *Tadić* Appeals Chamber Decision on Jurisdiction (n 4) (Separate Opinion of Judge Li on the Defence Motion for Interlocutory Appeal on Jurisdiction), para 12.
146   Meron (n 92) 80, repeating his journal article 'The Case for War Crimes Trials in Yugoslavia' published in 1993 (n 112).
147   *Tadić* Appeals Chamber Decision on Jurisdiction (n 4) (Separate Opinion of Judge Li on the Defence Motion for Interlocutory Appeal on Jurisdiction), paras 8-10.

The *Tadić* Appeals Chamber's analysis of individual liability for violations in non-international armed conflict is rather brief as compared to its discussion on customary rules of international humanitarian law.[148] The Appeals Chamber concluded that a customary rule existed at that time based on only scarce authorities. The Chamber heavily relied on *opinio juris* in the identification of a customary rule, leaving State practice as an indication of 'intention'.[149] Apart from some military manuals, there is limited evidence providing that serious violations of rules applicable in non-international armed conflict are punishable as 'war crimes' in international law at that time.[150] The Chamber also referred to 'substantive justice and equity' and national legislation of the former Yugoslavia to justify its finding.[151]

To sum up, individuals are criminally responsible for violations of Common Article 3 in non-international armed conflict before the ICTY and the ICTR. These violations may constitute crimes against humanity or genocide. This idea of individual criminal responsibility in non-international armed conflict does not show that a general agreement has been reached on criminalising violations in this context as 'war crimes' in international law. However, as Larissa van den Herik noted, the *Tadić* Appeals Chamber Decision indeed 'paved the way for future prosecution' of 'war crimes'.[152] The ICTY's subsequent decisions endorsed the interpretation of article 3 of the ICTY Statute in this Decision.[153] Its four requirements for the application of article 3 were also subscribed to in many subsequent ICTY cases.[154] After the delivery of the *Tadić* Appeals

---

148   *Tadić* Appeals Chamber Decision on Jurisdiction (n 4), paras 96-127.
149   T. Meron, 'The Continuing Role of Custom in the Formation of International Humanitarian Law' (1996) 90 *AJIL* 238, 242.
150   Manuals of the UK, Swiss, Norwegian, Federal Republic of Yugoslavia and Canadian. See M. Bothe, 'War Crimes in Non-International Armed Conflicts' in Y. Dinstein and M. Tabory (eds), *War Crimes in International Law* (Martinus Nijhoff Publishers 1996) 297.
151   *Tadić* Appeals Chamber Decision on Jurisdiction (n 4), paras 135-36.
152   For an analysis of the development of jurisprudence in the ICTY and the ICTR after this decision, see Van den Herik (n 113) 208–14.
153   *Prosecutor v Martić* (Decision on the Issuance of an International Arrest Warrant) Transcript of Oral Proceedings (8 March 1996), paras 135-36; *Prosecutor v Tadić* (Sentencing Judgement) ICTY-94-1-T (14 July 1997), paras 609, 613, 639; *Prosecutor v Mucić et al* (Judgement) ICTY-96-21-T (16 November 1998), para 306; *Mucić et al* Appeals Chamber Judgment (n 128), paras 143, 147, 154.
154   *Prosecutor v Prlić et al* (Judgement) ICTY-04-74-T (29 May 2013), para 142; *Prosecutor v Perišić* (Judgement) ICTY-04-81-T (6 September 2011), para 75; *Prosecutor v Delić* (Judgement) ICTY-04-83-T (15 September 2008), para 42; *Prosecutor v Boškoski & Tarčulovski* (Judgement) ICTY-04-82-T (10 July 2008), para 296; *Prosecutor v Krajišnik* (Judgement) ICTY-00-39-T (27 September 2006), para 842; *Prosecutor v Orić* (Judgement) ICTY-03-68-T (30 June 2006), para 257; *Prosecutor v Hadžihasanović & Kubura* (Judgement) ICTY-01-47-T (15 March 2006), para 17; *Prosecutor v Limaj et al* (Judgement)

Chamber Decision on jurisdiction, the early 1990s saw a shift towards including the notion of war crimes in non-international armed conflict.

3.3.4.3 Shifts Subsequent to the *Tadić* Appeals Chamber Decision on Jurisdiction

Before the delivery of the *Tadić* Appeals Chamber Decision, commentators differed on whether a rule of violations in non-international armed conflict entailing individual criminal responsibility for war crimes had been established in international law. Michael Bothe argued that there was ample basis for the punishment of individuals for their violations in non-international armed conflict as war crimes.[155] As observed above, some commentators contended that violations of these provisions involved individual liability, but it was unclear whether the perpetrators were liable for crimes against humanity or war crimes.[156] The majority of commentators, however, answered negatively.[157] James O'Brien was uncertain whether violations of Common Article 3 in non-international armed conflict gave rise to individual criminal responsibility.[158] Meron noted that even in 1995 the accepted wisdom was that Common Article 3 and Protocol II constituted an uncertain basis for individual criminal responsibility on the international plane.[159]

After the delivery of the *Tadić* Appeals Chamber Decision, commentators responded differently. Peter Rowe disagreed with the idea of considering violations of Common Article 3 in non-international armed conflict as war crimes.[160] He maintained that the *Tadić* Appeals Chamber Decision was not entirely consistent with treaty provisions and would create legal difficulties concerning the status of rebels. Even if the Decision was reached because of the development of customary law, disagreements also existed about the state of customary law.[161] By contrast, some commentators supported the Decision on the war

---

ICTY-03-66-T (30 November 2005), para 175; *Prosecutor v Halilović* (Judgement) ICTY-01-48-T (16 November 2005), para 30; *Prosecutor v Strugar et al* (Judgement) ICTY-01-42-T (31 January 2005), para 218; *Prosecutor v Blagojević et al* (Judgement) ICTY-02-53-T (17 January 2005), para 37.

155 Bothe (n 150) 251.
156 For other debates, see Meron (n 149); G. Aldrich, 'Jurisdiction of the International Criminal Tribunal for the Former Yugoslavia' (1996) 90 *AJIL* 64.
157 Meron (n 138) 82–83.
158 J. O'Brien, 'The International Tribunal for Violations of International Humanitarian Law in the Former Yugoslavia' (1993) 87 *AJIL* 639, 647.
159 Meron (n 138) 559.
160 P. Rowe, 'Liability for War Crimes during a Non-International Armed Conflict' (1995) 34 *Military L & L War Rev* 149, 155–56.
161 P. Rowe, 'Duress as a Defence to War Crimes after *Erdemović*: A Laboratory for a Permanent Court?' (1998) 1 *YIHL* 210, 222–25.

crimes issue. In 1996, Meron wrote that 'I entirely agree with the Tribunal's views that violations of Article 3 common to the Geneva Conventions entail individual criminal responsibility under customary law'.[162] Again, he did not refer to war crimes or crimes against humanity. But in 1998, he developed three strategies for the criminalisation of war crimes in non-international armed conflict.[163] An increasing number of scholars recognised then that criminal responsibility could be attached to individuals for war crimes committed in non-international armed conflict.[164] Judge Cassese, the presiding judge of the Appeals Chamber in the *Tadić* Appeals Chamber Decision, opined that 'particularly after *Tadić*', 'it is now widely accepted that serious infringements of customary or applicable treaty law on internal armed conflicts must also be regarded as amounting to war crimes'.[165]

The International Committee of the Red Cross (ICRC) also shifted its position that war crimes were limited to international armed conflict.[166] In its 1993 comments on the proposal to establish the ICTY, the ICRC contended that 'according to international humanitarian law as it stands today, the notion of war crimes is limited to situations of international armed conflict'.[167] It then gradually abandoned this position. In February 1997, the ICRC prepared a

---

162 Meron (n 149) 243.
163 T. Meron, 'Is International Law Moving towards Criminalisation?' (1998) 9 *EJIL* 18, 25–30.
164 C. Greenwood, 'International Humanitarian Law and the *Tadić* Case' (1996) 7 *EJIL* 265, 277–78; R. Müllerson, 'International Humanitarian Law in Internal Conflicts' (1997) 2 *J Armed Conflict L* 109, 122; A. McDonald, 'The Year in Review' (1998) 1 *YIHL* 113, 121–22; C. Cissé, 'The End of a Culture of Impunity in Rwanda? Prosecution of Genocide and War Crimes before Rwandan Courts and the International Criminal Tribunal for Rwanda' (1998) 1 *YIHL* 161,167; B. Simma and A. Paulus, 'The Responsibility of Individuals for Human Rights Abuses in Internal Conflicts: A Positivist View' (1999) 93 *AJIL* 302, 313; S. Boelaert-Suominen, 'Grave Breaches, Universal Jurisdiction and Internal Armed Conflict: Is Customary Law Moving towards a Uniform Enforcement Mechanism for All Armed Conflicts' (2000) 5 *J Conflict & Security L* 63; J.E. Aldykiewicz and G.S. Corn, 'Authority to Court-Martial Non-US Military Personnel for Serious Violations of International Humanitarian Law Committed During Internal Armed Conflicts' (2001) 167 *Military L Rev* 74, 101–43.
165 A. Cassese, *International Law* (2nd edn, OUP 2005) 437.
166 ICRC, DDM/JUR/442 b, para 4; ICRC, 'Statement in the 9th UN Congress on the Prevention of Crimes and Treatment of Offenders' (Cairo, 30 April 1995), UN Doc A/CONF.169/NGO/ICRC/1, 4, reprinted in Henckaerts and Doswald-beck (eds) (n 6) Vol II: Practices, 3703, § 405.
167 ICRC, 'Preliminary Remarks' (25 March 1993), DDM/JUR/442 b, reprinted in V. Morris and M. Scharf, *An Insider's Guide to the International Criminal Tribunal for the Former Yugoslavia: A Documentary History and Analysis*, Vol 2 (Transnational Publishers 1995) 391–92.

working paper regarding war crimes,[168] in which it classified war crimes into three categories, including other serious violations committed in international armed conflict and war crimes in non-international armed conflict.[169] In its 2005 ICRC *Study*, Rule 156 concludes that trials for war crimes before national and international tribunals support a customary rule of war crimes in non-international armed conflict.[170] Although the method employed in the 2005 ICRC *Study* has been criticised for its flexibility,[171] this critique is now insignificant with respect to war crimes in Rule 156.

In sum, after the delivery of the *Tadić* Appeals Chamber Decision, the positions of commentators and the ICRC changed quickly. Commentators and the ICRC tend to support that the view is outdated that individual responsibility for war crimes is limited to international armed conflict.[172] These academic and institutional demands for such a norm indirectly imply that a positive customary rule, providing individual responsibility for war crimes in non-international armed conflict, had not yet fully emerged in 1995.[173] After the *Tadić* Appeals Chamber Decision, a rule was emerging concerning war crimes in non-international armed conflict.

3.3.5 *The Work of the International Law Commission*

An overview of the ILC's work on the draft code of offences and security of mankind (Draft Code of Crimes (Offences)) and the drafts of the International Criminal Court Statute helps in understanding comments of State delegations at the Sixth Committee on these drafts related to the issue of war crimes in non-international armed conflict. This subsection also examines the viewpoint concerning the extension of war crimes occurring in non-international armed conflict among members of the ILC.

---

168 ICRC, 'War Crimes, Working Paper Prepared by the ICRC for the Preparatory Committee for the Establishment of an International Criminal Court' (13 February 1997).
169 Convention on the Protection of Cultural Property in the Event of Armed Conflict, 249 UNTS 215.
170 Henckaerts and Doswald-beck (eds) (n 6) Vol II.
171 D. Bethlehem, 'The Methodological Framework of the Study' and C. Garraway, 'War Crimes' and I. Scobbie, 'The Approach to Customary International Law in the Study' in E. Wilmshurst and S. Breau (eds), *Perspectives on the ICRC Study on Customary International Humanitarian Law* (CUP 2007) 3–49; C. Emanuelli, 'Comments on the ICRC Study on Customary International Humanitarian Law' (2006) 44 *Canadian Ybk Intl L* 437, 440.
172 A. Cassese, 'On the Current Trends towards Criminal Prosecution and Punishment of Breaches of International Humanitarian Law' (1998) 9 *EJIL* 2, 2–17.
173 New Zealand, Interim Law of Armed Conflict Manual 1992; Argentina, Law of War Manual 1989.

3.3.5.1 Draft Code of Crimes (Offences)

The ILC was re-entrusted by the General Assembly to prepare a Draft Code of Offences in 1981.[174] Doudou Thiam was appointed as the Special Rapporteur for this task.[175] In the 1980s and the early 1990s, the issue of war crimes was debated at many meetings of the ILC.[176] In the 1980s, governments did not discuss war crimes in non-international armed conflict.[177] In his fourth and seventh reports, Thiam did not include serious violations of Common Article 3 and other serious violations of Additional Protocol II in the scope of war crimes.[178] In his fourth report, he used the phrase 'non-international armed conflicts' to define war crimes in draft article 13.[179] Thiam, however, did not use the phrase in a technical way as we consider it at the present time. He might have intended to use the phrase to cover conflicts between States and non-State entities, including fighting against colonial domination, alien occupation or racist regimes in the exercise of self-determination, without noticing that article 1(4) of Additional Protocol I characterises these conflicts as international armed conflict instead of non-international armed conflict.[180] Later

---

174 'Draft Code of Offences against the Peace and Security of Mankind', GA Res 897 (IX) (1954), UN Doc A/RES/897 (IX); 'Draft Code of Offences against the Peace and Security of Mankind', GA Res 36/106 (1981), UN Doc A/RES/36/106, paras 1-2.

175 'Draft Code of Offences against the Peace and Security of Mankind' in 'Report of the International Law Commission', UN Doc A/37/10 (1982), Vol II (2), para 252; 'Draft Code of Offences against the Peace and Security of Mankind', UN Doc A/RES/37/102 (1982).

176 'Report of the International Law Commission', UN Doc A/38/10 (1983); 'Fourth report on the draft Code of Crimes against the Peace and Security of Mankind, by Doudou Thiam, Special Rapporteur', UN Doc A/CN.4/398 and Corr.1-3 (1986); 'Report of the International Law Commission', UN Doc A/41/10 (1986); 'Fifth report on the draft Code of Crimes against the Peace and Security of Mankind, by Doudou Thiam, Special Rapporteur', UN Doc A/CN.4/404 (1987); 'Report of the International Law Commission', UN Doc A/43/10 (1988); 'Draft Code of Crimes against the Peace and Security of Mankind', UN Doc A/RES/41/75 (1986), UN Doc A/RES/42/151(1987), UN Doc A/RES/43/164 (1988), UN Doc A/RES/44/32(1989); 'Seventh report on the draft Code of Crimes against the Peace and Security of Mankind, by Doudou Thiam, Special Rapporteur', UN Doc A/CN.4/419 and Add.1 (1989); UN Doc A/51/10 (1996).

177 'Comments and observations received pursuant to General Assembly resolution 37/102' (8 March 1983), Suriname.

178 UN Doc A/CN.4/398 and Corr.1-3 (1986); UN Doc A/CN.4/419 and Add.l (1989).

179 For discussions on nuclear weapons in 1986 and 1989, see 'Summary record of the 1958th meeting', UN Doc A/CN.4/SR.1958 (1986), para 23; 'Summary record of the 1960th meeting', UN Doc A/CN.4/SR.1960 (1986), para 20, 'Summary record of the 1961st meeting', UN Doc A/CN.4/SR.1961 (1986), para 28; 'Summary record of the 1962nd meeting', UN Doc A/CN.4/SR.1962 (1986), paras 13, 35; 'Summary record of the 1965th meeting', UN Doc A/CN.4/SR.1965 (1986), para 12; UN Doc A/41/10 (1986), paras 103-14; UN Doc A/CN.4/419 and Add.l (1989), paras 19, 25.

180 The 1977 Additional Protocol I, art 1(4).

he replaced the phrase 'non-international armed conflicts' with 'rules of international law applicable in armed conflict' in his seventh report.[181]

The issue of war crimes in non-international armed conflict emerged in discussing the seventh report in 1989, but the majority of Commission members did not contemplate the extension of war crimes to non-international armed conflict.[182] One member stated that the new phrase 'rules of international law applicable in armed conflict' was controversial and would raise a question whether offences committed in non-international armed conflict could be regarded as war crimes.[183] Some members argued that this new phrase indeed covered non-international armed conflict[184] and that serious violations of Common Article 3 and Additional Protocol II were included as war crimes.[185] However, Thiam suggested that the scope of 'rules of international law applicable in armed conflict' was limited to the 1907 Hague Convention, grave breaches of the 1949 Geneva Conventions, and articles 11 and 85 of Additional Protocol I.[186]

In the 1991 text of the Draft Code of Crimes, the definition of war crimes also referred to violations of international law applicable in 'armed conflict'.[187] The phrase 'armed conflict' did not limit itself to international armed conflict. One member insisted that war crimes were limited to serious violations in international armed conflict,[188] while three members upheld different views.[189] The Netherlands expressed its positive attitude towards the inclusion of war crimes in non-international armed conflict.[190] It 'agreed with the ILC that

---

181 UN Doc A/CN.4/419 and Add.1 (1989), 82–83, para 8.
182 UN Doc A/CN.4/SR.1962 (1986), para 34; 'Summary record of the 1963rd meeting', UN Doc A/CN.4/SR.1963 (1986), para 30.
183 'Summary record of the 2101st meeting', UN Doc A/CN.4/SR.2101 (1989), para 24 (Mr Jacovides).
184 'Summary record of the 2096th meeting', UN Doc A/CN.4/SR.2096 (1989), para 34 (Mr Roucounas); 'Summary record of the 2097th meeting', UN Doc A/CN.4/SR.2097 (1989), paras 22-23 (Mr Barsegov).
185 'Report of the International Law Commission', UN Doc A/44/10 (1989), paras 107-08.
186 UN Doc A/CN.4/419 and Add.1 (1989), 82–83, para 8.
187 'draft Code of Crimes against the Peace and Security of Mankind, Titles and texts of articles adopted by the Drafting Committee', UN Doc A/CN.4/L.459 and Corr.1 and Add.1 (1994), para 22. 'Thirteenth report on the Draft Code of Crimes against the Peace and Security of Mankind, by Doudou Thiam, Special Rapporteur', UN Doc A/CN.4/466 (1995), paras 95-110.
188 'Summary record of the 2240th meeting', UN Doc A/CN.4/SR.2240 (1991), paras 48-49, 73 (Mr Pellet).
189 UN Doc A/CN.4/SR.2240 (1991), paras 64 (Mr Graefrath), 66 (Mr Calero Rodrigues), 71 (Mr Eriksson).
190 'Comments and observations received from Governments', UN Doc A/CN.4/448 and Add.1(1993), Netherlands, 87–88.

[war crimes] should also be applicable to national armed conflicts, given that serious war crimes can likewise be committed in these circumstances'.[191] The chairperson of the Drafting Committee, established by the ILC to prepare the text of the Draft Code of Crimes, stated that 'this ambiguity is constructive, in light of the fact that Common Article 3 applied in non-international armed conflicts'.[192] Hence, the ambiguous text in the 1991 draft kept the door open for the inclusion of war crimes in non-international armed conflict, at the very least, including serious violations of Common Article 3.

In discussing war crimes in the 1995 ILC draft text, different views were expressed whether to expand the law of war crimes to non-international armed conflict. By citing the ICTR Statute, some Commission members argued that the notion of war crimes should be extended to non-international armed conflict.[193] Other members disagreed with such a construction.[194] At the Sixth Committee in February 1996, State delegations also expressed divergent views.[195] In June 1996, draft article 18 included serious violations in non-international armed conflict as war crimes.[196] Draft article 18 stated that:

> Any of the following war crimes constitutes a crime against the peace and security of mankind when committed in a systematic manner or on a large scale: (a) Any of the following acts committed in violation of international humanitarian law: [...] (b) Any of the following acts committed wilfully in violation of international humanitarian law and causing death or serious injury to body or health: [...] (c) Any of the following acts committed wilfully in violation of international humanitarian law: [...] (d) Outrages upon personal dignity in violation of international humanitarian law, in particular humiliating and degrading treatment, rape, enforced prostitution and any form of indecent assault; (e) Any of the

---

191   ibid.
192   UN Doc A/CN.4/SR.2240 (1991), para 29 (Mr Pawlak).
193   'Summary record of the 2384th meeting', UN Doc A/CN.4/SR.2384 (1995), paras 26 (Mr Fomba), 71 (Mr Rosenstock); 'Thirteenth report on the draft Code of Crimes against the Peace and Security of Mankind, by Doudou Thiam, Special Rapporteur', UN Doc A/CN.4/466 (1995), para 107.
194   UN Doc A/50/10 (1995), para 101.
195   'Topical summary of the discussion held in the Sixth Committee of the General Assembly during its 50th session', UN Doc A/CN.4/472 (1996), paras 139-40, 145.
196   'draft Code of Crimes against the Peace and Security of Mankind-Titles and texts of articles adopted by the Drafting Committee on second reading at the 47th and 48th sessions', reproduced in 'Summary record of the 2437th meeting', UN Doc A/CN.4/SR.2437 (1996), para 7.

following acts committed in violation of the laws or customs of war: [...] (f) Any of the following acts committed in violation of international humanitarian law applicable in armed conflict not of an international character: [...] (g) In the case of armed conflict, [...].[197]

Draft articles 18(d) and (g) covered violations in both kinds of armed conflict. Draft article 18(d) criminalised violations of fundamental guarantees embodied in Common Article 3 and article 4(2) of Additional Protocol II. Draft article 18(g) criminalised the method of warfare causing widespread, long-term and severe damage to the natural environment if these violations cause serious consequences to the population in armed conflict, whether of international or internal character.[198] In addition, draft article 18(f) listed seven acts committed in violation of international humanitarian law applicable in non-international armed conflict as war crimes.[199] The list is identical to the definition of war crimes in article 4 of the ICTR Statute. The ILC almost adopted draft article 18 in its entirety under draft article 20 of the final 1996 Draft Code of Crimes.[200]

The examination of the ILC's work on the Draft Code of Crimes shows that the view on war crimes in non-international armed conflict dramatically changed in the final 1996 Draft Code of Crimes. Based on the text of the 1996 Draft Code of Crimes, a new regime of war crimes in non-international armed conflict was emerging.

3.3.5.2 1993 and 1994 Drafts of the International Law Commission for an International Criminal Court

The General Assembly had also entrusted the ILC to consider the issue of an international judicial organ.[201] The ILC earnestly worked on this mandate, but the General Assembly later deferred this because the definitions of crimes were not completed.[202] In 1989, based on a proposal of Trinidad and Tobago

---

197 ibid, para 7.
198 ibid.
199 ibid.
200 'Draft Code of Crimes against the Peace and Security of Mankind with commentaries', UN Doc A/51/10 (1996), para 50, art 20.
201 'Prevention and Punishment of the Crime of Genocide, Study by the International Law Commission of the Question of an International Criminal Jurisdiction', UN Doc A/Res/260 B (III) (1948).
202 'Question of Defining Aggression', UN Doc A/RES/688 (VII) (1952); 'International Criminal Jurisdiction', UN Doc A/RES/687 (VII) (1952); 'International Criminal Jurisdiction', UN Doc A/RES/898 (IX) (1954); 'International Criminal Jurisdiction', UN Doc A/RES/1187 (XII) (1957).

and a request of the General Assembly, the ILC resumed its work on the issue of an international criminal court.[203] From 1989 to 1991, the ILC's work on an international criminal court was included as part of its work for the Draft Code of Crimes. The initial draft texts of the judicial organ focused on procedural matters instead of substantive definitions of crimes, which were covered by the Draft Code of Crimes.[204]

In 1992, a working group, established by the ILC to work on the issue of international criminal jurisdiction, submitted its proposals.[205] In discussing these proposals in the Sixth Committee, only the Italian delegate implicitly mentioned the issue of war crimes in non-international armed conflict.[206] In its written comments, the Italian government recommended that war crimes considered by the Geneva Conventions and its protocols be listed in the jurisdiction of the proposed court.[207]

In 1993, the working group submitted its preliminary but comprehensive text of a draft statute of an international criminal tribunal with commentary to the ILC.[208] The ILC then attached this Draft text to its report to the General Assembly for discussion.[209] Article 22 of the 1993 Draft text provided a list of crimes defined by treaties as international crimes. The working group's commentary on article 22 stated that the 1977 Additional Protocol II was not included in the list, as Protocol II contains no provision about grave breaches.[210] The Slovenian delegation, however, did not share the working group's view. Its delegate supported incorporating Additional Protocol II in the treaty list of article 22.[211] In his view, the 'notion of war crimes should be extended to crimes committed

---

203   UN Doc A/RES/44/39 (1989).
204   'Eleventh report on the draft Code of Offences against the Peace and Security of Mankind, by Doudou Thiam, Special Rapporteur', UN Doc A/CN.4/449 and Corr.1 (1993), 113–24.
205   'Working Group established pursuant to the request contained in General Assembly resolution 44/39 of 4 December 1989' (16 May 1990).
206   'Topical summary of the discussion held in the Sixth Committee of the General Assembly during its 47th session' [French], UN Doc A/CN.4/446 (1992), prepared by Secretariat.
207   'Comments of Governments on the report of the Working Group on the question of an international criminal jurisdiction', UN Doc A/CN.4/452 and Add.1-3 (1993), Italy, para 6.
208   'Revised report of the Working Group on a draft statute for an international criminal court', UN Doc A/CN.4/L.490 and Add.1(1993), as reproduced in UN Doc A/48/10 (1993), Vol II (2), annex.
209   UN Doc A/48/10 (1993), Vol II (2), annex, 100–31.
210   ibid, 107, art 22, para (3).
211   'Observations of Governments on the report of the Working Group on a draft statute for an international criminal court', UN Doc A/CN.4/458 and Add.1-8 (1994), in UN Doc A/CN.4/SER.A/1994/Add. l, para 4 (Slovenia); 'Topical summary of the discussion held in the Sixth Committee of the General Assembly during its 48th session', UN Doc A/CN.4/457

in internal armed conflicts'.[212] Slovenia recommended that the ILC should follow the approach of the ICTY Statute to cover war crimes for violations of international humanitarian law applicable in non-international armed conflict under article 22. Other delegates or governments, however, did not share the Slovenia's position.[213] In brief, it is inconclusive to argue that article 22 of the 1993 Draft text covered 'war crimes' in non-international armed conflict.

In addition, article 26(2)(a) of the 1993 Draft text required special acceptance of a jurisdictional clause for crimes 'under general international law' but not covered by article 22.[214] Some members of the ILC argued that article 26(2)(a) covered offences in non-international armed conflict, but the offences were only aggression and crimes against humanity that were not defined by treaties.[215] War crimes in non-international armed conflict, therefore, in their view, were not covered under this article. However, Slovenia claimed that in drafting article 26(2)(a), the working group considered crimes for violations of customary international law applying to non-international armed conflict, for example, Common Article 3 of the four Geneva Conventions.[216] Therefore, article 26(2)(a), at the very most, covered serious violations of Common Article 3 in non-international armed conflict, although the label of the offences is uncertain.

In 1994, the working group, re-established by the ILC and chaired by James Crawford,[217] submitted a report to the ILC.[218] The ILC adopted the 1994 Draft

---

(1994), para 84; 'Summary record of the 2330th meeting', UN Doc A/CN.4/SR.2330 (1994), para 23.

212 UN Doc A/CN.4/457 (1994), para 84.
213 UN Doc A/CN.4/458 and Add.1-8 (1994), 22–96 (Algeria, Australia, Austria, Belarus, Chile, Cuba, Cyprus, Czech Republic, Denmark, Finland, Germany, Hungary, Iceland, Japan, Kuwait, Malta, Mexico, New Zealand, Nordic countries, Norway, Panama, Romania, Spain, Sri Lanka, Sweden, Tunisia, UK, US, Yugoslavia); UN Doc A/CN.4/457 (1994), paras 84-88.
214 1993 Draft Statute, art 26(2)(a) reads: '[i]t was accepted and recognised by the international community of States as a whole as being of such a fundamental character that its violation gives rise to the criminal responsibility of individuals'.
215 'Report of the International Law Commission', UN Doc A/49/10 (1994), para 48 (Mr Crawford); UN Doc A/CN.4/SR.2330 (1994), paras 5 (Mr Crawford), 23 (Mr Villagran Kramer), 31–32 (Mr Kabatsi).
216 UN Doc A/CN.4/458 and Add.1-8 (1994), para 10 (Slovenia).
217 'Summary record of the 2331st meeting', UN Doc A/CN.4/SR.2331 (1994). The Working Group on a draft statute for an international criminal court held 27 meetings. The 1993 text was considered from the 2329th to 2334th meetings, held between 3 and 9 May 1994, UN Doc A/CN.4/SR.2329-2334 (1994).
218 'Report of the Working Group on the question of a Draft Statute for an International Criminal Court-Revision', UN Doc A/CN.4/L.491/Rev.2, UN Doc A/CN.4/L.491/Rev.2/Corr.1, and UN Doc A/CN.4/L.491/Rev.2/Add.1-3 (1994).

Statute accompanied by commentaries and then submitted it to the General Assembly.[219] Article 20(c) of the 1994 Draft Statute proposed 'serious violations of the laws and customs applicable in armed conflict'.[220] According to its commentary, the ILC shared the idea that a category of war crimes exists under customary international law which is distinct from the grave breaches regime.[221] The ILC was very cautious and did not address whether the term 'armed conflict' covered non-international armed conflict. State delegations in the Sixth Committee said that 'crimes associated with domestic armed conflicts [...] should not have been explicitly mentioned as falling within the jurisdiction of the Court'.[222]

Article 20(e) of the 1994 Draft Statute proposed 'exceptionally serious crimes of international concern' for violations of treaties in an Annex. The Annex provided an exhaustive list of treaty crimes, including 'grave breaches' of the 1949 Geneva Conventions and Additional Protocol I.[223] Similar to the 1993 Draft text, the ILC expressly excluded Additional Protocol II from the Annex[224] because that Protocol does not specifically contain a provision about grave breaches or criminalising serious violations as war crimes. Since Common Article 3 was not excluded from the Annex, one may argue that grave breaches of Common Article 3 in non-international armed conflict were implicitly included. Its drafters, however, did not contemplate criminalising 'grave breaches' of Common Article 3 in non-international armed conflict as war crimes. Except for some support by a few judges, the jurisprudence of the ICTY also did not support the idea of grave breaches of Common Article 3 in non-international armed conflict.[225] In contrast to its 1993 Draft text, the ILC's 1994 Draft Statute was more modest because it contemplated no offences committed in non-international armed conflict.

---

219   UN Doc A/49/10 (1994), paras 42-91.
220   ibid, para 91, art 20(c).
221   ibid.
222   'Topical summary of the discussion held in the Sixth Committee of the General Assembly during its 49th session', UN Doc A/CN.4/464/Add.1 (1995), para 89.
223   UN Doc A/49/10 (1994), para 91, Annex 'crimes pursuant to treaties'.
224   ibid, commentary (1)(j) to art 20(e).
225   *Tadić* Trial Chamber Decision on Jurisdiction (n 125), paras 46-52; *Tadić* Appeals Chamber Decision on Jurisdiction (n 4) (Separate Opinion of Judge Abi-Saab on the Defence Motion for Interlocutory Appeal on Jurisdiction), part IV, para 7; *Delalić/Mucić et al* Trial Chamber Judgment (n 153), para 203; *Prosecutor v Aleksovski* (Judgement, Dissenting Opinion of Judge Rodrigues) ICTY-95-14/1-T (25 June 1999), paras 27-49.

States and international organisations submitted their comments on the 1994 Draft Statute to the UN Secretary-General.[226] Belarus argued that Additional Protocol II should be included in the list of Annex in article 20(e),[227] while Switzerland cast doubt on this view by stating that:

> A fifth category of crimes is constituted by 'crimes established under or pursuant to the treaty provisions listed in the annex' (article 20, paragraph (e)), including, in particular, the Geneva Conventions of 12 August 1949 and Protocol I additional thereto of 8 June 1977 (perhaps also Protocol II?).[228]

The US opposed the inclusion of violations of Additional Protocol II in the jurisdiction of the proposed Court.[229] In connection with its position, as observed above in subsection 3.3.4.1, the US did not oppose the criminalisation of violations in non-international armed conflict. In addition, it was unknown what the positions of other States were from their comments on the issue of war crimes. They seemingly did not intend to apply the notion of war crimes to non-international armed conflicts at that time.[230]

The observation of the ILC's work on the ICC demonstrates that in 1995 the majority of UN member delegations were reluctant to consider war crimes committed in non-international armed conflict. The ILC did not specify to what extent it codified or progressively developed the notion of war crimes. Some observers of the ILC were ambitious about including violations in non-international armed conflict, but they were more prudent about labelling these offences as war crimes.

---

226 'Comments Received Pursuant to Paragraph 4 of General Assembly Resolution 49/53 on the Establishment of an International Court, Report of the Secretary-General', UN Doc A/AC.244/1(1995), Belarus, China, Singapore, Sweden, Switzerland, Venezuela, and the ICTY. See also 'Comments Received Pursuant to Paragraph 4 of General Assembly Resolution 49/53 on the Establishment of an International Court, Report of the Secretary-General, Addendum', UN Doc A/AC.244/1/Add.1(1995), Azerbaijan, Czech Republic, Sudan, and the Crime Prevention and Criminal Justice Branch and the United Nations International Drug Control Program; UN Doc A/AC.244/1/Add.2 (1995), Cyprus, France, and US; UN Doc A/AC.244/1/Add.3 (1995), Libya; UN Doc A/AC.244/1/Add.4 (1995), Barbados and Trinidad and Tobago.
227 UN Doc A/AC.244/1(1995), para 14 (Belarus).
228 ibid, para 6 (Switzerland).
229 UN Doc A/AC.244/1/Add.2 (1995), para 105 (US).
230 UN Doc A/50/10(1995), para 100.

3.3.6 Assessment and Conclusions

The exploration of the notion of war crimes and its evolution in the context of non-international armed conflict indicates that there is a remarkable trend of criminalising serious violations in non-international armed conflict in the UN Security Council and among scholars.[231] As shown above, first, after the First and Second World Wars, the practice of prosecution of war crimes emerged in international law. The establishment of international investigation commissions in 1919 and 1943, the criminalisation of violations of international humanitarian law by treaties, and war crimes trials at Nuremberg and Tokyo denoted the attempts of the international community to prosecute war crimes under international law. The issue of war crimes in non-international armed conflict, however, was not considered from 1919 to 1945.

Secondly, when Common Article 3 and Additional Protocol II were adopted, they did not indicate States' recognition of war crimes in non-international armed conflict. Despite some instances of national legislation, there was no criminalisation of violations in non-international armed conflict as war crimes at the international level until the early 1990s.[232] Thirdly, after the *Tadić* Appeals Chamber Decision on jurisdiction, the view emerged among scholars that serious violations of Common Article 3 and Additional Protocol II in non-international armed conflict were war crimes. The *Tadić* Appeals Chamber Decision and the ICTR Statute also shed light on the drafting of war crimes in the 1996 Draft Code of Crimes. The ICRC and the ILC remarkably accepted the idea of war crimes in non-international armed conflict in 1996. Their work inspired the drafting of article 8 of the Rome Statute.[233] Yet, a rule of war crimes in non-international armed conflict was not widely accepted under customary law at that time.[234]

One may notice that there have been some prosecutions carried out against individuals with respect to acts perpetrated before 1995 in non-international

---

231 Cameron *et al*, 'Article 3', para 522.
232 Australia, War Crimes Act 1945, amended 1988, § 5(c); Netherlands, Criminal Law in Wartime Act 1952, amended 1990, Preamble and § 1(3); Nicaragua, Military Penal Code 1996, art 47; Norway, Military Penal Code 1902, arts 107-108; Spain, Criminal Code 1995, amended 2015, arts 607-614; Thailand, Prisoners of War Act 1955, §§ 12-19. UN Doc S/1994/674, para 52.
233 R. Cryer *et al*, *An Introduction to International Criminal Law and Procedure* (3rd edn, CUP 2014).
234 ibid 27; Sivakumaran (n 81) 475–76; Meron (n 92) 82; D. Shraga and R. Zacklin, 'The International Criminal Tribunal for the Former Yugoslavia' (1994) 5 *EJIL* 360, 366 and fn 20; ICRC, Preliminary Remarks, 25 March 1993, para 4; W.J. Fenrick, 'The Prosecution of War Criminals in Canada' (1989) 12 *Dalhousie LJ* 256, 259 and fn 9.

armed conflict. For example, the Netherlands is active in prosecuting war crimes committed in civil wars in the 1970s and 1980s.[235] Spanish courts are considering prosecuting war crimes committed in Morocco in 1976.[236] The Extraordinary African Chambers in Senegal in 2016 decided that Hissène Habré, the former President of Chad, committed war crimes in the 1982–1990 civil wars. A Canadian court found Munyaneza responsible for war crimes committed in Rwanda in 1994 because in its view article 4 of the ICTR Statute reflects customary international law.[237] Most of these prosecutions are based on national legislation rather than customary international law. For instance, section 8 of the 1952 Dutch Wartime Offences Act clearly provides for violations of 'laws and customs of war'.[238] It is acceptable for these isolated prosecution of war crimes in civil wars by reference to national laws as 'it is the role of the domestic courts to interpret and apply relevant rules of domestic procedural or substantive law'.[239]

Alternatively, a few international practices support prosecution of war crimes in 1980s. In the *Van Anraat* case, Dutch courts charged a Dutch business person, Van Anraat, for war crimes during the Iran-Iraq war in 1988.[240] The Dutch Court of Appeal held that 'laws and customs of war' in its

---

235 Reuters, 'Dutchman put on trial for Ethiopian war crimes in 1970s' <https://www.reuters.com/article/us-netherlands-ethiopia-war-crimes/dutchman-put-on-trial-for-ethiopian-war-crimes-in-1970s-idUSKBN1CT27U?il=0> accessed 5 March 2020; *Public Prosecutor v Heshamuddin Hesam* (Judgment, District Court of The Hague, the Netherlands) LJN: AV1163 (14 October 2005); *Public Prosecutor v Heshamuddin Hesam* (Judgment, Supreme Court, the Netherlands) LJN: BG1476 (8 July 2008), paras 5.1, 5.3, 6.6. See also *Public Prosecutor v Habibullah Jalalzoy* (Judgment, Supreme Court, the Netherlands) LJN: BC7418 (8 July 2008); *Public Prosecutor v Abdullah Faqirzada* (Judgment, Supreme Court, the Netherlands) LJN: BR6598 (8 November 2011), para 40.
236 Spain, the *Sahara* case, see International Federation for Human Rights, 'Universal Jurisdiction Developments: January 2006 – May 2009', 2 June 2009.
237 *R v Munyaneza* (Judgment, Supreme Court of Quebec, Canada) 2009 ACCS 2201 (22 May 2009), paras 131-35, 147.
238 Wartime Offences Act of 10 July 1952, amendments to the law dated 27 March 1986 (Bulletin of Acts and Decrees, 1986, 139) and amendment by Act of Parliament of 14 June 1990 (Bulletin of Acts and Decrees, 1990, 369), replaced by the International Crimes Act of 19 June 2003.
239 *Van Anraat v the Netherlands* (Decision on admissibility, Third Section) ECtHR Application No. 65389/09 (6 July 2010), paras 93-96.
240 *Public Prosecutor v Van Anraat* (Judgment, District Court of The Hague, the Netherlands) LJN: AX6406 (23 December 2005), para 14; *Public Prosecutor v Van Anraat* (Judgment, Court of Appeal of The Hague, the Netherlands) LJN: BA6734 (9 May 2007), para 13; *Public Prosecutor v Van Anraat* (Judgment, Supreme Court, the Netherlands) LJN: BG4822 (30 June 2009).

Wartime Offences Act included Common Article 3 of the four 1949 Geneva Conventions in 'conflict not of an international nature'. Van Anraat complained to the European Court of Human Rights (ECtHR) about the imprecision of the term 'laws and customs of war'. The ECtHR concluded that the Dutch Court of Appeal's interpretation of national law was not a violation of article 7 of the European Convention on Human Rights concerning legal certainty. In addition to this, the ECtHR relied on the *Tadić* Appeals Chamber Decision on jurisdiction in stating that in customary law, a serious violation of Common Article 3 in non-international armed conflict was an international crime in the 1980s.[241] This authority is an isolated decision, which does not contradict the previous point that a rule of war crimes in non-international armed conflict was not well accepted in custom but isolated before the early 1990s.

Isolated examples of national prosecutions and legislation do not significantly weaken the general observation. States did not reach an agreement on criminalising serious violations in non-international armed conflict as war crimes in international law in late 1995. Some practice exists supporting that offences committed in a civil war before the 1990s can be prosecuted as war crimes in international law as we understand it at the present time. Whether this flaw is an obstacle for victims to claim compensation in civil litigation is a separate issue, which goes beyond the focus of this book.

3.4 War Crimes in Non-international Armed Conflict: Were Articles 8(2)(c) and (e) Declaratory of Custom?

When the ICC was being established, States and international organs vigorously debated the scope of war crimes, including whether the law of war crimes applies to non-international armed conflict.[242] This section depicts the evolution of the notion of war crimes in non-international armed conflict under articles 8(2)(c) and (e) of the Rome Statute to show whether a customary rule was codified or crystalised in the drafting, or at the adoption, of the Statute. The drafting history of war crimes is examined following three phases, in the *Ad Hoc* committee, the Preparatory Committee and at the Rome Conference.

---

241 *Van Anraat v the Netherlands* (n 239), para 94.
242 R. Cryer, *Prosecuting International Crimes: Selectivity and the International Criminal Law Regime* (CUP 2005) 45; M. Arsanjani, 'The Rome Statute of the International Criminal Court' (1999) 93 *AJIL* 22, 32.

3.4.1 Ad Hoc *Committee 1995 Sessions*

Two related issues were discussed at the *Ad Hoc* Committee. The first one was whether certain international humanitarian treaty rules formed part of customary law. The second issue was whether violations of these rules could give rise to individual criminal responsibility. After two meetings, the *Ad Hoc* Committee submitted a Report to the UN General Assembly in September 1995.[243] The Report mentioned that:

> There were different views as to whether the laws and customs applicable in armed conflict [...] should include those governing non-international armed conflicts, notably common article 3 of the 1949 Geneva Conventions and Additional Protocol II thereto. Those who favoured the inclusion of such provisions drew attention to the current reality of armed conflicts, the statute of the *ad hoc* Tribunal for Rwanda and the recent decision of the *ad hoc* Tribunal for the former Yugoslavia recognising the customary-law status of common article 3.[244]

The 'recent decision' mentioned here is the *Tadić* Trial Chamber decision on jurisdiction delivered in August 1995. In that decision, Common Article 3 was considered as a customary rule, and serious violations of it were criminalised as war crimes.[245]

The *Ad Hoc* Committee's Report went on to state that:

> However, other delegations expressed serious reservations concerning the possibility of covering non-international armed conflicts and questioned the consistency of such an approach with the principle of complementarity. As regards Additional Protocol II, the view was expressed that that instrument as a whole had not achieved the status of customary law and therefore was binding only on States parties thereto.[246]

The view was expressed that violations of Common Article 3 or Additional Protocol II in non-international armed conflict should not fall within the jurisdiction of the Court.[247] The Committee commented that 'the conduct would

---

243 'Report of the *Ad Hoc* Committee on the Establishment of an International Criminal Court', UN Doc A/50/22 (1995), para 74.
244 ibid (italics by the author).
245 *Tadić* Trial Chamber Decision on Jurisdiction (n 125), paras 57-74.
246 UN Doc A/50/22 (1995), para 74.
247 ibid.

universally be acknowledge[d] as wrongful [...] [, but] there was doubt [...] in respect of whether it constituted a crime'.[248] The Report concluded that most delegations supported the idea of including a rule about war crimes committed in non-international armed conflict in the Statute.[249] Some delegations feared that an 'inherent competence' of the proposed court over war crimes in non-international armed conflict would violate the principle of complementarity.[250]

In the Committee, delegations focused on the customary status of Common Article 3 and Additional Protocol II rather than the customary status of war crimes for violations thereof. In addition, views were divided concerning the customary status of treaty rules applicable in non-international armed conflict. Some delegations had doubts about the customary status of Additional Protocol II as a whole, but not about Common Article 3. And in some delegations' logic, individuals are only responsible for acts that violate international humanitarian rules with customary status.[251] They supported the inclusion of violations of Additional Protocol II in non-international armed conflict, but only if the rule violated was recognised as custom.

The Report indicates that if there were a customary rule of 'war crimes committed in non-international armed conflict' at that time, some of them would not argue that only States Parties to Additional Protocol II were subjected to treaty-based crimes. Doubts about the customary status of war crimes in non-international armed conflict also did not suddenly evaporate one month later in October 1995, when the *Tadić* Appeals Chamber Decision on jurisdiction was rendered. As will been seen below, article 8 of the Rome Statute incorporates part of the *Tadić* Appeals Chamber Decision into its definition of war crimes.[252]

3.4.2 *Preparatory Committee Sessions and Intersessional Meetings: 1996–1998*

From 1996 to 1998, the Preparatory Committee held six sessions and established different working groups.[253] Two working groups dealt with the

---

248   ibid, para 72.
249   ibid.
250   ibid, para 74.
251   This is not the place here to discuss the customary status of international humanitarian law in non-international armed conflict and its relevance with individual criminal responsibility, see Henckaerts and Doswald-beck (n 6) Vol I.
252   *Prosecutor v Milošević* (Decision on Motion for Judgement of Acquittal) ICTY-02-54-T (16 June 2004), para 20.
253   UN Doc A/AC.244/L.5; 'Preparatory Committee on Establishment of International Criminal Court, Provision Agenda', UN Doc A/AC.249/L.1; 'Establishment of an international

war crimes issue. Three intersessional meetings were also held during this period.

3.4.2.1   1996 Sessions

During the first session, views were divided on whether to include war crimes in non-international armed conflict and on the scope of the applicable international humanitarian law in this context. Some States upheld the opinion that war crimes in non-international armed conflict should be included as the 1996 Draft Code of Crimes provided. An Austria's draft text included violations of law applicable to non-international armed conflict in the definition of war crimes.[254] In light of the expansive interpretation of article 3 of the ICTY Statute, France also proposed including 'serious violations' of the laws and customs of war as war crimes in both international and non-international armed conflicts.[255] Italy proposed punishing infringements of the Geneva Conventions in both kinds of armed conflicts.[256] The Italian delegate added that the list of crimes enumerated in article 3 of the ICTY Statute was a useful guide.[257] Egypt's draft included violations of Common Article 3 and articles 4 and 18 of Additional Protocol II as war crimes.[258]

Other States neither expressed views nor intended to include crimes in non-international armed conflict within the jurisdiction of the Court. Singapore did not express a view about the inclusion of violations of Common Article 3 and Additional Protocol II because it was considering the Annex list of article 20(e) of the 1994 ILC Draft Statute.[259] A Japanese proposal limited the context of war crimes to international armed conflict. Japanese representatives said that it was a State's responsibility to ensure their militaries conformed to international law and to prosecute individuals under the national law.[260]

Criminal Court', GA Res 51/207 (1997), UN Doc A/RES/51/207, para 4. The other working groups: working group on general principle of criminal and penalties; working group on complementarity and trigger mechanism; working group on procedural matters; working group on individual cooperation and judicial assistance.

254   Austria, 'Serious violations of the laws and customs applicable in armed conflicts' (2 April 1996).
255   France, 'Draft Statute of the International Criminal Court: Working Paper' (6 August 1996), UN Doc A/AC.249/L.3, arts 27 and 31, 30-34.
256   UN Doc L/2764, 27 March 1996; Italy, 'Proposal on war crimes' (30 March 1996).
257   Italy, 'Proposal on war crimes' (30 March 1996).
258   Egypt, 'Draft: Optional Approaches to the Definition of War Crimes' (29 March 1996).
259   Singapore, 'Amendments to Article 20 footnote 3' (4 April 1996).
260   Japan, 'Proposal on the Definition of War Crimes' (27 August 1996), UN Doc A/AC.249/WP.48.

India and Russia also raised doubts about whether the Court should address non-international armed conflict.[261] The UK representative argued for clearly enumerated criminal acts that violated customary international law. An annex submitted by the UK about applicable customary international law excluded Common Article 3.[262] It appears that at the time the UK doubted whether violations of Common Article 3 in non-international armed conflict constituted war crimes under international law.

Considering different State proposals, the Chairman's informal text included violations of Common Article 3 and Additional Protocol II within square brackets.[263] Square brackets indicate that a consensus has not yet been reached on a proposal. The Chairman's revised text also put the phrases 'whether of an international or of a non-international character' and 'Additional Protocol II' within square brackets.[264] The Preparatory Committee summarised:

> Some delegations expressed the view that it was important to include violations committed in internal armed conflicts given their increasing frequency in recent years, that national criminal justice systems were less likely to be able to adequately address such violations and that individuals could be held criminally responsible for such violations as a matter of international law, [...]. Other delegations expressed the view that violations committed in internal armed conflicts should not be included, that the inclusion of such violations was unrealistic [...], that individual criminal responsibility for such violations was not clearly established as a matter of existing law [...], and that customary law had not changed in this respect since the Rwanda Tribunal Statute.[265]

Similar proposals and arguments for the notion of war crimes were also reflected when the Report of the *Ad Hoc* Committee was discussed in the Sixth Committee of the General Assembly. Delegations claimed that a customary

---

261 UN Doc L/2764 (1996).
262 UK, 'Graves Breaches, Customary international law – annex' (1 April 1996).
263 'Chairman's Informal Text No 4, Article 20*ter*, War Crimes', UN Doc A/AC.249/1996/WG.1/IP.4 (1996); 'Summary of the Proceedings of the Preparatory Committee during the Period 25 March-12 April 1996', UN Doc A/AC.249/1 (1996), Annex I, 65-67.
264 'Chairman's Revised Informal Text No 4', UN Doc A/AC.249/CRP.9/Add.4 (1996); 'Draft Summary of Proceedings of the Preparatory Committee during the Period 25 March-12 April 1996', UN Doc A/AC.249/CRP.2/Add.2/Rev 1(1996), 62.
265 'Report of the Preparatory Committee on the Establishment of an International Criminal Court', UN Doc A/51/22 (1996), Vol I, para 78; UN Doc A/AC.249/1 (1996), para 38.

rule existed regarding war crimes in international armed conflict, whereas divergent opinions existed concerning war crimes in non-international armed conflict.[266]

3.4.2.2   1997 February session

In February 1997, three States and the ICRC submitted proposals to the Preparatory Committee on the war crimes issue. New Zealand and Switzerland's joint working paper proposed serious violations of international humanitarian law applicable in non-international armed conflict as war crimes.[267] The US supported a restricted idea of war crimes in non-international armed conflict, extending war crimes to violations of Common Article 3 but not of Additional Protocol II.[268] The ICRC included violations in non-international armed conflict as war crimes. The ICRC proposal based on the joint working paper was much broader. Relying on the three State proposals, Working Group I on the definition of crimes worked out several texts on war crimes.[269] The final text also included many square brackets in Section C of war crimes, which provided that certain serious violations of Common Article 3 in non-international armed conflict could constitute war crimes.[270]

3.4.2.3   Subsequent Sessions and Intersessional Meetings

In June 1997, Germany convened the first intersessional workshop about the issue of war crimes for NATO experts in Bonn and provided an informal working paper (Bonn Text). The Bonn Text included serious violations of Common Article 3 in non-international armed conflict under Section C and other violations of the laws and customs applicable in non-international armed conflict

---

266 'Summary record of the 26th-30th meetings', UN Doc A/C.6/50/R.26-30 and 48-50 (1995); UN Doc A/C.6/50/R.30 (1995), paras 30 (Hungary), 50 (India), 80 (Argentina), 81 (Georgia).

267 'Working Paper submitted by the delegations of New Zealand and Switzerland' (14 February 1997), UN Doc A/AC.249/1997/WG.1/DP.2.

268 US, 'War Crimes: Proposal', UN Doc A/AC.249/1997/WG.1/DP.1(1997); C.K. Hall, 'The Third and Fourth Sessions of the UN Preparatory Committee on the Establishment of an International Criminal Court' (1998) 92 *AJIL* 124, 128.

269 'Preparatory Committee of an International Criminal Court approved work program for two-week session', UN Doc A/AC.249/1997/L.2 (1997); Working Group I, 'War crimes, Draft Consolidated Text', UN Doc A/AC.249/1997/WG.1/CRP.2(1997); Working Group I, 'War crimes Preliminary Text', UN Doc A/AC.249/1997/WG.1/IP/REV.1(1997); Working Group I, 'War crimes, Draft Consolidated Text', UN Doc A/AC.249/1997/WG.1/CRP.2/Corr.1(1997); 'Decision taken by the Preparatory Committee at its Session held from 11 to 21 February 1997', UN Doc A/AC.249/1997/L.5 (1997).

270 UN Doc A/AC.249/1997/WG.1/CRP.2 and Corr.1 (1997); 'Preparatory Committee on International Criminal Court Concluded Third Session', UN Doc L/2824 (1997).

under Section D.[271] Both sections remained in square brackets. States commented on the Bonn Text. Turkey said the two sections should remain in square brackets.[272] The UK held that

> At present, this [Section C] must remain in square brackets as our review [of the UK's position in relation to internal armed conflict] has not yet been completed. However, [...] there may be a change to their position.[273]

As to Section D, the UK was 'not yet convinced that this section in principle is reflective of customary international law. This section, therefore, should also remain in square brackets in its entirety'.[274] The ICRC, however, commented that the text missed war crimes committed in non-international armed conflict.[275]

The fourth session of the Preparatory Committee and the second intersessional meeting did not develop the issue of war crimes in non-international armed conflict. In that period, some States and the ICRC in the Sixth Committee and the General Assembly also expressed their demands for the inclusion of war crimes in non-international armed conflict in the Statute.[276]

The fifth session in December 1997 was fruitful with respect to war crimes.[277] Working Group I submitted a text on the definition of war crimes.[278] Its draft

---

[271] 'Informal working paper on war crimes and preliminary comments on Bonn's text', UN Doc A/AC.249/1997/WG.1/IP/REV.1.

[272] 'United Nations negotiations on the establishment of an International Criminal Court (ICC): Second Informal Inter-Sessional Workshop for experts from Member States of the Atlantic Alliance with regard to the issue of War Crimes', UN Doc A/AC.249/1997/WG.1/IP.

[273] 'Comments submitted by Partners', Annex to the 'Informal working paper on war crimes', UN Doc A/AC.249/1997/WG.1/IP/REV.1.

[274] ibid.

[275] Preparatory Committee, 'Preliminary comments on BONN's Text', UN Doc A/AC.249/1997/WG.1/IP/Rev.1.

[276] UN Doc A/C.6/52/SR.11 (1997), para 46 (Trinidad and Tobago, speaking on behalf of the 14 State members of the Caribbean community); 'Summary record of the 13th meeting', UN Doc A/C.6/52/SR.13 (1997), para 16 (Costa Rica); 'Summary record of the 14th meeting', UN Doc A/C.6/52/SR.14 (1997), paras 49 (Germany), 55 (Belarus); UN Doc A/C.6/52/SR.15 (1997), para 15 (ICRC); GAOR 52nd session, 23rd plenary meeting, UN Doc A/52/PV.23 (1997), Ethiopia.

[277] Report of the Working Group on the Definition of the Crime, 'Informal Working paper on war crimes' in 'Decision taken by the Preparatory Committee at its session held from 1 to 12 December 1997', UN Doc A/AC.249/1997/L.9/Rev.1, Annexe I; UN Doc A/AC.249/1997/WG.1/CRP.9. Other versions see UN Doc A/AC.249/1997/WG.1/CRP.7; UN Doc A/AC.249/1997/WG.1/CRP.7 Add.1; UN Doc A/AC.249/1997/WG.1/CRP.8; 'War Crimes, Article 20C', UN Doc A/AC.249/1997/WG.1/CRP.9.

[278] UN Doc A/AC.249/1997/WG.1/CRP.9.

article 20C provided five options on war crimes in non-international armed conflict. Option I contained two sections, Sections C and D. Option I proposed removing the square brackets in Sections C and D and added a new restrictive clause before the two sections. The text of Section C was not substantially distinct from article 8(2)(c) of the Rome Statute, while the text of Section D listed 12 acts of serious violations.[279] Germany and the UK both submitted a war crimes text that was similar to Option I.[280] Option I provided the original framework for the final version of articles 8(2)(c) and (e) of the Rome Statute.

Like the proposal in Option I, Option II further suggested inserting another four violations in Section D. Option III advised deleting the restrictive clause of Sections C and D. By contrast, Option IV proposed deleting Section D, and Option V proposed deleting both Sections C and D.[281] Draft article 20C with five options was well supported. Both the Report of the Zutphen Intersessional meeting and the Preparatory Committee's 1998 Draft Statute defined war crimes in non-international armed conflict with similar text and structure to draft article 20C.[282] All these documents with the Report of the Preparatory Committee were transmitted to the 1998 Rome Conference for discussion.[283]

3.4.2.4 Summary

The recapitulation of the drafting works of the Preparatory Committee shows that States' attitudes were changing with respect to criminalising serious violations in non-international armed conflict as war crimes. States switched their positions within months of the delivery of *Tadić* Appeals Chamber Decision in October 1995, despite the scarcity of prosecution practice. It seems that a customary rule of war crimes in non-international armed conflict was crystallised before 1998 concerning serious violations of Common Article 3. But there was no consensus on criminalising serious violations of Additional Protocol II

---

279   ibid.
280   'Reference Paper on War Crimes submitted by Germany', UN Doc A/AC.249/1997/WG.1/DP.23/Rev1; UK and Germany, 'Informal Working Paper on War Crimes Option B' (12 December 1997).
281   UN Doc A/AC.249/1997/WG.1/CRP.9.
282   'Inter-Sessional Meeting from 19 to 30 January 1998 in Zutphen, the Netherlands', UN Doc A/AC.249/1998/L.13; 'Report of the Preparatory Committee on the Establishment of an International Criminal Court', UN Doc A/CONF.183/2 (1998), 19–20.
283   UN Doc A/CONF.183/2 (1998).

and other rules applicable to non-international armed conflict as war crimes at that time.

The US stated that it 'strongly believe[d] that serious violations of the elementary customary norms reflected in Common Article 3 should be the centrepiece of the ICC's subject matter jurisdiction with regard to non-international armed conflicts'.[284] It 'urged' that 'there should be a section, in addition to Section C, covering other rules regarding the conduct of hostilities in non-international armed conflicts'. The US said it was 'eager to work with other delegations to build strong consensus on these matters'.[285] These concluding remarks indicate that in the US's view, no consensus had been reached on the subject matter jurisdiction in early 1998.[286] The US in 1996 had just passed an Act to cover war crimes in civil wars for 'grave breaches' of humanitarian rules.[287]

According to the German 'Working Paper on War Crimes', a consensus was reached on serious violations of Common Article 3 in non-international armed conflict during the third session of the Preparatory Committee in February 1997.[288] The ICRC in December 1997 observed that 'the emergence of *opinio juris* on a customary rule on criminal liability for violations of international humanitarian law committed in non-international armed conflict has recently been recognised'.[289] Indeed, States either supported or opposed the inclusion of war crimes in non-international armed conflict for several reasons. Only some of them argued that war crimes in non-international armed conflict was or was not part of international law. It is less convincing to argue that States' support for the inclusion of war crimes in non-international armed conflict manifests *opinio juris* for such a customary rule at that time. Discussions on war crimes in non-international armed conflict at the 1998 Rome Conference seem to enhance this conclusion and demonstrate the crystallisation of customary rule.

---

284 'Statement, United States Delegation to the Preparatory Committee on the Establishment of an International Criminal Court' (23 March 1998).

285 ibid.

286 US, War Crimes Act of 1996, 18 USC 2441(c)(3), as amended by Military Commissions Act of 2006, 10 USC 948a note.

287 ibid 18 USC 2441(c).

288 'German Synoptical Working Paper on War Crimes: Intersessional Workshop for experts from NATO countries with regard to the issue of war crimes' (Bonn, 24 and 25 June 1997).

289 ICRC, 'Commentary on the Definition of War Crimes Submitted to the Preparatory Committee for the Establishment of an International Criminal Court' (1-12 December 1997), 24.

3.4.3 Crystallisation of War Crimes Committed in Non-international Armed Conflict in Rome: 1998

Delegations debated war crimes in detail at the 1998 Rome Conference. During the Conference, three main issues were discussed with regard to war crimes in non-international armed conflict.[290] The first issue was whether to include provisions on war crimes in non-international armed conflict. The second issue was what acts should be added in addition to violations of Common Article 3 of the Geneva Conventions. The third issue was what the threshold is for war crimes in non-international armed conflict.[291] This subsection focuses on the inclusion issue in general and the threshold issue.

3.4.3.1 The Inclusion of War Crimes in Non-international Armed Conflict
Many delegations in the meetings addressed their positions on the inclusion of war crimes in non-international armed conflict.[292] This subsection looks into the attitude and explanations of States and organisations towards the inclusion of war crimes in non-international armed conflict.

As mentioned above, Working Group I drafted five options for war crimes in non-international armed conflict.[293] Its definition of war crimes was submitted to the Preparatory Committee and later included in the Committee's Draft Statute.[294] After the first round of discussions, the Bureau of the Committee of the Whole prepared a Discussion Paper, which re-organised the five options for Sections C and D to satisfy different concerns about war crimes.[295] The Discussion Paper proposed two options for Section C and two options for Section D. Option I of Section C proposed a list of violations of Common Article 3 in non-international armed conflict, whereas Option II of Section C recommended the deletion of the whole section. The two options of Section D were

---

290 'Summary Records of 3rd-5th meetings of the Committee of the Whole', UN Doc A/CONF.183/C.1/SR.3-5.

291 P. Kirsch and J. Holmes, 'The Rome Conference on an International Criminal Court: The Negotiating Process' (1999) 93 AJIL 2, 7.

292 From the 1st to 23rd meetings, the 1998 Draft Statute prepared by the Preparatory Committee was discussed in the Committee of the Whole. From the 24th to 32nd meetings, the Discussion Paper prepared by the Bureau of the Committee of the Whole was discussed. From the 33rd to 36th meetings, the Bureau Proposal was discussed. 'Summary Records of 3rd-5th, 25th-27th, 33rd-36th meetings of the Committee of the Whole', UN Doc A/CONF.183/C.1/SR.3-5, UN Doc A/CONF.183/C.1/SR.25-27, UN Doc A/CONF.183/C.1/SR.33-36.

293 Chapter 3.4.2.3.

294 UN Doc A/CONF.183/2 (1998), 19–20.

295 'Discussion Paper prepared by the Bureau' (6 July 1998), UN Doc A/CONF.183/C.1/L.53 [Discussion Paper], 205–07.

formulated similar to Section C. After the second round of discussions, the Committee of the Whole further prepared a Bureau Proposal, in which there was no option of removing either section and the square brackets in Sections C and D were deleted.[296] Sections C and D appears to be no longer options but were assumed as belonging clearly under the jurisdiction of the Court.

In the meetings, the majority of European States, Arab and Southern African States, Australia, Canada, Russia, the US, many Latin American States and some Asian States all expressed their support for the inclusion of Section C or both sections.[297] The French delegation said that accepting a restriction

---

296   'Proposal prepared by the Bureau' (11 July 1998), UN Doc A/CONF.183/C.1/L.59 and Corr.1 [Bureau Proposal], 215.

297   'Summary Records of Plenary meetings of the Conference', UN Doc A/CONF.183/SR.2, paras 13 (South Africa), 34 (UK), 54 (Sweden), 66 (Canada), 81 (Republic of Korea), 91 (Slovenia); UN Doc A/CONF.183/SR.3, paras 21 (Czech Republic), 48 (Lithuania), 74 (Costa Rica), 83 (Armenia); 114 (Observer for the European Community); UN Doc A/CONF.183/SR.4, paras 12 (Albania), 57 (Namibia), 66 (Chile); UN Doc A/CONF.183/SR.5, paras 5 (Slovakia), 13 (Brunei Darussalam), 21 (Hungary), 28 (Zambia), 47 (Estonia), 54 (Bulgaria), 61 (US); UN Doc A/CONF.183/SR.6, paras 2 (Belgium), 12 (Ireland), 77 (France); UN Doc A/CONF.183/SR.7, paras 26 (Bangladesh), 74 (Cape Verde); UN Doc A/CONF.183/SR.8, paras 3 (Denmark), 10–11 (Georgia), 20 (Russian Federation), 38 (Belarus), 45 (Bahrain), 62 (Ecuador), 68 (Uganda); UN Doc A/CONF.183/SR.9, para 21 (Philippines).

'Summary Records of meetings of the Committee of the Whole', UN Doc A/CONF.183/C.1/SR.3, paras 13-14 (Netherlands); UN Doc A/CONF.183/C.1/SR.4, paras 40-41 (Netherlands), 54 (US), 57 (Germany); UN Doc A/CONF.183/C.1/SR.5, paras 64 (Italy), 104 (Australia), 106 (Costa Rica), 108 (Canada), 109 (Belgium), 110 (New Zealand), 111 (Czech Republic), 112 (Ireland), 113 (Republic of Korea), 114 (Brazil), 117 (UK), 119 (Norway); UN Doc A/CONF.183/C.1/SR.6, paras 77 (France), 100 (US); UN Doc A/CONF.183/C.1/SR.25, paras 24 (New Zealand), 14 (Austria on behalf of the EU), 31 (Japan), 38 (Mozambique), 52 (Norway), 55 (Sierra Leone), 59 (Azerbaijan), 62 (Trinidad and Tobago), 65 (Mexico), 68 (UK), 71 (Germany), 73 (Botswana), 76 (Croatia), 78 (Australia), 80 (Senegal); UN Doc A/CONF.183/C.1/SR.26, paras 38 (Liechtenstein), 41 (Switzerland), 44 (Lithuania), 51 (Brazil), 54 (Republic of Korea), 58 (Chile), 66 (Mali), 69 (Italy), 72 (Togo), 78 (Cuba), 81 (Portugal), 107 (Ireland), 116 (Georgia), 118 (Lesotho), 123 (Greece), 126 (Cameroon), 131 (Slovakia); UN Doc A/CONF.183/C.1/SR.27, paras 9 (Uruguay), 13 (Colombia), 17 (Finland), 18 (Nicaragua), 21 (Bahrain), 23 (Slovenia), 27 (Hungary), 34 (Israel), 41 (Angola), 44 (Bosnia and Herzegovina), 49 (Denmark), 51 (Czech Republic), 54 (Poland), 55 (Congo), 58 (Benin), 69 (Cyprus), 81 (Gabon); UN Doc A/CONF.183/C.1/SR.28, paras 4 (Ethiopia), 7 (Burkina Faso), 22 (Brunei Darussalam), 26 (Namibia), 30 (Malta), 33 (Romania), 44 (France), 55 (Spain), 58 (Guatemala), 68 (Philippines), 71 (Ecuador), 73 (Andorra), 77 (Guinea-Bissau), 90 (Venezuela), 83 (Qatar); UN Doc A/CONF.183/C.1/SR.33, paras 18-19 (Switzerland), 24 (US), 68 (Germany), 80 (UK); UN Doc A/CONF.183/C.1/SR.34, paras 4 (Sweden), 22 (Trinidad and Tobago), 34 (Spain), 60 (South Africa), 75 (Jordan), 107–08 (Australia), 112 (Mexico); UN Doc A/CONF.183/C.1/SR.35, paras 8 (Sierra Leone); 15 (Italy), 23 (Uganda), 37 (Finland), 41 (Venezuela), 49 (Tanzania), 62 (Ethiopia), 67 (Canada), 68 (Denmark); 73 (Portugal); 76 (Estonia), 80 (Solomon Island), 84 (Botswana); UN Doc A/CONF.183/C.1/

of war crimes to international armed conflict would be a retrograde step.[298] In its view, in practice the 1998 Statute would reflect existing law.[299] But Germany stated that war crimes committed in non-international armed conflicts must be included 'in view of their increasing frequency and the inadequacy of national criminal justice systems in addressing such violations'.[300] Spain also supported the inclusion of the two sections because offences committed in non-international armed conflict should be dealt with and a consensus seemed to be emerging in that regard.[301] Venezuela said: 'what [sic] important was the nature and seriousness of the crimes, rather than the context in which it was [sic] committed'.[302] Bangladesh upheld the insertion of both sections to achieve 'high standards of justice', and urged that the list of violations in Section D should be extended.[303]

Despite voting against the Rome Statute and subsequently declaring that they would not ratify the Statute,[304] the US and Israel showed a positive attitude towards the inclusion of war crimes in non-international armed conflict.[305] The US supported the inclusion of crimes in non-international armed conflict and assisted in ensuring they would be covered by the Rome Statute.[306] The US strongly believed that:

> serious violations of the elementary customary norms reflected in common Article 3 should be the centrepiece of the ICC's subject matter jurisdiction with regard to non-international armed conflicts. Finally, the United States urges that there should be a section, in addition to Section C, covering other rules regarding the conduct of hostilities in non-international armed conflicts. It is good international law, and good

---

SR.36, paras 2 (Norway), 12 (Congo), 30 (Slovenia), 33 (Zimbabwe), 37 (Costa Rica), 39 (Andorra), 42 (Bosnia and Herzegovina).

298   UN Doc A/CONF.183/C.1/SR.6, para 77(France).
299   France, 'Statement by Director of the Legal Department of the French Ministry of Foreign Affairs' (22 April 1998).
300   UN Doc A/CONF.183/C.1/SR.4, paras 57, 60 (Germany).
301   UN Doc A/CONF.183/C.1/SR.28, para 55 (Spain).
302   UN Doc A/CONF.183/C.1/SR.35, para 41 (Venezuela).
303   Bangladesh, UN Doc A/CONF.183/C.1/SR.7, paras 26-7 and UN Doc A/CONF.183/C.1/SR.28, para 40.
304   Israel, 'Statement by Judge Eli Nathan' (17 July 1998).
305   UN Doc A/CONF.183/SR.9, paras 28 (US), 33 (Israel); UN Doc A/CONF.183/C.1/SR.27, para 34 (Israel).
306   US, 'Intervention on the Bureau's Discussion Paper (A/CONF.183/C.1/L.53)' (8 July 1998); D. Scheffer, 'The United States and the International Criminal Court' (1999) 93 AJIL 12, 14, 16; UN Doc A/CONF.183/SR.5, para 61 (US).

policy, to make serious violations of at least some fundamental rules pertaining to the conduct of hostilities in non-international armed conflicts a part of the ICC's jurisdiction.[307]

The US also stressed that concerning war crimes 'it was essential to cover internal armed conflicts, which were the most frequent and the most cruel. That area of law had been developed and clearly established and must be included in the Statute.'[308] In its view, the law of war crime in non-international armed conflict was well established under customary law.[309]

In addition, some States swiftly changed their positions on war crimes in non-international armed conflict. Japan once claimed that the context of war crimes was limited to international armed conflict. In the second plenary meeting, Japan only stated that 'war crimes that have not become part of customary international law should be excluded from the treaty'.[310] Yet, Japan kept silent on the inclusion of Sections C and D. In connection with the statement cited, its acquiescence might be interpreted as indicating that Japan doubted the customary status of some provisions in Section D or that Japan was willing to accept Section D but did not want to do so explicitly. Japan, thus, implicitly accepted that war crimes in non-international armed conflict, in general, had become part of customary law. Likewise, the UK changed its attitude towards violations of Additional Protocol II and 'strongly favoured the inclusion of Sections C and D'.[311] When a new threshold was introduced to limit the scope of non-international armed conflict, the UK even criticised this threshold for its potential effect to narrow the ICC's competence.[312] Russia also appreciated the inclusion of Section C, but it doubted the justification for including Section D.[313] Its suspicion of war crimes in non-international armed conflict was erased partly. This observation shows that these States did not object to war crimes in non-international armed conflict in general but concerned violations of Additional Protocol II.

At the Conference, many intergovernmental and non-governmental organisations also addressed the inclusion of war crimes in non-international armed

---

307   US, 'Statement, United States Delegation to the Preparatory Committee on the Establishment of an International Criminal Court' (23 March 1998).
308   UN Doc A/CONF.183/C.1/SR.6, para 100 (US).
309   ibid; US, UN Doc A/CONF.183/SR.5, para 61 and UN Doc A/CONF.183/C.1/SR.4, para 49.
310   UN Doc A/CONF.183/SR.2/Add.1 and Corr.1, para 44 (Japan).
311   UN Doc A/CONF.183/C.1/SR.5, para 117 (UK).
312   UN Doc A/CONF.183/C.1/SR.33, para 80 (UK).
313   UN Doc A/CONF.183/SR.7, para 20 (Russian Federation); UN Doc A/CONF.183/C.1/SR.28, para 20 (Russian Federation).

conflict.[314] The ICRC noted that crimes committed in non-international armed conflict were crimes under customary law.[315] In its view, 'the Court must have jurisdiction over war crimes committed in all types of armed conflict, international or otherwise'.[316] The ICRC further said that 'many of the acts listed in Section D were recognised as crimes by customary law'.[317]

It should also be noted that more than 20 States objected to the inclusion of Section C, or Section D, or both.[318] Firstly, some States concerned that the jurisdiction of the Court would prejudice their State sovereignty.[319] But some of them would accept the inclusion of Section C or both sections as long as the Court would not prejudice State sovereignty or its jurisdiction was complementary.[320] Secondly, in the first round of discussions, some States worried about the threshold of non-international armed conflict because how the Court would decide the existence of internal conflicts or internal disturbances was unclear.[321] Sudan was in favour of the inclusion of Section C, but it argued that Section D would hamper efforts at amnesty and domestic reconciliation.[322] Turkey called for a threshold of war crimes in both armed conflicts.[323] Sudan and Turkey did not object to war crimes in non-international armed conflict, but they either stressed the practical difficulties in identifying a threshold or claimed a higher threshold to restrain the ICC's competence.

---

314 UN Doc A/CONF.183/SR.2; UN Doc A/CONF.183/SR.3, para 115 (the European Community); UN Doc A/CONF.183/SR.4, paras 67 (League of Arab States), 72 (the Office of the United Nations High Commissioner for Refugees); UN Doc A/CONF.183/SR.5, para 72 (Women's Caucus); UN Doc A/CONF.183/SR.7, para 108 (Huma Rights Watch); UN Doc A/CONF.183/SR.8, para 75 (the Latin American Institute of Alternative Legal Services).
315 UN Doc A/CONF.183/C.1/SR.28, para 108 (ICRC).
316 UN Doc A/CONF.183/SR.4, para 68 (ICRC).
317 UN Doc A/CONF.183/C.1/SR.36, para 52 (ICRC).
318 'Summary record of the 3rd plenary meeting of the Conference', UN Doc A/CONF.183/SR.3, paras 13-14 (Thailand, Vietnam, Syria, Iraq, India, Libya, Saudi-Arabia, Pakistan, Qatar, Sudan, Algeria, Turkey, China, Egypt, Iran, Sri Lanka, Yemen, Comoros, Indonesia, Nepal, Oman, Burundi and Russian Federation).
319 UN Doc A/CONF.183/C.1/SR.5, para 115 (India); UN Doc A/CONF.183/C.1/SR.28, paras 88 (Saudi Arabia), 104 (Libya); UN Doc A/CONF.183/C.1/SR.28, para 9 (Pakistan); UN Doc A/CONF.183/C.1/SR.35, paras 54 (Pakistan), 57 (Qatar); UN Doc A/CONF.183/C.1/SR.36, para 6 (Libya).
320 UN Doc A/CONF.183/C.1/SR.27, paras 60 (Indonesia), 61 (Comoros), 73 (Nepal); UN Doc A/CONF.183/C.1/SR.36, para 20 (Oman).
321 UN Doc A/CONF.183/C.1/SR.4, para 76 (Sudan); UN Doc A/CONF.183/C.1/SR.5, para 107 (Turkey); UN Doc A/CONF.183/C.1/SR.27, para 5 (Algeria).
322 UN Doc A/CONF.183/C.1/SR.5, paras 101-03 (Sudan).
323 ibid, para 107 (Turkey).

Thirdly, some States addressed a variety of other considerations. Indonesia held that acts set out in both sections could be prosecuted as crimes against humanity.[324] India also noted that '[t]here is also no agreement about whether or not conflicts not of an international nature could be covered under the definition of such crimes under customary international law'.[325] Comoros mentioned that the content of both sections should be discussed.[326] Some other States expressed their concerns about the conflicts between international law and domestic law or policy, for example, the reference to 'enforced pregnancy'.[327] Iran, Saudi Arabia and some other Arab States argued that express recognition of a crime in non-international armed conflict would tend to legitimise abortion, which would be in conflict with the religious policy of prohibiting abortion in their States.[328]

Lastly, Iraq and Syria voiced their objections without giving reasons.[329] Thailand was not satisfied with the two sections, while Vietnam strongly advocated excluding them.[330] Some other States objected to the inclusion, while upholding a flexible view for further discussion. Iran and Sri Lanka firmly opposed the inclusion of Section D because it was not an expression of well-established customary law, whereas they were flexible concerning Section C.[331] China initially favoured the deletion of both sections, but it said it was open to any other suggestions.[332]

The observation demonstrates that States objected to the inclusion of war crimes in non-international armed conflict on different grounds. These States worried about specific crimes, the threshold of non-international armed

---

[324] UN Doc A/CONF.183/C.1/SR.27, para 60 (Indonesia).
[325] India, 'Statement, by Mr Dilip Lahiri, Head of the Indian Delegation at the United Nations Diplomatic Conference of Plenipotentiaries on the Establishment of an International Criminal Court' (16 June 1998), para 11.
[326] UN Doc A/CONF.183/C.1/SR.27, para 61 (Comoros).
[327] UN Doc A/CONF.183/C.1/SR.3, para 32 (Saudi-Arabia); UN Doc A/CONF.183/C.1/SR.4, paras 63 (Libya), 66 (United Arab Emirates); UN Doc A/CONF.183/C.1/SR.5, paras 21 (Saudi-Arabia), 71(Iran). However, abortion was not an issue in Jordan, see UN Doc A/CONF.183/C.1/SR.34, para 73 (Jordan).
[328] UN Doc A/CONF.183/C.1/SR.3, para 32 (Saudi-Arabia).
[329] UN Doc A/CONF.183/SR.4, para 18 (Syrian Arab Republic); UN Doc A/CONF.183/C.1/SR.27, para 2 (Iraq); 'Indonesia, Philippines, Thailand and Vietnam: Proposal regarding the Bureau Proposal', UN Doc A/CONF.183/C.1/L.59 and Corr.1, in UN Doc A/CONF.183/C.1/L.74, 14 July 1998.
[330] UN Doc A/CONF.183/C.1/SR.28, para 51 (Thailand); UN Doc A/CONF.183/C.1/SR.27, para 64 (Vietnam).
[331] UN Doc A/CONF.183//SR.5, para 102 (Iran); UN Doc A/CONF.183/C.1/SR.27, para 80 (Sri Lanka); UN Doc A/CONF.183/C.1/SR.34, paras 62-3 (Iran).
[332] China, UN Doc A/CONF.183/C.1/SR.5, para 120 and UN Doc A/CONF.183/C.1/SR.25, para 36.

conflict, and the relationship between the ICC's and their national courts' jurisdiction, instead of objecting to war crimes in non-international armed conflict in general. Some States were uneasy about war crimes in this context being tried by the Court. In their view, the complementarity mechanism reserved assessment of the unable and unwilling exclusively to the Court, which looked like a form of interference with their internal affairs.[333] Their concerns, however, implicitly confirmed their positive attitude towards the prosecution of war crimes in non-international armed conflict by national courts, although they objected to the inherent jurisdiction of the Court over such crimes.

Many of these opposing States also did not insist on their objections. A final compromise formula was agreed that 'enforced pregnancy' was changed to 'forced pregnancy', with the clarification that 'this definition shall not in any way be interpreted as affecting national laws relating to pregnancy'.[334] As will be seen below, the thresholds of non-international armed conflict also made the two sections less difficult to be accepted. Indonesia, Thailand and Vietnam finally all agreed to include serious violations of law in non-international armed conflict as war crimes.[335]

3.4.3.2   Thresholds of Non-international Armed Conflict

Option 1 of the 1998 Draft Statute contained a newly added restrictive clause for war crimes.[336] The provision stated: 'Sections C and D of this article apply to armed conflicts not of an international character and thus do not apply to situations of internal disturbances and tension, such as riots, isolated and sporadic acts of violence or other acts of a similar nature.'[337] This threshold was not adequately discussed in the first round of discussions. The Discussion Paper duplicated the restrictive clause cited above as an opening clause, which was applicable to both Sections C and D.[338] After the second round of discussions,

---

333   ICRC (ed) (n 75). For discussions on the principle of complementarity, C. Stahn and M.M. El Zeidy (eds), *The International Criminal Court and Complementarity: From Theory to Practice* (CUP 2011).

334   1998 Rome Statute, art 7(2)(f).

335   'Proposal Submitted by Indonesia, Philippines, Thailand and Viet Nam', UN Doc A/CINF.183/C.1/L.74 (1998).

336   'Report of the Working Group on the Definition of the Crime, Informal Working paper on war crimes, 18 December 1997' in 'Decision taken by the Preparatory Committee at its session held from 1 to 12 December 1997', UN Doc A/AC.249/1997/L.9/Rev1, annex I; UN Doc A/AC.249/1997/WG.1/CRP.9. See also UN Doc A/AC.249/1997/WG.1/CRP.7; UN Doc A/AC.249/1997/WG.1/CRP.7 Add.1; UN Doc A/AC.249/1997/WG.1/CRP.8.

337   UN Doc A/AC.249/1997/WG.1/CRP.9, 7.

338   Discussion Paper, UN Doc A/CONF.183/C.1/L.53, 205–07.

the restrictive opening clause was generally accepted for Section C. It was later wholly integrated into article 8(2)(d) to limit violations of Common Article 3 in article 8(2)(c).

In the Bureau Proposal, the restrictive clause cited above was relocated to the opening clause of Section D (the first safeguard for Section D).[339] A second safeguard was added to the opening clause of Section D in order to receive delegations' broader support for this section. The Bureau Proposal first added language drawn from article 1(1) of Additional Protocol II:

> It applies to armed conflicts that take place in a territory of a State Party between its armed forces and dissident armed forces or other organised armed groups which, under responsible command, exercise such control over a part of its territory as to enable them to carry out sustained and concerted military operations.[340]

In addition, the Bureau Proposal added a negative threshold of armed conflict, which states: '[n]othing in sections C and D shall affect the responsibility of a Government to maintain or re-establish law and order in the State or to defend the unity and territorial integrity of the State, by all means consistent with international law.'[341]

Delegations discussed the Bureau Proposal for a whole day on 13 July 1998. A few delegations, such as India, continued to insist that the Statute should not apply to war crimes in non-international armed conflict.[342] Turkey was not satisfied when limitations were inserted, and emphasised the exclusion of war crimes in non-international armed conflict.[343] Its concern was more focused on a high threshold for the exercise of the jurisdiction by the Court and the method for maintenance of national security, rather than whether serious violations in non-international armed conflict were punishable as war crimes.

After inserting the second safeguard for Section D and the negative threshold of non-international armed conflict, China did not resist the inclusion of Section D but still had doubts about some subparagraphs listed in this

---

339 Bureau Proposal, UN Doc A/CONF.183/C.1/L.59 and Corr.1, art 5*quarter* War Crimes, 215.
340 ibid 213.
341 UN Doc A/CONF.183/C.1/SR.33, para 7 (Netherlands).
342 ibid, paras 33 (Syrian Arab Republic), 37 (India); UN Doc A/CONF.183/C.1/SR.34, para 48 (Turkey); UN Doc A/CONF.183/C.1/SR.35, paras 2, 4 (Egypt), 54 (Pakistan), 64 (Iraq); UN Doc A/CONF.183/C.1/SR.36, para 6 (Libya).
343 UN Doc A/CONF.183/C.1/SR.34, para 48 (Turkey); UN Doc A/CONF.183/SR.9, para 43 (Turkey).

section.[344] Nevertheless, China at the end voted against the Rome Statute.[345] At the Rome Conference and after, China repeatedly explained that '[t]he definition of war crimes committed during domestic armed conflicts in the Statute had far exceeded commonly understood and accepted customary international law' and said that it 'opposed the inclusion of non-international armed conflicts in the jurisdiction of the Court'.[346] Egypt shared a similar view with China and said that the Statute should only deal with war crimes recognised under customary law. In its view, the content of Section D had not been recognised as customary law except for the paragraph relating to children.[347] Unlike China, Egypt did not show any resistance to the inclusion of Section D and even made a declaration to accept the ICC's jurisdiction.[348] Russia was not satisfied with the negative threshold of armed conflict, and suggested a reference to 'State sovereignty' after the wording 'affect'.[349] But Russia did not vote against the Rome Statute and signed it.

On the other hand, some others criticised the second safeguard for Section D and the negative threshold of armed conflict.[350] Some States argued that by introducing the second safeguard, the Bureau Proposal set up a high threshold for other serious violations of war crimes in non-international armed conflict.[351] Others claimed that the very high threshold would inhibit the capacity of the Court to prosecute war crimes committed in non-international armed conflict between armed groups.[352] The Italian delegation stated that 'the

---

344 UN Doc A/CONF.183/C.1/SR.33, para 40 (China).
345 UN Doc A/CONF.183/SR.9, para 38 (China).
346 ibid.
347 UN Doc A/CONF.183/C.1/SR.35, paras 2, 4 (Egypt).
348 *Situation in the Arab Republic of Egypt* (Decision on the 'Declaration under Article 12(3) and Complaint regarding International Crimes Committed in Egypt', OTP) OTP-CR-460/13 (23 April 2014).
349 UN Doc A/CONF.183/C.1/SR.34, para 82 (Russian Federation).
350 States did not support the requirements, see UN Doc A/CONF.183/C.1/SR.33, para 14 (Austria (on behalf of European Union)); UN Doc A/CONF.183/C.1/SR.34, para 34 (Spain); UN Doc A/CONF.183/C.1/SR.35, paras 8 (Sierra Leone), 114–15 (Croatia, Czech Republic, Estonia, Hungary, Iceland, Norway, Poland, Slovenia and Austria).
351 UN Doc A/CONF.183/C.1/SR.33, para 7 (the Netherlands, Coordinator).
352 ibid, paras 14 (Austria, on behalf of European Union); 18 (Switzerland), 24 (US), 68 (Germany), 80 (UK); UN Doc A/CONF.183/C.1/SR.34, paras 9 (Trinidad and Tobago), 22 (New Zealand), 34 (Spain), 60 (South Africa), 94 (Sudan), 107 (Australia), 112 (Mexico), 114 (Croatia, Czech Republic, Estonia, Hungary, Iceland, Norway, Poland, Slovenia); UN Doc A/CONF.183/C.1/SR.35, paras 8 (Sierra Leone), 23 (Uganda), 37 (Finland), 49 (Tanzania),60 (Lithuania), 67 (Canada), 68 (Denmark), 76 (Estonia), 77 (Romania), 79 (Solomon Islands); UN Doc A/CONF.183/C.1/SR.36, paras 2 (Norway), 30 (Slovenia), 33 (Zimbabwe), 37 (Costa Rica), 42 (Bosnia and Herzegovina), 52 (ICRC). 'Information conveyed by New Zealand on Behalf of the International Committee of the Red Cross' (13 July 1998), UN Doc

acceptability of the two substantial restrictions was contingent on the acceptance of the entire package of provisions contained in sections C and D'.[353] In the spirit of compromise, many States opposing the inclusion of Sections C and D finally gave up their objections.[354] Burundi initially opposed to including war crimes in non-international armed conflict,[355] but finally accepted its inclusion.[356] Sudan even recommended adding a reference to conflicts among armed groups to cover a broad scope of war crimes in non-international armed conflict.[357] The final package deleted the requirement of 'responsible command and control over territory' and included conflicts among armed groups for Section D.[358] The two safeguards for Section D with these slight changes were later incorporated into article 8(2)(f) of the Statute.[359] The negative threshold of non-international armed conflict finally applied to the entire article 8 and was integrated into article 8(3) of the Statute.[360]

Overall, summary records of meetings show that the majority of delegations supported the inclusion of war crimes in non-international armed conflict, in particular, Section C, albeit with different views. Section D is more controversial for its underlying acts and the threshold of non-international armed conflict as opposed to its inclusion in the Statute. In addition, discussions on the thresholds also reveal that war crimes in non-international armed conflict were widely accepted in international law. As Philippe Kirsch, the Chair of the Committee of the Whole, pointed out: 'those reactions [towards the two added restrictions in articles 8(2)(f) and 8(3)] ultimately proved useful, reflecting as they did widespread support for covering internal armed conflicts'.[361]

3.4.4 *Assessment and Conclusions*
This review of the preparatory works demonstrate that the majority of States generally accepted a rule of war crimes in non-international armed conflict.

A/CONF.183/INF/11; 'Sierra Leone: Proposal regarding the Bureau proposal in UN Doc A/CONF.183/C.1/L.59 and Corr.1' (13 July 1998), UN Doc A/CONF.183/C.1/L.62.
353 UN Doc A/CONF.183/C.1/SR.35, para 15 (Italy).
354 ibid, para 31 (Algeria); UN Doc A/CONF.183/C.1/SR.34, para 85 (Thailand). See also UN Doc A/CONF.183/C.1/SR.35, para 35 (Indonesia); UN Doc A/CONF.183/C.1/SR.27, para 80 (Sri Lanka); UN Doc A/CONF.183/C.1/SR.35, para 44 (Sri Lanka).
355 UN Doc A/CONF.183/C.1/SR.27, para 46 (Burundi).
356 UN Doc A/CONF.183/C.1/SR.35, para 20 (Burundi).
357 UN Doc A/CONF.183/C.1/SR.34, para 96 (Sudan).
358 Kirsch and Holmes (n 291) 10; 'Draft Statute for the International Criminal Court' (16 July 1998), UN Doc A/CONF.183/C.1/L.76 and Add.1.
359 1998 Rome Statute, the second sentence of art 8(2)(f).
360 ibid art 8(3).
361 Kirsch and Holmes (n 291) 7.

War crimes for violations of Common Article 3 in non-international armed conflict were generally accepted before the 1998 Rome Conference, while war crimes for other serious violations in non-international armed conflict were crystallised at the 1998 Rome Conference.

An overwhelming number of States generally recognised serious violations of war crimes in non-international armed conflict, despite some States' reluctance to expand its scope at the Conference. Kirsch also concluded:

> [Section C] [...] was supported by almost all delegations. Even some of those delegations that publicly stated that they did not think the statute should apply to internal armed conflicts indicated privately that if it did, they could accept a provision based on Common Article 3. The second section [Section D], which defined the other serious violations of the laws and customs of armed conflict to be governed by the statute, was more controversial. [362]

Considering States' support for the inclusion and their shifts, there is sufficient evidence showing widespread acceptance that in international law war crimes cover serious violations of Common Article 3 and other rules of international humanitarian law applicable to non-international armed conflict. After the adoption of the Rome Statute, satisfaction was also expressed in the UN General Assembly and the Sixth Committee about the inclusion of war crimes in non-international armed conflict in the Rome Statute.[363] Notwithstanding a few States' concerns, it cannot be denied that a customary rule was crystallised to criminalise serious violations of international humanitarian law in non-international armed conflict as war crimes in 1998.[364]

One State expressed its concern that the inclusion of serious violations of Additional Protocol II would cause difficulties for a State that is not a party to the Protocol.[365] This concern cannot be upheld now. Except for Andorra, Marshall Islands and Mexico, 120 of the 123 States Parties to the Rome Statute

---

362 ibid 7 and fn 17.
363 GAOR 53rd session, 10th plenary meeting, UN Doc A/53/PV.10 (1998), Finland; GAOR 53rd session, 22nd plenary meeting, UN Doc A/53/PV.22 (1998), Zambia; 'Summary record of the 10th meeting', UN Doc A/C.6/53/SR.10 (1998), para 14 (Greece); 'Summary record of the 11th meeting', UN Doc A/C.6/53/SR.11(1998), paras 87 (Liechtenstein), 95–6 (ICRC); 'Summary record of the 12th meeting', UN Doc A/C.6/53/SR.12 (1998), paras 42 (UK), 57 (Georgia); 'Summary record of the 12th meeting', UN Doc A/C.6/55/SR.12 (2000), para 34 (Libyan Arab Jamahiriya).
364 Kreß (n 86) 104–09, 175.
365 UN Doc A/CONF.183/C.1/SR.27, para 73 (Nepal).

were also States Parties to Additional Protocol II.[366] States accepted that when becoming a party to the Rome Statute, the situation would not be dependent upon the acceptance of legal instruments defining the substance of such crimes.[367] Thus, the three States will not be bound by Additional Protocol II, but their citizens are obliged indirectly not to exercise conducts of war crimes.

In short, with regard to war crimes in non-international armed conflict, article 8(2)(c) was a reflection of pre-existing customary law, and article 8(2)(e) was a crystallisation of customary law. The two provisions of the Rome Statute were declaratory of customary law concerning war crimes in non-international armed conflict at the adoption of the Statute in 1998.

3.5 Further Recognition of War Crimes in Non-international Armed Conflict: Are Articles 8(2)(c) and (e) Declaratory of Custom?

Post-Rome practice and statements further confirm the establishment of a customary rule of war crimes in non-international armed conflict and the custom status of articles 8(2)(c) and (e).

3.5.1 *Preparatory Commission: Elements of Crimes*

States at the Rome Conference decided to establish a Preparatory Commission for the International Criminal Court to further the operation and arrangements of the Court.[368] There were five sessions of the Preparatory Commission over the course of 1999 and 2000 during which some States submitted proposals and commented on the elements of war crimes in articles 8(2)(c) and (e).[369] By consensus, the Preparatory Commission in 2000 adopted the Elements

---

366   ICRC, 'States Parties to the Following International Humanitarian Law and Other Related Treaties as of 15-Dec-2020' <https://ihl-databases.icrc.org/ihl> accessed 28 December 2020.
367   'Declarations, Colombia' (5 August 2002), para 1.
368   'Final Act of the United Nations Diplomatic Conference of Plenipotentiaries on the Establishment of an International Criminal Court', UN Doc A/CONF.183/10, Annex, Resolution F.
369   C.K. Hall, 'The First Five Sessions of the UN Preparatory Commission for the International Criminal Court' (2000) 94 *AJIL* 773, 776–79; 'List of documents issued at the first, second and third sessions of the Preparatory Commission, held in 1999, Working Group on Elements of Crimes', UN Doc PCNICC/1999/L.5/Rev1, Annex I, the US, Costa Rica, Hungary and Switzerland, Republic of Korea, Colombia, China and the Russian Federation; 'Proposal submitted by China and the Russian Federation on the elements of article 8, paragraph 2(c)(i)', UN Doc PCNICC/1999/WGEC/DP.27.

of Crimes.[370] According to the summaries of the Sixth Committee proceedings: 'all the speakers expressed satisfaction with the conclusion of the finalised draft texts for the Elements of Crimes'.[371] The materials on the drafting of the Elements of Crimes, however, do not contribute anything significant to the debate.[372] The adoption of the Elements of Crimes by consensus and the fact that more than 110 States signed the Statute in 2000 further 'provided clear proof of the international community's commitment' to the recognition of war crimes in non-international armed conflict 'within the shortest possible time'.[373]

3.5.2 *Practice of States*
Before ratifying the Statute, several States passed national laws to bring their legislation into line with the provisions of the Statute. Canada passed the Crimes against Humanity and War Crimes Act, which stipulates: 'crimes described in [...] paragraph 2 of article 8 of the Rome Statute are, as of July 17, 1998, crimes according to customary international law, and may be crimes according to customary international law before that date'.[374] The 2004 UK Manual of the Law of Armed Conflict clearly states:

> Although the treaties governing internal armed conflicts contain no grave breach provisions, customary law recognises that serious violations of those treaties can amount to punishable war crimes. It is now recognised that there is a growing area of conduct that is criminal in both international and internal armed conflict. This is reflected in Article 8 of the Rome Statute.[375]

---

370 Elements of Crimes, ICC-ASP/1/3 and Corr.1, UN Doc PCNICC/2000/1/Add.2. See 'Proceedings of the Preparatory Commission at its fifth session (12–30 June 2000) (summary)' 123, UN Doc PCNICC/2000/L.3/Rev1, para 11; 'Summary record of the 9th meeting', UN Doc A/C.6/55/SR.9 (2000), para 9 (France, on behalf of the European Union, Bulgaria, Cyprus, Czech Republic, Estonia, Hungary, Latvia, Malta, Romania, Slovakia and Slovenia).
371 'Summary record of the 9th-13th meetings', UN Doc A/C.6/55/SR.9-13 (2000).
372 K. Dörmann, 'War Crimes under the Rome Statute of the International Criminal Court, with a Special Focus on the Negotiations on the Elements of Crimes' (2003) 7 *MPUNYB* 341, 396–402.
373 'Summary record of the 11th meeting', UN Doc A/C.6/54/SR.11 (1999), para 31 (Australia); UN Doc A/C.6/55/SR.9 (2000), para 14 (Columbia); UN Doc A/C.6/55/SR.11 (2000), para 19 (Trinidad and Tobago); 'Summary record of the 13th meeting', UN Doc A/C.6/55/SR.13 (2000), paras 1 (Croatia), 34 (Slovakia).
374 Canada, Crimes against Humanity and War Crimes Act 2000, amended 2019, § 6(4); Canada, LOAC at the Operational and Tactical Levels 2001, § 1725.2.
375 UK, LOAC Manual 2004, §§ 15.32, 15.32.1.

The German Code of Crimes against International Law is going even beyond the inclusion of war crimes for non-international armed conflict by almost completely abandoning the distinction between international and non-international armed conflict.[376] Except for a few States that have not enacted or drafted implementing legislation in their national laws,[377] many States Parties have implemented the Rome Statute and the 1949 Geneva Conventions by providing provisions of war crimes in non-international armed conflict.[378]

---

[376] Germany, Code of Crimes against International Law 2002, amended 2016, §§ 8-12; Australia, ICC (Consequential Amendments) Act 2002, §§ 268.69-268.94.

[377] Serbia, Criminal Code 2006, amended 2012, art 376; Peru, Presidential Decree on the National Human Rights Plan 2005, § 3.1.3 A1. 20 States have ratified the Rome Statute as of 1 January 2007. Mexico, Criminal Code 1931, amended 2013, art 149 (ratified in 2005); Estonia, Penal Code 2001, amended 2014, § 94 (ratified in 2002).

[378] Australia, ICC (Consequential Amendments) Act 2002, §§ 268.69-268.94; Belgium, Act of 23 April 2003, amending the act of 16 June 1993 concerning the punishment of Grave Breaches of the Geneva Conventions of 12 August 1949 and their Additional Protocols I and II of 18 June 1977, art 2; Bangladesh, International Crimes (Tribunals) Act 1973, amended 2013, art 3(2)(d); Bosnia and Herzegovina, Criminal Code 2003, amended 2018, arts 173-175, 177-179; Bulgaria, Criminal Code 1968, amended 2017, arts 411-415a; Burundi, Law on Genocide, Crimes against Humanity and War Crimes 2003, art 4; Cambodia, Law on the Establishment of the ECCC, art 1; Canada, Crimes against Humanity and War Crimes Act 2000, amended 2019, §§ 4 and 6; Central African Republic, Penal Code 2010, arts 156-157; Congo, Genocide, War Crimes and Crimes against Humanity Act 1998, arts 4(c) and 4(d); Croatia, Criminal Code 1998, amended 2011, art 91; Finland, Criminal Code 1889, amended 2015, chapter 11, § 5(1); France, Penal Code 1994, amended 2016, § 461-1; Germany, Code of Crimes against International Law 2002, §§ 8(1)-(2), 9(1), 10(1)-(2), 11(1)-(2), 12; Georgia, Criminal Code 1999, amended 2016, arts 411-412; Ireland, ICC Act 2006, § 6(1); Ireland, Geneva Conventions Act 1962, amended 1998, § 4; Jordan, Military Penal Code 2000, art 41; Kenya, International Crimes Act 2008, § 6(4); Latvia, Criminal Law 1998, amended 2013, § 78; Lesotho, Penal Code 2010, amended 2012, §§ 95(1)(c)-(d); Lithuania, Criminal Code 2000, amended 2015, arts 333-344; Malta, Criminal Code 1854, amended 2016, § 54D; Moldova, Criminal Code 2002, amended 2009, art 391; New Zealand, International Crimes and ICC Act 2000, § 11; Netherlands, International Crimes Act 2003, § 6; Nicaragua, Penal Code 1998, art 551; Niger, Penal Code 1961, amended 2003, art 208.8; Norway, Penal Code 1902, amended 2008, § 107; Rwanda, Law Setting up Gacaca Jurisdictions 2001, art 1; Senegal, Penal Code 1965, amended 2007, art 431-3(d); Slovenia, Criminal Code 2008, amended 2009, arts 102(3)-(4); South Africa, Implementation Act 2002, § 4(1); Spain, Criminal Code 1995, amended 2015, art 614; Sweden, Penal Code 1962, amended 1998, § 6; Switzerland, Military Criminal Code 1927, amended 2011, arts 111-112d; Switzerland, Criminal Code 1937, amended 2017, art 264b; Tajikistan, Criminal Code 1998, art 404; UK, ICC Act 2001, § 50; US, Military Commissions Act of 2006, 10 USC 948a § 6(b)(1)(A); Venezuela, Code of Military Justice 1998, art 474; Vietnam, Penal Code 1999, arts 313–314, 336–340, 343; The Socialist Federal Republic of Yugoslavia, Penal Code 1976, amended 2001, art 142.

Enactment of these national laws further confirmed the customary status of war crimes in non-international armed conflict.

National jurisprudence also enhances the customary status of war crimes in non-international armed conflict. For instance, German courts have examined whether war crimes were committed in recent civil wars in Afghanistan, Chechnya, the Democratic Republic of Congo (DRC) and Syria.[379] The German Federal Administrative Court in the *Chechnya* case had to determine whether a person is excluded from refugee protection for committing war crimes in a civil war. The court considered whether war crimes in civil war existed in 2002 by referring to article 8 of the Rome Statute.[380] The Dutch Public Prosecutor charged a Dutch national for war crimes committed during the Second Liberian War (1999–2003), although the charge was dismissed for lack of evidence.[381] In its *Liberation Tigers of Tamil Elam* (LTTE) case, one charge was war crimes in civil wars in Sri Lanka from 2003 to 2010. Referring to article 6(2)(f) of the International Crimes Act, The Hague District Court affirmed that it had jurisdiction over war crimes in internal armed conflict.[382]

In addition, the Constitutional Chamber of the Venezuelan Supreme Tribunal of Justice referred to the Rome Statute and held that war crimes 'refer to various acts against persons and objects that include' 'serious violations of article 3 common' in internal armed conflict.[383] A military court of the DRC relied on the Rome Statute indirectly to decide charges of war crimes committed in its internal armed conflict from 2003 to 2006.[384] Belgium, Finland, Sweden and other States have been engaged in prosecuting war crimes

---

379 *Prosecutor v Ignace Murwanashyaka* and *Straton Musoni* (Judgment, Higher Regional Court, Stuttgart, Germany) 3 StE 6/10 (28 September 2015); *Prosecutor v Ignace Murwanashyaka* and *Straton Musoni* (Decision, Federal Supreme Court, Germany) AK/13 (17 June 2010), paras 3(bb)(1)-(3); *Prosecutor v Klein* and *Wilhem* (Termination of proceedings pursuant to Penal Procedure Code, Federal Public Prosecutor General, Germany) 3 BJs 6/10-4 (16 April 2010), para D.II.4.a); *Prosecutor v Aria Ladjedvardi* (Decision, Federal Supreme Court, Germany) 3 StR 57/17 (27 July 2017), paras II (3)-(4); *Prosecutor v Abdelkarim El. B.* (Judgment, Higher Regional Court, Frankfurt am Main, Germany) 3 StE 4/16 (8 November 2016).

380 *Chechen Refugee* case (Judgment, Federal Supreme Administrative Court, Germany) 10.C.7.09 (16 February 2010), paras 26-27.

381 *Public Prosecutor v Kouwenhoven* (Judgment, District Court of The Hague, the Netherlands) LJN: AX7098 (7 June 2006).

382 *Public Prosecutor v Ramalingam/Liberation Tigers of Tamil Eelam (LTTE)* (Judgment, District Court of The Hague, the Netherlands) LJN: BU9716, 09/748802-09 (21 October 2011), 12–14.

383 *Recao* case (Judgment, Supreme Tribunal of Justice, Venezuela) (27 July 2004), 10–11.

384 *Garrison Military Auditor, Public Prosecutor's Office and civil parties v Kyungu Mutanga* (Judgment, Military Garrison Court of Haut-Katanga, DRC) (5 March 2009), 69–70.

committed in recent civil wars by exercising personal or universal jurisdiction.[385] The absence of objection to the exercise of universal jurisdiction and the support from other States through extradition of suspects, for instance, Chad, Ethiopia, Spain and Turkey, at the very least, indicate their practice of supporting a rule of war crimes in non-international armed conflict in international law.[386] In 2016 and 2018, three African States and Philippines notified the UN Secretary-General of their intention to withdraw from the Rome Statute. And two of them rescinded their withdrawal notifications.[387] The impact of their withdrawals or attempts should not be overstated with respect to the generally recognised rule of war crimes in non-international armed conflict.

Practice of other non-party States also indicates support for war crimes in non-international armed conflict.[388] National laws of some non-party States have confirmed war crimes in civil wars.[389] Some non-party States are preparing

---

385   *Public Prosecutor v Mouhannad Droubi* (Judgment, Svea Court of Appeal, Sweden) B 4770-16 (5 August 2016); *Public Prosecutor v Haisam Omar Sakhanh* (Judgment, District Court of Stockholm, Sweden) B 378716 (16 February 2017) for war crimes committed in Syria. For more details about complaints, investigations, arrests and prosecutions of war crimes committed in non-international armed conflict, see Human Rights Watch, 'These are the Crimes we are Fleeing' Justice for Syria in Swedish and German Courts and Annex, 3 October 2017; FIDH, ECCHR, REDRESS, FIBGAR, 'Make Way for Justice #3: Universal Jurisdiction Annual Review 2017', March 2017; TRIAL, ECCHR, FIDH, FIBGAR, 'Make Way for Justice #2: Universal Jurisdiction Annual Review 2016', February 2016; TRIAL, ECCHR, FIDH, 'Make Way for Justice: Universal Jurisdiction Annual Review 2015', April 2015; International Federation for Human Rights, Universal Jurisdiction Developments: January 2006-May 2009, 2 June 2009; ICRC, Customary IHL Database; *Repak* case (Judgment, Court of Appeal, Norway) 12 April 2010, 15; *Public Prosecutor v Momcillo Trajković* (Opinions on Appeals of Conviction of Momcillo Trajković, Office of the Public Prosecutor of Kosovo) 68/2000 (30 November 2001), Section II (D).

386   For instance, a Belgian citizen involved in the civil war in Sierra Leone, was arrested by Spain.

387   UN Doc C.N.805.2016.TREATIES-XVIII.10, UN Doc C.N.786.2016.TREATIES-XVIII.10, UN Doc C.N.62.2017.TREATIES-XVIII.10, UN Doc C.N.862.2016.TREATIES-XVIII.10, UN Doc C.N.121.2017.TREATIES-XVIII.10 and UN Doc C.N.138.2018.TREATIES-XVIII.10.

388   31 of these non-party States have signed the 1998 Rome Statute.

389   Signature States, see Angola, Constitution of the Republic of Angola 2010, amended 2013, art 61; Armenia, Criminal Code 2003, art 390; Belarus, Criminal Code 1999, amended 2012, arts 134-136, 138; Thailand, Prisoners of War Act 1955, §§ 12-19; Uzbekistan, Criminal Code 1994, amended 2012, art 152; US, War Crimes Act of 1996, 18 USC 2441(c)(3). Further information is not available due to the language of legislation text in Russia, Spanish and Indonesia. States have not signed or acceded, see Lebanon, Lebanese Criminal Code 1943, art 197; Nicaragua, Penal Code 1974, amended 1998, art 551; Vietnam, Penal Code 1999, art 343; Report on the Practice of Ethiopia (1998), Chapter 6.4, Ethiopia's Penal Code.

to accede to the Rome Statute.[390] The amendment of its Constitution for ratification of the Rome Statute and the two *ad hoc* declarations according to article 12(3) of the Rome Statute manifest Ukraine's positive attitude towards war crimes in civil war.[391] Despite its vote against the Statute, Israel did not object to war crimes in non-international armed conflict but expressed concerns about the inclusion of forced transfer.[392] The US declared that it would not ratify the Statute, and Russia withdrew its signature. However, they both have recognised war crimes in non-international armed conflict.[393] Pakistan voted for the Statute, and it did not consider war crimes in non-international armed conflict as an issue.

Rules 102, 151 and 156 of the 2005 ICRC *Study* concerning individual criminal responsibility and war crimes further confirmed that serious violations of international humanitarian law in non-international armed conflict constitute war crimes.[394] The 2005 ICRC *Study* demonstrates that some national military manuals address the issue of war crimes in non-international armed conflict,[395] although some of them limit war crimes to grave breaches in this context.[396] Trials for war crimes before international and national tribunals

---

390   Indonesia is considering joining the Statute. See Nepal, Asian Parliamentarians' Consultation on the Universality of the International Criminal Court, 'An action plan for the Working Group of the Consultative Assembly of Parliamentarians for the ICC and the rule of law on the universality of the Rome Statute in Asia' (16 August 2006), 5. e; Ukraine, Council of Ministers' decision No. 82 of 2003 on Approval of Accession to the Statute of the International Criminal Court (1 April 2003).

391   'Declaration by Ukraine lodged under Article 12 (3) of the Rome Statute' (9 April 2014); 'Declaration by Ukraine lodged under Article 12 (3) of the Rome Statute' (8 September 2015). The Ukraine's Criminal Code simply refers to war crimes in war. See Ukraine, Criminal Code 2001, amended 2010, arts 438, 441, 444.

392   'Statement by Judge Eli Nathan, Head of the Delegation of Israel' (17 July 1998); 'Summary record of the 14th meeting', UN Doc A/C.6/54/SR.14 (1999), para 49 (Israel).

393   GAOR 58th session, 95th plenary meeting, UN Doc A/58/PV.95 (2004), US; US, War Crimes Act of 1996, 18 USC 2441(c)(3), as amended by Military Commissions Act of 2006, 10 USC 948a note; Russian Federation, Criminal Code 1996, amended 2012, art 356.

394   Henckaerts and Doswald-beck (eds) (n 6) Rule 156 and its practice.

395   Australia, LOAC Manual 2006, § 13. 39; Cameroon, Instructor's Manual 2006, § 551; Canada, LOAC at the Operational and Tactical Levels 2001, §§ 1602-1603, 1610; Netherlands, Humanitarian Law of War Manual 2005, §§ 1131-1132, 1134; Sierra Leone, Instructor Manual 2007, at 65; Switzerland, Regulation on Legal Bases for Conduct during an Engagement 2005, § 152; UK, LOAC Manual 2004, § 16.26; Ukraine, IHL Manual 2004, § 1.8.4; US, Military Commissions Act of 2006, 10 USC 948a §6(b)(1)(A) cited in ICRC, Customary IHL Database.

396   Burundi, Regulations on International Humanitarian Law 2007, Part I*bis*; France, LOAC Manual 2001, §§ 44-46; Germany, Soldiers' Manual 2006, R113; Mexico, IHL Guidelines 2009, § 5; Nigeria, The Laws of War States (undated), § 6; Peru, IHL Manual 2004, § 31

support the conclusion as provided under Rule 156.[397] National laws, case law and many official statements from the early 1990s also endorse the view of criminal responsibility for war crimes in non-international armed conflict.[398]

3.5.3 *Post-Rome Instruments and Cases at the ICC and Other Tribunals*

Definitions of war crimes in non-international armed conflict have been adopted to prosecute war crimes in civil war in the following legal documents: Statute of the Special Court for Sierra Leone (SCSL),[399] Law on the Establishment of the Extraordinary Chambers in the Courts of Cambodia (ECCC),[400] the Iraqi High Criminal Court Law,[401] Regulation for East Timor's Special Panels for Serious Crimes,[402] and Statute of the Extraordinary African Chambers within the Senegalese Judicial System.[403] Articles 3 and 4 of the Statute of the SCSL[404] copy article 4 of the ICTR Statute. The Statute of the African Court of Justice and Human Rights includes war crimes in non-international armed conflict.[405] Post-Rome instruments for international and national tribunals further confirm the customary status of war crimes in non-international armed conflict.

The jurisprudence of the two *ad hoc* tribunals after the adoption of the Rome Statute endorses war crimes in non-international armed conflict under customary law.[406] An ICTY Trial Chamber even referred to article 8 of the Rome

---

a; Peru, IHL and Human Rights Manual 2010, § 32(a), cited in ICRC, Customary IHL Database.

[397] Henckaerts and Doswald-beck (eds) (n 6) Vol II.

[398] ibid 372-74, 553–54 and fn 12–14.

[399] Statute of the SCSL, arts 3-4.

[400] Law on the Establishment of the ECCC, arts 6-7.

[401] Iraq, Iraqi High Criminal Court Law 2005, art 13(a).

[402] East Timor, Regulation for Special Panels for Serious Crimes 2000, § 6.

[403] Statute of the Extraordinary African Chambers within the Courts of Senegal Created to Prosecute International Crimes Committed in Chad between 7 June 1982 and 1 December 1990 (African Union-Senegal) (unofficial translation) (2013) 52 *ILM* 1028, art 7(2).

[404] Statute of the SCSL.

[405] Protocol on Amendments to the Protocol on the Statute of the African Court of Justice and Human Rights (adopted 27 June 2014) STC/Legal/Min/7 (1) Rev 1, arts 28D(c) and (e).

[406] *Delalić/Mucić et al* Trial Chamber Judgment (n 153), paras 131-33; *Prosecutor v Furundžija* (Judgement) ICTY-95-17/1-T (10 December 1998), para 132; *Prosecutor v Blaškić* (Judgement) ICTY-95-14-T (3 March 2000), para 176; *Prosecutor v Naletilić & Martinović* (Judgement) ICTY-98-34-T (31 March 2003), para 228; *The Prosecutor v Akayesu* (Judgement) ICTR-96-4-T (2 September 1998), para 611; *The Prosecutor v Musema* (Judgement and Sentence) ICTR-96-13-T (27 January 2000), para 242; *The Prosecutor v Bagilishema* (Judgement) ICTR-95-1A-T (7 June 2001), paras 98-105; *The Prosecutor v Semanza* (Judgement and Sentence) ICTR-97-20-T (15 May 2003), paras 354-71; *The Prosecutor v Kamuhanda* (Judgement) ICTR-99-54A-T (22 January 2004), paras 721-24; *The Prosecutor v Ntagerura*

Statute to justify the consistency between the Rome Statute and the *Tadić* test about war crimes in non-international armed conflict.[407]

Most Situations present before the ICC for consideration today occurred in non-international armed conflict. The OTP of the Court also actively prosecuted serious violations in non-international armed conflict as war crimes, and these indicted include Lubanga,[408] Katanga and Ngudjolo,[409] Mbarushimana,[410] and Al Mahdi.[411] The Darfur Situation referred to the ICC by the Security Council implied the Security Council's willingness to hold individuals responsible for war crimes in internal armed conflicts, despite its mandate to guarantee international peace and security.

The list of war crimes in non-international armed conflict is substantially shorter than that in international armed conflict. In order to narrow the gap between war crimes in international and non-international armed conflicts, Belgium proposed harmonising them at the review conference.[412] At the 2010 Kampala Review Conference, another three serious violations were added to the list in article 8(2)(e).[413] By consensus, the Assembly of States Parties in 2017 decided to insert another three amendments into the list of war crimes in both categories of armed conflicts.[414]

---

et al (Judgement and Sentence) ICTR-99-46-T (25 February 2004), para 766. For further references, see Henckaerts and Doswald-beck (eds) (n 6) Vol II, Rule 156.

407   *Milošević* Decision on Acquittal Judgment (n 252), para 20.
408   *The Prosecutor v Lubanga* (Judgment pursuant to Article 74 of the Statute, TC I) ICC-01/04-01/06-2842 (14 March 2012), paras 531, 571.
409   *The Prosecutor v Katanga & Ngudjolo* (Decision on the confirmation of charges, PTC I) ICC-01/04-01/07-717 (30 September 2008), paras 21, 23-24, 26, 28-32.
410   *The Prosecutor v Mbarushimana* (Decision on the confirmation of charges, PTC I) ICC-01/04-01/10-465-Red (16 December 2011), paras 93, 103-07; *The Prosecutor v Mbarushimana* (Judgment on the appeal of the Prosecutor against the decision of Pre-Trial Chamber I of 16 December 2011 entitled Decision on the confirmation of charges, A Ch) ICC-01/04-01/10-514 (30 May 2012).
411   *The Prosecutor v Al Mahdi* (Decision on the confirmation of charges against Ahmad Al Faqi Al Mahdi, PTC I) ICC-01/12-01/15 (24 March 2016); *The Prosecutor v Al Mahdi* (Judgment and Sentence, TC I) ICC-01/12-01/15 (27 September 2016).
412   'Harmonization of the Competences of the ICC Relating to War Crimes in Case of International Armed Conflict and Armed Conflict not of an International Character', Non-paper of Belgium.
413   Amendment to Article 8 of the Rome Statute of the International Criminal Court, 2868 UNTS 195. See also 'Statement by Belgium', 'Statement by France', in Official Record of the Review Conference of the Rome Statute (Kampala, 31 May - 11 June 2010), RC/11, Annex VI; 'House of Lords debate on the Kampala Amendments to the ICC Statute' (22 July 2010).
414   'Resolution on Amendments to Article 8 of the Rome Statute of the International Criminal Court', Resolution ICC-ASP/16/Res 4, 14 December 2017, para 2 and Annexes.

3.5.4 *Assessment and Conclusions*

All the research about signing, ratification, amendments, national implementation legislation, international and national prosecutions as well as other specified tribunal instruments either echoes the view that article 8 is declaratory of custom about war crimes in non-international armed conflict, or implies that article 8 is generally recognised as a part of the corpus of customary law now. True, some non-party States continue to qualify war crimes as grave breaches of the Geneva Conventions,[415] and some States do not provide for war crimes in national law, not to mention war crimes in non-international armed conflict.[416] These facts are not sufficient to alter the status of current custom. In general, a customary rule is recognised that criminalising violations in non-international armed conflict as war crimes. The two provisions of the Rome Statute continue to be declaratory of customary law concerning war crimes in non-international armed conflict.

3.6 Concluding Remarks

Before the 1990s, the international community did not consider war crimes in non-international armed conflict as international crimes under customary law. In 1993, the UN Security Council adopted the ICTY Statute, which set up the first step for legal development. The Security Council expressly recognised serious violations in non-international armed conflict as a category of war crimes when it adopted the 1994 ICTR Statute. In October 1995, the ICTY in the *Tadić* Appeals Chamber Decision on jurisdiction further contributed to the formation of a customary rule, declaring that the law applied is pre-existing customary law. This Decision has to be seen as a starting point for the formation of a new customary rule.

States generally accepted the rule of war crimes in non-international armed conflict during the preparation and negotiation process of the 1998 Rome Statute. The examination in this chapter shows that war crimes in non-international armed conflict in general were and are part of the corpus of customary law. This chapter concludes that article 8(2)(c) of the Rome Statute

---

415 Somalia, Constitution of Somalia 1960, § 3.5.4.1; Ethiopia, Criminal Code 2005, arts 269–280; Azerbaijan, Criminal Code 1999, amended 2020, art 116; Kiribati, Geneva Conventions (Amendment) Act 2010, § 5; Kazakhstan, Criminal Code 1997, amended 2014, art 2; Sri Lanka, Geneva Conventions Act 2006; Zimbabwe, Geneva Conventions Act 1981, amended 1996.

416 China, Law Governing the Trial of War Criminals 1946, art 3.

was a codification of pre-existing customary law, while article 8(2)(e) was a crystallisation of an emerging customary rule concerning war crimes in non-international armed conflict. The two provisions, in general, were declaratory of customary law in 1998 with respect to war crimes in non-international armed conflict. They continue to be declaratory of custom to the present day.

CHAPTER 4

Crimes against Humanity

Article 7 of the Rome Statute and Custom

4.1 Introductory Remarks

This chapter analyses the relationship between article 7 of the Rome Statute and customary international law concerning crimes against humanity. In 2014, the International Law Commission (ILC) put the topic 'crimes against humanity' on its agenda aiming to adopt a convention on crimes against humanity, and appointed Sean Murphy as the Special Rapporteur.[1] In 2019, the ILC adopted the draft articles on crimes against humanity, together with commentaries, and recommended the draft articles to the UN General Assembly for examination.[2] Draft article 2 defines the notion of crimes against humanity. The first three paragraphs of draft article 2 are a replica of article 7 of the Rome Statute without any substantive modification.[3] The ILC deemed article 7 of the Rome Statute the legal basis for draft article 2.[4] One of its explanations is that article 7 of the Rome Statute has been widely accepted by more than 120 States Parties and 'marks the culmination of almost a century of development of the concept of crimes against humanity and expresses the core elements of the crime'.[5]

Despite the general assertion that the notion of crimes against humanity is accepted under customary law, its contextual requirements remain controversial.[6] Article 7 of the Rome Statute provides contextual requirements of

---

[1] UN Doc A/69/10 (2014), para 266; 'Resolution adopted by the General Assembly on 23 December 2015: Report of the International Law Commission on the work of its sixty-seventh session', UN Doc A/RES/70/236 (2015).

[2] 'Crimes against Humanity' in 'Report of the International Law Commission', UN Doc A/72/10 (2017), paras 34-45.

[3] 'Text of the draft articles on prevention and punishment of crimes against humanity' in 'Report of the International Law Commission', UN Doc A/74/10 (2019), paras 44–45.

[4] ibid, para 44.

[5] 'First report on Crimes against Humanity, by Sean D. Murphy, Special Rapporteur', UN Doc A/CN.4/680 (2015), para 8.

[6] D. Robinson, 'Defining "Crimes Against Humanity" at the Rome Conference' (1999) 93 *AJIL* 43; W.A. Schabas, 'State Policy as an Element of International Crimes' (2008) 98 *J Crim L & Criminology* 953; *Prosecutor v Tadić* (Opinion and Judgment) ICTY-94-1-T (7 May 1997), para 644. Cf. *Prosecutor v Kunarać et al* (Judgement) ICTY-96-23 and ICTY-96-23/

© YUDAN TAN, 2021 | DOI:10.1163/9789004439412_005

'widespread or systematic attack', 'directed against any civilian population', and 'State or organisational policy'. Judge Loucaides of the European Court of Human Rights (ECtHR) wrote: '[a]s regards the elements of crimes against humanity, one may take the recent Rome Statute of the International Criminal Court as declaratory of the international law definition of this crime'.[7] In contrast, Antonio Cassese wrote that: 'on some points, article 7 of the Rome Statute departs from customary law',[8] for instance, the 'policy' element goes beyond what is required under customary law.[9] A critical analysis is required on whether article 7 setting forth these elements was and is declaratory of custom.

This chapter analyses whether article 7 was, and if yes, still is declaratory of custom with regard to crimes against humanity. This chapter focuses on two related issues, the absence of a nexus with an armed conflict and the policy element.[10] The other elements of this crime are discussed when necessary. For this purpose, section 4.2 briefly analyses provisions of the Rome Statute to answer whether article 7 was intended by the drafters to be declaratory of custom concerning crimes against humanity. Section 4.3 elaborates on the development of the concept of crimes against humanity to show that crimes against humanity as defined in article 7, in general, were declaratory of custom.[11] The reiteration also serves to provide a common background for discussing the two contextual elements. Two consecutive sections (4.4–4.5) examine the two elements of crimes against humanity. Section 4.4 discusses the absence of the nexus with an armed conflict and section 4.5 considers policy as a distinct element in article 7 and under customary law. Finally, some concluding remarks are provided in section 4.6 on the nature of article 7 of the Rome Statute as evidence of customary law on these two issues.

1-A (12 June 2002), para 98 and fn 114; G. Mettraux, 'Crimes Against Humanity in the Jurisprudence of the International Criminal Tribunals for the Former Yugoslavia and for Rwanda' (2002) 43 *Harvard Intl LJ* 237.

[7] *Streletz, Kessler and Krenz v Germany* (Merits, Concurring Opinion of Judge Loucaides) ECtHR Application No. 34044/96, 35532/97 and 44801/98 (22 March 2001).

[8] A. Cassese *et al* (eds), *Cassese's International Criminal Law* (3rd end, OUP 2013) 106.

[9] ibid 107.

[10] K. Ambos, *Treatise on International Criminal Law, Vol II: The Crimes and Sentencing* (OUP 2014) 67.

[11] *Prosecutor v Tadić* (Sentencing Judgement) ICTY-94-1-T (14 July 1997), para 8, considering the crime of genocide as a specific form of crimes against humanity.

4.2 Provisions on Crimes against Humanity in the Rome Statute

Article 7 of the Rome Statute defines crimes against humanity. Article 7(1) provides a chapeau with an exhaustive list of underlying prohibited acts of crimes against humanity. Article 7(2) defines some terms used in paragraph 1, and article 7(3) further defines the term 'gender'. The chapeau in article 7(1) stipulates that '[f]or the purpose of this Statute, "crime against humanity" means any of the following acts when committed as part of a widespread or systematic attack directed against any civilian population, with knowledge of the attack'.[12] Article 7(2)(a) defines the term 'attack': 'attack directed against any civilian population' means 'a course of conduct involving the multiple commission of acts referred to in paragraph 1 against any civilian population, pursuant to or in furtherance of a State or organisational policy to commit such attack'.

Similar to article 8 about war crimes, the text of article 7 also does not expressly address whether this provision was declaratory of custom concerning the notion of crimes against humanity. The phrase 'for the purpose of this Statute' merely indicates that the Rome Statute is a self-contained regime. This view is reaffirmed by the 'without prejudice' clause in article 10 of the Rome Statute, which permits a discrepancy between the Rome Statute and customary law. In brief, the phrase 'for the purpose of this Statute' was not relevant to the issue of whether article 7 as a whole was of a declaratory nature. Likewise, as observed in chapter 3, other texts and the structure of the Rome Statute also do not definitively show that article 7 in its entirety was declaratory of a pre-existing custom before the adoption of the Statute.[13]

The preparatory works of article 7 seem to indicate that the notion of crimes against humanity was generally accepted before the 1998 Rome Conference. In discussing the 1996 Draft Code of Crimes in the Sixth Committee, States expressed positive views on whether to include crimes against humanity.[14] In the *Ad Hoc* Committee, discussions focused on the specification of this crime.[15] No State suggested excluding crimes against humanity from the Rome

---

12   1998 Rome Statute, art 7(1).
13   Chapter 3.2.
14   UN Press Release, 'Sixth Committee Hears Differing Views on Code of Crimes against International Peace and Security', UN Doc GA/L/2866 (1995).
15   'Question of the crimes to be covered and specification of the crimes, Rapporteur: Ms. Kuniko SAEKI (Japan)', UN Doc A/AC.244/CRP.6/Add.3 (1995), paras 6-9; 'Report of the *Ad Hoc* Committee on the Establishment of an International Criminal Court', UN Doc A/50/22 (1995), paras 77-80.

Statute.[16] In the Preparatory Committee, the UK, the US and Japan submitted their proposals for crimes against humanity.[17] Discussions in the Preparatory Committee were pertinent to the elements of crimes against humanity in custom. Some speakers said that the definition of crimes against humanity 'lay in aspects of customary international law'.[18] The chair's drafts provided many brackets in the compiled definition of crimes against humanity.[19] Further works focused on defining the elements of crimes against humanity and the list of prohibited acts.[20] The Canadian Minister of Citizenship and Immigration openly stated that crimes against humanity in the Statute are endorsed as customary law in Canada.[21] The ICJ and the Preamble of the ILC's 2019 Draft articles on crimes against humanity provide that the prohibition of crimes against humanity possesses the character of *jus cogens*.[22] As opposed to war crimes in non-international armed conflict, crimes against humanity had been recognised as international crimes under customary law before the adoption of

---

16   'Comments Received Pursuant to Paragraph 4 of General Assembly Resolution 49/53 on the Establishment of An International Criminal Court, Report of the Secretary-General' (20, 30–31 March 1995), and Addendums, UN Doc A/AC.244/1 and Add.1 and Add.2 (1995). See comments of China, 5 March 1995; Czech Republic, 22 March 1995; Sudan, 24 March 1995; US, 30 March 1995. 'Summary of the statement of the delegate of Japan, April 1995'; 'Summary of the Proceedings of the *Ad Hoc* Committee During the Period 3-13 April 1995', UN Doc A/AC.244/2 (1995), paras 32, 36.

17   'The UK Proposal on Crimes against Humanity' (March 1996); 'Japan Proposal Crimes against Humanity'; US, 'Crimes against Humanity, Lack of a Requirement for a Nexus to Armed Conflict' (26 March 1996).

18   UN Press Release, 'Preparatory Committee on Establishment of International Criminal Court First Session 1st Meeting', UN Doc GA/L/2761(1996), Australia and the Netherlands; id, 'Preparatory Committee for Establishment of International Criminal Court, Discussed Definitions of "Genocide", "Crimes against Humanity"', UN Doc GA/L/2762 (1996); id, '"Crimes against Humanity" Must be Precisely Defined Say Speakers in Preparatory Committee for International Court', UN Doc GA/L/2763 (1996); id, 'Preparatory Committee on International Criminal Court Concludes First Session', UN Doc GA/L/2787 (1996).

19   'Report of the Preparatory Committee on the Establishment of an International Criminal Court', UN Doc A/51/22 (1996), Vol I, paras 82-102; 'Compilation of Proposals', UN Doc A/51/22 (1996), Vol II, 65–69.

20   C.K. Hall, 'The First Two Sessions of the UN Preparatory Committee on the Establishment of an International Criminal Court' (1998) 91 *AJIL* 177, 180; id, 'The Third and Fourth Sessions of the UN Preparatory Committee on the Establishment of an International Criminal Court' (1998) 92 *AJIL* 124, 126–27.

21   *Sapkota v Canada*, [2013] FC 790, para 28.

22   *Jurisdictional Immunities of the State (Germany v Italy: Greece Intervening)*, Judgment, [2012] ICJ Rep 99, 141, para 95; 'Peremptory norms of general international law (*jus cogens*)' in 'Report of the International Law Commission', UN Doc A/74/10 (2019), para 57; 'Prevention and punishment of crimes against humanity', UN Doc A/74/10 (2019), para 45, commentary (5) to the preamble.

the Rome Statute.[23] Leena Grover also concluded that the provision on crimes against humanity in the Rome Statute was, in general, a codification of existing customary international law.[24] Observations in the next section further support such a preliminary finding.

4.3 Crimes against Humanity as International Crimes under Customary Law

This section first examines the origin of crimes against humanity to show that the concept was created by the Nuremberg Charter and that the crime was generally accepted as an international crime under customary law before 1998.[25] It then goes on to analyse various definitions of crimes against humanity to demonstrate that the divergences in the definitions of crimes against humanity do not negatively affect the customary status of this crime in international law.

4.3.1 Revisiting the Origin of Crimes against Humanity as International Crimes

The notion of crimes against humanity as international crimes was defined by the Nuremberg Charter. Article 6(c) of the Nuremberg Charter provided that:

> Crimes against Humanity: namely, murder, extermination, enslavement, deportation, and other inhumane acts committed against any civilian population, before or during the war, or persecutions on political, racial or religious grounds in execution of or in connection with any crime within the jurisdiction of the Tribunal, whether or not in violation of the domestic law of the country where perpetrated.[26]

---

23 For further national legislation and prosecution of crimes against humanity after World War II, see M.C. Bassiouni, *Crimes Against Humanity: Historical Evolution and Contemporary Application* (CUP 2011) 660–723.

24 L. Grover, *Interpreting Crimes in the Rome Statute of the International Criminal Court* (CUP 2014) 220–344.

25 *Prosecutor v Tadić* (Interlocutory Appeal Decision on Jurisdiction) ICTY-94-1-AR72 (2 October 1995), para 141; id, (Judgement) ICTY-94-1-A (15 July 1999), para 251; *Tadić* Opinion and Judgment (n 6), paras 618-23; UN Doc A/CN.4/680 (2015), para 51; Y. Dinstein, 'Case Analysis: Crimes Against Humanity after *Tadić*' (2000) 13 *LJIL* 373.

26 Nuremberg Charter, art 6(c), as amended by the Semi-colon Protocol.

The prohibited acts are not listed exhaustively[27] and are generally classified into two types: a murder type and a persecution type.[28] The former type includes all prohibited acts except for persecution.

In academia, there are debates about whether the concept of crimes against humanity was a creation of the Nuremberg Charter. One theory claims that the notion of this crime was created by the four powers (the UK, the US, France and the USSR).[29] The other theory argues that this concept was a codification of a pre-existing customary rule.[30] An American Military Tribunal in the *Justice* case was aware of the challenge to this new crime and argued that this concept had existed under customary law.[31] The Tribunal in the *Justice* case referred to academic writing of Charles Hyde and of Lassa Oppenheim, political messages before World War II, and the UK Chief Prosecutor's words before the IMT and the 1946 General Assembly Resolution regarding genocide. The Tribunal concluded that the notion of crimes against humanity (in particular, persecution) was the product of customary law before World War II.[32] The argumentation of the second theory, however, does not seem persuasive.

In contrast to war crimes with some precedents before World War II, crimes against humanity were first punished as a separate type of international crimes by the IMT.[33] After World War I, references to 'the laws of humanity' were made to the Preamble of the 1899 and 1907 Hague Conventions (Martens

---

27   'The Charter and Judgment of the Nuremberg Tribunal – History and Analysis: Memorandum submitted by the Secretary-General', UN Doc A/CN.4/5 (1949), 67, 81.
28   E. Schwelb, 'Crimes Against Humanity' (1946) 23 *British Ybk Intl L* 178, 191–95; United Nations War Crimes Commission (ed), *History of the United Nations War Crimes Commission and the Development of the Laws of War* (HMSO 1948) 178.
29   *Tadić* Opinion and Judgment (n 6), para 628; W.A. Schabas, *Unimaginable Atrocities Unimaginable Atrocities: Justice, Politics, and Rights at the War Crimes Tribunals* (OUP 2012) 53–54; *Polyukhovich v Commonwealth* (Order, High Court) [1991] HCA 32 (14 August 1991). See also L. Green, 'Canadian Law, War Crimes and Crimes Against Humanity' (1989) 59 *British Ybk Intl L* 217, 225–26; J. Kunz, 'The United Nations Convention on Genocide' (1949) 43 *AJIL* 738, 742.
30   *France et al v Göring et al*, Attorney General Sir Hartley Shawcross's Opening Speech (4 December 1945), (1948) 3 TMWC 91, 92; *Attorney General v Eichmann* (Judgment, District Court of Jerusalem, Israel) (11 November 1961), (1968) 36 ILR 5, 283.
31   *US v Altstötter et al* [The *Justice* case], (1951) 3 TWC 1, 966–68. See also *US v von Leeb et al* [The *High Command* case], (1950) 11 TWC 1, 476; *US v List et al* [The *Hostage* case], (1950) 11 TWC 757, 1239; *US v Flick et al* [The *Flick* case], (1952) 6 TWC 1, 1189; *US v Krupp et al* [The *Krupp* case], (1950) 9 TWC 1, 1331; *US v Ohlendorf et al* [The *Einsatzgruppen* case], (1950) 4 TWC 1, 154.
32   The *Justice* case, ibid 959–71.
33   Nuremberg Charter, art 6(c); UN Doc S/25704 (1993), para 47.

Clause). The Martens Clause in the Hague Conventions speaks of 'the laws of humanity, and the dictates of the public conscience'.[34] At that time, the laws of humanity were confined to the context of a war between States. The phrase 'the laws of humanity' was not used in a technical legal sense to formulate a separate set of rules different from the 'laws and customs of war'. Violations of 'the laws of humanity' would be deemed a category of 'war crimes' rather than a new crime at that time.

On 28 May 1915, the governments of France, Great Britain and Russia made a Declaration with respect to the offences committed by Turkey against Armenians.[35] The 1915 Declaration about the Armenian atrocities provided that:

> En présence de ces nouveaux crimes de la Turquie contre l'humanité et la civilisation [these new crimes of Turkey against humanity], les Gouvernements alliés font savoir publiquement à la Sublime Porte qu'ils tiendront personnellement responsables des dits crimes tous les membres du Gouvernement ottoman ainsi que ceux de ses agents qui se trouveraient impliqués dans de pareils massacres.[36]

This declaration referred to violations of the laws of humanity in the territory of a State (Turkey). Most scholars deemed this declaration the first expression of 'crimes against humanity' in a document of political and legal significance.[37] The reference to 'crimes of Turkey against humanity' in that context remained in common usage, which was a non-technical term and referred to moral condemnations. This declaration might be considered as the seed of the modern idea of prosecuting inhumane acts committed by a government against its citizens, which are internationally condemned.[38]

---

34   The Martens Clause states: 'Until a more complete code of the laws of war has been issued, the High Contracting Parties deem it expedient to declare that, in cases not included in the Regulations adopted by them, the inhabitants and the belligerents remain under the Protection and the rule of the principles of the law of nations, as they result from the usages established among civilized peoples, from the laws of humanity, and the dictates of the public conscience.'
35   M.C. Bassiouni, *Introduction to International Criminal Law: 2nd Revised Edition* (Brill | Nijhoff 2013) 544.
36   It was quoted in the Armenian Memorandum presented by the Greek Delegation to the Commission on Responsibilities, Conference of Paris, 14 March 1919, as reproduced in UNWCC (ed) (n 28) 35 (translation added); Schwelb (n 28) 181.
37   Cf. Schabas (n 29) 53.
38   ibid.

The 1919 Commission on Responsibilities, established after World War I, considered violations of the laws of humanity as a category of offences.[39] It is unclear whether the Commission deemed the notion of 'offences against the laws of humanity' an independent offence as opposed to war crimes.[40] At the Paris Peace Conference, States upheld different views about the offences against 'the laws of humanity' recommended by the Commission on Responsibilities.[41] The Memorandum of the UK supported prosecution of offences against the laws of humanity.[42] However, the US, which later insisted on crimes against humanity as a part of the mandate of the IMT,[43] strongly objected to the reference to 'the laws or principles of humanity'. The US delegation argued that this reference was a moral standard. In its view, 'there is no fixed and universal standard of humanity', and such breaches were not recognised in international law applicable at that time.[44] Japan also opposed prosecuting offences against the laws of humanity.[45] Finally, the reference to 'the laws of humanity' was omitted in the 1919 Treaty of Versailles. There was no charge of offences against the laws of humanity in the German Leipzig trials.

The 1920 Treaty of Sèvres also proposed prosecuting Turkish nationals, including those people whose victims were subjects of the Ottoman (Turkey) Empire, victims of the genocide of the Armenian people.[46] This idea might be the 'embryo' that was later called crimes against humanity.[47] Eventually, the Treaty of Sèvres was not ratified. There was also no actual prosecution based on this treaty, despite some charges for this crime. This treaty later was replaced by the 1923 Treaty of Lausanne, which did not contain a provision on

---

39   'Commission on the Responsibility of the Authors of the War and on Enforcement of Penalties, Report Presented to the Preliminary Peace Conference' reprinted in (1920) 14 *AJIL* 95, 121.
40   ibid 135; UNWCC (ed) (n 28) 35–36.
41   Report of the Commission on Responsibilities (n 39) Annex IV, art 1; Annex II, 135-36, 144-45 and Annex III.
42   Schabas (n 29) 53.
43   'Report of the President by Mr. Justice Jackson, June 6, 1945' in *Report of Robert H. Jackson, United States Representative to the International Conference on Military Trials* (USGPO 1949) 50–51.
44   'Memorandum of Reservations Presented by the Representatives of the United States to the Report of on the Commission on Responsibilities, 4 April 1919', annexed in Report of the Commission on Responsibilities (n 39) 135–36, 144, 146.
45   Bassiouni (n 35) 544.
46   Treaty of Peace between the Allied and Associated Powers and the Ottoman Empire [Treaty of Sèvres], (1920) UKTS 11, arts 215, 230; W.A. Schabas, *An Introduction to the International Criminal Court* (6th edn, CUP 2020) 4.
47   Schabas, ibid.

prosecuting Turkish nationals for this crime.[48] Cherif Bassiouni commented that political concerns prevailed over the pursuit of justice at that time.[49]

The definition of crimes against humanity was not further developed until the 1945 Nuremberg Charter. According to a 'Draft Statute for the Permanent International Criminal Court', presented at the 1924 ILA Conference by Huge Bellot, 'all offences committed contrary to the laws of humanity and the dictates of public conscience' was included in the jurisdiction of a proposed court.[50] The 1943 United Nations War Crimes Commission (UN War Crimes Commission) observed that the crimes committed against its population in Ethiopia during 1935–36 by the Italian government were qualified as war crimes and crimes against humanity.[51] Many official and semi-official declarations were issued concerning crimes against humanity, including the 1943 resolution passed by the London International Assembly.[52] These practices still do not support the existence of what are now called 'crimes against humanity' as opposed to war crimes.

The international prosecution of crimes against humanity first occurred after the end of World War II. There were discussions on crimes against humanity in the UN War Crimes Commission. Desiring to prosecute atrocities committed in Axis territory, including Germany and Austria, as well as in Axis satellite countries, such as Hungary and Romania, against nationals of those countries, in particular, the Jewish population, the UN War Crimes Commission intended to extend international crimes to cover offences not constituting war crimes *stricto sensu*.[53] The US representative designated the 'offences perpetrated on religious or racial grounds against stateless persons or against any persons' as 'crimes against humanity' which were 'justifiable as war crimes'. These offences 'were crimes against the foundations of civilisation, irrespective of place and time, and irrespective of the question as to whether they did or did not represent violations of the laws and customs of war'.[54]

---

48   Treaty of Peace with Turkey [Treaty of Lausanne], 28 LNTS 11; Bassiouni (n 23) 93–94.
49   Bassiouni (n 35) 544; M.C. Bassiouni, *The Perennial Conflict Between International Criminal Justice and Realpolitik* (2006) 22 *Ga St U L Rev* 541; M.C. Bassiouni, *Justice and Peace: The Importance of Choosing Accountability Over Realpolitik* (2003) 35 *Case W Res J Intl L* 191; M.C. Bassiouni, *Searching for Justice in the World of Realpolitik* (2000) 12 *Pace Intl L Rev* 213.
50   Nationality and Naturalisation Committee, 'Draft Statute for the Permanent International Criminal Court, by Huge Bellot' in International Law Association Report of the 33rd Conference (Stockholm 1924) (ILA, London 1924) 81, art 25 (2).
51   UNWCC (ed) (n 28) 189–90.
52   ibid 190–91.
53   ibid 11.
54   ibid 175. See also 'Statement by the President, March 24, 1944' in Report of Robert H. Jackson (n 43) 13.

Representatives of Czechoslovakia and the Netherlands supported this proposal because for them these offences were a matter of international concern.[55] In contrast, the British, Greek and Norwegian representatives objected to such an idea. They argued that the competence of the UN War Crimes Commission was limited to the punishment of 'war crimes', no matter how compelling it was that the other offences should be punished. In 1944, the Legal Committee of the UN War Crimes Commission, mandated to give legal opinions, submitted a draft resolution to the Commission and recommended that crimes against individuals on the ground of their race or religion should be considered as war crimes in a wider sense.[56] The British government insisted that the 'activities of the Commission should be restricted to the investigation of war crimes *stricto sensu* of which the victims have been Allied nationals'. As to crimes against Axis nationals, the perpetrators 'would one day have the punishment which their actions deserve'.[57] Given these different opinions, the UN War Crimes Commission abandoned the idea of adding another category of crimes to war crimes.[58]

In short, during this period, the UN War Crimes Commission considered 'crimes against humanity' as 'war crimes' in a broader, non-technical sense. No agreement was reached among States concerning persecution on religious, racial or political grounds in Axis territory until the Nuremberg Charter, which first recognised crimes against humanity as a separate type of international crimes.[59] In November 1945, the issue of crimes against humanity was raised again in the UN War Crimes Commission. By referring to the Nuremberg Charter, the Norwegian delegation suggested including 'crimes against humanity' as a category of war crimes in a wider sense. Many members of the UN War Crimes Commission supported this proposal, and there was no vote opposing.[60] The change of the Commission's attitude was mainly due to the Nuremberg Charter.

As examined in chapter 3 about war crimes, the UK, the US, France and the USSR adopted the London Agreement to which is annexed the Nuremberg

---

55 'Notes on Fifth Meeting of Committee III' (27 March 1944).
56 UNWCC (ed) (n 28) 75–76. See Schwelb (n 28) 179–80; The *Flick* case (n 31) 1187–212; The *Hostage* case, (1950) 11 TWC 757; *UK v Bruno Tesch et al* [The *Zyklon B* case] (1947) 1 LRTWC 93; *UK v Josef Kramer et al* [The *Belsen* case] (1947) 2 LRTWC 1; *The Prosecutor v Ongwen* (Decision on the confirmation of charges, PTC II) ICC-02/04-01/15-422-Red (23 March 2016), paras 69, 74, 79, 84.
57 UNWCC (ed) (n 28) 176.
58 ibid.
59 Nuremberg Charter, art 6(c).
60 UNWCC (ed) (n 28) 177; 'Minutes of Ninety-first Meeting, 9 January 1946', M. 91.

Charter in August 1945.[61] In the final days of the London Conference in 1945, the American delegate Robert Jackson proposed renaming the category of 'atrocities, persecutions and deportations' as 'crimes against humanity'.[62] Article 6(c) of the Nuremberg Charter first designed crimes against humanity as a distinct international crime to cover offences that are related to war but not wholly covered by war crimes.[63] The term 'crimes against humanity' was also employed in the judgment of the IMT.[64] In the IMT, 17 of the 24 defendants were indicted for crimes against humanity, and 15 of the 17 indicted were convicted of this crime. The IMT did not examine the legality of its inclusion and the pre-existence of the crime, as the defences did not challenge crimes against humanity as an innovation. Assuming the issue of retroactive application of the law was put before the IMT, two approaches might have been available for this tribunal. The first approach was used by the IMT to justify its prosecution for crimes against peace. The IMT held that retroactive prosecution could be morally justified in order to pursue 'substantive justice' at that time.[65] The second approach, as adopted by the military tribunal in the *Justice* case, was to argue that the definition of crimes against humanity was not an innovation but a reflection of a pre-existing customary rule.[66] This approach was employed by the IMT to justify its prosecution of war crimes.[67]

It appears that the IMT might have adopted the first approach to admit the creation of this new crime and justify its prosecution on grounds of substantive justice.[68] As Jackson stated at the London Conference:

> It has been a general principle of foreign policy of our Government from time immemorial that the internal affairs of another government are not ordinarily our business; that is to say, the way Germany treats its

---

61   London Agreement.
62   Schabas (n 29) 51; 'Minutes of Conference Session of July 23, 1945' and 'Revision of Definition of "Crimes" submitted by American Delegation, July 31, 1945' and 'Minutes of Conference Session of August 2, 1945' in Report of Robert H. Jackson (n 43) 332–33, 395, 399–419, 416.
63   M.C. Bassiouni, *Crimes Against Humanity in International Criminal Law* (Martinus Nijhoff Publishers 1992) 114–19.
64   Nuremberg Charter, art 6(c); *France et al v Göring et al*, Judgment and Sentence of the Nuremberg International Military Tribunals, (1948) 1 TMWC 171, 254.
65   ibid 219.
66   The *Justice* case (n 31) 966–68.
67   *France et al v Göring et al* (n 64) 253–54. UN Doc A/CN.4/5 (1949), 61–64.
68   Schabas (n 29) 49–50.

inhabitants, or any other country treats its inhabitants, is not our affair any more than it is the affair of some other government to interpose itself in our problems.[69]

Following the adoption of the Nuremberg Charter, in his letter to a legal officer in the Foreign Office, Hersch Lauterpacht described 'crimes against humanity' as an 'innovation'.[70] In addition, the 1991 UK War Crimes Act limited the jurisdiction to 'war crimes' committed between 1939 and 1945, leaving the issue of crimes against humanity untouched. The UK Parliament explained that 'in 1939 there was no internationally accepted definition of crimes against humanity [...] [,] while the moral justification for trying crimes against humanity at Nuremberg is understandable, the legal justification is less clear'.[71] In short, despite having some roots in international law, the notion of crimes against humanity as a category of international crimes was created by the drafters of the Nuremberg Charter.[72] Some subsequent national cases also endorsed this idea indirectly.[73]

On the whole, the concept of crimes against humanity existed before World War II. At the outset, this concept was not designed as a distinct international crime but as part of war crimes in either a strict sense or a broader sense. The above observation suggests that the notion of crimes against humanity in the Nuremberg Charter, as an international crime, was a creation of its drafters. Crimes against humanity as a separate type of international crimes were also first punished by the IMT.[74] The notion of crimes against humanity embedded in the Nuremberg Charter was the landmark for the formation of customary law.

After article 6(c) of the Nuremberg Charter and prior to the adoption of the Rome Statute, other international instruments formulated various definitions of crimes against humanity, for instance, article 5(c) of the Tokyo Charter,

---

69 'Minutes of Conference Session of July 23, 1945' in Report of Robert H. Jackson (n 43) 331.
70 Hersch Lauterpacht to Patrick Dean, 30 August 1945, FO 371/51034, cited in E. Lauterpacht, *The Life of Hersch Lauterpacht* (CUP 2010) 273–74, and quoted in Schabas (n 29) 58.
71 T. Hetherington and W. Chalmers, *War Crimes: Report of the War Crimes Inquiry*, Command Paper 744 (HMSO 1989), paras 5.43 and 6.44.
72 'Minutes of Conference Session of July 23, 1945' in Report of Robert H. Jackson (n 43) 332–33.
73 *R v Finta* (Judgment, Supreme Court), [1994] 1 SCR 701; *Polyukhovich* case (n 29), paras 62–63.
74 Nuremberg Charter, art 6(c); UN Doc S/25704 (1993), para 47.

article 11(1)(a) of Control Council Law No. 10, the ILC's Nuremberg Principles adopted in 1950,[75] articles 5 and 3 of the ICTY and ICTR Statutes, and the ILC's texts of the Draft Code of Crimes. Crimes against humanity were also confirmed by the 1946 General Assembly Resolution. The notion of crimes against humanity was generally recognised as part of customary law before the adoption of the Rome Statute.[76]

After the adoption of the Rome Statute, there were other international and national definitions of crimes against humanity adopted in the Statute of the Special Court for Sierra Leone (SCSL),[77] Law of the Extraordinary Chambers in the Courts of Cambodia (ECCC),[78] the Iraqi High Criminal Court Law,[79] Regulation for Special Panels of Serious Crimes in East Timor,[80] the amended Bangladesh International Crimes (Tribunals) Act[81] and the Statute of the Extraordinary African Chambers within the Senegalese Judicial System.[82] Other international and national cases prosecuting crimes against humanity as international crimes after World War II further enhance its customary status.[83] The work of the ILC on crimes against humanity shares the same feature.[84] Article 7 of the Rome Statute, in general, was and is declaratory of customary law about the notion of crimes against humanity.

---

75   UN Doc A/RES/94 (I) (1946); UN Doc A/RES/95 (I) (1946); 'Report of the Committee on the plans for the formulation of the principles of the Nuremberg Charter and judgment' (17 June 1947), UN Doc A/AC.10/52, para 2.
76   UN Doc A/RES/217 (III) A (1948); Convention for the Protection of Human Rights and Fundamental Freedoms (as amended) [ECHR], art 7(2); UN Doc S/25704 (1993), para 35; *Tadić* Appeals Chamber Decision on Jurisdiction (n 25), para 141.
77   Statute of the SCSL, art 6(1).
78   Law on the Establishment of the ECCC, art 5.
79   Iraq, Iraqi High Criminal Court Law 2005, art 12.
80   East Timor, Regulation for Special Panels for Serious Crimes 2000, § 5.
81   Bangladesh, International Crimes (Tribunals) Act 1973, as amended 2013, § 3(2)(a).
82   Statute of the Extraordinary African Chambers within the Senegalese Judicial System, arts 4(b) and 6.
83   Identifying crimes against humanity as one of the 'most frequently cited candidates for the status of *jus cogens*', see UN Doc A/CN.4/L.682 and Corr.1 (2006), para 374; *Almonacid Arellano et al v Chile* (Judgment, Preliminary Objections, Merits, Reparations and Costs, Inter-American CtHR), Series C No 154 (26 September 2006), para 96; *Jurisdictional Immunities of the State* Judgment (n 22), 141, para 95; *Tadić* Opinion and Judgment (n 6), paras 618-23; UN Doc A/CN.4/680 (2015), para 51.
84   'Topical summary of the discussion held in the Sixth Committee of the General Assembly during its seventy-second session, prepared by the Secretariat', UN Doc A/CN.4/713 (2018), para 93; 'Third report on Crimes against Humanity, by Sean D. Murphy, Special Rapporteur', UN Doc A/CN.4/704 (2017), para 3; UN Doc A/74/10 (2019), para 44.

4.3.2 The Definitions of Crimes against Humanity beyond the Nuremberg Charter

As shown above, after World War II, there were various definitions of crimes against humanity as international crimes. The ILC's 1991 Draft Code of Crimes even avoided using the term of 'crimes against humanity'.[85] All these definitions of crimes against humanity are different in specific aspects. For example, according to the Nuremberg and Tokyo Charters as well as the 1950 Nuremberg Principles, a nexus with an armed conflict was a legal requirement. By contrast, this nexus was omitted in the 1945 Control Council Law No. 10 and was abandoned in the 1998 Rome Statute. Article 5 of the ICTY Statute also explicitly referred to a link with an armed conflict; however, article 3 of the ICTR Statute did not refer to an armed conflict despite all offences being committed in the context of a civil war. The 1954, 1991, and 1996 versions of the Draft Code of Offences (Crimes) do not refer to a connection with an armed conflict.[86] In addition, with respect to the policy issue, neither the 1991 version of the Draft Code of Crimes nor article 5 of the ICTY Statute refer to a 'State or organisational' policy. The 1954 Draft Code of Offences omitted the condition that act were the required acts committed 'by the authorities of a State or by private individuals acting at the instigation or with the toleration of such authorities'.[87] And the 1996 Draft Code of Crimes requires acts committed 'in a systematic manner or on a large scale and instigated or directed by a Government or by any organisation or group'.[88] The definition of crimes against humanity for the ECCC does not require the policy element as set out in article 7(2)(a) of the Rome Statute. The treaty agreement for the Statute of the Extraordinary African Chambers also does not contain the term 'policy' in its definition of crimes against humanity.[89]

A view has been expressed that 'the existence of customary law on [the issue of a nexus with an armed conflict] was questionable in view of the conflicting definitions contained in the various instruments'.[90] Bassiouni pointed out that '[t]hese diverse definitions undermine the certainty of customary international

---

85 'Draft Code of Offences against the Peace and Security of Mankind' in 'Report of the International Law Commission', UN Doc A/46/10 (1991), para 176, art 21.
86 'Draft Code of Offences against the Peace and Security of Mankind' in 'Report of the International Law Commission', UN Doc A/2693 (1954), para 50, art 2(11); 1991 Draft Code of Crimes, art 21; 1996 Draft Code of Crimes, art 18.
87 1954 Draft Code of Offences, art 2(11).
88 1996 Draft Code of Crimes, art 18.
89 Statute of the Extraordinary African Chambers within the Senegalese Judicial System, art 6.
90 'Report of the *Ad Hoc* Committee on the Establishment of an International Criminal Court', UN Doc A/50/22 (1995), para 79.

law'.[91] Nevertheless, both statements should not be misinterpreted or exaggerated. On the one hand, the meanings of these definitions should be analysed by considering the jurisprudence of these international and national tribunals. For instance, the ICTY held that the reference to armed conflict in article 5 of the ICTY Statute was not a substantive element but a jurisdictional threshold for the tribunal.[92] On the other hand, some post-Rome definitions applicable at the national level have been limited in temporal scope. For example, the jurisdiction of the SCSL is confined to crimes committed during the period from 1996 to 2002. Likewise, the ECCC only has jurisdiction over crimes committed from 1975 to 1979. These post-Rome definitions indeed endorse the existence of crimes against humanity before 1998.

These definitions show a lack of uniformity of the text of crimes against humanity. The existence of different definitions would not inherently undermine the claim that there is a consensus on crimes against humanity as an international crime under customary law. However, the various definitions indicate different understandings of elements of these crimes in customary law. These understandings are related to the issue of what makes an inhumane act a crime against humanity. Competing views exist in academia on this question.[93] One viewpoint is that, from a historically descriptive perspective, most of the crimes were planned and committed by State actors, who are generally not the physical perpetrators who committed the crimes. It is likely that they would go unpunished without the availability of international jurisdiction.[94] After examining the establishment of the IMT and the IMTFE and the historic experience of mass crimes in Cambodia, in the former Yugoslavia and in Rwanda, Judge Kaul of the ICC concluded that 'historic origins are decisive in understanding the specific nature and fundamental rationale of the category of international crime'.[95] He added that 'a demarcation line must be drawn

---

91   M.C. Bassiouni, 'Revisiting the Architecture of Crimes Against Humanity' in L.N. Sadat (ed), *Forging a Convention for Crimes Against Humanity* (CUP 2011) 58.

92   *Tadić* Appeals Chamber Judgment (n 25), para 249; *Prosecutor v Stanišić & Simatović* (Judgement) ICYT-03-69-T (30 May 2013), para 960.

93   L. May, *Crimes Against Humanity: A Normative Account* (CUP 2005); M.M. deGuzman, 'Crimes Against Humanity' in W.A. Schabas and N. Bernaz (eds), *Routledge Handbook of International Criminal Law* (Routledge 2011) 121–38; *Situation in the Republic of Kenya* (Decision Pursuant to Article 15 of the Rome Statute on the Authorization of an Investigation into the Situation in the Republic of Kenya, PTC II) ICC-01/09-19-Corr (31 March 2010), fn 62. See also K. Ambos, *Treatise on International Criminal Law, Vol I: Foundations and General Part* (OUP 2013) 56–73.

94   For a thorough analysis of these views, see deGuzman, ibid 121–38.

95   *Kenya* Authorisation Decision 2010 (n 93) (Dissenting Opinion by Judge Hans-Peter Kaul to Pre-Trial Chamber II's Decision), paras 58–65.

between international crimes and human rights infractions; between international crimes and ordinary crimes; between those crimes subject to international jurisdiction and those punishable under domestic penal legislation'.[96]

The historical experience is vital to understanding what the fundamental rationale of crimes against humanity is and how the elements has come and changed. This chapter addresses the issues of the nexus with an armed conflict and the element of policy from an historical perspective.

4.3.3   Assessment and Conclusions

Observations of the development of crimes against humanity show that the notion of crimes against humanity was a new type of international crime in the Nuremberg Charter, as opposed to an existing customary rule. However, before the adoption of the Rome Statute, this crime had generally been recognised under customary law.[97] The observations further enhance the preliminary finding that article 7, in general, was declaratory of custom with respect to crimes against humanity. Various definitions of crimes against humanity do not affect the customary status of the crime but demonstrate controversial arguments about the contextual elements. The contextual element means that the underlying acts of crimes against humanity should be committed in this context and constitute part of the attack.[98] The next section focuses on the issue of the nexus with an armed conflict.

4.4   No Nexus with an Armed Conflict: Was and Is Article 7(1) Declaratory of Custom?

The text of article 7 of the Rome Statute does not use the phrases 'in connection with an armed conflict' or 'whether or not committed in time of armed conflict'.[99] It is argued that under customary law crimes against humanity can be committed in times of war and peace. This section first briefly interprets article 7 and provides a preliminary examination of the nexus with an armed

---

96   ibid, para 65.
97   See *Prosecutor v Marcelino Soares* (Judgment, District Court of Dili) SPSC-11/2003 (11 December 2003), paras 16-17.
98   *Prosecutor v Deronjić* (Judgement) ICTY-02-61-A (20 July 2005), para 109; *Prosecutor v Limaj et al* (Judgement) ICTY-03-66-T (30 November 2005), paras 180, 188; *Prosecutor v Blagojević & Jokić* (Judgement) ICTY-02-60-T (17 January 2005), para 547; *Prosecutor v Simić et al* (Judgement) ICTY-95-9-T (17 October 2003), para 41; *Tadić* Appeals Chamber Judgment (n 25), para 251.
99   UN Doc A/74/10 (2019), para 44, art 2.

conflict issue, and then analyses the removal of this nexus under customary law to show whether article 7(1) was and is declaratory of customary law on the nexus issue.

4.4.1 The Nexus Issue in Article 7(1) of the Rome Statute

For lack of a reference to the connection with an armed conflict, a plain reading of article 7 is impractical on the nexus issue. The aim to 'put an end to impunity for the perpetrators of these crimes' and other provisions of the Statute do not help in understanding this issue.[100] It seems that the strict construction requirement in article 22 supports a stringent interpretation requiring a nexus with an armed conflict. However, given the reference to armed conflict in many previous definitions of crimes against humanity, the omission of this link in article 7 indicates that such a nexus with an armed conflict is not a requirement for crimes against humanity in the Rome Statute. It is agreed that the armed conflict nexus requirement cannot be implied in article 7.[101] The ICC's interpretation that the 'attack' 'need not constitute a military attack' further indicates that the link with an armed conflict was not a requirement of crimes against humanity.[102]

The drafting history of article 7 also demonstrates that a nexus with an armed conflict is not a legal requirement for crimes against humanity. The *Ad Hoc* Committee in 1995 reported that 'in light of Nuremberg precedent and the two UN *ad hoc* tribunals, there were different views as to whether crimes against humanity could be committed in peace time'.[103] Australia said there is no longer any requirement of such a nexus between an armed conflict and crimes against humanity in customary law.[104] In the Preparatory Committee,

---

100 1998 Rome Statute, art 21(3).
101 W.A. Schabas, *The International Criminal Court: A Commentary on the Rome Statute* (2nd edn, OUP 2016) 148.
102 *The Prosecutor v Bemba* (Judgment pursuant to Article 74 of the Statute, TC III) ICC-01/05-01/08-3343 (21 March 2016), para 149; id, (Decision Pursuant to Article 61(7)(a) and (b) of the Rome Statute on the Charges, PTC II) ICC-01/05-01/08-424 (15 June 2009), para 75; *The Prosecutor v Katanga* (Judgment pursuant to Article 74 of the Statute, TC II) ICC-01/04-01/07-3436-tENG (27 March 2014), para 1101.
103 'Report of the *Ad Hoc* Committee on the Establishment of an International Criminal Court', UN Doc A/50/22 (1995), para 79. UN Press Release, 'Sixth Committee Hears Differing Views on Code of Crimes against International Peace and Security', UN Doc GA/L/2866 (1995); 'Summary of Interventions by the Australian Delegation on the Specification of Crimes' (17 August 1995).
104 'Summary of Interventions by the Australian Delegation on the Specification of Crimes' (17 August 1995).

there were debates about the nexus with an armed conflict.[105] It was generally agreed that the crime need not be limited to acts during international armed conflict.[106] The US strongly argued for removing a nexus with an armed conflict.[107] By contrast, China and Russia argued for retaining the nexus with an armed conflict.[108] There were proposals to incorporate the wording 'in time of peace or in time of war' in the chapeau of the provision about crimes against humanity. This proposal, however, did not survive in the 1998 Draft Statute adopted by the Preparatory Committee.[109] In the Draft Statute, one alternative of the definition of crimes against humanity retains the phrase 'in armed conflict' in a bracket.[110]

At the 1998 Rome Conference, opinions of States were divided on the issue of a nexus with an armed conflict. The majority of States supported the view that crimes against humanity can be committed both in wartime and in peacetime.[111] The UK clearly stated that 'in international customary law, no such nexus [between crimes against humanity and armed conflict] exists', whose

---

105 'Report of the Preparatory Committee on the Establishment of an International Criminal Court', UN Doc A/51/22 (1996), Vol I, paras 88-90; UN Doc GA/L/2787 (1996). For States supporting no armed conflict nexus, UN Doc GA/L/2761 (1996), Australia and Netherlands; 'Proposal by Japan on Crimes against Humanity' (25 March 1996); 'Proposal by the United Kingdom on Crimes against Humanity: Article 20 *quarter*' (25 March 1996); Netherlands, 'Crimes against Humanity' (27 March 1996); Denmark, 'Crime against Humanity: Chapeau and residual clause' (27 March 1996).
106 UN Doc GA/L/2762 (1996).
107 United States Delegation, 'Crimes against Humanity, Lack of a Requirement for a Nexus to Armed Conflict' (26 March 1996).
108 UN Doc GA/L/2763 (1996).
109 UN Doc A/51/22 (1996), Vol II, 66.
110 'Draft Statute for the International Criminal Court' in 'Report of the Preparatory Committee on the Establishment of an International Criminal Court', UN Doc A/CONF.183/2 (1998), 20–21. For a detailed analysis of the Preparatory Committee's drafts, see Schabas (n 101) 170.
111 UN Doc A/CONF.183/SR.1, paras 6-7 (Italy), UN Doc A/CONF.183/SR.8, para 62 (Ecuador); UN Doc A/CONF.183/C.1/SR.3, paras 21 (Germany), 36 (Czech Republic), 40 (Malta), 51 (Brazil), 55 (Denmark), 58 (Lesotho), 77 (Republic of Korea), 81 (Poland), 84 (Trinidad and Tobago), 87 (Australia), 89 (UK), 92 (Argentina), 95 (France), 101 (Cuba), 108 (Thailand), 109 (Slovenia), 112 (Norway), 114 (Côte d'Ivoire), 117 (South Africa), 120 (Egypt), 124 (Mexico), 133 (Colombia), 136 (Iran), 138 (US), 147 (Spain), 149 (Romania), 152 (Senegal), 154 (Sri Lanka), 158 (Venezuela), 162 (Italy), 167 (Ireland); UN Doc A/CONF.183/C.1/SR.4, paras 2 (Canada), 4 (Guinea), 7 (Switzerland), 8 (Sweden), 11 (Portugal), 12 (Yemen), 13 (Vietnam), 14 (Netherlands), 15 (Bahrain), 16 (Benin), 17 (Japan), 18 (Bangladesh), 19 (Niger), 20 (Austria), 21 (Uruguay), 23 (Sierra Leone), 25 (Israel), 27 (Chile), 29 (Kenya); UN Doc A/CONF.183/C.1/SR.5, para 51 (Venezuela); UN Doc A/CONF.183/C.1/SR.34, para 15 (Jamaica).

remarks were endorsed by other States.[112] Some States wished to limit the provision to crimes against humanity in the context of international armed conflict,[113] while some others claimed that this concept also applied to non-international armed conflict.[114] Some States in the latter group insisted on the nexus requirement,[115] but it is unclear whether others in this group also shared this view. In later discussions, negotiations focused less on the nexus issue of crimes against humanity.[116] The Discussion Paper prepared by the Bureau of the Committee of the Whole formulated the notion of crimes against humanity.[117] After informal consultation, an updated version of this concept was developed in the Recommendation of the Coordinator.[118] Both documents omitted the 'armed conflict' nexus. The Bureau Proposal further confirmed the omission of that phrase.[119] A large number of States expressed their satisfaction with the absence of an armed conflict nexus.[120] Also, other States did not openly complain about this.[121] Two States insisted on maintaining the reference to 'armed conflict' in the definition but admitted that crimes against humanity could be

---

112 Arguing for no nexus with an armed conflict under customary law, see UN Doc A/CONF.183/C.1/SR.3, paras 89 (UK), 92 (Argentina), 109 (Slovenia); UN Doc A/CONF.183/C.1/SR.4, paras 2 (Canada), 25 (Israel).

113 UN Doc A/CONF.183/C.1/SR.3, paras 22 (Syria), 24 (United Arab Emirates), 27 (Bahrain), 28 (Lebanon), 31 (Saudi Arabia), 34 (Tunisia), 39 (Morocco), 42 (Algeria), 68 (Sudan), 86 (Iraq).

114 UN Doc A/CONF.183/C.1/SR.3, paras 28 (Jordan), 30 (Belgium), 53 (Costa Rica), 66 (Malawi), 74 (China), UN Doc A/CONF.183/C.1/SR.4, paras 5 (Russian Federation), 9 (Ukraine), 10 (Syria).

115 UN Doc A/CONF.183/C.1/SR.3, para 74 (China); UN Doc A/CONF.183/C.1/SR.4, para 10 (Syria); UN Doc A/CONF.183/C.1/SR.27, para 64 (Vietnam).

116 UN Doc A/CONF.183/2/Add.1 and Corr.1; 'United States of America: proposal regarding an annexe on definitional elements for part 2 crimes', UN Doc A/CONF.183/C.1/L.10 (1998).

117 'Discussion Paper prepared by the Bureau', UN Doc A/CONF.183/C.1/L.53 (1998), 204–05.

118 UN Doc A/CONF.183/C.1/L.44 and Corr.1 (1998), 221–22.

119 'Proposal prepared by the Bureau', UN Doc A/CONF.183/C.1/L.59 and Corr. L (1998), 212–13.

120 UN Doc A/CONF.183/C.1/SR.25, paras 8 (South Africa), 39 (Mozambique), 41 (Sweden), 74 (Botswana), 76 (Croatia), 78 (Australia), 79 (Senegal); UN Doc A/CONF.183/C.1/SR.26, paras 34 (Uruguay), 35 (Turkey), 48 (Brazil), 63 (Ghana); UN Doc A/CONF.183/C.1/SR.27, paras 19 (Nicaragua), 74 (Sri Lanka); UN Doc A/CONF.183/C.1/SR.34, para 15 (Jamaica).

121 UN Doc A/CONF.183/C.1/SR.25, paras 22 (Belgium), 27 (Japan), 34 (China), 46 (Syria), 61 (Azerbaijan); UN Doc A/CONF.183/C.1/SR.26, paras 100 (Iran), 118 (Lesotho), 122 (Greece); UN Doc A/CONF.183/C.1/SR.27, paras 2 (Iraq), 57 (Congo), 60 (Indonesia), 61 (Comoros); UN Doc A/CONF.183/C.1/SR.28, paras 72 (Tunisia), 84 (Qatar), 87 (Saudi Arabia), 94 (Nigeria), 104 (Libya); UN Doc A/CONF.183/C.1/SR.34, paras 32 (Spain), 70 (Cuba), 73 (Jordan); UN Doc A/CONF.183/C.1/SR.35, paras 19-20 (Burundi), 38 (Finland), 53 (Liechtenstein), 64 (Iraq); UN Doc A/CONF.183/C.1/SR.36, paras 6 (Libya), 13 (Congo), 30 (Slovenia), 24 (Peru).

committed in peacetime.[122] A few States insisted on the retention of the armed conflict nexus for crimes against humanity.[123]

These observations show that article 7 of the Statute should be interpreted as not requiring a nexus with an armed conflict. The preparatory works also show that States widely accepted the absence of the nexus with an armed conflict at the Rome Conference. However, the text of article 7, the structure of the Statute and the preparatory works do not demonstrate a preliminary finding that article 7 of the Statute was declaratory of customary law on the absence of a nexus.

4.4.2 A Nexus with an Armed Conflict and Its Disappearance for Crimes Against Humanity in Custom

In order to determine whether article 7 was declaratory of custom on the nexus issue, it is necessary to discuss the removal of the nexus with an armed conflict under customary law. For this purpose, this subsection briefly analyses the jurisprudence and authorities after World War II to show whether a nexus with an armed conflict was a legal element of crimes against humanity under customary law.

4.4.2.1 The Nexus with an Armed Conflict

Currently, it is generally agreed that the notion of crimes against humanity does not require a nexus with an armed conflict. However, scholars' opinions differ with respect to a nexus with an armed conflict as a legal element for the crime in the past and the disappearance of such a nexus. On the one hand, commentators argue that the link with an armed conflict was never a legal but a jurisdictional requirement since the 1945 IMT in Nuremberg. On the other hand, some other commentators claim that the nexus with an armed conflict was a legal requirement before the IMT, while it disappeared at some time. The second view seems to be the appropriate interpretation of the nexus issue.

According to article 6(c) of the Nuremberg Charter, the definition of crimes against humanity was linked to 'any crime within the jurisdiction of the

---

122   UN Doc A/CONF.183/C.1/SR.3, para 27 (Bahrain), UN Doc A/CONF.183/C.1/SR.4, para 15 (Bahrain), UN Doc A/CONF.183/C.1/SR.27, para 22 (Bahrain); UN Doc A/CONF.183/C.1/SR.4, para 13 (Vietnam), UN Doc A/CONF.183/C.1/SR.27, para 64 (Vietnam). Bahrain and Vietnam supported crimes against humanity committed in peacetime, but they also intended to limit the Court's jurisdiction over this crime in the context of 'international' armed conflict or of 'armed conflict'.
123   UN Doc A/CONF.183/C.1/SR.28, paras 8 (Pakistan), 11 (Kuwait), 90 (Oman); UN Doc A/CONF.183/SR.9, para 38 (China).

Tribunal'.[124] It is understood that the phrase 'any crime within the jurisdiction of the Tribunal' refers to crimes against peace and war crimes.[125] In practice, ill-treatment and murder of non-German civilians in concentration camps committed by Germans during the war were charged mostly as both crimes against humanity and war crimes.[126] In addition, as Jackson addressed at the London Conference:

> The reason that this program of extermination of Jews and destruction of the rights of minorities becomes an international concern is this: it was a part of a plan for making an illegal war. Unless we have a war connection as a basis for reaching them, I would think we have no basis for dealing with atrocities. They were a part of the preparation for war or for the conduct of the war in so far as they occurred inside of Germany and that makes them our concern.[127]

Indeed, Streicher and von Schirach were found guilty only of crimes against humanity by the IMT. But the IMT judgment also established that the two defendants' conducts were associated with war crimes committed by others.[128] Thus, article 6(c) of the Nuremberg Charter required a link with crimes against peace or war crimes.

One may note that the reference to the phrase 'before or during the war' in article 6(c) of the Nuremberg Charter permits prosecutions of crimes against humanity before the war.[129] The IMT in some specific instances also referred to some acts before the war and admitted their connection with the planning of aggressive wars. Nevertheless, the IMT in practice only considered atrocities committed 'during the war' in connection with the aggressive wars as crimes against humanity.[130] For example, von Schirach was largely found guilty of crimes against humanity for acts after the beginning of the war, which were in connection with Austria's occupation.[131] According to the IMT, '[t]o constitute Crimes against Humanity, the acts relied on before the outbreak of war

---

124   Nuremberg Charter, art 6(c).
125   UN Doc A/CN.4/5 (1949), 68–69.
126   The *Flick* case (n 31) 1187–212; The *Hostage* case (n 31); The *Zyklon B* case (n 56); The *Belsen* case (n 56).
127   'Minutes of Conference Session of July 23, 1945' in Report of Robert H. Jackson (n 43) 331.
128   *France et al v Göring et al* (n 64) 302–04, 318–20.
129   Schwelb (n 28) 188, 193–95, 204.
130   *France et al v Göring et al* (n 64) 254; The *Flick* case (n 31) 1212. A. Goldstein, 'Crimes Against Humanity: Some Jewish Aspects' (1948) 1 *Jewish Ybk Intl L* 206, 221.
131   *France et al v Göring et al* (n 64) 302–04, 318–20; Schwelb (n 28) 205.

must have been in execution of, or in connection with, any crime within the jurisdiction of the Tribunal'.[132] In addition, the IMT also held that since many actions committed before the war were not proved in connection with any crime, it could not 'make a general declaration that the acts before 1939 were crimes against humanity within the meaning of the Charter'.[133] Therefore, it was potentially possible for the IMT to prosecute crimes against humanity before the war, but only if a nexus existed between the acts and aggressive wars.[134]

In the IMT, the essence of the linkage with war crimes or crimes against peace, in fact, was a connection with aggressive wars.[135] These observations indicate that acts committed in peacetime without any connection to the subsequent wars would not constitute crimes against humanity at that time. Only concrete acts committed in connection with an armed conflict would constitute crimes against humanity, regardless of whether they occurred before or during the war.

Nevertheless, some commentators consider that the nexus with aggressive wars was intentionally inserted by the Four Powers to limit the jurisdiction of the IMT over individuals of Axis countries.[136] Egon Schwelb and Roger Clark argued that the armed conflict linkage requirement in the Nuremberg Charter was a jurisdictional limit rather than an inherent substantive element of crimes against humanity.[137] In addition, the definition of crimes against humanity in the Nuremberg Charter was almost replicated in article 5(c) of the Tokyo Charter. According to the former Judge Röling of the IMTFE, 'the connection did not restrict *the scope of the crime,* but only *the scope of [the court's] jurisdiction*'.[138] Furthermore, the US and the ECCC also once argued that the nexus never existed. The US delegation in 1996 stated that '[t]he record of the development of the Nuremberg and Tokyo Charters does not [...] indicate that the drafters believed that the nexus was required as a matter of law'.[139] A Chamber

---

132   *France et al v Göring et al* (n 64) 254.
133   Goldstein (n 130) 221.
134   'Report of the International Law Commission', UN Doc A/1316 (1950), para 122.
135   Schwelb (n 28) 204; Dinstein (n 25) 383–84.
136   R.S. Clark, 'History of Efforts to Codify Crimes Against Humanity' in Sadat (ed) (n 91) 11; US, 'Crimes against Humanity, Lack of a Requirement for a Nexus to Armed Conflict' (26 March 1996).
137   Clark, ibid; Schwelb (n 28) 188, 194–95.
138   B.V.A. Röling and A. Cassese, *The Tokyo Trial and Beyond: Reflections of a Peacemonger* (Polity Press 1993) 56 (italics in original).
139   US, 'Crimes against Humanity, Lack of a Requirement for a Nexus to Armed Conflict' (26 March 1996), 2 and fn 4.

of the ECCC in the *Duch* case referred to the ICTY's *Tadić* Appeals Chamber Decision on jurisdiction to justify an argument that a nexus never existed.[140]

Clark first pointed out that in article II of the 1948 Genocide Convention, a nexus with aggressive wars was not required for the crime of genocide, which is closely related to the persecution type of crimes against humanity in the Nuremberg Charter.[141] In addition, he noted that the connection to the 'initiation of war and war crimes' was omitted in Control Council Law No. 10. Last, Clark clarified that in the original English and French texts of article 6(c) of the Nuremberg Charter adopted in August 1945, a semi-colon existed between 'before or during the war' and 'or persecutions'. However, in the original Russian text, a comma was used.[142] This semi-colon in the English and French texts was later amended to a comma in the 'Semi-colon Protocol' in October 1945.[143] Given the modification of this semi-colon, Clark concluded that the phrase 'in execution of or in connection with any crime within the jurisdiction of the Tribunal' was only a requirement for persecutions. With regard to crimes against humanity, acts of 'murder, extermination, enslavement, deportation, and other inhumane acts committed against any civilian population' are not required to be linked with the war.[144] As to acts of persecution, the 'crimes' mentioned in the phrase 'link with any crimes' refer to the murder type of underlying offences, such as 'murder, extermination or enslavement', instead of 'crimes against peace and war crimes' or aggressive wars. In his view, a link with these underlying offences is confirmed by the Rome Statute, which requires persecution to be 'in connection with any act referred to in this paragraph'.[145] Accordingly, Clark argued that the Nuremberg Charter did not acknowledge a substantive link with aggressive wars or an armed conflict for crimes against humanity in international law.[146]

---

140   *KAING Guek Eav alias Duch* (Trial Judgment) 001/18-07-2007/ECCC/TC (26 July 2010), para 292.

141   Clark (n 136) 12; R.S. Clark, 'Crimes against Humanity at Nuremberg' in G. Ginsburgs and V.N. Kudriavtsev (eds), *The Nuremberg Trial and International Law* (Martinus Nijhoff Publishers 1990) 190–92.

142   'Crimes against Humanity: namely, murder, extermination, enslavement, deportation, and other inhumane acts committed against any civilian population, before or during the war [;] or persecutions on political, racial or religious grounds in execution of or in connection with any crime within the jurisdiction of the Tribunal, whether or not in violation of the domestic law of the country where perpetrated.' See Clark (n 136) 11.

143   'Protocol Rectifying Discrepancy in Text of Charter, drawn up by the Governments who has concluded the Agreement of 8th August' (6 October 1945), (1948)1 TMWC 17.

144   ibid.

145   1998 Rome Statute, art 7(1)(h).

146   Clark (n 136) 11.

A different argument, however, is also tenable by reference to these same sources.[147] It is argued that the nexus with an armed conflict in the Nuremberg Charter was a substantive legal element rather than a jurisdictional limit for the following reasons. Firstly, it is the wording 'trial and punishment of the major war criminals of the European Axis' in article 1 and in the chapeau of article 6 of the Nuremberg Charter, rather than the nexus with war, that was inserted to limit the jurisdiction of the IMT.[148] Secondly, the semi-colon in the English and French texts has not been found in preceding drafts and where it came from is a puzzle. The 'Semi-colon Protocol' amended the semi-colon two months later. This slight revision has a high impact on the definition of crimes against humanity, which required all prohibited murder type acts to be linked to war. It is not persuasive to argue that the reviewers changed it mistakenly and failed to consider the impact of the revision. Thirdly, persecution as a crime against humanity requires a link with the underlying murder-type acts. Such a link for persecution does not exclusively exclude an alternative requirement of a link with any crime within the ICC's jurisdiction (war crimes, genocide, and the crime of aggression).[149] This link builds a relationship between murder type offences and persecution type offences. But this link between the two types of offences cannot justify the view that the concept of crimes against humanity in the Nuremberg Charter substantively required no link with war.

Fourthly, the US delegation might have mixed the factual 'context' of war or peace with the 'nexus' with aggressive wars. The Legal Committee of the UN War Crimes Commission once declared that '[i]t was irrelevant whether a crime against humanity had been committed before or during the war'.[150] By referring to the Nuremberg and Tokyo Charters,[151] the UN War Crimes Commission confirmed this clarification.[152] Nevertheless, the Legal Committee concluded that 'the inhumane acts committed against any civilian population before the war [...] fall under crimes against humanity' because the purpose of these clashes was in connection with the contemplated invasion of Czechoslovakia.[153] Thus, acts committed before the war (in peacetime) would be considered as crimes against humanity only if these acts were connected with the later aggressions

---

147   Schwelb (n 28) 195.
148   'Minutes of Conference Session of July 24, 1945' in Report of Robert H. Jackson (n 43) 361.
149   1950 Draft Code of Offences, art 2(10); 1954 Draft Code of Offences, art 2(11) and UN Doc A/2693 (1954), para 50.
150   UNWCC (ed) (n 28) 178–79.
151   ibid 522–24.
152   ibid 192–93.
153   ibid 178–79.

of war. In fact, the ILC in its 1950 Nuremberg Principles deleted the phrase 'before or during the war' in defining crimes against humanity, while it specifically referred to the connection with war crimes and aggressive wars. In its commentary to Principle VI(c), the ILC emphasised that crimes against humanity 'need not be committed during a war', but it maintained that 'such crimes may take place also before a war in [connection] with crimes against peace'.[154] This is the correct reading of the Nuremberg Charter and the IMT judgment.[155]

Additionally, the text of Control Council Law No. 10 did not refer to the nexus with war.[156] In practice, except for the *Justice* and the *Einsatzgruppen* cases, subsequent tribunals applying that law required a connection with the aggressive wars for acts committed before and during the war.[157] Suspects in the *Flick* and *Ministries* cases were charged with crimes against humanity committed in peacetime.[158] However, the tribunals in the two cases held that it would not contemplate offences committed before the war and having no connection with the war.[159] As shown above, the fact that crimes against humanity might be committed before the war does not indicate that the nexus with aggressive wars was not required. In discussion the relationships between genocide and crimes against humanity, the UN War Crimes Commission said that 'genocide is difference from crimes against humanity in that, to prove it, no connection with war need be shown'.[160] The US delegation went too far to argue that there was no nexus with an armed conflict in the Nuremberg Charter.[161]

Fifthly, the *Tadić* Appeals Chamber of the ICTY, in fact, supported a reading that a nexus with an armed conflict was a legal requirement in the Nuremberg Charter. Article 5 of the ICTY Statute provides a notion of crimes against

---

154 UN Doc A/1316 (1950), para 123.
155 Dinstein (n 25) 384. For delegations' debates on Principle VI(c), see 'Second report on the Draft Code of Offences against the Peace and Security of Mankind, by Mr J. Spiropoulos, Special Rapporteur', UN Doc A/CN.4/44 (1951), paras 116-24.
156 The *Justice* case (n 31) 972–73; The *Einsatzgruppen* case (n 31) 499.
157 The *Flick* case (n 31) 1212–13; The *Krupp* case (n 31); *US v Pohl et al* [The *Pohl* case], (1950) 5 TWC 195, 991–92; *US v von Weizaecker et al* [The *Ministries* case], (1953) 12 TWC 1. See also K.J. Heller, *The Nuremberg Military Tribunals and the Origins of International Criminal Law* (OUP 2011) 236–42.
158 The *Flick* case (n 31) Indictment, para 13; The *Ministries* case (n 157) Indictment, para 30.
159 The *Flick* case ((n 31) 1212; The *Ministries* case ((n 157) 116 and (1953) 14 TWC 1, 557. Heller (n 157) 236–42.
160 UNWCC (n 56) (1949)15 LRTWC 1, 38; *US v Greifelt et al* (1947) 13 LRTWC 1, 40.
161 Schabas (n 101) 170.

humanity committed in 'armed conflict'.[162] In the *Tadić* Appeals Chamber Decision on jurisdiction, the Chamber held that:

> [T]he nexus between crimes against humanity and either crimes against peace or war crimes, required by the Nuremberg Charter, was peculiar to the jurisdiction of the Nuremberg Tribunal. Although the nexus requirement in the Nuremberg Charter was carried over to the 1948 General Assembly resolution affirming the Nuremberg principles, there is no logical or legal basis for this requirement and it has been abandoned in subsequent State practice with respect to crimes against humanity. Most notably, the nexus requirement was eliminated from the definition of crimes against humanity contained in Article II (1)(c) of Control Council Law No. 10 of 20 December 1945.[163]
>
> It is by now a settled rule of customary international law that crimes against humanity do not require a connection to international armed conflict ... .[C]ustomary international law may not require a connection between crimes against humanity and any conflict at all. ... [T]he Security Council may have defined the crime in Article 5 more narrowly than necessary under customary international law. [164]

The literal meaning of the first paragraph is a bit ambiguous. By referring to 'peculiar to the jurisdiction of the Nuremberg Tribunal', the Chamber seems to imply that a nexus with an armed conflict for crimes against humanity was not a substantive but a jurisdictional requirement in the IMT.[165] At the same time, the Appeals Chamber said that the nexus requirement had been 'abandoned in subsequent state practice' and referred to Control Council Law No. 10 to indicate that the notion of crimes against humanity began to change on 20 December 1945.[166] If the nexus with an armed conflict was not a substantive requirement, how could it be 'abandoned in subsequent State practice'?[167]

In the second paragraph cited above, with reference to '[no] connection to international armed conflict' as 'a settled' customary rule, on the one hand, the Appeals Chamber held that the nexus with an armed conflict was expanded

---

162   1993 ICTY Statute, art 5.
163   *Tadić* Appeals Chamber Decision on Jurisdiction (n 25), para 140.
164   ibid, para 141. For an analysis of the case concerning the nexus requirement, see Dinstein (n 25) 386–87.
165   *Tadić* Appeals Chamber Decision on Jurisdiction (n 25), para 140.
166   ibid.
167   ibid.

to include a nexus with non-international armed conflict.[168] On the other hand, the Appeals Chamber held that the text of crimes against humanity with a nexus in article 5 of the ICTY Statute was narrower than what customary law required. The Appeals Chamber acknowledged that a nexus requirement existed, but it said it was 'obsolescent'.[169] There is a cross-reference to the two paragraphs cited, confirming the relationship between them. The Appeals Chamber stated that 'customary international law no longer requires any nexus between crimes against humanity and armed conflict [...] Article 5 was intended to reintroduce this nexus for the purposes of this Tribunal'.[170] The expressions of 'no longer' and of 'reintroduce' further discredit the idea that a nexus with an armed conflict was never a requirement. The clarification of the *Tadić* Appeals Chamber Decision demonstrates that a link with an armed conflict was a legal element. This clarification also indicates that the chamber of the ECCC in *Duch* misunderstood the *Tadić* case. Therefore, the ECCC decision in *Duch* is also less valuable on the interpretation of the nexus issue.

As the UN Secretary-General summarised, the nexus with war is a compromise between two ideas.[171] One is the traditional principle that the treatment of nationals is a matter of domestic jurisdiction. The competing principle is that inhumane treatment of human beings is wrong even if it is tolerated or practised by their States, in peace and war, and this wrong should be penalised in the interest of the international community. Without abandoning the traditional principle, the latter idea of guaranteeing a minimum standard of fundamental rights to all human beings was qualified by the nexus requirement at that time.[172] In other words, since aggressive wars affect the rights of other States, the nexus with an armed conflict justifies international prosecution. A construction of no nexus at that time means that acts of their governmental leaders against their citizens in peacetime might be charged with crimes against humanity. It would be going too far to conclude that States aimed to create the notion of crimes against humanity without any association with war.

The Four Powers knew that they were creating a new regime that would be binding on all States in the future. The American delegate Jackson stated that:

> If certain acts and violations of treaties are crimes, they are crimes whether the United States does them or whether Germany does them,

---

168 *Tadić* Appeals Chamber Decision on Jurisdiction (n 25), para 142.
169 ibid, para 140.
170 ibid, para 78.
171 UN Doc A/CN.4/5 (1949), 70–72.
172 ibid.

and we are not prepared to lay down a rule of criminal conduct against others which we would not be willing to have invoked against us.[173]

[...] [O]rdinarily we do not consider that the acts of a government toward its own citizens arrant our interference. We have some regrettable circumstances at times in our own country in which minorities are unfairly treated. We think it is justifiable that we interfere or attempt to bring retribution to individuals or to states only because the concentration camps and the deportations were in pursuance of a common plan or enterprise of making an unjust or illegal war in which we became involved. We see no other basis on which we are justified in reaching the atrocities which were committed inside Germany, under German law, or even in violation of German law, by authorities of the German state.[174]

These statements demonstrate that without a link with aggressive wars, the leaders of those countries that created the IMT might be at a real risk for murder or persecution of their own civilian populations. The UK Chief Prosecutor Hartley Shawcross shared this view of the nexus with war. The prosecutor believed that acts, not associated with aggressive wars and committed by a government against their civilian populations, should not constitute crimes against humanity as a distinct international crime.[175]

As shown above, the nexus with aggressive wars was required for crimes against humanity in the Nuremberg Charter and by the IMT. This nexus was not a jurisdictional link but a substantive element of crimes against humanity.[176] The IMT focused on the need to show a connection to aggressive wars.[177] This idea was confirmed by the ILC in its 1950 Nuremberg Principles and its 1950 Draft Code of Offences.[178]

---

173   'Minutes of Conference Session of July 23, 1945' in Report of Robert H. Jackson (n 43) 330.
174   ibid 333.
175   *France et al v Göring et al*, Sir Hartley Shawcross making Final Speech on behalf of Prosecution (26 July 1946), (1948) 19 TMWC 433, 470–71.
176   Schabas (n 29) 60; J. Brown, 'Australian Practice in International Law 1990 and 1991' (1990–1991) 13 *Australian Ybk Intl L* 195, 246.
177   *France et al v Göring et al* (n 64) 184.
178   'Formulation of the Nuremberg Principles, Report by Jean Spiropoulos, Special Rapporteur', UN Doc A/CN.4/22 (1950), 187; 'Text of a Draft Code of Offences against the Peace and Security of Mankind suggested as a working paper for the International Law Commission', UN Doc A/CN.4/SER.A/1950/Add.1.

4.4.2.2   The Disappearance of the Nexus with an Armed Conflict

As for commentators arguing for the nexus as a jurisdictional requirement in the Nuremberg Charter, it is not necessary to assess when this link disappeared as it never existed. For other commentators deeming the nexus a substantive legal element, the nexus with an armed conflict disappeared at some time. As observed above, the second viewpoint is the appropriate interpretation. William Schabas wrote: 'The nexus between armed conflict and crimes against humanity that existed at Nuremberg was part of the original understanding, and was only removed at some point subsequent to 1945'.[179] Scholars also differ with respect to the disappearance of a nexus with an armed conflict as a legal element at the material time. A further question is when that link with an armed conflict has disappeared under customary law.

The disappearance of the nexus remains crucial for tribunals in prosecuting crimes against humanity committed in the past. National courts can and do prosecute crimes against humanity that occurred decades ago, for instance, the International Crimes Tribunal in Bangladesh. According to the amended International Crimes (Tribunals) Act 1973, the International Crimes Tribunals in Bangladesh was established in 2010 and 2012 to deal with international crimes including crimes against humanity committed since the liberation war of 1971. In the absence of relevant treaty or national criminal prohibitions in Bangladesh at the material time before or in 1971, how can its tribunals prosecute crimes against humanity without violating the principle of non-retroactivity? The existing customary international rules play a vital role in this circumstance. The following paragraphs survey post-Nuremberg instruments, jurisprudence and the attitude of the UN organs to show the existing confusion about determining the moment of the disappearance of the nexus.

As shown above, the text of Control Council Law No. 10 did not refer to the nexus with war. However, in the application of Control Council Law No. 10, the Subsequent Proceedings required a link with an armed conflict. Additionally, the 1950 ILC Nuremberg Principles also upheld the requirement that the underlying acts of crimes against humanity, before or during the war, be connected to aggressive wars. The formulation of crimes against humanity in the 1951 Draft Code of Offences required that 'inhuman acts [...] are committed in execution of or in [connection] with other offences defined in this article'.[180] This formulation did not substantively remove the armed conflict nexus

---

179   Schabas (n 29) 59.
180   'Draft Code of Offences against the Peace and Security of Mankind', UN Doc A/CN.4/SER.A/1951, 136, art 2(10).

requirement.[181] The definition in the 1954 Draft Code of Offences, however, did not follow the essence of the 1951 version on the nexus issue but enlarged the scope of crimes against humanity to cover acts not committed in connection with other offences.[182] Article 1(b) of the 1968 Convention on the Non-Applicability of Statutory Limitations referred to '[c]rimes against humanity whether committed in time of war or in time of peace as they are defined in the Charter of the Nuremberg International Military Tribunal'.[183] Given its very ratification by States, article 1(b) of the Convention is less significant evidence to justify that a nexus was not required under customary law in 1968.

Jurisprudence of international and internationalised tribunals also does not show consistency on when the armed conflict nexus disappeared for crimes against humanity. The 2006 *Kolk and Kislyiy v Estonia* case before the ECtHR concerned the punishment against two individuals by Estonia based on the 1994 Estonia Penal Code for crimes against humanity committed in peacetime in 1949. The ECtHR rejected the two individuals' applications because article 7(1) of the European Convention on Human Rights prohibiting retroactive prosectuion of crimes under national or international law was not violated. The Chamber of the ECtHR implicitly upheld that by virtue of international law, the prosecution of deportation as a crime against humanity committed in peacetime in 1949 was not a violation of non-retroactive application of the law. In its logic, international law in 1949 did not require a nexus with an armed conflict for crimes against humanity.[184]

Cassese criticised the decision in the *Kolk and Kislyiy v Estonia* case and argued that the link with war was an indispensable element for prohibited acts of crimes against humanity before 1949. In his view, it is 'only later, in the late 1960s, that a general rule gradually began to evolve, prohibiting crimes against humanity even when committed in time of peace'.[185] By contrast, the Grand Chamber of the ECtHR in the 2008 *Korbely v Hungary* case held that the link with an armed conflict 'may no longer have been relevant by 1956'.[186]

---

181   ibid 136.
182   'Draft Code of Offences against the Peace and Security of Mankind', UN Doc A/CN.4/SER.A/1954/Add.1, 150, art 2(11).
183   Convention on the Non-Applicability of Statutory Limitations to War Crimes and Crimes against Humanity, 754 UNTS 73, 55 Parties and 9 Signatories.
184   *Kolk and Kislyiy v Estonia* (Decision, Fourth Section Court) ECtHR Application No. 23052/04 (17 January 2006).
185   A. Cassese, 'Balancing the Prosecution of Crimes Against Humanity and Non-Retroactivity of Criminal Law: The *Kolk and Kislyiy v Estonia* Case before the ECHR' (2006) 4 *JICJ* 410, 413.
186   *Korbely v Hungary* (Merits and Just Satisfaction, Grand Chamber) ECtHR Application No. 9174/02 (19 September 2008), para 82.

And, a Chamber of the ECCC found that 'customary international law between 1975 and 1979 required that crimes against humanity be committed in the context of an armed conflict.'[187] The observation on case law shows that different views exist about when the nexus with an armed conflict was or was not relevant.

The UN Secretary-General and the Security Council considered that the nexus with an armed conflict was not required for crimes against humanity under customary law in 1993. In 1993, the Report of the Secretary-General on the establishment of the ICTY stated that:

> Crimes against humanity were first recognised in the Charter and the Judgement of the Nuremberg Tribunal, as well as in Law No. 10 of the Control Council for Germany. Crimes against humanity are aimed at any civilian population and are prohibited regardless of whether they are committed in an armed conflict, international or internal in character.[188]

A plain reading indicates no nexus with an armed conflict. The Secretary-General held that the nexus with an armed conflict is not required for punishable acts constituting crimes against humanity under customary law.[189] The Secretary-General, however, proposed interpreting article 5 of the draft statute of the ICTY by restricting the crime 'when committed in armed conflict, whether international or internal in character'. The Secretary-General may have intentionally 'defined the crime in Article 5 more narrowly than necessary under customary international law'.[190] The UN Security Council adopted the draft statute of the ICTY without modification.[191] In its interpretative clarification of the ICTY Statute, the UK delegation also stated that:

> Articles 2 to 5 of the draft [ICTY] Statute describe the crimes within the jurisdiction of the Tribunal. The Statute does not, of course, create new law, but reflects existing international law in this field. [...] Article 5 covers acts committed in time of armed conflict.[192]

---

187 *Co-Prosecutors v Ieng Sary* (Decision on Appeals by Nuon Chea and Ieng Thirith Against the Closing Order) 002/19-09-2007-ECCC/OCIJ (PTC 145 & 146) (15 February 2011), para 144.
188 UN Doc S/25704 (1993), para 47 (citations omitted).
189 ibid, para 34.
190 *Tadić* Appeals Chamber Decision on Jurisdiction (n 25), para 141.
191 UN Doc S/RES/827 (1993).
192 UN Doc S/PV.3217 (1993), 19 (UK).

CRIMES AGAINST HUMANITY   165

This statement demonstrates that a notion of crimes against humanity in non-international and international armed conflict reflects part of 'existing international law'. In addition, the possibility that acts committed in peacetime constitute crimes against humanity under customary law at that time is not excluded.[193] The Security Council then implicitly confirms the absence of the nexus requirement in adopting the 1994 ICTR Statute.[194]

The 1995 *Tadić* Appeals Chamber Decision has a significant impact on the clarification of the absence of nexus in custom. As mentioned above, the Appeals Chamber in the *Tadić* decision on jurisdiction observed that the practice of States began to abandon the nexus requirement. The Appeals Chamber was confident in claiming no connection to an armed conflict under customary law in 1993. In its view, offences with no connection to an armed conflict constituted crimes against humanity in 1993, whereas the ICTY only has jurisdiction over crimes against humanity committed in armed conflicts or linked geographically and temporally with an armed conflict.[195] Subsequent ICTY cases upheld the view that there was no nexus with an armed conflict under customary law, at least at the material time in 1993.[196] The preparatory works of article 7 of the Rome Statute, as observed above in subsection 4.4.1, also demonstrate that States generally recognised the definition of crimes against humanity committed without association with an armed conflict at the 1998 Rome Conference.

To sum up, instruments and jurisprudence after World War II and the view of the UN organs further justify that the nexus with an armed conflict was a legal element in the Nuremberg Charter, but leave the moment of its disappearance more confusing in 1949, 1951, 1956, the 1960s, 1968 or later in 1993. For lack of practice in prosecuting crimes against humanity, it is inappropriate to conclude at what moment the customary rule of crimes against humanity was modified by dismissing the armed conflict nexus. However, it is reasonable

---

193 See also UN Doc S/25704 (1993), para 47 and fn 9.
194 Cf. Schabas (n 101) 169.
195 *Kunarać* Appeals Chamber Judgment (n 6) para 83; *Prosecutor v Šešelj* (Decision on the Interlocutory Appeal Concerning Jurisdiction) ICTY-03-67-AR72.1 (31 August 2004), para 14; id, (Decision on Motion for Reconsideration of the 'Decision on the Interlocutory Appeal Concerning Jurisdiction' Dated 31 August 2004) ICTY-03-67-AR72.1 (15 June 2006), para 25.
196 *Prosecutor v Furundžija* (Judgement) ICTY-95-17/1-T (10 December 1998), para 59; *Tadić* Appeals Chamber Judgment (n 25), paras 249, 251; *Kunarać* Appeals Chamber Judgment (n 6) paras 82-83; *Šešelj* Interlocutory Appeals Decision, ibid, para 13; *Šešelj* Motion for Reconsideration Decision, ibid, para 21; *Stanišić & Simatović* Trial Chamber Judgment (n 92), para 960.

to argue that the nexus requirement was removed, at the very latest, before the 1998 Rome Conference. To date, national legislation of almost 60 States, including the UK, the US, Canada, Germany, Australia, New Zealand, the Philippines, Vietnam and some African States, do not require a link with an armed conflict for crimes against humanity.[197] The ILC also endorsed the view of no nexus with an armed conflict in its recent draft articles on crimes against humanity.[198]

4.4.3 *Assessment and Conclusions*
Article 7 of the Rome Statute provides that underlying offences disassociated from an armed conflict constitute crimes against humanity.[199] These post-World War II cases and instruments show that the armed conflict nexus requirement was a substantive element for the notion of crimes against humanity in the Nuremberg Charter. Later on, the nexus with an armed conflict was disassociated from crimes against humanity under customary law. It remains unclear when this nexus disappeared under customary law. In conclusion, article 7 of the Rome Statute restated or, at the very least, crystallised the notion of crimes against humanity under customary law by excluding the armed conflict nexus. Article 7 was and is declaratory of custom on the nexus issue of crimes against humanity. The following section examines the policy issue of crimes against humanity.

4.5 The Policy Element: Was and Is Article 7(2)(a) Declaratory of Custom?

After the insertion of the word 'policy' in article 7(2)(a) of the Rome Statute, debates continued as to whether policy should be or is a legal requirement for crimes against humanity under customary law.[200] The issue of whether policy

---

[197] Vietnam, Penal Code 1999, art 342. See National Implementing Legislation Database.
[198] UN Doc A/74/10 (2019), paras 44-45, art 2 and its commentary.
[199] Schabas (n 101) 146–47; Amnesty International, 'The International Criminal Court: Making the Right Choices', Part I (1997), 33.
[200] For policy as an independent element, see Robinson (n 6) 48–52; Schabas (n 6); Bassiouni (n 23) 14–19; C. Hall and C. Stahn, 'Article 7' in O. Triffterer and K. Ambos (eds), *Commentary on the Rome Statute of the International Criminal Court: Observers' Notes, Article by Article* (3rd edn, Hart/Beck 2016) 157–58. Cf. Mettraux (n 6); L.N. Sadat, 'Preface' in Sadat (ed) (n 91) xxii; G. Sluiter, ' "Chapeau Elements" of Crimes Against Humanity in the Jurisprudence of the UN *ad hoc* Tribunals' in Sadat (ed) (n 91) 108; D. Hunt, 'The International Criminal Court: High Hopes, "Creative Ambiguity" and an Unfortunate Mistrust in International Judges' (2004) 2 *JICJ* 56, 65; Cassese *et al* (eds) (n 8) 107.

should or should not be a legal element goes beyond the focus of this section. This section analyses whether article 7(2)(a) of the Rome Statute was and is declaratory of custom on the policy element of crimes against humanity. This section first examines the concept of policy in the Rome Statute and then discusses the issue of the policy element under customary law.[201]

4.5.1 Policy as a Legal Element in Article 7(2)(a) of the Rome Statute

Article 7(2)(a) of the Rome Statute states that an 'attack directed against civilian population means a course of conduct [...] against any civilian population, pursuant to or in furtherance of a State or organisational policy to commit such attack'. This provision contains a threshold for crimes against humanity, requiring that the attack be pursuant to or in furtherance of a 'State or organisational policy'. The following paragraphs answer whether policy is a legal element for crimes against humanity as defined in article 7.

4.5.1.1   The Notion of Policy

The Rome Statute does not define the word 'policy' in article 7(2)(a). The *Oxford English Dictionary* defines 'policy' as 'senses related to public or politic practice'.[202] The Trial Chamber in *Bemba* held that policy need not be formalised and that it may be inferred from other factors. These factors include:

> (i) that the attack was planned, directed or organised; (ii) a recurrent pattern of violence; (iii) the use of public or private resources to further the policy; (iv) the involvement of the State or organisational forces in the commission of crimes; (v) statements, instructions or documentation attributable to the State or the organisation condoning or encouraging the commission of crimes; and/or (vi) an underlying motivation.[203]

Or 'the existence of preparations or collective mobilisation orchestrated and coordinated by that State or organisation'.[204] In addition, it is doubtful whether the policy-making entity is limited to 'States'.

---

201   G. Mettraux, 'The Definition of Crimes Against Humanity and the Question of a "Policy" Element' in Sadat (ed) (n 91) 156–66.
202   OED, the now usual sense is: 'A principle or course of action adopted or proposed as desirable, advantageous, or expedient; *esp.* one formally advocated by a government, political party, etc'.
203   *Bemba* Trial Chamber Judgment (n 102), para 160 (citations omitted).
204   *Katanga* Trial Chamber Judgment (n 102), para 1109; *The Prosecutor v Ntaganda* (Judgment, TC VI) ICC-01/04-02/06-2359 (08 July 2019), para 674.

A plain reading of the phrase 'State or organisational policy' in article 7(2)(a) seems to suggest that a State is not the solo policy-making entity involving in the attack of crimes against humanity. The English text 'organisational policy', however, does not require the policy to be authored by an entity of an 'organisation', but the policy is in essence organised and planned. By contrast, the French, Spanish and Arabic texts indicate policy to be adopted by an 'organisation'.[205] The Chinese text '组织的政策' shares the same meaning as the latter three equally authentic texts. The texts of the Rome Statute, therefore, do not provide guidance concerning the interpretation of the phrase 'State or organisational policy'.

It is also hard to know how the drafters understood 'State or organisational policy' by simply referring to their statements at the Rome Conference.[206] Reflections of scholars attending the Conference provide guidance to understand the meaning of organisation, but real intention and the purpose of Rome Statute's drafters on this phrase remain doubtful.[207] The Elements of Crimes provides that a 'policy of committing such attack' requires that 'the State or organisation actively promote or encourage such an attack against a civilian population'.[208] According to the ICC's jurisprudence, the phrase 'State or organisational policy' includes two concepts: 'policy of State' and 'policy of organisation'.[209] Debates at the ICC on the standard of qualifying a non-State actor as an organisation have further endorsed this interpretation implicitly.[210] These

---

205   *Kenya* Authorisation Decision 2010 (n 93) (Dissenting Opinion by Judge Hans-Peter Kaul), para 38.

206   UN Doc GA/L/2787 (1996); UN. Doc A/CONF.183/C.1/SR.27, para 74 (Sri Lanka); States did not comment on the meaning of organisational policy, see 'Discussion Paper prepared by the Bureau', UN Doc A/CONF.183/C.1/L.53 (1998), 204.

207   M.C. Bassiouni and W.A. Schabas (eds), *The Legislative History of the International Criminal Court* (2nd revised and expanded edn, Brill 2016) 169–70; Schabas (n 6) 972–74; Bassiouni (n 91) 57.

208   Elements of Crimes, UN Doc PCNICC/2000/1/Add.2, art 7, introduction, para 2. For further discussions on the policy, see R.S. Lee (ed), *The International Criminal Court, Elements of Crimes and Rule of Procedure and Evidence* (Transnational 2001) 75–76.

209   *Bemba* Decision on Confirmation of Charges (n 102), para 115; *Kenya* Authorisation Decision 2010 (n 93), para 89 and (Dissenting Opinion by Judge Hans-Peter Kaul), para 38; *Katanga* Trial Chamber Judgment (n 102), para 1108; *The Prosecutor v Gbagbo* (Decision on the Confirmation of Charges against Laurent Gbagbo, PTC I) ICC-02/11-01/11-656-Red (12 June 2014), para 216. For further discussions, see UN Doc A/74/10 (2019), para 45, commentaries (17)-(33) to draft art 2.

210   For capacity test, see *Kenya* Authorisation Decision 2010 (n 93), paras 90-92; *The Prosecutor v Muthaura et al* (Decision on the Confirmation of Charges Pursuant to Article 61(7)(a) and (b) of the Rome Statute, PTC II) ICC-01/09-02/11-382-Red (23 January 2012), paras 112-14; *The Prosecutor v Ruto et al* (Decision on the Confirmation of Charges

issues merit discussion but go beyond the focus of this chapter. This brief clarification sets out the basic understanding of policy. The following paragraphs analyse whether a 'policy' in general is a legal element for crimes against humanity under article 7 of the Rome Statute.

4.5.1.2 Policy as a Legal Element in the Rome Statute

The legal effect of the reference to 'policy' in article 7 of the Statute is not self-explanatory as to whether the policy is an independent legal element for crimes against humanity. Nevertheless, the Rome Statute leaves no room to argue against the policy element at the ICC. The Elements of Crimes explicitly notes that 'policy to commit such attack requires that the State or organisation actively promote or encourage such an attack against a civilian population' and 'in exceptional circumstances, [policy may] be implemented by a deliberate failure to take action, which is consciously aimed at encouraging such attack'.[211]

The preparatory works of article 7 also indirectly clarify the distinct status of the policy element in discussing the relationship between the 'widespread or systematic' test and the policy element.[212] The Preparatory Committee considered 'a policy, plan, conspiracy or a campaign' as a potential element of crimes against humanity.[213] In its report, the Preparatory Committee summarised that:

Pursuant to Article 61(7)(a) and (b) of the Rome Statute, PTC II) ICC-01/09-01/11-373 (23 January 2012), para 184; *Katanga* Trial Chamber Judgment (n 102), paras 1119-20; *Bemba* Trial Chamber Judgment (n 102), para 149. Cf. State-like organisation test, see *Kenya* Authorisation Decision 2010 (n 93) (Dissenting Opinion by Judge Hans-Peter Kaul), para 51; *The Prosecutor v Ruto et al* (Dissenting Opinion by Judge Hans-Peter Kaul to Pre-Trial Chamber II's 'Decision on the Prosecutor's Application for Summons to Appear for William Samoei Ruto, Henry Kiprono Kosgey and Joshua Arap Sang') ICC-01/09-01/11-2 (15 March 2011), paras 2-15; *The Prosecutor v Muthaura et al* (Dissenting Opinion by Judge Hans-Peter Kaul to Pre-Trial Chamber II's 'Decision on the Prosecutor's Application for Summonses to Appear for Francis Kirimi Muthaura, Uhuru Muigai Kenyatta and Mohammed Hussein Ali') ICC-01/09-02/11-3 (15 March 2011), paras 2-15; *Ruto et al* Decision on Confirmation of Charges (n 210) (Dissenting Opinion by Judge Hans-Peter Kaul), paras 8-10; *Muthaura et al* Decision on Confirmation of Charges (n 210) (Dissenting Opinion by Judge Hans-Peter Kaul) ICC-01/09-02/11-382-Red (26 January 2012), paras 8-10; *Bemba* Trial Chamber Judgment (n 102) (Separate Opinion of Judge Kuniko Ozaki) ICC-01/05-01/08-3343-AnxII, para 29. Cf. *Ntaganda* Trial Chamber Judgment (n 204), para 675 and fn 2135.

211 Elements of Crimes, UN Doc PCNICC/2000/1/Add.2, 5 and fn 6; *Ntaganda* Trial Chamber Judgment (n 204), para 673.
212 *Kenya* Authorisation Decision 2010 (n 93) (n 93), para 94; *Bemba* Decision on Confirmation of Charges (n 102), para 82.
213 UN Doc A/51/22 (1996), Vol I, para 85.

There was general support for the widespread or systematic criteria to indicate the scale and magnitude of the offences. The following were also mentioned as elements to be taken into account: an element of planning, policy, conspiracy or organisation; a multiplicity of victims; acts of a certain duration rather than a temporary, exceptional or limited phenomenon; and acts committed as part of a policy, plan, conspiracy or a campaign rather than random, individual or isolated acts in contrast to war crimes. Some delegations expressed the view that this criterion could be further clarified by referring to widespread and systematic acts of international concern to indicate acts that were appropriate for international adjudication; acts committed on a massive scale to indicate a multiplicity of victims in contrast to ordinary crimes under national law; acts committed systematically or as part of a public policy against a segment of the civilian population; acts committed in application of a concerted plan to indicate the necessary degree of intent, concert or planning; acts committed with the consent of a Government or of a party in control of territory; and exceptionally serious crimes of international concern to exclude minor offences, as in article 20, paragraph (e). Some delegations expressed the view that the criteria should be cumulative rather than alternative.[214]

At the 1998 Rome Conference, delegations agreed that 'not every inhumane act amounts to a crime against humanity' and a threshold is required.[215] Similar to the situation in the Preparatory Committee, views of State delegations were divided as to the relationship between the two qualifiers 'widespread' and 'systematic': a conjunctive test, i.e., widespread and systematic; or a disjunctive test, i.e., widespread or systematic.[216] By referring to the jurisprudence of the two UN *ad hoc* tribunals and the ICTR Statute, a large number of delegations favoured the disjunctive test.[217] In contrast, many other delegations supported

---

214   ibid.
215   ibid, para 84.
216   Robinson (n 6); Hall (1998a) (n 20).
217   'Summary Records of the Plenary Meetings and of the Meetings of the Committee of the Whole', UN Doc A/CONF./183/C.1/SR.3, paras 21 (Germany); 36 (Czech Republic), 61 (Greece), 66 (Malawi), 77 (Korea), 88 (Australia), 93 (Argentina), 109 (Slovenia),112 (Norway), 114 (Côte d'Ivoire), 117 (South Africa), 124 (Mexico), 130 (Finland), 148 (Spain), 150 (Romania), 158 (Venezuela), 162 (Italy), 168 (Ireland); UN Doc A/CONF.183/C.1/SR.4, paras 7 (Switzerland), 8 (Sweden), 11(Portugal), 13 (Vietnam), 14 (Netherlands), 18 (Bangladesh), 20 (Austria), 23 (Sierra Leone), 27 (Chile); UN Doc A/CONF./183/C.1/SR.25, paras 27 (Japan), 78 (Australia), 118 (Lesotho); UN Doc A/CONF./183/C.1/SR.27, para 57 (Congo).

a conjunctive test.[218] Supporters of the conjunctive test doubted whether the 'widespread' test was sufficient to exclude unrelated crimes, such as serial killings, from crimes against humanity. Delegations favouring a disjunctive test responded that this doubt was addressed by the phrase 'an attack directed against any civilian population'. Despite their different positions, State delegations acknowledged that the two qualifiers were not sufficient to define the scope of crimes against humanity. Another qualifier is required under the disjunctive test. Those objecting to the disjunctive test proposed describing the third qualifier explicitly. Article 7(2)(a) was therefore drafted during the Rome Conference, and only two States objected to the inclusion of the third qualifier, the policy.[219] Accordingly, if the attack is not shown to be systematic, the policy requirement serves to exclude widespread but unrelated acts from the scope of crimes against humanity.

Discussions at the Rome Conference indicate political compromise between those worrying about the limitation of national sovereignty and those working for a definition reflecting positive developments.[220] The insertion of the policy paragraph in article 7(2)(a) shares this feature. The final threshold with the policy element in article 7, as Darryl Robinson has noted, is the 'middle ground' between the too restrictive conjunctive test and the too extensive disjunctive test. Judge Kaul pointed out that 'drafters of the Rome Statute confirmed in 1998 in article 7(2)(a) of the Statute the policy requirement [...] as a decisive, characteristic and indispensable feature of crimes against humanity'.[221] 'It is a fundamental rationale of crimes against humanity to protect the international community against the extremely grave threat emanating from such policies.'[222] The ICC's jurisprudence further confirms that the policy is

---

218 'Summary Records of the Plenary Meetings and of the Meetings of the Committee of the Whole', UN Doc A/CONF./183/C.1/SR.3, paras 45 (India), 90 (UK), 96 (France), 108 (Thailand), 120 (Egypt), 136 (Iran), 144 (Indonesia), 172 (Turkey); UN Doc A/CONF.183/C.1/SR.4, paras 5 (Russian Federation), 15 (Bahrain), 17 (Japan), 21 (Uruguay), 30 (Peru); UN Doc A/CONF./183/C.1/SR.25, para 46 (Syria); UN Doc A/CONF./183/C.1/SR.27, paras 11 (Uruguay), 22 (Bahrain).
219 'Discussion Paper prepared by the Bureau', UN Doc A/CONF.183/C.1/L.53 (1998); 'Summary Records of the Plenary Meetings and of the Meetings of the Committee of the Whole', UN Doc A/CONF.183/C.1/SR.34, para 15 (Jamaica); UN Doc A/CONF.183/C.1/SR.36, para 13 (Congo).
220 *Tadić* Opinion and Judgment (n 6), para 654; Robinson (n 6).
221 *Kenya* Authorisation Decision 2010 (n 93) (Dissenting Opinion by Judge Hans-Peter Kaul), para 63.
222 ibid.

an independent requirement for crimes against humanity, directly or indirectly.[223] The ICC in *Bemba* found that the course of conduct 'must reflect a link with the State or organisational policy'.[224] The policy is a threshold to exclude 'spontaneous or isolated acts of violation' from the ambit of crimes against humanity.[225]

Some commentators argue that only if the requirement of either widespread or systematic attack is satisfied, may offences constitute crimes against humanity. In their view, the 'widespread or systematic' disjunctive test is sufficient 'to exclude isolated offences from crimes against humanity'.[226] Some tribunals held that the policy is an evidentiary factor in establishing a systematic character of an attack.[227] These interpretations are contestable as to article 7 of the Rome Statute. As shown above, an independent status of the policy element was established by the drafters of the Statute. The jurisprudence of the ICC has repeatedly clarified that the terms 'policy' and 'systematic' are not

---

223   *Ntaganda* Trial Chamber Judgment (n 204), paras 673, 689; *The Prosecutor v Ongwen* (Decision on the confirmation of charges, PTC II) ICC-02/04-01/15-422-Red (23 March 2016), para 63; *Katanga* Trial Chamber Judgment (n 102), para 1112; *Gbagbo* Decision on Confirmation of Charges (n 209), paras 211-12, 215; *The Prosecutor v Gbagbo* (Judgment on the appeal of the Prosecutor against the decision of Pre-Trial Chamber I of 3 June 2013 entitled 'Decision adjourning the hearing on the confirmation of charges pursuant to Article 61(7)(c)(i) of the Rome Statute', A Ch) ICC-02/11-01/11-572 (16 December 2013), paras 51, 53; id, (Decision adjourning the hearing on the confirmation of charges pursuant to Article 61(7)(c)(i) of the Rome Statute, PTC I) ICC-02/11-01/11-432 (3 June 2013), para 36; *Muthaura et al* Decision on Confirmation of Charges (n 210), para 111; *Ruto et al* Decision on Confirmation of Charges (n 210), paras 181-221; *The Prosecutor v Mbarushimana* (Decision on the confirmation of charges, PTC I) ICC-01/04-01/10-465-Red (16 December 2011), paras 261-63; *Situation in the Republic of Côte d'Ivoire* (Decision Pursuant to Article 15 of the Rome Statute on the Authorisation of an Investigation into the Situation in the Republic of Côte d'Ivoire, PTC III) ICC-02/11-14-Corr (15 November 2011), paras 96-101; *Kenya* Authorisation Decision 2010 (n 93), paras 83-93; *The Prosecutor v Katanga & Ngudjolo* (Decision on the confirmation of charges, PTC I) ICC-01/04-01/07-717 (30 September 2008), paras 396, 398.

224   *Bemba* Trial Chamber Judgment (n 102), para 161; *Katanga* Trial Chamber Judgment (n 102), para 1097.

225   *Bemba* Decision on Confirmation of Charges (n 102), para 81.

226   Mettraux (n 201) 163; G. Werle and F. Jeßberger, *Principles of International Criminal Law* (3rd edn, OUP 2014) 345; *Ntakirutimana* Appeals Chamber Judgment, para 93 and fn 883; *Prosecutor v Kordić & Čerkez* (Judgment) ICTY-95-14/2-A (17 December 2004), para 93; *Prosecutor v Blaškić* (Judgement) ICTY-95-14-A (29 July 2004), para 98; *Kunarać et al* Appeals Chamber Judgment (n 6), para 97.

227   *Katanga* Trial Chamber Judgment (n 102), para 1111; *The Prosecutor v Muhimana* (Judgement) ICTR-95-1B-T (28 April 2005), para 527; *The Prosecutor v Semanza* (Judgement and Sentence) ICTR-97-20-T (15 May 2003), para 512; *Semanza v The Prosecutor* (Judgement) ICTR-97-20-A (20 May 2005), para 269.

synonymous.[228] If policy were only an evidentiary factor of the systematic test, the 'widespread' practice of gang activities would be considered as a crime against humanity in international law.[229] The element of policy also serves the function of excluding ordinary national crimes committed by individuals, for example, serial killings, from being considered as crimes against humanity.[230]

All these observations indicate that policy is a distinct element for crimes against humanity set out in article 7 of the Rome Statute. Policy is considered as a requisite legal element, rather than an evidentiary factor in identifying the systematic character of an attack.

4.5.2 *Policy as a Legal Element of Crimes against Humanity in Custom*
The examination of the preparatory works of article 7 provides no preliminary indication of whether the element of policy was declaratory of customary law in 1998. The texts and the structure of the Rome Statute also offer no hint on this point. Based on the finding that policy is an independent legal element, this subsection endeavours to analyse post-World War II instruments and cases and the jurisprudence of the two UN *ad hoc* tribunals to assess whether article 7(2)(a) was and is declaratory of custom on the element of policy.[231]

4.5.2.1   Policy as a Legal Element before 1998
Several instruments have been referred to in arguing for or against policy as a distinct element under customary law.[232] These documents include article 6(c) of the Nuremberg Charter, the judgment of the IMT, the Report of the Secretary-General on the establishment of the ICTY, the draft ICTY Statute, various versions of the Draft Code of Crimes, and national cases of Australia, Israel, Canada and Yugoslavia.[233] An analysis of whether the policy was a distinct element of this crime in these instruments mostly overlaps with the identification of its customary status because many of these authorities also indicate the formation of a customary rule. The following paragraphs mainly focus on these instruments and cases to show whether the element of policy

---

228 *Katanga* Trial Chamber Judgment (n 102), para 1112; *Gbagbo* Decision on Confirmation of Charges (n 209), para 208.
229 Bassiouni (n 91) 54.
230 Robinson (n 6); D. Robinson, 'Crimes Against Humanity' in R. Cryer *et al*, *An Introduction to International Criminal Law and Procedure* (3rd edn, CUP 2014) 229, 239; Hall and Stahn (n 200) 157–58.
231 Schabas (n 6) 972–74, 982; G. Werle and B. Burghardt, 'Do Crimes Against Humanity Require the Participation of a State or a "State-like" Organisation?' (2012) 10 *JICJ* 1151, 1169.
232 Mettraux (n 6) 270–82.
233 *Kunarać et al* Appeals Chamber Judgment (n 6), para 98 and fn 114.

was generally recognised as a distinct element of crimes against humanity before 1998.

Both the Nuremberg and Tokyo Charters did not expressly refer to a plan or policy. The absence of an express reference to 'policy' does not lead to the conclusion that policy was not required. A literal reading approach should be adopted carefully. For instance, based on a literal reading, it might be said that the 'widespread or systematic' test, which was not explicitly contained in the ICTY Statute, is not a requirement for crimes against humanity.[234] This idea is not correct. Therefore, a further examination of the two Charters is required on the issue of policy.

Three main points deserve attention. It should be first noted that the Nuremberg and Tokyo Charters were illustrative rather than exhaustive attempts at definition, which means that they may not provide a complete definition of crimes against humanity. Second, the drafters of the Nuremberg Charter designed crimes against humanity, as observed above, connected with an armed conflict, as a part of 'a plan' for aggressive wars committed by Germany against German nationals. At the London Conference, Jackson said:

> The reason that this program of extermination of Jews and destruction of the rights of minorities becomes an international concern is this: it was a part of a plan for making an illegal war. [...] They were a part of the preparation for war or for the conduct of the war in so far as they occurred inside of Germany and that makes them our concern.[235]

Third, the two Charters were adopted to deal with crimes committed by the aggressive regimes of Germany and Japan. The existence of the policy of aggressive wars was not an issue in the two tribunals.[236] The IMT did state that:

> The policy of terror was certainly carried out on a vast scale, and in many cases was organised and systematic. The policy of persecution, repression, and murder of civilians in Germany before the war of 1939, who were likely to be hostile to the Government, was most ruthlessly carried out. The persecution of Jews during the same period is established beyond all doubt.[237]

---

234   *Tadić* Opinion and Judgment (n 6), para 656.
235   'Minutes of Conference Session of July 23, 1945' in Report of Robert H. Jackson (n 43) 331.
236   Schabas (n 6).
237   *France et al v Göring et al* (n 64) 254.

The IMT, therefore, recognised the existence of a 'policy of persecution and murder' of political opponents and Jewish population for crimes against humanity. The historical reality that most crimes against humanity were committed in furtherance of a plan or policy might justify that the drafters of the Nuremberg Charter considered this contextual element in creating the notion of crimes against humanity.[238]

Two examples are frequently referred to argue for the non-existence of the element of policy in the Nuremberg Charter. Streicher and von Schirach were convicted only of crimes against humanity by the IMT. Stretcher as a Nazi propagandist was found guilty of crimes against humanity for his incitement to persecution, which was connected with war crimes committed by others.[239] Von Schirach was found guilty of crimes against humanity for his participation in the deportation plan in occupied Austria since 1940.[240] The two examples in effect indicate the existence rather than the non-existence of the policy element because the policy of aggressive wars was the background for all charges of crimes against humanity before the IMT. In the *Belsen* case, the military tribunal also stated that 'the concentration camp system was in any case intended to further the German war effort'.[241] On the whole, the 'policy' underlying crimes against humanity was implicit in the Nazi Party policy of aggressive wars.[242]

One different view should be addressed. Some commentators argue that the reference to policy simply recognises a form of criminal participation, by which the furtherance of policy is equally applied to war crimes and crimes against peace.[243] Jean Graven explained that:

> The confusion of the 'conspiracy' condition resulted from the last paragraph of article 6 of the Nuremberg Charter, stipulating that '[l]eaders, organisers, instigators and accomplices participating in the formulation or execution of a common plan or conspiracy to commit any of the foregoing crimes are responsible for all acts performed by any persons in execution of such plan.' However, it does not mean that the perpetrator of crimes against humanity is punishable only if a crime results from such a plan.[244]

---

238 Cf. deGuzman (n 93) 121–38.
239 *France et al v Göring et al* (n 64) 318–20.
240 ibid 302–04.
241 The *Belsen* case (n 56) 1–2, 73.
242 'Minutes of Conference Session of July 24, 1945' in Report of Robert H. Jackson (n 43) 361.
243 Mettraux (n 201) 165.
244 J. Graven, 'Les Crimes contre l'Humanité' (1950) 76 *Recueil des cours* 427, 560 and fn 4.

According to Graven, the reference to a 'plan' stipulated in the concluding paragraph of article 6 concerns individual responsibility of leaders and members of an organisation for acts in execution of the aggressive plan. In the *Justice* case, the military tribunal considered participation in a common plan or conspiracy to commit crimes against humanity as a mode of liability.[245] The existence of the plan/policy is an essential factor for the assessment of individual contributions to offences of crimes against peace, war crimes and crimes against humanity, rather than a unique requirement for crimes against humanity. By referring to a plan, the focus of the authority is the mode of liability.[246] Therefore, the existence of policy is not a contextual element to convict a person of crimes against humanity.[247] This idea reveals an alternative function of a plan/policy as a material element of the complicity liability.[248] Yet, this alternative function of policy does not lead to a conclusive finding that policy does not serve as an element of crimes against humanity.

The Nazi and Japanese policies of aggressive wars were not only the background facts. The UN War Crimes Commission once concluded that '[n]ot only the ringleaders, but also the actual perpetrators of crimes against humanity were criminally responsible',[249] which recognised the leaders' role in the policy of aggressive wars from a top-to-bottom perspective, and indirectly affirmed the policy requirement for crimes against humanity. Further evidence tends to enhance this viewpoint and develop the notion of crimes against humanity under customary law. The ILC's Drafts Code of Crimes implicitly endorsed the element of policy in its drafts of 1950, 1951, 1954, 1991 and 1996. For instance, the words 'by the authorities of a State or by private individuals' were added in the 1951 Draft Code of Crimes.[250] The phrase 'private individuals' initiated a debate about whether this crime requires a connection to a State or group, which is a 'threshold requirement'[251] in recent discussions that was not used in the 1950s debates. The 1954 formulation of crimes against humanity confirmed the reference to 'authorities of a State or private individuals' and added the phrase 'acting at the instigation or with the toleration of such authorities'.[252] This new insertion shows great strength of

---

245   The *Justice* case (n 31) 954, 1063.
246   ibid.
247   Graven (n 244) 560.
248   *Poland v Goeth* (1948) 7 LRTWC 1; *Poland v Hoess Commandant of the Auschwitz Camp* (1948) 7 LRTWC 11, 24.
249   UNWCC (ed) (n 28) 178–79.
250   1951 Draft Code of Offences, UN Doc A/CN.4/SER.A/1951, art 2 (9).
251   Chapter 4.5.1.1.
252   1954 Draft Code of Offences, in UN Doc A/CN.4/SER.A/1954/Add.1, Vol II, 150.

a plan or policy as a contextual element. The 1991 and 1996 Drafts included the new phrase of 'instigation by Government, organisation and groups'.[253] This phrase is a modified version of the State involvement requirement. The phrase 'involvement or toleration of State authorities' was introduced for the notion of crimes against humanity.[254] The drafting committee and commentaries on the 1996 Draft Code of Crimes explained that this phrase was added to exclude random acts or an isolated inhumane act.[255] In short, a logical conclusion is that policy was a contextual legal element for crimes against humanity at its creation.

Several post-World War II cases also deemed policy a legal element for crimes against humanity. The military tribunal in the *Justice* case expressly stated that only criminals who consciously participated in 'systematic governmentally organised or approved procedures' would be punished for crimes against humanity.[256] The tribunal in *Ministries* held that 'governmental participation is a material element of crimes against humanity.'[257] Additionally, the French Court of Appeal in the *Barbie* case stated that crimes against humanity within the meaning of article 6(c) of the Nuremberg Charter are 'inhuman acts and acts of persecution committed by the State pursuing a policy of ideological supremacy in a systematic way against individuals'.[258] In contrast, the Australian High Court held that with respect to 'systematic governmental procedures', the idea in the *Justice* case 'had not been accepted as an authoritative statement of customary international law'.[259] This decision, however, does not discredit the view of policy as a legal element. The purpose of the High Court was not to reject the element of policy but rather to include the policy of non-State actors. All other cases or claims, aiming to extend the scope of policy-making entities or dissatisfying with a narrow scope of policy-making entities, implicitly acknowledged that the element of policy was required for crimes against humanity.

---

253   1996 Draft Code of Crimes, art 18.
254   ibid art 18.5; 1954 Draft Code of Offences, art 2.
255   Schabas (n 6).
256   The *Justice* case (n 31) 954, 982, 984. See also UNWCC, Notes on the Justice Case, (1947) 6 LRTWC 76, 83, fn 3; 'Draft Code of Offences against the Peace and Security of Mankind, Report by Mr J. Spiropoulos, Special Rapporteur', UN Doc A/CN.4/25 (1950), para 65.
257   The *Ministries* case (n 157) 984.
258   *Advocate General v Klaus Barbie* (Judgement, Court of Cassation, France) 86–92714 (25 November 1986) 3. See also *Advocate General v Klaus Barbie* (Judgement, Court of Cassation, France) 85–95166 (20 December 1985) 14–15, (1985) 78 ILR 124; *Advocate General v Touvier* (Judgment, Court of Cassation, France), (1995) 100 ILR 337.
259   *Polyukhovich* case (n 29).

Further confirmation of the element of policy in international law can be found in recent national laws and courts prosecuting crimes against humanity or genocide committed before 1998. The Dutch Supreme Court in the *Menten* case interpreted that the element of policy is embedded in the definition of article 6(c) of the Nuremberg Charter.[260] The Iraqi High Tribunal in the *Al-Dujail* case affirmed the policy requirement for crimes against humanity in 1982.[261] A Panama court recognised the policy requirement for crimes against humanity committed from 1968 to 1989.[262] Colombia and Chile in the *Pinochet* cases also endorsed the necessity of policy.[263] A Peruvian court held that '[t]he murders and severe bodily harm inflicted in Barrios Altos and La Cantuta also constitute crimes against humanity, fundamentally because they were committed within the framework of a State policy for the selective but systematic elimination of alleged members of subversive groups.'[264] The Canadian Supreme Court in the *Finta* case affirmed that the policy was an element of crimes against humanity.[265]

In national legislation, there is more discrepancy than consistency concerning the policy requirement. The criminal codes of some States referred to a premeditated plan.[266] Australia, Bangladesh and other States' criminal codes did

---

260   *Public Prosecutor v Menten* (Judgment, Supreme Court, the Netherlands), (1981) 75 ILR 331, 362–63.
261   *The Public Prosecutor in the High Iraqi Court et al v Saddam Hussein Al Majeed et al* (Opinion, Appeals Commission, IHT) 29/c/2006 (26 December 2006), 7–8.
262   *Cruz Mojica Flores* Case (Appeal motion, Supreme Court, Panama) (List of Judgments 11.c), in X. Medellín-Urquiaga, *Digest of Latin American Jurisprudence on International Crimes*, Vol I (Due Process of Law Foundation 2010) 37.
263   *Clandestine Detention Centres of DINA* case (Application for revocation of immunity of Augusto Pinochet Ugarte, Supreme Court, Chile) 21 April 2006 (List of Judgments 3.c), Whereas 3, in Medellín-Urquiaga (n 262) 38–39 and fn 39; *José Rubén Peña Tobón et al* case (Ruling and motion for comprehensive reparations, Colombia) 1 December 2011 (List of Judgments 2.b), in X. Medellín-Urquiaga, *Digest of Latin American Jurisprudence on International Crimes*, Vol II (Due Process of Law Foundation 2013) 4–5.
264   *Prosecutor v Alberto Fujimori* (Judgment, Supreme Court of Justice, Special Criminal Chamber, Peru) A.V 19-2001 (7 April 2009) (List of Judgments 13.j), in Medellín-Urquiaga (n 262) 40: whereas 717.
265   *R v Finta* (Judgment, Supreme Court), [1994] 1 SCR 701, paras 814, 823. For comments on this case, see Mettraux (n 201) 166.
266   Cambodia, Provisions relating to the Judiciary and Criminal Law and Procedure Applicable in Cambodia during the Transitional Period 1992, art 188; Albania, Criminal Code 1995, art 74; Spain, Criminal Code 1995, amended 2015, art 607*bis*; Finland, Criminal Code 1889, amended 2015, chapter 1, §§ 7(3) and (4).

not refer to the wording 'policy' or 'plan'.[267] The texts of national law with or without a reference to policy do not exclusively demonstrate State practice and attitude towards the element of 'policy' for crimes against humanity. Further interpretation and application of these provisions are needed from an international law perspective. For instance, the Australian Criminal Code did not refer to the term policy, but Australian courts supported the element of policy.[268] In addition, despite a reference to 'premeditated plan' in the definition of crimes against humanity, the Bangladesh International Tribunals argued for no policy in custom.[269] National law alone is less valuable for the assessment of the element of policy.

It is true that the policy in the definition of crimes against humanity was first explicitly mentioned in the Rome Statute. However, as shown above, these post-World War II authorities indicate that evidence of practice and opinions at the international and national levels support policy as an element for crimes against humanity. The work of the ILC also tends to require the policy element in its draft codes of crimes.[270] Schabas claims that sufficient authorities confirm policy as an element of crimes against humanity.[271] Robinson also argues that 'the applicability of the policy element is supported by the bulk of authority [including decisions of national courts] since Nuremberg'.[272] These authorities seem to reveal that policy was a distinct element under customary law before 1998.

The drafting of article 7 of the Rome Statute mentioned above further provides evidence of *opinio juris* as to the development of custom when recommendations of States were adopted in 1998. States attending the Rome Conference widely recognised this element. A recent instance can be found in the Crimes against Humanity and War Crimes Act of Canada, which provides that crime under article 7 of the Rome Statute are, 'as of 17 July 1998, crimes according to customary international law', and 'may be crimes according to

---

267 Australia, Criminal Code 1995, §§ 268.8-268.23; Croatia, Criminal Code 1998, amended 2011, art 157a; Latvia, Criminal Law 1998, amended 2013, § 71(2); Bangladesh, International Crimes (Tribunals) Act 1973, amended 2013, § 3(2)(a).
268 *Polyukhovich* case (n 29).
269 *Chief Prosecutor v Delowar Hossain Sayeedi* (Judgment, International Crimes Tribunal-1) ICT-BD 01 of 2011 (28 February 2013), para 30(4); *Chief Prosecutor v Salauddin Quader Chowdhury* (Judgment, International Crimes Tribunal-1) ICT-BD 02 of 2011 (1 October 2013), para 36(4).
270 UN Doc A/74/10 (2019), paras 44-45, art 2 and commentary.
271 ibid; Schabas (n 6) 972–74.
272 Robinson (n 6) 48.

customary international law before that date'.[273] Overwhelming evidence shows that the element of policy was required for crimes against humanity. Article 7 of the Statute crystallised the element of policy for crimes against humanity under customary law at the very least in 1998.

4.5.2.2 Policy as a Legal Element in the Jurisprudence of the Two UN Ad Hoc Tribunals

The following paragraphs analyse the jurisprudence of the ICTY and the ICTR to show whether article 7(2)(a) was not declaratory of custom on the element of policy. Most of these decisions were delivered after the adoption of the Rome Statute, but they dealt with crimes committed prior to 1998.

The jurisprudence of the ICTY shows two trends on the issue of policy. At the outset, the ICTY case law required the 'policy' element for crimes against humanity. In interpreting the phrase 'attack against any civilian population', the Trial Chamber in the *Tadić* case confirmed that 'there must be some form of a governmental, organisational or group policy to commit these acts'.[274] The Chamber considered policy as a distinct requirement aside from the widespread and systematic tests.

The Trial Chamber in the *Blaškić* case, however, held that policy was a legal element implied in the 'systematic' requirement.[275] The *Blaškić* Trial Chamber Judgment led subsequent chambers to doubt the independent status of the element of policy. For instance, the *Kupreškić* Trial Chamber held that 'there is some doubt as to whether [policy] is strictly a *requirement*, as such, for crimes against humanity.'[276] By endorsing the *Kupreškić* decision, the *Kordić* Trial Chamber concluded that 'the existence of a plan or policy should better be regarded as indicative of the systematic character of offences charged as crimes against humanity'.[277]

In the *Kunarać et al* case, the Trial Chamber commented that 'there has been some difference of approach [...] as to whether a policy element is required under existing customary law'. In that case, the defendants were held responsible for crimes against humanity for sexual assault or rape of detained Muslim

---

273   Canada, Crimes against Humanity and War Crimes Act 2000, amended 2019, §§ 4(4) and 6(4).
274   *Tadić* Opinion and Judgment (n 6), para 644.
275   *Prosecutor v Blaškić* (Judgement) ICTY-95-14-T (3 March 2000), paras 203-05, 254; *Blaškić* Appeals Chamber Judgment (n 226), paras 119-20.
276   *Prosecutor v Kupreškić et al* (Judgement) ICTY-95-16-T (14 January 2000), para 551 (emphasis in original).
277   *Prosecutor v Kordić & Čerkez* (Judgment) ICTY-95-14/2-T (26 February 2001), paras 181–82.

women. Deeming that the policy requirement was satisfied, the Trial Chamber did not decide on this issue. However, in a footnote, the Chamber wrote that 'it was open to question whether the [...] sources often cited by Chambers of the ICTY and of the ICTR support[ed] the existence of such a requirement'.[278] Later on, by citing the footnote quoted and without providing further interpretations, the Trial Chamber in the *Krnojelac* case asserted that 'there is no requirement under customary international law that the acts of the accused person [...] be connected to a policy or plan'.[279]

A door was opened at the Appeals Chamber in *Kunarać et al* to consider policy as an evidentiary factor in establishing the systematic character of an attack instead of an independent legal requirement. The Appeals Chamber in the *Kunarać et al* case concluded that:

> [...] the attack [does not need] to be supported by any form of 'policy' or 'plan'. There was nothing in the [ICTY] Statute or in customary international law at the time of the alleged acts which required proof of the existence of a plan or policy to commit these crimes.[280]

According to the Chamber:

> [...] proof that the attack was directed against a civilian population and that it was widespread or systematic, are legal elements of the crime. But to prove these elements, it is not necessary to show that they were the result of the existence of a policy or plan. It may be useful in establishing that the attack was directed against a civilian population and that it was widespread or systematic (especially the latter) to show that there was in fact a policy or plan, but it may be possible to prove these things by reference to other matters. Thus, the existence of a policy or plan may be evidentially relevant, but it is not a legal element of the crime.[281]

After the *Kunarać et al* Appeals Chamber judgment, the jurisprudence of the ICTY did not support the element of policy for crimes against humanity under

---

278 *Prosecutor v Kunarać et al* (Judgement) ICTY-96-23-T and ICTY-96-23/1-T (22 February 2001), paras 432, 479 and fn 1109.
279 *Prosecutor v Krnojelac* (Judgment) ICTY-97-25-T (15 March 2002), para 58.
280 *Kunarać et al* Appeals Chamber Judgment (n 6), paras 98, 101.
281 ibid, para 98.

customary law.[282] The ICTY Chambers deemed the 'policy' an evidentiary factor rather a distinct element of crimes against humanity.[283]

The jurisprudence of the ICTR followed in the ICTY's footsteps on the issue of the element of policy.[284] The ICTR's earlier decisions held that '[a] systematic attack is one carried out pursuant to a preconceived policy or plan',[285] and that the element of policy effectively excludes acts carried out outside of a broader policy or plan for purely personal motives.[286] By endorsing the *Kunarać et al* Appeals Chamber judgment of the ICTY, its later cases abandoned the view of policy as a legal requirement.[287] Subsequent trials of the ICTR also treated

282 *Prosecutor v Vasiljević* (Judgement) ICTY-98-32-T (29 November 2002), para 36; *Simić et al* Trial Chamber Judgment (n 98), para 44; *Prosecutor v Galić* (Judgement) ICTY-98-29-T (5 December 2003), para 147; *Blaškić* Appeals Chamber Judgment (n 226), paras 119-20; *Prosecutor v Brđanin* (Judgement) ICTY-99-36-T (1 September 2004), para 137; *Kordić & Čerkez* Appeals Chamber Judgment (n 226), para 98; *Blagojević & Jokić* Trial Chamber Judgment (n 98), para 546; *Limaj et al* Trial Chamber Judgment (n 98), para 212; *Prosecutor v Krajišnik* (Judgement) ICTY-00-39-T (27 September 2006), para 706.

283 *Limaj et al* Trial Chamber Judgment (n 98) paras 184, 212; *Galić* Trial Chamber Judgment (n 282), para 147; *Simić et al* Trial Chamber Judgment (n 98), para 44; *Blagojević & Jokić* Trial Chamber Judgment, ibid; *Prosecutor v Martić* (Judgement) ICTY-95-11-T (12 June 2007), para 49; *Prosecutor v Perišić* (Judgement) ICTY-04-81-T (6 September 2011), para 86; *Prosecutor v Tolimir* (Judgement) ICTY-05-88/2-T (12 December 2012), para 698; *Prosecutor v Stanišić & Župljanin* (Judgement) ICTY-08-91-T (27 March 2013), para 28; *Stanišić & Simatović* Trial Chamber Judgment (n 92), para 963.

284 *The Prosecutor v Akayesu* (Judgement) ICTR-96-4-T (2 September 1998), paras 579-80; *The Prosecutor v Kayishema & Ruzindana* (Judgment) ICTR-95-1-T (21 May 1999), paras 122-24 and fn 28; *The Prosecutor v Rutaganda* (Judgement and Sentence) ICTR-96-3-T (6 December 1999), paras 69, 71; *The Prosecutor v Musema* (Judgement and Sentence) ICTR-96-13-T (27 January 2000), para 204; *The Prosecutor v Ruggiu* (Judgement and Sentence) ICTR-97-32-T (1 June 2000), para 20; *The Prosecutor v Bagilishema* (Judgement) ICTR-95-1A-T (7 June 2001), paras 77-78.

285 *Akayesu* Trial Chamber Judgment, ibid. Followed by *Mugesera v Canada*, [2003] FCA 325, para 52; *Bukumba v Canada*, [2004] FC 93, para 15.

286 *Kayishema & Ruzindana* Trial Chamber Judgment (n 284), paras 122-24 and fn 28.

287 *Semanza* Trial Chamber Judgment and Sentence (n 227), para 329; *Semanza* Appeals Chamber Judgment (n 227), para 269; *The Prosecutor v Kajelijeli* (Judgment and Sentence) ICTR-98-44A-T (1 December 2003), para 872; *The Prosecutor v Kamuhanda* (Judgement) ICTR-99-54A-T (22 January 2004), para 665; *The Prosecutor v Ntagerura et al* (Judgement and Sentence) ICTR-99-46-T (25 February 2004), para 698; *The Prosecutor v Gacumbitsi* (Judgement) ICTR-01-64-T (17 June 2004), para 299; *Gacumbitsi v The Prosecutor* (Judgement) ICTR-01-64-A (7 July 2006), para 512; *The Prosecutor v Seromba* (Judgement) ICTR-01-66-T (13 December 2006), para 356; *The Prosecutor v Seromba* (Judgement) ICTR-01-66-A (12 March 2008) para 149; *Nahimana et al v The Prosecutor* (Judgement) ICTR-99-52-A (28 November 2007), para 922.

policy as an evidentiary factor for the assessment of attack.[288] It is worthwhile noting that the policy issue are insignificant in these Rwanda cases because the existence of a policy was never in doubt. But the issue of policy is substantial in the *Kunarać et al* case because in that case no policy existed in the background.[289]

According to the *Kunarać et al* Appeals Chamber, the element of policy for crimes against humanity never existed under customary law. This view has been subscribed to not only by the ICTR but also by other tribunals, for example, the SCSL.[290] Some national courts simply relied on the *Kunarać et al* Appeals Chamber judgment to argue for no policy element for crimes against humanity.[291] The Appeals Chamber only briefly explained its argument in a footnote, which said: 'although there has been some debate[s] in the jurisprudence of this Tribunal as to whether a policy or plan constitutes an element of the definition of crimes against humanity; [t]he practice [...] overwhelmingly supports the contention that no such requirement exists under customary international law'.[292] The Chamber, however, failed to provide a detailed explanation as to how the authorities addressed in the footnote support its position.[293]

Some commentators have endorsed its conclusion by referring to similar authorities.[294] In contrast, Bassiouni pointed out that this Chamber

> misapplied the law with respect to a State policy [...] on the basis of a misstatement of precedential authority. [...] [T]he Tribunal relied on precedents that held to the contrary of the proposition of which these precedents were cited.[295]

---

288 *Semanza* Trial Chamber Judgment and Sentence, ibid; *Semanza* Appeals Chamber Judgment, ibid.
289 *Kunarać et al* Appeals Chamber Judgment (n 6), para 75.
290 *Prosecutor v Brima et al* (Judgment) SCSL-04-16-T (20 June 2007), para 215; *Prosecutor v Fofana & Kondewa* (Judgment) SCSL-2004-14-T (2 August 2007), para 113; *Prosecutor v Fofana & Kondewa* (Judgment) SCSL-2004-14-A (28 May 2008), para 246; *Prosecutor v Sesay et al* (Judgment) SCSL-04-15-T (2 March 2009), para 79.
291 *Mugesera v Canada*, [2005] 2 SCR 100, para 158; *Chief Prosecutor v Delowar Hossain Sayeedi* (Judgment, International Crimes Tribunal-1) ICT-BD 01 of 2011 (28 February 2013), para 30(4); *Chief Prosecutor v Salauddin Quader Chowdhury* (Judgment, International Crimes Tribunal-1) ICT-BD 02 of 2011 (1 October 2013), para 36(4).
292 *Kunarać et al* Appeals Chamber Judgment (n 6), para 98 and fn 114.
293 ibid (emphasis in original).
294 Mettraux (n 6); D. Hunt, 'The International Criminal Court – High Hopes, Creative Ambiguity and an Unfortunate Mistrust in International Judges' (2004) 2 *JICJ* 56.
295 Bassiouni (n 91) 54.

The observations in subsection 4.5.2.1 show that the authorities cited in the *Kunarać et al* Appeals Chamber judgment have been misinterpreted. Some authorities are not closely relevant to the issue of policy, while some authorities recognise policy as a legal element for crimes against humanity.[296] The Appeals Chamber in *Kunarać et al* cited three Canadian cases from lower courts but ignored the 1994 Supreme Court *Finta* case. The *Kunarać et al* Appeals Chamber judgment is less persuasive on the point of policy.[297]

In sum, the two UN *ad hoc* tribunals confirmed policy as an element of crimes against humanity in their early jurisprudence. The two tribunals in their subsequent decisions held that customary law requires no policy for crimes against humanity. The *Kunarać et al* Appeals Chamber judgment is the turning point on the issue of the element of policy. The fact that the *Kunarać et al* Appeals Chamber judgment has repeatedly been endorsed by later jurisprudence cannot make it a convincing authority or guarantee that the debate about the element of policy is well settled under customary law. The above observations tend to support the finding in the initial jurisprudence of the two UN *ad hoc* tribunals that the element of policy was a legal requirement under customary law. Thus, article 7(2)(a) was declaratory of customary law on the element of policy.

4.5.2.3 Policy as a Legal Element in Customary International Law after 1998

It is noteworthy that the *Kunarać et al* Appeals Chamber judgment is not conclusive evidence for the status of customary law on the element of policy at present.[298] The *Kunarać et al* Appeals Chamber reached its conclusion by qualifying the time 'at which the crimes occurred' in 1992 to 1993, although subsequent cases citing this decision did not cautiously restate this phrase. These ICTY decisions did not examine the text of article 7(2)(a) of the Rome Statute despite that they were delivered after the Statute's entry into force. Chambers of these decisions also did not consider the impact of article 7(2)(a) on the formation of customary international law as other chambers did.[299] Therefore, by merely referring to the *Kunarać et al* Appeals Chamber judgment, it is unclear

---

296 C.C. Jalloh, 'What Makes Crimes Against Humanity Crimes Against Humanity?' (2013) 28 *Am U Intl L Rev* 381, 400–01.
297 ibid; Schabas (n 6) 959–64.
298 *Furundžija* Trial Chamber Judgment (n 196), para 227.
299 ibid, paras 227, 231; *Tadić* Appeals Chamber Judgment (n 25), paras 222-23, 255-71; *Blaškić* Appeals Chamber Judgment (n 226), para 653, fn 1366; *Prosecutor v Šainović et al* (Appeal Judgement) ICTY-05-87-A (23 January 2014), paras 1626-50.

CRIMES AGAINST HUMANITY

whether the policy element outlined in the Rome Statute is declaratory of a customary rule now. The following paragraphs address this issue.

At the present time, the Rome Statute has been adopted and signed by more than two-thirds of the States in the world. The ICC itself has interpreted policy as an element of crimes against humanity. After the adoption of the Rome Statute, most national implementation legislation further supports policy as a legal element for crimes against humanity. Much of the implementation legislation refers to policy. Some legislation refers to the phrase 'instigated or directed by a State or an organisation' used in the 1996 version of the Draft Code of Crimes.[300] Some others directly or indirectly incorporate article 7(2)(a) of the Rome Statute into their national law with small revisions.[301] But many other national laws merely incorporate the definition of crimes against humanity set out in article 7(1) of the Statute. Thus, they do not refer to the policy requirement as provided for in article 7(2)(a).[302]

Furthermore, most legislation supports policy as a legal requirement for crimes against humanity as to underlying acts. For example, the Swiss Criminal

---

300   Estonia, Penal Code 2001, amended 2014, § 89; Greece, Law on the adaptation of internal law to the provisions of the ICC Statute 2002, amended 2011, art 8.

301   Bosnia and Herzegovina, Criminal Code 2003, amended 2018, art 172; Ireland, ICC Act 2006; Kenya, International Crimes Act 2008, § 6(4); Lesotho, Penal Code 2010, amended 2012, § 94(2); Liechtenstein, Act on Cooperation with the ICC and other International Tribunals 2004, art 3; Lithuania, Criminal Code 2000, amended 2015, art 100; Malta, Criminal Code 1854, amended 2016, § 54C(2)(a); Mauritius, ICC Act 2011, § 2; Netherlands, International Crimes Act 2003, § 4(2); New Zealand, International Crimes and ICC Act 2000, § 10(2); Republic of Korea, Act on the Punishment of Crimes within the Jurisdiction of the ICC 2007, art 9; Samoa, ICC Act 2007, § 6; Slovakia, Criminal Code 2005, amended 2009, § 425; South Africa, Implementation Act 2002, § 1; Uganda, ICC Act 2010, § 8; UK, ICC Act 2001, § 50.

302   Australia, ICC (Consequential Amendments) Act 2002, Subdivision C; Azerbaijan, Criminal Code 1999, amended 2020, arts 105-113; Belgium, Act of 16 June 1993 concerning the punishment of Grave Breaches of the Geneva Conventions of 12 August 1949 and their Additional Protocols I and II of 18 June 1977, amended 2003, art 7; Canada, Crimes against Humanity and War Crimes Act 2000, amended 2019, §§ 4(3), 6(3) and 6(5); Costa Rica, Criminal Prosecution to Punish War Crimes and Crimes against Humanity 2002, art 2; Croatia, Criminal Code 1998, amended 2011, art 90; Fiji, Crimes Decree 2009, Part 12, Division 3; Finland, Criminal Code 1889, amended 2015, Chapter 11, § 3; Germany, Code of Crimes against International Law 2002, § 1(7); Georgia, Criminal Code 1999, amended 2016, art 408; Latvia, Criminal Law 1998, amended 2013, § 71(2); Montenegro, Criminal Code 2003, amended 2012, art 427; Philippines, Act on Crimes against IHL, Genocide, and Other Crimes against Humanity 2009, § 6; Poland, Criminal Code 1997, amended 2016, arts 118-120; Romania, Criminal Code 2009, amended 2012, art 439; Slovenia, Criminal Code 2008, amended 2009, art 101; Timor-Leste, Penal Code 2009, art 124; Trinidad and Tobago, ICC Act 2006, § 10.

Code provides that the act of enforced disappearance of persons should be committed on behalf of or with the acquiescence of a State or political organisation.[303] However, different views remain. The Turkish Criminal Code regards plan as factual evidence to show the existence of specific intent for acts of persecution.[304] But a plain reading should be carefully employed. Instances in national legislation where there is no reference to policy do not exclusively amount to substantial evidence of *opinio juris* on the issue of the element of policy. These national laws do not discredit the view that crimes against humanity require the element of policy under customary law.

In contrast to national laws, some national cases have taken a clear position on the issue of policy. In interpreting article 7(2)(a) of the Rome Statute, the Supreme Court of Argentina concluded that the facts of the case must be linked with a sort of 'policy', understanding this term as directions and guidelines followed by an entity's practice on a specific ground.[305] An Indonesian court reaffirmed the policy element by saying that 'the accused had knowledge of, and sympathised with, the policy to carry out crimes [against humanity], and this is an essential element that distinguishes him from an ordinary criminal'.[306] The court in Bosnia and Herzegovina requires an attack 'pursuant to or in furtherance of a State or organisational policy'.[307] It seems that the idea of the element of policy in customary law is further enhanced following the adoption of the Rome Statute. The ILC's recent work on crimes against humanity also supports the policy element.[308]

On the other hand, other evidence implies that the element of policy is not a part of customary law at a particular moment. By citing article 7(2)(a) of the Rome Statute, the Supreme Court of Canada in 2005 once concluded that 'it seems that there is currently no requirement in customary international law

---

303   Switzerland, Criminal Code 1937, amended 2017, art 264a(1)(E). For similar provisions, see Norway, Penal Code 1902, amended 2008, §§ 101-110; Portugal, Adaptation of Criminal Legislation to ICC Statute 2004, art 9.
304   Turkey, Penal Code 2016, art 77(1); Cassese *et al* (eds) (n 8) 126.
305   *René Jesús Derecho* case (Decision about incidental proceeding on the extinguishment of a criminal complaint, Supreme Court, Argentina) Case No. 24079 (11 July 2007) 10-12; *René Jesús Derecho* case (Judgment, Argentina) Case No. 24079 (29 November 2011).
306   *Prosecution v Abílio Soares* (Judgment, Indonesian *Ad Hoc* Human Rights Court for East Timor, Central Jakarta District Court) 01/PID.HAM/AD.Hoc/2002/ph.JKT.PST (14 August 2002).
307   *Prosecutor's Office v Rašević and Todović* (First Instance Verdict, Court of Bosnia and Herzegovina) (28 February 2008), 37–38. This case was cited in *Prosecutor's Office v Bundalo et al* (Second Instance Verdict, Court of Bosnia and Herzegovina) X-KRŽ-07/419 (28 Jan 2011), para 289.
308   UN Doc A/74/10 (2019), paras 44-45, art 2 and commentary.

that a policy underlies [sic] the attack, though we do not discount the possibility that customary international law may evolve over time so as to incorporate a policy requirement'.[309] Following its logic, article 7 of the Statute was not declaratory of custom on the element of policy in 1998; in addition, the element of policy had not developed into customary law in 2005. However, the position of the Supreme Court should be given less weight for its reference to the *Kunarać et al* Appeals Chamber judgment and its inconsistency with Canadian law. In contrast to the Supreme Court, Canada's legislation maintains that the element of policy has been crystallised into custom since 1998.

To conclude, further evidence after the adoption of the Rome Statute shows that the element of policy continues to be a legal element for crimes against humanity in international law. At present, the element of policy as a requirement is widely recognised. This leads to the conclusion that article 7(2)(a) is declaratory of custom on the issue of the element of policy.

4.5.3 *Conclusions*

The wording 'policy' was explicitly inserted in article 7(2)(a) of the Rome Statute. Policy is considered a distinct legal requirement for crimes against humanity. The Rome Statute did not depart from customary international law but declared existing customary law with respect to the issue of policy. The *Kunarać et al* Appeals Chamber judgment of the ICTY, which deemed policy an evidentiary factor in establishing an attack, is not persuasive on this point. The Elements of Crimes further confirmed this idea. Sufficient evidence suggests that the element of policy was embedded in customary international law in 1998 and that it continues to be a legal element of crimes against humanity under customary law. In short, article 7(2)(a) was and is declaratory of customary law about the element of policy.

4.6 Concluding Remarks

Crimes against humanity was a new type of international crime in the Nuremberg Charter. Before the adoption of the Rome Statute, which provides for crimes against humanity in its article 7, this crime, in general, had already been recognised as a crime under customary law. This chapter critically analysed two related contextual requirements in article 7, the removal of the nexus with an armed conflict and the recognition of the element of policy. As Kai

---

309 *Mugesera v Canada*, [2005] 2 SCR 100, para 158 (citations omitted).

Ambos wrote, the 'codification' of the element of policy in the article 7 'reflects the international element's move from the war nexus requirement, to state or organizational authority'.[310]

This chapter first argues that the texts and the preparatory works of the Rome Statute preliminarily show that article 7 was declaratory of customary law on the nexus issue. Second, this chapter observes that the armed conflict nexus requirement was a substantive element for the notion of crimes against humanity in the Nuremberg Charter. Later on, as a departure from pre-existing customary law, the link with an armed conflict disassociated itself from crimes against humanity. It remains unclear when this nexus disappeared under customary law, but it indeed occurred before 1998. Article 7 of the Rome Statute codified or, at the very least, crystallised crimes against humanity under customary law by excluding the nexus with an armed conflict. Chapter 4 concludes that article 7(1) of the Statute was and is declaratory of custom concerning the disassociation with an armed conflict for crimes against humanity.

Chapter 4 also looked into the notion of policy, arguing that policy is a legal element articulated in article 7 of the Rome Statute. The texts and the preparatory works do not assist in answering whether article 7 was declaratory of custom on the issue of the element of policy. Authorities after World War II indicate that policy of aggressive wars was always in the background of prosecution as a contextual element. In addition to this, the *Kunarać et al* Appeals Chamber judgment of the ICTY deemed policy an evidentiary factor instead a distinct legal element to establish an attack. The authorities prior to this judgment, however, do not assist its conclusion. Its reasoning is not convincing on the policy point. In short, Article 7(2)(a) of the Rome Statute was declaratory of pre-existing custom on the issue of policy. Far from indicating a trend towards removal of the element of policy under customary law, practice since the adoption of the Rome Statute confirms its validity. Therefore, article 7(2)(a) is also declaratory of custom about the element of policy.

---

310   Ambos (n 10) 50–52, 67.

CHAPTER 5

The Crime of Aggression
*Articles 8*bis *and 25(3*bis*) of the Rome Statute and Custom*

5.1   Introductory Remarks

This chapter analyses the relationship between articles 8*bis* and 25(3*bis*) of the Rome Statute and customary international law concerning the leadership element of the crime of aggression. The 1998 Rome Conference provided for the ICC's jurisdiction over the crime of aggression but deferred its definition and enforcement.[1] In 2010, the Kampala Review Conference adopted a definition of the crime of aggression but again deferred its enforcement.[2] Article 8*bis* of the Rome Statute defines the crime of aggression and article 25 paragraph 3*bis* restricts the application of article 25 to persons who shall be responsible for that crime.[3] The provisions on the crime of aggression entered into force in 2013.[4] In December 2017, the Assembly of States Parties (ASP) finally adopted a resolution activating the ICC's jurisdiction over the crime of aggression as of 17 July 2018.[5] Under this resolution, leaders 'in a position effectively to exercise control over or to direct the political or military action of a State' might be held liable for the crime of aggression at the ICC.[6]

---

1   1998 Rome Statute, art 5.
2   1998 Rome Statute, as amended by resolution RC/Res.6 of 11 June 2010, Annex I, art 8*bis*. see Official Record of the Review Conference of the Rome Statute (Kampala, 31 May - 11 June 2010), RC/11, part II.
3   For negotiating on the definition of the crime of aggression, see S. Barriga, 'Negotiating on the Amendments on the crime of aggression' in S. Barriga and C. Kreß (eds), *The Travaux Préparatoires of the Crime of Aggression* (CUP 2012) 3–57. For the relationship between article 8*bis* and article 25(3*bis*), see A. Zimmermann and E. Freiburg 'Article 8*bis*' in O. Triffterer and K. Ambos (eds), *Commentary on the Rome Statute of the International Criminal Court: Observers' Notes, Article by Article* (3rd edn, Hart/Beck 2016) 585.
4   1998 Rome Statute, art 121(5).
5   Activation of the jurisdiction of the Court over the crime of aggression, ICC-ASP/16/Res.5 of 14 December 2017, see Official Record of the sixteenth session of the Rome Statute (New York, 4–14 December 2017), ICC-ASP/16/20/Vol. I, 35. See also C. McDougall, 'Introductory Note to Report on the Facilitation on the Activation of the Jurisdiction of the International Criminal Court over the Crime of Aggression (Int'l Crim. Ct.) & Resolution ICC-ASP/16/RES. 5 on the Activation of the Jurisdiction of the Court over the Crime of Aggression' (2018) 57 *ILM* 513.
6   For discussions on the activation of the ICC's jurisdiction over aggression, see J. Trahan, 'From Kampala to New York – The Final Negotiations to Activate the Jurisdiction of the

---

© YUDAN TAN, 2021 | DOI:10.1163/9789004439412_006

It is generally accepted that the concept of the crime of aggression as the 'supreme international crime' is part of customary law.[7] However, debates exist as to the precise definition of the crime of aggression and its material and mental elements, in particular, the leadership element.[8] Scholars believed that the existence of the leadership element as part of the definition of the crime of aggression is recognised under customary law.[9] Nevertheless, it remains unsettled whether the specific 'control or direct' threshold for the leadership element in the Rome Statute was and is declaratory of custom. Some commentators argued that the leadership crime of aggression may only be committed

International Criminal Court over the Crime of Aggression' (2018) 18 *ICLR* 197; J. Sarkin and J. Almeida, 'Understanding the Activation of the Crime of Aggression at the International Criminal Court: Progress and Pitfalls' (2018) 36 *Wis Intl LJ* 518; C. Kreß, 'On the Activation of ICC Jurisdiction over the Crime of Aggression' in P. Šturma (ed), *The Rome Statute of the ICC at Its Twentieth Anniversary: Achievements and Perspectives* (Brill | Nijhoff 2019) 43–64. For discussions on the legal effect of the resolution in determining the ICC's jurisdiction, see D. Akande and A. Tzanakopoulos, 'Treaty Law and ICC Jurisdiction over the Crime of Aggression' (2018) 29 *EJIL* 939.

7   *France et al v Göring et al*, Judgment and Sentence of the Nuremberg International Military Tribunals, (1948) 1 TMWC 171, 186 the 'supreme international crime'. Lord Goldsmith, Attorney General, 'Iraq: Resolution144' (7 March 2003), para 34: *R v Jones et al* (29 March 2006) [2006] UKHL 16, [12–19] (Lord Bingham), [44, 59] (Lord Hoffmann), [99] (Lord Mance); S. Glaser, 'The Charter of the Nuremberg Tribunal and New Principles of International Law' in G. Mattraux (ed), *Perspectives on the Nuremberg Trial* (OUP 2008) 67–69; A.R. Coracini, 'Evaluating Domestic Legislation on the Customary Crime of Aggression Under the Rome Statute's Complementarity Regime' in C. Stahn and G. Sluiter (eds), *The Emerging Practice of the International Criminal Court* (Brill | Nijhoff 2009) 725; A. Cassese et al (eds), *Cassese's International Criminal Law* (3rd edn, OUP 2013) 142–43; G. Werle and F. Jessberger, *Principles of International Criminal Law* (3rd edn, OUP 2014) 27; A. Zimmermann, 'Article 5' in Triffterer and Ambos (eds) (n 3) 119.

8   H.H. Koh, Legal Adviser, US Department of State, 'Statement at the Review Conference of the International Criminal Court' (Kampala, Uganda, 4 June 2010); B.B. Jia, 'The Crime of Aggression as Custom and the Mechanisms for Determining Acts of Aggression' (2015) 109 *AJIL* 569, 571–72; W.A. Schabas, *The International Criminal Court: A Commentary on the Rome Statute* (2nd edn, OUP 2016) 303. For discussions on the State act, individual conduct and the scope of acts of aggression, see C. McDougall, *The Crime of Aggression under the Rome Statute of the International Criminal Court* (CUP 2013) 137–54, 178–83; Werle and Jessberger (n 7) 534–38; A.R. Coracini and P. Wrange, 'Specificity of the Crime of Aggression' in S. Barriga and C. Kreß (eds), *The Crime of Aggression: A Commentary* (CUP 2017) 309–50. For arguing the 'control or direct' test as a codification of Nuremberg standard, see A. Danner, 'The Nuremberg Industrialist Prosecutions and Aggressive War' (2007) 46 *Va J Intl L* 651, 675.

9   Schabas (n 8) 309; Werle and Jessberger (n 7) 542; Coracini and Wrange (n 8) 310–11; S. Sayapin, *The Crime of Aggression in International Criminal Law: Historical Development, Comparative Analysis and Present State* (Springer 2014) 202. Cf. K. Ambos, 'The Crime of Aggression after Kampala' (2010) 53 *German Ybk Intl L* 463, 478.

by persons 'in a position effectively to exercise control over or to direct the political or military action of a State', which 'is consistent with customary international law as derivable from' the Nuremberg standard.[10] By contrast, Kevin Heller commented that the 'control or direct' requirement in the Rome Statute, as amended by the 2010 ASP resolution 6, retreated from that in the Nuremberg principles.[11]

The 2010 Kampala Amendments on the crime of aggression assimilated the legal nature of the provisions in the 1998 Rome Statute. The central issue here is whether article 8*bis* and article 25 paragraph 3*bis* of the updated Rome Statute were or are declaratory of custom about the 'control or direct' leadership requirement for the crime of aggression, leading to exclude persons who simply shape or influence the action of a State from the scope of persons who shall be liable for the crime of aggression. The sub-questions are whether: (1) articles 8*bis* and 25(3*bis*) were declaratory of a pre-existing customary rule requiring persons in a position 'to control or direct' the action of a State, which committed the act of aggression, at the time when the two provisions were adopted in 2010; and (2) articles 8*bis* and 25(3*bis*) are declaratory of a customary rule now.

This chapter first reviews the crime of aggression in international law in section 5.2, and then interprets and observes provisions concerning the crime of aggression in the Rome Statute in section 5.3. Section 5.3 aims to provide a preliminary answer to the question of whether articles 8*bis* and 25(3*bis*) were articulated as being declaratory of custom concerning the scope of perpetrators for the crime of aggression and then interprets the leadership clause 'to control or direct'. Section 5.4 carefully revisits international instruments and the jurisprudence of international tribunals after World War II to show whether the leadership element for the crime of aggression was inserted as a reflection of customary law. This section will cover, first of all, the Charters and trials of the Nuremberg and Tokyo, and three subsequent trials. Secondly, the work of the International Law Commission (ILC) on the Draft Code of Crimes (Offences), and the drafting and negotiating history of the definition of the crime of aggression, particularly, positions of States on the leadership clause will be examined. Section 5.5 explores further developments of the crime of aggression after the insertion of articles 8*bis* and 25(3*bis*). Section 5.6 concludes with closing remarks based on the examination of the relationship

---

10   Werle and Jessberger (n 7) 550.
11   K.J. Heller, 'Retreat from Nuremberg: The Leadership Requirement in the Crime of Aggression' (2007) 18 *EJIL* 477, 480–88.

between custom and articles 8*bis* and 25(3*bis*) of the Rome Statute on the leadership element of the crime of aggression.

5.2 The Crime of Aggression in International Law

This section briefly surveys aggression and the crime of aggression in international law for a better understanding of the notions used in this chapter.

5.2.1 *The Prohibition of Aggression*

The prohibition of aggression is a requirement for the criminalisation of aggression. International law has not developed in a short time from war being a legitimate tool to the prohibition of aggressive war.[12] The 1928 Kellogg–Briand Pact provides a ban on war, but it did not totally prevent the outbreak of World War II.[13] However, as scholars observed, it is agreed that by the end of the 1930s, States' attitude towards war had changed dramatically, and aggressive wars were restricted if not totally outlawed in international law.[14] The 1945 UN Charter then provides the prohibition of 'the threat or use of force', grants the right of the Security Council to take measures where 'acts of aggression' occur, and also recognises the right of self-defence against an 'armed attack'.[15] The 1974 UN General Assembly Resolution 3314 (XXIX) defines aggression and employs the term 'act of aggression', which covers aggressive wars and acts of less intensive than war.[16] The UN Security Council, the General Assembly and

---

[12] Y. Dinstein, *War, Aggression and Self-Defence* (5th edn, CUP 2012) 85–123; Sayapin (n 9) 1–38; S. Barriga and C. Kreß (eds), *The Crime of Aggression: A Commentary* (CUP 2017).

[13] General Treaty for Renunciation of War (signed 27 August 1928) [Kellogg–Briand Pact], 94 LNTS 57, 63.

[14] For discussions on the development of prohibition of aggression, Werle and Jessberger (n 7) 530–34; G. Kemp, *Individual Criminal Liability for the International Crime of Aggression* (2nd edn, Intersentia 2016) chapters 2–3; M.C. Bassiouni, 'The Status of Aggression in International Law from Versailles to Kampala – and What the Future Might Hold' in L.N. Sadat (ed), *Seeking Accountability for the Unlawful Use of Force* (CUP 2018) 5–57.

[15] The UN Charter, arts 2(4), 39 and 51.

[16] 'Definition of Aggression', GA Res 3314 (XXIX) (1974), UN Doc A/RES/3314 (XXIX). E. Wilmshurst, 'Introductory Note to Definition of the Crime of Aggression: General Assembly resolution 3314 (XXIX)' (August 2008), UN Audiovisual Library of International Law, Historical Archives <https://legal.un.org/avl/ha/da/da.html> accessed 20 January 2021. For a history of the committees on aggression's work, see B.B. Ferencz, *Defining International Aggression: The Search for World Peace (A Documentary History and Analysis)*, Vol 2 (Oceana Publications 1975) 77–540; B. Broms, 'The Definition of Aggression' (1977) 154 *Recueil des cours* 299.

the International Court of Justice have previously determined several situations involving State acts of aggression.[17]

5.2.2 The Criminalisation of Aggression

Aside from the prohibition of State act of aggression in public international law, individual criminal responsibility for the crime of aggression also slowly develops in international criminal law.[18] The crime of aggression is an extrapolation of the notion of crimes against peace in international law. The term 'crime of aggression' in article 8*bis* of the Rome Statute was not used in 1945. Acts of crimes of aggression have been first prosecuted as 'crimes against peace' after World War II by the Nuremberg and Tokyo International Military Tribunals.[19] Article 6(a) of the Nuremberg Charter defined that '[c]*rimes against peace*: namely, planning, preparation, initiation or waging of a war of aggression, or a war in violation of international treaties, agreements or assurances, or participation in a common plan or conspiracy for the accomplishment of any of the foregoing'.[20] This definition with a slight change was repeated in article 5(a) of the Tokyo Charter.[21] Additionally, according to the last concluding paragraph of article 6 of the Nuremberg Charter and article 5(c) of the Tokyo Charter, individual criminal liability extends to 'leaders, organisers, instigators and accomplices participating in the formulation or execution of a common plan or conspiracy to commit' crimes against peace 'for all acts performed by any persons in execution of such plan'.[22]

---

17   'Historical Review of Developments relating to Aggression', Prepared by the Secretariat, UN Doc PCNICC/2002/WGCA/L.1 and Add.1 (18 and 24 January 2002), paras 379–450.

18   For a summary of origins of criminalising aggression, see Cassese *et al* (eds) (n 7) 136–38; K.E. Sellars, 'The First World War, Wilhelm II and Article 227: The Original of the Idea of "Aggression" in International Criminal Law' in Barriga and Kreß (eds) (n 12) 21–48; id, 'Definitions of Aggression as Harbingers of International Change' in Sadat (ed) (n 14) 122–53; W.A. Schabas, 'Nuremberg and Aggressive War' in Sadat (ed) (n 14) 58–79. For discussions on the normative assumptions of the crime of aggression, see L. May, *Aggression and Crimes Against Peace* (CUP 2008); id, 'The Just War in Ancient Legal Thought' in Sadat (ed) (n 14) 103–21.

19   For comments on Nuremberg and Tokyo precedents, see C.A. Pompe, *Aggressive War: An International Crime* (Springer 1953) 202–88; Dinstein (n 12) 125–34; K.E. Sellars, '*Crimes Against Peace*' *and International Law* (CUP 2013); Schabas, ibid; R. Cryer, 'The Tokyo International Military Tribunal and Crimes Against Peace (Aggression): Is There Anything to Learn?' in Sadat (ed) (n 14) 80–102.

20   Nuremberg Charter, art 6(a).

21   Tokyo Charter, art 5(a).

22   For further discussions on the two provisions, chapter 6.4.2.1 of the present book.

A preliminary comparison of the two notions' legal construction first shows that the State act element of the crime of aggression differs from that of crimes against peace.[23] In defining the crime of aggression, article 8*bis* of the Rome Statute uses the term 'act of aggression' rather than the phrase 'war of aggression'. Thus, the 'crime of aggression' contains aggressive wars and acts of less intensive than war, but crimes against peace cover two branches of acts, aggressive wars and war in violation of treaties, agreements or assurances. Secondly, the crime of aggression in the Rome Statute contains a 'manifest violation' threshold, which was not referred to in the notion of crimes against peace. Thirdly, a leadership clause is specified in the definition of the crime of aggression and its modes of participation; but the phrase 'leaders or organisers' was only stipulated to hold persons liable for participating in a conspiracy for crimes against peace. At present, the notion of the crime of aggression has replaced the term 'crimes against peace'. The concept of 'crimes against peace' and the term 'the crime of aggression' are used interchangeably in this chapter.

The crime of aggression has been well recognised as a part of customary international law, despite that its legal construction is rather complex. In the IMT and IMTFE, all defendants were charged with crimes against peace for participation in the conspiracy to waging aggressive wars or in preparing, initiating or waging aggressive wars. Two issues on the crime have been discussed in the two tribunals: (1) whether the crime against peace was a crime in customary law and; (2) whether individuals should be responsible for the war of aggression in international law. As the former Judge Mei Ju-ao of the IMTFE analysed, the two tribunals gave positive and affirmative answers to the two questions.[24]

Notwithstanding the declaratory nature of the two Charters concerning crimes against peace, it is agreed that the crime of aggression is a crime in international law from 1945 forward.[25] Article 5(2) of Resolution 3314 (XXIX) states that '[a] war of aggression is a crime against international

---

23 For a detailed comparison of the two notions, see Y. Dinstein, 'The Crime of Aggression under Customary International Law' in Sadat (ed) (n 14) 295–99.

24 Mei Ju-ao, *The Tokyo Trial and War Crimes in Asia* (Shanghai Jiao Tong University Press 2018) 21–30; Glaser (n 7) 69. Cf. B.V.A. Röling, 'The Nuremberg and Tokyo Trials in Retrospect' in Mattraux (ed) (n 7) 455, 459–60; id and A. Cassese, *The Tokyo Trial and Beyond: Reflections of a Peacemonger* (Polity Press 1993) 98; Pompe (n 19) 245–62; Dinstein (n 23) 286–88 and fns 22–25. For a summary of these debates, Sellars (n 19) 113–34, 166–67.

25 UN Doc A/51/10 (1996), para 50, commentary (5) to art 16; McDougall (n 8) 139–55; Werle and Jessberger (n 7) 536–38; Dinstein (n 23) 291, 302; Sayapin (n 9) 160, stating that the Nuremberg Charter and Judgment create 'instant custom'. Cf. May (2008) (n 18) 146–49; Sellars (n 19) 262.

peace. Aggression gives rise to international responsibility'.[26] Article 16 of the 1996 ILC's Draft Code of Crimes confirmed this view.[27] In addition to this, from 1995 to 1998, as will be seen below, States debated the issue of the inclusion of the crime of aggression in the ICC's jurisdiction.[28] The crime of aggression was included in the ICC's jurisdiction, despite that its definition was dropped at the 1998 Rome Conference.[29] Article 5(1)(d) of the Rome Statute not only indicates that there was no consensus on the definition of the crime of aggression, but also confirms that the crime of aggression is an international crime. Furthermore, after reviewing the developments of law since World War II, in 2006, the British House of Lords in *R v Jones et al* held that the crime of aggression was established in customary international law.[30] Lord Bingham said that 'the core elements of the crime of aggression have been understood, at least since 1945, with sufficient clarity to permit the lawful trial (and, on conviction, punishment) of those accused of this most serious crimes'.[31] The Kampala Amendments adopted at the 2010 Review Conference further echoed the view that the crime of aggression is recognised as an international crime under customary law.[32] This conclusion, however, does not touch on issues of the precise definition and elements of the crime of aggression.[33]

5.3   Provisions on the Crime of Aggression in the Rome Statute

Four provisions on the crime of aggression, articles 8*bis*, 15*bis* and 15*ter* and article 25(3*bis*), were added to the 1998 Rome Statute at the 2010 Kampala Review Conference. Apart from the four provisions, the Elements of Crimes and

---

26   UN Doc A/RES/3314 (XXIX) (1974). See also 'Declaration on Principles of International Law Concerning Friendly Relations and Co-operation Among States in Accordance with the Charter of the United Nations', GA Res 2625 (XXV) (1970), UN Doc A/RES/2625 (XXV).
27   UN Doc A/51/10 (1996). On this resolution, Cassese *et al* (eds) (n 7) 136–37.
28   'Report of the *Ad Hoc* Committee on the Establishment of an International Criminal Court', UN Doc A/50/22 (1995), paras 63-65; 'Summary of the Proceedings of the Preparatory Committee during the Period 25 March – 12 April 1996', UN Doc A/AC.249/1 (1996), para 10.
29   1998 Rome Statute, art 5(1)(d).
30   *R v Jones et al* (n 7).
31   ibid [19] (Lord Bingham).
32   Schabas (n 8) 302 and fn 7.
33   For a detailed discussion on the State act and individual act of aggression, see Sayapin (n 9).

Understandings of the crime are also part of the 2010 Kampala Amendments.[34] Article 8*bis* constitutes two parts. Article 8*bis* paragraph 1 defines the crime of aggression and modalities of the crime of aggression,[35] and paragraph 2 provides a definition of 'act of aggression' 'for the purpose of paragraph 1'. Articles 15*bis* and 15*ter* stipulate the ICC's exercise of jurisdiction over the crime of aggression.[36] And a paragraph 3*bis* was added to article 25 of the Rome Statute that restates the scope of persons for the crime of aggression.

Article 8*bis*(1) of the Rome Statute provides that:

> For the purpose of this Statute, 'crime of aggression' means the planning, preparation, initiation or execution, by a person in a position effectively to exercise control over or to direct the political or military action of a State, of an act of aggression which, by its character, gravity and scale, constitutes a manifest violation of the Charter of the United Nations.

This paragraph shows that the material elements of the crime of aggression comprise three types of elements: State act element (consequences), individual conduct element (conducts), and the leadership element (circumstances).[37] The mental element of the crime is covered by article 30 of the Rome Statute and the Elements of Crimes.[38] The 'control or direct' leadership element will be the main focus of this chapter. This section first interprets the 'control or direct' test of the leadership element and then examines the provisions of the Rome Statute and Understandings of the crime of aggression to show whether this leadership test restates a pre-existing customary rule.

5.3.1   *Meaning of Articles 8*bis *and 25(3*bis*): 'Control or Direct'*

A plain reading of article 8*bis* shows that the scope of perpetrators who might commit the crime of aggression is limited to 'a person in a position effectively to exercise control over or to direct the political or military action of a State'.[39]

---

34   S. Barriga and C. Kreß (eds), *The Travaux Préparatoires of the Crime of Aggression* (CUP 2012) 58–97; J. Trahan, 'The Crime of Aggression and the International Criminal Court' in Sadat (ed) (n 14) 304–28.

35   For a detailed analysis of this provision, see Zimmermann and Freiburg (n 3) 583–618.

36   1998 Rome Statute, arts 15*bis* and 15*ter*.

37   For comments on art 8*bis* (1), see Zimmermann and Freiburg (n 3) 514–86; Elements of Crimes, as amended by resolution RC/Res.6 of 11 June 2010, Annex II, art 8*bis*. For discussions on the three types elements, see 1998 Rome Statute, art 30; 'Elements of the Crime of Aggression: Proposal Submitted by Samoa', UN Doc PCNICC/2002/WGCA/DP.2 (21 June 2002), paras 4, 8–10.

38   Elements of Crimes, art 8*bis*, Elements 4 and 6.

39   1998 Rome Statute, art 8*bis*; Elements of Crimes, art 8*bis*, Elements 1-3.

By referring to 'effectively to exercise control over or to direct', the leadership element for the crime of aggression in the Rome Statute is formulated as the 'control or direct' test. The Elements of Crimes explained in a footnote that more than one person could satisfy the leadership criteria.[40] Article 25 paragraph 3*bis* duplicates the leadership clause and specifies that for the crime of aggression, the provision of article 25 'shall apply only to persons in a position effectively to exercise control over or to direct the political or military action of a State'. Article 25 paragraph 3*bis*, as a part of a provision concerning modes of participation, does not expand the scope of persons who shall be responsible for the crime of aggression, but rather reaffirms the 'control or direct' requirement for that crime.[41]

Apart from articles 8*bis* and 25(3*bis*) of the Rome Statute, the leadership phrase is reiterated in Element 2 of the Amendments to the Elements of Crimes, which provides that '[t]he perpetrators was a person in a position effectively to exercise control over or to direct the political or military action of the State which committed the act of aggression'.[42] The drafting history of article 8*bis* shows that the leadership phrase is not a jurisdictional limitation for the ICC over the crime of aggression, but was intentionally inserted by the drafters as a substantial legal element for that crime.[43] The leadership element requires potential perpetrators to be persons 'in a position effectively' to 'exercise control over or to direct' 'the political or military action of a State'. This leadership element 'describes the circumstance in which the conduct', planning, preparing, initiating or executing an act of aggression, 'is to have taken place'.[44] This circumstance element is a crucial factor in which the actor operates. For example, if a person kills a living being, it cannot be murder unless the being is a human one. The deceased is human here is a circumstance element. The persons indicted for the crime of aggression must satisfy the leadership

---

40 Elements of Crimes, art 8*bis*, Element 2 and fn 2.
41 For discussion on the individual criminal responsibility in art 25 (3*bis*), see K. Ambos, *Treatise on International Criminal Law, Vol I: Foundations and General Part* (OUP 2013) 171.
42 Elements of Crimes, art 8*bis*, Element 2.
43 Barriga (n 3) 23. See also Report of the Special Working Group on the Crime of Aggression, ICC-ASP/5/35, Annex II [2007 SWGCA Report (January)], para 11; Informal inter-sessional meeting of the Special Working Group on the Crime of Aggression, ICC-ASP/6/SWGCA/INF.1 (25 July 2007) [2007 Princeton Report], paras 9-10; 'Non-Paper by the Chairman on Defining the Individual's Conduct' in 'Report of the Special Working Group on the Crime of Aggression', ICC-ASP/6/ SWGCA/1, Annex, [2007 Chairman's Paper on Defining the Individual's Conduct], para 6.
44 Informal inter-sessional meeting of the Special Working Group on the Crime of Aggression, ICC-ASP/8/INF.2 [2009 Princeton Report], para 14; 'Explanatory note' in id, Annex II, Appendix II, para 14.

element.[45] Clearly, the leadership element will also significantly limit the ICC's jurisdiction *ratione personae* over that crime.

The 'control or direct' test is not a low standard, although the conjunctive 'or' indicates that this test could be satisfied alternatively. The two terms 'control' and 'direct' are thesaurus in English. The English Dictionary defines 'control' as 'to determine', 'to supervise' or 'to direct the behaviour or the course of events';[46] 'to exercise power or influence over'.[47] The phrase 'to exercise control over' indicates that the perpetrator has the power to determine the action of a State. Besides, the English Dictionary defines 'direct' as 'to control the operations'; 'to manage or govern';[48] 'to cause to turn, move, or point undeviating' on a particular course;[49] and 'to instruct (someone) with authority'.[50] It is noteworthy that the ILC has also interpreted the meaning of the two expressions, although its reference was relating to State responsibility.[51] In its commentary to the 2001 'Draft Articles on Responsibilities of States for Internationally Wrongful Acts', the ILC addressed that:

> the term 'controls' refers to cases of domination over the commission of wrongful conduct and not simply the exercise of oversight, still less mere influence or concern. Similarly, the word 'directs' does not encompass mere incitement or suggestion but rather connotes actual direction of an operative kind. [...] The choice of the expression, common in English, 'direction and control', raised some problems in other languages, owing in particular to the ambiguity of the term 'direction' which may imply, as is the case in French, complete power, whereas it does not have this implication in English.[52]

---

45 For comments on the phrase 'a State', C. Kreß, 'The German Chief Federal Prosecutor's Decision Not to Investigate the Alleged Crime of Preparing Aggression against Iraq' (2004) 2 *JICJ* 245, 251–54 concerning the responsibility of the leaders of third-States aiding or assisting the aggressor State; Heller (n 11) 492–97.

46 Oxford English Dictionary online.

47 B.A. Garner (ed), *Black's Law Dictionary* (8th edn, Thomson West 2004) 998.

48 ibid.

49 Merriam-Webster online.

50 Garner (n 47) 1383.

51 For the differences between criminal liability of individuals and State responsibility, see Cassese *et al* (eds) (n 7) 142–45.

52 UN Doc A/56/10 (2001), para 77, art 17 and its commentary (7). Article 17, entitled 'Direction and control exercised over the commission of an internationally wrongful act', states that 'A State which directs and controls another state in the commission of an internationally wrongful acts by the latter is internationally responsible for that act if: (a) that State does so with knowledge of the circumstances of the internationally wrongful act; and (B) the act would be internationally wrongful if committed by that State'.

This quoted paragraph shows that the term 'control' is not simply 'mere influence', and 'direction' in English does not imply 'complete power'.

The difference between 'control' and 'direct' is rather slight to a small degree. The concept 'control' covers a broader scope of the persons concerned, because this concept hints that the crime of aggression can also be committed through a way of supervision by the person who has guided the political or military action of a State.[53] In addition to this, the phrase 'control or direct' excludes persons, whom mere shaped or influenced the action of the State, outside the scope of potential persons. For instance, legal advisers of a Head of State might directly or indirectly affect and influence the decision-making of the State, but they are not in a position to control or direct the political or military action of that State. The 'control or direct' test is an extremely restrictive standard compared to the shape or influence formula.

The phrase 'in a position effectively' suggests that *de facto* positions, rather than the formal rank, title or *de jure* status, in a State are subject to the ICC's jurisdiction concerning the crime of aggression.[54]

With respect to persons satisfying the 'control or direct' test, it is generally agreed that these leaders of States include political and military leaders. Scholars, however, uphold slightly different views about whether business or religious leaders were included as potential perpetrators. The majority of scholars argued that the crime of aggression is committed and attributed to leaders of a State.[55] And industrialists who 'exercise a control over or direct the political or military action of a State' is *per se* not excluded from article 8*bis* of the Rome Statute.[56] A literal reading of 'control or direct the political or military action of State' does not restrict these potential persons prosecuted under article 8*bis* to governmental or military leaders. However, Carrie McDougall argued that although industrialists are *per se* not excluded, they

---

53   Cf. McDougall (n 8) 180.
54   Zimmermann and Freiburg (n 3) 591; McDougall (n 8) 179–81. For a discussion on the 'effective control' or 'overall control' on the leadership element, see N. Hajdin, 'The Nature of Leadership in the Crime of Aggression: The ICC's New Concern?' (2017) 17 *ICLR* 543, 560–63.
55   Zimmermann and Freiburg (n 3) 590.
56   ibid 592; Werle and Jessberger (n 7) 550; R.S. Clark, 'Negotiating Provisions Defining the Crime of Aggression, Its Elements and the Conditions for ICC Exercise of Jurisdiction' (2009) 20 *EJIL* 1103, 1105; Ambos (n 9) 490; R. Heinsch, 'The Crime of Aggression after Kampala: Success or Burden for the Future?' (2010) 2 *GoJIL* 713, 723; Sayapin (n 9) 225–26, 260; Kemp (n 14) 180. See 'Report of the Special Working Group on the Crime of Aggression', ICC-ASP/7/SWGCA/2, in ASP Official Records, ICC-ASP/7/20/Add.1, Annex II [2009 SWGCA Report], para 25.

are not capable of exercising the *de facto* control or direction of the political or military action of a State.[57] In her view, the broad interpretation of article 8*bis* to including private actors was not supported among the majority in the Special Working Group on the Crime of Aggression.[58]

As will be seen below in subsection 5.4.5, the high leadership test was intentionally inserted by the drafters to avoid evidential difficulties and to restrict the potential perpetrators to a small number of persons.[59] And a plain reading of the 'control or direct' clause does not exclude industrialists as potential perpetrators, which is consistent with the view suggested from its negotiating history.[60] It is rare but possible for these private economic actors or religious leaders to be able to 'control or direct' the 'political or military action of a State' at the present time.[61] It is the ICC that will ultimately deal with the issue of whether suspected persons who are private leaders satisfy the leadership element. Other concepts of the leadership element also merit discussions but go beyond the scope of this chapter.

This brief interpretation of the 'control or direct' test sets out the basis of analysing. The next subsection endeavours to analyse whether the 'control or direct' test in articles 8*bis* and 25(3*bis*) of the Rome Statute was declaratory of custom.

5.3.2   *'Control or Direct' as a Legal Element in the Rome Statute*

Similar to articles 7 and 8 of the Rome Statute about war crimes and crimes against humanity, the texts in articles 8*bis*, 15*bis* and 15*ter* and article 25 paragraph 3*bis* of the updated Rome Statute and the Elements of Crimes do not explicitly say whether articles 8*bis*, 8*bis* paragraph 1 or 25(3*bis*) were declaratory of custom concerning the definition of the crime of aggression or its 'control or direct' requirement. The phrase 'for the purpose of this Statute' in article 8*bis* (1) and the language in Understanding 4 for the Resolution on the crime of aggression that 'the amendments that address the definition of [...] the crime of aggression do so for the purpose of this Statute only' and its 'without prejudice' clause simply indicate the possibility of a discrepancy between the Rome Statute and customary law on the definition of the crime of aggression.[62]

---

57   McDougall (n 8) 181, 203; Heller (n 11) 489.
58   McDougall (n 8) 182.
59   ibid 183 and chapter 5.4 of the present book.
60   Coracini and Wrange (n 8) 311; Barriga (n 3) 22; 2007 Chairman's Paper on Defining the Individual's Conduct, para 9; 2009 SWGCA Report (n 56) para 25. Cf. Heller (n 11) 488–92.
61   Sayapin (n 9) 224–26.
62   'Understandings regarding the amendments to the Rome Statute of the International Criminal Court on the crime of aggression', Resolution RC/Res.6 of 11 June 2010, Annex III.

Neither the texts nor the structure of the Statute shows a consensus on this leadership element as a reflection of custom.

A close observation on the drafting history, as will be seen below in section 5.4, indicates that in the Special Working Group on the Crime of Aggression, there was no suggestion on the relationship between the definition of the crime of aggression and customary law. Claus Kreß correctly pointed out that it is unclear whether the Special Working Group was guided to confine the definition of the crime of aggression to existing customary law.[63] The specific leadership clause as a negotiation compromise was intentionally inserted to narrow the scope of persons responsible for the crime of aggression.[64]

One may note that the language in Understanding 4 was initially designed to address the relationship between customary law and the new treaty definition on the crime of aggression. Understanding 4 was inserted to address the US's concern on the definition of crimes of aggression.[65] At the 2010 Review Conference, the US legal adviser addressed that:

> adopting Article 8*bis* as the definition of aggression does not truly reflect customary international law. [...] [A]s yet, no authoritative definition of aggression exists under customary international law. If the Article 8*bis* language is not adopted to bring it into conformity with customary international law, it should be made clear that the language is being adopted for the purposes of implementing the Rome Statute and is not intended as an authoritative statement of customary international law.[66]

The US proposed one draft suggestion as follows:

> The amendments shall, in accordance with article 10 of the Rome Statute, not be interpreted as limited or prejudicing in any way existing or developing rules of international law for purposes other than this Statute, *and*

---

[63] C. Kreß and L. von Holtzendorf, 'The Kampala Compromise on the Crime of Aggression' (2010) 8 *JICJ* 1179, 1189.

[64] M. Scharf, 'Universal Jurisdiction and the Crime of Aggression' (2012) 53 *Harvard Intl LJ* 358, 363; McDougall (n 8) 182–83; Ambos (n 9) 490–91; Barriga (n 3) 22; Hajdin (n 54). For critics of the leadership element, M.A. Drumbl, 'The Push to Criminalize Aggression: Something Lost Amid the Gains' (2009) 41 *Case W Res J Intl L* 291.

[65] C. Kreß *et al*, 'Negotiating the Understandings on the Crime of Aggression' in Barriga and Kreß (eds) (n 34) 91–93; Statement of Koh (n 8).

[66] Statement of Koh (n 8).

shall not be interpreted as constituting a statement of the definition 'crime of aggression' or 'act of aggression' under customary international law.[67]

After consultations, the German delegation recognised that the quoted sentence in italics would not be accepted by a large number of delegations who opposed such an explicit separation between the treaty definition and customary law.[68] Ultimately, a more general term borrowed from article 10 of the Rome Statute was adopted in Understanding 4. The delegations' opposition to such a draft suggestion should not be overemphasised, for their opposition was more related to the definition of 'act of aggression' in article 8*bis*, thus, leaving the relationship between the Amendments and custom on the leadership element untouched.

In brief, by referring to the texts and the structure of the Rome Statute, and the drafting history of provisions concerned, it appears that articles 8*bis* and 25(3*bis*) were not authoritative declarations of customary law on the 'control or direct' leadership element.

5.4 The Leadership Element for the Crime of Aggression: Were Articles 8*bis* and 25(3*bis*) Declaratory of Custom?

This section analyses whether the 'control or direct' leadership clause in articles 8*bis* and 25(3*bis*) were inserted as a reflection of customary law or were of norm-making nature for the crime of aggression at the adoption of the 2010 Amendments. The consecutive subsections 5.4.1–5.4.3 examine pre-Rome trials and work on the crime of aggression, including the judgments of the IMT and the IMTFE, trials in tribunals established pursuant to Control Council Law No. 10 and the work of the ILC. The negotiating and drafting history of the crime of aggression will be divided into two phrases, pre-Rome phrase (1995–1998) and Rome-Kampala phrase (1999–2010), and will be analysed in subsections 5.4.4–5.4.5. Subsection 5.4.6 observes national criminal codes and case law relating to the leadership clause of the crime of aggression.[69]

---

[67] '2010 Non-Paper by the United States' (7 June 2010), cited in Barriga and Kreß (eds) (n 34) 751 (italics by the author).
[68] Kreß *et al* (n 65) 93.
[69] For documented negotiation history for the crime of aggression, see M.C. Bassiouni and W.A. Schabas (eds), *The Legislative History of the International Criminal Court* (2nd Revised and expanded edn, Brill 2016); Barriga and Kreß (eds) (n 12); Barriga and Kreß (eds) (n 34).

5.4.1 Any Leadership Test in the IMT and IMTFE?

Articles 6 and 5 of the Nuremberg and Tokyo Charters did not address the high-level position as a requirement for crimes against peace, but all defendants prosecuted by the IMT and IMTFE were major (or Class A) war criminals.[70]

Defendants were indicted for two counts relating to crimes against peace at the IMT. Count one addressed participating in the common plan or conspiracy to commit crimes against peace; count two charged the defendants with crimes against peace by the planning, preparation, initiation, and waging wars of aggression, which were also wars in violation of international treaties, agreements or assurances.[71]

22 defendants were indicted for count one, and 16 of the 22 defendants were charged with count two.[72] After reviewing all the defendants' high-level positions, knowledge of the aggressive plans and participation in preparing, planning or initiating war, the IMT ultimately found that 8 of the 22 indicted were convicted of count one, and 12 of the 16 indicted were convicted of count two. 8 of the 22 defendants were convicted of both counts of crimes against peace. All the defendants convicted were either leaders, policy-makers, decision-makers or influenced high-level foreign policy officials in political and military sectors of German at some point before or during the aggressive wars. The convictions of these defendants at high-level positions do not explicitly show that the IMT considered the leadership position as an independent element for the crime of aggression.[73]

However, the reasons for some acquittals may assist in understanding the leadership issue for crimes against peace at the IMT. Firstly, Schacht was acquitted of counts one and two. He was the central figure in the German Rearmament. The IMT acquitted Schacht under count one, because he was not in the inner circle around Hitler and he lost 'influence as the central figure' in 1936. No sufficient evidence showed that Schacht had knowledge of the aggressive wars or that he carried out the rearmament as a part of the common plan to wage aggressive wars. Additionally, the IMT acquitted Schacht of count two for lack of involvement in the planning for waging wars.[74] The acquittals of Schacht indicate that the IMT have contemplated the defendants' leadership status and their influence over the plan.

---

70 London Agreement, art 3.
71 *France et al v Göring et al*, Judgment and Sentence of the Nuremberg International Military Tribunals, (1948) 1 TMWC 171, 171.
72 2002 Historical Review (n 17), para 63.
73 Cf. Hajdin (n 54) 548–50.
74 *France et al v Göring et al* (n 7) 309.

Secondly, Fritzsche and Bormann were not charged with count two and were acquitted of count one. The IMT examined Fritzsche's 'position and influence' and found that he never achieved sufficient high position to attend the conferences which planned and led to aggressive wars, and that he had no knowledge of decisions taken at the conferences.[75] The IMT also analysed Bormann's position, power and influence to infer whether he had knowledge of the aggressive plans. The Tribunal found that a conclusive finding of knowledge could not be inferred from Bormann's position during the common plan or conspiracy.[76] The acquittals of Fritzsche and Bormann demonstrate that the IMT considered the position or influence as an important factor to infer the knowledge of aggressive wars under count one.

Thirdly, Funk and Dönitz were acquitted of count one and convicted of count two. The IMT acquitted Funk of count one because he was not a leading figure 'in originating the Nazi Plans for aggressive war'.[77] After considering his high-level positions, his knowledge of the plans and his participation in the planning and preparing of the aggressive wars, the IMT then convicted Funk for participation in preparing for aggressive wars under count two.[78] Again, the acquittal of Funk shows that the IMT considered the defendants' positions. More importantly, the IMT seems to set out different levels of leadership standards for the charges. A 'leading figure' level was required to convict the defendant for participating in the conspiracy to wage aggressive war; while a high-level position was sufficient for the conviction of preparing for aggressive wars. The IMT, however, did not further clarify these standards.

With respect to Dönitz, the IMT acquitted him of participation in the conspiracy to wage aggressive wars under count one for lack of knowledge of the plan.[79] Additionally, the IMT observed his 'positions and duties at the time' to show that he had no knowledge of the aggressive plans, and acquitted him of participation in preparing or initiating aggressive wars under count two.[80] After analysing his high-level position, his leadership role and significant contribution to waging aggressive wars, the IMT ultimately convicted Dönitz of participation in waging aggressive wars under count two.[81] The acquittals and conviction of Dönitz hint that the high-level position plays different roles with

---

75   ibid 526.
76   ibid 527.
77   ibid 304–05.
78   ibid 304–05, 307; 2002 Historical Review (n 17), para 84.
79   *France et al v Göring et al* (n 7) 310; 2002 Historical Review (n 17), para 85.
80   ibid.
81   *France et al v Göring et al* (n 7) 310–11, 315; 2002 Historical Review (n 17), paras 86-87.

regard to charges of crimes against peace under count two. On the one hand, for crimes against peace by participating in preparing for aggressive wars, his position was considered as an evidentiary factor of the knowledge of the aggressive plans; on the other hand, for crimes against peace by waging aggressive wars, his leadership role was regarded as an indicator of the defendants' participation in waging wars.

In the Tokyo trial, the IMTFE considered each of 25 accused stood trial concerning crimes against peace. After considering the positions of the indicted in the Government and the military, their knowledge of the aggressive plans and their participation in the conspiracy, in preparing for and waging aggressive wars, the IMTFE have convicted all the accused of crimes against peace for the conspiracy to wage aggressive wars and/or the waging of aggressive wars against several countries. Kimura was not a high-level officer, but the IMTFE also found that his contribution was crucial and sufficient to hold him liable for conspiracy to wage aggressive wars in China and the Pacific.[82] The IMTFE have acquitted some defendants of waging aggressive wars because they did not occupy official positions that would hold them liable.[83] It appears that the Tribunal did not clarify the importance of high official positions.

The conviction of Sato closely pertains to the leadership issue. The IMTFE analysed the necessity of the high-level position to influence the policy-making and found that Sato did not 'attained a position which by itself enabled him to influence the making of policy' until 1941.[84] Additionally, the Tribunal examined the knowledge of the criminal nature of Japan's policy and found that Sato had the knowledge of aggressive war against China based on his speech in 1938.[85] The Tribunal finally convicted Sato for participation in the conspiracy to wage aggressive wars from 1941 forward.[86] It seems that the IMTFE considered the high-position to influence the policy-making as an indicator of the *actus reus* element, paralleled with the knowledge requirement.

After observing these convictions and acquittals, McDougall concluded that the IMT considered crimes against peace as a leadership crime but it did not

---

[82] *US et al v Araki et al*, Judgment, 1 November 1948, in United Nations War Crimes Commission (ed), *Transcripts of Proceedings and Documents of the International Military Tribunals for the Far East (Tokyo Trials)*: Judgment, 1174–76; 2002 Historical Review (n 17), para 346.

[83] *US et al v Araki et al*, Judgment, ibid; Hajdin (n 54) 553–55.

[84] *US et al v Araki et al*, Judgment, 1190–91; 2002 Historical Review (n 17), para 360.

[85] *US et al v Araki et al*, Judgment, 1190–91; 2002 Historical Review (n 17), para 359.

[86] ibid; Hajdin (n 54) 553–54.

formulate a leadership standard.[87] However, the observations above show that in determining individual criminal responsibility for crimes against peace, the IMT and the IMTFE convicted the accused where evidence of two elements, the *mens rea* and the *actus reus*, or knowledge and active participation, was conclusive. They did not consider the defendants' positions or influence over the policy-making as a formal legal element. Instead, with regard to the charges of participating in the conspiracy and planning of aggressive wars, the IMT regarded the high-level position or influence as an evidentiary factor to infer the knowledge of the aggressive wars; while the IMTFE considered the position to influence the making of policy as evidence of active participation. With respect to the charge of participating in waging aggressive wars, the IMT considered the high-level position as an indicator to infer the defendant's participation. The determination of their positions was based on their 'ability to actually exercise power' in leadership or influencing positions.[88] In a nutshell, the leadership position was not considered as an independent legal element but evidentiary indicators of the two elements for crimes against peace in the IMT and the IMTFE.

5.4.2   *The Leadership Requirement in Tribunals Established under Control Council Law No. 10*

The definition of crimes against peace in article II(1)(a) of the Control Council Law No. 10 was largely based on the Nuremberg Charter, which said that:

> Initiation of invasions of other countries and wars of aggression in violation of international laws and treaties, including but not limited to planning, preparation, initiation or waging a war of aggression, or a war in violation of international treaties, agreements or assurances, or participation in a common plan or conspiracy for the accomplishment of any of the foregoing.

In addition, article II (2) added that:

> Any person without regard to nationality or the capacity in which he acted, is deemed to have committed a crime as defined in paragraph 1

---

[87]   McDougall (n 8); Hajdin (n 54) 550. For the reasons of no leadership standard in the IMT, see Hajdin (n 54) 548.

[88]   A.R. Coracini, 'National Legislation on Individual Responsibility for Conduct Amounting to Aggression' in R. Bellelli (ed), *International Criminal Justice: Law and Practice from the Rome Statute to its Review* (Ashgate Publishing 2010) 555.

of this Article, if he was (a) a principal or (b) was an accessory to the commission of any such crime or ordered or abetted the same or (c) took a consenting part therein or (d) was connected with plans or enterprises involving its commission or (e) was a member of any organization or group connected with the commission of any such crime or (f) with reference to paragraph 1 (a) if he held a high political, civil or military (including General Staff) position in Germany or in one of its Allies, co-belligerents or satellites or held high position in the financial, industrial or economic life of any such country.[89]

The Control Council Law No. 10 intended to provide a basis for the prosecution of less senior leaders as compared to major war criminals.[90] The text of article II did not impose a leadership requirement that the person should be in a leadership position to 'influence or affect' or 'direct or control' the waging of aggressive wars. A literal reading of article II (2) shows that a principal 'or' an accessory 'or' persons at 'high political, civil or military position' or at 'high position in the financial, industrial and economic life' were deemed to have committed crimes against peace.[91]

However, the US and French tribunals established pursuant to Law No. 10 imposed a leadership threshold and some tribunals required the accused should be in a position to 'shape or influence' the making of war policy. Five trials involved charges with crimes against peace, namely, the *I.G. Farben* case, the *Krupp* case, the *High Command* case, the *Ministries* case, and the *Roechling* case.[92] In the five trials, the defendants were not very high-level Government and Military leaders as those in the IMT and IMTFE, but key industry leaders and less high-level decision-makers in Government and Nazi Party. All the defendants but three in the *Ministries* case were acquitted for the charges of participation in the initiation, preparation, planning and waging of aggressive wars. The following paragraphs focus on the *I.G. Farben*, *High Command* and *Ministries* cases.

---

89   Control Council Law No. 10, art II (2).
90   For a comparison of the definitions in the Nuremberg Charter and in CC Law No. 10, see K.J. Heller, *The Nuremberg Military Tribunals and the Origins of International Criminal Law* (OUP 2011) 180–84; 2002 Historical Review (n 17), paras 72-153.
91   Control Council Law No. 10, art II (2).
92   For summaries of the NMTs judgments and observations for crimes against peace, see 2002 Historical Review (n 17), paras 72-153; Sayapin (n 9) 180–90; Heller (n 90) 179–202.

5.4.2.1 The US *I.G. Farben* Case

The Nuremberg Military Tribunals (NMTs) first dealt with crimes against peace in the *I.G. Farben* case. In the *Farben* case, 24 high-level members of the German industrial firm I.G. Farben were charged with participating in a conspiracy to commit crimes against peace and participating in the planning, preparing, initiating, and waging aggressive wars for their production and distribution of poison gas used in the concentration camps. The Tribunal stressed that proofs of both knowledge of and actual participation in the aggressive plans are required to hold an accused liable for crimes against peace. Finally, all the defendants stood trial were acquitted for the two charges of crimes against peace.

The Tribunal first found that before the war initiated, these industrialists did not know that the rearmament 'was a part of the plan or was intended to be used in waging aggressive war'.[93] The *Farben* Tribunal then imposed a leadership standard of participation with regard to the charge of waging aggressive war. The Tribunal believed that the words 'waging a war of aggression' used in article II(a) of the Control Council Law No. 10 were not 'intended to apply to any and all person who aided, supported, or contributed to the carrying on of an aggressive war'.[94] The Tribunal, thus, had to determine who may be held responsible for an aggressive war. In its words, it was

> faced with the problem of determining the guilt or innocence with respect to the waging of aggressive war on the part of men of industry who were not makers of policy but who supported their government during its period of rearmament and who continued to serve that government in the waging of war.[95]

The Tribunal believed that 'individuals who plan and lead a nation into and in an aggressive war should be held guilty of crimes against peace, but not those who merely follows the leaders'.[96] The Tribunal explained that '[i]f we lower the standard of participation to include [these followers], it is difficult to find a logical place to draw the line between the guilty and the innocent among the great mass of German people'. And it is 'unthinkable' that the majority of Germans were condemned as guilty of crimes against peace, which

---

93   *US v Kraunch et al* [The *I.G. Farben* case], (1952) 8 TWC 1, 1123.
94   ibid 1124.
95   ibid 1125.
96   *France et al v Göring et al* (n 7) 330.

would amount to a collective guilty.[97] The Tribunal found that these industrialists were neither high officials in the government nor high military officers. Despite that these industrialist' participation in the rearmament was of great importance in waging of war, their participation through producing arms was of followers rather than leaders.[98]

Some points in the *Farben* case need to be noted. Firstly, the decision in the *Farben* case implies that a leadership requirement is required for waging aggressive wars. As McDougall noted, some of the defendants convicted by the IMT, Funk and Dönitz, for instance, maybe acquitted under the leadership element imposed in the *Farben* Tribunal.[99] The *Farben* Tribunal did not define the leadership requirement clearly, but simply noted that persons 'in the political, military, and industrial fields' who were 'responsible for the formulation and execution of policies' qualified as leaders.[100] The *Farben* Tribunal thus required leaders to 'formulate' 'and' 'execute' the policy. The scope of perpetrators in the *Farben* Tribunal seems to be narrower than that defined in the *Roechling* case in relation to the execution of the policy.

In the *Roechling* case, a French General Tribunal of the Military Government once convicted Hermann Roechling, a director of the Roechling firm, for crimes against peace.[101] However, the Superior Military Government Tribunal believed that 'it is only the principal originators of the crimes committed against peace who are to be prosecuted and punished' and 'the degree of participation necessary to make an originator of a crime against peace punishable' is very high.[102] The Superior Military Court ultimately acquitted Roechling for lack of participation.[103] The Superior Military Court defined these 'principal originators' as 'prominent persons' whose actions bore the character of 'planning and carrying out' their national aggressive ambitions.[104]

Secondly, the *Farben* decision interpreted the 'or' preceding sub-paragraph (f) of article 11 (2) of the Control Council Law No. 10 as an 'and', requiring the defendants, either as principals or accessories, controlled the policy or participated in the activities as of leaders. This interpretation was reaffirmed in

---

97   For a discussion on this slippery slope argument, see A. Cassese *et al* (eds), *International Criminal Law: Cases and Commentary* (OUP 2013) 251.
98   The *I.G. Farben* case (n 93) 1123, 1126.
99   McDougall (n 8) 173; C. McDougall, 'The Crimes Against Peace Precedent' in Barriga and Kreß (eds) (n 12) 90.
100 The *I.G. Farben* case (n 93) 1124.
101 *French v Roechling et al* [The *Roechling* case], (1953) 14 TWC 1066, 1104.
102 ibid 1108.
103 ibid 1107–10.
104 ibid 1108.

the *Roechling* case. Thirdly, the decision does not indicate that persons outside the government and military would never be held liable for crimes against peace. Persons in industrial fields who were makers of policy may be qualified as leaders. Lastly, the opinion of the Tribunal did not say that the leadership requirement applied to all forms of participation but waging aggressive war as crimes against peace.

5.4.2.2 The US *High Command* Case

In the *High Command* case, 14 high-level military officers were charged with crimes against peace. The Tribunal dismissed the conspiracy count and analysed the participation in the planning, preparation, initiation and waging of aggressive wars. The Tribunal analysed three essential elements to convict a person for aggressive wars, namely: the person had the actual knowledge of the intention to initiate aggressive wars, the person must have the power to shape or influence the policy of the aggressive wars, and the person must use the power to actually participate in the policy at any stage.[105] In its view, common soldiers and officers below the policy level are 'the policy maker's instrument'.[106] 'The acts of commanders and staff officers below the policy level' do not constitute acts 'that international law denounces as criminal.'[107] Ultimately, all of the defendants in the *High Command* case were acquittal on the charge of crimes against peace because they were not in the position to shape or influence the Nazi war policy.[108]

The *High Command* Tribunal explicitly confirmed the leadership element by saying that 'the criminality [...] should be confined to those who participate in at the policy level'.[109] The Tribunal also found that customary law 'had not [yet] developed to the point of making the participation of military officers below the policy making or policy influencing level into a criminal offense in and of itself'.[110] In addition, the *High Command* Tribunal defined the leadership threshold as that the persons should be at a position to 'shape or influence' the policy of initiating or continuing aggressive wars. Furthermore, leaders were defined as those 'who participate at the policy making level in planning, preparing or initiating war. After the war is initiated, and is being waged, the policy question then involved becomes one of extending, continuing or discounting

---

105   *US v von Leeb et al* [The *High Command* case], (1950) 11 TWC 1, 488–89.
106   ibid 488, 490–91.
107   ibid 491.
108   ibid; *US v von Leeb et al* (1949) 12 LRTWC 11, 12.
109   The *High Command* case (n 105) 486.
110   ibid 489.

the war. The crime at this stage likewise must be committed at the policy making level'.[111] This qualification of leaders implies that the leadership threshold is satisfied as long as the defendant are able to shape or influence the policy at any stage. Lastly, the *High Command* Tribunal stressed that the persons should not be convicted or relieved of responsibility for aggression 'simply by reasons of their military positions', although occupying a high-level position is an important indication of a person's ability to shape or influence the policy.[112] Part of this opinion suggests that a person not at a high-level position could also be convicted for crimes against peace.

5.4.2.3 The US *Ministries* Case

In the *Ministries* case, 17 of the 21 high-level officials of the German government and the Nazi Party were charged with crimes against peace. Five of them were first convicted, and in response to defence motions, only three of the five were ultimately convicted for crimes against peace.[113] In the judgment, the terms of 'policy-making' and 'policy-shaping' were mentioned to convict Lammers and Koerner.[114] However, the *Ministries* Tribunal did not follow the *High Command* Tribunal to adopt the 'shape or influence' leadership test, but required these perpetrators played a role in 'the administration or execution' of the policy.[115] The conviction and acquittal of von Weizsaecker may cast a light on this view.[116]

Von Weizsaecker was at a high-level position in the Foreign Ministry but not at a policy-making position. The Tribunal initially convicted him for participation in the aggression against Czechoslovakia and later overturned this conviction based on an examination of his connection with the aggression.[117] Concerning his acquittal of aggression against Poland, the Tribunal said:

> While [von Weizsaecker's] position was one of prominence and he was one of the principal cogs in the machinery which dealt with foreign

---

111   ibid 490.
112   ibid 486.
113   *US v von Weizsäcker et al*, Orders and Memoranda of the Tribunal and Memoranda of Individual Members of the Tribunal on Defense Motions to Set Aside the Judgment or for the Correction of Alleged Errors of Fact and Law in the Judgment, (1953) 14 TWC 946, 946–1102.
114   ibid 974; *US v von Weizsäcker et al* [The *Ministries* case], (1953) 14 TWC 323, 409, 425.
115   The *Ministries* case, ibid, 338 and 406.
116   For another example of Woermann, see McDougall (n 99) 93.
117   The *Ministries* case (n 114) 354; *US v von Weizsäcker et al*, Orders and Memoranda (n 113) 953–56.

policy, nevertheless, as a rule, he was an implementor and not an originator. He could oppose and object, but he could not override. Therefore, we seek to ascertain what he did and whether he did all that lay in his power to frustrate a policy which outwardly he appeared to support. [...] [T]he defendant used every means in his power to prevent the catastrophe. [...] Although these efforts were futile, his lack of success is not the criteria.[118]

The Tribunal believed that a person not at the 'policy-shaping' or 'policy-influencing' level could also be held liable for crimes against peace. Judge Powers in his dissenting judgment explicitly addressed the leadership element, which read '[w]as his position and influence, or the consequences of his activity such that his action could properly be said to have had some influence or effect in bringing about the initiation of the war on the part of his government?'[119] The power to frustrate or prevent the policy in the *Ministries* case further shows the inconsistency of the NMTs' judgments on the leadership requirement.

5.4.2.4   Observations
In the Subsequent Proceedings, the NMTs were facing a task to decide who can be liable for crimes against peace. First, the Tribunals imposed a leadership requirement for crimes against peace. The leadership requirement played important roles in the failure of waging aggressive wars charges in the *Farben, Krupp*[120] and *High Command* cases. But who are leaders? In the *Farben* case, the Tribunal referred to leaders in several places and held that the individuals whose participation were that of leaders were guilty of waging aggressive wars. The *Farben* Tribunal, however, did not clarify the leadership requirement in precise but required the person in a position in 'the formulation and execution' of the policy. In the *High Command*, the Tribunal adopted a 'shape or influence' standard to clarify the leadership element. The Tribunal in the *Ministries* case required the person in a position in 'the administration or execution' of the policy.[121]

Secondly, whether industrialists outside the very high policy-making circles are included as the leaders? The Tribunal in the *Farben* case believed that these

---

118   The *Ministries* case (n 114) 369.
119   ibid, Dissenting Judgment of Judge Powers, 889.
120   *US v Krupp et al* [The *Krupp* case], (1950) 9 TWC 1, 449, Anderson Concurrence and 465–66, Wilkins Concurrence.
121   The *Ministries* case (n 114) 409; *US v von Weizsäcker et al*, Orders and Memoranda (n 113) 972, 974. For a comparison of the two judgments, see McDougall (n 99) 90.

persons could be qualified as leaders to be held liable for crimes against peace, which was echoed by the *Roechling* Superior Military Court and the US *Krupp* Tribunal. In the *Krupp* case, 12 defendants were in high-level management positions of their businesses. All the defendants were acquitted for the two charges of crimes against peace due to lack of sufficient evidence. Nonetheless, the *Krupp* Tribunal emphasised that '[w]e do not hold that industrialists, as such, could not under any circumstances be found guilty upon such charges'.[122] This statement indicates that the *Krupp* Tribunal also did not require the persons responsible for crimes against peace to be in the governmental and military circles.

In conclusion, in these subsequent trials, the persons responsible for crimes against peace were limited to people at the policy-making level. A leadership element as a third element to the knowledge and participation elements were developed and considered by these NMTs. However, as observed by Mark Drumble, Poland and Chinese military tribunals in the *Greiser* and *Skai* cases did not incline to impose a leadership element. Similar to Kimura in the IMTFE, Greiser and Skai were both found guilty of crimes against peace but their leadership role as a policy-maker or high-level leader was not evident.[123]

Besides, the NMTs were divided in clarifying the leadership standard. The *Farben* Tribunal implied a narrower range of persons with the power to influence the policy by requiring the leaders to be responsible for the 'formulation and execution' of policy.[124] By contrast, the *High Command* Tribunal believed that the leaders could 'shape or influence' the policy at any stage. The *High Command* Tribunal even considered these implementors' power 'to frustrate' a policy. In addition, as compared to the *Farben* Tribunal, the *High Command* Tribunal imposed the 'shape or influence' leadership threshold not only to waging aggressive wars but to all forms of participation for crimes against peace.[125] Compared to the IMT and IMTFE, the leadership element was considered and more elaborated in the NMTs, but it was still a vague element.

5.4.3 *The International Law Commission's Works*

The ILC worked on the definitions of aggression and the crime of aggression for a long period.[126] After World War II, the ILC was entrusted by the UN

---

122 The *Krupp* case (n 120) 393.
123 Drumbl (n 64) 299–304; *China v Takashi Sakai* (1949) 14 LRTWC 1, 3–7; *Poland v Artur Greiser* (1949) 13 LRTWC 70, 102–03.
124 McDougall (n 8) 174.
125 The *High Command* case (n 105) 491.
126 For a detailed analysis on the ILC's work on the definition of aggression, see McDougall (n 8) 3–9.

General Assembly to formulate the Nuremberg Principles, to work on the Draft Code of Offences (Crimes) and on the possibility of an international criminal tribunal.[127]

The General Assembly Resolutions 95(I) and 177(II), together with the Principle VI (a) of the Nuremberg Principles, the inclusion of crimes against peace in the 1951 Draft Code of Offences, and positive comments of governments about the Draft Code do contribute to the formation of customary law concerning the crime of aggression.[128] However, these authorities do little help in understanding the leadership requirement. The ILC in 1950 adopted a formulation of the Nuremberg Principles, together with comments.[129] Principle VI(a) defined crimes against peace. Concerning the potential perpetrators for waging aggressive wars, some of the ILC members 'feared that everyone in uniform who fought in a war of aggression might be charged with the "waging" of such a war. The Commission understands the expression [waging of a war of aggression] to refer only to high-ranking military personnel and high State officials'.[130] This restriction of the circle of perpetrators in the comments is rather rough. Britain and Belgian delegations thought that the terms of 'waging of a war of aggression' and 'high officials' should be further defined.[131]

In addition, Principle VII provided that '[c]omplicity in the commission of a crime against peace, a war crime, or a crime against humanity as set forth in Principle VI is a crime under international law'.[132] The ILC commented that, for crimes against peace, the complicity rule was limited to participation in a common plan or conspiracy to prepare, initiate and wage aggressive war.[133] The Netherlands delegation highly criticised the formulation of Principle VII. In his view,

---

127 'Formulation of the Principles Recognised in the Charter of the Nuremberg Tribunal and in the Judgment of the Tribunal', GA Res 177(II) (1947), UN Doc A/RES/177(II); 'Prevention and Punishment of the Crime of Genocide, Study by the International Law Commission of the Question of an International Criminal Jurisdiction', GA Res 260 B (III) (1948), UN Doc A/RES/260 B (III); 'Draft Code of Offences Against the Peace and Security of Mankind', UN Doc A/RES/897 (IX), UN Doc A/RES/36/106, UN Doc A/RES/37/102.

128 McDougall (n 8) 142.

129 'Formulation of the Nuremberg Principles' in 'Report of the International Law Commission', UN Doc A/1316 (1950), paras 95-127.

130 ibid, para 117.

131 'Views expressed by delegations in the Sixth Committee on the text of the Nuremberg principles formulated by the International Law Commission' in 'Second Report on the Draft Code of Offences Against the Peace and Security of Mankind, by Mr J. Spiropoulos, Special Rapporteur', UN Doc A/CN.4/44 (1951), paras 108, 110.

132 UN Doc A/1316 (1950), para 124.

133 ibid, para 126.

The judgment took care to limit the scope of crimes against peace. [...] According to the formulation of principle VII as it stood, not only industrialists, but all workers in munitions factories, not only the chief of staff but also all soldiers in the field from generals to privates, would be considered as criminals. That was a flagrant violation of the rules laid down in the charter and applied by the Tribunal.[134]

By contrast, the Belgian delegation accepted the wording 'complicity' 'only if the idea of complicity included co-authors, instigators and provocators'.[135] Other delegations at the Sixth Committee did not express the view that the notion of complicity was too wide and general, and this formulation of complicity was accepted.[136] Principles VI(a) and VII also did not provide a delicate formula to limit the scope of potential perpetrators.

The 1951 and 1954 versions of the Draft Code of Offences did not restrict the group of perpetrators but simply provided a list of acts for crimes against peace.[137] However, commentary to article 2(8) of the 1951 Draft Code of Offences concerning annexation of territory suggests that 'the offence defined in this paragraph can be committed only by the authorities of a State. Criminal responsibility of private individuals under international law may, however, arise under the provisions of paragraph (12) of the present article'.[138] The commentary to article 2(12) continues that with respect to complicity in the commission of all crimes in article 2, '[t]here can be no question of punishing as accomplices in such an offence all the members of the armed forces of a State or the works in war industries'.[139] The commentaries suggest that State officials qualify as principal perpetrators of the crime of aggression, but private individuals could also be punished for that crime as participators.

At the invitation of the UN General Assembly, the ILC resumed its work on the Draft Code of Offences in 1982.[140] This Draft Code did not provide a limitation on the scope of perpetrators. In its 1988 session, the ILC provisionally adopted a draft article 12 on aggression. It was provisional, as the commentary explained, partly because

---

134 UN Doc A/CN.4/44 (1951), paras 126-27.
135 ibid, para 129.
136 ibid, para 131.
137 1951 Draft Code of Offences, art 2(1)-(8); 1954 Draft Code of Offences, art 2(1)-(9).
138 1951 Draft Code of Offences, commentary to art 2(8).
139 1951 Draft Code of Offences, commentary to art 2(12).
140 UN Doc A/RES/35/106 (1981).

the question as to what category of individuals is involved is still unsettled. It remains to be decided whether only government officials are concerned, or also other persons having political and military responsibility and having participated in the organization and planning of aggression. It will also have to be decided whether article 12 applies to private persons who place their economic or financial power at the disposal of the authors of the aggression. In addition, that question is linked with the notions of complicity and conspiracy and will have to be studied later in relation to those notions.[141]

The later changes of the definition of the crime of aggression and its comments indicate that the ILC tried to strike a balance between a too wide term and a too narrow scope of perpetrators. In the 1991 ILC Draft Code of Crimes, the Commission identified the potential perpetrators of the crime of aggression as 'leaders or organisers'. In its view, acts of crimes of aggression

> are always committed by, or on orders from, individuals occupying the highest decision-making positions in the political or military apparatus of the State or in its financial or economic life. For those crimes, the Commission has restricted the circle of potential perpetrators to leaders and organizers, a phrase which is found in the Charter of the Nuremberg Tribunal and in the Charter of the Tokyo Tribunal.[142]

In observing the 1991 Draft Code of Crimes, some ILC members briefly discussed the leadership threshold for the crime of aggression from 1993 to 1995.[143] In discussing the notions of complicity, and aiding and abetting, some members thought that 'by applying the notion of complicit of traditional criminal law, it unduly widened the circle of offenders [of aggression]. What was needed was to strike at the leaders and organisers, since it was impossible to prosecute a whole people' or 'every soldier'.[144] However, some members expressed that 'the scope of criminal liability with respect to a "leader or organiser" was too narrow and should be expanded to include other decision-makers in the national

---

141 1988 Draft Code of Crimes, in UN Doc A/43/10 (1988), para 280, commentary (1) to art 12.
142 1991 Draft Code of Crimes, in UN Doc A/46/10 (1991), para 176, draft art 15 and commentary (4) to Part Two.
143 UN Doc A/48/10 (1993), Annex, III.
144 1990 Draft Code of Crimes, in UN Doc A/45/10 (1990), para 47; 'Report of the International Law Commission', UN Doc A/49/10 (1994), discussing 1991 Draft Code of Crimes, para 127.

hierarchy with sufficient authority and power to initiate conduct constituting a crime of aggression'.[145]

The final article 16 of the 1996 ILC Draft Code of Crimes provided that '[a]n individual who, as leader or organizer, actively participates in or orders the planning, preparation, initiation or waging of aggression committed by a State shall be responsible for a crime of aggression.'[146] The ILC's commentary to article 16 noted that:

> The perpetrators of an act of aggression are to be found only in the categories of individuals who have the necessary authority or power to be in a position potentially to play a decisive role in committing aggression. These are the individuals whom article 16 designates as "leaders" or "organizers", an expression that was taken from the Charter of the Nuremberg Tribunal. These terms must be understood in the broad sense, that is to say, as referring, in addition to the members of a Government, to persons occupying high-level posts in the military, the diplomatic corps, political parties and industry, as recognized by the Nurnberg Tribunal.[147]

In addition, article 2(2) of the 1996 Draft Code of Crimes deals with individual criminal responsibility for the crime of aggression, and its article 2(3) addresses the various ways of participation in other crimes. The commentary to article 2(2) wrote that:

> In relation to the crime of aggression, it was not necessary to indicate these different forms of participation [as provided in article 2(3)] which entail the responsibility of the individual, because the definition of the crime of aggression in article 16 already provides all the elements necessary to establish the responsibility. According to that article, an individual is responsible for the crime of aggression when, as a leader or organizer, he orders or actively participates in the planning, preparation, initiation or waging of aggression committed by a State. The crime of aggression has particular features which distinguish it from the other offences under the Code. Aggression can be committed only by individuals who are

---

145 'Report of the International Law Commission', UN Doc A/50/10 (1995), para 62, discussing 1991 Draft Code of Crimes.
146 1996 Draft Code of Crimes, in UN Doc A/51/10 (1996), paras 42-43.
147 ibid, para 43, commentary (2) to art 16.

agents of the State and who use their power to give orders and the means it makes available in order to commit this crime.[148]

Both commentaries echoed the view that the 'leaders or organisers' must be understood in a broad sense to include persons in the industry, only if they have the 'necessary authority' or 'power' or 'play a decisive role' in planning, preparing, initiating or waging aggression.[149]

The observation on the ILC's work indicates that a leadership element of the crime of aggression was not recognised by members of the Commission until 1991. Nonetheless, the ILC did not provide a clear distinction between the potential persons responsible for the crime of aggression and innocent persons. Although private individuals may be considered as 'organisers', the meanings of 'agents of the State' and 'power to give orders and the means' require further clarifications.

5.4.4 The Pre-Rome Work on the Crime of Aggression and the Rome Conference: 1995–1998

In the *Ad Hoc* Committee and the Preparatory Committee, States mainly debated the inclusion of the crime of aggression to the ICC's jurisdiction and the issue of the responsibility of the UN Security Council in determinations of the act of aggression.[150] Besides, two intersessional meetings were held in Siracusa in 1995 and 1996. This subsection mainly examines the work of the Preparatory Committee from 1996 to 1998 to show how the choice for the leadership clause came about, although this process did not yield any meaningful achievement on the definition of the crime of aggression.[151]

The *Ad Hoc* Committee's summary only noted that for the crime of aggression, 'the personal jurisdiction of the court with respect to individuals was

---

148   ibid, commentary (5) to art 2.
149   ibid, commentary (4) to art 16.
150   'Report of the *Ad Hoc* Committee on the Establishment of an International Criminal Court', UN Doc A/50/22 (1995), paras 63-71, 122-23; 'Report of the Preparatory Committee on the Establishment of an International Criminal Court', UN Doc A/51/22 (1996), Vol I, paras 65-73, 103-15; UN Press Release, 'Eight Speakers Comment on Draft Code of Crimes against Peace and Security', UN Doc GA/L/2865 (1995); id, 'Committee is Told Aggression Should be Within Jurisdiction of Proposed International Criminal Court', UN Doc GA/L/2877 (1995). For a summary of debates, see McDougall (n 8) 9–11; Kemp (n 14) 135; Bassiouni and Schabas (eds) (n 69) Vol II, 120-31; Schabas (n 8) 303–04.
151   For negotiating amendments on the crime of aggression, see Barriga and Kreß (eds) (n 34).

limited'.[152] The contour of the leadership element in article 8*bis* (1) of the Rome Statute was initially contained in the Report of the Preparatory Committee.[153] In the Preparatory Committee, some States submitted proposals for the definition of the crime of aggression.[154] The 1996 Preparatory Committee summarised and complied these illustrative texts of definitions for the crime of aggression.[155]

Two proposals with several alternatives for the crime of aggression were presented in the 1996 Report of the Preparatory Committee. Concerning the scope of potential perpetrators, one option restricted the potential perpetrators to be 'leaders or organisers', which was identical to the term used in the last clause of article 6 the Nuremberg Charter, the ILC's final Draft Code of Crimes and the 1995 Siracusa-Draft.[156] The 1995 Siracusa-Draft, prepared by a committee of experts in the first intersessional meeting, modified the 1994 ILC's draft text for the statute of an international criminal court and restricted the scope of perpetrators for the crime of aggression to 'a leader or organiser'. In the view of this committee,

> [it] firmly believed that [the crime of aggression] should not be limited to state officials, as private individuals and groups in today's society have clearly developed the ability, as well as possessing the means and

---

[152] 'Summary of the Proceedings of the Ad Hoc Committee During the Period 3 – 13 April 1995', UN Doc A/AC.244/2 (1995), para 32; R.S. Clark, 'Negotiations on the Rome Statute, 1995–98' in Barriga and Kreß (eds) (n 12) 244–70.

[153] 'Report of the Preparatory Committee on the Establishment of an International Criminal Court', UN Doc A/CONF.183/2 (1998), 14–15.

[154] Egypt, 'Draft Proposed Definition of Aggression' (29 March 1996); France, 'Draft Statute of the International Criminal Court' (6 August 1996), UN Doc A/AC.249/L.3, Art 30; 'Proposal, Submitted by Egypt and Italy on the Definition of Aggression'(21 February 1997), UN Doc A/AC.249/1997/WG.1/DP.6; Germany, 'Proposal for a definition of the crime of aggression'(19 February 1997), UN Doc A/AC.249/1997/WG.1/DP.3; 'Proposal by Germany, Article 20 the Crime of Aggression, An Informal Discussion Paper' (11 December 1997), UN Doc A/AC.249/1997/WG.1/DP.20; 'Revised proposal submitted by a group of integrated States including Germany' (1 April 1998), UN Doc A/AC.249/1998/DP.12.

[155] 'Report of the Preparatory Committee on the Establishment of an International Criminal Court', UN Doc A/51/22 (1996), Vol I, paras 70-73; 'Report of the Preparatory Committee on the Establishment of an International Criminal Court', UN Doc A/51/22 (1996), Vol II (Compilation of proposals), 58–59; 'Summary of the Proceedings of the Preparatory Committee during the Period 25 March – 12 April 1996', UN Doc A/AC.249/1 (1996), 60–61.

[156] 'Report of the Preparatory Committee on the Establishment of an International Criminal Court', UN Doc A/51/22 (1996), Vol II (Compilation of proposals), 58–59.

opportunity, to undertake acts that would otherwise constitute aggression were they to have been committed by a State.[157]

They aimed to include industrialists and business leaders or organisers as potential perpetrators. Another option referred to 'a person who is in a position of exercising control or capable of directing political/military action in his State'. Roger Clark noted that the source of this language was not proposed by delegation but exactly contained in the 1996 updated Siracusa-Draft.[158]

The 'leaders or organisers' alternative text for the crime of aggression was later abandoned by States. In the 1997-February session, Germany proposed to replace the term 'leaders or organisers' with 'exercising control or capable of directing political/military action in his State'. Germany explained that '[s]everal delegations were of the opinion that the term "as leader or organiser" [...] might be too broad in defining potential perpetrators of the crime of aggression'.[159] The proposal by Egypt and Italy repeated the same leadership text as that in the German proposal.[160] The 1997 draft definition of the crime of aggression placed the text of the crime of aggression between several square brackets, and referred to 'a person who is in a position of exercise control or capable of directing political/military action in his State'.[161] Delegations of States did not discuss the leadership text but addressed their general views on the inclusion of the crime of aggression.[162]

In the 1997-December session, after consultation among delegations on the crime of aggression, Germany submitted an informal discussion paper, which addressed its approach and position on the crime of aggression as follows:

---

157   Draft Statute for an International Criminal Court, Alternative to the ILC-Draft Statute (Siracusa-Draft), prepared by a committee of experts on an international criminal court, Siracusa/Freiburg, July 1995, art 20(3).
158   Clark (n 152) fn 62.
159   Germany, 'Proposal for a definition of the crime of aggression' (19 February 1997), UN Doc A/AC.249/1997/WG.I/DP.3.
160   'Proposal, Submitted by Egypt and Italy on the Definition of Aggression' (21 February 1997)., UN Doc A/AC.249/1997/WG.1/DP.6.
161   'Decisions Taken by the Preparatory Committee at Its Session Held from 11 to 21 February 1997', UN Doc A/AC.249/1997/L.5, 14–15; Working Group on Definition of Crimes, 'Draft Consolidated Text, Crime of aggression', UN Doc A/AC.249/1997/WG.1/CRP.6 and Corr.l.
162   UN Press Release, 'International Criminal Court Should be Independent Body, And Not Subsidiary of Security Council, Speakers Tell Legal Committee', UN Doc GA/L/3044 (1997); id 'United Stated Representative Tells Legal Committee International Criminal Court Should Not be Direct Part of United Nations', UN Doc GA/L/3046 (1997); id, 'Delegates Differ on Whether Statute of Proposed International Criminal Court Should Cover Crime of "Aggression" ', UN Doc GA/L/3047 (1997).

> Not to include [the crime of aggression] would [...] also amount to a refusal to draw an appropriate conclusion from recent history. The German side believes that we need the inclusion of this crime for reasons of deterrence and prevention, and in order to reaffirm in the most unequivocal manner that the waging of an aggressive war is a crime under international law. [...]
>
> In (the probably more frequent) cases where aggression entails war crimes and crimes against humanity, the importance of such a provision [for the crime of aggression] lies in the individual criminal responsibility it establishes for the political and/or strategic military leadership of a state: [...] [A] provision on aggression aims exclusively and directly at those responsible for the war as such. In such a situation, it may prove to be the only basis for holding them responsible. Aggression is, in our view, by definition a "leadership crime".[163]

The quoted paragraphs show that in the view of Germany, the crime of aggression is a leadership crime and it is necessary to learn lessons from 'history'. It is unclear whether Germany aimed to codify existent customary law on the crime of aggression or on the leadership element into the Statute.

The informal discussion paper employed nearly the same language of the leadership text as that in the German proposal (February): 'an individual who is in a position of exercising control or capable of directing political or military action of a State'.[164] The 1998 Zutphen draft used an identical text.[165] In the 1998-March/April session of the Preparatory Committee, Germany submitted a revised proposal, which was a result of consultations and 'supported by a number of States', to supersede its earlier text for the crime of aggression. The leadership text was kept in the 1998 revised proposal without any change.[166] In 1998, the Preparatory Committee presented three options for the definition of the crime of aggression to the Rome Conference.[167] All the three options restricted the potential perpetrators to be 'a person who is in a position of

---

163 'Proposal by Germany, Article 20 the Crime of Aggression, An Informal Discussion Paper' (11 December 1997), UN Doc A/AC.249/1997/WG.1/DP.20 (bold deleted).
164 ibid.
165 'Report of the Inter-Sessional Meeting from 19 to 30 January 1998 in Zutphen', Netherlands, UN Doc A/AC.249/1998/L.13, 19.
166 'Revised proposal submitted by a group of integrated States including Germany', UN Doc A/AC.249/1998/DP.12; UN Press Release, 'Netherlands Reiterates Offer to Host Seat of International Criminal Court', UN Doc GA/L/2860 (1998).
167 'Report of the Preparatory Committee on the Establishment of an International Criminal Court', UN Doc A/CONF.183/2 (1998), 14–15.

exercising control or capable of directing political/military action' in a/his State.[168] At the 1998 Rome Conference, delegations of States did not discuss the leadership issue but addressed their preferences for the definition of the crime of aggression.[169] The Rome Conference included the crime of aggression into the listed crime under the jurisdiction of the ICC in article 5(2).

This survey illustrates the drafting work of the leadership text for the crime of aggression in article 8*bis* of the Rome Statute. This survey shows that the phrase 'leaders or organisers' was considered broader than the leadership clause in article 8*bis* of the Rome Statute to capture potential perpetrators for the crime of aggression. Most delegations supported the inclusion of the crime of aggression in the proposed Statute, and some delegations intended to restrict the scope of persons by inserting the wording of 'effectively' and 'control or direct'.[170] The Preparatory Committee seems to reflect a consensus on the leadership nature of the crime, but not on the threshold of the leadership element.

5.4.5 *The Rome-Kampala Work on the Crime of Aggression: 1999–2009*

Following the Rome Conference, the Preparatory Commission (1999–2002), established under the Final Act of the Rome Conference,[171] and later a Special Working Group on the Crime of Aggression (Special Working Group 2003–2009), established by the ASP,[172] continued negotiating issues concerning the crime of aggression. In 2009, the Special Working Group adopted a set of proposals for a provision for aggression,[173] which was submitted to the ASP through Liechtenstein and later forwarded to the 2010 Kampala Review Conference.[174] This subsection explores post-Rome negotiations on the leadership clause in

---

168   UN Doc A/AC.249/1997/L.5, 14; UN Doc A/AC.249/1997/WG.1/DP.20.

169   'Summary records of meetings of the Committee of the Whole', UN Doc A/CONF.183/C.1/SR.6, UN Doc A/CONF.183/C.1/SR.25, UN Doc A/CONF.183/C.1/SR.26, UN Doc A/CONF.183/C.1/SR.27 and UN Doc A/CONF.183/C.1/SR.28.

170   'Decisions Taken by the Preparatory Committee at Its Session Held From 11 to 21 February 1997', UN Doc A/AC.249/1997/L.5. See also Working Group on Definition of Crimes, 'Draft Consolidated Text, Crime of aggression', UN Doc A/AC.249/1997/WG.1/CRP.6 and Corr. L.

171   'Final Act of the United Nations Conference of Plenipotentiaries on the Establishment of an International Criminal Court', UN Doc A/CONF.183/10 (1998), Annex I, resolution F, para 7.

172   Resolution ICC-ASP/I/Res.1 (2002), in ASP Official Records, ICC-ASP/1/3, 328. For discussions on the work of the SWGCA, see Kemp (n 14) 147–75.

173   2009 SWGCA Report (n 56), Appendix I (Proposals for a provision on aggression elaborated by the Special Working Group on the Crime of Aggression, Draft Resolution).

174   Resolution ICC-ASP/8/Res.6 (2009), para 3 and Annex II: Liechtenstein, 'Proposals for a provision on aggression'.

articles 8*bis* and 25(3*bis*) of the Rome Statute, in particular, the work of the Special Working Group, to show whether that leadership clause reflected an emerging customary law.[175]

5.4.5.1 Preparatory Commission: 1999–2002

In the Preparatory Commission, many States submitted their proposals and notes on the definition of the crime of aggression.[176] In the 2002 Coordinator's Paper (July), the leadership clause of the crime of aggression as that in article 8*bis* required the person being 'in a position effectively to exercise control over or to direct the political or military action of a State'.[177] This leadership clause was substantially unchanged in future negotiations on the crime of aggression. As Stefanie Barriga observed, few delegations participated in the Preparatory Commission actively, and the 2002 Coordinator's Paper (July) also did not reflect a consensus on the definition of the crime of aggression.[178] States, however, widely supported to incorporate the crime of aggression as a leadership crime into its definition.[179]

---

175 For a summary of the evolution of the leadership element, see Hajdin (n 54).
176 Barriga and Kreß (eds) (n 34) 335–419; Bassiouni and Schabas (eds) (n 69) Vol I, 112–23; 'Incorporating the Crime of Aggression as a Leadership Crime into the Definition – Proposal Submitted by Belgium, Cambodia, Sierra Leone and Thailand' (8 July 2002), UN Doc PCNICC/2002/WGCA/DP.5.
177 'Discussion Paper Proposed by the Coordinator' (11 July 2002), UN Doc PCNICC/2002/WGCA/RT.1/Rev.2 [2002 Coordinator's Paper (July)].
178 Barriga (n 3) 10.
179 'Proposal Submitted by Bahrain, Iraq, Lebanon, the Libyan Arab Jamahiriya, Oman, the Sudan, the Syrian Arab Republic and Yemen on the Crime of Aggression' (26 February 1999), UN Doc PCNICC/1999/DP.11; 'Proposal Submitted by Germany: Definition of the Crime of Aggression' (30 July 1999), UN Doc PCNICC/1999/DP.13; 'Proposal Submitted by Greece and Portugal' (7 December 1999), UN Doc PCNICC/1999/WGCA/DP.1; 'Proposal Submitted by Colombia on the Definition of the Crime of Aggression and on Conditions for the Exercise of the Jurisdiction of the Court with regard to this Crime' (1 March 2000), UN Doc PCNICC/2000/WGCA/DP.1; 'Considerations by Colombia Regarding its Proposal on Aggression Contained in Document PCNICC/2000/WGCA/DP.1' (17 March 2000), UN Doc PCNICC/2000/WGCA/DP.1/Add.1; 'Proposal Submitted by Germany: the Crime of Aggression: a Further Informal Discussion Paper' (13 November 2000), UN Doc PCNICC/ 2000/WGCA/DP.4 [2000 Proposal by Germany], para 24(3); 'Proposal Submitted by Greece and Portugal' (28 November 2000), UN Doc PCNICC/2000/WGCA/DP.5, para 1 and Explanatory note; 'Proposal Submitted by Bosnia and Herzegovina, New Zealand and Romania: Definition of the Crime of Aggression' (27 August 2001), UN Doc. PCNICC/2001/WGCA/DP.2, para 1 and commentary (a); 'Proposal by the Netherlands Concerning PCNICC/2002/WGCA/RT.1' (17 April 2002), UN Doc. PCNICC/2002/WGCA/DP.1; 'Proposed Text on the Definition of the Crime and Act of Aggression: Proposal Submitted by the Delegation of Colombia' (1 July 2002), UN Doc PCNICC/2002/WGCA/DP.3, Element 5 and para 15.

In discussing the appropriate definition of the crime, Germany in its 2000 proposal suggested that 'an approach based on experiences, conclusions and lessons to be drawn from [...] historical precedents of this crime will be the best way to reflect the relevant customary international law'.[180] But this approach was not fully discussed.

A few States concerned whether the leadership clause in the 2002 Coordinator's Paper (July) covers the same scope of perpetrators as that in the Nuremberg precedents. Colombia proposed that the persons should 'being in a position to contribute to or effectively cooperate in shaping in a fundamental manner political or military action by a State'.[181] In discussing the elements of crimes of aggression, Samoa proposed that:

> The perpetrator, who need not formally be a member of the Government of the military, [was in] [occupied] and [actual] [effective] position to exercise control over or direct the political or military action of the State which [was responsible for] [committed] the act of aggression.[182]

Its explanatory note to this proposed element further stated that:

> The 'need not formally' phrase is aimed at catching the essence of the Nuremberg decisions in the *I.G. Farben* and *Krupp* industrialist cases. The tribunals held there that it *may* be possible to convict non-governmental actors for a crime against peace (although there were acquittals on the facts of those cases).[183]

The explanatory note clearly shows Samoan concern that whether the leadership language reflects the jurisprudence of the NMTs to include persons who are non-government actors but 'shape or influence' the act of aggression of the State.[184]

In addition to this, some States stressed that:

> '[s]ince it is already given and supported by the jurisprudence of the Nuremberg Tribunal and the Tribunals established pursuant to Control

---

180   2000 Proposal by Germany, ibid, paras 7, 23.
181   2002 Proposal by Samoa (n 37).
182   ibid, Element 5.
183   ibid (italics in original).
184   2002 Proposal by Samoa (n 37); see also 'Proposal Submitted by Cuba' (4 September 2003), ICC-ASP/2/SWGCA/DP.1.

Council Law No. 10 that the crime of aggression is a leadership crime which may only be committed by persons who have effective control of the State and military apparatus on a policy level, it is crucial to reflect this principle in the definition of the Crime of Aggression; otherwise it might be subsequently diluted, among other things, by the application of article 10 of the Rome Statute.'[185]

This statement indicates these States' acceptance of the 'control' test. However, they misunderstood the Nuremberg precedents. As discussed above, neither the Nuremberg IMT nor NMTs adopted a 'control' test. The NMTs sometimes followed a 'shape or influence' test for crimes against peace. No substantial attention was paid to these concerns.

The 2002 Coordinators' Paper (July) suggested that article 25(3) of the Rome Statute should not apply to the crime of aggression.[186] As mentioned above, Samoa also proposed draft elements of the crime of aggression. Delegations discussed little on the application of article 25(3) to the crime of aggression and the elements of that crime in the Preparatory Commission. But the draft elements in the 2002 Coordinator's Paper (July) were substantially drawn from the Samoan proposal.[187] Its Element 1 provided that '[t]he perpetrator was in a position effectively to exercise control over or to direct the political or military action of a State which committed an act of aggression'. The main language of this draft leadership element was retained in the final Elements of Crimes.

5.4.5.2 Special Working Group and Princeton Process on the Crime of Aggression: 2003–2009

In 2003, the torch of the work on the crime of aggression was passed to a Special Working Group.[188] In addition to the formal sessions in the Special Working Group, informal intersessional meetings were held from 2004 to 2007 at Princeton University (Princeton Process on the Crime of Aggression).[189] The Special Working Group dealt with the drafting of Elements of Crimes for the crime of aggression on several occasions, but it did not discuss the substantive

---

185 'Incorporating the Crime of Aggression as a Leadership Crime into the Definition: Proposal Submitted by Belgium, Cambodia, Sierra Leone and Thailand' (8 July 2002), UN Doc PCNICC/2002/WGCA/DP.5.
186 2002 Coordinator's Paper (July) (n 177).
187 ibid.
188 2009 SWGCA Report, Appendix I (n 173).
189 For the work of the SWGCA and an assessment of the Princeton Process, see S. Barriga, 'Against the Odds: The Results of the Special Working Group on the Crime of Aggression' in Bellelli (ed) (n 88) 621–43; Kreß and Von Holtzendorf (n 63) 1186–88 and fn 29, fn 30.

leadership element.[190] The following paragraphs focus on the meaning of the leadership clause, its placement and the applicability of article 25(3) to the crime of aggression.[191] Delegations also debated the conduct verbs for the crime of aggression and the relevance of other provisions in the Rome Statute. Some of these discussions further stressed the leadership nature of the crime of aggression, but are not relevant to the issue of the leadership threshold.

The Princeton Process did not provide an alternative formulation to the leadership clause for the definition of the crime.[192] The language of the leadership clause in the 2002 Coordinators' Paper (July) was widely supported and it seems that 'there was limited interest in exploring alternative formulations'.[193] In the 2007–2009 Special Working Group proposals, the same formulation of the leadership clause was retained in the definition of the crime of aggression.[194] The 2008 Report of the Special Working Group noted that '[t]he first part of [article 8*bis*], ending with "act of aggression which", reflects the progress made in previous discussions regarding the definition of the individual's conduct [...] and the leadership clause. This part of the paragraph met with general agreement.'[195] The Special Working Group finished its work on the definition of the crime of aggression in February 2009.[196] There was an agreement on the leadership clause for the crime of aggression.[197]

As opposed to the meaning of the leadership clause in article 8*bis*, the Princeton Process discussed details of the application of article 25(3) to the crime of aggression and the placement of the leadership clause. In the 2004

---

190 F. Anggadi *et al*, 'Negotiating the Elements of the Crime of Aggression' in Barriga and Kreß (eds) (n 34) 61–62.

191 For discussions on general principles and the crime of aggression, see R.S. Clark, 'General Principles of International Criminal Law' in Barriga and Kreß (eds) (n 12) 590–620.

192 'Informal inter-sessional meeting of the Special Working Group on the Crime of Aggression', ICC-ASP/4/SWGCA/INF.1 [2005 Princeton Report], Appendix I; 'Informal inter-sessional meeting of the Special Working Group on the Crime of Aggression', ICC-ASP/5/SWGCA/INF.1 [2006 Princeton Report], Annex I.

193 Barriga (n 3) 22.

194 2007 SWGCA Report (January) (n 43), Annex; 'Non-paper by the Chairman on defining the individual's conduct' in 'Report of the Special Working Group on the Crime of Aggression', ICC-ASP/6/SWGCA/1 (December 2007) [2007 SWGCA Report (December)], Annex; 'Discussion paper on the crime of aggression proposed by the Chairman (revision June 2008)' in 'Report of the Special Working Group on the Crime of Aggression' (June 2008) [2008 SWGCA Report (June)], Appendix; 2009 SWGCA Report, Appendix I (n 173), 30, 32.

195 2008 SWGCA Report (June), ibid, para 17.

196 2009 SWGCA Report, Appendix I (n 173), art 8*bis*.

197 'Report of the Working Group on the Crime of Aggression', RC/5 of 10 June 2010, in RC/11, Annex III, para 4.

Princeton Process, the leadership nature of the crime of aggression was reaffirmed.[198] In discussing the exclusion or non-exclusion of applicability of article 25(3), it was suggested that:

> all persons in a position to exert decisive influence over the policies of the State should be held criminally responsible, so that political, social, business and spiritual leaders could be included within the leadership group. This point was made that the preliminary definition has been crafted in a manner broad enough to encompass most influential leaders. However, another view held that responsibility for the crime of aggression should be understood to be rather restrictive, basically limited to political leaders, excluding for example advisers who clearly would lack any effective control over the actions of a State.[199]

The limitation of responsibility to the restrictive scope of leaders ensures the leadership nature of the crime, thus it is not necessary to exclude the applicability of article 25(3).

The 2005 Princeton Process decided to abandon the exclusion approach and suggested to apply article 25(3) to the crime of aggression.[200] In discussing how to apply article 25(3) to the crime of aggression, participants expressed different views concerning the adding of a new paragraph 3*bis* to article 25.[201] However, they generally agreed that only leaders would be liable for the crime of aggression,[202] 'thereby excluding participants who could not influence the policy of carrying out the crime, such as soldiers executing orders'.[203] According to the 2005 Report of the Coalition for the International Criminal Court on the crime of aggression:

> The proponent of the policy level requirement explained that it would be wider than the leadership clause. It would reach beyond the high command and cover also involved industrialists and financiers. In answer, the Chair pointed out that it had been always understood that the leadership

---

198 'Informal inter-sessional meeting of the Special Working Group on the Crime of Aggression', ICC-ASP/3/SWGCA/INF.1 [2004 Princeton Report], paras 35, 37, 52–53.
199 2004 Princeton Report, ibid, para 49.
200 2005 Princeton Report (n 192), paras 18-31 and Appendix I. See also 2006 Princeton Report (n 192), para 84 and Annex I.
201 2005 Princeton Report (n 192), para 24.
202 ibid, paras 31.
203 ibid, paras 19-20.

clause would reach just as far and that it had never been limited to heads of state or individuals in the military.[204]

In the 2006 Princeton Process, some participations suggested again that the leadership clause 'should refer to the ability to influence policy'.[205] But the 'influence' test was never adopted.

In the 2007 (January and December) Special Working Group, 2007 Princeton Process, and 2009 Special Working Group, delegations discussed the content of the leadership clause in article 25(3*bis*). It was constantly asked whether the scope of perpetrators in the text of the leadership clause would encompass persons outside the military and political leadership, who had the power to shape or influence the actions of a State.[206] In response, some delegations argued that the language of article 25(3*bis*) was sufficiently broad to capture persons outside formal government circles, such as industrialists.[207] In their view, this interpretation was consistent with the NMTs precedents,[208] which 'referred to persons outside formal government circles who could shape or influence the State's action'.[209] Another view was also repeatedly expressed in the debates that 'the responsibility of persons beyond the direct leaders would be difficult to prove',[210] and widening the wording of the leadership clause might create 'more problems than it would solve'.[211]

Heller has suggested replacing 'to control or direct' with 'to shape or influence' under article 25(3*bis*), while to keep the leadership clause unchanged in the definition of the crime of aggression under article 8*bis*.[212] He compared the scope of potential persons covered under the leadership clause 3*bis* and the range of persons prosecuted in post-World War II trials. In his view, the scope of potential persons covered by the 'shape or influence' formula includes private economic leaders, who are excluded under the 'control or direct' test. But the Chairman responded and remarked that the 'control or direct' formula, in any event, covers private economic leaders, such as industrialists.[213]

---

204   Cited in Heller (n 11) 490 and fn 86.
205   2006 Princeton Report (n 192), para 88.
206   2007 SWGCA Report (January) (n 43), para 13; 2007 Princeton Report (n 43), para 12; 2007 SWGCA Report (December) (n 194), para 9; 2009 SWGCA Report (n 56), para 25.
207   2007 SWGCA Report (December) (n 194), para 9; 2009 SWGCA Report (n 56), para 25.
208   2007 SWGCA Report (December) (n 194), para 9.
209   2007 Princeton Report (n 43), para 12.
210   ibid, para 12.
211   2007 SWGCA Report (December) (n 194), para 9.
212   Heller (n 11) 497.
213   ibid 490 and fn 86.

In discussing the applicability of article 25(3), some delegations in the 2005 Princeton Process refered 'to the jurisprudence of the Nuremberg and Tokyo tribunals, which might be said to have codified customary international law'.[214] However, this view was not thoroughly discussed. Some participants in the 2007 Princeton Process expressed their views concerning the placement of the leadership clause in article 25 that:

> The absence of such a clause in article 25 might lead to jurisdiction over secondary perpetrators and thus undermine the leadership nature of the crime. The leadership clause in article 25, paragraph 3*bis*, would, furthermore, be useful for implementing legislation at the national level, and could also have an impact on customary law.[215]

In their view, such a duplication of the leadership clause in paragraph 3*bis* could 'have an impact on customary law'. The reference to an 'impact on customary law' here shows that they realised the non-existence of such a customary rule on the leadership element, which restricted the scope of potential participators for the crime of aggression as that in article 25(3*bis*).[216]

In the Princeton Process and the Special Working Group, it was agreed that the leadership element is a restrictive test, which excludes 'advisers' and 'soldiers' from the scope of perpetrators covered by the 'control or direct' formula under article 8*bis*. Some scholars correctly observed that, with regard to the executing of the crime of aggression, the legal argument is unconvincing that the leadership nature is inherently linked to the crime of aggression. Sovereignty and criminal policy might be the main reasons why States preferred to contain a leadership clause for the crime of aggression because they did not want their soldiers to be given a reason to review orders or decisions of their States relating to the use of force.[217]

In the Special Working Group, delegations questioned whether the scope of persons satisfying the leadership element for the crime of aggression is broad enough to cover industrialists. The chairman of the Special Working Group gave an affirmative reply. True, a plain reading of the leadership text also did not exclude non-governmental actors. The remarks of the Chairman and the views expressed in the Special Working Group also supported that the control or direct test is broad enough to encompass non-governmental leaders, for

---

214 2005 Princeton Report (n 192), para 26.
215 2007 Princeton Report (n 43), para 11.
216 For discussions on the limitation of article 25(3*bis*), Kreß (n 45); Heller (n 11) 492–97.
217 Coracini and Wrange (n 8) 310–11.

example, industrialists. The inclusion of industrialists does not mean that the 'control or direct' test is a restatement of the 'shape or influence' formula.[218] The leadership element, either 'control or direct' test or 'shape or influence' test, denotes the legal grounding for the prosecution of these persons for the crime of aggression. Either the 'control or direct' test or 'shape or influence' test encompasses private economic actors. But the range of private economic leaders potentially covered by the 'shape or influence' test may be wider than that contained by the phrase 'control or direct'. For instance, top-level managers of companies might indirectly influence the action of a State through affecting the decision-making of a State's leading industrial leaders; but these top-level managers are not in a position as those industrial leaders who may control or direct the State's action.

Heller has commented on the leadership clause in article 25(3*bis*) and argued that 'the control of direct' standard in this clause is 'a significant retreat from the Nuremberg principles – not their codification'.[219] McDougall agreed with Heller's finding on this point.[220] However, their views are divided on whether the retreat was a result of a misunderstanding of the Nuremberg and Tokyo precedents or was intentionally designed by delegations in the Special Working Group. Heller argued that the Special Working Group misunderstood the differences between the 'control or direct' test and the 'shape or influence' test. In the view of McDougall, though not all delegations presenting with full knowledge of Nuremberg and Tokyo jurisprudence, the 'key negotiators were aware of the distinction between the definition proposed and its precedent and made a conscious choice to narrow the scope of perpetrators captures'.[221]

As observed above in subsection 5.4.5.1, some States believed that the NMTs adopted a control test, which was a misunderstanding. But I agree with McDougall that the 'control or direct' test was intentionally inserted to restrict the persons who shall be responsible for the crime of aggression, given the 2002 UN *Historical Review of Developments relating to Aggression* and Heller's suggestion to the Special Working Group. Discussions on the meaning of the leadership clause under article 8*bis* indicate an intentional opposition to the view that the persons responsible for the crime of aggression are at the position to 'shape or influence' the State's political or military actions. The insertion and placement of article 25(3*bis*) further stressed the leadership nature of the crime of aggression. In this way, both potential perpetrators and participants

---

218   Cf. Heller (n 11) fn 86.
219   Heller (n 11) 497.
220   McDougall (n 8) 182.
221   ibid 182–83.

of the crime of aggression are limited to the persons in the leadership positions to effectively control or direct actions of a State.[222]

5.4.5.3 2009 Montreux and Princeton Meetings on the Elements of Crimes

The negotiations on the elements of crimes of aggression were not proceeding substantively in the Special Working Group. Since the Special Working Group concluded its mandate in February 2009, it was envisaged to discuss the Elements of Crimes at another informal intersessional Princeton meeting in June 2009. In April 2009, an informal experts' meeting was held beforehand in Montreux to exchange thoughts on drafting the elements of crimes.

Discussions at the Montreux meeting were based on the 2009 Montreux Draft Elements of Crimes (March), which suggested proposals for updated Elements since the 2002 Coordinator's Paper (July).[223] After three readings, twenty-three experts in the Montreux meeting agreed on a set of refined Elements, which was forwarded to the Chairman on negotiating the crime of aggression.[224] The proposed Elements and their explanatory note were incorporated into the appendixes of the Chairman's Non-Paper on the Elements of Crimes,[225] prepared for the Princeton meeting in June 2009. The proposed Elements were well received at the 2009 Princeton meeting and the 2010 Review Conference.[226]

With regard to the leadership element, Draft Element 2 of the 2009 Montreux Draft Elements of Crimes (March) read as follows:

> The perpetrator was in a position effectively to exercise control over the political or military action of the State which committed an act of aggression.[227]

This draft element reiterated the leadership element as that in the 2002 Coordinator's Paper (July). At the Montreux meeting, it was suggested to add

---

222 V. Nerlich, 'The Crime of Aggression and Modes of Lability – Is There Room Only for Principals?' (2017) 58 *Harvard Intl LJ* 44.
223 'Discussion Paper on Elements of the Crime of Aggression' (March 2009), cited in Barriga and Kreß (eds) (n 34) 673.
224 Summary to Retreat on the Elements of Crimes for the crime of aggression Montreux, Switzerland, 16 to 18 April 2009.
225 'Draft Elements of Crimes' in "Non-paper by the Chairman on the Elements of Crimes' (28 May 2009), Appendix I. See 2009 Princeton Report (n 44), Annex II, Appendix I.
226 'Draft Elements of Crimes' in 2009 Princeton Report (n 44), Annex I.
227 '2009 Montreux Draft Elements of Crimes (March)' (n 223) 673.

a footnote to clarify that the crime of aggression could also be committed by industrialists. However, 'some cautioned that there had not been a clear consensus on the matter in the Special Working Group and there might be some danger of inadvertently widening the scope of the definition's leadership requirement'.[228] This issue was not discussed in further meetings.

These experts attended the meeting in their capacity, rather than as governmental representatives. The abandonment of this proposal, thus, should not be exaggerated. The abandonment also does not mean that industrialists are excluded from the scope of persons satisfying the control or direct test. It was agreed that the Montreux meeting should not reopen issues but should reflect what has been agreed on its definition.[229] Some of the experts sought to clarify the elements with clear words, while others in the group aimed to leave room for judicial interpretation. The matter was not further discussed, partly because Element 2 was a result of a balance between clear law and flexible law.

These experts' discussion on Element 2 assists in understanding the meaning of the leadership element, but does not assist in establishing whether the control or direct test was inserted as a declaratory of custom. Other suggestions about Element 2 at the Montreux and Princeton meetings were not relevant to the issue here.[230] The final suggestion for Element 2 added 'a person' before 'in a position' and added a footnote '[w]ith respect to an act of aggression, more than one person may be in a position which meets these criteria'.[231] This text of Element 2 was unchanged and accepted at the 2009 Princeton meeting, and then adopted at the 2010 Review Conference.[232] The Review Conference adopted by consensus a comprehensive package of amendments on the crime of aggression, including the definition of the crime and its elements.[233]

5.4.5.4   Observations

The observation of the negotiating history and drafting work of the crime of aggression in the Rome-Kampala phase shows that the Nuremberg and Tokyo trials were guidelines for these discussions.[234] But delegations neither follow the framework of the Nuremberg and Tokyo Charters nor adopt a 'shape or

---

228 Anggadi *et al* (n 190) 67.
229 ibid 63.
230 ibid 64–68; 2009 Princeton Report (n 44), paras 14-15.
231 'Draft Elements of Crimes' in "Non-paper by the Chairman on the Elements of Crimes" (28 May 2009), Appendix I.
232 2009 Princeton Report (n 44), paras 14-15.
233 ICC-ASP/I/Res. 6.
234 2005 Princeton Report (n 192), para 26; 2007 Princeton Report (n 43), para 12.

influence' leadership test as that used by some NMTs. Also, it remains unclear whether delegations aimed to define the crime of aggression as a reflection of customary law. Departing from the NMTs precedents and the 1996 ILC's view, the 'control or direct' leadership element was intentionally inserted into the Rome Statute for the crime of aggression under articles 8*bis* and 25(3*bis*).

It was generally agreed that a leadership element was substantially required for the crime of aggression. Nevertheless, States seem to disagree that the 'control or direct' leadership element for potential perpetrators and participators of the crime of aggression has been well-formed under customary law. Since there was no customary rule of a 'shape or influence' leadership element, it is inappropriate to conclude that the 'control or direct' formula in the two articles departs from pre-existing customary law on the leadership element of the crime of aggression.[235] No evidence suggests that the two provisions reflect an emerging customary rule on the leadership threshold. The next subsection turns to national practice.

5.4.6 *National Practice*

Despite the recognition of the crime of aggression in international criminal law and the reinforcement of regulation of the use of force, there were international armed conflicts since 1946.[236] However, there was no substantial prosecution of the crime of aggression, except for trials after World War II at the Nuremberg and Tokyo. In 2003, German Prosecutor decided not to investigate the use of force against Iraq pertaining to the crime of preparing a war of aggression under German criminal law.[237] The Iraqi High Criminal Court Law includes 'the abuse of position and the pursuit of policies' that may lead to the threat of war or the use of Iraqi force against an Arab country as a domestic crime, leaving the alleged crime of aggression against Iraq in 2003 untouched.[238] As will be seen below in section 5.5, the British House of Lords in the *R v Jones et al* case have decided not to adjudicate on the issue of the crime of aggression for the invasion of Iraq by the UK and/or the US. It was also said that the Investigative Committee of the Russian Federation

---

235 Cf. Hajdin (n 54) 543; Heller (n 11).
236 UCDP/PRIO Armed Conflict Dataset <https://www.prio.org/Data/Armed-Conflict/UCDP-PRIO/> accessed 13 December 2020. See also 2002 Historical Review (n 17), paras 379–450; E. Greppi, 'State Responsibility for Acts of Aggression Under the United Nations Charter: A Review of Cases' in Bellelli (ed) (n 88) 499–517.
237 On this decision, see Kreß (n 45).
238 Iraq, Iraqi High Criminal Court Law 2005, art 14(3); C. Kreß, 'The Iraqi Special Tribunal and the Crime of Aggression' (2004) 2 *JICJ* 347, 348.

investigated the crime of aggressive war in the 2008 South Ossetia event based on its Criminal Code. But it seems that this crime was not on its list now.[239] In addition to this, the majority of national criminal codes do not contain the crime of aggression under international law. The following paragraphs examine some national provisions concerning the leadership element of the crime of aggression before the adoption of the Amendments in 2010 to show whether a leadership threshold for the crime of aggression was emerging.

After surveying 25 examples of definitions of the crime of aggression under international law in 90 countries' statutory legislation, Astrid Reisinger Coracini observed that the formulations of definitions in these national legislation are divided.[240] Sergey Sayapin also observed national provisions relative to the crime of aggression in 26 States Parties to the 1998 Rome Statute.[241] Sayapin summarised four models of prosecuting the crime of aggression at the national level, namely, 'Nuremberg and Tokyo model', 'territory integrity or political independence model', 'objective war model' and 'treason model'. Sayapin correctly noted that the 'treason model' is not a model of a crime of aggression under international law for its special 'internal' nature between a State and its nationals.[242] A close observation of these national provisions first shows that the title of the crime of aggression is divergent. The terms used include 'crimes against peace', 'aggression', 'criminal offences against the values protected by international law', 'endangering peace', 'crimes against the peace and security' and 'crime of aggression', which partly suggested the model applied. The majority of these provisions adopted the Nuremberg model.

Some scholars observed that these States have criminalised the crime of aggression 'under customary international law' so as 'to protect values of the international community as a whole'.[243] In fact, few States clarified their reasons or sources of revisions. When revising its criminal law in 2001, Estonia said it criminalised aggression for its obligation under customary law and international treaties.[244] Croatia explained that the crime of aggression was

---

239 S.V. Glotova, 'Russia' in Barriga and Kreß (eds) (n 12) 933–34 and fn 38.
240 Coracini (n 7) 726; Coracini (n 88) 550 and fn 22.
241 S. Sayapin, 'The Compatibility of the Rome Statute's Draft Definition of the Crime of Aggression with National Criminal Justice Systems' (2010) 81 *RIDP* 165. Also see Sayapin (n 9) 199.
242 Sayapin (n 9) 199–222.
243 Coracini (n 7) 726; Coracini (n 88) 550 and fn 22.
244 Explanator memorandum to the draft of the penal code, cited from A. Parmas, 'Estonia' in Barriga and Kreß (eds) (n 12) 897 and fn 8.

'formulated according to the general principles of international criminal law'.[245] In general, it is difficult to discern whether their legislators believed that they are obliged to fulfil the obligation derived from customary law or treaty obligations. These national legislation reaffirmed that the crime of aggression as an international crime is well accepted in international law. However, this finding does not apply to the leadership element.

With regard to the leadership element, most of these national provisions do not refer to a leadership clause. The formulations of these national provisions employ general terms, such as 'any person', 'any national' or 'whoever'. Coracini noted that commentaries to some Nuremberg Model provisions offer guidelines for interpretation, which suggest that these provisions have to be read in accordance with customary law definition of the crime. Potential perpetrators have to be capable of perpetrating and in the position to carry out the conduct elements of the crime of aggression.[246] These interpretation guidelines indicate that potential persons at the bottom of a chain will not be covered. In addition to this, the conduct verbs 'order' or 'command' in some criminal codes imply that there is a restriction to potential perpetrators for the crime of aggression.[247] Furthermore, judges of domestic courts are empowered to determine who are the potential perpetrators of these crimes. The final result might be that the majority of persons prosecuted are leaders, by virtue of the authority or function, who are aware of the acts of aggression.

Nevertheless, the presumption that only leaders are prosecuted in practice does not justify a view that the leadership element is required for the legal construction of the crime of aggression. Exceptionally, the 2001 Estonia Penal Code followed the Nuremberg model for the crime of aggression and explicitly qualified the circle of potential perpetrators for that crime.[248] Its commentary appears to suggest that for the alternative of participating in the act of aggression, the 2001 Penal Code has followed the 'shape or influence' test. With respect to the alternative of threatening a war of aggression, the possible perpetrators were limited to formal representatives of the State.[249] It is also notable that legal persons would be held responsible for the crime of aggression in the Estonian Penal Code.[250] In some countries, individuals 'who advise' the

---

245   Croatia, Criminal Code 1998, art 157. On this Code, see K. Turković and M.M. Vajda, 'Croatia' in Barriga and Kreß (eds) (n 12) 864 and fn 8.
246   Coracini (n 88) 553; Turković and Vajda (n 245) 866.
247   Coracini (n 7) 737–38; Coracini (n 88) 553.
248   Estonia, Penal Code 2001, § 91.
249   Parmas (n 244) 900–02.
250   Estonia, Penal Code 2001, amended 2014, § 91 (2).

carrying on of any war are also considered as potential persons to be prosecuted for the crime of aggression.[251] As for the crime of propaganda of war or public calls for aggressive wars, the perpetrator's State position is considered as an aggravating circumstance for punishment in some national criminal codes.[252]

These national legislation seems to testify that a leadership element of the crime of aggression was not firmly established under customary law. National provisions with a leadership text do not adopt the 'control or direct' test for potential perpetrators; and a leadership element is not required for prosecuting potential participators of the crime of aggression, which is at odds with article 25(3*bis*) of the Rome Statute.

5.4.7 *Assessment and Conclusions*

It is difficult to draw a line between the persons who are guilty of committing the crime of aggression from innocent persons. The exploration of the crime of aggression and the leadership text in post-World-War II trials shows that the crime of aggression was recognised as an international crime under customary law. However, the Nuremberg and Tokyo Charters did not contain an explicit leadership clause. A clear leadership standard was also not imposed by the IMT and the IMTFE to convict individuals of guilty for crimes against peace. In the NMTs, the leadership threshold was clearly affirmed for crimes against peace, but these tribunals were divided over the definition of leaders and the formula of the leadership test.

Neither the work of the ILC on the formulation of the Nuremberg Principles nor the Draft Code of Crimes (Offences) before 1991 provided a precise formulation of the leadership threshold for the crime of aggression. The 1991 and 1996 versions of the Draft Code of Crimes referred to leaders or organisers for the crime of aggression. The ILC's chairman summarised that 'the form of individual involvement was limited to leaders or organizers, recognising the fact that aggression was always committed by individuals who occupied the

---

251 Botswana, Penal Code 1964, amended 2005, § 38; Kenya, Criminal Code 1930, amended 2010, § 44.

252 Armenia, Criminal Code 2003, art 385(2) 'the highest State authority'; Georgia, Criminal Code 1999, art 405(2) 'a public political official'; Kazakhstan, Criminal Code 1997, art 161 'civil servant'; Mongolia, Criminal Code 2002, art 298.2 'a civil servant'; Russian Federation, Criminal Code 1996, art 354 (2) 'holding a State office of the Russian Federation or a State office of a subject of the Russian Federation'; Tajikistan, Criminal Code 1998, art 396 'hold state positions'.

highest decision-making positions in the political or military.'[253] A leadership clause was introduced, but the 'control or direct' test was not considered in these authorities. The phrase 'leaders or organisers' in the ILC's final Draft Code of Crimes covers a broader scope of potential persons as opposed to the 'control or direct' leadership test.

In the pre-Rome work on the crime of aggression, the leadership nature of the crime of aggression was generally accepted, but the leadership threshold was not discussed. In the Rome-Kampala work, the Preparatory Commission provided the text of the leadership clause like that in article 8*bis*. The leadership nature of the crime of aggression was widely and generally recognised by States, but the specific leadership element 'control or direct' was also not thoroughly discussed. The Special Working Group substantially contributed to the drafting of the leadership clauses under articles 8*bis* and 25(3*bis*). Delegations deliberately inserted the 'control or direct' leadership clause into article 8*bis* to guarantee that possible perpetrators of the crime of aggression are qualified to certain leaders. Except for some concerns about the scope of persons captured by the leadership clause, the leadership test was also placed in article 25 paragraph 3*bis* as a compromise. The 'control or direct' test for potential persons requires further clarifications by the ICC judges.

At the 2010 Review Conference, delegations focused on the conditions for the exercise of jurisdiction by the ICC over the crime of aggression and discussed little on the leadership element of this crime.[254] The 2010 Review Conference established the Working Group on the Crime of Aggression. The Chair of that Working Group noted that his conference room paper on the crime of aggression brought all the elements together and also reflected the agreement on the leadership clause.[255] No discussion on the definition of the crime of aggression and the draft Elements was reopened at the Review Conference, partly because of the support for the drafts among many delegations.[256] A resolution on the crime of aggression was adopted by consensus at the 2010 Review Conference.[257] Amendments to the Elements of Crimes in that Resolution restated the leadership element under articles 8*bis* and 25(3*bis*).[258]

---

253   UN Press Release, 'Draft Code of Crimes against Peace, Security and Mankind under Consideration in Legal Committee', UN Doc GA/L/3014 (1996).
254   Barriga (n 3) 46–57.
255   'Report of the Working Group on the Crime of Aggression', RC/5 of 10 June 2010, in RC/11, Annex III.
256   ibid, para 4.
257   Resolution RC/Res.6 of 11 June 2010.
258   Elements of Crimes, art 8*bis*.

Before and after the adoption of the resolution on the crime of aggression at the 2010 Review Conference, the five Permanent States of the UN Security Council and some other States addressed their concerns about the determination of the existence of an act of aggression[259] and about the acts of aggression.[260] The European Parliament also stressed the need to promote the ratification of the Rome Statute as amended and called for the EU to adopt a common position on the crime of aggression.[261] The remarks of the US might indicate its disagreement with the definition of the crime of aggression in general, but does not clearly show its attitude towards the leadership issue. All these statements did not specifically refer to the leadership clause. This observation indicates that States generally agreed on the leadership element compromise for the crime of aggression, although States might also believe that this issue is less attractive and significant from a political consideration.

At the national level, there was no prosecution of crimes against peace or the crime of aggression, except for subsequent trials after World War II. National provisions scarcely refer to a leadership element. A lack of national provisions and prosecution does not discredit the customary status of the crime of aggression in international law. However, this situation indicates divergences between national and international prosecutions of the crime of aggression, and the issue of complementarity may be arising.

The drafting of articles 8*bis* and 25(3*bis*) was a combination of codification and progressive development of customary law.[262] There existed no customary rule on the specific leadership element of the crime of aggression. States neither codify nor depart from a so-called pre-existing rule. They intentionally inserted the 'control or direct' leadership test into the Kampala Amendments. All these discussions show that a consensus on the leadership nature of the crime of aggression was reached before the 2010 Review Conference. But the

---

259 Statement of Koh (n 8); 'Statement by Japan', 'Statement by the United Kingdom', 'Statement by France', 'Statement by China', 'Statement by the Russian Federation', 'Statement by the United States of America', in RC/11, Annexes VII, VIII and IX; 'House of Lords debate on the Kampala Amendments to the ICC Statute' (22 July 2010). For a jurisdiction chart, see 'Report on the facilitation on the activation of the jurisdiction of the International Criminal Court over the crime of aggression', ICC-ASP/16/24 (2017), 23.

260 'Statement by Norway', 'Statement by Cuba', 'Statement by the Islamic Republic of Iran', 'Statement by Israel', 'Statement by the United States of America', in RC/11, Annexes VIII and IX; South Africa, 'Statement of the Republic of South Africa on the occasion of the Workshop on Ratification and Implementation of the Kampala Amendments' (13 April 3013).

261 European Parliament, Resolution on the crime of aggression, 17 July 2014, Resolution 2014/2714.

262 Jia (n 8) 571–72, 581.

'control or direct' leadership element of the crime of aggression, in particular, under article 25(3*bis*) in the Rome Statute, was not a crystallisation of an emerging customary law. The US once posited that article 25(3*bis*), modifying the attributing responsibility for the crime of aggression, could have been inserted into article 5.[263] Were its view adopted, the leadership clause for potential participators of the crime of aggression might be considered as a jurisdictional restriction rather than a substantial material element. Overall, articles 8*bis* and 25(3*bis*) are not law-declaring but norm-making, and they were not declaratory of customary law concerning the 'control or direct' leadership element of the crime of aggression.

5.5 The Leadership Element for the Crime of Aggression: Are Articles 8*bis* and 25(3*bis*) Declaratory of Custom?

States discussed the ICC's jurisdiction over the crime of aggression, its activation, and the opt-in regime in subsequent ASP sessions.[264] They did not aim to re-open the issue on the definition of that crime, including its leadership element. Their attitude reaffirms the finding that a leadership element in general is well accepted for the crime of aggression. This section observes national implementation laws and (potential) development of national practice to show whether the 'control or direct' leadership element of the crime of aggression as provided in articles 8*bis* and 25(3*bis*) is established under customary law now.

Liechtenstein first ratified the Kampala Amendments and the Amendments on the crime of aggression entered into force in 2013. As of 30 January 2021, 41 States have accepted or ratified the aggression Amendments.[265] All these States are also States Parties to the 1998 Rome Statute, despite that States not parties to the Statute can also ratify the Kampala Amendments. Accepting the jurisdiction of the ICC over the crime of aggression by 41 States does not demonstrate a general acceptance of the 'control or direct' leadership test for

---

263 H.H. Koh and T. F. Buchwald, 'The Crime of Aggression: The United States Perspective' (2015) 109 *AJIL* 257, 281.

264 'Position papers submitted by delegations', in ICC-ASP/16/24 (2017), Annex II; 'Statements concerning the adoption of the resolution on activation of the jurisdiction of the Court over the crime of aggression to the Assembly at its 13th plenary meeting, on 14 December 2017', in ICC-ASP/16/20 (2017), Annex VII, 80-90.

265 United Nations Treaty Collection <https://treaties.un.org/pages/ViewDetails.aspx?-src=TREATY&mtdsg_no=XVIII-10-b&chapter=18&clang=_en> accessed 12 March 2021.

the crime of aggression in international criminal law. In addition, two States declared that they will not accept the ICC jurisdiction regarding the crime of aggression. Kenya argued that the definition of the crime of aggression, in particular, the acts of aggression in article 8*bis* paragraph 2, is ambiguous and may be misused. Guatemala addressed that it will not accept the jurisdiction until it completed its internal process of ratification of the Amendments.[266] Thus, their concerns are irrelevant to the leadership element.

Most of the 41 ratifiers of the Kampala Amendments have not criminalised the crime of aggression in their national laws. States Parties to the Amendments are also not obliged to do so, despite that the Rome Statute affirms in its Preamble that for the most serious crimes, including the crime of aggression, 'effective prosecution must be ensured by taking measures at the national level'.[267] Understanding 5 in Annex III to the Resolution on Aggression explicitly acknowledges that 'the amendments shall not be interpreted as creating the right or obligation to exercise domestic jurisdiction with respect to an act of aggression committed by another State'.

In fact, a few States Parties to the Amendments have criminalised the crime of aggression in their national criminal codes before 2010, for instance, Botswana, Croatia, Estonia, Georgia, Germany, Lithuania, Poland and Slovakia.[268] Finland criminalised incitement to war as a treason offence but rejected to criminalise aggression in domestic law because aggression was a matter between States.[269] Before or after ratifying the Amendments, Croatia, Estonia, Slovenia, Georgia and Germany have also revised national provisions on the crime of aggression in their national criminal codes or special laws. Malta introduced the crime

---

[266] 'Declarations of the Government of Kenya' (30 November 2015); 'Declaration of the Government of Republic of Guatemala' (2 February 2018).

[267] 1998 Rome Statute, the Preamble, para 4; Werle and Jessberger (n 7) 29 and fn 163. Cf. 1998 Rome Statute, art 70(4); J.K. Kleffner, 'The Impact of Complementarity on National Implementation of Substantive International Criminal law' (2003) 1 *JICJ* 86. For discussions on the implementation of international core crimes, Werle and Jessberger (n 7) 29 and fn 165; M. Bergsmo *et al* (eds), *Importing Core International Crimes into National Criminal Law* (2nd edn, TOAEP 2010); A. Eser *et al* (eds), *National Prosecution of International Crimes, Vols 1–7* (Ed. Iuscrim 2003–2006).

[268] See National Implementing Legislation Database. Botswana, Penal Code 1964, amended 2005, § 38; Croatia, Criminal Code 1998, art 157; Estonia, Penal Code 2001, § 91; Georgia, Criminal Code 1999, amended 2006, arts 404-405; Germany, Criminal Code 1998, §§ 80, 80a; Lithuania, Criminal Code 2000, art 110; Mongolia, Criminal Code 2002, arts 297-298; Poland, Penal Code 1997, art 117; Slovenia, Criminal Code 2008, amended 2009, art 103; Slovakia, Criminal Code 2005, amended 2009, § 417(1).

[269] Finland, Criminal Code 1889, amended in 1995, chapter 12, § 2; Coracini (n 7) 736 and fn 72.

of aggression into its national penal code.[270] Other States Parties have not decided to align national legislation with the Kampala Amendments' definition.[271] Apart from these States Parties, some other 35 States have criminalised waging aggressive wars or the acts of aggression in their national penal codes.[272] The number of domestic codes containing the crime of aggression, however, is still few. Few national provisions restrict the scope of perpetrators responsible for the crime of aggression.

It seems that the definition of the crime of aggression in the Kampala Amendments does provide an impetus for some States to criminalise acts of aggression at the national and international level. Some national revisions need to be noted. First of all, Estonia revised its Nuremberg model definition of crimes against peace contained in the 2001 Penal Code to be in conformity with the Kampala model in article 8*bis*. The amended article 91 of 2014 Estonian Penal Code provides that participation in the management, execution or preparation of an act of aggression by a person 'controlling or directing

---

270 Croatia, Criminal Code 1998, amended 2011, art 89; Estonia, Penal Code 2001, § 91 (amended in 2014); Slovenia, Criminal Code 2008, art 103 (amended in 2013); Georgia, Criminal Code 1999, arts 404-405 (amended in 2014); Germany, Criminal Code 1998, § 80a (amended in 2016); id, Code of Crimes against International Law 2002, amended 2016, § 13; Malta, Criminal Code 1854, § 82C (2) (amended in 2012).

271 They are Botswana, Lithuania, Mongolia, Poland and Slovakia.

272 Albania, Criminal Code 1995, amended 2013, arts 211-212; Argentina, Criminal Code 1984, amended 2016, art 215; Armenia, Criminal Code 2003, amended 2013, arts 384–385; Azerbaijan, Criminal Code 1999, amended 2020, arts 100-101; Bangladesh, International Crimes (Tribunals) Act 1973, amended 2013, § 3(2)(b); Belarus, Penal Code 1999, amended 2012, art 122; Bosnia and Herzegovina, Criminal Code 2003, amended 2018, art 157; Bulgaria, Criminal Code 1968, amended 2017, arts 407-409; Cabo Verde, Penal Code 2003, art 267(2); Ethiopia, Criminal Code 2005, art 246; Guinea, Criminal Code 1998, art 80; Hungary, Criminal Code 1978, amended 2012, § 153; India, Penal Code 1860, amended 2013, §§ 121-121A, 122; Indonesia, Penal Code 1999, art 111; Kazakhstan, Criminal Code 1997, amended 2014, arts 160-161; Kenya, Criminal Code 1930, amended 2010, § 44; Latvia, Criminal Law 1998, amended 2013, § 72; Malawi, Penal Code 1930, § 40; Macedonia, Criminal Code 1996, amended 2009, art 415; Mauritius, Criminal Code, § 51; Moldova, Criminal Code 2002, amended 2009, art 139; Montenegro, Criminal Code 2003, amended 2012, art 442; Niger, Criminal Code 1961, amended 2003, art 72; Norway, Penal Code 1902, amended 2008, §§ 83-84; Pakistan, Penal Code 1860, amended 2017, §§ 121-121A, 122; Russian Federation, Criminal Code 1996, arts 353-354; Senegal, Criminal Code 1965, amended 2007, art 66; Serbia, Criminal Code 2005, amended 2014, art 386; Switzerland, Criminal Code 1937, amended 2017, art 266(2); Tajikistan, Criminal Code 1998, arts 395-396; Tanzania, Criminal Code 1945, amended 2007, § 43; Turkey, Criminal Code 2016, art 300; Ukraine, Criminal Code 2001, amended 2010, art 437; Uzbekistan, Criminal Code 1994, amended 2012, art 151; Vietnam, Penal Code 1999, art 341. See also Sayapin (n 9) 199, further observing national provisions of non-party States to the Rome Statute.

the activities of the State' or threatening with an act of aggression 'by a representative of the State' is punishable for crimes of aggression.[273] Compared to the 'shape or influence' test in the 2001 Penal Code, the 2014 Penal Code adheres to the 'control or direct' test with regard to the interpretation of the possible perpetrators for participating in an act of aggression.[274]

In addition, article 89 of the 2011 Croatian Criminal Code closely mirrors the definition of the crime of aggression in the Kampala Amendments. Article 89 explicitly repeats the leadership clause and says that for the crime of aggression, 'whoever, being in a position effectively to exercise control over or to direct the political or military action of a State, uses the armed forces of one state' against another state, shall be punished.[275] The drafting group for the new code says that 'this is a novelty' as anyone can commit the crime of aggression under the 1998 Croatian Criminal Code.[276] However, article 89 of the 2011 Croatian Criminal Code further provides that 'whoever takes part in the operations of the armed forces' and 'whoever directly and publicly incites to the crime of aggression' shall be punished.[277] Similarly, a note in article 404 of the 2014 Criminal Code of Georgia indicates that 'a person who, due to his/her position, is able to exercise efficient control or management over the state political or military actions, shall incur criminal liability' for planning, preparation, commencement or execution of an act of aggression.[278] Again, with regard to 'calling for planning, preparation, commencement or execution of an act of aggression', no limitation exists for the scope of persons prosecuted in Georgia.[279] Thus, private individuals and ordinary soldiers may also be prosecuted as participators of the crime of aggression.

In 2016, the German Code of Crimes against International Law implements the crime of aggression in international law and its section 13 provides that 'only persons in a position effectively to exercise control over or to direct the political or military action of a State' may be punished for planning, preparing, imitating or waging aggressive wars or any other act of aggression.[280]

---

273   Estonia, Penal Code 2001, § 91 (amended in 2014). On section 91 in the 2001 and 2014 Criminal Codes, see Parmas (n 244) 895–922.
274   Parmas (n 244) 900–02.
275   Croatia, Criminal Code 1998, amended 2011, art 89(1). For comments on Croatian Criminal Codes, see Turković and Vajda (n 245) 863–67.
276   Report of the expert group, cited from Turković and Vajda (n 245) 866.
277   Croatia, Criminal Code 1998, amended 2011, arts 89(2)-(3). See also Croatia, Criminal Code 1998, art 157(3).
278   Georgia, Criminal Code 1999, amended 2016, art 404.
279   ibid art 405.
280   Germany, Code of Crimes against International Law 2002, amended 2016, § 13(4).

Considering its customary approach in drafting the final definition of the crime of aggression in the Kampala Amendments, the repeal of a controversial provision for the crime of aggression under section 80 of the German Criminal Code indicates that German legislators believed that section 13 restates the 'control or direct' leadership element in customary law. Nevertheless, the German Criminal Code also reserves a provision that 'whoever, within the territorial scope of this statue' may be punished in Germany for incitement to crime of aggression.[281] Potential participants responsible for the crime of aggression, therefore, are also not limited to persons who control or direct the action of a State.

Apart from these national revisions, the Protocol on Amendments to the Protocol on the Statute of the African Court of Justice and Human Rights also includes the crime of aggression. Article 28M of the African Union Protocol repeated the Kampala Amendments on the definition of the crime of aggression under article 8*bis*.[282] However, the African Union Protocol does not insert an identical leadership clause like that in article 25(3*bis*), thus, leaving the scope of potential participators of the crime of aggression to include any persons beyond leaders.[283] These provisions observed show that the 'control or direct' leadership clause is accepting as a legal threshold for prosecuting principal perpetrators of the crime of aggression. With respect to the participators for the crime of aggression, the scope of potential persons to be prosecuted by these national courts or by the African Court of Justice will be much broader than that at the ICC.

Except for statutory legislation, customary law forms part of some States' domestic law, for instance, the UK and Canada.[284] However, the House of Lords in the *R v Jones et al* case held that the crime of aggression established in customary law was not a crime in the UK domestic law. In the *R v Jones et al* criminal case, the defendants were charged for their acts of unauthorised entry on military land and disruption of activities in the preparation of the invasion of Iraq in 2003. They argued that their acts were justified because they had been acting to prevent the commission of the crime of aggression by the UK

---

281 Germany, Criminal Code 1998, amended 2016, § 80a. On the repealed section 80 of 1998 Criminal Code, see E. Hoven, 'Germany' in Barriga and Kreß (eds) (n 12) 880–94.
282 Protocol on Amendments to the Protocol on the Statute of the African Court of Justice and Human Rights, arts 28M.
283 ibid, arts 28N.
284 *R v Jones et al* (n 7); Lord Goldsmith (n 7), para 34; R. O'Keefe, 'United Kingdom' in Barriga and Kreß (eds) (n 12) 940–41; T. Gut and M. Wolpert, 'Canada' in Eser *et al* (eds) (n 267), Vol 5 (Ed. Iuscrim 2005) 33.

and/or the US against Iraq. Two issues appealed to the House of Lords by the defendants were whether the crime of aggression, if established in customary law, formed part of English criminal law and whether the crime of aggression is justiciable in a criminal case.[285]

The House of Lords dismissed the appeals. Lord Bingham firstly concluded that the crime of aggression is established in customary law, which is one of sources of the English law.[286] However, customary law is applicable in the English courts only if the crime of aggression had 'been assimilated into the domestic criminal law'.[287] Customary law without statutory incorporation or judicial decision has not become a domestic crime and is not automatically applicable in the English courts.[288] With respect to the crime of aggression, since the courts have surrendered the power to create crimes, the sole source in the UK is statutory legislation. The democratic principle is very important in the UK. There is no very compelling reason for the courts to depart from that principle to create a crime.[289] Because, '[i]n the present context', the adjudication on the responsibility of a leader for the crime of aggression would involve a determination of whether (foreign) States have acted unlawfully, which is an area the courts are reluctant to inquire.[290] In conclusion, the crime of aggression is neither a statutory crime nor common law crime in domestic law and the power to make war is non-justiciable in the English courts.[291] The judgments suggest that, were the crime of aggression a statutory crime, the English courts are unlikely to determine the crime of aggression for the non-justiciability of the power to make war.[292] However, as Roger O'Keefe argued, should the UK legislature enact the crime of aggression, there would be no inherent legal barriers for its prosecution.[293] At present, the UK neither sent a message to ratify the Kampala Amendments on aggression nor intended to legislate that crime in its International Criminal Court Act.[294]

---

285   *R v Jones et al* (n 7) [2, 4, 10] (Lord Bingham). On this decision and the decision at the British Court of Appeal, see C. Villarino Villa, 'The Crime of Aggression before the House of Lords: Chronicle of a Death Foretold' (2006) 4 *JICJ* 866; R. Cryer, 'Aggression at the Court of Appeal' (2005) 10 *Journal of Conflict & Security Law* 209; O'Keefe, ibid.
286   *R v Jones et al* (n 7) [13–19] (Lord Bingham), [59] (Lord Hoffmann), [99] (Lord Mance).
287   ibid, [23, 30] (Lord Bingham).
288   ibid, [23] (Lord Bingham), [59–64] (Lord Hoffmann).
289   ibid, [28–30] (Lord Bingham), [67] (Lord Hoffmann), [101–03] (Lord Mance).
290   ibid, [30] (Lord Bingham), [65] (Lord Hoffmann).
291   ibid, [29] (Lord Bingham), [60–67] (Lord Hoffmann).
292   C.f. O'Keefe (n 284) 945–54, for critics of Lord Hoffmann's and Lord Bingham's views on the non-justiciability.
293   O'Keefe (n 284) 957.
294   *R v Jones et al* (n 7); O'Keefe (n 284) 939–40.

In South Africa, the crime of aggression was referred to in the Preamble of its 2002 ICC Act as a crime 'in terms of international law' but was not a crime in domestic law.[295] Since Section 2 of the ICC Act provides that any competent court 'must also consider and where, appropriate, may apply' customary law, the crime of aggression under customary law might be regarded as a crime under domestic law.[296] As Gerhard Kemp observed, a provision of the South African Constitution suggests that customary law crime of aggressive wars is directly applicable. However, it is unlikely that individuals would be prosecuted relying on the Constitution for practical and criminal justice obstacles.[297] The 2005 Iraqi High Criminal Court Law also makes trials against individuals for the invasion of Kuwait possible.[298] It is unclear to what extent the Kampala leadership clauses will be adopted by the UK, South Africa and other States.

The immunities in customary law continue to constitute procedural barriers to prosecution crimes under international law, including the crime of aggression, thus, former or sitting high-rank governmental leaders who may invoke the immunities for prosecuting the crime of aggression before foreign national courts.[299] In addition to this, considering the difficulties in obtaining evidence or getting hold of former or sitting senior leaders of a foreign State, the prosecution of the crime of aggression over governmental leaders who are 'in a position effectively to exercise control over or to direct' State acts will consequently rather exceptional at the national level.[300] As a result, the most frequently prosecuted persons at national courts might be non-governmental leaders or private individuals. Given the immunities and other potential legal or political

---

295 South Africa, Implementation Act 2002, the Preamble, para 1.
296 ibid, § 2.
297 G. Kemp, 'Implementing at national level the amendments to the Rome Statute of the International Criminal Court with respect to the crime of aggression: A South African perspective' in K. Ambos and O.A. Maunganidze (eds), *Power and Prosecution – Challenges and Opportunities for International Criminal Justice in Sub-Saharan Africa* (Göttingen University 2012) 47–49, 55.
298 Iraq, Iraqi High Criminal Court Law 2005, art 14(3); Kreß (n 238) 348.
299 Coracini (n 7) 727–31, 734; Coracini (n 88) 547–49; P. Wrange, 'The Crime of Aggression and Complementarity' in Bellelli (ed) (n 88) 593–95, 598; Dinstein (n 12) 156–62; P. Wrange, 'The Crime of Aggression, Domestic Prosecutions and Complementarity' in Barriga and Kreß (eds) (n 12) 721–24. For discussions on the jurisdiction of national courts, see Report of the International Law Commission, UN Doc A/50/10 (1995), para 70; 1996 Draft Code of Crimes, para 50, art 8 and its commentary (13), reserving the exception of the national jurisdiction of 'the State which has committed aggression'; B. Van Schaack, '*Par in Parem Imperium Non Habet* – Complementarity and the Crime of Aggression' (2012) 10 *JICJ* 133; Scharf (n 64); Werle and Jessberger (n 7) 545; Koh and Buchwald (n 263) 273–77.
300 Wrange (2017) ibid, 724–30; Coracini (n 88) 547–48.

obstacles to the prosecution of senior officials, it seems that national prosecution of the crime of aggression is extremely unlikely in the foreseeable future.

It seems that the more practice of national prosecution of the crime of aggression, the less support for a restricted scope of potential persons responsible for that crime in domestic law, which may affect the leadership nature of the crime of aggression in international law. At present, little evidence of national legislation and practice demonstrates that the 'control of direct' leadership test is well established under customary law. In sum, articles 8*bis* and 25 (3*bis*) are not declaratory of customary law concerning the 'control or direct' leadership element for the crime of aggression.

5.6   Concluding Remarks

It is accepted that the crime of aggression as an international crime is part of customary law. With regard to the leadership element, the Nuremberg and Tokyo trials did not establish a leadership standard for crimes against peace. The prosecution of crimes against peace by the IMT and the IMTFE may not be valuable 'precedents' for future trials of 'leaders' for the crime of aggression. The Tribunals established pursuant to the Control Council Law No. 10 also did not adopt the 'shape or influence' test in a consistent way in prosecuting crimes against peace. However, these trials indicate that not everyone could be convicted of crimes against peace. In the ILC, the Draft Code of Crimes did not restrict the scope of potential persons responsible for the crime of aggression in its definition until 1991. The 1991 and 1996 versions of the Draft Code of Crimes identify the 'leaders or organisers' as potential perpetrators and participators of the crime of aggression. It appears that a specific leadership condition for the crime of aggression was not generally recognised in custom.

Departing from the 'leaders or organisers' clause, the 2010 Kampala Amendments adopted a 'control or direct' leadership clause. The preparatory works of the 1998 Rome Statute and the negotiating and drafting history of the Kampala Amendments on the crime of aggression show that States generally agreed that the crime of aggression requires a leadership condition. However, no sufficient evidence suggests that the 'control or direct' leadership clause for the crime of aggression have crystallised an emerging customary rule in the drafting and negotiating process. It was less agreed that an identical leadership element applies to participators of the crime of aggression. Further evidence does not show that the 'control or direct' leadership element for the perpetrators or participators of the crime of aggression has been established under customary law. It is submitted that articles 8*bis* and 25(3*bis*) were and are not declaratory of customary rule on the 'control or direct' leadership threshold for the crime of aggression.

CHAPTER 6

Indirect Co-perpetration
Article 25(3)(a) of the Rome Statute and Custom

6.1   Introductory Remarks

This chapter focuses on article 25(3)(a) of the Rome Statute concerning a mode of liability for individuals at the leadership level. Judge Van den Wyngaert questioned whether the ICC could draw on custom for modes of liability.[1] Larissa van den Herik also claims that the role of customary law as a ground for rules on modes of liability is limited because the domestic origins of these rules.[2] In her view, there are blocks to the formation of customary law for these rules. Theories of modes of liability in civil and common law traditions are coexistent, and domestic courts usually attach domestic modes of liability in prosecuting international crimes. It will be difficult to establish the shared practice of States and it seems impossible to 'make either theory part of customary law', as Judge Shahabuddeen of the ICTY noted.[3] Thus, general principles of law might be the source of law for modes of liability universally recognised by all jurisdictions.[4] However, the fragmentation of national legal systems, as well as different theories and standards among international tribunals, is also not incompatible with the formation of custom, in particular, in light of custom's continued importance in domestic and international courts.[5] It remains also controversial whether indirect co-perpetration liability is considered a form

---

1   *The Prosecutor v Ngudjolo* (Judgment pursuant to Article 74 of the Statute–Concurring Opinion of Judge Christine Van den Wyngaert) ICC-01/04-02/12-4 (18 December 2012), para 17.
2   L.J. van den Herik, 'The Decline of Customary International Law as a Source of International Criminal Law' in C.A. Bradley (ed), *Custom's Future: International Law in a Changing World* (CUP 2016) 248–49. See also C. Steer, *Translating Guilt: Identifying Leadership Liability for Mass Atrocity Crimes* (TMC Asser Press 2017) 3–4, 345–49.
3   ibid; *Gacumbitsi v The Prosecutor* (Judgement) ICTR-01-64-A (7 July 2006) (Separate opinion of Judge Shahabuddeen), para 51.
4   Van den Herik (n 2); K. Amobs, *Treatise on International Criminal Law, Vol I: Foundations and General Part* (OUP 2013) 123 (concerning co-perpetration).
5   A. Bufalini, 'The Principle of Legality and the Role of Customary International Law in the Interpretation of the ICC Statute' (2015) 14 *LPICL* 233, 247–52; O.A. Hathaway *et al*, 'Aiding and Abetting in International Criminal Law' (2019) 104 *Cornell L Rev* 1593, 1627–30. Text to synthesis in chapter 8.

of co-perpetration or an independent (*sui generis*) mode of liability.[6] Article 25(3)(a) still has evidential value of a customary rule.

The attribution of liability to high-level leaders is complicated in international criminal law. Different approaches are developed to hold the accused of non-physical perpetrators at the leadership level accountable for the crimes committed by others (direct perpetrators/executors). This chapter explores the relationship between article 25(3)(a) of the Rome Statute and custom concerning the liability of indirect co-perpetration. The ICC has interpreted that indirect co-perpetration (jointly with another through another person) liability is subsumed in article 25(3)(a).[7] Some commentators claimed that indirect co-perpetration 'may well have support in customary international law'.[8] The *Stakić* Appeals Chamber of the ICTY, however, held that this liability lacked support under customary law.[9] The central issue here is whether article 25(3)(a) of the Rome Statute was and is declaratory of customary law about indirect co-perpetration.

For this purpose, section 6.2 briefly discusses the necessity and different approaches to attribute liability to leaders. Section 6.3 analyses the text of article 25(3)(a) and the *Katanga & Ngudjolo* case to see whether the controversial indirect co-perpetration is encompassed in article 25(3)(a) of the Statute. Section 6.4 covers the practice of post-World War II tribunals and the drafting history of article 25(3)(a) to examine whether this mode of liability was deemed a way to attribute liability. Conspiracy liability and commission through association are briefly commented on in this section. Section 6.5 examines practice after the adoption of the Rome Statute to show whether indirect co-perpetration has generally been accepted at the present time. The jurisprudence of the UN *ad hoc* tribunals concerning the notion of *Tadić* joint criminal enterprise (JCE), indirect co-perpetration, and the JCE as established in *Brđanin* are covered. Other instruments for international crimes, national cases and implementation laws are also examined. It seems that rare evidence shows acceptance of indirect co-perpetration liability. This unique mode of

---

6 Steer (n 2) 353–55; Amobs (n 4) 124 and fn 140.
7 *The Prosecutor v Katanga & Ngudjolo* (Decision on the confirmation of charges, PTC I) ICC-01/04-01/07-717 (30 September 2008), paras 506-08; *The Prosecutor v Ruto et al* (Decision on the Confirmation of Charges Pursuant to Article 61(7)(a) and (b) of the Rome Statute, PTC II) ICC-01/09-01/11-373 (23 January 2012), para 290.
8 G. Boas *et al, International Criminal Law Practitioner Library: Vol 1, Forms of Responsibility in International Criminal Law* (CUP 2007) 121.
9 *Prosecutor v Milutinović et al* (Decision on Dragoljub Ojdanić's Motion Challenging Jurisdiction: Indirect Co-perpetration) ICTY-05-87-PT (22 March 2006), para 40; *Prosecutor v Stakić* (Judgement) ICTY-97-24-A (22 March 2006), para 62.

liability has not been generally recognised as a customary rule. Chapter 6 concludes that article 25(3)(a) is not declaratory of a customary rule with regard to indirect co-perpetration.

6.2   The Attribution of Liability to Individuals at the Leadership Level

This section first analyses the basis of attributing a crime to an accused at the leadership level and then discusses approaches to attribute liabilities to high-level leaders.

6.2.1   *The Rationale to Attribute Liability to High-Level Leaders*
The notion of modes of liability assists in establishing a link between the crime committed and the accused.[10] An individual is held liable for his/her physical acts or omissions if all elements of that crime have been satisfied. This is the basic mode of liability.[11] In practice, if a plurality of individuals is involved in multiple acts of an offence, this leads to the 'systematic criminality' nature of international crimes.[12] Apart from the physical acts or omissions, each person may contribute to a crime through different forms of perpetration and participation. International criminal tribunals and authorities have adopted different approaches to attribute liability to an accused (a non-physical perpetrator) for the crime where others (direct perpetrators/executors) performed the physical acts.[13] Several modes of liability exist in international criminal law, such as command responsibility, aiding and abetting, planning, ordering, instigation and incitement.

Ringleaders, 'masterminds' or intellectual culprits, as non-physical perpetrators are usually physically distant from the execution of the crime. Post-World War II trials revealed that leaders were held responsible for the crimes executed by others.[14] Different grounds support prosecution of these non-physical

---

10   JM. Henckaerts and L. Doswald-beck (eds), *Customary International Humanitarian Law*, Vols I and II (CUP 2005), Rules 102 and 151 and accompanying commentary.

11   1998 Rome Statute, art 7(2). *Prosecutor v Tadić* (Opinion and Judgement) ICTY-94-1-T (7 May 1997), paras 663-69.

12   *Prosecutor v Tadić* (Judgement) ICTY-94-1-A (15 July 1999), paras 191-92; J. Kleffner, 'The Collective Accountability of Organised Armed Groups for System Crimes' in A. Nollkaemper and H. Van der Wilt (eds), *System Criminality in International Law* (CUP 2009) 238–69.

13   For a detailed analysis of leadership liability in international criminal tribunals, see Steer (n 2) 249–324.

14   M.C. Bassiouni, *Introduction to International Criminal Law: 2nd Revised Edition* (Brill | Nijhoff 2013) 263.

perpetrators at the political or military leadership level. One viewpoint is that they are criminalised because of their contribution to the crimes committed. These intellectual leaders designed a common criminal plan, which was later performed through physical executors' acts.[15] A Report of the UN Secretary-General stated that 'all persons who participate in the planning, preparation or execution of serious violations of international humanitarian law in the former Yugoslavia contribute to the commission of the violation and are, therefore, individually responsible'.[16]

Another view claims that these masterminds are punishable for the moral gravity of their participation in systemic international crimes.[17] 'The moral gravity of such participation in a JCE [joint criminal enterprise] is often no [...] different from that of those actually carrying out the acts in question.'[18] These leaders are deemed the 'most responsible' one, specifically for the crime of aggression.[19] In its commentary to the 1996 Draft Code of Crimes against the Peace and Security of Mankind (Draft Code of Crimes), the International Law Commission (ILC) stated that: '[a] government official may [...] be considered to be even more culpable than the subordinate who actually commits the criminal act'.[20] In contrast to the first legal ground, the second ground is of a moral and supplementary basis. For example, the US representative at the London Conference, Robert Jackson, once stated:

> We are prepared to show that as against the top men, not merely against the little soldiers who were out in the field and did these things, but against the top Nazis who ordered them. [...] [T]hey [the top Nazis] were guilty [...] because they personally knew and directed and planned these violations as their deliberate method of conducting war.[21]

---

15 *Tadić* Appeals Chamber Judgment (n 12), para 191; *Attorney General v Eichmann* (Judgment, District Court of Jerusalem, Israel) (11 November 1961) (1968) 36 ILR 5, para 194; S. Manacorda and C. Meloni, 'Indirect Perpetration versus Joint Criminal Enterprise Concurring Approaches in the Practice of International Criminal Law?' (2011) 9 *JICJ* 159.

16 UN Doc S/25704 (1993), para 54.

17 *Tadić* Appeals Chamber Judgment (n 12), para 191; *Prosecutor v Kvočka et al* (Judgement) ICTY-98-30/1-A (28 February 2005), para 80; *Prosecutor v Blagojević & Jokić* (Judgement) ICTY-02-60-T (17 January 2005), para 695. See also Steer (n 2) 9–19.

18 *Tadić* Appeals Chamber Judgment (n 12); *Kvočka et al* Appeals Chamber Judgment, ibid; N. Piacente, 'Importance of the Joint Criminal Enterprise Doctrine for the ICTY Prosecutorial Policy' (2004) 2 *JICJ* 446, 446–54.

19 1998 Rome Statute, arts 8*bis*(1) and 25 (3)*bis*; Steer (n 2) 18–19. Chapter 5 of the present book.

20 UN Doc A/51/10 (1996), 26.

21 'Minutes of Conference Session of July 23, 1945' in *Report of Robert H. Jackson, United States Representative to the International Conference on Military Trials* (USGPO 1949) 332.

The practice of international tribunals has also developed prosecution of leaders mainly based on the first ground. This gives rise to the question of how to attribute liability to high-level leaders who are far from the crimes committed by executors.[22]

6.2.2 Approaches to Attribute Liability to High-Level Leaders

National criminal law might enlighten the establishment of a link between the crimes and a leader, such as co-perpetration, aiding and abetting liability.[23] With regard to the detailed approaches to attribute liability to the accused for crimes physically executed by others, more differences than similarities exist in various national criminal legal systems for various national legislative considerations and policies.[24] Recent Statutes and jurisprudence of international criminal tribunals also progressively develop unique modes of liability in international criminal law.[25] For instance, article 25(3)(b) of the Rome Statute stipulates the liability for ordering the commission of crimes. Article 28 clearly provides 'responsibility of commanders and other superiors', which has been developed since the IMT and its subsequent trials. Another way to attribute liability is the idea of JCE established by the ICTY jurisprudence.[26]

This chapter focuses on indirect co-perpetration as defined by the ICC. In contrast to other provisions or drafts of individual liability for international crimes,[27] article 25 of the Rome Statute provides many explicit rules of

---

22 Manacorda and Meloni (n 15).
23 E. van Sliedregt, *Individual Criminal Responsibility in International Law* (OUP 2012) 65.
24 ibid; Steer (n 2) 238–43; M.C. Bassiouni, *Crimes Against Humanity: Historical Evolution and Contemporary Application* (CUP 2011) 472.
25 1993 ICTY Statute, art 7(1); 1994 ICTR Statute, art 6(1); Statute of the SCSL, art 6(1); Law on the Establishment of the ECCC, art 29(1); Protocol on Amendments to the Protocol on the Statute of the African Court of Justice and Human Rights, art 28N; as well as 1998 Rome Statute, arts 25 and 28; *Tadić* Appeals Chamber Judgment (n 12), para 192; *Blagojević & Jokić* Trial Chamber Judgment (n 17), para 695. E. van Sliedregt, 'Joint Criminal Enterprise as a Pathway to Convicting Individuals for Genocide' (2006) 5 *JICJ* 184, 199; Steer (n 2) 249–324.
26 *Tadić* Appeals Chamber Judgment (n 12), para 192; 1993 ICTY Statute, art 7(1).
27 Nuremberg Charter, art 6(2); Control Council Law No. 10, art 2(2); 1950 ILC Nuremberg Principles, Principles I, VI (a)(ii), and VII; 1948 Genocide Convention, art III; 1949 Geneva Conventions (GC: art 49 of GC I; art 50 of GC II; art 129 of GC III; and art 146 of GC IV); the 1977 Additional Protocol I, art 86; 1991 Draft Code of Crimes, arts 3(1)-(2); 1996 Draft Code of Crimes, art 2(3); 1993 ICTY Statute, art 7(1); 1994 ICTR Statute, art 6(1); Statute of the SCSL, art 6(1); Law on the Establishment of the ECCC, art 29(1); and Protocol on Amendments to the Protocol on the Statute of the African Court of Justice and Human Rights, art 28N.

individual criminal responsibility.[28] Article 25(3)(a) provides the ways of committing a crime: 'commits such a crime, whether as an individual, jointly with another or through another person, regardless of whether that other person is criminally responsible'. Based on the phrases 'jointly with another person' and 'through another person', Chambers of the ICC interpreted that article 25(3)(a) covers a way of commission 'jointly with another through another person', or indirect co-perpetration, or joint indirect perpetration.[29] The concept of indirect co-perpetration allows the ICC to attach liability to the accused at the leadership level for crimes committed by the physical perpetrators, who were used by these accused's co-perpetrators.[30]

The ICC's chambers in their recent decisions frequently employed indirect co-perpetration to attribute liability to the accused.[31] Prosecutions and the ICTY's Trial Chamber in *Stakić* have also relied on indirect co-perpetration to attach liability to defendants.[32] Some commentators even contended that indirect co-perpetration 'may well have support in customary international law'.[33] The *Stakić* Appeals Chamber, however, rejected this liability for its lack of basis in customary international law.[34] This chapter explores the relationship between article 25(3)(a) of the Rome Statute and the (possible)

---

28   1998 Rome Statute, arts 25, 25(3)(e) and 25(3) *bis*. See A. Eser, 'Individual Criminal Responsibility' in A. Cassese *et al* (eds), *The Rome Statute of the International Criminal Court: A Commentary*, Vol I (OUP 2002) 767; Ambos (n 4) 144–76; id, 'Article 25' in O. Triffterer and K. Ambos (eds), *Commentary on the Rome Statute of the International Criminal Court: Observers' Notes, Article by Article* (3rd edn, Hart/Beck 2016) 983–85; W.A. Schabas, *The International Criminal Court: A Commentary on the Rome Statute* (2nd edn, OUP 2016) 562; Van Sliedregt (n 23) 61–65.

29   *Katanga & Ngudjolo* Decision on the Confirmation of Charges (n 7), paras 491-92; *The Prosecutor v Lubanga* (Judgment on the Appeal of Thomas Lubanga Dyilo against his Conviction, A Ch) ICC-01/04-01/06-3121-Red (1 December 2014), paras 458, 460.

30   *Katanga & Ngudjolo* Decision on the Confirmation of Charges (n 7), para 492.

31   ibid, paras 491-92; *The Prosecutor v Katanga* (Judgment pursuant to Article 74 of the Statute, TC II) ICC-01/04-01/07-3436-tENG (27 March 2014), para 1416; *The Prosecutor v Ntaganda* (Decision Pursuant to Article 61(7)(a) and (b) of the Rome Statute on the Charges of the Prosecutor against Bosco Ntaganda, PTC II) ICC-01/04-02/06-309 (9 June 2014), paras 104, 121; *The Prosecutor v Gbagbo* (Decision on the Confirmation of Charges against Laurent Gbagbo, PTC I) ICC-02/11-01/11-656-Red (12 June 2014), para 241; *Lubanga* Conviction Appeals Chamber Judgment (n 29), paras 458, 460; *The Prosecutor v Blé Goudé* (Decision on the Confirmation of Charges against Charles Blé Goudé, PTC I) ICC-02/11-02/11-186 (11 December 2014), paras 136-37; *The Prosecutor v Ongwen* (Decision on the confirmation of charges, PTC II) ICC-02/04-01/15-422-Red (23 March 2016), para 41.

32   *Prosecutor v Stakić* (Judgement) ICTY-97-24-T (31 July 2003), paras 438-42.

33   Boas *et al* (n 8) 121.

34   *Milutinović et al* Trial Chamber Decision on Indirect Co-perpetration 2006 (n 9), para 40; *Stakić* Appeals Chamber Judgment (n 9), para 62.

customary law concerning indirect co-perpetration. The first step is to clarify whether indirect co-perpetration is embedded in article 25(3)(a) as a way of perpetration.

6.3 Is Indirect Co-perpetration Encompassed in Article 25(3)(a) of the Rome Statute?

This section first analyses article 25(3)(a) and then jurisprudence of the ICC to seek whether article 25(3)(a) contains indirect co-perpetration as a way of perpetration.

6.3.1 *The Text of Article 25(3)(a): Three Forms of Perpetration*

Article 25(3)(a) stipulates that an individual will be responsible if s/he commits a crime, whether 'jointly with another or through another person, regardless of whether that other person is criminally responsible'. It is generally commented that article 25(3)(a) depicts three alternatives of committing a crime: direct perpetration, co-perpetration and indirect perpetration.[35]

6.3.1.1 Direct Perpetration and Co-perpetration

Direct perpetration (commission as an individual) means that the accused physically executed all acts of the crime. If the individual fulfilled all material and mental elements of the crime, s/he is held liable as a direct perpetrator. Co-perpetration (commission jointly with another) means that individuals jointly committed a crime, in which all offenders exercise control over their own offences. Co-perpetration requires that all offenders acted together in a common plan and their essential functional divisions in the accomplishment of that crime.[36] Co-perpetrators, those individuals who did not carry out all material elements of the crime, can be held liable as principals for that crime, due to the mutual attribution between them.[37] The co-perpetrators can only realise their plan insofar as they act together, but each can ruin the whole plan

---

35   D. Robinson, 'Crimes Against Humanity' in R. Cryer *et al* (eds), *An Introduction to International Criminal Law and Procedure* (3rd edn, CUP 2014) 302; Schabas (n 28) 568-69; *Katanga & Ngudjolo* Decision on the Confirmation of Charges (n 7), para 488; *Katanga* Trial Chamber Judgment (n 31), para 1396.

36   Schabas (n 28) 568–69.

37   A. Eser, 'Individual Criminal Responsibility' in A. Cassese *et al* (eds), *The Rome Statute of the International Criminal Court: A Commentary* (OUP 2002) 789–95; *Katanga & Ngudjolo* Decision on the Confirmation of Charges (n 7), para 492.

if s/he does not carry out her/his part. To this extent, the individual is in control of the act.[38]

6.3.1.2 Indirect Perpetration

Article 25(3)(a) also contains the liability of indirect perpetration (commission through another person, regardless of whether that other person is criminally responsible), which is the result of a struggled compromise of common law and civil law at the Rome Conference.[39] Indirect perpetration had not been considered as a mode of liability in previous international instruments until the Rome Statute. Indirect perpetration, in its classic form, means that the accused (indirect perpetrators) as masterminds or men in the background committed a crime through another by exerting their will over that person to complete the crime, in which that person is considered as the accused' instrument or tool.[40]

One issue arises how to understand the phrase 'regardless of whether that other person is criminally responsible' in article 25(3)(a). It is first generally agreed that this phrase is irrelevant to co-perpetration but was inserted to restrict the wording 'commission through another person'. The drafting history of this provision confirms this view.[41] A plain reading of this phrase indicates that the liability of indirect perpetrators does not depend on the responsibility of the physical perpetrators for the criminal act. The persons used are not limited to innocent agents but include responsible persons. However, it is unclear to what extent the person is 'responsible'. Can that person be fully

---

38   *Stakić* Trial Chamber Judgment (n 32), paras 440-41. For comments on the joint control approach to interpreting co-perpetration, see L.D. Yanev and T. Kooijmans, 'Divided Minds in the Lubanga Trial Judgment: A Case Against the Joint Control Theory' (2013) 13 ICLR 789.

39   Bassiouni (n 14) 286.

40   *The Prosecutor v Lubanga* (Decision on the Confirmation of Charges, PTC I) ICC-01/04-01/06-803-tEN (29 January 2007), para 332; *Katanga & Ngudjolo* Decision on the Confirmation of Charges (n 7), paras 495, 499 and fn 660; Ambos (n 4) 154.

41   'Informal Group on General Principles of Criminal Law, Proposed new Part [III *bis*] for the Statute of an International Criminal Court General principles of Criminal Law' (26 August 1996), UN Doc A/AC.249/CRP.13, 4-8; 'Report of the Preparatory Committee on the Establishment of an International Criminal Court', UN Doc A/51/22 (1996), Vol II, 80–85; 'Working paper submitted by Canada, Germany, the Netherlands and the United Kingdom' (14 February 1997), UN Doc A/AC.249/1997/WG.2/DP.1; 'Chairman's Text, Article B b., c. and d.1, Individual criminal responsibility' (19 February 1997), UN Doc A/AC.249/1997/WG.2/CRP.2/Add.2; 'Report of the Preparatory Committee on the Establishment of an International Criminal Court' (14 April 1998), UN Doc A/CONF.183/2, 30–31, art 23(7)(a).

responsible and culpable for the crimes committed? The text of the Rome Statute and the drafting history of article 25(3)(a) were silent on this issue. ICTY Judge Schomburg, who advocates indirect perpetration, held that the direct perpetrator was used as a mere 'instrument'. He added that 'a particular "defect" on the part of the direct perpetrator' is required because the will or the act is controlled, although the phrase 'perpetrators behind perpetrators' seems to include an entirely responsible perpetrator.[42] The accused are considered as indirect perpetrators, if they used the physical executors, for example, children and persons acting under duress who are innocent or held partly responsible for any deficiency, to perform criminal acts. The jurisprudence of the ICC, relying on the term '(indirect) perpetrators behind (direct) perpetrators', recognised that the persons used cover both innocent agents and full responsible executors.[43]

The doctrine of 'control over an organisation', proposed by German jurist Claus Roxin, was employed to construct the indirect perpetration alternative in article 25(3)(a).[44] The idea of perpetration by means through 'control over an organisation' is that the accused in a leading position in an organised structure of power used the organisation as an instrument to commit the crime indirectly, and the accused is liable for all crimes committed by members of the organisation. Kai Ambos observed that the doctrine of control over an organisation has received widespread support in national jurisdictions.[45] Judge Schomburg also noted that there is a new trend of punishing organised crimes through the term 'indirect perpetration'.[46] Relying on the doctrine of 'control over an organisation', the ICC held that indirect perpetration contains 'commission through another person by means of control over the organisation'.[47]

---

42   *Gacumbitsi* Appeals Chamber Judgment (n 3) (Separate Opinion of Judge Schomburg), para 20 and fn 36; *Prosecutor v Simić et al* (Judgement) ICTY-95-9-A (28 November 2006) (Dissenting Opinion of Judge Schomburg), para 19. See also *The Prosecutor v Seromba* (Judgement) ICTR-01-66-A (12 March 2008) (Dissenting Opinion of Judge Liu), para 8 and fn 17.

43   *Katanga & Ngudjolo* Decision on Confirmation of Charges (n 7), paras 495-99; Ambos (n 4) 155–56.

44   ibid, para 498 and fn 659. For an explanation on this theory, see G. Werle and B. Burghardt, 'Claus Roxin on Crimes as Part of Organized Power Structures' (2011) 9 *JICJ* 191, 198–99.

45   Ambos (n 4) 117–18, 156 and fn 456. Cf. China, Criminal Law of the People's Republic of China 1997, amended 2020, art 26(3).

46   *Simić et al* Appeals Chamber Judgement (n 42) (Dissenting Opinion of Judge Schomburg), fn 32.

47   *The Prosecutor v Al Bashir* (Public Redacted Version of the Prosecution's Application under Article 58, OTP) ICC-02/05-157-AnxA (12 September 2008), para 248; *Katanga & Ngudjolo* Decision on Confirmation of Charges (n 7), para 525; *First Warrant of Arrest Decision for Al Bashir*, para 223; *The Prosecutor v Bemba* (Decision Pursuant to Article

The ICC's formulation of indirect perpetration 'by means of control over an organisation' is reminiscent of leaders' liability for their formulation of the common plan and the criminal organisation issues embedded in the Nuremberg Charter.[48] The ICC's construction of indirect perpetration by 'control over an organisation' appears to disregard the fact that the Rome Statute bears no provision similar to that in the Nuremberg Charter to impose liability on organisations' leaders.[49] As Judge Van den Wyngaert pointed out:

> Article 25(3)(a) only speaks of commission 'through another person'. It is hard to see how this could be read to mean that this form of criminal responsibility also attaches when an accused commits crimes through an organisation. [...] In this instance, there is no indication that the States Parties meant the word 'person' to mean 'organisation'. [...] [T]he type of control over an organisation that is envisaged by the Pre-Trial Chamber could be an important evidentiary factor to demonstrate that an accused did in fact dominate the will of certain individuals who were part of this organisation. However, in such cases, the level of discipline within an organisation and the accused's role in maintaining it are elements of proof and not legal criteria. [...] The words 'commission through another person' in Article 25(3)(a) [...] should be given their ordinary meaning.[50]

6.3.2   *Indirect Co-perpetration at the ICC*

Apart from the three alternatives, the ICC interprets that indirect co-perpetration is also subsumed in article 25(3)(a). At the ICC, the concept of indirect co-perpetration was introduced through an expansive interpretation to deal with the liability of the accused at the leadership level for the crime executed by a person belonging to another group. The following paragraphs

---

61(7)(a) and (b) of the Rome Statute on the Charges, PTC II) ICC-01/05-01/08-424 (15 June 2009), paras 350-51; *The Prosecutor v Abu Garda* (Decision on the Confirmation of Charges, PTC I) ICC-02/05-02/09-243-Red (8 February 2010), paras 162, 216; *Katanga* Trial Chamber Judgment (n 31), para 1404; *Lubanga* Conviction Appeals Chamber Judgment (n 29), para 465; *Blé Goudé* Decision on Confirmation of Charges (n 31), para 136. For comments on indirect perpetration in the *Katanga* Trial Chamber Judgment, see C. Stahn, 'Justice Delivered or Justice Denied? The Legacy of the *Katanga* Judgment' (2014) 12 *JICJ* 809, 823–25.

48   Nuremberg Charter, arts 9 and 10.
49   Argentina, Code of Military Justice, art 514; Argentina, Penal Code, art 45.
50   *Ngudjolo* Trial Chamber Judgment (Concurring Opinion of Judge Christine Van den Wyngaert) (n 1), paras 52, 55, 57.

first analyse the *Katanga & Ngudjolo* case in 2008 as to the interpretation of article 25(3)(a) and then briefly evaluate indirect co-perpetration.

6.3.2.1   A 'Literal' Reading of Article 25(3)(a) in *Katanga & Ngudjolo*

In *Katanga & Ngudjolo*, both accused were rebel military leaders in the Democratic Republic of Congo (DRC).[51] Katanga and Ngudjolo were alleged to have designed a plan to 'wipe out' the village of Bogoro in the Ituri district, DRC. The prosecutor charged both of the accused with crimes committed by members of their two troops in implementing that plan, during and after the attack on civilians.[52]

Pre-Trial Chamber I confirmed the charges based on indirect co-perpetration.[53] The Pre-Trial Chamber first stated that the accused jointly controlled the two organised troops based on the hierarchical relations between the accused and their subordinates. The accused, as indirect perpetrators behind perpetrators (their subordinates), both mobilised their power within troops to secure automatic compliance with their orders to achieve the plan.[54] The Chamber further claimed that the crime committed by the accused with an agreement was mutually imputed to both of them. In its wording, 'if he acts jointly with another individual – one who controls the person used as an instrument – these crimes can be attributed to him on the basis of mutual attribution.'[55] Accordingly, through a combination of joint perpetration at the senior level and perpetration 'through other persons by means of control over an organisation', the Chamber introduced the notion of indirect co-perpetration. The accused at the leadership level were held liable for committing a crime through other persons (subordinates) at the executive level, by means of joint control over the troops. In other words, the accused was liable for the crime indirectly committed by his co-perpetrator, who used a third person to execute that crime.[56]

Defences have constantly challenged that the liability of indirect co-perpetration neither exists in the Rome Statute nor is supported by customary law.[57] The ICC rejected this argument. Pre-Trial Chamber I in *Katanga & Ngudjolo* interpreted the wording 'or' in article 25(3)(a) by addressing:

---

51   *Katanga & Ngudjolo* Decision on Confirmation of Charges (n 7), para 492.
52   ibid, para 33.
53   ibid, para 466.
54   ibid, paras 513-14.
55   ibid, para 492.
56   ibid, paras 492-93.
57   *The Prosecutor v Katanga & Ngudjolo* (Defence Written Observations Addressing Matters that Were Discussed at the Confirmation Hearing, Defence) ICC-01/04-01/07-698 (28

article 25(3)(a) uses the connective 'or', a disjunction (or alternation). Two meanings can be attributed to the word 'or'-one known as weak or *inclusive* and the other strong or *exclusive*. An inclusive disjunction has the sense of 'either one or the other, and possibly both' whereas an exclusive disjunction has the sense of 'either one or the other but not both'. Therefore, to interpret the disjunction in article 25(3)(a) of the Statute as either 'inclusive' or 'exclusive' is possible from a strict textualist interpretation. In the view of the Chamber, basing a person's criminal responsibility upon the joint commission of a crime through one or more persons is therefore a mode of liability 'in accordance with the Statute'.[58]

The Chamber in a footnote referred to the element of 'widespread or systematic' attack in article 7 of the Rome Statute to support its inclusive disjunctive interpretation.[59] The Chamber concluded that indirect co-perpetration is encompassed in article 25(3)(a) through the wording 'jointly through another person'.[60] Trial Chambers in the *Katanga* and *Ngudjolo* cases both confirmed this finding.[61]

However, a textual reading of article 25(3)(a) does not to lead to such a construction. The reasoning behind the interpretation of the wording 'or' is misguided. In the *Ngudjolo* case, Judge Van den Wyngaert in her concurring opinion noted that the term 'inclusive disjunction' is not an ordinary language interpretation but a concept of formal logic. The term in this Statute should be interpreted 'in accordance with the ordinary meaning' rather than through its formal logic formulation.[62] In her view, '[t]his combined reading leads to a radical expansion of Article 25(3)(a) of the Statute, and indeed is a totally new mode of liability'.[63] Pre-Trial Chamber I also held that 'the attack can be

---

July 2008), paras 13-32; *Katanga & Ngudjolo* Decision on Confirmation of Charges (n 7), para 474; *The Prosecutor v Katanga & Ngudjolo* (Defence for Germain Katanga's Pre-Trial Brief on the Interpretation of Article 25(3)(a) of the Rome Statute, Defence) ICC-01/04-01/07-1578-Corr (30 October 2009), paras 2, 7, 9-26; *Katanga* Trial Chamber Judgment (n 31), paras 1373-76.

58 *Katanga & Ngudjolo* Decision on Confirmation of Charges (n 7), para 491 (emphasis in original and citations omitted).
59 ibid, para 491 and fn 652.
60 ibid, para 493.
61 *Katanga* Trial Chamber Judgment (n 31), para 1381; *The Prosecutor v Ngudjolo* (Judgment pursuant to Article 74 of the Statute, TC II) ICC-01/04-02/12-3-tENG (20 December 2012), paras 58-64.
62 *Ngudjolo* Trial Chamber Judgment (Concurring Opinion of Judge Christine Van den Wyngaert) (n 1), para 60 and fn 76.
63 ibid, paras 60-61.

widespread, or systematic, or both' concerning the element of 'widespread or systematic' attack. This Chamber conflated legal element of 'widespread or systematic' with the factual coincidence of a 'widespread and systematic' attack. This factual situation does not denote a legal requirement of 'widespread and systematic' for crimes against humanity.[64] Likewise, the factual situation that two persons may jointly commit crimes through another person, does not lead to the liability of indirect co-perpetration.[65] The 'textual' interpretation of the term 'or' in article 25(3)(a) is not persuasive. The ordinary meaning of article 25(3)(a) is that three alternatives of perpetrations are listed.

The drafting history also appears to show that the drafters did not intend to give the term 'or' a special meaning to include indirect co-perpetration. In the *Ad Hoc* Committee, a special working group summarily listed some general principles for discussion.[66] In the early two sessions of the Preparatory Committee, some States submitted several proposals.[67] These proposals contained direct perpetration and co-perpetration categories but did not contain commission through another person as a form of perpetration. Later on, the informal group re-organised States' submissions and provided possible proposals for further discussion,[68] with an additional paragraph inserted. This additional paragraph introduced indirect perpetration by addressing that a person 'shall be deemed to be a principal where that person commits the crime through an innocent agent who is not aware of the criminal nature of the act committed'. In addition, a proposal suggested combining responsibility of principal liability and responsibility of participation/complicity, which stated that '(b) those who commit such crimes; (c) those who jointly commit such crimes; (d) those who commit such crimes by means of a third person' are

---

64 ibid, para 60 and fn 76.
65 Cf. T. Weigend, 'Perpetration through an Organisation: The Unexpected Career of a German Legal Concept' (2011) 9 *JICJ* 91, 110–11.
66 'Guidelines for consideration of the question of general principles of criminal law', annexed in 'Report of the *Ad Hoc* Committee on the Establishment of an International Criminal Court', UN Doc A/50/22 (1995), 58.
67 'Report of the Preparatory Committee on the Establishment of an International Criminal Court', UN Doc A/51/22 (1996), Vol I, paras 191-92, 202-03; Canada, 'Applicable Law: non-paper' (27 March 1996); 'General Rules of Criminal Law: Non-Paper, submitted by Sweden' (4 April 1996).
68 'Informal Group on General Principles of Criminal Law, Proposed new Part [111*bis*] for the Statute of an International Criminal Court General principles of Criminal Law', UN Doc A/AC.249/CRP.13 (1996), 4–8; 'Report of the Preparatory Committee on the Establishment of an International Criminal Court', UN Doc A/51/22 (1996), Vol II, 80–85.

perpetrators of the crime.[69] This combinatory proposal detours the original shape of article 25(3)(a) of the Rome Statute.

In the Preparatory Committee's third session, a text, which supported the combinatory proposal and refined its wording, emerged.[70] Canada, Germany, the Netherlands and the UK submitted that: 'a person is criminally responsible and liable for punishment for a crime defined [...] if that person: (a) commits such a crime, whether as an individual, jointly with another, or through a person who is not criminally responsible'. This text was widely supported by the Preparatory Committee after revising the third category of the commission to 'through another person regardless of whether that person is criminally responsible'.[71] The final adopted text of the Preparatory Committee is that 'commits such a crime, whether as an individual, jointly with another, or through another person regardless of whether that person is criminally responsible'.[72] This text is nearly identical to the final version of article 25(3)(a) except for minor changes. This text was neither discussed at the Rome Conference nor amended by the working group on General Principles of Criminal Law.[73] This text was slightly refined by the Drafting Committee, who removed the comma between the phrase 'jointly with another' and the phrase 'or through another' and added a comma before 'regardless'.[74] The Drafting Committee's refined text was wholly adopted and incorporated in the 1998 Draft Statute, which was transmitted to the final plenary meeting of the Rome Conference for voting.[75]

The examination of the drafting history first indicates that the liability for commission 'jointly with another person' and the liability for commission 'through another person' were designed separately. The idea of indirect co-perpetration as a form of perpetration was neither in the mind of civil law lawyers nor consistent with the knowledge of common law representatives at

---

69   UN Doc A/51/22 (1996), Vol II, 80–85.
70   'Working paper submitted by Canada, Germany, the Netherlands and the United Kingdom', UN Doc A/AC.249/1997/WG.2/DP.1.
71   'Chairman's Text, Article B b., c. and d., Individual criminal responsibility', UN Doc A/AC.249/1997/WG.2/CRP.2/Add.2; 'Decision taken by the Preparatory Committee at its Session held from 11 to 21 February 1997', UN Doc A/AC.249/1997/L.5.
72   'Report of the Preparatory Committee on the Establishment of an International Criminal Court', UN Doc A/CONF.183/2 (1998), 30–31, art 23(7)(a).
73   UN Doc A/CONF.183/C.1/SR.1, A/CONF.183/C.1/SR.8, A/CONF.183/C1/SR.23, A/CONF.183/C1/SR.24, A/CONF.183/C1/SR.26; 'Report of the Working Group on General Principles of Criminal Law', UN Doc A/CONF.183/C.1/WGGP/L.4 and Corr.1 (1998), 254.
74   'Report of the Drafting Committee, Draft Statute for the International Criminal Court', UN Doc A/CONF.183/C.1/L.65/Rev.1 (1998).
75   'Report of the Committee of the Whole, Draft Statute for the International Criminal Court', UN Doc A/CONF.183/8 (1998).

the Rome Conference. Alternatively, the removal of the comma by the Drafting Committee did not aim to include an alternative of commission 'jointly through another person' as defined by the ICC. The above observation reveals that indirect co-perpetration is not encompassed in article 25(3)(a) as a new form of perpetration.

6.3.2.2 Observations and Assessment of Indirect Co-perpetration

Other issues merit further discussions to understand the notion of indirect co-perpetration. The first issue is the way to establish a link between the accused and the crime committed by subordinates. In the *Katanga* & *Ngudjolo* case, Katanga was a top commander of Ngiti ethnicity armed forces, while Ngudjolo was the military leader of Lendu ethnicity fighters. Based on 'indirect perpetration of commission through control over the organisation', the accused as the armed group's leader may be held liable for the commission of crimes through subordinates by means of control over their own troops. The question of how to prove a crime was executed by an individual is closely related to evidence. In practice, it is sometimes difficult to ascertain which member of which troop executed a specific crime because the two troops implemented plans together. One may suggest imputing all offences committed by members of both troops to the accused if a link exists between the accused and the other troop. Nevertheless, the fact, in this case, is that despite a shared common plan between the two accused, subordinates of each troop belonging to different ethnic origins are 'unlikely to comply with orders of a leader not of their own ethnicity'. In this circumstance, based on indirect perpetration, both accused would not be held liable for crimes executed by the other troop due to their lack of control over that other troop. It seems that if there is any doubt about the membership of the executor, both accused might not be liable for that offence committed. The difficulty in locating the physical perpetrators in each troop seems to be a motivation for the prosecutor to introduce indirect co-perpetration to attribute liability to the accused. By setting aside evidentiary problems, each indirect co-perpetrator is liable for all crimes.

According to the Pre-Trial Chamber, the accused and his co-perpetrators contributed to the crime through their joint control of the fulfilment of the material elements of a crime. It means that Ngudjolo had control over the Lendu troop and is liable for the crimes committed by the Lendu troop's subordinates; the accused Katanga would also be liable for the crime attached to his co-perpetrator Ngudjolo based on mutual attribution. Thus, Katanga is liable for the crimes committed by the Lendu troop's subordinates, despite no direct link between him and the Lendu troop. The creation of indirect co-perpetration liability establishes a link between the accused at the higher leadership level and the crime committed by a lower-level perpetrator of another group.[76]

Secondly, the Pre-Trial Chambers of the ICC even applies this liability to a crime committed outside the common plan. In *Katanga & Ngudjolo*, aside from the charge against the offence of attack on civilians, the prosecution also charged both of the accused with sexual offences committed by soldiers after the attack on Bogoro. The Chamber relied on indirect co-perpetration liability and held that although the sexual offences were not a part of the common plan, as a consequence of the plan, the accused knew that these sexual offences 'would occur in the ordinary course of the events'.[77] The ICC further clarified the material and mental elements of indirect co-perpetration. The Trial Chambers in the *Katanga* and *Ngudjolo* cases combined the two elements of indirect perpetration and co-perpetration to flesh out the elements of indirect co-perpetration. The mental elements are:

> (i) the suspect must satisfy the subjective elements of the crimes; (ii) the suspect must be aware of the factual circumstances enabling him to exercise joint control over the commission of the crime through another person(s); and (iii) the suspect and the other co-perpetrators must be mutually aware and accept that implementing the common plan will result in the fulfilment of the objective elements of the crime.[78]

The material elements are:

> (i) the suspect must be part of a common plan or an agreement with one or more persons; (ii) the suspect and the other co-perpetrators must carry out essential contributions in a coordinated manner which result in the fulfilment of the material elements of the crime; (iii) the suspect must have control over the organisation; and (iv) the suspect and the other co-perpetrators' joint control is actually possible.[79]

---

76   *The Prosecutor v Muthaura & Kenyatta* (Prosecutions Submissions on the Law of Indirect co-perpetration under Article 25(3)(a) of the Statute and Application for Notice to be Given under Regulation 55 (2) with respect to the Individual's Individual Criminal Responsibility, OTP) ICC-01/09-01/11-433 (3 July 2012), paras 5-6, 8-35.

77   *Katanga & Ngudjolo* Decision on Confirmation of Charges (n 7), paras 565, 567.

78   ibid, paras 495-537; *Ruto et al* Decision on Confirmation of Charges (n 7), para 292; *Bemba* Decision on Confirmation of Charges (n 47), paras 350-51.

79   ibid. Cf. *The Prosecutor v Ntaganda* (Judgment, TC VI) ICC-01/04-02/06-2359 (08 July 2019), para 774.

Thirdly, apart from interpreting indirect co-perpetration as the fourth way of perpetration, a different construction of it was illustrated by the *Lubanga* Appeals Chamber. Bearing in mind Judge Van den Wyngaert's different view,[80] the *Lubanga* Appeals Chamber pointed out that divergent views exist at the ICC and held that there are only three rather than four forms of perpetration embedded in article 25(3)(a). In interpreting co-perpetration liability, the *Lubanga* Appeals Chamber found that 'co-perpetrators need [not] to carry out the crime personally and directly'.[81] The Appeals Chamber implicitly endorsed 'joint commission through another person' as a form of co-perpetration instead of using the label of indirect co-perpetration. Subsequent cases subscribed to this extended interpretation of co-perpetration.[82] After the *Katanga & Ngudjolo* confirmation of charges decision, indirect co-perpetration was confirmed in the *Al Bashir, Bemba, Abu Garda, Ruto et al, Gaddafi et al, Muthaura et al, Lubanga, Ntaganda, Ongwen,* and most recently the *Gbagbo* and *Blé Goudé* cases.[83]

Relying on the construction of indirect perpetration 'by control over an organisation', indirect co-perpetration not only covers commission jointly 'through another person' but also includes commission 'by means of joint

---

80   *Ngudjolo* Trial Chamber Judgment (Concurring Opinion of Judge Christine Van den Wyngaert) (n 1), paras 62-64; *Katanga* Trial Chamber Judgment (n 31) (Minority Opinion of Judge Christine Van den Wyngaert) ICC-01/04-01/07-3436-AnxI, para 278.

81   *Lubanga* Conviction Appeals Chamber Judgment (n 29), paras 458, 460, 465.

82   *Bemba* Decision on Confirmation of Charges (n 47), para 348; *Ruto et al* Decision on Confirmation of Charges (n 7), para 292; *Ongwen* Decision on Confirmation of Charges (n 31), paras 38-41; *Ntaganda* Trial Chamber Judgment (n 79), para 772.

83   *First Warrant of Arrest* Decision for *Al Bashir* (n 47), paras 209-13; *Bemba* Decision on Confirmation of Charges (n 47), paras 350-51; *Abu Garda* Decision on Confirmation of Charges (n 47), para 169; *The Prosecutor v Gaddafi et al* (Decision on the "Prosecutor's Application Pursuant to Article 58 as to Muammar Mohammed Abuminyar Gaddafi, Saif Al-Islam Gaddafi and Abdullah Al Senussi", PTC I) ICC-01/11-01/11-1 (30 June 2011), para 69; *Ruto et al* Decision on Confirmation of Charges (n 7), paras 280-90, 299, 349; *The Prosecutor v Muthaura et al* (Decision on the Confirmation of Charges Pursuant to Article 61(7)(a) and (b) of the Rome Statute, PTC II) ICC-01/09-02/11-382-Red (23 January 2012), paras 298-99; *Ngudjolo* Trial Chamber Judgment (n 61), paras 7, 58-64; *Katanga* Trial Chamber Judgment (n 31), paras 1381, 1416; *The Prosecutor v Ntaganda* (Decision Pursuant to Article 61(7)(a) and (b) of the Rome Statute on the Charges of the Prosecutor against Bosco Ntaganda, PTC II) ICC-01/04-02/06-309 (9 June 2014), paras 104, 121; *Gbagbo* Decision on Confirmation of Charges (n 31), para 241; *Lubanga* Conviction Appeals Chamber Judgment (n 29), paras 458, 460; *Blé Goudé* Decision on Confirmation of Charges (n 31), paras 136-37; *Ongwen* Decision on Confirmation of Charges (n 31), para 41; *The Prosecutor v Gbagbo & Blé Goudé* (Public Redacted Version of Reasons of Judge Geoffrey Henderson, TC I) ICC-02/11-02/15-1263-AnXB-Red (16 July 2019), para 1921.

control over an organisation'. This construction of indirect co-perpetration serves to attribute liability to a leader of an organisation for the crimes performed by physical executors belonging to another organisation, regardless of whether offences were a part of the common plan shared between the accused and their co-perpetrators. Jens Ohlin remarks that indirect co-perpetration liability is a form of 'double vicarious liability', a by-product of co-perpetration and indirect perpetration liabilities.[84] From a moral perspective, the ICC's construction of indirect co-perpetration would be highly desirable in proceedings against high-ranked leaders; nonetheless, moral arguments should not be the primary reason for introducing such a new mode of liability. We cannot say that prosecution of these leaders based on other modes of liability is not an effort to prevent and narrow the impunity gap.

6.3.3   *Assessment and Conclusions*

The above analysis reveals that three categories of perpetration are encompassed in article 25(3)(a). The ICC created indirect co-perpetration in a way either by combining co-perpetration and indirect perpetration as the fourth way of perpetration, or by expansively interpreting co-perpetration to cover a new form of co-perpetration 'through another person by control over an organisation'. Indirect co-perpetration is in nature a creation by combining co-perpetration and indirect perpetration. Consequently, relying on indirect co-perpetration, the accused might be held liable for all crimes 'indirectly' committed by their co-perpetrators who used physical executors to perform criminal acts, regardless of whether the crime committed is a part of the plan. This expansive interpretation is not consistent with a textual reading, nor was it especially defined by the drafters. Since a treaty provision dealing with a specific subject matter is a starting point for this book, it seems that it is not a real issue now concerning the relationship between article 25(3)(a) and custom with regard to indirect co-perpetration. Nonetheless, a further examination of whether article 25(3)(a) is declaratory of custom to date is valuable, as it is possible that the view of indirect co-perpetration embedded in article 25(3)(a) is subsequently well accepted. The following sections evaluate whether article 25(3)(a) is declaratory of customary law concerning indirect co-perpetration.

---

84   J.D. Ohlin, 'Second-Order Linking Principles: Combining Vertical and Horizontal Modes of Liability' (2012) 25 *LJIL* 771.

6.4 Non-acceptance of Indirect Co-perpetration in Post-World War II Trials

An analysis of the form and the structure of the text, and the preparatory works of article 25(3)(a) does not assist in assessing whether article 25(3)(a) is declaratory of custom on indirect co-perpetration. Commentators have closely examined proposals about conspiracy debated in the drafting of the Nuremberg Charter and in subsequent World War II cases.[85] This section looks into post-World War II instruments and cases to survey whether indirect co-perpetration was emerging under customary law before 1998.

6.4.1 *Post-World War II Instruments*

Previous provisions or drafts of individual criminal responsibility for international crimes did not use wording similar to that in article 25(3)(a).[86] The concluding paragraph of article 6 of the Nuremberg Charter focused on the liability of leaders, organisers, instigators and accomplices participating in the formulation or execution of a common plan or conspiracy to commit crimes for the acts performed by any person in the execution of the crime.[87] Article 5 of the Tokyo Charter contained a provision similar to that in the Nuremberg Charter.[88] Article 7(1) of the ICTY Statute provides that a person 'who planned, instigated, ordered, committed or otherwise aided and abetted in the planning, preparation or execution of a crime' is responsible. Article 6(1) of the ICTR Statute provides a similar construction. The 1994 ILC Draft Statute of the court did not contain a provision about individual criminal responsibility.[89] Article 2(3) of the 1996 ILC Draft Code of Crimes addressed various forms of perpetration and participation,[90] including intentionally committing, ordering, aiding and abetting, direct participation in planning or conspiring, incitement and

---

85 L.D. Yanev, 'A Janus-Faced Concept: Nuremberg's Law on Conspiracy vis-à-vis the Notion of Joint Criminal Enterprise' (2015) 26 *CLF* 419, 456.
86 Control Council Law No. 10, art 2(2); 1950 ILC Nuremberg Principles, Principles I, VI (a) (ii), and VII; 1948 Genocide Convention, art III; 1949 Geneva Conventions (GC: art 49 of GC I; art 50 of GC II; art 129 of GC III; and art 146 of GC IV); the 1977 Additional Protocol I, art 86; 1991 Draft Code of Crimes, arts 3(1)-(2); 1996 Draft Code of Crimes, art 2(3); 1993 ICTY Statute, art 7(1); 1994 ICTR Statute, art 6(1); Statute of the SCSL, art 6(1); Protocol on Amendments to the Protocol on the Statute of the African Court of Justice and Human Rights, art 28N.
87 Nuremberg Charter, art 6(2); Bassiouni (n 24) 382–83.
88 Tokyo Charter, art 5.
89 'Report of the International Law Commission on the Work of its Forty-sixth Session, Note by the Secretary-General', UN Doc A/49/355 (1994), 3-31.
90 1996 Draft Code of Crimes, art 2(3).

attempts.[91] Article 25(3)(a) seems to contain no trace of this Draft Code of Crimes. In short, no precedent in international treaties has explicitly set out indirect co-perpetration.

6.4.2 Post-World War II Trials

The absence of the term 'indirect co-perpetration' in post-World War II instruments is not conclusive evidence of its lack of customary basis. A mode of liability in a different label or terminology may fulfil the same function of indirect co-perpetration. Supporters of indirect co-perpetration under customary law have referred to post-World War II trials to justify their claims.[92] This subsection surveys post-World War II cases relating to conspiracy liability, complicity through organisation and concerted actions to explore whether indirect co-perpetration can trace its roots to these cases.

6.4.2.1 The Offence of Conspiracy and Conspiracy Liability

The wording 'common plan or conspiracy' was contained in two paragraphs of the Nuremberg Charter, article 6(a) and the concluding paragraph of article 6. The IMT differentiated the meaning of conspiracy in the two paragraphs. The drafters of the Nuremberg Charter and the IMT both considered the notion of conspiracy to wage aggressive wars in article 6(a) as a separate inchoate crime.[93] The IMT interpreted the concluding paragraph of article 6 as a liability provision stipulating individual criminal responsibility for any crimes listed in articles 6(a)-(c).[94] Based on this liability, leaders and organisers who were involved in the formulation of a plan to commit war crimes and crimes against humanity would also be punished. Conspiracy as an inchoate crime is familiar to common law lawyers, whereas conspiracy as a form of complicity is more familiar to civil law lawyers.

Article 5 of the Tokyo Charter provided a similar construction of conspiracy. But the concluding paragraph of article 6 in the Nuremberg Charter was

---

91   See also 'Fourth report on the Draft Code of Offences against the Peace and Security of Mankind, by Mr Doudou Thiam, Special Rapporteur', UN Doc A/CN.4/398 and Corr.1-3 (1986), paras 89-145; 'Report of the International Law Commission', UN Doc A/42/10 (1987), para 66, commentary to art 3.

92   *Simić et al* Appeals Chamber Judgement (n 42) (Dissenting Opinion of Judge Schomburg), para 14.

93   Nuremberg Charter, art 6(a). See Yanev (n 85) 419.

94   *France et al v Göring et al*, Judgment and Sentence of the Nuremberg International Military Tribunals, (1948) 1 TMWC 171, 226; 'The Charter and Judgment of the Nuremberg Tribunal – History and Analysis: Memorandum submitted by the Secretary-General', UN Doc A/CN.4/5 (1949), 73-74.

incorporated in the definition of crimes against humanity in article 5(c) of the Tokyo Charter. The IMTFE did not clarify the meaning of the two words 'conspiracy' in article 5 of the Tokyo Charter.[95] Control Council Law No. 10 did not contain a provision similar to the concluding clause of article 6. Its article 11 (2)(d) stipulated criminal responsibility of individuals 'connected with plans or enterprises' involving the commission of a crime. The defences argued that article 11 (2)(d) deemed 'enterprise liability' a mode of liability. It seems that the tribunals in the Nuremberg Subsequent Proceedings supported the defences' view and endorsed the distinction between conspiracy as a separate crime and conspiracy liability by interpreting the phrase 'connected with plans or enterprises' in article 11 (2)(d) as a form of liability.[96]

Thus, the function of conspiracy in the post-World War II trials is twofold. The first is to define a separate crime for a concrete plan to crimes against peace. The second function is as a mode of liability to attribute liability to defendants for their contribution to offences of crimes against peace, war crimes and crimes against humanity committed by others.[97] At the IMT, conspiracy liability was originally designed to attribute liability to leaders and planners at the planning level. The IMT judgment and the Nuremberg Subsequent Proceedings concerning the conspiracy liability issue might be relevant to the examination of indirect co-perpetration.

The IMT provided little opportunity for discussion on the elements of conspiracy liability. According to the text of the concluding paragraph of article 6, conspiracy liability first requires offences 'committed' by any persons in the execution of a common plan. Secondly, the drafting history of the Nuremberg Charter indicates a shared common plan between the physical perpetrators and leaders, although article 6 includes no explicit reference to such a requirement.[98] The IMT did not adopt that mere agreement to a conspiracy suffices to charge the leaders.[99] Thirdly, simply participation in a conspiracy initiated

---

95   *US et al v Araki et al*, Indictment, counts 37, 38, 44, 53.

96   *US v Brandt et al* [The *Medical* case], (1949) 1TWC 1, 10; *US v Altstötter et al* [The *Justice* case], (1951) 3 TWC 1, 17; *US v Pohl et al* [The *Pohl* case], (1950) 5 TWC 195, 201. See also K.J. Heller, *The Nuremberg Military Tribunals and the Origins of International Criminal Law* (OUP 2011) 276–80.

97   A. Danner and J. Martinez, 'Guilty Associations: Joint Criminal Enterprise, Command Responsibility, and the Development of International Criminal Law' (2005) 93 *Cali L Rev* 75, 119; J.D. Ohlin, 'Joint Intentions to Commit International Crimes' (2011) 11 *Chicago J Intl L* 693, 702–03; H. Van der Wilt, 'Joint Criminal Enterprise: Possibilities and Limitations' (2007) 5 (1) *JICJ* 91, 96.

98   Yanev (n 85) 437–42.

99   ibid 434–36.

by others is not enough.[100] In the IMT's view, when statesmen, military leaders and diplomats, with knowledge of the common plan, willingly co-operate and facilitate the plan initiated by original conspirators, they make themselves parties to the common plan. At the IMT, conspiracy liability requires the knowledge of the common plan and the accused's actual acts of furthering that plan.

The above clarification of the conspiracy liability for the common plan reveals that conspiracy liability is distinct from modern indirect co-perpetration liability in several aspects. First, participation in the conspiracy to commit crimes at the IMT is regarded as a form of complicity. The current idea of indirect co-perpetration liability is considered as a form of commission; therefore, these accused are deemed principals instead of accessories. This difference is a choice of the way to solve a similar issue. Second, at the IMT, defendants' contribution at the preparatory stage sufficed to attribute liability for conspiracy. However, whether indirect co-perpetration requires the accused's essential contribution to crimes at the execution stage or the preparatory stage is controversial.[101] The third and main difference is that conspiracy liability requires a shared plan between the leaders and physical executors at a vertical level, whereas indirect co-perpetration requires no such shared common purpose. These cases about conspiracy liability did not show that the indirect co-perpetration liability was well rooted.

6.4.2.2   Liability for Complicity through Association

Apart from the introduction of conspiracy liability, articles 9 and 10 of the Nuremberg Charter deal with membership in a criminal organisation. The American Chief Prosecutor explained that both articles aimed to make subsequent trials of minor war criminals more expeditious.[102] The IMT clarified the characteristics of criminal organisation:

> A criminal organisation is analogous to a criminal conspiracy in that the essence of both is cooperation for criminal purposes. There must be a

---

100   ibid.
101   A.G. Gil and E. Maculan, 'Current Trends in the Definition of "Perpetrator" by the International Criminal Court: From the Decision on the Confirmation of Charges in the *Lubanga* Case to the *Katanga* Judgment' (2015) 28 *LJIL* 349; *Lubanga* Decision on Confirmation of Charges (n 40), para 367; *Ongwen* Decision on Confirmation of Charges (n 31), para 44; *The Prosecutor v Al Mahdi* (Decision on the Confirmation of Charges against Ahmad Al Faqi Al Mahdi, PTC I) ICC-01/12-01/15-84-Red (24 March 2016), para 27.
102   *France et al v Göring et al*, Supplementary statement of the United States Prosecution, (1948) 1 TMWC 144.

group bound together and organised for a common purpose. The group must be formed or used in connection with the commission of crimes denounced by the Charter. Since the declaration with respect to the organisations and groups will [...] fix the criminality of its members, that definition should exclude persons who had no knowledge of the criminal purposes or acts of the organisation and those who were drafted by the State for membership, unless they were personally implicated in the commission of acts declared criminal by Article 6 of the Charter as members of the organisation. Membership alone is not enough to come within the scope of these declarations.[103]

This explanation indicates that the declaration of a criminal organisation is not collective punishment.[104] As Kevin Heller noted, the membership in a criminal organisation is a combination of conspiracy and criminal association liability.[105] In connection with conspiracy liability, the declaration of an organisation as a criminal opens the door to hold leaders of an organisation responsible for all crimes committed by members of that organisation. However, such a combinatory reading should not go too far. This idea does not give any hint that liability would be imposed on the leader for the crime committed by an individual who is a member of the criminal organisation but lacks the knowledge of the common purpose. A shared intention, for the common design of the organisation, is required.

In the Subsequent Proceedings, tribunals considered both small and large criminal enterprises. In the *Ministries* case, the enterprise was limited to the campaign of persecution of the Catholic Church; however, in the *Justice* case, the enterprise was a nationwide government-organised system of cruelty and injustice.[106] The case law did not emphasise the membership of direct perpetrators but rather the shared common plan between the accused and physical executors.[107] If the size of a group was extended, the executors who were not in the same group as the accused would be included as a member of the large group. For crimes committed within the scope of the common design of a large group, these post-World War II cases about complicity through association are

---

103   *France et al v Göring et al* (n 94) 256.
104   Yanev (n 85) 427–28.
105   Heller (n 96) 275.
106   The *Ministries* case, (1953) 14 TWC 1, 520; The *Justice* case, (1951) 3 TWC 1, 985. For a discussion on this liability, see Ambos (n 4) 111.
107   For a detailed analysis, see L.D. Yanev, *Theories of Co-perpetration in International Criminal Law* (Brill | Nijhoff 2018) 385–91.

a good start for ascertaining the contours of indirect co-perpetration at the leadership level. However, if the crimes committed were outside the common plan, these cases are irrelevant to the assessment of the emergence of indirect co-perpetration under customary law. Thus, it is inconclusive to argue that these cases evidence the indirect co-perpetration liability with the required mental and material elements.

Much more recently, the interpretation of the IMT has been followed by national courts.[108] In 1994, the Canadian Federal Court, in *Sivakumar*, held:

> [...] the starting point for complicity in an international crime was 'personal and knowing participation'. This is essentially a factual question that can be answered only on a case-by-case basis, but certain general principles are accepted.[109]

In its view, based on complicity through association, leaders may be rendered responsible for the acts of others because of their close association with the principal actors. The court held that: '[t]his view of leadership within organisation constituting a possible basis for complicity in international crimes committed by the organisation is supported by Article 6 of the Charter of the International Military Tribunal'.[110] Article 2(3)(e) the 1996 Draft Code of Crimes confirmed this liability, which provided for liability of an individual who 'directly participates in planning or conspiring to commit such a crime which in fact occurs'.[111] This complicity liability through association might be the origin of indirect perpetration 'through an organisation', instead of indirect co-perpetration 'through jointly control over an organisation'.[112]

6.4.2.3 'Concerted Actions' in Hong Kong Trials and Australia's War Crimes Trials

Regulation 8(ii) of the Regulation Annexed to the British Royal Warrant provided that:

---

108 *Naredo and Arduengo v Canada*, (1990) 37 FTR 161; *Rudolph v Canada*, [1992] 2 FC 653; *Moreno v Canada*, [1994] 1 FC 298; *Ramirez v Canada*, [1992] 2 FC 306, 317–18.
109 *Sivakumar v Canada*, [1994] 1 FC 433.
110 ibid.
111 UN Doc A/51/10 (1996), para 50, 21, commentary (14) to art 2(3).
112 'Memorandum of Proposals for the Prosecution and Punishment of Certain War Criminals and Other Offenders, April 30, 1945' in Report of Robert H. Jackson (n 21) 31. For an analysis of these proposals, see Yanev (n 85) 432–33.

> Where there is evidence that a war crime has been the result of concerted action upon the part of a unit or group of them, then evidence given upon any charge relating to that crime against any member of such unit or group may be received as *prima facie* evidence of the responsibility of each member of that unit or group for that crime.
>
> In any such case all or any members of any such unit or group may be charged and tried jointly in respect of any such war crime and no application by any of them to be tried separately shall be allowed by the Court.[113]

Writing on the Hong Kong war crimes trials and British Military trials, Nina Jørgensen found that by referring to Regulation 8(ii) prosecutors considered 'concerted action' as an evidentiary rule, rather than the notion of common plan/common intent.[114] The British Royal Warrant was the model for Australia's war crimes legislation. The two paragraphs in Regulation 8(ii) were repeated in Australia's 1945 Regulations for the Trial of War Criminals.[115] Section 9(2) of Australia's 1945 War Crimes Act was also similar to the first paragraph of Regulation 8(ii) with the phrase '*prima facie*' deleted. In some cases of Australia's war crimes trials, section 9(2) was interpreted to support a charge of criminal responsibility for joint participation; however, in other cases that section was interpreted as an evidentiary provision for crimes committed by a group of people.[116] At the very least, the Hong Kong war crimes trials, British Military trials and Australia's war crimes trials do not make the contemporary indirect co-perpetration more rooted and accessible.

6.4.3 *Assessment and Conclusions*

This idea of complicity liability for participation in a common plan or through association is not as expansive as indirect co-perpetration whereby leaders can be held liable for crimes committed by others, who neither are members of the group nor share a common purpose. In addition, cases

---

113 'Regulations for the Trial of War Criminals, Royal Warrant 0160/2498, Army Order 81/1845 (War Office, 18 June 1945)' in Telford Taylor, *Final Report to the Secretary of the Army on the Nuremberg War Crimes Trials under Control Council Law No. 10* (USGPO 1949) 254–56.
114 N. Jørgensen, 'On Being "Concerned" in a Crime: Embryonic Joint Criminal Enterprise?' in S. Linton (ed), *Hong Kong's War Crimes Trials* (OUP 2013) 137–67. Cf. Danner and Martinez (n 97) 108; S. Linton, 'Rediscovering the War Crimes Trials in Hong Kong, 1946–48' (2012) 13 *Melbourne J Intl L* 284.
115 Appendices I and II in G. Fitzpatrick *et al* (eds), *Australia's War Crimes Trials 1945–51* (Brill | Nijhoff 2016) 810–23.
116 G. Boas and L. Lee, 'Command Responsibility and Other Grounds of Criminal Responsibility' in Fitzpatrick *et al* (eds), ibid 160; Jørgensen (n 114) 137–67.

concerning concerted actions do not support an expansive interpretation of co-perpetration to include the form of indirect co-perpetration. Post-World War II cases do not evince the emergence of indirect co-perpetration in general. In short, indirect co-perpetration has not generally been accepted or practised in post-World War II trials. The next section further examines authorities to show whether indirect co-perpetration liability is now well accepted under customary law.

6.5 Indirect Co-perpetration: Is Article 25(3)(a) Declaratory of Custom?

One may note that the jurisprudence of the ICTY and ICTR had less influence on the substantive content of article 25(3)(a), since the ICTY's remarkable *Tadić* Appeals Chamber judgment dealing with the issue of JCE was delivered in 1999, i.e., one year after the adoption of the 1998 Rome Statute. Yet, it appears that JCE and indirect co-perpetration overlap each other in a certain context: the ICC Appeals Chamber in *Katanga* deemed indirect co-perpetration a form of co-perpetration; and some Chambers of the ICTY upheld JCE as 'a form of co-perpetration'.[117] As Elies van Sliedregt has noted, recent practice of the ICTY seems to reintroduce indirect co-perpetration liability under the label of JCE.[118] Thus, it is necessary to analysis the jurisprudence of the two UN *ad hoc* tribunals concerning indirect co-perpetration and JCE.

The consecutive subsections 6.5.1–6.5.3 first look into the jurisprudence of the two *ad hoc* tribunals. Subsections 6.5.1 and 6.5.3 mainly comment on the state of indirect co-perpetration under customary law through the lens of JCE liability, in particular, the JCE formulation in *Brđanin*. Subsection 6.5.2 covers case law of the two *ad hoc* tribunals concerning indirect co-perpetration. These cases are analysed chronologically. Subsections 6.5.4–6.5.5 observe and evaluate case law of other international and national criminal tribunals, and national legislation relating to co-perpetration.

---

117   *Stakić* Trial Chamber Judgment (n 32), para 441; *Prosecutor v Milutinović et al* (Decision on Dragoljub Ojdanić's Motion Challenging Jurisdiction: Joint Criminal Enterprise) ICTY-99-37-AR72 (21 May 2003) (Separate Opinion of Judge David Hunt on Challenge by Ojdanić to Jurisdiction Joint Criminal Enterprise), para 13; *Prosecutor v Kupreškić et al* (Judgement) ICTY-95-16-T (14 January 2000), paras 772, 782; *Prosecutor v Simić et al* (Judgement) ICTY-95-9-T (17 October 2003) (Separate and Partly Opinion of Judge Per-Johan Lindholm), para 2.

118   Van Sliedregt (n 23) 162–63.

6.5.1 Tadić *JCE liability: 1999 Appeals Chamber Judgment*

Case law of the two *ad hoc* tribunals has established the JCE liability.[119] In the ICTY, the *Furundžija* Trial Chamber firstly referred to JCE liability with respect to the liability of co-perpetrators who participate in a JCE of torture.[120] The *Tadić* Appeals Chamber judgment is widely known for confirming the customary status of JCE liability applicable in the Yugoslavia tribunal. In the famous *Tadić* case, the accused Dusko Tadić was a reserve police officer who had participated in the collection and forced transfer of civilians after the control of Bosnian Serb forces in 1992. In one count, five men were killed in the execution of the removal plan. Evidence showed that members of the armed group to which Tadić belonged committed the killing, but no evidence proved that Tadić had personally killed any of them.[121]

The Appeals Chamber analysed whether the killing could give rise to criminal culpability of Tadić who participated in the execution of that common plan, and what the requirements of the accused's mental and material

---

119 *Tadić* Appeals Chamber Judgment (n 12), paras 185-229; *Prosecutor v Furundžija* (Judgement) ICTY-95-17/1-A (12 July 2000), paras 118-20; *Prosecutor v Mucić et al* (Judgement) ICTY-96-21-A (20 February 2001), paras 365-66; *Prosecutor v Brđanin & Talin* (Decision on Form of Further Amended Indictment and Prosecution Application to Amend) ICTY-99-36-PT (26 June 2001); *Prosecutor v Krstić* (Judgement) ICTY-98-33-T (2 August 2001), para 601; *Prosecutor v Šainović et al* (Decision on Dragoljub Ojdanić's Preliminary Motion to Dismiss for Lack of Jurisdiction: Joint Criminal Enterprise) ICTY-99-37-PT (13 February 2003); *Prosecutor v Šešelj* (Decision on Motion by Vojislav Šešelj Challenging Jurisdiction and Form of Indictment) ICTY-03-67/PT (26 May 2004), paras 52; *Prosecutor v Kvočka et al* (Judgement) ICTY-98-30/1-T (2 November 2001), paras 265, 289; *Milutinović et al* Appeals Chamber Decision on Jurisdiction 2003 (n 117), paras 18-20, 41; *Krnojelac* Appeals Chamber Judgment, paras 28-32; *Prosecutor v Vasiljević* (Judgement) ICTY-98-32-A (25 February 2004), paras 99, 101; *Prosecutor v Brđanin* (Judgement) ICTY-99-36-T (1 September 2004), para 258; *Blagojević & Jokić* Trial Chamber Judgment (n 17), paras 695-703; *Kvočka et al* Appeals Chamber Judgment (n 17), para 83; *Prosecutor v Prlić et al* (Decision to Dismiss the Preliminary Objections against the Tribunal's Jurisdiction) ICTY-04-74-PT (26 September 2005), paras 16-17; *Prosecutor v Limaj et al* (Judgement) ICTY-03-66-T (30 November 2005), paras 511-12; *Prosecutor v Brđanin* (Judgement) ICTY-99-36-A (1 April 2007), para 405; *Prosecutor v Tolimir* (Decision on preliminary motions on the indictment pursuant to Rule 72 of the Rules) ICTY-05-88/2-PT (14 December 2007), para 53; *Prosecutor v Haradinaj et al* (Judgement) ICTY-04-84-T (3 April 2008), paras 135, 137-79; *Prosecutor v Milutinović et al* (Judgement) ICTY-05-87-T (26 February 2009), Vol 3, para 9; *Prosecutor v Haradinaj et al* (Retrial Judgement) ICTY-04-84*BIS*-T (29 November 2012), paras 618, 621; *Prosecutor v Tolimir* (Judgement) ICTY-05-88/2-A (8 April 2015), para 281; *Prosecutor v Prlić et al* (Judgement) ICTY-04-74-A (29 November 2017), Vol II, para 591.
120 *Prosecutor v Furundžija* (Judgement) ICTY-95-17/1-T (10 December 1998), para 216.
121 *Tadić* Appeals Chamber Judgment (n 12), paras 178-84.

elements were. The Appeals Chamber held that the commission of a crime might occur through different forms of participation aiming to achieve a common purpose,[122] which is encompassed in the ICTY Statute.[123] The Appeals Chamber then turned to customary law to clarify the mental and material elements of JCE liability.[124] In its view, JCE liability includes three forms: the basic form (JCE I), the systematic form (JCE II), and the extended form (JCE III).[125]

The facts in the *Almelo* trial after World War II present a good example of JCE I.[126] In this case, three people each played a role in the killings: one fired the actual shots, another gave the order, and a third waited near the car to prevent people from coming near. All three knew what they were doing. In this scenario, except for the one who fired the shots, the other two did not fulfil all the elements of the killings for lack of criminal acts. Relying on JCE I, the other two were also convicted of committing the killings.

A good illustration of JCE II is the cases of 'concentration camp' crimes committed by groups of persons acting pursuant to a concerted plan.[127] In the British *Belsen* case, members of military or administrative systems, such as concentration camps, physically mistreated prisoners.[128] The accused were held liable for the crimes committed by others who mistreated prisoners and detainees because the accused had intended to contribute to the crime through active participation in the enforcement of that system. The accused held a 'position of authority' in the system when the crimes were committed. JCE II is in nature a variant of JCE I.[129]

The scenario in *Tadić* illustrates JCE III. Tadić with other members participated in the execution of the removal plan, but five men were killed by other members during the execution of that plan. Based on JCE III, Tadić was also found guilty for the killing of the five men. Another example is provided by a situation where a group with a common plan shared the intention to forcibly remove members of one ethnicity from a town with the consequence that many members were shot and killed in the course of the execution of that plan.[130] The acts of killing were not envisaged in the ethnic cleansing plan. The accused was held responsible for the acts of killing committed by other

---

122   ibid, para 188.
123   ibid, paras 189-93.
124   ibid, para 194.
125   ibid, paras 196-203; *Kvočka et al* Appeals Chamber Judgment (n 17), para 198.
126   *UK v Otto Sandrock and Three Others* (1947) 1 LRTWC 35.
127   *Tadić* Appeals Chamber Judgment (n 12), para 202.
128   *UK v Josef Kramer et al* (1947) 2 LRTWC 1.
129   *Tadić* Appeals Chamber Judgment (n 12), paras 203, 228.
130   *Brđanin & Talin* Decision on Amended Indictment 2001 (n 119), para 25.

members of the group because the accused who participated in the group had foreseen the killing in carrying out the plan of ethnic cleaning. Other cases have also been frequently cited to illustrate JCE III.[131]

Two requirements have to be fulfilled for JCE liability: mental and material elements, both of which are said to be found in customary international law.[132] Three forms of JCE liability share the same material elements, requiring the existence of a joint criminal enterprise consisting of a plurality of persons with a common criminal plan and the participation of the accused in that enterprise.[133] As to the mental element of JCE I, the accused has to share the intent to commit the crime. JCE II requires that the accused had knowledge of the criminal nature of the system and had intended to further the common design of the system. The mental element of JCE III is that:

> [...] the *intention* to participate in and further the criminal activity or the criminal purpose of a group and to contribute to the joint criminal enterprise or in any event to the commission of a crime by the group. In addition, responsibility for a crime other than the one agreed upon in the common plan arises only if, under the circumstances of the case, (i) it was *foreseeable* that such a crime might be perpetrated by one or other members of the group and (ii) the accused *willingly took that risk*.[134]

After analysing post-World War II cases and some customary indicators, the *Tadić* Appeals Chamber concluded that JCE liability was 'firmly established in customary international law'.[135]

The defences in some subsequent cases challenged the customary status of JCE liability or its mental elements. Appeals Chambers of the ICTY, however, declined to revisit the *Tadić* findings in this regard for lack of a cogent reason.[136]

---

131 For example, the *Essen Lynching* and *Borkum Island* cases. *UK v Erich Heyer and Six Others*, (1945) 1 UNWCC 88, 89; M. Koessler, 'Borkum Island Tragedy and Trial' (1957) 47 *J Crim L & Criminology* 183.
132 *Tadić* Appeals Chamber Judgment (n 12), para 194; *Šainović et al* Trial Chamber Decision 2003 (n 119).
133 *Tadić* Appeals Chamber Judgment (n 12), para 227.
134 ibid, para 228 (emphasis in original).
135 ibid, para 220.
136 *Prosecutor v Karadžić* (Decision on prosecution's motion appealing trial chamber's decision on JCE III foreseeability) ICTY-95-5/18-AR72.4 (25 June 2009), para 19; *Prosecutor v Karadžić* (Judgement) MICT-13-55-A (20 March 2019), paras 431-37; *Milutinović et al* Appeals Chamber Decision on Jurisdiction 2003 (n 117), para 18; *Karemera et al v The Prosecutor* (Decision on Jurisdictional Appeals: Joint Criminal Enterprise) ICTR-98-44-AR72.5, ICTR-98-44-AR72.6 (12 April 2006), para 13; *Prosecutor v Prlić et al* (Judgement)

The ICTY also convicted the accused for JCE III liability in other cases: *Krstić, Babić, Stakić, Martić, Krajišnik, Šainović et al, Đorđević, Popović et al, Stanišić & Simatović*, and the recent *Stanišić & Župljanin* cases.[137] The customary status of JCE liability is confirmed, directly or indirectly, by subsequent ICTR cases.[138]

ICTY-04-74-T (29 May 2013), Vol 1, para 220; *Prosecutor v Đorđević* (Judgement) ICTY-05-87/1-A (27 January 2014), paras 48-53. For commentators' critics, see M. Boot, *Genocide, Crimes Against Humanity, War Crimes: Nullum Crimen Sine Lege and the Subject Matter Jurisdiction of the International Criminal Court* (Intersentia 2008) 597; A. Zahar and G. Sluiter, *International Criminal Law: A Critical Introduction* (OUP 2008) 221–57; J.D. Ohlin, 'Three Conceptual Problems with the Doctrine of Joint Criminal Enterprise' (2007) 5 *JICJ* 69; K. Ambos, 'Joint Criminal Enterprise and Command Responsibility' (2007) 5 *JICJ* 159; E. van Sliedregt, 'Joint Criminal Enterprise as a Pathway to Convicting Individuals for Genocide' (2007) 5 *JICJ* 184; A. Cassese, 'The Proper Limits of Individual Responsibility under the Doctrine of Joint Criminal Enterprise' (2007) 5 *JICJ* 109; A. Bogdan, 'Individual Criminal Responsibility in the Execution of a "Joint Criminal Enterprise" in the Jurisprudence of the *ad hoc* International Tribunal for the Former Yugoslavia' (2006) 6 *ICLR* 63, 119; S. Powles, 'Joint Criminal Enterprise: Criminal Liability by Prosecutorial Ingenuity and Judicial Creativity?' (2004) 2 *JICJ* 606, 615–18. For a summary of critics, see Boas *et al* (n 8); Ambos (n 4) 123–27.

137 *Krstić* Trial Chamber Judgment (n 119), para 616; *Prosecutor v Krstić* (Judgement) ICTY-98-33-A (1 July 2003), paras 144, 151; *Šainović et al* Trial Chamber Decision 2003 (n 119), 6–7; *Prosecutor v Babić* (Sentencing Judgement) ICYT-03-72-S (29 June 2004), para 33; *Stakić* Appeals Chamber Judgment (n 9), para 87; *Prosecutor v Martić* (Judgement) ICTY-95-11-A (8 October 2008), para 80; *Prosecutor v Krajišnik* (Judgement) ICTY-00-39-A (17 March 2009), paras 215-18; *Prosecutor v Šainović et al* (Appeal Judgement) ICTY-05-87-A (23 January 2014), para 1157; *Đorđević* Appeals Chamber Judgment (n 136), para 81; *Prosecutor v Popović et al* (Judgement) ICTY-05-88-A (30 January 2015), paras 1672, 1674; *Prosecutor v Stanišić & Simatović* (Judgement) ICTY-03-91-A (9 December 2015), para 77; *Prosecutor v Stanišić & Župljanin* (Judgement) ICTY-08-91-A (6 March 2016), para 599. For an analysis of the *Krstić* case, see H. Van der Wilt, 'Joint Criminal Enterprise: Possibilities and Limitations' (2007) 5 *JICJ* 91, 97–98.

138 *The Prosecutor v Karemera et al* (Decision on the Preliminary Motions by the Defence of Edouard Karemera *et al*, Challenging Jurisdiction in Relation to Joint Criminal Enterprise) ICTR-98-44-T (11 May 2004), para 38; *Karemera et al v The Prosecutor* (Decision on Jurisdictional Appeals: Joint Criminal Enterprise) ICTR-98-44-AR72.5, ICTR-98-44-AR72.6 (12 April 2006), paras 14-17; *Karemera et al v The Prosecutor* (Decision on Interlocutory Appeal of Edouard Karemera *et al* against Oral Decision of 23 August 2010) ICTR-98-44-AR50 (24 September 2010), para 16; *Rwamakuba v The Prosecutor* (Decision on Interlocutory Appeal on Joint Criminal Enterprise to the Crimes of Genocide) ICTR-98-44-AR72.4 (22 October 2004), paras 10, 17; *The Prosecutor v Uwinkindi* (Decision on Defence Appeal against the Decision Denying Motion Alleging Defects in the Indictment) ICTR-01-75-AR72 (C) (16 November 2011), paras 11-12; *Mugenzi & Mugiraneza v The Prosecutor* (Judgement) ICTR-99-50-A (4 February 2013), fn 290; *Nizeyimana v The Prosecutor* (Judgement) ICTR-00-55C-A (29 September 2014), para 325; *Ngirabatware v The Prosecutor* (Judgement) MICT-12-29-A (18 December 2014), para 249; *Karemera & Ngirumptse v The Prosecutor* (Judgment) ICTR-98-44-A (29 September 2014), para 623.

Both the Special Tribunal for Lebanon (STL) and the Special Court for Sierra Leone (SCSL) also supported JCE liability.[139] JCE liability has been crystallised into an international liability theory and has frequently been endorsed as a firmly established rule under customary law,[140] despite controversy about the customary status of JCE III.[141]

Cases of JCE I/II may be illustrations of traditional civil law co-perpetration at the executive level. Judge Schomburg claimed that JCE I is similar to co-perpetration in article 25(3)(a) of the Rome Statute.[142] Judge Lindholm also said that JCE I was 'nothing more than a new label affixed to a since long well-known concept or doctrine in most jurisdictions as well as in international criminal law, namely co-perpetration'.[143] In additional to this, the expression of 'joint criminal enterprise' can also be found in the UK's common law doctrine of joint enterprise (venture).[144] The UK joint enterprise doctrine requires the existence of a plurality of persons comprising the accused, regardless of whether they shared a common purpose.[145] In the context of an accused act with an implicit or explicit agreement, *Tadić* JCE I is similar to two categories of the UK joint enterprise, in which the accused jointly with the executor commits a single crime or the accused assists or encourages the executor to commit a crime. *Tadić* JCE III is also similar to one derivation of the UK joint enterprise or parasitic accessory liability, in which the accused and the

---

139   Interlocutory Decision on the Applicable Law: Terrorism, Conspiracy, Homicide, Perpetration, Cumulative Charging, STL-11/01/1 (16 February 2011), paras 237, 244-49; *Prosecutor v Brima et al* (Judgment, A Ch) SCSL-2004-16-A (22 February 2008), paras 66-87; *Prosecutor v Sesay et al* (Judgment, A Ch) SCSL-2004-15-A (26 October 2009), paras 98-110.
140   Van Sliedregt (n 23) 9; *Furundžija* Trial Chamber Judgment (n 120), para 216; *Tadić* Appeals Chamber Judgment (n 12), paras 185-229.
141   Schabas (n 28) 566–67; Ambos (n 4) 172–76.
142   *Gacumbitsi* Appeals Chamber Judgment (n 3) (Separate Opinion of Judge Schomburg on the Criminal Responsibility of the Appellant for Committing Genocide), para 25; *Simić et al* Trial Chamber Judgment (n 117) (Separate and Partly Opinion of Judge Per-Johan Lindholm), para 2; A. Cassese et al (eds), *Cassese's International Criminal Law* (3rd end, OUP 2013) 175.
143   *Simić et al* Trial Chamber Judgment, ibid.
144   UK, House of Commons Justice Committee, 'Report on Joint Enterprise, Eleventh Report of Session 2010–12' (11 January 2012); UK, House of Commons Justice Committee, 'Report on Joint Enterprise, Fourth Report of Session 2014–15' (10 December 2014); *Gacumbitsi* Appeals Chamber Judgment (n 3) (Separate Opinion of Judge Shahabuddeen), para 40; D. Ormerod and K. Laird, *Smith and Hogan's Criminal Law* (14th edn, OUP 2015) 239–61; A. Simester et al, *Simester and Sullivan's Criminal Law: Theory and Doctrine* (5th edn, Hart 2013) 232–49; *Karadžić* Appeals Chamber Judgement (n 136), paras 425-32.
145   UK, 'CPS Guidance On: Joint Enterprise Charging Decisions', December 2012, paras 4-11.

executor participated in one crime but the executor committed a second crime in carrying out the offence of the first crime.[146] The *Tadić* Appeals Chamber appears to have relied on the UK joint enterprise liability to depict JCE I, JCE II and JCE III.[147]

The *Tadić* Appeals Chamber, however, was not confronted with a comparable situation as the ICC was in the *Katanga & Ngudjolo* case. The formulation of JCE in *Tadić*, as a description of civil law and common law liability regimes, provides that a member of an enterprise without physical involvement is held liable for a crime contemplated and physically committed by other members of the enterprise. Based on this formulation, members of an enterprise would be liable for the offences committed by their co-perpetrators who shared the common plan related to a crime and participated in the commission of that crime.[148] By contrast, indirect co-perpetration requires no shared agreement between the accused and direct perpetrators, nor the same membership of direct perpetrators as the accused. Therefore, cases based on the *Tadić* formulation of JCE are not relevant to the analysis of the customary status of indirect co-perpetration at the leadership level.

6.5.2   *Indirect (Co-)perpetration in the UN* Ad Hoc *Tribunals*

Scenarios similar to that in the *Katanga & Ngudjolo* case occurred in subsequent ICTY and ICTR cases. This subsection surveys their practice about indirect co-perpetration.

6.5.2.1   Co-perpetratorship in *Stakić*: 2003 Trial Chamber Judgment and 2006 Appeals Chamber Judgment

The Trial Chamber of the ICTY in the *Stakić* case relied on 'co-perpetratorship' liability to convict the accused.[149] In this case, the accused Stakić was a civilian leader of the Prijedor Municipal Crisis Staff in Bosnia and Herzegovina. Murder, extermination and other atrocities were committed against non-Serbs in Prijedor by members of Crisis Staffs, the police and the army acting in coordination to achieve the goal of establishing a Serb controlled territory. The prosecution charged Stakić on the basis of participation in a joint criminal enterprise. The defence argued that participation in a JCE was limited to

---

146   *R v Chan Wing-siu* (21 June 1984) [1985] 1 AC 168, [1984] UKPC 27, 8; J. Smith, 'Criminal Liability of Accessories: Law and Law Reform' (1997) 113 *LQR* 453.

147   *Tadić* Appeals Chamber Judgment (n 12), paras 201, 203. Cf. *Karadžić* Appeals Chamber Judgement (n 136), paras 433-36.

148   *Milutinović et al* Appeals Chamber Decision on Jurisdiction 2003 (n 117), paras 25-56.

149   *Stakić* Trial Chamber Judgment (n 32), para 468.

participating directly, or being present at the commission of the crime, or acting in furtherance of a system.[150]

The Trial Chamber firstly held that 'joint criminal enterprise is only one of several possible interpretations of the term "commission"' and that other definitions of co-perpetration should be considered.[151] The Chamber defined the term 'commission' as that 'the accused participated, physically or otherwise directly or indirectly, in the material elements of the crime charged through positive acts or, based on a duty to act, omissions, whether individually or jointly with others'.[152] In addition, the Chamber addressed that:

> For co-perpetration it suffices that there was an explicit agreement or silent consent to reach a common goal by coordinated co-operation and joint control over the criminal conduct. [...] [T]he accused must also have acted in the awareness of the substantial likelihood that punishable conduct would occur as a consequence of coordinated co-operation based on the same degree of control over the execution of common acts. Furthermore, the accused must be aware that his own role is essential for the achievement of the common goal.[153]

The Trial Chamber found that Stakić shared joint control over these offences with his co-perpetrators (associates) who were in charge of the Crisis Staff, the police and the army. In its view, Stakić and his co-perpetrators acted with a mutual awareness that crimes would occur in the course of achieving the common goal. The accused Stakić, as a (co-)perpetrator behind the direct perpetrators was held liable for the crimes committed by his co-perpetrators.[154] According to Judge Schomburg, the presiding judge in this case, 'co-perpetratorship' was a part of customary law.[155]

Neither the accused nor the prosecutor appealed the decision on this liability issue. The *Stakić* Appeals Chamber, however, intervened in examining this liability to avoid uncertainty and to ensure respect for the consistency and coherence in the application of law. Based on factual findings in the Trial Chamber judgment, the Appeals Chamber convicted Stakić on the basis of

---

150 ibid, paras 429.
151 ibid, paras 438.
152 ibid, para 439 (citations omitted).
153 ibid, paras 440, 442.
154 ibid, paras 468-98, 629.
155 *Simić et al* Appeals Chamber Judgment (n 42) (Dissenting Opinion of Judge Schomburg), paras 9-23 and fn 20.

JCE.[156] The Appeals Chamber expressly rejected indirect (co-)perpetration liability because it did not form part of customary law.[157]

Scholars differ on the understanding of *Stakić's* co-perpetratorship liability. Some commentators argued for a limited reading of the co-perpetratorship in *Stakić*.[158] In their view, the prosecutor and the Trial Chamber in *Stakić* did not aim to construe co-perpetratorship to impose liability on Stakić for crimes 'committed by/attributable to' his co-perpetrators, who used the physical perpetrators to commit crimes. Due to this restrictive definition, *Stakić's* co-perpetratorship is different from indirect co-perpetration, in which the accused's co-perpetrators used the physical perpetrators. The rejection of the restricted customary status of co-perpetratorship in the *Stakić* Appeals Chamber judgment, therefore, does not affect further prosecution based on indirect co-perpetration.[159]

Another view seems to be more persuasive. This view claims that a broad reading of co-perpetratorship was confirmed in *Stakić*.[160] The *Stakić* Trial Chamber judgment and its factual analysis implicitly confirmed the finding that an accused might be held liable as a 'perpetrator behind perpetrators' for the crimes attributable to his/her co-perpetrators. The Trial Chamber recognised a broad interpretation of co-perpetration to attribute liability to the accused for their 'indirect' perpetration 'through acts jointly with others'. This broad understanding of co-perpetratorship is similar to the ICC's idea of indirect co-perpetration, although their mental elements are different.

In rejecting the customary status of co-perpetratorship, it is unclear whether the *Stakić* Appeals Chamber bore in mind a narrow or broad understanding of co-perpetratorship for lack of its reasoning on this point. At the very least, the *Stakić* Appeals Chamber did not recognise liability labelled 'co-perpetratorship' or 'indirect co-perpetration' but used the term 'JCE'. In light of the *Stakić* Appeals Chamber judgment, the ICTY prosecution amended several indictments.[161] For instance, the prosecution amended its indictment in *Popović et al* by replacing 'direct and/or indirect co-perpetration' with JCE

---

156 *Stakić* Appeals Chamber Judgment (n 9), paras 61-98, 104.
157 ibid, paras 59, 62.
158 Boas *et al* (n 8) 121–22.
159 ibid.
160 Cassese *et al* (eds) (n 142) 179.
161 *Prosecutor v Gotovina et al* (Decision on Prosecution's Consolidated Motion to Amend the Indictment and Joinder) ICTY-03-73-PT, ICTY-01-45-PT (14 July 2006), paras 25-26; *Prosecutor v Prlić et al* (Decision on Petković's Appeal on Jurisdiction) ICTY-04-74-AR72.3 (23 April 2008), para 21. For more analysis of these cases, see Boas *et al* (n 8) 104-23.

liability. The Trial Chamber allowed that amendment.[162] These amendments at least support the view that JCE, in effect, was used as a substitute for indirect co-perpetration for the crime committed by the physical perpetrators, who were outside the enterprise as the accused and were used by the accused's fellow co-perpetrators.

6.5.2.2 Indirect Co-perpetration: 2006 *Milutinović et al* Trial Chamber Decision

The *Stakić* Appeals Chamber did not give any reasons for its finding on the customary status of indirect co-perpetration as the *Milutinović et al* Trial Chamber did. In the *Milutinović et al* case, deportations, murders and other offences were committed by members of the forces of FRY and Serbia in the course of the expulsion of the Kosovo Albanian populations. Those accused were either civilian or military commanders of FRY and Serbia. In the indictment, where the physical perpetrators were not participants in the JCE, the accused were charged based on indirect co-perpetration, as an alternative form of liability, for their 'joint control over the criminal conduct of forces of the FRY and Serbia'. The mental element of indirect co-perpetration in *Milutinović et al* was identical to that of co-perpetratorship in the *Stakić* Trial Chamber judgment.[163] Indirect co-perpetration in this way allows the prosecution to attribute liability to the accused for indirect commission of crimes through persons who do not form part of the accused's group.

One of the accused, Ojdanić, challenged the 'indirect co-perpetration' form of responsibility for its lack of basis in the ICTY Statute or in customary international law. He argued that 'there is insufficient *opinio juris* in respect of indirect co-perpetration'.[164] Also, the accused submitted that indirect co-perpetration is not enshrined in article 25(3)(a) of the Rome Statute. State practice did not exist in 1992 to substantiate the existence of indirect co-perpetration under customary law.[165] The prosecution relied on the *Stakić* Trial Chamber judgment to support its indictment of indirect co-perpetration and

---

162 *Prosecutor v Popović et al* (Decision on Motions Challenging the Indictment pursuant to Rule 72 of the Rules) ICTY-05-88-PT (31 May 2006), paras 17, 22.
163 *Prosecutor v Milutinović et al* (Prosecution's Notice of Filing Amended Joinder Indictment and Motion to Amend the Indictment with Annexes) ICTY-05-87-PT (16 August 2005), paras 18-23; *Prosecutor v Milutinović et al* (Decision on Dragoljub Ojdanić's Motion Challenging Jurisdiction: Indirect Co-perpetration) ICTY-05-87-PT (22 March 2006), para 11.
164 *Milutinović et al* Trial Chamber Decision on Indirect Co-perpetration 2006, ibid, para 28.
165 ibid, para 29.

argued that 'indirect co-perpetration is part of customary international law or a general principle of law'.[166]

The Trial Chamber in the *Milutinović et al* case considered whether a customary rule of indirect co-perpetration existed at the relevant time.[167] The Chamber first narrowed down its question for examination. The Chamber said that:

> [It] will not perform an exhaustive investigation of all the available sources in order to ascertain what forms of responsibility exist in customary international law that might arguably be given the label 'indirect co-perpetration' [...]. Instead, the Chamber will limit its analysis to the more focused questions of whether a form of responsibility with the physical and mental elements alleged [...] existed under customary international law, [...].[168]

According to the Chamber, the 'awareness of the substantial likelihood that crimes would occur', which describes the mental element of indirect co-perpetration, is similar to that for planning or ordering liability. In its view, the *Stakić* Trial Chamber judgment in defining this formulation of the mental element may have relied on the jurisprudence of planning rather than on that element under customary law.[169] Additionally, 'indirect co-perpetration' liability had not been established as part of customary law at the critical times, despite judicial authorities in several legal systems of the world have recognised indirect perpetration and co-perpetration.[170] The Chamber dismissed that indirect co-perpetration with the specific mental element existed under customary law. As in *Stakić*, liability was imposed on the basis of JCE.

6.5.2.3 Co-perpetratorship: 2006 *Gacumbitsi* Appeals Chamber Judgment

In interpreting the term 'commission', the majority of the Appeals Chamber in two later cases of the ICTR, i.e., the *Gacumbitsi* and *Seromba* cases, accepted a broad interpretation of co-perpetration.[171] The accused in the two cases were

---

166 ibid, paras 30-31.
167 ibid, para 25.
168 ibid, para 26.
169 ibid, para 38.
170 ibid, para 39.
171 *Gacumbitsi* Appeals Chamber Judgment (n 3), paras 59-61; *Seromba* Appeals Chamber Judgment (n 42), paras 161, 171–172, rendering the decision by citing the *Gacumbitsi* judgment. For discussions on the two cases, see R.C. Clarke, 'Together Again? Customary Law and Control over the Crime' (2015) 26 *CLF* 457, 490; F.Z. Giustiniani, 'Stretching the

described either as indirect perpetrators or as co-perpetrators.[172] In *Gacumbitsi*, the Appeals Chamber held that the accused supervised and directed refugees to carry out killings as an 'integral part of the massacre plan'. The accused's supervision and direction constituted 'committing' genocide for his 'direct participation in the *actus reus* of the crime' (co-perpetratorship).[173] The same reasoning was applied in *Seromba* to charge the commission of extermination.[174] The ICTR followed *Gacumbitsi* and *Seromba* in subsequent cases.[175] In the *Simić et al* case, Judge Lindholm supported charging the accused on the basis of co-perpetration.[176] The Appeals Chamber in *Simić et al*, however, relied on JCE liability to convict the accused.[177]

In *Gacumbitsi*, Judge Schomburg in his separate opinion cited a series of national provisions, case law and scholarly works to argue that 'international criminal law has accepted co-perpetratorship and indirect perpetratorship (perpetration by means) as a form of "committing"'.[178] Article 25(3)(a) of the Rome Statute was also cited to support a conviction based on both indirect perpetration and co-perpetration. Judge Schomburg in another case further expressed his position that co-perpetration and indirect perpetration are firmly entrenched in customary law.[179] Judge Güney in his dissenting opinion argued that the majority of the Appeals Chamber departed from case law of JCE liability and adopted a novel approach of 'direct participation in the material elements of the crime' without providing an analysis of whether this form is recognised in customary law.[180] Judge Shahabuddeen, however, contended that: '[s]ince several states adhere to one theory [JCE] while several

---

Boundaries of Commission Liability: The ICTR Appeal Judgment in *Seromba*' (2008) 6 JICJ 783.

172 *Gacumbitsi* Appeals Chamber Judgment (n 3) (Separate Opinion of Judge Schomburg), para 28.
173 *Gacumbitsi* Appeals Chamber Judgment (n 3), para 60.
174 *Seromba* Appeals Chamber Judgment (n 42), paras 161-63, 171-72, 189-90.
175 *Kalimanzira v The Prosecutor* (Judgement) ICTR-05-88-A (20 October 2010), paras 218-19; *Rukundo v The Prosecutor* (Judgement) ICTR-2001-70-A (20 October 2010), paras 15-16, 38; *Prosecutor v Munyakazi* (Judgment) ICTR-97-36A-A (28 September 2011), paras 135-36.
176 *Simić et al* Trial Chamber Judgment (n 117) (Separate and Partly Opinion of Judge Per-Johan Lindholm), para 2.
177 *Simić et al* Trial Chamber Judgment (n 117), para 62.
178 *Gacumbitsi* Appeals Chamber Judgment (n 3) (Separate Opinion of Judge Schomburg), paras 2-28.
179 *Simić et al* Appeals Chamber Judgment (n 42) (Dissenting Opinion of Judge Schomburg), paras 9-23 and fn 20.
180 *Gacumbitsi* Appeals Chamber Judgment (n 3) (Partially dissenting opinion of Judge Güney), paras 2-8; *Seromba* Appeals Chamber Judgment (n 42) (Dissenting Opinion of Judge Liu), paras 7, 9, 15, 18.

other states adhere to the other theory [co-perpetration], it is possible that the required State practice and *opinio juris* do not exist so as to make either theory part of customary international law'.[181]

6.5.2.4 Observations and Summary

Jurisprudence of the ICTY and the ICTR demonstrates that indirect (co-)perpetration liability was less widely accepted by the two *ad hoc* tribunals. Rare cases of two *ad hoc* tribunals support its customary status, and some decisions have stated that indirect co-perpetration does not exist under customary law.[182] The Trial Chamber in the *Milutinović et al* case was silent on the form of liability labelled 'indirect co-perpetration' under customary law in general, but rejected indirect co-perpetration with the specific mental element.[183] In addition, rejecting indirect co-perpetration liability in these cases does not mean that the accused were not liable. Instead, JCE liability was employed to convict them. The tribunals rejected the use of the term 'indirect co-perpetration' for lack of customary basis, rather than the way of imposing liability on the accused in these scenarios. This way of solving issues in these decisions demonstrates that indirect co-perpetration and JCE deal with similar situations.

In conclusion, indirect co-perpetration with specific mental elements was not recognised as a customary rule by the ICTY. These cases ascertaining or rejecting the customary status of indirect co-perpetration confirm the way of attributing liability to the accused for the crimes committed by non-members of his/her group who were indirectly used by the accused's co-perpetrators. The ICTY labelled this mode of liability with different elements as JCE rather than indirect co-perpetration. The ICTY's formulation of JCE in these cases, in effect, is a substitute for the construction of indirect co-perpetration in general.

6.5.3 Brđanin *JCE Liability*

This subsection examines indirect co-perpetration through the lens of *Brđanin* JCE liability. In *Brđanin*, the accused was President of a 'War Presidency' of the

---

181 *Gacumbitsi* Appeals Chamber Judgment (n 3) (Separate Opinion of Judge Shahabuddeen), para 51; M. Shahabuddeen, 'Judicial Creativity and Joint Criminal Enterprise' in S. Darcy and J. Powderly (eds), *Judicial Creativity at the International Criminal Tribunals* (OUP 2010) 184–203.

182 ibid, para 40; *Stakić* Appeals Chamber Judgment (n 9), para 622; *Prosecutor v Gotovina et al* (Decision on Prosecution's Consolidated Motion to Amend the Indictment and Joinder) ICTY-03-73-PT, ICTY-01-45-PT (14 July 2006), para 26.

183 *Milutinović et al* Trial Chamber Decision on Indirect Co-perpetration 2006 (n 163), para 39.

Autonomous Region of Krajina (ARK) in Bosnia and Herzegovina. Based on JCE (I and III), Radoslav Brđanin was charged for the acts of deportation, forcible transfer of civilians and persecution committed by members of the police, the army and Serb paramilitary forces, which were used by the ARK Crisis Staff to implement a Strategy Plan of creating a separate Bosnian Serb state. Where direct perpetrators (members of the army and Serb paramilitary forces) outside the enterprise (ARK) committed the crimes, the Trial and Appeals Chambers in *Brđanin* clarified the formulation of JCE in two different ways.

6.5.3.1 JCE: 2004 *Brđanin* Trial Chamber Judgment and Subsequent Constructions

The issues of *Brđanin* JCE may be analysed in three aspects: (i) what is the size of the enterprise, small or large-scale; (ii) must the physical executors be members of the same enterprise as the accused; and (iii) is an agreement required between the accused and the physical executor?

The *Brđanin* Trial Chamber first considered that JCE liability does not apply to a large-scale enterprise, where the physical perpetrators and the accused Brđanin are far from each other.[184] After analysing the evidence, the Trial Chamber found that an enterprise between Brđanin and the executors outside ARK could not be established.[185] In its view, the prosecution failed to prove that: (i) all physical executors were members of the same JCE as Brđanin, and (ii) there was a mutual understanding or agreement between the accused and physical executors to commit a specific crime in furtherance of the common purpose.[186] The Chamber concluded that JCE was not an appropriate mode of liability to describe the responsibility of the accused and held the accused liable for aiding and abetting the crimes.[187]

This Trial Chamber judgment is an attempt to limit the application of JCE liability. Its reasoning implies that the size of the enterprise is small, that physical executors must be a part of the same JCE as the accused, and that an agreement is required between the accused and direct perpetrators. The *Brđanin* Trial Chamber rendered the judgment out of the concern that 'it is

---

184 *Brđanin* Trial Chamber Judgment (n 119), para 355.
185 ibid, paras 346-47.
186 ibid, paras 341-42, 344, 351-54. See also *Prosecutor v Krnojelac* (Judgment) ICTY-97-25-T (15 March 2002), para 84; *Brđanin & Talin* Decision on Amended Indictment 2001 (n 119), para 44; *Furundžija* Appeals Chamber Judgment (n 119), paras 120-21. *Prosecutor v Krnojelac* (Judgement) ICTY-97-25-A (17 September 2003), paras 84-97, supporting a common purpose, but rejecting a required proof of agreement.
187 *Brđanin* Trial Chamber Judgment (n 119), paras 355-56, 367-69.

inappropriate to impose liability on an accused where the link between the accused and those who physically perpetrated the crimes for which the accused is charged is too tenuous'.[188] The agreement requirement ensures a close link between the accused and direct perpetrators, thus, excluding the accused's responsibility for the crimes that occurred independently to achieve the common plan but are attributable to other JCE members.[189] In the Chamber's view, an accused is not liable for the crime directly executed by individuals outside the enterprise ARK under the liability of JCE.

However, several indictments and decisions of the ICTY dismissed the ideas implied in the *Brđanin* Trial Chamber judgment.[190] Firstly, it is argued that the size of the enterprise is irrelevant to the applicability of JCE. In some circumstances, 'crimes committed by other participants in a large-scale enterprise will not be foreseeable to an accused'.[191] But only if the mental element of foreseeability has been satisfied, JCE III applies to both small and large-scale enterprises in customary law.[192]

Secondly, the notion of membership and the shared agreement viewpoint were gradually dismissed.[193] The two issues occurred in the *Milutinović et al* case. In *Milutinović et al*, aside from indirect co-perpetration as an alternative form of responsibility as analysed above, the accused were also indicted for 'participation in a joint criminal enterprise as a co-perpetrator' for the crimes committed by the physical perpetrators who were non-participants of the JCE but were used by the participants in the JCE to implement the common plan. An accused challenged the ICTY's jurisdiction and argued that:

---

188   ibid, para 418.
189   Boas *et al* (n 8) 84–88, 89–95.
190   *Milutinović et al* Trial Chamber Decision on Indirect Co-perpetration 2006 (n 163) (Separate Opinion of Judge Iain Bonomy); *Prosecutor v Krajišnik* (Judgement) ICTY-00-39-T (27 September 2006).
191   *Karemera et al v The Prosecutor* (Decision on Jurisdictional Appeals: Joint Criminal Enterprise) ICTR-98-44-AR72.5, ICTR-98-44-AR72.6 (12 April 2006), para 17.
192   *Rwamakuba v The Prosecutor* (Decision on Interlocutory Appeal on Joint Criminal Enterprise to the Crimes of Genocide) ICTR-98-44-AR72.4 (22 October 2004), para 25; *Karemera et al* Appeals Chamber Decision on Jurisdiction 2006 (n 191), paras 12, 16-17; *The Prosecutor v Karemera et al* (Decision on Defence Motion Challenging the Jurisdiction of the Tribunal – Joint Criminal Enterprise Rules 72 and 73 of the Rules of Procedure and Evidence) ICTR-98-44-R72 (5 August 2005), paras 7, 15-16; *Krajišnik* Trial Chamber Judgment (n 190), para 876; *Milutinović et al* Trial Chamber Decision on Indirect Co-perpetration 2006 (n 163), para 22.
193   *Prosecutor v Haradinaj et al* (Amended Indictment) ICTY-04-84-PT (25 October 2006), paras 20-21; *Prosecutor v Haradinaj et al*, (Revised Second Amended Indictment) ICTY-04-84-PT (11 Jan 2007), para 29; *Krajišnik* Trial Chamber Judgment (n 190), para 883.

neither the Statute nor customary international law recognise[s] the proposition that an accused may be held responsible for his participation in a joint criminal enterprise ('JCE') where one or more of the JCE participants use persons outside the JCE to physically perpetrate the crime or crimes which constitute the JCE's common criminal purpose.[194]

The Trial Chamber simply noted that: 'the concept of JCE does not extend to circumstances in which the commission of a crime is said to have been effected through the hands of others whose *mens rea* is not explored and determined, and who are not shown to be participants in the JCE'.[195] The Chamber did not decide whether JCE liability applied in this context because these issues were not related to the tribunal's jurisdiction but to the contours of JCE liability, which were matters to be addressed at trial.[196]

Judge Bonomy, in his separate concurring opinion in *Milutinović et al*, argued that membership of the physical perpetrators in the same JCE as the accused was not necessary for the attribution of liability. Fellow members of the accused may 'order' or 'induce' non-members to commit crimes.[197] After reviewing other ICTY's jurisprudence, Judge Bonomy concluded that:

> it is not inconsistent with the jurisprudence of the Tribunal for a participant in a JCE to be found guilty of commission where the crime is perpetrated by a person or persons who simply act as an instrument of the JCE, and who are not shown to be participants in the JCE.[198]

Judge Bonomy also analysed post-World War II cases and general principles of law, and posited that where evidence established a close and direct link between the accused the physical perpetrators, the physical perpetrators' mental state for the crime was not material for the interpretation of JCE liability.[199]

---

194 *Milutinović et al* Trial Chamber Decision on Indirect Co-perpetration 2006 (n 163), para 3.
195 ibid, para 23.
196 ibid, paras 23-24. The majority of the *Popović et al* Trial Chamber followed the *Milutinović et al* approach to dismissing the request on the issue of the physical perpetrator in the JCE, see *Popović et al* Trial Chamber Decision (n 162), paras 20-22. For an analysis of this case, see M. Gatenacci, 'The Principle of Legality' in F. Lattanzi and W.A. Schabas (eds), *Essays on the Rome Statute of the International Criminal Court* (Editrice il Sirente 1999) 85–89, 91–93.
197 *Milutinović et al* Trial Chamber Decision on Indirect Co-perpetration 2006 (n 163) (Separate Opinion of Judge Iain Bonomy), paras 3-13.
198 ibid, para 13.
199 ibid, paras 14-30.

It suggests that he disagreed with the viewpoint of a requirement of 'shared agreement'. The Trial Chamber in *Krajišnik* also rejected the requirements of membership and a shared agreement.[200]

In the *Popović et al* case, the prosecution proposed replacing 'direct and/or indirect co-perpetration' with that of 'JCE with common purpose' in the indictment.[201] According to the prosecution, 'JCE with common purpose' did not require the physical perpetrators in the same JCE. The Trial Chamber allowed this amendment and missed the opportunity to discuss the membership and agreement issues, in particular, whether a shared agreement is necessary between the accused and the non-member physical perpetrators.[202] The Appeals Chamber in *Brđanin* rejected the two requirements.

6.5.3.2 The *Brđanin* Formulation of JCE: 2007 *Brđanin* Appeals Chamber Judgment

The *Brđanin* Trial Chamber judgment was appealed. The prosecutor claimed that an enterprise might exist only at a leadership level. Also, no basis supported a conclusion that the physical perpetrators must be members of the JCE, and that no requirement of agreement existed under customary law.[203] The defence submitted that the prosecutor's arguments would create new law instead of applying existing customary law.[204] Considering jurisprudence of the post-World War II tribunals and the ICTY, the *Brđanin* Appeals Chamber dismissed the Trial Chamber's findings on the size, membership and agreement issues of JCE.[205]

The Appeals Chamber held: first, that an enterprise is not static and JCE liability applies to a large-scale enterprise, including region-wide JCEs.[206] Second, to establish a link between the accused and the crime, the decisive matter is whether a member of the JCE used the physical perpetrators to further the common purpose, even if that member is not the accused and that the crime needs to be attributable to the accused's fellow member. The existence of such a link is a case-by-case issue. Thus, the physical perpetrators may be non-members of an enterprise.[207]

---

200 *Krajišnik* Trial Chamber Judgment (n 190), paras 883-84, 1082, 1085. For an analysis of this decision, see Boas *et al* (n 8) 100–03.
201 *Popović et al* Trial Chamber Decision (n 162), para 11.
202 ibid, para 21.
203 *Brđanin* Appeals Chamber Judgment (n 119), paras 367-70, 377-82.
204 ibid, paras 371-73, 383-84.
205 ibid, paras 393-404, 411, 418-19.
206 ibid, paras 420-25; *Krajišnik* Trial Chamber Judgment (n 190), para 876; *Kvočka et al* Trial Chamber Judgment (n 119), para 307.
207 *Brđanin* Appeals Chamber Judgment (n 119), paras 367, 410-15, 430.

Third, an agreement to commit a specific crime is not required between the accused and the (non)-member physical perpetrators. According to the Appeals Chamber, if the physical executor is a JCE member, an agreement requirement is superfluous for JCE I because that member has already shared the common purpose. However, if the physical perpetrator is a non-member of the JCE, the accused and his/her fellow members must share an intent to further that crime. In the latter situation, the key issue is whether 'the crime forms part of the common purpose', which is an evidential matter rather than a legal requirement.[208] The mental element of JCE III is that the accused has foreseen the commission of the offence. The Appeals Chamber dismissed an agreement between the non-member physical perpetrator and the accused. Judge Van den Wyngaert in her declaration also took a view similar to that of the majority on these issues.[209]

The *Brđanin* Appeals Chamber held that:

> [The accused] has the intent to commit a crime, he has joined with others to achieve this goal, and he has made a significant contribution to the crime's commission. Pursuant to the jurisprudence, which reflects standards enshrined in customary international law when ascertaining the contours of the doctrine of joint criminal enterprise, he is appropriately held liable not only for his own contribution, but also for those actions of his fellow JCE members that further the crime (first category of JCE) or that are foreseeable consequences of the carrying out of this crime, if he has acted with *dolus eventualis* (third category of JCE). It is not decisive whether these fellow JCE members carried out the *actus reus* of the crimes themselves or used principal perpetrators who did not share the common objective.[210]

The centre of the three aspects of JCE in *Brđanin* seems to be the dismissal of an agreement between the accused and the physical perpetrators. The formulation of JCE in *Brđanin* appears to deconstruct the basis of JCE: common purpose or joint intention.[211] Dissenting opinions were expressed on this *Brđanin* formulation of JCE. Judge Meron declined to rely on the expansive employment of JCE liability to hold the accused liable for a crime attributable

---

208 ibid, paras 415-19.
209 *Brđanin* Appeals Chamber Judgment (n 119) (Declaration of Judge Van den Wyngaert), para 1.
210 *Brđanin* Appeals Chamber Judgment (n 119), para 431.
211 Ohlin (n 84).

to another JCE member.[212] Judge Shahabuddeen disagreed with the majority on the membership issue and restricted the application of JCE. In his view, an agreement between the accused and physical perpetrators is required, while an individual would be considered as a member of the JCE if s/he 'acquiesces in the JCE and perpetrates the crime within its common purpose'.[213] In this logic, the physical perpetrators would be considered as members in a large-size JCE if the enterprise were sufficiently large.[214] These controversies also indicate the difficulty in attributing liability to an accused at the leadership level, who has no personal contact with these perpetrators and victims, for a crime committed by the physical perpetrators at the executive level.

6.5.3.3 Observations and Summary

The *Brđanin* formulation of JCE shows a trend of expanding the application of JCE liability at the ICTY. It should be noted that the factual scenarios in the *Brđanin* case were different from the circumstance in the *Tadić* case. In the *Tadić* case, the accused was a reserve police officer and Tadić's enterprise comprised a small group of active participants. By contrast, Brđanin was a political figure at the leadership level, Brđanin's alleged enterprise co-participants at the leadership level were also not physically involved in the crimes, and the lower-ranking members of the army and Serb paramilitary forces were not participants in his enterprise. If the physical perpetrators did belong to the same enterprise as the accused, it is presumed that they shared the common purpose of the enterprise.[215] If the physical perpetrators are non-members of the accused's enterprise, but have reached an agreement with the accused to commit a crime in furthering a common plan of the accused's enterprise, this construction of JCE remains within the scope of *Tadić* JCE.

The *Brđanin* formulation of JCE, however, went further. *Brđanin* JCE removed the membership requirement, which is in nature a dismissal of a preliminary agreement between the accused and the physical perpetrators. In addition, a common purpose is not required when the person is a non-member of the accused's enterprise. By virtue of *Brđanin* JCE, an accused is held liable for crimes committed by non-members of the same JCE, who were merely 'used' by the accused's fellow members of the JCE and shared no common purpose with the accused to commit the crimes. The essential link of this liability is

---

212 *Brđanin* Appeals Chamber Judgment (n 119) (Separate Opinion of Judge Meron), paras 6-8.
213 ibid (Partly Dissenting Opinion of Judge Shahabuddeen), paras 2-18.
214 ibid, paras 2, 4.
215 For discussions on the membership, see C. Farhang, 'Point of No Return: Joint Criminal Enterprise in *Brđanin*' (2010) 23 *LJIL* 137, 153.

that the accused's fellow members in the JCE acted with a common plan when using the physical perpetrators as tools. In this way, *Brđanin* JCE is employed to impute liability to the accused at the leadership level of that enterprise for the crimes committed by these non-member physical perpetrators.

The *Brđanin* formulation of JCE opens the door to hold leaders liable. *Brđanin* JCE enables convictions of all other members at intermediate and low levels of the enterprise. It also provides a way to prosecute masterminds who are far from the physical perpetrators and the crime. *Brđanin* JCE has been called 'leadership level' JCE, which is a new form of liability.[216] As shown above, *Brđanin* JCE holds the leader of an enterprise without physical involvements to be legally responsible for a crime perpetrated by persons who were used by the accused's fellow members. Also, the accused's fellow members are not limited to those who committed the crime directly and physically by themselves. It suffices that the fellow members indirectly 'used' others to commit the crime in accordance with the common plan. Furthermore, the crimes committed may either form part of or exceed the common plan; and, the physical perpetrators need not be a member of the accused's enterprise, nor share an understanding with the accused. The Appeals Chamber in *Brđanin* viewed the leadership level JCE as a reflection of customary law.[217]

Subsequent jurisprudence of the ICTY and the ICTR has endorsed *Brđanin* JCE and further clarified its construction.[218] In *Đorđević*, the defendant

---

216   H. Olásolo, *The Criminal Responsibility of Senior Political and Military Leaders as Principals to International Crimes* (Hart Publishing 2009) 182–84, 202–07, 227; Van Sliedregt (n 23) 136, 157.

217   *Brđanin* Appeals Chamber Judgment (n 119), para 431.

218   For confirming the physical perpetrators as non-JCE members, see ibid, para 367; *Prosecutor v Haradinaj et al* (Third Amended Indictment) ICTY-04-84-PT (7 September 2007), paras 25-29; *Prosecutor v Limaj et al* (Judgement) ICTY-03-66-A (27 September 2007), para 120; *Martić* Appeals Chamber Judgment (n 137), paras 168-169; *Krajišnik* Appeals Chamber Judgment (n 137), paras 664-65; *Prosecutor v Gotovina & Markač* (Judgement) ICTY-06-90-A (16 November 2012), para 89; *Haradinaj et al* Retrial Judgment (n 119), para 618; *Prlić et al* Appeals Chamber Judgment (n 119), Vol 1, paras 218-19; *Đorđević* Appeals Chamber Judgment (n 136), paras 72, 165; *Karemera & Ngirumptse* Appeals Chamber Judgment (n 138) (Partially Dissenting Opinion of Judge Tuzmukhamedov), para 14; *Ngirabatware* Appeals Chamber Judgment (n 138), para 325.

For endorsing the dismissal of an agreement requirement, see *Kvočka et al* Appeals Chamber Judgment (n 17), para 168; *Martić* Appeals Chamber Judgment (n 137), paras 171-72, 195; *Krajišnik* Appeals Chamber Judgment (n 137), paras 225-26, 235-36; *Haradinaj et al* Retrial Judgment (n 119), para 621; *Prosecutor v Karadžić* (Judgement) ICTY-95-5/18-AR98BIS.1 (11 July 2013), para 79; *Prosecutor v Stanišić & Simatović* (Judgement) ICTY-03-69-T (20 May 2013), para 1259; *Prlić et al* Trial Chamber Judgment (n 136), Vol 1, paras 202-05, 210, 220; *Šainović et al* Appeals Chamber Judgment (n 137), paras 1256-60; *Đorđević* Appeals Chamber Judgment (n 136), para 165; *Popović et al* Trial Chamber Decision (n

submitted that in the leadership cases *Brđanin* JCE was not clearly established in customary law when the physical perpetrators are not members of the JCE.[219] Also, it was argued that *Brđanin* JCE was 'indirect co-perpetration by another name'.[220] The Appeals Chamber rejected the first argument because there is no cogent reason for it to depart from its consistent jurisprudence.[221] The second argument was also dismissed. The Appeals Chamber did not clarify the meaning of 'use' in the *Brđanin* formulation of JCE but held that it is not equivalent to 'the use of a tool'. Other chambers tried to identify how the accused members 'used the forces' to which these physical perpetrators belonged.[222] The Appeals Chambers in *Martić* employed the approach of 'control over the armed force' to identify the essential link of 'acted with common purpose' to establish *Brđanin* JCE liability.[223] Relying on the 'control over the armed force' approach, the Chamber concluded that Martić's fellow members acted with the common purpose when they used the members of another armed force to carry out the crimes.[224] The *Brđanin* formulation of JCE, thus, also tends to cover using 'the armed forces' or 'organisation' as a way of 'use'. Despite a missing reference to the notion of indirect perpetration (through an organisation), the ICTY in some cases, in effect, combined *Tadić* JCE with indirect perpetration to attribute liability to the accused at the leadership level.[225]

The *Brđanin* formulation of JCE seems to cover a scenario similar to what occurred in the *Katanga & Ndjudjlo* case.[226] At the ICTY, *Brđanin* JCE dates from 2007. In 2008, the Pre-Trial Chamber of the ICC in *Katanga & Ndjudjlo* introduced indirect co-perpetration. The Chamber held that indirect

---

162), para 1050; *Stanišić & Župljanin* Appeals Chamber Judgment (n 137), para 119; *Prosecutor v Mladić* (Judgment) ICTY-09-92-T (22 November 2017), para 3561; *Prlić et al* Appeals Chamber Judgment (n 119), Vol II, paras 584-91; *Karemera & Ngirumptse* Appeals Chamber Judgment (n 138), para 605.

219 *Prosecutor v Đorđević* (Vlastimir Đorđević's Appeal Brief) ICTY-05-87/1-A (15 August 2011), para 75.

220 *Đorđević* Appeals Chamber Judgment (n 136), para 61 and fn 194.

221 ibid, paras 59-72.

222 ibid, paras 63, 165; *Brđanin* Appeals Chamber Judgment (n 119), paras 412-13, 418; *Martić* Appeals Chamber Judgment (n 137), paras 168-69; *Krajišnik* Appeals Chamber Judgment (n 137), paras 225-26.

223 *Martić* Appeals Chamber Judgment (n 137), paras 169, 187; *Stakić* Appeals Chamber Judgment (n 9), paras 59, 62-63, 79-85; *Đorđević* Appeals Chamber Judgment (n 136), paras 69, 165.

224 *Milutinović et al* Trial Chamber Judgment (n 119) Vol 3.

225 Yanev (n 107) 353–57.

226 C. Meloni, 'Fragmentation of the Notion of Co-Perpetration in International Criminal Law' in C. Stahn and L.J. van den Herik (eds), *The Diversification and Fragmentation of International Criminal Law* (Brill | Nijhoff 2012) 498–99.

co-perpetration is encompassed in the Rome Statute. One reason why the Pre-Trial Chamber in this case employed 'indirect co-perpetration' rather than the expression of '*Brđanin* JCE', which is said to be enshrined under customary law, to depict liability for 'joint commission of a crime through one or more persons', might be that the Chamber was aiming at legal consistency.[227] In a preceding decision, the *Lubanga* Pre-Trial Chamber employed the 'widely recognised' theory of 'control over the act' in interpreting perpetration.[228] The *Lubanga* Pre-Trial Chamber deemed JCE a liability derived from a purely subjective approach, which requires a shared intent and neglects objective factors relating to the commission of the crime.[229] Therefore, the Pre-Trial Chamber in *Katanga & Ndjudjlo* adhered to the control theory and did not employ the subjective-oriented *Brđanin* JCE liability to address the scenario.

The ICTY and the ICC have developed the concepts of *Brđanin* JCE and indirect co-perpetration. The *Brđanin* JCE is reminiscent of the rejected rulings of the ICTY on co-perpetratorship and indirect co-perpetration. The *Stakić* Appeals Chamber rejected the use of the term 'indirect co-perpetration' because of its lack of customary status with specific elements but employed JCE to hold the accused responsible. The construction of *Brđanin* JCE seems to revive the rejected indirect co-perpetration, although under the label of JCE, for crimes physically committed by an individual who is outside the enterprise.[230] Van Sliedregt writes that '[i]ndirect (co-) perpetration seems to have recently gained recognition in ICTY case law, albeit in the context of JCE liability.'[231] William Schabas also notes that the two approaches seem to 'lead to much the same result in [their] ability to facilitate convictions'.[232] Ohlin points out that they may function in a similar way to convict the accused for the crimes committed by the physical perpetrators.[233] As Lachezar Yanev's research has shown, if the standard that the physical perpetrators are deemed 'tools' is accepted, *Brđanin* JCE at the leadership level as a combination of JCE and indirect perpetration would allow to brand the JCE members as indirect

---

227   *Katanga & Ndjudjlo* Decision on Confirmation of Charges (n 7), para 486.
228   *Lubanga* Decision on Confirmation of Charges (n 40), para 330. For a discussion on the claim of 'widely recognised', see J.D. Ohlin, 'Co-Perpetration: German *Dogmatik* or German Invasion?' in C. Stahn (ed), *The Law and Practice of the International Criminal Court* (OUP 2015) 517, 523–24.
229   *Lubanga* Decision on Confirmation of Charges (n 40), para 329.
230   *Haradinaj et al* Revised Second Amended Indictment (n 193), paras 25, 29; Van Sliedregt (n 23) 158–63.
231   Van Sliedregt (n 23) 93.
232   Schabas (n 28) 568.
233   Ohlin (n 84).

co-perpetrators of the crimes committed by the non-members of the enterprise.[234] Barbara Goy points out that, compared to the *Brđanin* JCE of the ICTY, indirect co-perpetration at the ICC has 'more onerous material requirements, and different mental requirements'.[235]

With regard to the liability of an accused at the leadership level, the material elements of the two notions share some similarities: (i) a common plan between the accused and the co-perpetrators; (ii) a level of contribution to the commission of the crime; (iii) the physical perpetrators who may not belong to the same enterprise as the accused or to the organisation under direct control of the accused;[236] and (iv) no requirement of an agreement between the accused and the physical executors.[237] Differences also exist between the two notions. Indirect co-perpetration is constrained by 'the control over the act' doctrine and the 'essential contribution' requirements as opposed to *Brđanin* JCE. Indirect co-perpetration requires the joint control over the organisation and the accused's *condition sine qua non* contribution to the commission of the crime.[238] In contrast, *Brđanin* JCE requires the co-perpetrators 'acting with common purpose' and a significant contribution. The similarities and differences in the elements merit further detailed discussions but go beyond the focus of this book.[239]

The differences above indicate that the jurisprudence of the two *ad hoc* tribunals concerning *Brđanin* JCE plays less of a role in interpreting indirect co-perpetration at the ICC. The quarrels seem to be about detailed elements rather than a different way of attributing liability. Commentators debated whether the link between the accused and the physical perpetrator in *Brđanin* JCE is too loose, and proposed alternative theories and qualifications to fill a linkage gap in dealing with the *Brđanin* scenario, such as functional perpetration (perpetration by means) theory.[240] This functional perpetration idea is closely linked to indirect co-perpetration at the ICC. Furthermore, the convergences demonstrate that both liabilities allow establishing a link to charge

---

234   Yanev (n 107) 390.
235   B. Goy, 'Individual Criminal Responsibility before the International Criminal Court: A Comparison with the *Ad Hoc* Tribunals' (2012) 12 ICLR 1, 49–50.
236   *Brđanin* Appeals Chamber Judgment (n 119), para 413.
237   Van Sliedregt (n 23) 170–71.
238   *Lubanga* Decision on Confirmation of Charges (n 40), paras 342, 347.
239   Goy (n 235) 26–50; Yanev (n 107) chapters 3 and 5.
240   For discussions on alternatives in dealing with the circumstance, see Yanev (n 107) 328–94; Van der Wilt (n 137); K. Gustafson, 'The Requirement of an "Express Agreement" for Joint Criminal Enterprise Liability: A Critique of *Brđanin*' (2007) 5 JICJ 134; Cassese *et al* (eds) (n 142) 169; Steer (n 2) 339–43.

the accused at the leadership level for crimes committed by an individual who was not in the same enterprise or organisation but used by the accused's fellow members.[241] The two notions deal with a similar factual scenario: a crime was committed by physical executors at the executive level who were used by the accused's co-perpetrators at the leadership level to carry out a common plan of an enterprise/organisation, and these executors were non-members of the enterprise/organisation to which the accused belongs.

In conclusion, case law of the ICTY relating to *Brđanin* JCE evidences a departure from *Tadić* JCE but serves a similar function of indirect co-perpetration in the context where a leader is far from the physical perpetrators. After the delivery of the *Brđanin* Appeals Chamber judgment, an expansive JCE liability for international crimes has developed to deal with the scenario covered by indirect co-perpetration, although with different material and mental elements. To establish a link between the accused and the crime in this scenario, *Brđanin* JCE and indirect co-perpetration would attribute the liability to the accused for a crime committed by or imputed to his/her fellow member of the enterprise at the leadership level through a non-JCE member perpetrator at the executive level. The ICC jurisprudence and decisions of the two *ad hoc* tribunals that combined *Tadić* JCE and indirect perpetration seem to support this unique mode of liability, indirect co-perpetration, in general, but not this mode of liability with specific elements. Yet, rare practice and *opinio juris* of States acknowledge such a liability in custom as will be seen below.

6.5.4   *National Legislation and Cases*

International crimes are punishable in different ways at the national level.[242] War crimes in a State might be covered by a special law, but crimes against humanity might be punishable as an ordinary crime enumerated in a criminal code; and genocide might be covered by special provisions in a criminal code.[243] Likewise, the liability provisions in a national criminal code might apply to international crimes that were set out in the code and a special law. For example, Australia's War Crimes Act 1945, as amended in 2010, provides

---

241   A. Smeulers, 'A Criminological Approach to the ICC's Control Theory' in K.J. Heller *et al* (eds), *The Oxford Handbook of International Criminal Law* (OUP 2020) 379–81, 396–98.

242   A. Eser *et al* (eds), *National Prosecution of International Crimes*, Vols 1–7 (Ed. Iuscrim 2003–2006).

243   In some States, their penal codes cover all the three crimes, for example, Croatia, Costa Rica, Czech Republic, Estonia, Finland, Georgia, Hungary, Lesotho and Panama, Poland, Romania, Serbia and Spain, see National Implementing Legislation Database. In US and Israel, crimes against humanity are deemed ordinary criminal offence, while genocide is regulated as a special criminal offence.

that 'Chapter 2 of the Criminal Code [concerning the general principles of criminal responsibility] applies to all offences [of war crimes] against this Act'.[244] Due to different ways of national prosecution for international crimes, the applicable laws in attributing liability are mainly covered by special implementation laws, penal codes and military manuals.

In fact, some States Parties have only implemented international crimes in their criminal codes or special laws.[245] And several penal codes of non-party States of the Rome Statute only deal with ordinary crimes. These national laws are not valuable for the identification of a customary rule in this regard. The majority of national cases about ordinary crimes are also not relevant to the analysis of custom. This subsection focuses on the practice of States concerning complicity for joint commission or common purpose. It analyses attribution of liability for a crime committed by several persons in available national law (criminal codes and case law) and special implementation legislation of States to show whether indirect co-perpetration is well accepted.

6.5.4.1   National Criminal Codes and Implementation Legislation

At the national level, there are different kinds of national provisions that may be relevant to indirect co-perpetration. Firstly, some national laws provide liability for joint commission with or without prior agreement.[246] These States provide a provision similar or identical to the following paragraph that:

---

244   Australia, War Crimes Act 1945, amended 2010, § 3A; Australia, Geneva Conventions Act 1957, amended 2016, § 6A.

245   See National Implementing Legislation Database.

246   Afghanistan, Penal Code 1976, art 39(2), art 49; Australia, Criminal Code 1995, § 11.2A; Bangladesh, Penal Code 1860, amended 1973, arts 34-35, 37; Botswana, Penal Code 1964, amended 2005, § 22; Brunei Darussalam, Penal Code 1951, amended 2001, §§ 34-35, 37; Canada, Criminal Code 1985, amended 2020, § 21(2); Cook Islands, Criminal Act 1969, § 68(2); Cyprus, Criminal Code 1959, § 21; Ethiopia, Criminal Code 2005, art 38; Fiji, Crimes Decree 2009, § 46; India, Penal Code 1860, amended 2013, §§ 34-35, 37; Kenya, Criminal Code 1930, amended 2010, § 21; Kiribati, Criminal Code 1965, amended 1977, art 22; Lesotho, Penal Code 2010, amended 2012, § 26; Malaysia, Penal Code 1936, amended 2014, §§ 34-35, 37; Myanmar, Penal Code 1861, amended 2016, §§ 34-35, 37; Malawi, Penal Code 1930, § 22; Nauru, Criminal Code 1899, amended 2011, § 8; New Zealand, Criminal Code 1961, amended 2013, § 66(2); Nigeria, Criminal Code 1916, amended 1990, § 8; Pakistan, Penal Code 1860, amended 2017, §§ 34-35; Philippines, Act on Crimes against IHL, Genocide, and Other Crimes against Humanity 2009, § 8(a)(3); Papua New Guinea, Criminal Code 1974, § 8; Samoa, Crimes Act 2013, § 33(2); Seychelles, Penal Code 1955, amended 2014, § 23; Singapore, Penal Code 1871, amended 2015, §§ 34-35, 37; Solomon Islands, Penal Code 1996, amended 2016, § 22; Sri Lanka, Penal Code 1883, amended 2006, §§ 32-33, 35; Sudan, Criminal Act 1991, § 21; Tanzania, Code of Criminal Law 1945, amended 2007, § 23; Tuvalu, Penal Code 2008, § 22; Uganda, Penal Code 1950, amended 1998, § 20; UK, Penal Code 1990, amended 2014, § 20; Ukraine, Criminal Code 2001, amended 2010, art

When two or more persons form a common intention to prosecute an unlawful purpose in conjunction with one another, and in the prosecution of such purpose an offence is committed of such a nature that its commission was a probable consequence of the prosecution of such purpose, each of them is deemed to have committed the offence.[247]

These rules concerning joint commission with shared purpose are limited to joint commission of the crimes at the execution stage. They are similar to *Tadić* JCE liability, but distinct from indirect co-perpetration or *Brđanin* JCE at the leadership level. Therefore, they do not indicate the way of attributing liability as depicted by indirect co-perpetration.

Secondly, a large amount of national legislation supports the liability of co-perpetration[248] and indirect

---

28(2); Vanuatu, Penal Code 1981, amended 2016, § 31; Zambia, Penal Code 1931, amended 2011, § 22.

247 Identical provisions in Botswana, Penal Code 1964, amended 2005, § 22; Cyprus, Criminal Code 1959, § 21; Kenya, Criminal Code 1930, amended 2010, § 21; Kiribati, Criminal Code 1965, amended 1977, art 22; Nauru, Criminal Code 1899, amended 2011, § 8; New Zealand, Criminal Code 1961, amended 2013, § 66(2); Nigeria, Criminal Code 1916, amended 1990, § 8; Papua New Guinea, Criminal Code 1974, § 8; Samoa, Crimes Act 2013, § 33(2); Solomon Islands, Penal Code 1996, amended 2016, § 22; Seychelles, Penal Code 1955, amended 2014, § 23; Tanzania, Code of Criminal Law 1945, amended 2007, § 23; Uganda, Penal Code 1950, amended 1998, § 20; UK, Penal Code 1990, amended 2014, § 20; Zambia, Penal Code 1931, amended 2011, § 22.

248 More than 90 State legislation provide provisions of co-perpetration. See Afghanistan, Penal Code 1976, art 38(1); Afghanistan, Law on Combat against Terrorist Offences 2008, art 18; Armenia, Criminal Code 2003, amended 2013, art 41(2); Andorra, Penal Code 2005, amended 2008, art 21; Austria, Criminal Code 1974, amended 2015, § 12; Azerbaijan, Criminal Code 1999, amended 2020, arts 32.2, 33.2; Bahamas, Penal Code 1924, amended 2014, art 14(2); Bolivia, Criminal Code and Criminal Procedural Code 1997, amended 2010, art 20; Bosnia and Herzegovina, Criminal Code 2003, amended 2018, art 31; Burundi, Penal Code 2009, art 37(1); Belarus, Penal Code 1999, amended 2012, arts 16(1), 17; Cabo Verde, Penal Code 2003, art 25; Cambodia, Provisions relating to the Judiciary and Criminal Law and Procedure Applicable in Cambodia during the Transitional Period 1991, art 27; Cameroon, Penal Code 1967, amended 2016, art 96; Chile, Criminal Code 2011, art 15(3); China, Criminal Law 1997, amended 2020, art 25; Colombia, Penal Code 2000, art 29(2); DRC, Criminal Code 1940, amended 2004, art 21(1); Costa Rica, Penal Code 1970, amended 2002, art 45; Côte d'Ivoire, Penal Code 1981, amended 1995, arts 26, 29; Croatia, Criminal Code 1998, amended 2011, art 36(2); Cuba, Penal Code 1987, amended 1997, art 18(2)(ch); Czech Republic, Criminal Code 2009, amended 2011, § 23; Ecuador, Penal Code 1997, amended 2013, art 42; El Salvador, Penal Code 1997, amended 2010, art 33; Estonia, Penal Code 2001, amended 2014, § 21(2); Eritrea, Penal Code 2015, art 37(3); Finland, Criminal Code 1889, amended 2015, Chapter 5, § 3; Georgia, Criminal Code 1999, amended 2016, arts 22, 25(2), 27(2); Germany, Criminal Code 1998, amended 2016, § 25(2); Ghana, Criminal

perpetration.[249] Judge Schomburg argued that both co-perpetration and

---

Code 1960, art 13(2); Greece, Penal Code 1950, amended 2003, art 45; Grenada, Criminal Code 1987, amended 1993, § 14(2); Guatemala, Penal Code 1973, art 36; Guinea, Criminal Code 1998, art 52; Haiti, Penal Code 1995, art 44; Honduras, Penal Code 1983, amended 2008, art 32; Hungary, Criminal Code 1978, amended 2012, § 13(3); Iraq, Iraqi High Criminal Court Law 2005, art 15(2)(a); Iraq, Penal Code 1969, § 47(2); Iran, The Islamic Penal Code 2013, art 125; Israel, Penal Code 1977, amended 1990, § 29(b); Italy, Criminal Code 1930, amended 2017, art 113; Japan, Criminal Code 1907, amended 2006, art 60; Kazakhstan, Criminal Code 1997, amended 2014, art 29(2); Kyrgyzstan, Criminal Code 1997, amended 2006, art 30(3); Latvia, Criminal Law 1998, amended 2013, § 19; Liechtenstein, Criminal Code 1988, amended 2013, § 12; Lithuania, Criminal Code 2000, amended 2015, art 24(3); Luxembourg, Criminal Code 1879, amended 2016, art 66(1); Maldives, Penal Code 1968, amended 2004, § 10; Malta, Criminal Code 1854, amended 2016, § 45; Macedonia, Criminal Code 1996, amended 2009, art 22; Mexico, Criminal Code 1931, amended 2013, art 13(3); Moldova, Criminal Code 2002, amended 2009, art 44; Mongolia, Criminal Code 2002, art 36.2; Montenegro, Criminal Code 2003, amended 2012, art 23(2); Morocco, Penal Code 1962, amended 2016, art 128; Netherlands, Criminal Code 1881, amended 2012, § 47(1)(1); Nicaragua, Penal Code1974, amended 1998, art 24.3; Panama, Penal Code 2007, art 44; Paraguay, Penal Code 1997, art 29(2); Peru, Penal Code 1991, amended 2010, art 23; Philippines, Penal Code 1930, amended 2012, art 17(3); Poland, Criminal Code 1997, amended 2016, art 18 § 1; Portugal, Criminal Code 2006, amended 2015, art 26; Republic of Korea, Criminal Act 1953, amended 2005, art 30; Romania, Criminal Code 2009, amended 2012, art 46; Rwanda, Penal Code 1977, amended 2012, art 90; Russian Federation, Criminal Code 1996, amended 2012, arts 33(2), 34(2); Serbia, Criminal Code 2006, amended 2012, art 33; Singapore, Penal Code 1871, amended 2015, § 37; Sao Tome and Principe, Penal Code 2012, art 26(c); Spain, Criminal Code 1995, amended 2015, art 28; Slovakia, Criminal Code 2005, amended 2009, § 20; Slovenia, Criminal Code 2008, amended 2009, art 20(2); Somalia, Penal Code 1963, art 72; Tajikistan, Criminal Code 1998, arts 36(2), 37(2); Thailand, Penal Code 1956, amended April 2016, § 83; Timor-Leste, Penal Code 2009, art 30(2); Turkmenistan, Penal Code 1997, amended 2013, art 33(2); Turkey, Penal Code 2016, art 37(1); Ukraine, Criminal Code 2001, amended 2010, arts 28(1)-(2); Uruguay, Criminal Code 1933, amended 2010, art 61; Uzbekistan, Criminal Code 1994, amended 2012, art 27; Vietnam, Penal Code 1999, art 20(3); Yemen, Republican Decree for Law No 12 for the Year 1994 Concerning Crimes and Penalties, art 21.

249 More than 70 State legislation provide indirect perpetration. See Andorra, Penal Code 2005, amended 2008, art 21; Austria, Criminal Code 1974, amended 2015, § 12; Azerbaijan, Criminal Code 1999, amended 2020, art 32.2; Bahamas, Penal Code 1924, amended 2014, arts 14(1), 14(4); Belize, Criminal Code 2000, § 11(4); Bolivia, Criminal Code and Criminal Procedural Code 1997, amended 2010, art 20; Burundi, Penal Code 2009, art 20; Cabo Verde, Penal Code 2003, art 25; Chile, Criminal Code 2011, art 15(3); China, Criminal Law 1997, amended 2020, art 25; Colombia, Penal Code 2000, art 29(1); DRC, Criminal Code 1940, amended 2004, art 21(3); Costa Rica, Penal Code 1970, amended 2002, art 45; Côte d'Ivoire, Penal Code 1981, amended 1995, art 25; Croatia, Criminal Code 1998, amended 2011, art 36(1); Cuba, Penal Code 1987, amended 1997, art 18(2)(d); Czech Republic, Criminal Code 2009, amended 2011, § 22(2); Djibouti, Penal Code 1995, art 23(3); Ecuador, Penal Code 1997, amended 2013, art 42; El Salvador, Penal Code 1997, amended 2010, art 34; Estonia, Penal Code 2001, amended 2014, § 21(1); Eritrea, Penal Code 2015, art 37(1)(c);

indirect perpetration were accepted as modes of liability in customary international law.[250] However, there is certainly nothing that suggests that indirect co-perpetration as a merger of the two notions is a form of liability recognised as customary law.[251] An empirical inductive overview of these provisions in penal codes shows that they do not demonstrate an expansive understanding of (co-)perpetration or indirect perpetration to cover the form of 'joint commission through an organisation'.[252]

A special form of liability for offences of criminal association and conspiracy should be noted. The liability for criminal association stipulates that leaders/organisers of a criminal organisation (group/community/association/society)

Ethiopia, Criminal Code 2005, art 32(1)(c); Finland, Criminal Code 1889, amended 2015, Chapter 5, § 4; France, Penal Code 1994, amended 2016, § 121-7; Ghana, Criminal Code 1960, art 13(1); Georgia, Criminal Code 1999, amended 2016, art 22; Germany, Criminal Code 1998, amended 2016, § 25(1); Guatemala, Penal Code 1973, art 36; Honduras, Penal Code 1983, amended 2008, art 32; Hungary, Criminal Code 1978, amended 2012, § 13(2); Iran, The Islamic Penal Code 2013, art 128; Iraq, Iraqi High Criminal Court Law 2005, art 15(2)(a); Israel, Penal Code 1977, amended 1990, § 29(c); Italy, Criminal Code 1930, amended 2017, art 112; Kyrgyzstan, Criminal Code 1997, amended 2006, art 30(3); Liberia, Criminal Code 1976, § 3.1(a); Latvia, Criminal Law 1998, amended 2013, § 17; Liechtenstein, Criminal Code 1988, amended 2013, § 12; Lithuania, Criminal Code 2000, amended 2015, art 24(3); Luxembourg, Criminal Code 1879, amended 2016, art 66(3); Maldives, Penal Code 1968, amended 2004, § 14; Malta, Criminal Code 1854, amended 2016, § 47(b); Mexico, Criminal Code 1931, amended 2013, art 13(4); Moldova, Criminal Code a 2002, amended 2009, art 42(2); Montenegro, Criminal Code 2003, amended 2012, art 23(1); Netherlands, Criminal Code 1881, amended 2012, § 47(1)(1); Nicaragua, Penal Code 1974, amended 1998, art 24.2; Panama, Penal Code 2007, art 43; Paraguay, Penal Code 1997, art 29(1); Peru, Penal Code 1991, amended 2010, art 23; Poland, Criminal Code 1997, amended 2016, art 18 § 1; Portugal, Criminal Code 2006, amended 2015, art 26; Rwanda, Law Setting up Gacaca Jurisdictions 2001, art 51; Slovenia, Criminal Code 2008, amended 2009, art 20(1); Spain, Criminal Code 1995, amended 2015, art 28; Sri Lanka, Geneva Conventions Act 2006, §§ 2-3; Sao Tome and Principe, Penal Code 2012, art 26(a); Somalia, Penal Code 1963, art 73; Tajikistan, Criminal Code 1998, art 36(2); Turkmenistan, Penal Code 1997, amended 2013, art 33(2); Turkey, Penal Code 2016, art 37(2); Timor-Leste, Penal Code 2009, art 30(1); Togo, Criminal Code 1992, amended 2012, art 247; Ukraine, Criminal Code 2001, amended 2010, art 27(2); Uruguay, Criminal Code 1933, amended 2010, art 60(2); Uzbekistan, Criminal Code 1994, amended 2012, art 28(2); US, Criminal Justice Code 1967, § 46.3207; Venezuela, Penal Procedure Code 2009, art 124; Yemen, Republican Decree for Law No 12 for the Year 1994 Concerning Crimes and Penalties, art 21.

250 *Gacumbitsi* Appeals Chamber Judgment (n 3) (Separate Opinion of Judge Schomburg), para 21; *Simić et al* Appeals Chamber Judgment (n 42) (Dissenting Opinion of Judge Schomburg), para 14 and fn 20. For critics of the control doctrine, Yanev and Kooijmans (n 38) 808.
251 Yanev (n 107) 390, 490.
252 For a review of the domestic approach to co-perpetration liability, ibid 497–513.

are liable for all crimes committed by members of the group if the crimes committed were embraced by the intention of the accused.[253] For instance, the Criminal Code of Uzbekistan explicitly provides that: '[h]eads for crime, as well as members of a criminal group organised by the previous concert, organised criminal group, or criminal community shall be subject to liability for all crimes, of which preparation or commission they participated'.[254] The Criminal Law of the People's Republic of China (PRC) also provides that organisational leaders are criminally liable for all crimes committed by members of the organisation.[255] After analysing 43 legal systems worldwide, researchers of the Max-Planck-Institute project *General Legal Principles of International Criminal Law on the Criminal Liability of Leaders of Criminal Groups and Networks* concluded:

> A result of this comparison of the various rules of complicity is that structurally differing concepts of the doctrine of complicity yield results that are, to a large extent, functionally equivalent. [...] the classification of the organiser of a network who directs the activities from the background as the primarily responsible offender of a crime does not fail due to the fact that the person who directly commits the crime, a 'little cog in the big wheel', has no knowledge of the crime's overriding goals or of its specific character and magnitude. In contrast, the various legal systems treat very differently the issue of the attributability [...] to hierarchically superior participants of actions by individual group

---

253   Armenia, Criminal Code 2003, amended 2013, arts 38(3), 41(4)-(5); Albania, Criminal Code 1995, amended 2013, arts 27-28; Azerbaijan, Criminal Code 1999, amended 2020, art 34.6; Belarus, Penal Code 1999, amended 2012, arts 18(2), 19(4); Bosnia and Herzegovina, Criminal Code 2003, amended 2018, art 342(3); Canada, Criminal Code 1985, amended 2020, §§ 467.1, 467.13; China, Criminal Law 1997, amended 2020, art 26; Georgia, Criminal Code 1999, amended 2016, art 27(4); Honduras, Penal Code 1983, amended 2008, art 34(1); Iran, The Islamic Penal Code 2013, art 130; Kazakhstan, Criminal Code 1997, amended 2014, art 31(4); Kyrgyzstan, Criminal Code 1997, amended 2006, arts 29(3), 34(1); Latvia, Criminal Law 1998, amended 2013, § 21(2); Lithuania, Criminal Code 2000, amended 2015, art 26(4); Moldova, Criminal Code 2002, amended 2009, art 47(4); Mongolia, Criminal Code 2002, § 37.2; Russian Federation, Criminal Code 1996, amended 2012, arts 35(5); Slovenia, Criminal Code 2008, amended 2009, art 41(3); Tajikistan, Criminal Code 1998, art 39(6); Ukraine, Criminal Code 2001, amended 2010, art 30(1); Uzbekistan, Criminal Code 1994, amended 2012, art 30.
254   Uzbekistan, Criminal Code 1994, amended 2012, arts 29-30; Kazakhstan, Criminal Code 1997, amended 2014, art 31(3).
255   China, Criminal Law 1997, amended 2020, art 26(3).

members that are not (expressly) encompassed by the common crime plan.[256]

These national provisions also indicate that 'clear differences exist as far as the issue of minimum requirements regarding the *mens rea* of those who themselves remain inactive is concerned'. These laws and other legislation evidence a liability similar to the expansive interpretation of 'indirect perpetration through an organisation',[257] rather than indirect co-perpetration. These provisions do not suggest a consensus on the liability of a head of the organisation for crimes that neither are committed by members of the organisation nor fall within the scope of the common plan.

Some national legislation provides that: '[a] crime is considered committed by a criminal association, if it was committed [...] by a member (members) of the association [...], as well as, committal of a crime by a person not considered a member of the association, by instruction of the criminal association'.[258] The Criminal Code of Uzbekistan provides a similar rule and stipulates that: '[c]riminal community shall be a previous association of at least two groups for criminal activity'.[259] Combining the liability of the leaders for offences committed by a criminal association with the notion of criminal community, these provisions evince support for the construction of indirect co-perpetration (or *Brđanin* JCE I). The head of one group would be held liable for the crime committed by a person of another group. These provisions, however, do not extend to crimes that fall outside the scope of the common design. These few instances are not sufficient to support a rule of indirect co-perpetration under customary law.

Another liability for the offences of conspiracy exists in national legislation.[260] One example is the US 2010 Manual for Military Commissions, which provides that

---

256 MPICC, 'General Legal Principles of International Criminal Law on the Criminal Liability of Leaders of Criminal Groups and Networks', Project Coordination: Ulrich Sieber, Hans-Georg Koch and Jan Michael Simon <https://csl.mpg.de/en/research/projects/general-legal-principles-of-international-criminal-law-on-the-criminal-liability-of-leaders-of-criminal-groups-and-netwo/> accessed 15 January 2021.
257 T. Weigend, 'Perpetration through an Organisation: The Unexpected Career of a German Legal Concept' (2011) 9 *JICJ* 91, 106.
258 Armenia, Criminal Code 2003, amended 2013, art 41(4); Azerbaijan, Criminal Code 1999, amended 2020, art 34.5; Moldova, Criminal Code 2002, amended 2009, art 47(2); Tajikistan, Criminal Code 1998, art 39(5); Uzbekistan, Criminal Code 1994, arts 29-30.
259 Uzbekistan, Criminal Code 1994, arts 29-30; Kazakhstan, Criminal Code 1997, amended 2014, art 31(3).
260 Belize, Criminal Code 2000, § 24(1).

> Any person [...] who conspires to commit one or more substantive offences triable by military commission under this chapter, and who knowingly does any overt act to effect the object of the conspiracy, shall be punished. [...] Each conspirator is liable for all offences committed pursuant to or in furtherance of the conspiracy by any of the co-conspirators, after such conspirator has joined the conspiracy and while the conspiracy continues and such conspirator remains a party to it.[261]

These provisions on conspiracy offer a different solution to crimes committed in an organised way at the offence level, instead of at the liability level. Article 5 of the UN Convention against Transnational Organised Crime also provides for the offence of 'participation in an organised criminal group', which stipulates that the action of the heads of a criminal organisation, who plan, coordinate and manage the commission of the crimes committed, is criminalised.[262] The head of the organisation would be held liable for the crimes committed based on direct perpetration through his/her plan or coordinated actions. This provision indicates an attitude to expand the scope of responsible persons through an extensive criminalisation of offences. By contrast, the ICC tends to expand that scope through an expansive interpretation of liability because the Rome Statute does not generally criminalise all plans or coordinated actions. The practice of States in implementing this Convention against Transnational Organised Crime does not further contribute to the development of indirect co-perpetration liability at the international level.

There are more distinctions than similarities in national laws concerning liability. Some national criminal laws provide a distinction between principals (perpetrators) and accessories (accomplices), while some others do not distinguish principals from accessories.[263] The former is generally classified as a differentiation system, while the latter is called a unitary system.[264] In the unitary system, liability is attributed to an accused through criminalising actions of plan, encouragement and execution as the commission of offences. In the differentiation system, divergent approaches exist to hold an individual liable for

---

261 US, Manual for Military Commissions of 2010, Part IV Crimes and Elements, § 950v (29), IV 23–24. See also US, Military Commissions Act of 2006, 10 USC 948a, § 6(b)(1)(A); *US v Harman* (Judgment, US Army Court of Criminal Appeals) Army 20050597 (30 June 2008); Australia, War Crimes Act 1945, amended 2001, § 6(1)(k).
262 United Nations Convention against Transnational Organised Crime, 2225 UNTS 209.
263 K. Ambos, 'Is the Development of a Common Substantive Criminal Law for Europe Possible? Some Preliminary Reflections' (2005) 12 *MJECL* 173, 182–86.
264 Van Sliedregt (n 23) 65–67.

a crime committed by others, for example, JCE and complicity through association, as well as aiding and abetting liability. The above analysis of national laws indicates that without the employment of indirect co-perpetration, the accused would also not go unpunished. Taking these various regimes and approaches into consideration, it appears that indirect co-perpetration liability would not frequently be used in prosecuting international crimes.

Indeed, military manuals of States do not help much in assessing the customary status of indirect co-perpetration.[265] States Parties' special implementation legislation also does not evince the acceptance of indirect co-perpetration. Some implementation legislation of the Geneva Conventions and the 1948 Genocide Convention follows the mode of liability either in article 7 of the ICTY Statute or in that provided in the Genocide Convention.[266] Some implementation legislation merely repeats the text in article 25(3)(a) of the Rome Statute,[267] while other laws only implement the rule in article 25(3)(d) of the Rome Statute.[268] A large number of national laws and implementation legislation concerning joint commission, co-perpetration, indirect perpetration and unique forms of liability in various national jurisdictions, do not evidence the acceptance of indirect co-perpetration under customary law.

6.5.4.2   National Case Law

It appears that scarce national case law employs indirect co-perpetration in prosecuting international crimes. Canadian courts endorsed the view of complicity through association in dealing with the issue of refugee protection. The Canadian courts argued that: 'the broadest modes of commission recognised under current international criminal law are most relevant to our complicity

---

[265] For sources of military manuals concerning individual criminal responsibility, see Henckaerts and Doswald-beck (eds) (n 10), Vol II: Practice, practice concerning Rules 102 and 151. Some military manuals, see Australia, LOAC Manual 2006, § 13.39; Canada, LOAC at the Operational and Tactical Levels 2001, § 1610; Netherlands, Humanitarian Law of War Manual 2005, §§ 1147-1148; Sierra Leone, Instructor Manual 2007, at 65; UK, LOAC Manual 2004, § 16.35; US, Field Manual 2004, § 500.

[266] ICTY Mode: Australia, Geneva Conventions Act 1957, amended 2002, § 7(1); Burundi, Law on Genocide, Crimes against Humanity and War Crimes 2003, art 5; Ireland, Geneva Conventions Act 1962, amended 1998, § 4; Rwanda, Law on Repressing the Crime of Genocide, Crimes against Humanity and War Crimes 2003, art 17; UK, Geneva Conventions Act 1957, amended 1995, § 1(1).

[267] Philippines, Act on Crimes against IHL, Genocide, and Other Crimes against Humanity 2009, § 8(a)(3).

[268] ibid § 8(a)(3); Mauritius, ICC Act 2011, § 4(2)(b); Iraq, Iraqi High Criminal Court Law 2005, art 15(2)(d); Sri Lanka, Geneva Conventions Act 2006, § 2(1); UK, Geneva Conventions Act 1957, amended 1995, § 1(1).

analysis, namely, common purpose liability under art. 25(3)(d) of the Rome Statute and joint criminal enterprise developed in the *ad hoc* tribunals' jurisprudence'.[269] In the *Peters* case, the Canadian Immigration and Refugee Protection Board clarified the liability of complicity through a shared common purpose.[270] In its view, complicity liability may arise either from facilitating the organisation's mission by aiding and abetting or from 'the existence of a shared common purpose and knowledge that all parties in question may have of the purpose of the organisation'.[271] Also, the Canadian Supreme Court in *Ezokola* openly stated:

> While individuals may be complicit in international crimes without a link to a *particular crime*, there must be a link between the individuals and the *criminal purpose* of the group [...]. [T]his link is established where there are serious reasons for considering that an individual has voluntarily made a significant and knowing contribution to a group's crime or criminal purpose.[272]

With reference to the *Brđanin* Appeals Chamber judgment, the Canadian Supreme Court adhered to the *Brđanin* JCE liability. Therefore, if no shared common purpose exists between the accused and the executors, 'a significant and knowing contribution' will suffice to hold the accused liable by virtue of complicity through association. The Canadian case law cited above shows that an accused at the leadership level would be responsible for crimes committed by the executors. Depending on the facts of each case, the accused would be held liable for aiding and abetting the crimes or for complicity through the shared common purpose. The Canadian courts did not rely on article 25(3)(a) of the Rome Statute to broaden the forms of perpetration or use the label of indirect co-perpetration.

According to the UK Crown Prosecution Service, the common law doctrine of joint enterprise 'can apply where two or more persons are involved in an offence or offences. The parties to a joint enterprise may be principals (P) or secondary parties (accessories/accomplices) (D)'.[273] When a joint enterprise

---

269   *Ezokola v Canada*, [2013] 2 SCR 678, 2013 SCC 40, paras 52-67.
270   *Peters v Canada* (Record of an Admissibility Hearing under the Immigration and Refugee Protection Act, Immigration and Refugee Protection Board) 0003-B2-02557 (29 January 2013).
271   *Ramirez v Canada*, [1992] 2 FC 306, 318; *Sivakumar v Canada*, [1994] 1 FC 433.
272   *Ezokola v Canada*, [2013] 2 SCR 678, para 8 (emphasis in original).
273   UK, 'CPS Guidance On: Joint Enterprise Charging Decisions', December 2012, para 5.

is pre-planned, a category of the UK joint enterprise is similar to *Tadić* JCE. However, as analysed above, cases supporting *Tadić* JCE do not show the practice of *Brđanin* JCE in attributing liability to the person at the leadership level. Additionally, if there is no shared purpose, the accused who was convicted based on joint enterprise has to 'act' in concert, or the accused ought to be acquitted. Cases from the UK concerning joint enterprise, therefore, are not valuable evidence for the assessment of indirect co-perpetration under customary law. The UK in recent decisions re-set a threshold of the mental element of JCE III by arguing that it was 'illegitimate' 'to treat foresight as an inevitable yardstick of common purpose'.[274] According to the English courts, 'the correct approach is to treat [foresight] as evidence of intent.'[275] The accused must have intended rather than foreseen the offences that was not agreed upon but committed. This change shows a more restrictive attitude of the UK towards the expansion of responsible persons by virtue of joint enterprise.

The Administrative Appeals Tribunal of Australia has also dealt with some cases concerning international crimes attributable to refugee applicants who did not directly or physically commit offences of war crimes or crimes against humanity.[276] In the *SAH* case, the accused was a member and an administrative officer of the Iraqi Army when war crimes and crimes against humanity were committed. The Administrative Appeals Tribunal held that: 'under the Rome Statute, a person need not have directly committed the act him or herself.' The Tribunal recognised that to bear criminal responsibility, a person must have 'aided, abetted or otherwise assisted' in the commission by persons acting with a common purpose.[277] The Appeals Tribunal, however, did not rely on an interpretation of article 25(3)(a) of the Rome Statute to hold the accused liable.[278] The Tribunal in interpreting article 25(3)(d) also noted that 'there must be a *shared common purpose*, as between the perpetrator and the accomplice, to

---

274 *Jogee and Ruddock v R* (Jamaica) (Judgment) (18 February 2016) [2016] UKSC 8, [2016] UKPC 7, para 87.
275 ibid. For debates on the *Jogee* case at the ICTY, see *Karadžić* Appeals Chamber Judgement (n 136), paras 425-37.
276 Australia, War Crimes Act 1945, amended 2010, § 9(1); *AXOIB v Australia* [2002] AATA 365 (17 May 2002), para 33. For other cases after World War II, see D. Blumenthal and T. McCormack (eds), *The Legacy of Nuremberg: Civilising Influence or Institutionalised Vengeance?* (Brill | Nijhoff 2007).
277 *SAH v Australia* [2002] AATA 263 (18 April 2002), paras 58-59.
278 *SAL v Australia* [2002] AATA 1164 (2 November 2002), para 85; *VAG v Australia* [2002] AATA 1332 (23 December 2002), para 66; *SHCB v Australia* [2003] FCAFC 308 (22 December 2003), para 13; *SZCWP v Australia* [2006] FCAFC 9 (20 February 2006), para 107; *WBR v Australia* [2006] AATA 754 (5 September 2006), para 28.

engage in conduct which constitutes a crime'.[279] Currently, the Australian tribunals adhere to the narrow interpretation of *Tadić* JCE, instead of adopting *Brđanin* JCE or indirect co-perpetration.

In the DRC *Barnaba Yonga Tshopena* case, the accused was considered the supreme leader of the Ngiti combatants of this political-military movement. The Military Garrison Court held that 'in this capacity, together with other commanders of this political-military movement, he organised, planned or encouraged in any way the successive attacks.'[280] Military, police and political leaders used their power to initiate the crimes committed by executors. They were liable because they were the ones who conceived the crime.[281] This case does not support attributing liability to the accused for the crimes committed by the executors who were not affected by the accused's power. Liability of indirect co-perpetration is not rooted in this approach to attributing liability.

In the *Fujimori* case, Peru's Supreme Court of Justice examined whether former Peruvian president Alberto Fujimori was liable for crimes against humanity carried out by State officials.[282] The prosecution argued that the crimes committed could be attributed to the ex-president 'by recourse to the mode of criminal liability of perpetration-by-means'. The court held that the liability of perpetration-by-means through control over an organised apparatus of power is 'a form of commission which, however, is transferred from an order issued at the highest strategic level to the concrete execution of the ordered act by a proxy'.[283] This case only supports the interpretation of indirect perpetration through an organisation, which has been supported by several civil law criminal systems as mentioned above.[284] Kai Amobs observed that other cases in Latin American jurisdictions also supported this form of indirect

---

279 *WBR v Australia*, ibid (emphasis added).
280 *Garrison Military Auditor, Public Prosecutor's Office and civil parties v Barnaba Yonga Tshopena* (Judgment, Military Garrison Court of Ituri-Bunia, DRC) RP No 071/09, 009/010 and 074/010, RMP No 885/EAM/08, RMP No 1141/LZA/010, RMP No 1219/LZA/010 and RMP No 1238/LZA/010 (9 July 2010), para 132.
281 DRC, 'Training manual by the Prosecutor at the Military High Court for magistrates on techniques for investigating sexual crimes, adopted as part of the Programme on Investigating Sexual Crimes of the Democratic Republic of the Congo, Military Justice seminar', 2008, 8–9.
282 K. Ambos, 'The *Fujimori* Judgment, A President's Responsibility for Crimes Against Humanity as Indirect Perpetrator by Virtue of an Organised Power Apparatus' (2011) 9 JICJ 137; Ambos (n 4) 116–17.
283 *Prosecutor v Alberto Fujimori* (Judgment, Supreme Court of Justice, Special Criminal Chamber, Peru) A.V 19-2001 (7 April 2009), para 744.
284 ibid.

perpetration,[285] and that indirect co-perpetration has been employed by a Chilean court for the crime of murder.[286] The majority of these cases, thus, do not support indirect co-perpetration.[287]

National practice relating to individual criminal responsibility for war crimes, as shown in Rules 102 and 151 of the 2005 ICRC *Study*, does not show a trend of accepting indirect co-perpetration liability.[288] The analysis of case law above concerning complicity through association, aiding, abetting or assisting, complicity through a shared common purpose, joint enterprise and indirect perpetration, shows that few national cases support indirect co-perpetration, especially where the crimes committed are outside the common plan of the organisation.

6.5.5 Other International Tribunals and Special National Tribunals or Chambers: Instruments and Cases

Differences also exist in instruments in other international and national tribunals specially designed for the prosecution of international crimes. Article 15(2) of the 2005 Iraqi High Criminal Court Law is similar to article 25(3) of the Rome Statute. It provides that:

> [...] a person shall be criminally responsible if that person: A. Commits such a crime, whether as an individual, jointly with another or through another person, regardless of whether that this person is criminally responsible.[289]

The text of article 15 appears to leave no room for the tribunal to interpret a mode of liability for crimes 'by contribution via another individual'. In practice, the Iraqi High Tribunal in the *Al-Dujail* case systematically interpreted article 15(2), which addressed that:

> [...] the actor, despite his role and legal-official description, is reckoned in-charge in perpetrating one of the crimes which falls under the court's

---

285   Ambos (n 4) 114–16. For an analysis of indirect perpetration through organisation, see F. Muñoz-Conde and H. Olásolo, 'The Application of the Notion of Indirect Perpetration through Organised Structures of Power in Latin America and Spain' (2011) 9 *JICJ* 113, 114; H. Olásolo, *Essays on International Criminal Justice* (Hart Publishing 2012) 102–42.
286   Ambos (n 4) 116.
287   *Simić* Appeals Chamber Judgment (n 42) (Dissenting Opinion of Judge Schomburg), fn 32.
288   Henckaerts and Doswald-beck (eds) (n 10), practice of Rules 102 and 105.
289   Iraq, Iraqi High Criminal Court Law 2005, art 15(2)(a). For discussions on the case law of the IHT, Ambos (n 4) 141–42.

jurisdiction, whether the offender [...] committed the crime by personal attribution, contribution or via another individual, even if the latter was not criminally responsible (for any reason), enticed, urged, assisted, instigated, or helped in whatsoever mean, to facilitate the execution of the crime, provided its tools, instigated or contributed with other individuals, aiming a joint criminal contribution conditioned by premeditation and effectively granting [...].[290]

In its view, 'the legislator goes to the equilibrium of all factors contributing to create the crime's result'. All actors would be charged for perpetrating the crime, regardless of the degree of contribution to the crime.[291] This interpretation indicates that an accused would be held liable for committing the crime via another person. On the other hand, the tribunal would not attribute crimes 'jointly committed via another individual' to an accused through indirect co-perpetration, or an expansive interpretation of co-perpetration, because the accused would also be held liable as an offender based on the other way of contribution. The Iraqi High Tribunal did not follow the ICC's notion of indirect co-perpetration.

In addition, the text of section 14(3)(a) of the Regulation for Special Panels of East Timor is identical to article 25(3)(a) of the Rome Statute.[292] The Special Panels adopted diverse approaches in interpreting section 14(3)(a). The Special Panels in some cases cited the *Tadić* Appeals Chamber judgment and employed JCE to interpret liability for commission jointly with another under section 14(3)(a).[293] For instance, Salvador Soares was held 'responsible for committing the crime of murder as a crime against humanity pursuant to a joint criminal enterprise to murder the pro-independence supporters'.[294] Additionally, the Special Panels simply relied on the literal reading of the phrase 'jointly with another' for incurring co-perpetration liability of physical perpetrators.[295]

---

290   *The Public Prosecutor in the High Iraqi Court et al v Saddam Hussein Al-Majeed et al* (Verdict, Second Criminal Court, IHT)1/C Second/2006 (24 June 2007), 8.
291   ibid 128–31.
292   East Timor, Regulation for Special Panels for Serious Crimes 2000, § 14.3. For the applicable law and case law of the Special Panels, Ambos (n 4) 136–38.
293   *Prosecutor v Jose Cardoso* (Judgment, District Court of Dili) SPSC-4c/2001 (5 April 2003), paras 367-71; *Prosecutor v Salvador Soares* (Judgment, District Court of Dili) SPSC-7a/2002 (9 December 2003), paras 187-89. For decisions of joint criminal enterprise under section 14(3)(d), see *Prosecutor v Sisto Barros and Cesar Mendonca* (Judgment, District Court of Dili) SPSC-1/2004 (12 May 2005), paras 123-24, 134.
294   *Salvador Soares* Judgment, ibid, para 189.
295   *Prosecutor v João Sarmento* (Judgment, District Court of Dili) SPSC-18a/2001 (12 August 2003), paras 81-82; *Prosecutor v Domingos Mendonca* (Judgment and Dissenting Opinion,

These different approaches at a minimum do not show an expansive interpretation of co-perpetration to include indirect co-perpetration. In fact, in the Special Panels, the accused were mostly mid-to-low-level militants who participated in the killing of civilians. These cases would be less helpful for the construction of indirect co-perpetration to hold the high-level leaders responsible.

Other international instruments and case law also do not tend to support indirect co-perpetration. Bangladesh's International Crimes (Tribunal) Act 1973, as amended in 2013, provides that conspiracy to commit and complicity in the commission of international crimes are criminalised.[296] The Bangladesh tribunals criminalised the act of conspiracy and complicity, instead of attributing liability to the accused for the crimes committed by other perpetrators. Leaders are liable for the crime of conspiracy directly committed by themselves. This Act with a broad scope of offences leaves no room for the development of indirect co-perpetration liability. Also, although the Extraordinary Chambers in the Courts of Cambodia (ECCC) aims to try senior leaders, the Law on the Establishment of the ECCC provides no general rule on liability as to different crimes falling under the jurisdiction of the court.[297] In practice, the two UN ad hoc tribunals' *Tadić* JCE doctrine played a vital role in the cases of the ECCC.[298] Furthermore, article 3 of the Statute of the STL and article 6(1) of the Statute of SCSL[299] provide rules similar to those in article 7(1) of the ICTY Statute concerning liability.[300] The STL denied the customary status of perpetration by means and the application of JCE III to special intent crimes.[301] Trial Chamber I of the SCSL concurred with the opinion of the Appeals Chamber

---

District Court of Dili) SPSC-18b/2001 (12 October 2003), paras 110-02; *The Prosecutor v de Carvalho* (Judgment, District Court of Dili) SPSC-10/2001 (18 March 2004), para 61.

[296] Bangladesh, International Crimes (Tribunals) Act 1973, amended 2013, §§ 3(2)(g) – (h), 4(1).

[297] Law on the Establishment of the ECCC, 27 October 2004, arts 1-2, 4-8.

[298] L.D. Yanev, 'The Theory of Joint Criminal Enterprise at the ECCC: A Difficult Relationship' in S. Meisenberg and I. Stegmiller (eds), *The Extraordinary Chambers in the Courts of Cambodia* (TMC Asser Press 2016) 203–54; Ambos (n 4) 140–41.

[299] Statute of the SCSL, art 6(1).

[300] Statute of the Special Tribunal for Lebanon (Statute of the STL), attached to the Agreement between the United Nations and the Lebanese Republic on the Establishment of a Special Tribunal for Lebanon annexed to UN Security Council Resolution 1757, 30 May 2007, art 3(1). See Rwanda, Law Setting up Gacaca Jurisdictions 2001, art 51.

[301] M. Scharf, 'Introductory Note to the Decision of the Appeals Chamber of the Special Tribunal for Lebanon on the Definition of Terrorism and Modes of Participation' (2011) 50 *ILM* 509, 601; Interlocutory Decision on the Applicable Law: Terrorism, Conspiracy, Homicide, Perpetration, Cumulative Charging, STL-11/01/1 (16 February 2011), paras 249, 255-56; Ambos (n 4) 143.

on the *Brđanin* formulation of JCE, while its Trial Chamber II rejected the JCE doctrine.[302]

6.5.6 *Assessment and Conclusions*

The two UN *ad hoc* tribunals adopted the JCE approach. The ICTY and the ICTR first clarified and developed the liability of *Tadić* JCE. The tribunals in their subsequent cases rejected the liability of co-perpetratorship and indirect co-perpetration but introduced the liability of *Brđanin* JCE. *Brđanin* JCE has been adhered to in subsequent cases of the two tribunals. *Brđanin* JCE has also been accepted as a part of customary law by the two *ad hoc* tribunals, whereas it is highly criticised in academia. By contrast, the ICC appears to interpret article 25(3)(a) as achieving a function similar to *Brđanin* JCE by using the notion of indirect co-perpetration. It should be emphasised that legal elements of *Brđanin* JCE are different from those of indirect co-perpetration required at the ICC.

The observations above show that case law of the two *ad hoc* tribunals supporting *Tadić* JCE is irrelevant to the analysis of indirect co-perpetration. Jurisprudence based on *Brđanin* JCE, which combined *Tadić* JCE with indirect perpetration, generally supports indirect co-perpetration imposing liability on the accused at the leadership level. National criminal codes, implementation legislation and case law share more divergence than convergence, and few instances support for indirect co-perpetration. Instruments and cases of other international and national tribunals share the same feature.

These few instances of practice, as well as the ICC's adherence to indirect co-perpetration, would be helpful in the development of a similar way to attribute liability under customary law. But the liability of indirect co-perpetration is not widely recognised by States at the present time. Thus, it is inconclusive to argue that these instances suffice to evince a firmly established customary rule, in particular, with all these elements set out by the ICC. Indirect co-perpetration is not part of the corpus of customary law. Even if indirect co-perpetration is subsumed in article 25(3)(a) of the Rome Statute through subsequent practice, this provision is not declaratory of customary law concerning indirect co-perpetration.

---

302   Ambos (n 4) 139–40 and fn 310; *Prosecutor v Fofana & Kondewa* (Judgment) SCSL-2004-14-T (2 August 2007), para 216; *Prosecutor v Sesay et al* (Judgment) SCSL-04-15-A (26 October 2009), paras 394, 400.

6.6 Concluding Remarks

The way to assign liability to leaders, who are far from the scene of offences committed by physical executors, is a demanding issue in international criminal law. This chapter focused on article 25(3)(a) of the Rome Statute and indirect co-perpetration liability under customary law. The above analysis shows that article 25(3)(a) contains three forms of perpetration: direct perpetration, indirect perpetration and co-perpetration. The notion of indirect co-perpetration is not subsumed in article 25(3)(a). Nevertheless, through an interpretation of article 25(3)(a) and by relying on the idea of joint control over an organisation, the ICC introduced indirect co-perpetration to deal with a situation in which the identities of the physical perpetrators are unclear. Indirect co-perpetration is deemed a form of commission, and its legal elements derive from the elements of indirect perpetration and co-perpetration. This (interpretation) practice should not be ignored.

After analysing the post-World War II instruments and subsequent trials, this chapter observes that only few cases support indirect co-perpetration. Indirect co-perpetration was not firmly established in international criminal law before the adoption of the Rome Statute. If the crime committed falls within the scope of the common plan among the leaders, the newly developed indirect co-perpetration is very similar to part of *Brđanin* JCE I, but with different standards of material and mental elements. After analysing the cases of international and national tribunals, and national laws, the conclusion that a customary rule concerning indirect co-perpetration or an expansive construction of co-perpetration with the specific elements is emerging at the international level cannot be sustained. In conclusion, even assuming article 25(3)(a) of the Rome Statute contains indirect co-perpetration now, article 25(3)(a) is not declaratory of a customary rule on indirect co-perpetration.

CHAPTER 7

An Exception to Personal Immunity for International Crimes

Article 27(2) of the Rome Statute and Custom

7.1 Introductory Remarks

This chapter analyses the relationship between article 27(2) of the Rome Statute and customary international law on the issue of an exception to personal immunity for the commission of international crimes. Article 27(2) of the Rome Statute clearly provides that international immunities cannot bar the ICC from exercising its jurisdiction.[1] Some commentators have argued that 'the non-availability of international immunity rights *ratione materiae et personae* with respect to persons, as articulated in article 27(2), is declaratory of customary international law'.[2] In contrast, the African Union (AU) commented that under customary law sitting heads of State are granted immunities before an international court.[3] And the ICJ in its 2002 *Arrest Warrant* case said that

---

1   1998 Rome Statute, art 27.
2   *The Prosecutor v Al Bashir* (Judgment in the Jordan Referral re Al-Bashir Appeal, A Ch) ICC-02/05-01/09-397-Corr (6 May 2019), paras 103, 122; id, (Judgment in the Jordan Referral re Al-Bashir Appeal, A Ch) ICC-02/05-01/09-397-Anx1-Corr (17 May 2019) (Joint Concurring Opinion of Judges Eboe-Osuji, Morrison, Hofmański and Bossa), para 446; id, (Request by Professor Claus Kreß with the assistance of Erin Pobjie for leave to submit observations on the merits of the legal questions presented in 'The Hashemite Kingdom of Jordan's appeal against the "Decision under Article 87(7) of the Rome Statute"') ICC-02/05-01/09-346 (30 April 2018), para 5; C. Kreß and K. Prost, 'Article 98' in O. Triffterer and K. Ambos (eds), *Commentary on the Rome Statute of the International Criminal Court: Observers' Notes, Article by Article* (3rd edn, Hart/Beck 2016) 2125; P. Gaeta and P.I. Labuda, 'Trying Sitting Heads of State: The African Union versus the ICC in the Al Bashir and Kenyatta Cases' in C.C. Jalloh and I. Bantekas (eds), *The International Criminal Court and Africa* (OUP 2017) 149.
3   Extraordinary Session of Assembly of the African Union, 'Decision on Africa's Relationship with the International Criminal Court (ICC)', Ext/Assembly/AU/Dec.1 (October 2013), §§ 9-10; *The Prosecutor v Al Bashir* (The African Union's Submission in the Hashemite Kingdom of Jordan's Appeal against the Decision under Article 87(7) of the Rome Statute on the Non-Compliance by Jordan with the Request by the Court for the Arrest and Surrender [of] Omar Al-Bashir) ICC-02/05-01/09-370 (16 July 2018), para 10.

it could not 'conclude that any such an exception exists in customary international law in regard to national courts'.[4] A question may arise whether a customary rule exists claiming non-availability of personal immunity for committing international crimes.

The central issue here is whether article 27(2) of the Rome Statute was and is declaratory of a customary rule about non-availability of personal immunity. The sub-questions are whether: (1) article 27(2) was declaratory of a pre-existing or emerging customary rule permitting an exception to personal immunity at the time of the adoption of the Statute; and (2) article 27(2) is declaratory of a customary rule leading to a denial of personal immunity for committing international crimes.

For this purpose, section 7.2 briefly addresses the regime of immunity in international law and examines challenges to this legal system. The text of article 27(2) of the Statute is discussed in section 7.3, which stipulates an exception to the customary rule respecting personal immunity of senior officials. The preparatory works of article 27 and other texts relating to immunity are also analysed in this section. It appears that article 27(2) was not declaratory of a 'pre-existing customary rule' permitting an exception to personal immunity. Section 7.4 examines the practice of personal immunity before 1998 and argues that a rule of no personal immunity was not established or emerging in custom. Lastly, section 7.5 observes positions and practice after 1998 to evaluate whether the practice enshrined in the text of article 27(2) has been sufficiently developed and accepted as a modified (new) customary rule. The evidence examined in this section includes the jurisprudence of international criminal tribunals, national legislation and cases, as well as the resolutions of the UN Security Council and the International Law Commission's work. Section 7.5 argues that it is now immature for a rule as set out in article 27(2) to emerge under customary law, providing an exception to personal immunity for the commission of international crimes. Chapter 7 concludes that article 27(2) of the Rome Statute neither was declaratory nor is declaratory of a customary rule providing an exception to absolute personal immunity from arrest for committing international crimes.

---

4   *Arrest Warrant of 11 April 2000* (*Democratic Republic of the Congo v Belgium*), Judgment, [2002] ICJ Rep 3, 24, para 58.

7.2 Immunity under International Law

This section first briefly examines the well-developed regime of immunity under international law and then explains challenges to immunities for the commission of international crimes.

7.2.1 Regime of Immunity in International Law

State immunity as a limit to national jurisdiction is generally considered as a doctrine of customary international law.[5] It derives from the principle of sovereignty and equality that '*par in parem imperium non habet*'.[6] In the 1812 *Exchange v McFaddon*, the US Chief Justice Marshall explained that:

> This perfect equality and absolute independence of sovereigns, and this common interest impelling them to mutual intercourse, and an interchange of good offices with each other, have given rise to a class of cases in which every sovereign is understood to waive the exercise of a part of that complete exclusive territorial jurisdiction which has been stated to be the attribute of every nation.[7]

Thus, States and their property are exempted from the local jurisdiction of another State.[8]

In the modern era, the ruler of a State is separated from a State entity under international law. In order to ensure the function of foreign States, such as serving diplomats and other officials abroad for specific missions, individuals are also entitled to immunity from the jurisdiction of receiving States.[9] The immunity a person enjoys is divided into two categories: functional immunity (immunity *ratione materiae*) relating to acts of agents of State, and personal immunity (immunity *ratione personae*) attaching to particular officeholders. Functional immunity means that all State officials enjoy immunity for their

---

5 X. Yang, *State Immunity in International Law* (CUP 2012) 34; Institut de Droit International, 'Resolution on Immunity from Jurisdiction of the State and of Persons Who Act on Behalf of the State in case of International Crimes', Resolution of the Third Commission (2009); UN Doc A/CN.4/631 (2011), paras 56-70.

6 B. de Saxoferrato, *Tractatus de regimine civitatis* (1354), cited in PT. Stoll, 'State Immunity' in R. Wolfrum (ed) (2011) *MPEPIL*, para 4. Cf. Yang, ibid 44–58.

7 *Schooner Exchange v McFaddon*, 11 U.S. 116 (1812), 137; *Al-Adsani v UK* (Judgment) ECtHR Application No. 35763/97 (21 November 2001), para 54.

8 Stoll (n 6) paras 4-12.

9 C. Wickremasinghe, 'Immunities Enjoyed by Officials of States and International Organisations' in M. Evans (ed), *International Law* (OUP 2010) 381–82.

acts of State in connection with the exercise of their official functions, and receiving States must respect their immunity from local jurisdiction. Personal immunity indicates that sitting senior officials are immune from legal proceedings of foreign courts for their acts in office, including their actions on behalf of the State and private acts.[10] Compared with functional immunity, personal immunity covers a narrower range of actors, but a wider range of acts. Personal immunity is practically absolute in criminal cases. In addition, functional immunity never ceases for shielded people, while personal immunity exists as long as the person is in office and lapses when the person leaves office.[11]

Although personal immunity is controversial for high-ranking diplomats, generally serving senior State officials, namely, foreign ministers, heads of governments and heads of State enjoy it.[12] As Arthur Watts has written, heads of State enjoy immunity for their functional need and the 'considerations that they are the personification of their States' in international relations.[13] Sitting heads of State abroad enjoy both functional and personal immunities. They can invoke immunities to challenge criminal proceedings of other States for their official and private acts carried out before or during their period of office. If a head of State was out of office, s/he cannot enjoy full personal immunity but may still invoke functional immunity for the official acts during his/her period of office.

Some of these ideas are restated in international instruments, such as the Vienna Convention on Diplomatic Relations,[14] the UN Convention on Special Missions[15] and the UN Convention on Jurisdictional Immunities of States and Their Property.[16] The rule of personal immunity of senior officials is generally

---

10 *Prosecutor v Blaškić* (Judgement on the request of the Republic of Croatia for review of the Decision of Trial Chamber II of 18 July 1997) ICTY-95-14-AR108BIS (29 October 1997), para 38; A. Bianchi, 'Immunity versus Human Rights: The *Pinochet* Case' (1999) 10 *EJIL* 237, 262–65; Institut de Droit International (n 5), art II (1).

11 UN Doc A/CN.4/661 (2013), paras 47-79.

12 'Report of the International Law Commission', UN Doc A/63/10 (2008), para 307; A. Watts, 'The Legal Position in International Law of Heads of States, Heads of Governments and Foreign Ministers' (1994) 247 *Recueil des cours* 100, Chapter III; 2002 *Arrest Warrant* case (n 4), 20, para 51; UN Doc A/CN.4/661 (2013), paras 56-68; UN Doc A/CN.4/722 (2017), Annex, 'Draft articles on immunity from foreign criminal jurisdiction of State officials provisionally adopted by the Commission', art 3. For further discussions, M. Shaw, *International Law* (8th edn, CUP 2017) 1211–13.

13 A. Watts, 'Heads of State' in R. Wolfrum (ed) (2010) *MPEPIL*, paras 1-4.

14 Vienna Convention on Diplomatic Relations, 500 UNTS 95, arts 39(2) and 29.

15 Convention on Special Missions, 1400 UNTS 23, arts 21 and 29.

16 United Nations Convention on Jurisdictional Immunities of States and Their Property, adopted on 2 December 2004, but has not yet entered into force.

recognised in customary international law, although it has not been stipulated in a multilateral treaty.[17] The immunity from foreign criminal jurisdiction under international law is, by nature, procedural and is a veil protecting officials for their acts from the jurisdiction of other States, rather than their domestic authority.[18] Local legal proceedings would also be permitted when appropriate authorities have expressly waived these immunities.[19] Additionally, no question of international immunity will arise at all if their home States decide to initiate proceedings against these person at their national courts. However, challenges to immunities have arisen.

7.2.2 *Challenges to Immunity for Committing International Crimes*

Alongside the development of international criminal law and the prosecution of international crimes, there has been controversy about the material scope and the applicability of absolute immunity.[20] If senior officials are alleged to have committed core international crimes, such as war crimes, crimes against humanity, genocide and aggression, do they continue to enjoy immunity?

---

17   *Jurisdictional Immunities of the State (Germany v Italy: Greece Intervening)*, Judgment, [2012] ICJ Rep 99, 122, para 53; *Case concerning Certain Questions of Mutual Assistance in Criminal Matters (Djibouti v France)*, Judgment, [2008] ICJ Rep 177, 236, 238, paras 170, 174; 2002 *Arrest Warrant* case (n 4), 11, 21, paras 20-21, 52; *Al-Adsani v UK* (n 7) para 54; A. Kiyani, 'Al-Bashir & the ICC: The Problem of Head of State Immunity' (2013) 12 *Chinese J Intl L* 467, 472–74; 'Second report on immunity of State officials from foreign criminal jurisdiction, by Roman Anatolevich Kolodkin, Special Rapporteur', UN Doc A/CN.4/631 (2011), paras 90-93, 'preliminary report', UN Doc A/CN.4/601, paras 30-31; X.M. Wang, 'The Immunity of State Officials from Foreign Criminal Jurisdiction' (2010) 30 *Journal of Xi'an Jiaotong University (Social Sciences)* 67, 69; R.B. Baker, 'Customary International Law in the 21st Century: Old Challenges and New Debates' (2010) 21 *EJIL* 173, 189; D. Singerman, 'It's Still Good to Be the King: An Argument for Maintaining the *Status Quo* in Foreign Head of State Immunity' (2007) 21 *Emory Intl L Rev* 413; K.C. O'Neill, 'A New Customary Law of Head of State Immunity?: Hirohito and Pinochet' (2002) 38 *Stanford J Intl L* 291; Watts (n 12) 36–37; P. Gaeta, 'Official Capacity and Immunities' in A. Cassese *et al* (eds), *The Rome Statute of the International Criminal Court: A Commentary* (OUP 2002) 979; Bianchi (n 10); M.N. Leich, 'Contemporary Practice of the United States Relating to International Law' (1983) 77 *AJIL* 298, 306. For more discussions in recent literature, see R. van Alebeek, *The Immunity of States and Their Officials in International Criminal Law and International Human Rights Law* (OUP 2008); R. Pedretti, *Immunity of Heads of State and State Officials for International Crimes* (Brill | Nijhoff 2015) 304–07. Cf. 2002 *Arrest Warrant* case (n 4) (Dissenting Opinion of Judge *ad hoc* Van den Wyngaert), paras 8-39.

18   Bianchi (n 10); UN Doc A/CN.4/661 (2013), paras 36-46.

19   Vienna Convention on Diplomatic Relations, art 33. UN Doc A/CN.4/722 (2017), paras 25-63 (about procedural aspects of immunity).

20   Bianchi (n 10); UN Doc A/CN.4/631 (2011), paras 90-93.

One argument is that it would be too great an interference with other States and the conduct of international relations of sitting senior officials to be subject to other States' jurisdiction.[21] By contrast, Antonio Cassese explained that:

> In the present international community respect for human rights and the demand that justice be done wherever human rights have been seriously and massively put in jeopardy, override the principle of respect for state sovereignty. The new thrust towards protection of human dignity has shattered the shield that traditionally protected state agents.[22]

The ILC in its commentary to the 1996 Draft Code of Crimes also observed that:

> It would be paradoxical to allow the individuals who are, in some respects, the most responsible for the crimes covered by the Code to invoke the sovereignty of the State and to hide behind the immunity that is conferred on them by virtue of their positions particularly since these heinous crimes shock the conscience of mankind, violate some of the most fundamental rules of international law and threaten international peace and security.[23]

Some scholars have also argued that the person who initiates and plans these crimes should be prosecuted,[24] whereas the immunity enjoyed by the ringleader seems to be inconsistent with the goal to end impunity. These challenges are not merely theories. An evaluation of these challenges may occur in certain contexts. For example, the immunity issue arose when Belgium planned to exercise universal jurisdiction over a foreign minister of Congo for alleged international crimes.[25] Senior serving officials' immunities seem to prevent the exercise of universal jurisdiction to narrow the impunity gap.[26] In addition, the ICC Pre-Trial Chamber once addressed that 'when the exercise of jurisdiction by the Court entails the prosecution of a Head of State of a

---

21 *R v Bartle, Evans and Another and the Commissioner of Police for the Metropolis and Other, Ex Parte Pinochet* (Judgment) [2000] 1 AC 147 (24 March 1999), [1999] UKHL 17, (1999) 38 ILM 581 [644] (Lord Millett).
22 A. Cassese *et al* (eds), *Cassese's International Criminal Law* (3rd end, OUP 2013) 246.
23 UN A/51/10 (1996), para 50, commentary (1) to art 7.
24 2002 *Arrest Warrant* case (n 4) (Joint Separate opinion of Judges Higgins, Kooijmans and Buergenthal), para 8.
25 2002 *Arrest Warrant* case (n 4).
26 2002 *Arrest Warrant* case (n 4) (Dissenting Opinion of Judge *ad hoc* Van den Wyngaert), paras 16-19.

non-State Party, the question of personal immunities might validly arise'.[27] The former Sudan's President Al Bashir is the first sitting head of State to be wanted by the ICC. The issue of whether Al Bashir as head of State enjoyed immunity before the ICC was highly debated.[28] These challenges call for an analysis of proposals that disregard international immunities in specific situations.[29]

7.2.3 Theories of Repudiating Immunities

There are some theories about lifting international immunities for committing international crimes.[30] One view argues that former senior officials cannot invoke functional immunity as a challenge in criminal proceedings before a competent court.[31] There are differing rationales for abrogating functional immunity. One argument claims that committing international crimes are not within the ambit of governmental functions but are private acts falling outside immunity protection.[32] Thus, functional immunity cannot be invoked for committing international crimes.[33] Other commentators argue that functional immunity cannot be circumvented through the idea of private acts. In their view, an exception exists to the customary rule of respecting functional immunity for the commission of international crimes.[34] Cassese neither supported

---

27 *The Prosecutor v Al Bashir* (Decision on the Cooperation of the Democratic Republic of the Congo Regarding Omar Al Bashir's Arrest and Surrender to the Court, PTC II) ICC-02/05-01/09-195 (9 April 2014), para 26.

28 *The Prosecutor v Al Bashir* (Warrant of Arrest for Omar Hassan Ahmad Al Bashir, PTC I) ICC-02/05-01/09-1 (4 March 2009); id, (Second Warrant of Arrest for Omar Hassan Ahmad Al Bashir, PTC I) ICC-02/05-01/09-95 (12 July 2010); H. Van der Wilt, 'Immunities and the International Criminal Court' in T. Ruys *et al* (eds), *The Cambridge Handbook of Immunities and International Law* (CUP 2019) 595–613.

29 For other scenarios, see O. Triffterer and C. Burchard, 'Article 27' in Triffterer and Ambos (eds) (n 2)1042.

30 A. Clapham, *Brierly's the Law of Nations* (7th edn, OUP 2012) 273–77.

31 2002 *Arrest Warrant* case (n 4), 25–26, para 61; Kreß and Prost (n 2) 2126–27.

32 *R v Ex Parte Pinochet et al* (No 3), (1999) 38 *ILM* 581 (n 21) [595] (Lord Browne-Wilkinson), [638] (Lord Hutton). See also R. van Alebeek, 'National Courts, International Crimes and the Functional Immunity of State Officials' (2015) 59 *Netherlands Intl L Rev* 5, 18–19; 'Report of the International Law Commission', UN Doc A/46/10 (1991), 12, 15, 18 and 22; 2002 *Arrest Warrant* case (n 4), 25–26, para 61. Cf. 2002 *Arrest Warrant* case (n 4) (Joint Separate opinion of Judges Higgins, Kooijmans and Buergenthal), 63–90; id, (Dissenting Opinion of Judge *ad hoc* Van den Wyngaert), para 36; C. Kreß, 'Reflections on the *Iudicare* Limb of the Grave Breaches Regime' (2009) 7 *JICJ* 789, 803–04; UN Doc A/CN.4/722 (2017), para 14 (Netherlands and Switzerland).

33 For criticism of this view, see A. Gattini, 'War Crimes and State Immunity in the *Ferrini* Decision' (2005) *JICJ* 224, 234 and fn 41.

34 *R v Ex Parte Pinochet et al* (No 3), (1999) 38 *ILM* 581 (n 21) [626] (Lord Hope of Craighead), [643] (Lord Saville of Newdigate), [651] (Lord Millett), [661] (Lord Phillips of Worth

the private acts argument nor adopted the idea of an exception.[35] He argued that if there is a new rule of customary law for committing international crimes, offences of international crimes are not immune from jurisdiction by invoking functional immunity. The private acts, exceptional idea and Cassese's view, in effect, are similar to each other. But the onus of proof for (no) personal immunity will different in practice. In addition, an exception to the traditional customary rule respecting absolute immunity could be based on either a treaty or a customary rule;[36] while Cassese's viewpoint demands the establishment of a new customary rule. Although no consensus exists among scholars on the lifting approach, it seems to be generally agreed that State officials should not invoke functional immunity for committing international crimes before foreign national authorities.[37]

The ICC and academics have also developed several avenues to deal with the tension between personal immunity and impunity, for example, waiver of immunity through signing treaties or through UN Security Council resolutions,

---

Matravers); 2002 *Arrest Warrant* case (n 4) (Dissenting Opinion of Judge *ad hoc* Van den Wyngaert), para 36; 2002 *Arrest Warrant* case (n 4) (Dissenting Opinion of Judge Al-Khasaweh), para 6; *Jones v Ministry of Interior for the Kingdom of Saudi Arabia et al* (Opinions of the Lords of Appeal for Judgement in the Cause) (14 June 2006) [2006] UKHL 26, [2006] 2 WLR 1424, [2007] 1 AC 270 [85] (Lord Hoffmann); A. Cassese, 'When May Senior State Officials be Tried for International Crimes? Some Comments on the *Congo v Belgium* Case' (2002) 13 *EJIL* 853, 866–69.

35   Cassese, ibid 864, 870–75; Cassese *et al* (eds) (n 22) 247–48.
36   UN Doc A/CN.4/722 (2017), para 14.
37   Institut de Droit International (n 5), art III (1); UN Doc A/CN.4/631 (2011), para 33 and fn 75; D. Robinson, 'Immunities' in R. Cryer *et al* (eds), *An Introduction to International Criminal Law and Procedure* (3rd edn, CUP 2014) 540–65; Clapham (n 30) 276–77; Triffterer and Burchard (n 29) 1052; Kreß and Prost (n 2) 2127; D. Akande, 'International Law Immunities and the International Criminal Court' (2004) 98 *AJIL* 407, 413; Gaeta (n 17) 981–83; Kreß (n 32) 803–05; Pedretti (n 17) 156–91, 307–08; Cassese *et al* (eds) (n 22) 240–47. *Prosecutor v Milošević* (Decision on Preliminary Motions) ICTY-02-54-PT (8 November 2001); *Prosecutor v Krstić* (Judgement) ICTY-98-33-A (1 July 2003), para 26; *Mario Luiz Lozano v General Prosecutor* (Sentence, Supreme Court of Cassation) 31171/2008, ILDC 1085 (IT 2008), paras 6-7; *Re Hilao and ors v Estate of Ferdinand Marcos* (Interlocutory Appeal Decision), 25F 3d 1467 (9th Cir 1994), para 28; *R v Bow Street Metropolitan Stipendiary Magistrate, Ex Parte Pinochet Ugarte* (Opinions of the Lords of Appeal for Judgement in the Cause) (25 November 1998) [1998]3 WLR 1456, [1998] UKHL 41; *R v Ex Parte Pinochet et al* (No 3), (1999) 38 *ILM* 581 (n 21) [595] (Lord Browne-Wilkinson), [652] (Lord Millett); Institute of International Law, Immunities from Jurisdiction and Execution of Heads of State and of Government in International Law, Vancouver 2001/II (IIL Vancouver Resolution), art 13 (2). Cf. J. Crawford, *Brownlie's Principles of Public International Law* (8th edn, OUP 2012) 500.

and a new customary rule of non-availability of personal immunity.[38] One viewpoint is that 'the non-availability of international immunity rights [...] *ratione personae* with respect to persons, as articulated in article 27(2), is declaratory of customary international law'.[39] They claim that, with regard to crimes under customary international law, a new customary rule that no personal immunity can be invoked before certain international criminal tribunals, the jurisdiction of which is 'direct enforcement of the *jus puniendi* of the international community'.[40] This new customary rule is based on the nature of the crimes

---

38 *The Prosecutor v Al Bashir* (Corrigendum to the Decision Pursuant to Article 87(7) of the Rome Statute on the Failure by the Republic of Malawi to Comply with the Cooperation Requests Issued by the Court with Respect to the Arrest and Surrender of Omar Hassan Ahmad Al Bashir, PTC I) ICC-02/05-01/09-139-Corr (13 December 2011), para 43; id, (Decision Pursuant to Article 87 (7) of the Rome Statute on the Refusal of the Republic of Chad to Comply with the Cooperation Requests Issued by the Court with Respect to the Arrest and Surrender of Omar Hassan Ahmad Al Bashir, PTC I) ICC-02/05-01/09-140-tENG (13 December 2011); id, (Transcript, A Ch) ICC-02/05-01/09-T-4-ENG, ICC-02/05-01/09-T-5-ENG, ICC-02/05-01/09-T-6-ENG (10–12 September 2018); *Al Bashir Jordan* Cooperation Appeals Chamber Judgment 2019 (n 2), paras 80-94, 149; *Al Bashir Jordan* Cooperation Appeals Chamber Judgment 2019 (Joint Concurring Opinion of Judges Eboe-Osuji, Morrison, Hofmański and Bossa) (n 2), paras 65-75, 446; D. Jacobs, 'The Frog That Wanted to Be an Ox: The ICC's Approach to Immunities and Cooperation' in C. Stahn (ed), *The Law and Practice of the International Criminal Court* (OUP 2015) 281–304.

For a waiver-based approach, see Akande (n 37); D. Akande, 'The Legal Nature of Security Council Referrals to the ICC and Its Impact on Al Bashir's Immunities' (2009) 7 *JICJ* 333; C. Ryngaert and M. Blommestijn, 'Exploring the Obligations for States to Act upon the ICC's Arrest Warrant for Omar Al-Bashir: A Legal Conflict between the Duty to Arrest and the Customary Status of Head of State Immunity' (2010) 5 *ZIS* 428, 435–38; *The Prosecutor v Al Bashir* (Decision on the Cooperation of the Democratic Republic of the Congo Regarding Omar Al Bashir's Arrest and Surrender to the Court, PTC II) ICC-02/05-01/09-195 (9 April 2014).

For a custom-based approach, see P. Gaeta, 'Does President Al Bashir Enjoy Immunity from Arrest?' (2009) 7 *JICJ* 315, 320; J. Paust, 'Genocide in Rwanda, State Responsibility to Prosecute or Extradite, and Nonimmunity for Heads of State and Other Public Officials' (2011) 34 *Houston J Intl L* 57, 71–84; Kreß and Prost (n 2) 2125, 2128–39; Watts (n 13), paras 10-11; C. Kreß, 'The International Criminal Court and Immunities under International Law for States Not Party to the Court's Statute' in M. Bergsmo and Y. Ling (eds), *State Sovereignty and International Criminal Law* (TOAEP 2012) 223; id, 'Preliminary Observations on the ICC Appeals Chamber's Judgment of 6 May 2019 in the Jordan Referral re Al-Bashir Appeal' (2019) Occasional Paper Series No. 8; Triffterer and Burchard (n 29) 1041–42, 1053–54.

39 Kreß and Prost (n 2) 2125; *Al Bashir Jordan* Cooperation Appeals Chamber Judgment 2019 (n 2), paras 103-119.

40 UN Doc A/51/10 (1996), para 50, commentary (6) to art 7, fn 69; Pedretti (n 17); Kreß and Prost (n 2) 2128–33; Gaeta and Labuda (n 2) 146–47; Triffterer and Burchard (n 29) 1041–42; Kreß (2019) (n 38).

and the nature of the proceedings.[41] The Appeals Chamber of the ICC in its 2019 *Jordan* decision also agreed that in customary law there was no head of State personal immunity before international courts.[42] The Appeals Chamber simply addressed that 'international courts' 'are adjudicating international crimes, do not act on behalf of a particular State or States. Rather, international courts act on behalf of the international community as a whole.'[43] The Special Court for Sierra Leone (SCSL) once also upheld an interpretation that personal immunity under customary law can be disregarded before an 'international' court.[44] In the view of the SCSL, 'these tribunals are not organs of a State, but derive their mandate from the international community'.[45] And 'States have considered the collective judgment of the international community to provide a vital safeguard against the potential destabilizing effect of unilateral judgment in that area'.[46]

In addition to this, scholars propose that once the default absence of personal immunity in international criminal tribunals becomes a customary rule, the rule 'must be construed to include the horizontal (co-operation) limb of the triangular legal relationship' between States.[47] This extended construction enables a requested State Party of the Rome Statute to justify its arrest or detention of a sitting senior official of another State, including a non-party State, for committing international crimes.[48] Alternatively, the Appeals Chamber of the ICC adopted another approach to dealing with the horizontal personal immunity issue.[49] In its view, the State requested by the ICC to arrest the person it sought is 'merely acting as jurisdictional surrogates of the ICC, for the purposes

---

41 Pedretti (n 17); Gaeta and Labuda (n 2); Kreß and Prost (n 2) 2132–33.

42 *Al Bashir Jordan* Cooperation Appeals Chamber Judgment 2019 (n 2), paras 2, 114, 116; Kreß (2019) (n 38) 5–26.

43 ibid, para 115. See also ICC (Decision on the "Prosecution's Request for a Ruling on Jurisdiction on Article 19(3) of Statute", PTC) ICC-RoC46(3)-01/18-37 (6 September 2018), para 48. Cf. Kreß (2019) (n 38).

44 For comments on the *Taylor* decision, see C. Kreß, 'Decision on Immunity from Jurisdiction, Prosecutor v. Taylor, Case No. SCSL-2003-01-I, A. Ch., 31 May 2004: Commentary' in A. Klip and G. Sluiter (eds), *Annotated Leading Cases of International Criminal Tribunals: The Special Court for Sierra Leone 2003–2004*, Vol 9 (Intersentia 2010) 202–08; M. Frulli, 'Piercing the Veil of Head-of-State Immunity: The Taylor Trial and Beyond' in C.C. Jalloh (ed), *The Sierra Leone Special Court and its Legacy: The Impact for Africa and International Criminal Law* (CUP 2013) 327.

45 *Prosecutor v Charles Taylor* (Decision on Immunity from Jurisdiction, A Ch) SCSL-2003-L-AR72 (E) (31 May 2004), para 51.

46 ibid.

47 Kreß (2019) (n 38).

48 *Al Bashir Malawi* Cooperation Decision 2011 (n 38), para 42.

49 *Al Bashir Jordan* Cooperation Appeals Chamber Judgment 2019 (n 2).

of enabling it to exercise its jurisdiction effectively'.[50] The ICC seems to be discomfort for that extended construction of a customary rule.

In my view, the idea of invalidating personal immunity for international crimes on the basis of the distinction between national and international proceedings is not convincing. True, personal immunity is mainly designed to protect 'international relations' between or among States, instead of the relations between a State and an international tribunal. A new construction of a customary rule of no personal immunity for the crimes under international law is a good proposition. Nevertheless, the reason for the distinction between national courts and international courts is unconvincing. National courts can also act on behalf of the international community when they exercise universal jurisdiction over crimes under international law. The nature of certain international proceedings alone cannot account for the unavailability of personal immunity.

Secondly, the argument that international tribunals are a direct enforcement of the right to punish on behalf of the international community is rather ambiguous due to the vagueness of the concept of 'international community'. States may collectively do what they are not allowed to do individually without risk of violation, such as the member States of the UN Security Council establishing the ICTY and the ICTR to exercise jurisdiction over sitting senior officials of former Yugoslavia and Rwanda.[51] Apart from the power of the Security Council, States in most cases are not allowed to do collectively what they individually have no power to do, for example, to remove personal immunity of senior officials of a State by establishing an international criminal tribunal without receiving the consent or a waiver of immunity by that State.[52] The principle of sovereign equality is not the only basis for personal immunity, which also aims to protect international relations without interfering with high ranking representatives. As the extended construction of customary law suggested, a new rule of no personal immunity is impractical without a change of the traditional customary rule concerning horizontal personal immunity.

A new theory of a customary rule with no personal immunity for crimes under international law in international proceedings would not simplify the practice between States, but somewhat complicates the practice and the regime of immunity. The new theory does not sufficiently address why

---

50   ibid (Joint Concurring Opinion of Judges Eboe-Osuji, Morrison, Hofmański and Bossa), para 445.
51   W.A. Schabas, 'The Special Tribunal for Lebanon: Is a 'Tribunal of an International Character' equivalent to an 'International Criminal Court'?' (2008) 21 *LJIL* 513, 527–28.
52   Pedretti (n 17) 295.

individuals cannot invoke personal immunity before a national court when an international tribunal issues the arrest warrant, whereas they can still invoke personal immunity before another national court when that national court issues the warrant for committing international crimes.[53] If a modified (new) customary international rule concerning personal immunity is emerging, better construction of its content should only rely on the nature of the crimes. In other words, 'the practice that sitting senior officials are subject to the jurisdiction of other States for committing international crimes is universally upheld as a modified customary rule, regardless of whether such proceedings are brought before national or international courts'.[54] Once an exception to personal immunity for committing international crimes comes into a customary rule, personal immunities would not be bars for the exercise of jurisdiction in international criminal tribunals.[55]

Finally, yet equally important, some tribunals have rejected the construction that relies on the nature of the court. The Appeals Chamber of the ICTY in *Blaškić* recognised that functional immunity does not disappear simply because the tribunal is international.[56] In the *Krstić* case, Judge Shahabuddeen in his dissenting opinion argued that 'there is no substance in the suggested automaticity of the disappearance of the immunity just because of the establishment of international criminal courts'.[57] Both cases refer to functional immunity from testifying based on an order issued by the ICTY, but their findings are equally true as to personal immunity. No tendency seems to indicate that personal immunity of senior officials would be abrogated simply due to the international nature of the criminal court.[58]

This chapter examines the relationship between article 27(2) of the Rome Statute and custom concerning personal immunity for committing international crimes. The nature of crimes is the main concern in the following analysis, whereas evidence concerning the international nature of the court is assessed when necessary. This chapter qualifies personal immunity enjoyed by senior serving officials: heads of State, heads of government or ministers of foreign affairs. The premise of this chapter is that competent authorities

---

53   Cf. *Amicus Curiae* Brief of Kreß (n 2), paras 12-14.
54   2002 *Arrest Warrant* case (n 4) (Dissenting Opinion of Judge *ad hoc* Van den Wyngaert), para 31.
55   Cassese (n 34) 864.
56   *Prosecutor v Blaškić* (Decision on the Objection of the Republic of Croatia to the Issue of *subpoena duces tecum*) ICTY-95-14-PT (18 July 1997), paras 38-45.
57   *Krstić* Appeals Chamber Judgment (n 37) (Dissenting Opinion of Judge Shahabuddeen), para 11.
58   Akande (n 37).

must respect personal immunity of sitting senior officials under customary law unless appropriate authorities collectively agree to remove it or separately waive it through a treaty or an explicit declaration.[59] The issues of functional immunity and whether violations of *jus cogens* repudiate immunity also deserve discussion but digress from the focus of this chapter.[60]

7.3 Personal Immunity: Article 27(2) of the Rome Statute

This section analyses different understandings of article 27 to survey whether article 27(2) departs from or restates a customary rule. Article 27 of the Rome Statute under the title of 'the irrelevance of official capacity' stipulates that:

> 1. This Statute shall apply equally to all persons without any distinction based on official capacity. In particular, official capacity as a Head of State or Government, a member of a Government or parliament, an elected representative or a government official shall in no case exempt a person from criminal responsibility under this Statute, nor shall it, in and of itself, constitute a ground for reduction of sentence.
> 2. Immunities or special procedural rules which may attach to the official capacity of a person, whether under national or international law, shall not bar the Court from exercising its jurisdiction over such a person.

This section first reviews the interpretation of article 27(2) in connection with article 27(1) and then observes the scope of personal immunity embedded in article 27(2). Last, it examines the structure of the Rome Statute about immunity.

7.3.1 *Understanding of Articles 27(1) and (2): Personal Immunity*

A plain reading of article 27(2) shows that 'immunities under international law' do not 'bar the Court from exercising its jurisdiction' over the person who

---

59 Van Alebeek (n 17); 2002 *Arrest Warrant* case (n 4), 20–21, paras 51-52. Cf. *Al Bashir Jordan Cooperation* Appeals Chamber Judgment 2019 (n 2).

60 For discussions, see *Al-Adsani v UK* (n 7) para 54; *Armed Activities on the Territory of the Congo (Democratic Republic of the Congo v Rwanda)*, Jurisdiction and Admissibility, Judgment, [2006] ICJ Rep 6, 32, para 64; *Jones v Saudi Arabia and et al*, [2006] UKHL 26; *Jurisdictional Immunities of the State Judgment* (n 17), 140–41, paras 93, 95; B.B. Jia, 'Immunity for State Officials from Foreign Jurisdiction for International Crimes' in Bergsmo and Ling (eds) (n 38) 88–92.

enjoys such immunities. This reading means that personal immunities attaching to an individual in international law are irrelevant to the ICC's jurisdiction for alleged crimes falling within its jurisdiction. By comparison with article 27(1), further clarification of the purport of article 27(2) is necessary to clarify which provision covers the personal immunity issue.

Different views exist among scholars about the interpretation of the two paragraphs in article 27. Some commentators argue that article 27(1) includes both the principle of individual criminal responsibility and the principle of no immunity for international crimes.[61] Others consider that article 27(1) denotes the consent of States Parties to remove either personal or functional immunity of their representatives, while article 27(2) affirms the absence of immunities in ICC proceedings.[62] Both viewpoints, however, do not reflect the drafters' intention. The text of article 27(1) echoes the principle of individual criminal responsibility.[63] This principle has repeatedly been provided in: article 7 of the Nuremberg Charter,[64] article 6 of the Tokyo Charter,[65] the judgments of the IMT and the IMTFE, Principle III of 1950 ILC Nuremberg Principles, articles 7(2) and 6(2) of the Statutes of the ICTY and the ICTR, and article 7 of the ILC's 1996 Draft Code of Crimes.[66] These rules concern official capacity as a substantive defence for individual criminal responsibility as opposed to State responsibility.

In contrast to article 27(1), no predecessor of article 27(2) existed in these instruments mentioned above.[67] It seems that article 27(2) was initially inserted to avoid immunities prejudicing the principle of individual criminal responsibility before the ICC as set out in article 27(1). During the Preparatory Committee's first two sessions, some States expressed concerns about the 'question of diplomatic or other immunity from arrest and other procedural measures taken by or on behalf of the Court'.[68] The Preparatory Committee compiled two proposals on this issue.[69] The first proposal provided that '[i]n

---

61 Clapham (n 30) 274 and fn 162.
62 Pedretti (n 17) 248–50; Cassese *et al* (eds) (n 22) 240–47, 318–19.
63 Triffterer and Burchard (n 29) 1043–47.
64 'Charter of the International Military Tribunal – Annex to the Agreement for the prosecution and punishment of the major war criminals of the European Axis' (8 August 1945) [Nuremberg Charter], 82 UNTS 284.
65 Tokyo Charter.
66 UN Doc A/51/10 (1996), para 50, commentaries (4)-(5) to art 7.
67 UN Doc A/49/10 (1994), 20–73.
68 'Report of the Preparatory Committee on the Establishment of an International Criminal Court', UN Doc A/51/22 (1996), Vol I, para 85.
69 ibid.

the course of investigation or procedures performed by, or at request of the Court, no person may make a plea of immunity from jurisdiction irrespective of whether on the basis of international or national law'. The second proposal stated that '[t]he special procedural rules, the immunities and the protection attached to the official capacity of the accused and established by internal law or by international conventions or treaties may not be used as a defence before the Court'.[70]

Later on, this paragraph was rephrased as '[a]ny immunities or special procedural rules [...] may not be relied upon to prevent the Court from exercising its jurisdiction in relation to that person'. In a footnote to this paragraph, the Preparatory Committee pointed out that it 'would be required in connection with procedure as well as international judicial cooperation'.[71] This paragraph with the text of the footnote was repeated in subsequent drafts, while the phrase 'procedure as well as' was deleted in a later footnote.[72] The examination of the preparatory works indicates that article 27(2) was inserted to remove immunities in national and international law as a potential substantive defence to individual liability, but it was finally included to remove immunities or other procedural bars of State officials.

In discussing article 27(1), the drafters also mentioned 'immunity'.[73] However, it is unclear what mode of immunity the drafters had in mind: immunity in national or in international law. Since functional immunity amounts to a substantive defence to liability, the immunities under international law might be considered.[74] The drafters may have considered the removal of functional immunity for the violation of international law.[75] This viewpoint explains why some scholars support an interpretation whereby article 27(1)

---

70 ibid.
71 'Decision taken by the Preparatory Committee at its Session held from 11 to 21 February 1997', UN Doc A/AC.249/1997/L.5, 22 and fn 14.
72 'Report of the Inter-Sessional Meeting from 19 to 30 January 1998 in Zutphen', the Netherlands, UN Doc A/AC.249/1998/L.13, 54–55 and fn 86; 'Report of the Preparatory Committee on the Establishment of an International Criminal Court', UN Doc A/CONF.183/2 (1998), 31–32 fn 77.
73 W.A. Schabas, *The International Criminal Court: A Commentary on the Rome Statute* (2nd edn, OUP 2016) 595.
74 Jacobs (n 38); Cassese *et al* (eds) (n 22) 240–47, 318–19; Princeton Project on Universal Jurisdiction, 'The Princeton Principles on Universal Jurisdiction' (2001), 48–49.
75 The *Prosecutor v Kenyatta* (Decision on Defence Request for Conditional Excusal from Continuous Presence at Trial, TC V (b)) ICC-01/09-02/11-830 (18 October 2013), paras 66, 70, 98; E. La Haye, 'Article 49' in ICRC (ed), *Commentary on the First Geneva Convention: Convention (I) for the Amelioration of the Condition of the Wounded and Sick in Armed Forces in the Field* (CUP 2016), para 2877.

includes immunity in international law.[76] In addition, it may be noted that the ILC considered the issue of personal immunity in its commentary on the 1996 Draft Code of Crimes. Article 7 of the Draft Code of Crimes concerning 'official position and responsibility' provides that 'the official position of an individual who commits a crime against the peace and security of mankind, even if he acted as head of State or Government, does not relieve him of criminal responsibility or mitigate punishment'. The ILC observed that

> Article 7 is intended to prevent an individual who has committed a crime against the peace and security of mankind from invoking his official position as a circumstance absolving him from responsibility or conferring any immunity upon him [...]. The absence of any procedural immunity with respect to prosecution or punishment in appropriate judicial proceedings is an essential corollary of the absence of any substantive immunity or defence. It would be paradoxical to prevent an individual from invoking his official position to avoid responsibility for a crime only to permit him to invoke this same consideration to avoid the consequences of this responsibility.[77]

Based on this interpretation, one may argue that the absence of personal immunity is contemplated by article 27(1) of the Rome Statute, while article 27(2) merely confirms the non-availability of personal immunity.

Yet, the ILC's commentary does not strongly support this conclusion. Firstly, the IMT judgment does not indicate that the absence of procedural immunity is also embedded in article 7 of the Nuremberg Charter. The doctrine of State consent, indicating Germany's waiver of personal immunity, played a role in establishing the IMT and its prosecution, which will be clarified in detail below in section 7.4. Secondly, the ILC proposed disregarding procedural immunities in 'appropriate judicial proceedings', for example, 'before an international criminal court' for committing international crimes.[78] This idea of the absence of personal immunity is expressly articulated in article 27(2) rather than article 27(1) of the Rome Statute. Relying upon the preparatory works of the Rome

---

76 Clapham (n 30) 274 and fn 162; Pedretti (n 17) 248–50; Cassese *et al* (eds) (n 22) 240–47, 318–19.
77 UN Doc A/51/10(1996), para 50, commentary (6) to art 7 (citations omitted). For a similar view, see *The Prosecutor v Ruto & Sang* (Decision on Defence Applications for Judgments of Acquittal, TC V(A)) ICC-01/09-01/11-2027-Red-Corr (4 April 2016) (Reasons of Judge Eboe-Osuji), paras 263, 286–87.
78 *Ruto & Sang* Acquittal Decision 2016 (n 77), fn 69.

Statute, it is more persuasive to conclude that article 27(2) instead of article 27(1) directly affects personal immunity.[79]

Further explanations of the relationship between individual criminal responsibility and the ICC's jurisdiction provide another perspective to understand the two paragraphs of article 27. As pointed out by Judge Liu, '[w]hile [...] a head of state cannot escape criminal responsibility and that this can be considered a rule of customary international law, it does not mean that person no longer has immunity from the jurisdiction of the ICC'.[80] The existence of jurisdiction is a precondition for the exercise of jurisdiction, and the existence of jurisdiction does not mean that jurisdiction would be exercised. The immunity from jurisdiction indicates the protection from the exercise of jurisdiction.

Likewise, the recognition of individual criminal responsibility does not mean that all senior State officials as the most responsible persons would be held liable for international crimes.[81] The Rapporteur of the ILC on the subject of 'Immunity of State officials from foreign criminal jurisdiction' noted that the regime of immunity contains normative elements and procedural aspects.[82] The immunity from criminal jurisdiction is, by nature, eminently 'procedural and not substantive' and it means 'immunity from criminal process or from criminal procedure measures and not from the substantive law of the foreign State'.[83] The ILC's Rapporteur echoed that the immunity 'has no effect on [...] the individual criminal responsibility of the person who enjoys immunity'.[84] It is undeniable that sitting senior officials shall be criminally responsible for conducts, regardless of their official capacity.[85] However, recognising individual criminal responsibility does not mean that immunity is automatically lifted before national authorities and an individual would be arrested and prosecuted by disregarding personal immunity to exercise jurisdiction. A competent local jurisdiction cannot arrest or detain a person unless personal immunity

---

79 Kreß and Prost (n 2) 2125; Jacobs (n 38); Gaeta (n 17) 978; Akande (n 37) 419–20; S. Zappalà, 'Do Heads of State in Office Enjoy Immunity from Jurisdiction for International Crimes? The *Gaddafi* Case before the French Cour de Cassation' (2001) 12 *EJIL* 595.

80 D. Liu, 'Has Non-Immunity for Heads of State Become a Rule of Customary International Law?' in Bergsmo and Ling (eds) (n 38) 64.

81 *Krstić* Appeals Chamber Judgment (n 37) (Dissenting Opinion of Judge Shahabuddeen), paras 7-9.

82 UN Doc A/CN.4/646 (2011), paras 11-57; UN Doc A/CN.4/722 (2017), paras 23-44; UN Doc A/CN.4/729 (2018), paras 26-168.

83 'Preliminary Report on immunity of State officials from foreign criminal jurisdiction, by Special Rapporteur Roman Anatolevich Kolodkin', UN Doc A/CN.4/601 (2008), paras 102 (f)-(g); UN Doc A/CN.4/661 (2013), para 45; UN Doc A/CN.4/722 (2017), paras 28-108.

84 UN Doc A/CN.4/661 (2013), para 45.

85 Jacobs (n 38).

is waived or removed by appropriate authorities or through a treaty[86] or by a Security Council resolution.[87] The immunities, in effect, prevent a tribunal from exercising jurisdiction to determine liability for crimes.[88] This statement does apply to international criminal jurisdiction. Article 27(2) indirectly confirms the idea that a person enjoying functional immunity and acting in an official capacity cannot invoke immunities to oppose individual responsibility or to reduce punishment. The text of article 27(2) mainly serves a function in removing procedural immunity before the ICC.[89] The distinction between article 27(1) (irrelevance of official capacity to individual responsibility) and article 27(2) (irrelevance of personal immunity to the exercise of jurisdiction) should be kept in mind.[90]

To sum up, article 27 covers two different issues. Article 27(1) addresses the removal of a substantive defence to individual criminal responsibility, while article 27(2) concerns immunities as procedural barriers to the ICC's exercise of jurisdiction.[91] The drafting history of article 27 confirms this distinction. Article 27(1) endorses the principle of individual criminal responsibility for international crimes and dismissed immunity derived from national law and international law, at most, including functional immunity.[92] The text of article 27(2) addresses the idea of non-availability of personal immunity.

7.3.2 Scope of Personal Immunity in Article 27(2)

Another issue concerns the scope of personal immunity in article 27(2). As the text of article 27(2) suggests, possible invocation of personal immunity is *de facto* rejected at the ICC. By ratifying the Rome Statute, States Parties agreed to end absolute personal immunity before the ICC ('vertical personal immunity').[93] Another issue is whether article 27(2) also includes a derogation

---

86 Cassese *et al* (eds) (n 22) 321–22; 2002 *Arrest Warrant* case (n 4), 24–26, paras 59-61.
87 R v Ex Parte Pinochet et al (No 1) [1998] 3 WLR 1456 (n 37) [1474] (Dissenting opinion of Lord Slynn of Hadley); R v Ex Parte Pinochet et al (No 3), (1999) 38 ILM 581 (n 21) [599] (Dissenting opinion of Lord Goff of Chieveley).
88 Jacobs (n 38); Liu (n 80).
89 2002 *Arrest Warrant* case (n 4), 24–25, paras 58-60.
90 C. Lind, 'Article 27' in M. Klamberg (ed), *The Commentary on the Law of the International Criminal Court* (TOAEP 2017), confusing the two paragraphs.
91 Cassese (n 34) 863; Akande (n 37); Jacobs (n 38); Schabas (n 51) 526; Schabas (n 73) 596–600; Cassese *et al* (eds) (n 22) 240–47, 318–22; Protocol on Amendments to the Protocol on the Statute of the African Court of Justice and Human Rights, arts 46A*bis* (Immunities) and 46B (individual criminal responsibility).
92 *Krstić* Appeals Chamber Judgment (n 37) (Dissenting Opinion of Judge Shahabuddeen), paras 7-9.
93 Akande (n 37) 424.

from the customary rule of 'personal immunity from arrest' between or among States Parties ('horizontal personal immunity').

The first view is that personal immunity under article 27(2) is limited to vertical personal immunity. It means that no personal immunity may be invoked in the ICC's preliminary proceedings of investigation and its issuance of arrest warrants, as well as prosecution once the person concerned is before the ICC. The horizontal personal immunity from arrest by a State Party is therefore untouched in article 27(2).[94] The second opinion argues that personal immunity under article 27(2) contains both vertical personal immunity before the ICC and horizontal personal immunity between or among ICC States Parties. Supporters interpret the immunities in a general sense, including any immunities for the purpose of ICC proceedings.[95]

The jurisprudence of the ICC has never supported the first restrictive interpretation of personal immunity in article 27(2). For the effectiveness of ICC proceedings, States Parties vertically waived immunities enjoyed by their senior officials before the ICC, and they also waived the horizontal personal immunity before other States Parties in proceedings governed by the Rome Statute. The ICC has generally upheld the second interpretation.[96] In its recent decisions, the ICC has supported the two-fold function of immunity in article 27(2). In its view, article 27(2) serves two functions:

> (i) it prevents States Parties from raising any immunity belonging to it under international law as a ground for refusing arrest and surrender of a person sought by the Court (vertical effect); and (ii) it prevents States Parties from invoking any immunity belonging to them when cooperation

---

94 H. Kreicker, *Völkerrechtliche Exemtionen Grundlagen und Grenzen Völkerrechtlicher Immunitäten Und Ihre Wirkungen Im Strafrecht* (International Law Exemptions: Fundamentals and Limitations of International Immunities and their Effects in Criminal Law), Vol II (Berlin: Max Planck Institute 2007) 1391, cited in Kreß and Prost (n 2) 2125 and fn 43; Gaeta and Labuda (n 2) 147–48; *The Prosecutor v Al Bashir* (The Hashemite Kingdom of Jordan's appeal against the "Decision under article 87(7) of the Rome Statute on the non-compliance by Jordan with the request by the Court for the arrest and surrender [of] Omar Al-Bashir") ICC-02/05-01/09-326 (12 March 2018), paras 15-21; *The Prosecutor v Al Bashir* (The League of Arab States' Observations on the Hashemite Kingdom of Jordan's appeal against the "Decision under Article 87(7) of the Rome Statute on the non-compliance by Jordan with the request by the Court for the arrest and surrender [of] Omar Al-Bashir") ICC-02/05-01/09-367 (16 July 2018), para 26.

95 Triffterer and Burchard (n 29) 1053; Kreß and Prost (n 2) 2125; B. Broomhall, *International Justice and the International Criminal Court: Between Sovereignty and the Rule of Law* (OUP 2004) 144.

96 *Al Bashir DRC Cooperation Decision 2014* (n 27), para 26.

in the arrest and surrender of a person to the Court is provided by another State Party (horizontal effect).[97]

The vertical effect means that States Parties cannot invoke the personal immunity of their senior officials from arrest or detention for the ICC proceedings.[98] The horizontal effect indicates that a State Party also cannot invoke personal immunity from arrest enjoyed by officials of other States Parties.[99] The Chambers held that article 27(2) excludes immunity.[100] The ICC has no means to arrest a suspect, and it has to rely on States to do so. The Pre-Trial Chamber of the ICC has implicitly held that a non-party State can continue to invoke personal immunity from arrest enjoyed by its sitting senior officials in international law to challenge the exercise of jurisdiction by other States. When it comes to heads of a non-party State, in the ICC's wording, 'the irrelevance of immunities [...] as enshrined in article 27(2) of the Statute has no effect on their rights under international law'.[101] In addition, the Pre-Trial Chamber has restricted the removal of horizontal personal immunity from arrest amongst States Parties for the purpose of ICC proceedings, thus leaving horizontal personal immunities from arrest/detention/prosecution in national proceedings intact. In other words, article 27(2) does not cover the personal immunities

---

[97] *The Prosecutor v Al Bashir* (Decision under article 87(7) of the Rome Statute on the non-compliance by South Africa with the request by the Court for the arrest and surrender of Omar Al-Bashir, PTC II) ICC-02/05-01/09-302 (6 July 2017), paras 76-80; id, (Decision under Article 87(7) of the Rome Statute on the non-compliance by Jordan with the request by the Court for the arrest and surrender of Omar Al-Bashir, PTC II) ICC-02/05-01/09-309 (11 December 2017), para 33. See also *Al Bashir Jordan* Cooperation Appeals Chamber Judgment 2019 (n 2), paras 117-25, 130, 132.

[98] *Al Bashir South Africa* Cooperation Decision 2017, ibid, paras 77-78.

[99] *Al Bashir South Africa* Cooperation Decision 2017 (n 97) paras 79-80. See also *The Prosecutor v Al Bashir* (Request by Professors Robinson, Cryer, deGuzman, Lafontaine, Oosterveld, Stahn and Vasiliev for Leave to Submit Observations) ICC-02/05-01/09-337 (26 April 2018), paras 2, 6; id, (Request by Max du Plessis, Sarah Nouwen and Elizabeth Wilmshurst for leave to submit observations on the legal questions presented in 'The Hashemite Kingdom of Jordan's appeal against the "Decision under Article 87(7) of the Rome Statute on the non-compliance by Jordan with the request by the Court for the arrest and surrender [of] Omar Al-Bashir"') ICC-02/05-01/09-338 (27 April 2018), paras 4-5.

[100] *Al Bashir South Africa* Cooperation Decision 2017 (n 97), paras 74-75; *Al Bashir Jordan* Cooperation Decision 2017 (n 97), para 33.

[101] *Al Bashir South Africa* Cooperation Decision 2017 (n 97), para 82; Schabas (n 73) 600; Liu (n 80); M. Ssenyonjo, 'The International Criminal Court Arrest Warrant Decision for President Al Bashir of Sudan' (2010) 59 *ICLQ* 205, 210; R.H. Steinberg (ed), *Contemporary Issues Facing the International Criminal Court* (Brill | Nijhoff 2016) 73–137.

attaching to serving senior officials in traditional customary law before local jurisdictions of other States, including party and non-party States. Heads of States continue to enjoy personal immunity from another State's national criminal proceedings for committing international crimes.

To conclude, article 27(2) of the Rome Statute covers personal immunity between States Parties as well as personal immunity between a State Party and the ICC. This provision covers the issue of non-availability of personal immunity from arrest by local authorities of States Parties for the ICC proceedings. Article 27(2) evidences a departure from the pre-existing traditional customary rule respecting personal immunity between States. An examination of article 98(1) of the Rome Statute and article 19 of the *Relationship Agreement* between the ICC and the UN further confirms this finding.

7.3.3 Structure of the Rome Statute and Article 19 of the Relationship Agreement

A brief elaboration of article 98(1) of the Rome Statute is required on the issue of 'cooperation with respect to waiver of immunity'. Article 98(1) reads:

> The Court may not proceed with a request for surrender or assistance which would require the requested State to act inconsistently with its obligations under international law with respect to the State or diplomatic immunity of a person or property of a third State, unless the Court can first obtain the cooperation of that third State for the waiver of the immunity.

Article 98(1) addresses the ICC's act and how a requested State cooperates with the ICC's requests for surrender or assistance. It is not the place here to address the procedural aspects of the request for surrender or assistance and the obligations to cooperate.[102] Article 98(1) does mention the terms 'immunity' and 'waiver of the immunity' under 'international law'. The phrase 'international law' means that immunity derived from national law is excluded, while personal immunity and diplomatic immunity of property under customary law are included. A plain reading of article 98(1) shows that this provision covers 'waiver of immunity' by a third State. This rule applies when a third State's waiver of immunity is required.

---

102 D. Jacobs, 'Commentary' in A. Klip and G. Sluiter (eds), *Annotated Leading Cases of the International Criminal Court: 2005–2007*, Vol 23 (Intersentia 2010) 113–21; D. Tladi, 'The ICC Decisions on Chad and Malawi: On Cooperation, Immunities and Article 98' (2013) 11 *JICJ* 199, 205–18.

Article 98(1) was included without sufficient time for a thorough discussion during the 1998 Rome Conference.[103] The preparatory works do not aid in understanding the meaning of 'third State'. This has become clear in the context of the *Al Bashir* case, in which Sudan is a non-party State. Some States repeatedly cited article 98(1) to justify refusal to cooperate. Although a State Party is not empowered by article 98(1) to determine unilaterally whether its cooperation is inconsistent with international law, States' practice implies that these States support an interpretation of 'third State' by including non-party States. Consequently, the usage of the wording 'waiver' signifies that senior officials of a non-party State continue to enjoy personal immunity under traditional international law. Article 98(1) itself, therefore, gives strength to the existence of the traditional customary rule respecting personal immunity.[104] Articles 27(2) and 98(1) further indicate the recognition of the drafters that they did not intend to override but did intend to respect personal immunity in traditional customary law.[105] By accepting the two articles, States Parties did not aim to create a new general rule of non-availability of personal immunity in article 27(2). Heads of non-party States continue to enjoy personal immunity before other States under customary law.[106]

This interpretation is also supported in the negotiations of article 19 of the Relationship Agreement between the Court and the UN. Belgium wanted to confirm that there existed a customary rule of no immunity for international crimes and proposed a provision to deny personal immunity of UN officials for war crimes, crimes against humanity and genocide. Its proposal stated that '[p]aragraph 1 of this article [article 19] shall be without prejudice to the relevant norms of international law, particularly [...] article 27 of the Statute, in respect of the crimes that come under the jurisdiction of the Court'.[107] Belgium's proposal, however, was rejected by the UN representative. The final version of article 19 of the Agreement confirms that UN officials are entitled to immunities, and the UN should agree to 'waive' immunity. Article 19 reads:

---

103 H.-P. Kaul and C. Kreß, 'Jurisdiction and Cooperation in the Statute of the International Criminal Court: Principles and Compromises' (1999) 2 *YIHL* 143, 164.
104 Crawford (n 37) 501.
105 Liu (n 80) 66. Cf. *Al Bashir Jordan* Cooperation Appeals Chamber Judgment 2019 (n 2), paras 130-31.
106 Schabas (n 73) 600; W.A. Schabas, *An Introduction to the International Criminal Court* (6th edn, CUP 2020) 67–68.
107 'Proposal submitted by Belgium Concerning document PCNICC/2000/WGICC-UN/L.1', PCNICC/2000/WGICC-UN/DP.18.

[...] the United Nations undertakes to cooperate fully with the Court and to take all necessary measures to allow the Court to exercise its jurisdiction, in particular by waiving any such privileges and immunities in accordance with the Convention on the Privileges and Immunities of the United Nations and the relevant rules of international law.[108]

Had the text of article 27(2) reflected a customary rule denying personal immunity for committing international crimes, there would be no need for such a provision under article 19.[109]

As mentioned above, the form of article 27(2) indicates a departure from a pre-existing customary rule respecting personal immunity. The structure of the Rome Statute further gives strength to this conclusion. The clause in article 27(2) is a treaty exception to the traditional customary rule respecting personal immunity.[110]

7.3.4 *Conclusions*

Article 27(2) concerns immunities as procedural barriers to the ICC's jurisdiction. This provision serves a two-fold function about personal immunity. The text of article 27(2) rejects a possible invocation of personal immunity by a State Party to challenge another State Party for the effectiveness of the ICC proceedings. It evinces an exception to or a departure from traditional customary law. This exclusion of application of customary law through a treaty is acceptable.[111] The preparatory works show that its drafters indirectly recognised the existence of traditional customary law.[112] They did not aim to modify the pre-existing customary rule respecting personal immunity with an exception, or to create a new customary rule of non-availability of personal immunity between States for committing international crimes. The drafters employed the waiver approach through article 27(2) of the Statute to remove personal immunity from arrest between States Parties for the purpose of ICC proceedings. Article

---

108   Negotiated Relationship Agreement between the International Criminal Court and the United Nations, art 19.
109   Schabas (n 73) 601.
110   *The Prosecutor v Al Bashir* (Request by Prof. Flavia Lattanzi for leave to submit observations on the merits of the legal questions presented in "The Hashemite Kingdom of Jordan's appeal against the 'Decision under Article 87(7) of the Rome Statute on the non-compliance by Jordan with the request by the Court for the arrest and surrender" [of] Omar Al-Bashir) ICC-02/05-01/09-341 (30 April 2018), para 3.
111   *Jones v Saudi Arabia and et al*, [2006] UKHL 26 [33] (Lord Bingham); Cassese *et al* (eds) (n 22) 154; Jia (n 60) 86–87.
112   Schabas (n 73) 600–01; Liu (n 80) 66; Ssenyonjo (n 101) 210–11.

98(1) of the Statute and article 19 of the *Relationship Agreement* also support such a finding.

After examining the text, the form, the preparatory works and the structure of the Rome Statute, it is appropriate to conclude that article 27(2) was an exception to the pre-existing customary rule respecting personal immunity in 1998. This clause was not of a norm-making nature because such an intent cannot be identified. The examination above does not evince whether article 27(2) was declaratory of a customary rule of non-availability of personal immunity for core international crimes in 1998. Article 27(2) in its plain meaning stipulates that personal immunity in international law enjoyed by a senior official of a State Party cannot bar prosecution against that person by the ICC, once it has adjudicatory jurisdiction.[113]

7.4 Non-availability of Personal Immunity for International Crimes: Was Article 27(2) Declaratory of Custom?

The main issue in this section is whether article 27(2) was declaratory of a customary rule about non-availability of personal immunity from arrest for committing international crimes before 1998. This section looks into the 1919 Report of the Commission on the Responsibility of the Authors of the War and on Enforcement of Penalties (1919 Report of the Commission on Responsibilities), the 1919 Treaty of Versailles, article 7 of the Nuremberg Charter and other post-World War II practice to show that article 27(2) was not declaratory of such a customary rule in 1998.

7.4.1 *1919 Report of the Commission on Responsibilities and Treaty of Versailles*

The Commission on Responsibilities in its 1919 Report said that it desired:

> [...] to state expressly that in the hierarchy of persons in authority, there is no reason why rank, however exalted, should in any circumstances protect the holder of it from responsibility when that responsibility has been established before a properly constituted tribunal. This extends even to the case of heads of states. An argument has been raised to the contrary based upon the alleged immunity, and in particular the alleged inviolability, of a sovereign of a state. But this privilege, where it is recognised, is

---

113   2002 *Arrest Warrant* case (n 4), 24–25, paras 58-60; Schabas (n 73).

one of practical expedience [sic] in municipal law, and is not fundamental. However, even if, in some countries, a sovereign is exempt from being prosecuted in a national court of his own country the position from an international point of view is quite different.[114]

This paragraph, however, cannot stand as hard supporting evidence for non-availability of personal immunity. The first two sentences are relevant to substantive individual criminal responsibility.[115] The view in the last two sentences is also contestable. Immunities under international law are not only of practical expediency in municipal law but also a customary rule in contemporary international law. International immunities also do not aim to prevent people from being prosecuted in their own country. The last sentence simply stresses the difference between immunities under national and international law, which is irrelevant to the issue of personal immunity.

The following paragraphs of the 1919 Report should not be disregarded. The Report further stated that '[w]e have [...] proposed the establishment of a high tribunal [...] and included the possibility of the trial before that tribunal of a former head of a state with the consent of that state itself secured by articles in the Treaty of Peace'.[116] What the Commission finally proposed was not the removal of immunity enjoyed by a sitting head of State without consent, but rather a removal of immunity of 'a former head of State [the Kaiser of Germany] with the consent of that State'. The 1919 Report removed the functional immunity of former heads of States, far from disregarding personal immunity of a head of a State.

According to article 227 of the 1919 Treaty of Versailles, the former German Kaiser William II was indicted for prosecution before a special tribunal. The indictment was achieved through Germany's waiver of immunity by signing the Treaty of Versailles, despite the fact that Germany may have had little choice.[117] More details about this indictment are significant. William II was a former head of State who did not enjoy personal immunity. Practices of prosecution of former heads of States exist, but the consent of their States should

---

114 'Commission on the Responsibility of the Authors of the War and on Enforcement of Penalties, Report Presented to the Preliminary Peace Conference' reprinted in (1920) 14 *AJIL* 95, 116; *Al Bashir Malawi* Cooperation Decision 2011 (n 38), para 23.

115 Princeton Project on Universal Jurisdiction, 'The Princeton Principles on Universal Jurisdiction' (2001), 48–51, Principle 5 and its commentary; 2002 *Arrest Warrant* case (n 4), 24, para 58.

116 Report of the Commission on Responsibilities (n 114), 116.

117 Cf. *Ruto & Sang* Acquittal Decision 2016 (n 77) (Reasons of Judge Eboe-Osuji), para 261.

not be ignored. Even for a former head of State who has been deposed and whose monarchy no longer exists, he still enjoyed functional immunity, not to mention personal immunity, if he was in office.

The Commission on Responsibilities proposed a text on responsibility in article III of its draft provisions for the special tribunal, which was a predecessor of article 7 of the Nuremberg Charter and article 27(1) of the Rome Statute. Article III provided that 'all persons belonging to enemy countries, however high their position may have been, without distinction of rank, including chiefs of states, who have been guilty of offences against the laws and customs of war or the laws of humanity, are liable to criminal prosecution'. The US delegate reserved for this article.[118] The US objected to the idea of individual responsibility of a sitting head of State in international law because 'no precedents are to be found in the modern practice of nations'. The US also referred to the *Schooner Exchange v McFaddon* case and argued that 'proceedings against [a head of a State] might be wise or unwise, but in any event they would be against an individual out of office and not against a [person in his position] and thus in effect against the state'.[119] This statement show that even the principle of individual responsibility for a head of State such as article 27(1) of the Rome Statute provides had not yet been generally recognised at that time. It is not persuasive to argue that States would begin to acknowledge a rule of non-availability of personal immunity of a sitting head of State before such a 'high tribunal'. These sources support the view that in 1919 States continued to recognise personal immunity of heads of State, even for international crimes.

7.4.2 Article 7 of the Nuremberg Charter and Article 6 of the Tokyo Charter

Article 7 of the Nuremberg Charter provides that '[t]he official position of Defendants, whether as heads of State, or responsible officials in Government departments, shall not be considered as freeing them from responsibility, or mitigating punishment.' The text of article 6 of the Tokyo Charter is a bit different from that of article 7. Article 6 adds that 'official position and the fact that an accused acted pursuant to order of his government or of a superior may be considered in mitigation of punishment if the Tribunal determines'. Article 6 of the Tokyo Charter did not refer to a head of State, presumably because the decision not to prosecute the Japanese Emperor Hirohito.[120] Articles 6 and 7 of the two Charters, which are similar to article 27(1) of the Rome Statute, are

---

118   Report of the Commission on Responsibilities (n 114) 127–53.
119   ibid 135–36.
120   Gaeta (n 17) 981 and fn 18; Pedretti (n 17) 252; Triffterer and Burchard (n 29) 1044; O'Neill (n 17).

often deemed supporting evidence for a customary rule of non-availability of personal immunity.

Indeed, with reference to article 7, the IMT judgment wrote:

> Crimes against international law are committed by men, not by abstract entities, and only by punishing individuals who commit such crimes can the provisions of international law be enforced. [...] The principles of international law, which under certain circumstances, protects the representatives of States, cannot be applied to acts which are condemned as criminal by international law. The authors of these acts cannot shelter themselves behind their official position in order to be freed from punishment in appropriate proceedings. Article 7 of the Charter expressly declares [...] [h]e who violates the laws of war cannot obtain immunity while acting in pursuance of the authority of the state if the state in authorising action moves outside its competence under international law.[121]

These sentences of the judgment show that individuals cannot hide behind the veil of acting on behalf of a State, because in the IMT's view, acts of international crimes were beyond the competence of a State. A systematic observation of these sentences suggests that the IMT aimed to enforce its view of individual responsibility for international crimes, and article 7 was referred to pierce the veil of functional immunity in international law. An examination of the draft proposals of article 7 of the Nuremberg Charter further affirms this interpretation.

At the London Conference, the US made Draft Proposals for the later London Agreement.[122] An Annex regarding modes of liability and defences stated that '[a]ny defence based upon the fact that the accused is or was the head or purported head or other principal official of a State is legally inadmissible and will not be entertained'.[123] The Soviet Union also proposed a

---

121 *France et al v Göring et al*, Judgment and Sentence of the Nuremberg International Military Tribunals, (1948) 1 TMWC 171, 223.

122 'American Draft of Definitive Proposal, Presented to Foreign Ministers at San Francisco, April 1945'; 'Revision of American Draft of Proposed Agreement, June 14, 1945'; and 'Revised Draft of Agreement and Memorandum Submitted by American Delegation, June 30, 1945' in *Report of Robert H. Jackson, United States Representative to the International Conference on Military Trials: London, 1945* (USGPO 1949).

123 'Revised Draft of Agreement and Memorandum Submitted by American Delegation, June 30, 1945' in Report of Robert H. Jackson (n 122) 124, 180–81.

draft.[124] Article 28 of the Soviet draft proposed that '[t]he official position of persons guilty of war crimes, their position as heads of States or as heads of various departments shall not be considered as freeing them from or in mitigation of their responsibility'.[125] The British draft of the later Nuremberg Charter provided that '[t]he official position of defendants, whether as heads of State or responsible officials in various Departments, shall not be considered as freeing them from responsibility or mitigating punishment'.[126] Except for a minor change, this draft text was retained substantially in article 7 of the Nuremberg Charter.

The reference to the accused as a sitting head of a State and the general references to 'heads of States' seem to suggest that personal immunities were also considered. However, these drafts about the issues of responsibilities and defences aimed to remove a potential defence for acting on behalf of the State in national law to free an individual from responsibility. Individuals cannot take refuge in the doctrine that their crimes were acts of States. They did not cope with the issue of personal immunity in international law as we discuss it now. Article 7 of the Nuremberg Charter was initially designed to distinguish individual criminal responsibility from State responsibility for committing international crimes.[127] Article 6 of the Tokyo Charter itself shared the same function as article 7. The two provisions pertain to substantive defences of official position. They do not directly answer whether personal immunities were automatically lifted before the two tribunals for committing international crimes.

7.4.3 Post-World War II Practice

After World War II, no evidence shows that the IMTFE and the IMT prosecuted 'sitting' senior State officials without consent. The Japanese Emperor Hirohito was never indicted. The highest indicted state officials in IMTFE were former prime ministers. Hitler, as a leader of Nazi Germany, committed suicide. The IMT prosecuted Dönitz, who was the sitting head of State of Germany, for

---

124 'Draft of Agreement Presented by the Soviet Delegation, July 2, 1945'; 'Draft Showing Soviet and American Proposals (in Parallel Columns)' in Report of Robert H. Jackson (n 122) 180.
125 UN Doc A/CN.4/22 (1950), 183.
126 Report of Robert H. Jackson (n 122) 352; 'Draft Code of Offences against the Peace and Security of Mankind, Report by Mr J. Spiropoulos, Special Rapporteur', UN Doc A/CN.4/25 (1950), paras 129-138.
127 W.A. Schabas, *Genocide in International Law, The Crime of Crimes* (2nd edn, CUP 2009) 369–71; 'Formulation of Nuremberg Principles, Report by Jean Spiropoulos, Special Rapporteur', UN Doc A/CN.4/22 (1950), 192.

crimes against peace and war crimes.[128] Dönitz was convicted for acts of waging aggressive wars committed after he was appointed as a Commander-in-Chief of the Navy. When Dönitz was prosecuted, Germany did not raise any objection to the prosecution by virtue of personal immunity. Article 1 of the London Agreement provided that '[t]here shall be established after consultation with the Control Council for Germany an International Military Tribunal'.[129] The Control Council had the capacity as local sovereign of Germany authority at that time, although it was created by the Allied powers acting as a *de facto* legislator.[130] The phrase 'consultation with the Control Council for Germany' implies that Germany consented to remove the personal immunity of senior officials.

The sentence of the IMT judgment on immunities wrote that '[h]e who violates the laws of war cannot obtain immunity while acting in pursuance of the authority of the state if the state in authorising action moves outside its competence under international law'.[131] In the IMT's view, the principle of immunity in international law does not apply to international crimes, and individuals cannot obtain immunity if they committed international crimes.[132] One may argue that the 'immunity' here also covers personal immunities. If Germany had objected to the prosecution of Dönitz, the personal immunity held by Dönitz would also be generally rejected by the IMT. However, as observed above, this sentence should be read in the context that the IMT sought to establish individual criminal responsibility in international law. The IMT intended to specify that an act was committed in the official capacity would not constitute a defence or mitigate punishment. It appears that the IMT adopted the private acts approach to reject potential defence of the accused by virtue of functional immunity. It is inappropriate to conclude that a potential plea of head of State personal immunity was also contemplated by the IMT here.

Besides, one may note that the IMTFE also held that 'this immunity has no relation to crimes against international law charged before a tribunal having jurisdiction'.[133] The 'immunity' here was not expressly confined to diplomatic immunity. However, the IMTFE aimed to reject the special defence of Hiroshi

---

128   *France et al v Göring et al* (n 121).
129   London Agreement.
130   The *Justice* case, (1951) 3 TWC 1, 964–65.
131   *France et al v Göring et al* (n 121) 223.
132   ibid.
133   *US et al v Araki et al*, Judgment, 1 November 1948, in United Nations War Crimes Commission (ed), *Transcripts of Proceedings and Documents of the International Military Tribunals for the Far East (Tokyo Trials)*: Judgment, 1189.

Ōshima that he was protected by diplomatic privilege for his activities in Germany as he was the Japanese ambassador to Germany.[134] The wording 'this immunity' does not directly show that the IMTFE generally considered the irrelevance of personal immunity for international crimes. Accordingly, the practice of post-World War II confirms individual responsibility of senior officials, instead of supporting a denial of personal immunity of senior officials.

7.4.4   *1946 GA Resolution and 1950 Nuremberg Principle III*

Other sources frequently referred to in this context are 1946 UN General Assembly Resolution 95(I),[135] and Principle III of the ILC's 'Principles of International Law Recognised in the Charter of the Nuremberg Tribunal and the Judgment of the Tribunal' (1950 ILC Nuremberg Principles).[136] The legal status of the two documents should be noted. The 1946 Resolution 95(I) did not attach or refer to a consolidated text of the Nuremberg principles, and the General Assembly never adopted the 1950 ILC Nuremberg Principles. The irrelevance of official capacity under article 7 of the Nuremberg Charter was recognised by the General Assembly in Resolution 95(I).[137] Principle III of the 1950 ILC Nuremberg Principles, which was also based on article 7 of the Nuremberg Charter,[138] provided that 'the fact that a person who committed an act which constitutes a crime under international law acted as head of State or responsible government official did not relieve him from responsibility under international law'.[139] As noted above, both documents do not deal with personal immunity as a procedural bar, but rather the issue of acting on behalf of a State as a defence to individual responsibility.

7.4.5   *Assessment and Conclusions*

Article IV of the 1948 Genocide Convention also merits brief discussion.[140] Article IV reads that '[p]ersons committing genocide or any of the other acts enumerated in article III shall be punished, whether they are constitutionally responsible rulers, public officials or private individuals'. William Schabas

---

134 ibid.
135 UN Doc A/RES/95 (I).
136 'Formulation of the Nuremberg Principles' in 'Report of the International Law Commission covering its second session, 5 June – 29 July 1950', UN Doc A/CN.4/34 (1950), 374–78; 'Formulation of the Nuremberg Principles', GA Res 488 (V) (1950), UN Doc A/RES/488 (V), para (1).
137 UN Doc A/RES/95 (I).
138 'UN Doc A/CN.4/34 (1950), 375, para 104.
139 ibid.
140 Convention on the Prevention and Punishment of the Crime of Genocide, 78 UNTS 277.

comments that the drafters of the Convention in that article only provide responsibility for genocide, instead of depriving senior officials of immunity who are in office.[141] In contrast, commentators and an ICC Judge Perrin De Brichambaut have argued that personal immunities were 'removed' or 'waived' by States Parties to the Genocide Convention.[142] In their view, personal immunities were not attached to senior officials in accordance with article IV.[143] This argument implicitly recognises the rule of respecting personal immunities.

The above authorities provide no similar wording to that provided in article 27(2). Immunities constitute no bar for the exercise of jurisdiction in the IMT and the IMTFE, while personal immunities were not expressly removed in their founding instruments. This factual situation does not lead to the conclusion that a rule of non-availability of personal immunity existed for international crimes. In fact, most individuals involved in the proceedings were not sitting senior officials. The issue of personal immunity did not arise before the two tribunals. The evaluation of these sources demonstrates that they are all echoed in article 27(1) of the Rome Statute. Similarly, article 7(2) of the 1993 ICTY Statute and article 6(2) of the 1994 ICTR Statute share the same feature. All these instruments are irrelevant to personal immunity but confirm either a rule of functional immunity by removing that immunity with 'consent' or a rule of individual criminal responsibility in international law. Relying on the authorities referred to above, commentators supporting an exception to immunity seem to conflate the issue of no defence for official acts with the issue of no exception to personal immunity. In establishing these tribunals to exercise jurisdiction over international crimes, these States did not intend to abrogate personal immunity in traditional customary law.

The observations demonstrate a lack of support for an emerging customary rule before 1998 recognising non-availability of personal immunity from arrest for committing international crimes. No sufficient practice or *opinio juris* exists to support a pre-existing or an emerging customary rule that there was no personal immunity in national or international proceedings for committing international crimes. Exceptionally, the commentary to article 7 of

---

141 Schabas (n 127) 54–55, 369–71.
142 *Al Bashir South Africa* Cooperation Decision 2017 (n 97) (Minority Opinion of Judge Marc Perrin De Brichambaut), paras 8, 30.
143 Akande (n 38) 350–51; G. Sluiter, 'Using the Genocide Convention to Strengthen Cooperation with the ICC in the Al Bashir Case' (2010) 8 *JICJ* 365, 378; *Al Bashir South Africa* Cooperation Decision 2017 (n 97), paras 21-37 and fn 16.

the 1996 ILC Draft Code of Crimes about 'official position and responsibility' wrote that

> The absence of any procedural immunity with respect to prosecution or punishment in appropriate judicial proceedings is an essential corollary of the absence of any substantive immunity or defence. It would be paradoxical to prevent an individual from invoking his official position to avoid responsibility for a crime only to permit him to invoke this same consideration to avoid the consequences of this responsibility.[144]

This passage restates that the non-availability of procedural immunity 'is an essential corollary' of the absence of substantive defence. The purposive reading of the inclusion of person immunity in article 7 reflects the ILC members' ambition to end impunity through no immunity, because the personal immunity might bar the prosecution before a specific court or over a period of time. But this instance does not challenge the main finding. The construction of article IV of the Genocide Convention also does not undermine this finding. This section concludes that article 27(2) was not declaratory of a customary rule of non-availability of personal immunity from arrest for committing international crimes before the adoption of the 1998 Rome Statute.

7.5 Non-availability of Personal Immunity for Committing International Crimes: Is Article 27(2) Declaratory of Custom?

By lifting personal immunity from arrest for international crimes, article 27(2) of the Rome Statute provides an exception to the existing customary rule respecting personal immunity. The new customary rule is formed unless sufficient evidence of State practice and *opinio juris* support an exception to absolute personal immunity for committing international crimes.[145] After the adoption of the Rome Statute, some national and international decisions seem to show a denial of immunity for international crimes. This section examines practice and new trends after 1998 to answer whether article 27(2) is declaratory of a modified (new) customary rule with respect to personal immunity to date.

---

144 UN Doc A/51/10(1996), para 50, commentary (6) to art 7 (citations omitted). For a similar view, see *Ruto & Sang* Acquittal Decision 2016 (Reasons of Judge Eboe-Osuji) (n 77), paras 263, 286–87.
145 Robinson (n 37) 562–64.

7.5.1   *Immunity for International Crimes: 1999* Pinochet *Case (the UK)
and 2001* Gaddafi *Case (France)*

The 1999 *Pinochet* (*No 3*) case was the first challenge to immunity for torture before the UK's House of Lords.[146] When Augusto Pinochet, the former Head of State of Chile, was visiting the UK for medical treatment in 1998, Spain requested the UK to extradite him for charges of torture in the Spanish Court. The UK issued two warrants for his arrest. The High Court quashed one of the warrants because Pinochet was immune from prosecution as a former head of State.[147] During the appeal before the House of Lords, the majority agreed that Pinochet enjoyed no functional immunity for acts of torture as defined in the 1984 Convention against Torture.[148] Despite different grounds for the dismissal of immunity, the *Pinochet* case represents a change of direction for the issue of immunity.[149] This case, however, dealt with functional immunity of former senior officials rather than personal immunities of sitting senior officials. The majority of the House of Lords supported the view that incumbent senior State officials still enjoy personal immunity before national courts, even if they committed torture.[150] In 2004, a UK district court rejected an application for an arrest warrant for then sitting President of Zimbabwe Robert Mugabe for alleged torture.[151] The judge held that:

> Whilst international law evolves over a period of time international customary law which is embodied in our Common Law currently provides absolute immunity to any Head of State. [...] Robert Mugabe is President and Head of State of Zimbabwe and is entitled whilst he is Head of State to that immunity. He is not liable to any form of arrest or detention [...].[152]

French courts held a slightly different view on the matter of personal immunity. In the 2001 *Gaddafi* case, the Court of Cassation of France examined

---

146   *R v Ex Parte Pinochet et al* (No 3), (1999) 38 ILM 581 (n 21).
147   Bianchi (n 10).
148   *R v Ex Parte Pinochet et al* (No 3), (1999) 38 ILM 581 (n 21) [595] (Lord Browne-Wilkinson), [626] (Lord Hope of Craighead), [643] (Lord Saville of Newdigate), [651] (Lord Millett). Convention against Torture and Other Cruel, Inhuman or Degrading Treatment or Punishment, 1465 UNTS 85.
149   For an analysis of this case, see A. Gattini, '*Pinochet* Cases' in R. Wolfrum (ed) (2007) MPEPIL, paras 13-18.
150   *R v Ex Parte Pinochet et al* (No 3), (1999) 38 ILM 581 (n 21) [643] (Lord Saville of Newdigate).
151   *Application for a Warrant for the Arrest of Robert Mugabe* (First instance) (14 January 2004), ILDC 96 (UK 2004).
152   ibid, paras 5, 7.

whether Gaddafi as a serving head of State was immune from the national court of France for complicity in acts of terrorism.[153] In the beginning, the Court of Appeal ruled that since the end of World War II the principle of immunity admits some exceptions for acts outside the realm of the duties of a head of State. In addition, considering the gravity of the crime, Gaddafi could not enjoy immunity from jurisdiction.[154] The Prosecutor appealed on the interpretation of personal immunity. The Prosecutor argued that a sitting head of State enjoys absolute immunity from jurisdiction and no exception could be made, no matter how grave the crime charged. The Court of Cassation of France overturned the Court of Appeal's ruling. The Court of Cassation in its judgment held that 'in international law, the reported crime [acts of terrorism], regardless of its gravity, does not provide exceptions to the principle of the immunity from jurisdiction of foreign heads of State in office, the indictment division failed to consider the above-mentioned principle'.[155]

The Court of Cassation implicitly upheld that 'exceptions to the principle of the immunity of jurisdiction of a sitting head of State' before a national court exist, but these exceptions 'in international law' do not include 'the reported crime', acts of terrorism.[156] Nevertheless, it is unclear what exceptions the Court had considered, treaty derogations from custom for committing international crimes or the gravity of core international crimes. The *Gaddafi* case, therefore, does not directly support the contention that core international crimes provide exceptions to absolute personal immunity before an international tribunal.

7.5.2 The ICJ: 2002 Arrest Warrant Case (Belgium v Congo)

Both the *Pinochet* and *Gaddafi* cases were cited by Belgium in the 2002 *Arrest Warrant* or *Yerodia* case before the ICJ.[157] In the *Arrest Warrant* case, Belgium issued an international arrest warrant for the incumbent Minister for Foreign Affairs of Congo, Mr Abdulaye Yerodia Ndombasi, for inciting racial hatred when he was a personal secretary of the Congolese President.

---

153 *General Prosecutor v Gaddafi* (Appeal Judgment, Court of Cassation, France) 00-87215 (13 March 2001), ILDC 774 (FR 2001); Zappalà (n 79).
154 *General Prosecutor v Gaddafi* (n 153) para 1; T. Marguerite, 'General Prosecutor *v* Gaddafi' in A. Nollkaemper and A. Reinisch (eds), *Oxford Reports on International Law in Domestic Courts* (28 October 2008), Facts, F4 and F5.
155 *General Prosecutor v Gaddafi* (n 153) paras 1, 10.
156 Y. Kerbrat and T. Marguerite, '*General Prosecutor v Gaddafi*' in Nollkaemper and Reinisch (eds) (n 154) Analysis, A6.
157 2002 *Arrest Warrant* case (n 4) (Counter Memorial of the Kingdom of Belgium) (28 September 2001), paras 3.5.92–3.5.93.

Congo contended that Belgium violated rules of international law including the principle of immunity from jurisdiction, which is absolute and subject to no exception.[158] Belgium argued that the immunities attaching to incumbent ministers of foreign affairs could not be invoked to protect them when they are suspected of having committed war crimes or crimes against humanity.[159] Based on a distinction between the immunity for ordinary crimes and the immunity for international crimes, Belgium argued that 'an exception to the immunity rule was accepted in the case of serious crimes under international law'. Congo insisted that 'under international law as it currently stands, there is no basis for asserting that there is any exception to the principles of absolute immunity from criminal process of an incumbent Minister for Foreign Affairs where he or she is accused of having committed crimes under international law'.[160]

The majority of the ICJ rejected Belgium's arguments about personal immunity.[161] The ICJ held that no exception to personal immunity exists under customary law before the jurisdiction of other States, regardless of the nature of crimes. The ICJ found that:

> It has been unable to deduce from this practice that there exists under customary international law any form of exception to the rule according immunity from criminal jurisdiction and inviolability to incumbent Ministers for Foreign Affairs, where they are suspected of having committed war crimes or crimes against humanity.[162]

This finding was affirmed in a subsequent case before the ICJ.[163] The ICJ also cited articles 6 and 7 of the Tokyo and Nuremberg Charters, articles 6(2) and 7(2) of the ICTR and ICTY Statutes and article 27 of the Rome Statute. The ICJ concluded that 'these rules do not enable it to conclude that any such an exception exists in customary international law in regard to national courts'.[164] The ICJ affirmed the immunity of sitting foreign ministers for committing

---

158   2002 *Arrest Warrant* case (n 4), 8, paras 11-12, 20-21, paras 47-48.
159   2002 *Arrest Warrant* case (n 4) (Counter Memorial of the Kingdom of Belgium), para 0.26 (d).
160   2002 *Arrest Warrant* case (n 4), 24, para 57.
161   2002 *Arrest Warrant* case (n 4) (Dissenting Opinion of Judge *ad hoc* Van den Wyngaert).
162   2002 *Arrest Warrant* case (n 4), 24, para 58.
163   *Questions of Mutual Assistance* Judgment (n 17).
164   2002 *Arrest Warrant* case (n 4), 24, para 58.

international crimes as a customary rule. Without a doubt, its conclusion also extends to heads of State and heads of government.[165]

A statement in paragraph 61 of the judgment of the *Arrest Warrant case* is significant. It stated that:

> [...] an incumbent or former Minister for Foreign Affairs may be subject to criminal proceedings before certain international criminal courts, where they have jurisdiction. Examples include the International Criminal Tribunal for the former Yugoslavia, and the International Criminal Tribunal for Rwanda, established pursuant to Security Council resolutions under Chapter VII of the United Nations Charter, and the future International Criminal Court created by the 1998 Rome Convention. The latter's Statute expressly provides, in article 27, paragraph 2, that [...].[166]

This statement seems to open a door for non-availability of personal immunity before 'certain international courts'.[167] This statement should be understood systemically, and other reasoning of the ICJ should not be overlooked.

The ICJ first noted that 'jurisdiction does not imply absence of immunity'.[168] It then clarified that immunity from jurisdiction does not automatically mean impunity for crimes committed, 'irrespective of their gravity'. In its wording, '[j]urisdictional immunity may well bar prosecution for a certain period or for certain offences'.[169] Consequently, the ICJ described in paragraph 61 some plausible circumstances in which immunity does not bar criminal prosecution. The first three ways are prosecution by their own countries, waiver of immunity and prosecution of former senior officials. For the first two alternatives: personal immunity in international law is never a bar for prosecution by the State to which the suspect belongs and the waiver of immunity ceases personal immunity as a bar. Despite the fact that Belgium only charged Mr Yerodia for his acts performed before he assumed the Minister for Foreign Affairs, the third alternative indicates that when Mr Yerodia left the office and enjoyed no personal immunity in international law, a foreign State may try him not only

---

165 Cassese *et al* (eds) (n 22) 320; Kreicker, *Völkerrechtliche Exemtionen Grundlagen Und Grenzen Völkerrechtlicher Immunitäten Und Ihre Wirkungen Im Strafrecht*, cited in Kreß and Prost (n 2) 2128 and fn 58; 2002 *Arrest Warrant* case of the ICJ (Dissenting Opinion of Judge *ad hoc* Van den Wyngaert), paras 16-19.
166 2002 *Arrest Warrant* case (n 4), 25, para 61.
167 Akande (n 38) 334.
168 2002 *Arrest Warrant* case (n 4), 24–25, para 59.
169 ibid 25, para 60.

for acts performed before or subsequent to his office, but also for acts 'in a private capacity' committed during his office.

The fourth alternative, as cited above, is the prosecution of an incumbent minister for foreign affairs for international crimes by international criminal tribunals, if they have jurisdiction.[170] The ICJ referred to three examples of the ICTY, the ICTR and the ICC. The ICJ noted that the UN Security Council established the former two tribunals, while the procedural bar to the ICC was deprived by virtue of article 27(2) of the Rome Statute. The ICJ, however, did not clarify why personal immunity may not be a bar to proceedings 'before certain international criminal courts, where they have jurisdiction': denied automatically for the nature of international courts and the nature of the crimes, waived by signing a treaty, or deprived by the UN Security Council.

By virtue of its reasoning, the ICJ may agree that personal immunity is not a bar before the two *ad hoc* tribunals due to the removal of immunity by the Security Council.[171] The ICJ may also support the view that States Parties cannot invoke personal immunity before the ICC pursuant to article 27(2). Alternatively, it may be noted that the passage cited suggests a different rule of personal immunity in prosecuting international crimes before certain international courts, for instance, the ICC. Because if the reference to the ICC suggests States Parties' waivers by signing a treaty, the second alternative (waiver-exception) would be unnecessary. However, the separate waiver-exception alternative seems to be closely linked to a court of foreign State, and a specific waiver-exception before the ICC through accepting a treaty provision, therefore, is not superfluous. In addition, the ICJ in the *Arrest Warrant* case stated that 'although various international conventions […] requiring [States] to extend their criminal jurisdiction, such extension […] in no way affects immunities under customary international law'.[172] It seems that the ICJ would disagree with the idea that the horizontal personal immunity from arrest under customary law is disregarded as long as the arrest warrant was issued by a competent 'international' court. Judge Van den Wyngaert in her dissenting opinion also did not argue for a distinction of immunity based on the nature of the court.[173] The ICJ did not aim to rely on the nature of certain international courts to deny personal immunity for international crimes.

---

170   ibid 25–26, para 61. For comments on the ICJ's view concerning the prosecution of former State officials, see 2002 *Arrest Warrant* case (n 4) (Joint Separate opinion of Judges Higgins, Kooijmans and Buergenthal), para 85; Cassese (n 34) 867–74.
171   Chapter 7.5.6.
172   2002 *Arrest Warrant* case (n 4), 24–25, para 59.
173   2002 *Arrest Warrant* case (n 4) (Dissenting Opinion of Judge *ad hoc* Van den Wyngaert), paras 8-39.

To sum up, the ICJ provided certain avenues for States to narrow the impunity gap arising from an invocation of personal immunity. By rejecting Belgium's arguments, personal immunity in customary law was acknowledged by the ICJ for committing crimes, regardless of their gravity.

7.5.3 *The SCSL and the ICTY:* Taylor *and* Milošević *Cases*

Some cases of international criminal tribunals show a trend of eroding the customary rule respecting personal immunity, notably the *Slobodan Milošević* case at the ICTY,[174] the *Charles Taylor* case at the SCSL,[175] and several ICC decisions in the *Al Bashir* case.[176] The following paragraphs focus on the *Taylor* and *Milošević* cases.

In the *Taylor* case, an indictment and an arrest warrant were issued when Charles Taylor was the sitting President of Liberia. The issue before the Appeals Chamber of the SCSL was whether he was entitled to immunity from the court's jurisdiction.[177] The Appeals Chamber considered the international nature of the SCSL[178] and emphasised the ICJ's finding in the *Arrest Warrant* case that personal immunity could not prevent Taylor from being subject to international proceedings.[179] The Appeals Chamber drew a distinction between international and national courts on the issue of personal immunity. The Chamber concluded that 'the principle seems now established that the sovereign equality of states does not prevent a Head of State from being prosecuted before an international criminal tribunal or court'.[180] The *Taylor* decision seems to indicate removal of personal immunity of a sitting head of State for committing international crimes.[181]

The Appeals Chamber's reasoning is, however, not sound.[182] Firstly, article 6(2) of the Statute of the SCSL substantially used the same wording as article 7(2) of the ICTY Statute and article 27(1) of the Rome Statute, which are less relevant to the personal immunity issue. Secondly, the *Taylor* decision relied heavily on the last alternative in paragraph 61 of the ICJ's *Arrest Warrant* case to

---

174   2001 *Milosević* Decision on Preliminary Motions (n 37), paras 28-33.
175   2004 *Charles Taylor* Jurisdiction Decision (n 45).
176   *Al Bashir Malawi* Cooperation Decision 2011 (n 38); *Al Bashir Chad* Cooperation Decision 2011 (n 38); *Al Bashir DRC* Cooperation Decision 2014 (n 27).
177   2004 *Charles Taylor* Jurisdiction Decision (n 45), para 20.
178   ibid, paras 41-42.
179   ibid, para 52.
180   ibid, paras 51-52.
181   ibid.
182   Cf. Kreß and Prost (n 2) 2136. For an analysis of the international nature of a court, see Schabas (n 51) 523.

uphold an emerging trend of no personal immunity before international criminal tribunals.[183] As mentioned above, the last alternative cannot be exclusively construed as depriving personal immunity for the nature of international proceedings. The waiver-exception and the power of the Security Council are also grounds for the non-availability of personal immunity before international tribunals. That passage does not directly support the non-availability of personal immunity for committing international crimes before international courts. The SCSL was established through the Agreement between the UN and Sierra Leone. It is thus less convincing to argue that the SCSL was at a position similar to the ICC. Thirdly, the Chamber also referred to the opinion of Lord Millett in the *Pinochet (No 3)* case.[184] But Lord Millett's idea was that in the future the rank of a person accused of committing international crimes affords no defence, which evidences the irrelevance of official capacity as a defence. Lord Millett also wrote that:

> Immunity *ratione personae* is a status immunity. [...] If he [Pinochet] were [a serving head of State], he could not be extradited. It would be an intolerable affront to the Republic of Chile to arrest him or detain him. [...] The nature of the charge is irrelevant; his immunity [*ratione personae*] is personal and absolute.[185]

The Appeals Chamber of the SCSL also cited other sources to support its argument. It indeed mixed the issue of individual responsibility with the issue of personal immunity.[186] In brief, the reasoning in the *Taylor* decision does not support a new rule of non-availability of personal immunity for committing international crimes.

In the *Milošević* case, the ICTY indicted Slobodan Milošević, a sitting head of State of the Federal Republic of Yugoslavia (FRY), for crimes committed in Kosovo. Judge Hunt confirmed the indictment and ordered the issuance and transmission of arrest warrants to the FRY in 1999.[187] In 2001, the Republic of Serbia surrendered the former FRY president Milošević to the ICTY. The *amicus curiae* and Milošević raised objections to the jurisdiction of the ICTY partly

---

183   2004 *Charles Taylor* Jurisdiction Decision (n 45), para 50.
184   *R v Ex Parte Pinochet et al* (No 3), (1999) 38 *ILM* 581 (n 21) [652] (Lord Millett).
185   ibid [644], [651] (italics by the author).
186   2004 *Charles Taylor* Jurisdiction Decision (n 45), paras 44-49.
187   *Prosecutor v Milošević et al* (Decision on Review of Indictment and Application for Consequential Orders) ICTY-99-37-PT (24 May 1999), paras 5, 20, 38 (2).

by reason of Milošević's status as former president.[188] The Trial Chamber dismissed the reason because in its view article 7(2) of the Statute of ICTY reflected a customary international rule.[189] The Trial Chamber referred to the ICTR's prosecution of Kambanda, a former Prime Minister of Rwanda, as well as other international instruments. Since the legality of the issuance of the international arrest warrant for a sitting head of State was not challenged, the Trial Chamber actually dealt with the functional immunity instead of personal immunity. It seems that the Trial Chamber also oversimplified the issue without distinguishing a defence of official capacity from the procedural immunity. As will be seen below in subsection 7.5.6, personal immunity was not a problematic issue for the indictment and surrender of Milošević before the ICTY.[190] This *Milošević* case, therefore, does not support a rule of non-availability of personal immunity under customary law.

7.5.4 Al Bashir *Cooperation Decisions before the ICC*

Debates have occurred in the ICC's Darfur Situation as to personal immunities of Al Bashir, who was a sitting head of State that is not a party to the Rome Statute.[191] The Darfur Situation was referred to the ICC by the Security Council.[192] It is undeniable that the ICC can exercise jurisdiction over the alleged crimes. However, Al Bashir as a serving head of State enjoys personal immunity embedded under customary law, leading to his protection from arrest by foreign authorities.[193] A question arises whether Al Bashir can invoke personal immunities from arrest before the ICC and national authorities of States Parties.

The legality of the ICC's issuance of warrants also concerns the issue of personal immunity. In the *First Warrant of Arrest* Decision, Pre-Trial Chamber I of the ICC concluded that Al Bashir did not enjoy personal immunity before the

---

188 *Prosecutor v Milošević* (Preliminary Protective Motion) ICTY-99-37-PT (9 August 2001), 5; 2001 *Milošević* Decision on Preliminary Motions (n 37), paras 26-34.
189 2001 *Milošević* Decision on Preliminary Motions (n 37), paras 28, 34.
190 ibid, paras 42-45. The *Milošević* case in connection with the position of the Security Council is analysed in detail in chapter 7.5.6.
191 1998 Rome Statute, art 27; L. Condorelli and S. Villalpando, 'Can the Security Council Extend the ICC's Jurisdiction?' in A. Cassese *et al* (eds), *The Rome Statute of the International Criminal Court: A Commentary* (OUP 2002) 634; *The Prosecutor v Al Bashir* (Warrant of Arrest for Omar Hassan Ahmad Al Bashir, PTC I) ICC-02/05-01/09-1 (4 March 2009).
192 UN Doc S/RES/1593 (2005).
193 Van Alebeek (n 17); Pedretti (n 17) 57–100.

ICC because article 27(2) applies to a non-party State.[194] The Chamber relied on the treaty provision to remove his personal immunity without explaining why this provision prevails over existing customary law respecting personal immunity. It remained silent on whether article 27(2) is a declaration of customary law recognising an exception to personal immunity. The *First Warrant of Arrest* Decision, therefore, may not be relevant to ascertaining a customary rule with an exception to personal immunity.[195]

In analysing the reasoning behind this decision, Paola Gaeta argues that article 27(2) may apply to senior officials of non-party States by virtue of its customary nature.[196] In her view, no personal immunity before the ICC exists since article 27(2) is a reflection of customary law acknowledging non-availability of personal immunity. Her idea seems to have been partly followed by subsequent decisions of the ICC. Pursuant to article 87(7) of the Rome Statute, the ICC has made several decisions for failure to comply with the cooperation requests for the arrest and surrender of Al Bashir.[197] Some of these decisions

---

194 *The Prosecutor v Al Bashir* (Decision on the Prosecution's Application for a Warrant of Arrest against Omar Hassan Ahmad Al Bashir, PTC I) ICC-02/05-01/09-3 (4 March 2009), para 41.

195 For observations of the Chamber's four reasons, see Gaeta (n 38) 322–25; Kreß (2012) (n 38) 241–42.

196 Gaeta (n 38) 322–25. See also *The Prosecutor v Al Bashir* (Request by Professor Paola Gaeta for leave to submit observations on the merits of the legal questions presented in the Hashemite Kingdom of Jordan's appeal against the "Decision under Article 87 (7) of the Rome Statute on the non-compliance by Jordan with the request by the Court for the arrest and surrender [of] Omar Al-Bashir" of 12 March 2018) ICC-02/05-01/09-349 (30 April 2018), para 1.

197 As of 31 December 2020, there are 13 States Parties' non-cooperation decisions in the *Al Bashir* case. Kenya Cooperation Decision 2010, ICC-02/05-01/09-107; Chad Cooperation Decision 2010, ICC-02/05-01/09-109; Djibouti Cooperation Decision 2011, ICC-02/05-01/09-129; *Al Bashir* Malawi Cooperation Decision 2011 (n 38); *Al Bashir Chad* Cooperation Decision 2011 (n 38); The Prosecutor v *Al Bashir* (Decision on the Non-compliance of the Republic of Chad with the Cooperation Requests Issued by the Court Regarding the Arrest and Surrender of Omar Hassan Ahmad Al-Bashir, PTC II) ICC-02/05-01/09-151 (26 March 2013); *Al Bashir Nigeria* Cooperation Decision 2013, ICC-02/05-01/09-159; *Al Bashir* DRC Cooperation Decision 2014 (n 27); *Al Bashir Sudan* Cooperation Decision 2015, ICC-02/05-01/09-227; *The Prosecutor v Al Bashir* (Decision on the non-compliance by the Republic of Djibouti with the request to arrest and surrender Omar Al-Bashir to the Court and referring the matter to the United Nations Security Council and the Assembly of the States Parties to the Rome Statute) ICC-02/05-01/09-266 (11 July 2016); id, (Decision on the non-compliance by the Republic of Uganda with the request to arrest and surrender Omar Al-Bashir to the Court and referring the matter to the United Nations Security Council and the Assembly of States Parties to the Rome Statute) ICC-02/05-01/09-267 (11 July 2016); *Al Bashir South Africa* Cooperation Decision 2017 (n 97); *Al Bashir*

are closely related to the present issue of personal immunity under customary law.[198]

7.5.4.1 *Malawi* Decision: Personal Immunity before the ICC

In 2011, Pre-Trial Chamber I of the ICC in the *Malawi* decision held that in international law no personal immunity can be invoked to oppose a prosecution by an international court.[199] It also concluded that in international proceedings there is a customary exception to absolute personal immunity from arrest recognised in traditional customary law.[200] The following paragraphs focus on the 2011 *Malawi* decision.

In the *Malawi* decision, two issues merit discussion. The first issue here is whether Omar Al Bashir enjoys personal immunity from arrest and prosecution before the ICC. Malawi argued that article 27 of the Rome Statute does not apply to Sudan, and Al Bashir as a sitting head of non-party State to the Statute enjoyed immunity from arrest and prosecution in accordance with principles of international law.[201] Pre-Trial Chamber I agreed that the acceptance of article 27(2) implies no immunity, but it rejected the idea that 'with respect to non-party State to the Rome Statute, international law provides immunity to Heads of State in proceedings'.[202] The Chamber concluded that 'the principle in international law is that immunity [...] cannot be invoked to oppose a prosecution by an international court'.[203]

It is disputable whether Pre-Trial Chamber I reasonably justified its conclusions. First and foremost, the provisions and instruments (i.e., the 1919 Report of the Commission on Responsibilities, articles 7 and 6 of the Nuremberg and Tokyo Charters, the judgments of the IMT and IMTFE, Principle III of Nuremberg Principles, articles 7(2) and 6(2) of the Statutes of the ICTY and the ICTR, and article 7 of the 1996 Draft Code of Crimes) referred to in this case are related to the issue of individual responsibility rather than the issue of personal immunity. Most examples here, as mentioned above, are evidence of

---

Jordan Cooperation Decision 2017 (n 97); *Al Bashir Jordan* Cooperation Appeals Chamber Judgment 2019 (n 2).

198 Watts (n 13) paras 10-11; Kreß and Prost (n 2) 2128-39; *Al Bashir Malawi* Cooperation Decision 2011 (n 38), para 43; *Al Bashir Chad* Cooperation Decision 2011 (n 38); *Al Bashir Jordan* Cooperation Appeals Chamber Judgment 2019 (n 2). For a critical analysis of the *Malawi* and *Chad* decisions, see Tladi (n 102) 204-05.

199 *Al Bashir Malawi* Cooperation Decision 2011 (n 38), para 36.
200 ibid, para 43.
201 ibid, paras 13, 18.
202 ibid, para 18.
203 ibid, para 36.

a substantial defence. Schabas commented that '[n]ot only was the reference rather inexact, when the report [of the Commission on Responsibilities] is read as a whole it is actually rather more supportive of the position opposite to that taken by the Pre-Trial Chamber'.[204] The Pre-Trial Chamber conflated the substantive defences with the procedural personal immunities. A defence of official capacity, belonging to an individual, is distinct from the invocation of personal immunity of a head of State, only waived by a State.[205] These sources are not relevant to the ongoing debate about non-availability of personal immunity at the ICC.[206]

In addition, it seems that the Pre-Trial Chamber also misunderstood the reasoning of the ICJ in the *Arrest Warrant* case. The Chamber held that the ICJ's judgment confirmed a customary international rule respecting personal immunity. It explained that the ICJ only affirmed immunity under customary law 'before national courts of foreign States'. In its view, it adhered to the ICJ's reasoning with respect to personal immunity before international criminal tribunals.[207] Thus, similar to the SCSL in *Taylor*, this Pre-Trial Chamber of the ICC upheld an exception to personal immunity by differentiating between international courts and national courts, instead of resorting to Belgium's argument in distinguishing the nature of the crimes. The ICC Pre-Trial Chamber's interpretation of the ICJ's *Arrest Warrant* case went too far.

To support its contention, the Pre-Trial Chamber also cited the *Milošević* case and the *Taylor* case. The Chamber held that international tribunals are 'totally independent of states and subject to strict rules of impartiality'.[208] It added that 'the rationale for foreign state officials being entitled to raise personal immunity before national courts is that otherwise, national authorities might use prosecutions to unduly impede or limit a foreign state's ability to engage in international action'. By referring to the impartiality of international courts and the risk of abusing State authorities by national courts, the Chamber aimed to establish a new customary rule recognising no personal immunity before international courts for international crimes. However, this argument is less supported for non-availability of personal immunity before international courts. The impartiality and independence of international courts does not justify automatically invalidating personal immunity enjoyed by senior officials of a State, although they may be stimuli for States to waive

---

204   Schabas (n 73) 602.
205   UN Doc A/CN.4/631 (2011), para 19.
206   Kiyani (n 17) 487–500.
207   *Al Bashir Malawi* Cooperation Decision 2011 (n 38), paras 33-34.
208   ibid, para 34; Cassese *et al* (eds) (n 22) 312.

immunities before these courts. The reasoning based on the potential abuse of State authority and the impartiality of international courts does not provide sound legal grounds for modification of a customary rule before international tribunals.[209]

7.5.4.2 *Malawi* Decision: Personal Immunity from Arrest by National Authorities

The second issue in the *Malawi* decision remains whether such a customary rule, of no personal immunity before international courts, extends to an arrest and surrender where international courts seek an arrest. This issue relates to horizontal personal immunity from arrest at the national level. The Chamber held that a modified customary international rule is formed denying absolute personal immunity from arrest. The Chamber provided four reasons. Firstly, the Chamber held that personal immunity does not constitute an admissible plea in international proceedings. Secondly, the Chamber referred to several cases of the ICC and the ICTY in holding that 'initiating international prosecutions against Heads of State have gained widespread recognition as accepted practice'.[210] Thirdly, the Chamber held that about two-thirds of all UN member States have ratified the Rome Statute evidence a significant erosion of personal immunity before the ICC. Lastly, in its view, the relinquishing of personal immunity is required for the ICC's exercise of jurisdiction.[211] The Chamber concluded that 'the international community's commitment to rejecting immunity in circumstances where international courts seek arrest for international crimes has reached a critical mass'.[212]

The first consideration relies on the conclusion of the first issue that article 27(2) is a reflection of customary international law for the absence of personal immunity in international proceedings. Its second argument simply referred to the fact of prosecution, leaving aside the legal basis for prosecution untouched. The first two considerations are not relevant to the issue of personal immunity from arrest by States Parties. The third ground that about two-thirds of the States are parties to the Statute showing a denial of personal immunity from arrest among these States, does not automatically imply a general and consistent rule under customary law. As examined above, the voluntary waiver requirement implies that States Parties respect personal immunity in custom. The last argument is appealing but not sufficient to prove that

---

209   Gaeta (n 38) 321.
210   *Al Bashir Malawi* Cooperation Decision 2011 (n 38), para 39.
211   ibid, paras 38-41.
212   ibid, para 42.

personal immunity from arrest enjoyed by senior officials of non-party States is removed. Based on irrelevant evidence and flawed arguments, Pre-Trial Chamber I concluded that current customary international rule recognises 'an exception to the traditional customary rule on absolute personal immunity before international proceedings seeking arrest for the commission of international crimes'.[213] In short, most sources mentioned in the *Malawi* decision are irrelevant, and some decisions are rendered with flawed arguments. Its reasoning does not lead to its conclusion.

7.5.4.3 Other Decisions of the ICC

The ICC's jurisdiction is a preliminary question for further practical issues regarding individual criminal responsibility and cooperation among States. Three questions should not be confused: (1) can the ICC exercise jurisdiction over senior officials benefiting from personal immunity; (2) is the ICC empowered to issue an arrest warrant against that person; and (3) is a State Party as a host State obliged to arrest and surrender that person? The Pre-Trial Chamber disregarded personal immunity from arrest before national authorities of other States by concluding that Malawi is obliged to arrest Al Bashir. An identically-composed Pre-Trial Chamber I reached the same conclusions in the 2011 *Chad* decision.[214]

Trial Chamber V (A) in the *Kenyatta* case in 2013 followed the rulings of the *Malawi* decision.[215] In this case, Kenyatta as President of the Republic of Kenya since 2013 was charged with crimes against humanity.[216] In 2014, he appeared before the ICC for a status conference. Since Kenya is a party to the Rome Statute, personal immunity was not an issue before the Chamber. The Chamber also relied on the evidence referred to in the *Malawi* decision. The Chamber confirmed the ruling of the *Malawi* decision and suggested that personal immunity is denied before international judicial bodies under customary law.[217] The *Kenyatta* case does not firmly evince the customary law of non-availability of personal immunity.

---

213 ibid, para 43.
214 *Al Bashir Chad* Cooperation Decision 2011 (n 38).
215 *The Prosecutor v Muthaura et al* (Decision on the Confirmation of Charges Pursuant to Article 61(7)(a) and (b) of the Rome Statute, PTC II) ICC-01/09-02/11-382-Red (23 January 2012).
216 *The Prosecutor v Kenyatta* (Transcript, TC V) ICC-01/09-02/11-T-22-ENG (14 February 2013), 6, lines 4-11.
217 The *Prosecutor v Kenyatta* (Decision on Defence Request for Conditional Excusal from Continuous Presence at Trial, TC V(b)) ICC-01/09-02/11-830 (18 October 2013), para 32. For further reading, see L.N. Sadat and B. Cohen, 'Impunity through Immunity: The Kenya

Subsequent decisions of the ICC do not adhere to the conclusions in the *Malawi* decision.[218] In the 2014 *DRC* decision, Pre-Trial Chamber II stated that under international law, a sitting head of State enjoys personal immunities from criminal jurisdiction and inviolability before national courts of foreign States even when suspected of having committed the crimes that fall within the jurisdiction of the ICC.[219] Pre-Trial Chamber II added that as provided in article 27(2) of the Rome Statute, 'there is an exception to personal immunities of Heads of State for prosecution before an international criminal jurisdiction'.[220] This statement indirectly recognised the customary rule respecting personal immunity. Alternatively, the Pre-Trial Chamber held that the Security Council implicitly waived the immunity of Al Bashir.[221] The word 'waiver' enhances the contention that the Chamber acknowledged personal immunity under current international law. Other ICC non-cooperation decisions followed the same approach to show that the immunity has been removed.[222] These ICC non-cooperation decisions did not reject a general customary rule respecting personal immunity for international crimes but indirectly affirmed the idea of the non-existence of a new customary rule. The Pre-Trial Chambers of the ICC in the *South Africa* and *Jordan* decisions held that an incumbent head of a State still enjoys personal immunity under customary law. They agreed that the immunity was not available as a consequence of the Security Council resolution.[223]

Judge Eboe-Osuji in his separate opinion in *Kenyatta* Decision declared that 'customary international law does not recognise immunity for a head of state against prosecution before an international tribunal'.[224] In the 2016 *Ruto & Sang* acquittal decision, Judge Eboe-Osuji reviewed history and argued that 'article 27 is quite simply a codification of customary international law'.[225] His

---

Situation and the International Criminal Court' in E.A. Ankumah (ed), *The International Criminal Court and Africa: One Decade On* (Intersentia 2016) 101.
218   *Al Bashir Chad* Cooperation Decision 2013 (n 197), para 21.
219   *Al Bashir DRC* Cooperation Decision 2014 (n 27), para 25.
220   ibid.
221   ibid, para 29.
222   *Al Bashir Djibouti* Cooperation Decision 2016 (n 197), para 11; *Al Bashir Uganda* Cooperation Decision 2016 (n 197), para 11.
223   *Al Bashir South Africa* Cooperation Decision 2017 (n 97), para 68; id, (Minority Opinion of Judge Marc Perrin De Brichambaut); *Al Bashir Jordan* Cooperation Decision 2017 (n 97), para 27.
224   *The Prosecutor v Kenyatta* (Separate further opinion of Judge Eboe-Osuji) ICC-01/09-02/11-830-Anx3-Corr (18 October 2013), para 32.
225   *Ruto & Sang* Acquittal Decision 2016 (n 77) (Reasons of Judge Eboe-Osuji), paras 238-94.

crucial requirement for the absence of personal immunity is also the international character of the court. The viewpoint of Judge Eboe-Osuji is endorsed by the Appeals Chamber of the ICC.

In its 2019 *Jordan* decision, the Appeals Chamber further dealt with the head of State immunity issue before the ICC. The legal proposition of the Appeals Chamber Judgment and the Joint Concurring Opinion is that the traditional customary law of immunity has not been developed to cover head of State facing international crimes prosecution before international tribunals.[226] In the view of the Appeals Chamber,

> 'given the fundamentally different nature of an international court as opposed to domestic court exercising jurisdiction over a head of State, it would be wrong to assume that an exception to the customary international law on Head of State immunity applicable in the relationship between States has to be established'.[227]

After studying 'consistent and repeated rejection of immunity [even for Heads of States] in sundry instruments of international law since World War II', and by reason of certain international courts that are 'act on behalf of the international community as a whole', the Appeals Chamber concluded that under customary law there was no head of State immunity *ratione personae vis-à-vis* international criminal tribunals over crimes under international law.[228] The customary law of absence of immunity *vis-à-vis* international courts will justify the legality of the issuance of an international arrest warrant and the arrest of a head of State by States acting as jurisdictional 'surrogates' of the courts.[229] The Appeals Chamber also wrote that

> no rule of customary international law that recognises immunity for high officials of states, including Heads of State, before an international criminal tribunal that has jurisdiction to try suspects of crimes under

---

226 *Al Bashir Jordan* Cooperation Appeals Chamber Judgment 2019 (n 2), paras 115-16; id, (Joint Concurring Opinion of Judges Eboe-Osuji, Morrison, Hofmański and Bossa), paras 66, 196, 198-218.
227 *Al Bashir Jordan* Cooperation Appeals Chamber Judgment 2019 (n 2), para 116.
228 ibid, paras 103-13, 115; id, (Joint Concurring Opinion of Judges Eboe-Osuji, Morrison, Hofmański and Bossa), paras 56-64, 66, 76-174, 414-18, 446.
229 *Al Bashir Jordan* Cooperation Appeals Chamber Judgment 2019 (n 2), paras 114; id, (Joint Concurring Opinion of Judges Eboe-Osuji, Morrison, Hofmański and Bossa), paras 441-45.

international law. Article 27 of the Rome Statute appropriately reflects this reality of customary international law.[230]

This judgment further endorses the view in the *Malawi* decision. However, its determination seems to make article 98(1) superfluous.[231] Also, as analysed above, these post-World War II instruments and practice referred to by the Appeals Chamber does not show an independent status of vertical personal immunity, but a dependent status of it based on the consent (waiver) of States.[232] The reasoning of the nature of an international court in the Judgment and the Joint Concurring Opinion is also less clear and convincing.[233] When a national criminal court exercises universal jurisdiction, the court adjudicating international crimes may also 'act on behalf of the international community as a whole'. The judicial debate in the ICC appears to be at an end because of the trial of Al Bashir by the Sudanese Authorities.[234] But it seems that the *Jordan* Appeals Chamber judgment was not the final word on the immunity matter, because as proposed by African States, the UN General Assembly was determining whether to request an advisory opinion from the ICJ on the consequences of legal obligations under different sources with respect to personal immunities.[235] Several States Parties and non-party States to the Rome Statute have also raised doubts on the reasoning of immunities in this judgment.[236]

In sum, most of the ICC's *Al Bashir* non-cooperation decisions did not claim non-availability of personal immunity for international crimes under customary law but recognise the existence of personal immunity from arrest at the national level. The case law of the ICC does not persuade that a customary rule of an exception to head of State immunity, or a new customary rule of no immunity, for committing international crimes has been established.

---

230 *Al Bashir Jordan* Cooperation Appeals Chamber Judgment 2019 (Joint Concurring Opinion of Judges Eboe-Osuji, Morrison, Hofmański and Bossa) (n 2), para 446. See also *Al Bashir Jordan* Cooperation Appeals Chamber Judgment 2019 (n 2), paras 103.
231 Cf. Schabas (n 106) 70.
232 Cf. Kreß (2019) (n 38) 9.
233 ibid 12-15.
234 ibid; ICC, 'Thirty-Second Report of the Prosecutor of the International Criminal Court to the UN Security Council Pursuant to UNSCR 1593 (2005)' (10 December 2020), para 11.
235 'Resolutions and Decisions adopted by the General Assembly during its seventy-third session' (16 September 2019), UN Doc A/DEC/73/568, in UN Doc A/73/49 (2019), Vol III, 229.
236 'Reports of the Secretary-General on the Sudan and South Sudan', UN SCOR, 8554th meeting, UN Doc S/PV.8554 (2019), 7 (France), 7-8 (Russia), 13 (the US), 16 (Sudan).

7.5.5 National Reactions to Personal Immunity for Committing International Crimes

Following the adoption of the Rome Statute, and decisions in the *Pinochet* case, the *Arrest Warrant* case and the *Al Bashir* case, States Parties to the Rome Statute and non-party States responded in different ways to the issue of immunity. Recent national cases and legislation seem to show that States did not intend to erode the customary rule respecting personal immunity or to modify the rule with an exception for committing international crimes.

7.5.5.1 National Laws

A few States specifically regulate personal immunity from criminal proceedings in international law in their national legislation.[237] This subsection surveys States Parties' legislation concerning international crimes and their implementing laws of the Rome Statute to show that national laws have either echoed or reaffirmed the finding that customary law respects personal immunity, regardless of the nature of the crimes committed.

Belgium was the most active and leading State denying personal immunity for sitting heads of State for committing international crimes. Its national law seems to shows a contrary direction after the 2002 *Arrest Warrant* case.[238] Belgium's Act of 16 June 1993 allowed its courts to prosecute persons for genocide, war crimes and crimes against humanity based on universal jurisdiction, even *in absentia*.[239] After the adoption of the Rome Statute, article 5(3) of the 1993 Act was amended in 1999.[240] It provided that '[t]he immunity attributed to the official capacity of a person, does not prevent the application of the present Act.'[241] Based on this amended Act, Belgian courts accepted judicial complaints against some senior leaders of States, including Israeli Prime Minister Ariel Sharon, Cuban President Fidel Castro, the US former President George H.W. Bush and Vice President Richard Cheney, as well as former Chadian President Hissène Habré.[242]

---

237 UN Doc A/CN.4/701, paras 43-46, Privileges and Immunities of Foreign States, International Organisations with Headquarters or Offices in Spain and International Conferences and Meetings held in Spain. Spain, Organic Act 2015, art 22; Hungary, Criminal Code 1978, amended 2012, § 4(5); Ireland, Criminal Code 1997, art 2(2); Latvia, Criminal Law 1998, amended 2013, § 2(2); Lithuania, Criminal Code 2000, amended 2015, art 4(4).

238 2002 *Arrest Warrant* case (n 4) (Dissenting Opinion of Judge Oda), para 5.

239 Belgium, Act of 16 June 1993 concerning the punishment of Grave Breaches of the Geneva Conventions of 12 August 1949 and their Additional Protocols I and II of 18 June 1977, art 7.

240 Belgium, Act of 16 June 1993, as modified by the Act of 10 February 1999, (1999) 38 *ILM* 921.

241 ibid art 5(3).

242 M. Halberstam, 'Belgium's Universal Jurisdiction Law: Vindication of International Justice or Pursuit of Politics Faculty Issue' (2003) 25 *Cardozo L R* 247.

In contrast to its court, the Belgian Ministry of Foreign Affairs was less advanced for the concern about political abuse of the law by prosecuting senior officials.[243] Since the entry into force of the Rome Statute, Belgium has modified the respective Act twice with respect to the issue of immunity under article 5(3).[244] Article 5(3) of the 1993 Act as amended by the Law of April 2003 reads: 'International immunity derived from a person's official capacity does not prevent the application of the present law except under those limits established under international law'.[245] Belgium's Code of Criminal Procedure[246] as modified by the Law of August 2003 confirmed that '[i]n accordance with international law, sitting foreign heads of state, heads of government and ministers of foreign affairs, whose immunity is recognised by international law, are immune from criminal prosecution'.[247] Accordingly, the provision that removed immunity for committing international crimes has been substantially repealed.[248]

The implementing legislation in the Netherlands interpreted international law regarding personal immunity.[249] The 2003 Dutch International Crimes Act criminalised genocide, crimes against humanity and war crimes in conformity with the Rome Statute. The Act provides that 'foreign heads of state, heads of government and ministers of foreign affairs, *as long as* they are in office, and other persons in so far as their immunity is recognised under customary international law' are exempt from prosecution for international crimes.[250] The 2011 Netherlands Government Advisory Committee held that functional immunity should yield to the prosecution of international crimes. However, the Advisory Committee did not suggest that personal immunity would also cease to apply for the prosecution of international crimes. The Advisory Committee argued that 'the underlying reason for this [personal] immunity is to facilitate the smooth conduct of international relations'.[251] It even recommended amending

---

243 ibid 250–51.
244 Belgium, Act of 23 April 2003, amending the Act of 16 June 1993 and Article 144*ter* of the Judicial Code, (2003) 42 *ILM* 749 [Act of 23 April 2003], art 4; id, Act of 5 August 2003, amending the Act of 16 June 1993 [Act of 5 August 2003], art 13.
245 Belgium, Act of 23 April 2003, art 4.
246 Belgium, Code of Criminal Procedure 1878, amended 2007.
247 ibid, art 1*bis*.
248 Pedretti (n 17) 112-14. For similar provisions, Latvia, Criminal Code 1998, amended 2013, § 2(2); Hungary, Criminal Code 1978, amended 2012, § 4(5).
249 Netherlands, International Crimes Act 2003.
250 ibid, § 16(a).
251 'Immunity for Foreign State Official: Advisory Report by the Netherlands Government Advisory Committee on Issues of Public International Law' (2011) 58 *Netherlands Intl L Rev* 461.

the Dutch Disposal of Criminal Complaints (Offences under the International Crimes Act) Instructions with a more extended scope of persons who enjoy immunities recognised by customary law.[252]

A number of States Parties have not substantially implemented the rule of the Rome Statute in their national law. Several States' implementing laws implicitly support that in case of unsatisfactory consultation with the ICC, personal immunity under customary law could bar the request of the ICC for arrest.[253] In contrast, some States have stated that personal immunity is not a bar for the request of the ICC to arrest and surrender. The 1999 Extradition Act of Canada provides that '[d]espite any other law, no person who is the subject of a request for surrender by the International Criminal Court or by any international criminal tribunal that is established by resolution of the Security Council of the United Nations, may claim immunity under common law or by statute'.[254]

Kenya's implementing provisions stipulated that '[t]he existence of any immunity or special procedural rule attaching to the official capacity of any person is not a ground for refusing the execution of a request for surrender made by the ICC'.[255] Similar provisions were enshrined in the implementing laws of France, Germany, New Zealand, Norway, Switzerland, Trinidad and Tobago and Uganda.[256] In their view, immunity cannot be invoked for non-compliance with an ICC request. The implementing laws were closely connected with article 98(1) of the Statute. All these provisions indicate the attitude that these States can or cannot reject the request to cooperate with the ICC when there is no waiver of immunity or necessary consent. However, the provisions do not address the issue of personal immunity in custom. Without further observation, it is inappropriate to conclude that these rules evidence the belief of national legislators that an exception to personal immunity is an accepted practice in international law. For example, Kenya in 2014 proposed

---

252 ibid.
253 For national laws, see Austria, Cooperation with the ICC 2002, § 9.1.3; Australia, ICC (Consequential Amendments) Act 2002, § 12(4); Argentina, Act Implementing the Rome Statute of the ICC 2001, arts 40 and 41; Liechtenstein, Act on Cooperation with the ICC and other International Tribunals 2004, arts 10.1(c) and 10.3.
254 Canada, Extradition Act 1999, § 6.1.
255 Kenya, International Crimes Act 2008, § 27(1)(a); Uganda, ICC Act 2010, § 25.
256 France, Code of Criminal Procedure 2002, art 627.8; Germany, Law on Cooperation with the ICC 2002, § 70; Kenya, Act on International Crimes 2008, art 27; New Zealand, International Crimes and ICC Act 2000, § 31 (1); Norway, Implementation Act 2001, § 2; Switzerland, Federal Law on Cooperation with the ICC 2001, art 6; Trinidad and Tobago, ICC Act 2006, § 31(1)(a); Uganda, ICC Act 2010, § 25.

amending article 27 of the Rome Statute by adding a new paragraph to 'pause' prosecution of 'sitting' senior officials.[257] Although the proposal was unsuccessful, this instance demonstrates that Kenya, in fact, supports the ICC prosecuting sitting senior officials only after leaving office.

Few national laws intend to invalidate personal immunity. The respective Croatian law stipulates that 'immunities and privileges shall not apply in procedures involving the crimes' within the jurisdiction of the ICC.[258] The laws in Burkina Faso, Comoros, Mauritius and South Africa shared a similar feature.[259] Article 27(2) was also duplicated in East Timor's Regulation for Special Panels to deal with international crimes from 1974 to 1999.[260]

Many national laws seem to confirm personal immunity under customary law. Some national implementing laws repeated the provision under article 27(2) that the personal immunity is not a bar for the proceeding of the ICC, for instance, the laws in Ireland, the Philippines, Samoa and the UK.[261] These implementing provisions also qualify the immunity by stressing 'a connection with a State party to the ICC Statute'. The UK Act stipulates:

> Where –
> (a) state or diplomatic immunity attaches to a person by reason of a connection with a state other than a state party to the ICC Statute, and
> (b) waiver of that immunity is obtained by the ICC in relation to a request for that person's surrender,
>
> the waiver shall be treated as extending to proceedings under this Part in connection with that request.[262]

---

257 The ICC ASP, 'Report of the Working Group on Amendments', ICC-ASP/13/31 (7 December 2014), para 12. Proposal of amendments by Kenya to the Statute (14 March 2014), C.N.1026.2013.TREATIES-XVIII.10.
258 Croatia, Law on the Implementation of the Statute of the ICC and the Prosecution of Crimes against International Law of War and Humanitarian Law 2003, art 6.4.
259 Burkina Faso, Act on the determination of competence and procedures for application of the Rome Statute of the ICC 2009, arts 7 and 15.1; Comoros, Act concerning the application of the Rome Statute 2011, art 7.2; Mauritius, ICC Act 2001, § 4; South Africa, Implementation Act 2002, §§ 4(2)(a)(i) and 4(3)(c).
260 East Timor, Regulation for Special Panels for Serious Crimes 2000, § 15.2.
261 Samoa, ICC Act 2007, § 32(1); UK, ICC Act 2001, § 23(1); Ireland, ICC Act 2006, § 61(1); Iceland, Act on the ICC 2003, art 20.1; Malta, Extradition Act 1982, amended 2010, art 26S; Philippines, Act on Crimes against IHL, Genocide, and Other Crimes against Humanity 2009, § 9(b); Estonia, Code of Criminal Procedure 2004, para 492(6).
262 UK, ICC Act 2001, art 23(2).

The Philippine legislation clearly states that '[i]mmunities that may be attached to the official capacity of a person under international law may limit the application of this [Philippine] Act'.[263] These implementing provisions dismiss personal immunity of nationals of a State Party to the Rome Statute. A waiver of immunity is required with regard to a person of a State not a party to the Statute. These implementing provisions, therefore, evince the continuation of personal immunity rather than a denial of it under customary law.

7.5.5.2 Practice of States Parties

Through the ratification of the Rome Statute, States Parties consent to waive any immunity before the ICC and before the jurisdiction of other States Parties. This implies that personal immunity is not a bar to such proceedings with the consent of States Parties. Also, some States Parties claim that personal immunity of senior non-party State officials remains under international law. This part focuses on the practice, statements and reactions of States to personal immunity for international crimes.

Analysing the practice of States that frequently exercise universal jurisdiction over international crimes, Belgium, Spain and Switzerland, would provide hints for their attitude towards the issue of personal immunity.

Rulings of Belgian courts demonstrate the same direction as its two amendments of law do. In the 2002 *Arrest Warrant* case, Belgium's proposal was rejected by the ICJ that no immunity exists before Belgian courts for serious crimes.[264] Belgium then withdrew the arrest warrant for Yerodia and declared that the case was inadmissible because of his immunity. The Belgian delegation said that the majority of complaints concerning senior leaders who enjoyed immunity were declared inadmissible.[265] In the 2003 *Sharon et al* case, the defendants appealed to the Belgian Court of Cassation about an Indictments Chamber's ruling.[266] The Court of Cassation upheld that criminal actions against Ariel Sharon were inadmissible. According to the Court of Cassation, the 'principle of customary international criminal law relative to jurisdictional immunity was not impaired by article 27(2) of the Rome Statute

---

263   Philippines, Act on Crimes against IHL, Genocide, and Other Crimes against Humanity 2009, § 9(b).

264   2002 *Arrest Warrant* case (n 4), 32, para 78.

265   'Summary record of meeting with the Human Rights Committee of 13 July 2004 in relation to the fourth periodic report under the International Covenant on Civil and Political Rights', UN Doc CCPR/C/SR.2199, 23 July 2004, Belgium, para 10.

266   *H.A.S. et al v Ariel Sharon, Amos Yaron et al* (Decision Related to the Indictment of Ariel Sharon, Amos Yaron and others, Court of Cassation, Belgium) Case No. P.02.1139.F/1 (12 February 2003), (2003) 42 *ILM* 596.

before national courts of a third State claiming universal jurisdiction in *absentia* over genocide'.[267] The exercise of universal jurisdiction does not imply non-entitlement to personal immunity for international crimes. In addition, Sharon's personal immunity before Belgian courts was not removed by virtue of the 1948 Genocide Convention.[268] The Court upheld that any trial against Sharon would have to wait for his departure from office. Later on, the Court of Appeals cited the *Sharon et al* case and declared that Belgium lacked jurisdiction over Fidel Castro. One reason was also that Castro as a then sitting head of State could not be tried.[269] In 2005, a Belgian judge issued an international arrest warrant for Habré for alleged international crimes.[270] As a matter of fact, Habré was a former Chadian president at that time, and Chad waived his functional immunity.[271] All these rulings further demonstrate that Belgium changed its active position on personal immunity.

Spain is also advanced in exercising universal jurisdiction.[272] Unlike Belgium's view in the *Arrest Warrant case*, Spain always stresses that an incumbent head of State who enjoys personal immunity in international law cannot be prosecuted for international crimes in Spain based on universal jurisdiction. The Central Criminal Court in its 1999 finding argued that Castro could not be prosecuted in Spain because he was an incumbent head of State. The Court also stated that this finding did not conflict with its ruling in *Pinochet*[273] because Pinochet was a former head of State.[274] The Central Criminal Court in 2005 further rejected the complaint against Castro by virtue of the immunity of a sitting head of State.[275] The Swiss Federal

---

267   ibid 600.
268   ibid 599.
269   *José J. Basulto et al v Fidel Castro Ruz et al* (Court of Cassation, Belgium) (29 July 2003).
270   *Questions relating to the Obligation to Prosecute or Extradite (Belgium v Senegal)*, Judgment, [2012] ICJ Rep 422, 432, para 21.
271   Letter from the Minister of Justice of Chad on the Immunity of Hissène Habré to Belgium, 7 October 2002 (unofficial translation).
272   Belgium, Judicial Power Organisation Act 1985, amended 1999, art 23.4. Limitations to its universal jurisdiction, see art 1 of the Organisation Act No 1/2009.
273   *Augusto Pinochet* case (Order, Central Criminal Court, Spain) No 1998/22605 (5 November 1998) and No 1999/28720 (24 September 1999), cited in Cassese (n 34) 860 and fn 19. For summaries of this case, see 'Order of the Criminal Chamber of the Spanish Audiencia Nacional Affirming Spain's Jurisdiction, 5 November 1998 (unofficial translation)' in R. Brody and M. Ratner (eds), *The Pinochet Papers: The Case of Augusto Pinochet Ugarte in Spain and Britain* (Kluwer Law International 2000) 95–107.
274   *The Foundation for Human Rights v Fidel Castro* (Order, Central Criminal Court, Spain) No 1999/2723 (4 March 1999), cited in Cassese (n 34) 860–61 and fn 21.
275   For other decisions of Spain, see *Al Bashir South Africa* Cooperation Decision 2017 (n 97) (Minority Opinion of Judge Marc Perrin De Brichambaut), para 86 and fn 119.

Criminal Court in 2012 held that the four alternatives mentioned in the ICJ's *Arrest Warrant* case highlighted the emergence of exceptions to immunity from jurisdiction for international crimes.[276] However, the Swiss court also affirmed that an incumbent minister still enjoys personal immunity during the period in which s/he held office.[277]

The African Union (AU), of which 33 of the 55 member States are States Parties to the Rome Statute, collectively adopted a resolution to confirm the customary rule respecting personal immunity of senior officials before the ICC.[278] In addition, the AU in 2014 approved an amendment to the Protocol on the Statute of the African Court of Justice and Human Rights to respect immunities of serving African senior State officials for prosecution of international crimes. It provides that '[n]o charges shall be commenced or continued before the Court against any serving African Union Head of State or Government, or anybody acting or entitled to act in such capacity, or other senior state officials based on their functions, during their tenure of office'.[279] In recent years, the AU in its *amicus curiae* observation reaffirmed personal immunity under customary law in national and international proceedings.[280] As mentioned before, Congo objected to the idea of the denial of personal immunity for war crimes and crimes against humanity in the *Arrest Warrant* case of the ICJ.[281] This discrepancy between treaty provisions at least shows that no consensus

---

276 *A v Public Ministry of the Confederation, B and C* (Decision, Federal Criminal Court, Switzerland) BB. 2011.140 (25 July 2012), paras 5.3.3-5.3.5.

277 ibid, para 5.4.2.

278 Assembly of the African Union, 'Decision on the Meeting of African States Parties to the Rome Statute of the International Criminal Court (ICC)', Assembly /AU/Dec.245 (XIII) 1–3 July 2009; 'Decision on the Progress Report of the Commission on the Implementation of Decision Assembly/AU/Dec.270 (XIV) on the Second Ministerial Meeting on the Rome Statute of the International Criminal Court (ICC)', Assembly/AU/Dec.296 (XV), 25–27 July 2010; African Union Press Release, 'On the Decision of the Pre-Trial Chamber of the ICC Informing the UN Security Council and the Assembly of the States Parties to the Rome Statute About the Presence of President Omar Hassan Al-Bashir of the Sudan Territories in the Republic of Chad and the Republic of Kenya' (29 August 2010); Extraordinary Session of Assembly of the African Union, 'Decision on Africa's Relationship with the International Criminal Court (ICC)', Ext/Assembly/AU/Dec.1(Oct. 2013), §§ 9-10. See also Gaeta and Labuda (n 2) 139–41.

279 Protocol on Amendments to the Protocol on the Statute of the African Court of Justice and Human Rights, arts 28A and 46A*bis*.

280 *The Prosecutor v Al Bashir* (Order inviting expressions of interest as *amici curiae* in judicial proceedings (pursuant to Rule 103 of the Rules of Procedure and Evidence), AC) ICC-02/05-01/09-330 (29 March 2018), para 1; African Union's Submission to the ICC (n 3), paras 10-12.

281 2002 *Arrest Warrant* case (n 4), 12, para 25.

exists among African States Parties to the Rome Statute concerning a customary rule with an exception to personal immunity.

Furthermore, responses of States to Al Bashir's travels indicate their attitude towards the issue of denial of personal immunity. Al Bashir has frequently travelled abroad and been allowed access to 30 States in Africa, Arab countries and Asia despite warrants for his arrest.[282] Some of the States he has visited are Parties to the Rome Statute.[283] Chad consistently allowed Al Bashir to visit it and refused to arrest him and surrender him to the ICC.[284] Malawi claimed that since article 27(2) of the Rome Statute does not apply to a head of non-party State to the Rome Statute, Al Bashir was immune from arrest under customary law. Jordan and the League of Arab States[285] shared the same view as Malawi.[286] These States' persistent refusal to arrest Al Bashir suggest that, in their view, personal immunity remains a rule of customary law for the prosecution of international crimes, even if an arrest warrant was issued by an international tribunal.

Recent national decisions of South Africa also merit attention. In 2015, the Southern Africa Litigation Centre (SALC) applied to examine South Africa's government decision to respect the immunity of all State representatives to the AU Summit before the High Court of South Africa. The High Court admitted that customary law is a source for an individual to enjoy immunity.[287] Additionally, the Court relied on Security Council Resolution 1593 to remove the personal immunity of Al Bashir.[288] This decision was appealed to the South

---

282   See ICC (Report of the Registry on information received regarding Omar Al Bashir's travels to States Parties and Non-States Parties from 5 October 2016 to 6 April 2017 and other efforts conducted by the Registry regarding purported visits, Registry) ICC-02/05-01/09-296 (11 April 2017); id, 'Twenty-Eighty Report of the Prosecutor of the International Criminal Court to the UN Security Council Pursuant to UNSCR 1593 (2005)' (14 December 2018), paras 15-16, 21; id, 'Twenty-Ninth Report of the Prosecutor of the International Criminal Court to the UN Security Council Pursuant to UNSCR 1593 (2005)' (19 June 2019), paras 13-14, 20. These States were Algeria, Bahrain, Chad, China, Democratic Republic of Congo, Djibouti, Egypt, Equatorial Guinea, Eritrea, Ethiopia, Jordan, India, Iran, Iraq, Kenya, Kuwait, Libya, Malawi, Mauritania, Morocco, Nigeria, Qatar, Russian Federation, Rwanda, Saudi Arabia, South Africa, and South Sudan, Turkey, Uganda, United Arab Emirates. 21 of 30 States are not States Parties to the Rome Statute.
283   ibid. These States are Chad, Kenya, Djibouti, Malawi, Nigeria, DRC, Uganda, South Africa, Jordan.
284   ibid.
285   The Arab League consists of 22 Member States.
286   *Al Bashir Jordan* Cooperation Decision 2017 (n 97), paras 7, 14-15; Jordan's Appeal (n 94), paras 15-21; The League of Arab States' Observations (n 94), para 26.
287   *The Southern Africa Litigation Centre v The Minister of Justice and Constitutional* (27740/2015) [2015] ZAGPPHC 402, para 2.
288   ibid.

African Supreme Court. All judges in the Supreme Court supported personal immunity of heads of State under customary law. Also, the Supreme Court held that according to the 2002 South African ICC Act, when a person is prosecuted in South Africa for genocide, war crimes and crimes against humanity, international immunities have been removed, irrespective of whether the person is a sitting head of State not a party to the Rome Statute. In interpreting its national law, it seems that the Supreme Court follows Belgium's position prior to the ICJ's *Arrest Warrant* case.[289] Two concurring judges in the Supreme Court said that this decision 'would create an intolerable anomaly' because 'South Africa was taking a step that many other nations have not yet taken'.[290] It is unknown whether South Africa would follow in the Belgium's footsteps to exercise universal jurisdiction, and even widely investigate and prosecute sitting heads of State for committing international crimes. In short, South African domestic courts do not show an active position on a new customary rule with an exception to personal immunity for committing international crimes.

Indeed, Al Bashir has been denied access to some States. Botswana, France, Malaysia and Zambia announced that if Al Bashir visited, they would comply with the Rome Statute to arrest him. Their denial of access may indicate either their support for a new customary rule or an obligation to cooperate pursuant to the Rome Statute. The fact that some of the States Parties he has visited sometimes have not hosted him is also not persuasive evidence to show that these States accepted an exception to personal immunity in custom. Some States changed their plans to host him in reaction to political pressure or to avoid potential immunity disputes. For instance, Malawi, Nigeria and Uganda first denied but later allowed him access.[291] Accordingly, a new customary rule that provides an exception to personal immunity for committing international crimes is at least not widely acknowledged by States Parties.

7.5.5.3 Practice of Non-party States

Non-party States also play a role in modifying or creating a customary rule. Non-party States are not bound by the new immunity regime set out in article 27(2). Al Bashir has travelled to 21 non-party States, including Russian Federation and China. They all abstained from arresting him when he visited.[292] Some States

---

289 *The Minister of Justice and Constitutional Development v The Southern African Litigation Centre* (867/15) [2016] ZASCA 17, para 103.
290 ibid, paras 103, 122.
291 ibid.
292 28th and 29th Reports of the OTP to the UN Security Council (n 282).

have never accepted the waiver of immunity enshrined in the Rome Statute.[293] The statement of the Russian Federation in the Security Council meeting implicitly confirmed Al Bashir's immunity,[294] which stated: '[t]he ICC must respect the provisions of international law relating to the immunity accorded Heads of State and other senior officials during their tenure'.[295] On an occasion, the Chinese delegation also expressed in the UN General Assembly that 'China does not believe that the provisions of draft article 7 [the ILC's draft article concerning exceptions to functional immunity about international crimes] qualify as codification or progressive development of customary international law'.[296] China does not share the view that a new customary rule denying personal immunity is emerging, or current customary law provides an exception to personal immunity for committing international crimes.[297]

Despite the US's supportive attitude towards the ICC in recent years,[298] it would be less convincing to say that the US also supports a denial of personal immunity.[299] The US 1976 Foreign Sovereign Immunities Act only allows the US to deny functional immunity in civil cases in relation to acts of torture and international crimes.[300] The US State Department also observed that 'the doctrine of head of state immunity is applied in the United States as a matter of customary international law'.[301] The US Court of Appeal in the 2012 *Samantar*

---

[293] 'Report of the Security Council Mission to Djibouti (on Somalia), the Sudan, Chad, the Democratic Republic of the Congo and Côte d'Ivoire, 31 May to 10 June 2008', UN Doc S/2008/460, para 60; 'Reports of the Secretary-General on the Sudan and South Sudan', UN SCOR, 7963rd meeting, UN Doc S/PV.7963 (2017).

[294] UN Doc S/PV.7963 (2017).

[295] ibid.

[296] China, 'Statement by Director-General XU Hong at the 72nd Session of the UN General Assembly on Agenda Item 81: Report of the International Law Commission on the work of its 69th session' (27 October 2017). For a similar idea see GAOR 69th session, 35th plenary meeting, UN Doc A/69/PV.35 (2014), Algeria.

[297] China, 'Statement by HU Bin, Head of the Chinese Observer Delegation and Deputy Director-General of the Department of Treaty and Law, Ministry of Foreign Affairs of China, 18th Session of the ASP to the Rome Statute of the ICC' (3 December 2019).

[298] W.A. Schabas, 'International War Crimes Tribunals and the United States' (2011) 35 *Diplomatic History* 769.

[299] 'Statement of the United States of America Delivered by David Scheffer, US Ambassador at Large for War Crimes Issues before the Sixth Committee of the UN General Assembly, Agenda Item: The International Criminal Court' (19 October 2000); UN Doc S/PV.8554 (2019).

[300] US, Foreign Sovereign Immunities Act 1976, 28 USC 1605A (a)(1), amended by the Torture Victim Protection Act of 1991, 28 USC 1350.

[301] J. Crook, 'Contemporary Practice of the United States Relating to International Law' (2006) 100 *AJIL* 219, 219–20; Singerman (n 17); M. Tunks, 'Diplomats or Defendants? Defining the Future of Head-of-State Immunity' (2002) 52 *D Law J* 651.

case held that 'American courts have generally followed the foregoing trend, concluding that *jus cogens* violations are not legitimate official acts and therefore do not merit foreign official immunity but still recognising that head-of-state immunity, based on status, is of an absolute nature and applies even against *jus cogens* claims'.[302] The US is also less reluctant to accept such a new customary rule.

7.5.6   *The UN Security Council and Its Resolutions*

This subsection analyses the Security Council's binding resolutions to discover its attitude towards personal immunity. Security Council Resolution 827 and Resolution 1593, which created the ICTY and referred the Darfur Situation to the ICC respectively, are examined to show whether the Security Council intended to override the traditional customary rule of personal immunity or to confirm a new customary rule.

It should first be clarified whether the Security Council is empowered to override or derogate from customary law. Some commentators argue that the Security Council has the power to remove personal immunity through a resolution backed up by the Chapter VII authority of the UN Charter.[303] Other commentators doubt the power of the Security Council, in particular, the impact of the Security Council on the application of the ICC legal framework.[304] Schabas argues that it is necessary to note the differences between the ICC and the UN *ad hoc* tribunals on the establishing mechanism.[305] The Security Council may have the power to deprive senior officials of the UN member States of personal immunity before *ad hoc* tribunals established by it; however, its power is strictly restrained by the Rome Statute about immunities, even acting by virtue of Chapter VII of the UN Charter.[306] Serving as a trigger mechanism

---

302   *Yousuf and ors v Samantar*, 699 F 3d 763 (4th Cir 2012), para 35. Cf. *Belhas et al v Ya'alon* (Appeal from the US District Court for the District of Columbia) (15 February 2008) [2008] USCADC 15, 6–8, 13.

303   D. Akande, 'The Effect of Security Council Resolutions and Domestic Proceedings on State Obligations to Cooperate with the ICC' (2012) 10 *JICJ* 299; Ssenyonjo (n 101) 211; Kiyani (n 17) 474–80; *Amicus Curiae* Brief of Professors Robinson *et al* (n 99), para 6. For more discussions, see *The Prosecutor v Al Bashir* (Transcript, AC) ICC-02/05-01/09-T-4-ENG, ICC-02/05-01/09-T-5-ENG, ICC-02/05-01/09-T-6-ENG (10-12 September 2018).

304   Schabas (n 73) 604.

305   ibid 603; *Milošević* Decision on Preliminary Motions, paras 28-33; Liu (n 80).

306   For discussions, see Kiyani (n 17) 474–80.

under the Rome Statute, the Security Council has no more power than a State Party does.[307]

UK national law, however, provides that:

> The power conferred by section 1 of the United Nations Act 1946 (c. 45) (power to give effect by Order in Council to measures not involving the use of armed force) includes power to make in relation to any proceedings such provision corresponding to the provision made by this section in relation to the proceedings, but with the omission [...] of the words 'by reason of a connection with a state party to the ICC Statute' [in section 23(1)], and of [sections 23(2)-(3)], as appears to Her Majesty to be necessary or expedient in consequence of such a referral as is mentioned in article 13(b) [of the Rome Statute].[308]

This provision enables a Security Council resolution to override any immunities of State, including non-party States, 'depending upon their wording'.[309] This provision confirms the power of the Security Council to remove personal immunity of non-party States of the Rome Statute but with an emphasis on the importance of the wording. The Pre-Trial Chamber of the ICC has also implicitly confirmed the power of the Security Council to override immunity of a head of State under customary law.[310]

The following analysis is based on the assumption that the Security Council can override personal immunity by virtue of a resolution under Chapter VII of the UN Charter. Resolution 827 was adopted without a vote but by a general agreement of the Security Council under Chapter VII of the UN Charter.[311] Resolution 827 stated that 'all States shall cooperate fully with the Tribunal [...] in accordance with the present resolution [...] all States shall take any measures necessary under their domestic law to implement the provisions of the present resolution and the Statute'.[312]

---

307 *The Prosecutor v Ahmad Harun & Ali Kushayb* (Decision on the Prosecution Application under Article 58(7) of the Statute (2), PTC I) ICC-02/05-01/07-1-Corr (29 April 2007), para 16; Condorelli and Villalpando (n 191) 575.
308 UK, ICC Act 2001, art 23(5).
309 UK, ICC Act 2001 (Isle of Man) Order 2004, Explanatory Note.
310 *Al Bashir* DRC Cooperation Decision 2014 (n 27); *Al Bashir South Africa* Cooperation Decision 2017 (n 97).
311 UN Doc S/RES/827 (1993); J. O'Brien, 'The International Tribunal for Violations of International Humanitarian Law in the Former Yugoslavia' (1993) 87 *AJIL* 639.
312 UN Doc S/RES/827 (1993), para 4.

The Security Council kept silent regarding the issue of immunity in its Resolution 827 and the annexed ICTY Statute. Also, the Federal Republic of Yugoslavia (FRY) did not claim that the ICTY violated personal immunity under customary law by issuing an arrest warrant and an indictment against Milošević.[313] Cassese wrote that 'the absence of any challenge to issuance of the ICTY of an arrest warrant, and the absence of any derogation provision regarding personal immunities indicate that States considered that it is unnecessary to include such a provision with regard to the exercise of jurisdiction by an international criminal court'.[314] Nevertheless, it is debatable why it is 'unnecessary' to include a provision derogating from personal immunity, such as article 27(2) of the Rome Statute. The element of 'unnecessary' could be explained for several reasons.

The first possible interpretation of 'unnecessary' might be that in the Resolution the Security Council implicitly intended to confirm a new customary rule for committing international crimes. This idea is not credible because the Security Council had no specifically targeted suspect in mind during the establishment of the ICTY. The Security Council would not have intended to confirm a customary rule eroding personal immunity for committing international crimes. The second interpretation is that the traditional rule of personal immunity does not apply to certain international courts 'acting on behalf of international community'. This idea was mentioned in the *Taylor* decision of the SCSL and the *Malawi* and *Jordan* decisions of the ICC.[315] This argument is also less convincing as analysed above. It seems that Cassese would not support such a rule that is merely based on a distinction between international courts and national courts.[316] The third construction is that a customary rule derogating from personal immunity for committing international crimes exists. Thus, it is not necessary to include this provision. Accordingly, the FRY's absence of a challenge to the ICTY indictment based on Milošević's personal immunity further indicates that the FRY behaved in that way with a conviction of recognising the invalidation of personal immunity under customary law. The third interpretation is possible but not exclusive.

---

313   ICTY Press Release, 'Justice Minister of the Federal Republic of Yugoslavia gives Commitment to serve ICTY Arrest Warrant on Slobodan Milošević' (6 April 2001), J.L./P.I.S./585-e; *Prosecutor v Milošević* (Decision on Preliminary Motion) ICTY-99-37-PY (8 November 2001).
314   Cassese *et al* (eds) (n 22) 322 and fn 26.
315   *Prosecutor v Milošević* (Decision on Preliminary Motion) ICTY-99-37-PY (8 November 2001), para 35; *Al Bashir Malawi* Cooperation Decision 2011 (n 38), para 34; *Al Bashir Jordan* Cooperation Appeals Chamber Judgment 2019 (n 2), para 115 and fn 338.
316   Cassese (n 34) 864.

A more appropriate understanding might be that it is 'unnecessary' because the UN Security Council Resolution under Chapter VII of the UN Charter implicitly obliges States to waive personal immunity for the exercise of jurisdiction by the UN *ad hoc* tribunals.[317] This is an indirect legal effect of Security Council Resolution 827. According to article 25 of the UN Charter, these Security Council decisions have to be accepted and carried out by members of the UN. All States were obliged to enforce Resolution 827 and the Statute through any possible measures.[318] The FRY, as a UN member as a successor to the Socialist Federal Republic of Yugoslavia, waived personal immunity enjoyed by its former head of State Milošević.[319] This interpretation indicates that the practice of non-availability of personal immunity is not sufficiently accepted to become a customary rule by the Security Council.

At the ICC, the drafters of the Rome Statute did not want States or the Security Council to pre-determine the focus of the ICC on targeted conduct and suspects. The Security Council can only refer a Situation rather than a case to the ICC.[320] The term 'immunity' was also absent from Resolution 1593 referring the Darfur Situation to the ICC. Resolution 1593 decided that:

> [...] nationals, current or former officials or personnel from a contributing State outside Sudan which is not a party to the Rome Statute of the International Criminal Court shall be subject to the exclusive jurisdiction of that contributing State for all alleged acts or omissions arising out of or related to operations in Sudan established or authorised by the Council or the African Union, unless such exclusive jurisdiction has been expressly waived by that contributing State.[321]

In the 2017 *South Africa* non-cooperation decision, Judge Perrin De Brichambaut in his minority opinion thoroughly examined the interpretation of Resolution 1593 by observing its ordinary meaning, context, object

---

317 W.A. Schabas, 'Kosovo, *Prosecutor v Milošević*, Decision on preliminary motions Case No IT-99-37-PT' in *Oxford Reports on International Law*, 21 May 2010.
318 1993 ICTY Statute, art 29.
319 This argument is supported by the *Prosecutor v Blaškić* (Decision on the Objection of the Republic of Croatia to the Issue of *subpoenae duces tecum*) ICTY-95-14-PT (18 July 1997), paras 83-86, 89.
320 'Report of the Preparatory Committee on the Establishment of an International Criminal Court', UN Doc A/51/22 (1996), Vol I, para 146; R. Rastan, 'Jurisdiction' in C. Stahn (ed), *The Law and Practice of the International Criminal Court* (OUP 2015) 158.
321 UN Doc S/RES/1593 (2005), para 6. Similar formulations repeated in UN Doc SC/RES/1970 (2014), para 6 and UN Doc S/2014/348 (22 May 2014), para 7.

and purpose, statements by members of the Security Council and other UN Security Council's resolutions, as well as the subsequent practice of relevant UN organs and affected States. He concluded that a definite answer could not be reached regarding the removal of Al Bashir's immunity by virtue of Resolution 1593.[322]

The Appeals Chamber of the ICC in the 2019 *Jordan* decision held that for the principle of effectiveness, the wording 'full cooperation' in paragraph 2 of Resolution 1593 imposed upon Sudan the same obligation of cooperation that the Rome Statute imposed on ICC States Parties, including the application of article 27(2) of the Rome Statute, which does not recognise immunities *vis-à-vis* ICC States Parties. Since no immunity could be invoked in the ICC proceedings, Resolution 1593 did not deprive the non-existent head of immunity *vis-à-vis* ICC States Parties.[323] The reasoning of the Appeals Chamber on this point seems to be a slippery slope argument. When the ICC Prosecutor reported to the Security Council about the non-cooperation issue in the *Al Bashir* case, the Russian Federation openly commented that 'the obligation to cooperate, as set forth in resolution 1593 (2005), does not mean that the norms of international law governing the immunity of the [sic] Government officials of those States not party [to] the Rome Statute can be repealed, and presuming the contrary is unacceptable'.[324] This statement further confirms the view that no implied agreement exists among members of the Security Council to refuse personal immunity.[325] It is doubtful that the Security Council intended to indirectly override it and lift Al Bashir's personal immunity *vis-à-vis* ICC States Parties through the wording of Resolution 1593.

In short, Resolutions 827 and 1593 are not enough credible evidence to demonstrate the Security Council's intention to override traditional customary law or to confirm a modified customary rule derogating from personal immunity. The absence of personal immunity in the Resolutions was not intended to alter or to override but instead to respect personal immunity under customary law. The following paragraphs analyse the work of the ILC to show its view on an exception to absolute personal immunity.

---

322   *Al Bashir South Africa* Cooperation Decision 2017 (n 97) (Minority Opinion of Judge Marc Perrin De Brichambaut), paras 64-83; *Al Bashir Jordan* Cooperation Decision 2017 (n 97) (Minority Opinion of Judge Marc Perrin De Brichambaut) ICC-02/05-01/09-309-9-Anx-tENG (11 December 2017), para 3.
323   *Al Bashir Jordan* Cooperation Appeals Chamber Judgment 2019 (n 2), paras 133-49.
324   UN Doc S/PV.7963 (2017).
325   *Al Bashir DRC* Cooperation Decision 2014 (n 27), para 29.

7.5.7 The Work of the International Law Commission

The ILC's recent work has expressed its attitude towards the exception to the rule of personal immunity for committing international crimes. In the ILC's work on the issue of 'Immunity of State officials from foreign criminal jurisdiction', Roman A. Kolodkin and Concepción Hernández were appointed as Special Rapporteurs.[326] The first Rapporteur Kolodkin held that the 2002 ICJ judgment in the *Arrest Warrant* case was a correct landmark decision.[327] He supported that '[i]mmunity from international criminal jurisdiction appears to be fundamentally different from immunity from national criminal jurisdiction' and '[t]he principle of sovereign equality of States [...] cannot be the rationale for immunity from international jurisdiction'.[328] However, in his viewpoint, the ILC's topic only concerns immunity from foreign criminal jurisdiction. A principle of immunity of State officials exists, and it is uncertain whether there is a trend of asserting the existence of a new rule for the exception to immunity.[329] Some members held that this argument is outdated,[330] and that he did not take into account the new development of international law about international crimes. Kolodkin emphasised that his ultimate goal was not to 'formulate abstract proposals as to what international law might be, but to work on the basis of evidence of the existing international law in the field'. Divergent views exist in the Commission concerning the issue of exception.[331]

The second and present Rapporteur Hernández has submitted seventh reports to the ILC.[332] Her fifth report concluded that 'it had not been possible to determine the existence of a customary rule that allowed for the application of limitations or exceptions in respect of immunity *ratione personae*, or to identify a trend in favour of such a rule'.[333] She still believed that it was 'not necessary or useful' for the current Commission to discuss the 2019 *Jordan* decision.[334]

---

326 UN Doc A/61/10 (2006), paras 257, 386; UN Doc A/62/10 (2007), para 376.
327 UN Doc A/63/10 (2008), para 311.
328 UN Doc A/CN.4/601 (2008), para 103.
329 ibid; UN Doc A/CN.4/631 (2011), paras 90-93.
330 H. Huang, 'On Immunity of State Officials from Foreign Criminal Jurisdiction' (2014) 13 *Chinese J Intl L* 1.
331 UN Doc A/63/10 (2008), paras 295-98.
332 'Fourth Report on immunity of State officials from foreign criminal jurisdiction, by Special Rapporteur Concepción Escobar Hernández', UN Doc A/CN.4/686 (2015); UN Doc A/CN.4/701 (2016).
333 UN Doc A/CN.4/701 (2016), para 240; UN Doc A/72/10 (2017), para 83.
334 UN Doc A/74/10 (2019), paras 147, 181.

Now, the ILC has provisionally adopted seven draft articles with commentary.[335] Its draft article 7 provides exceptions to functional immunity in respect of crimes under international law. Views in the ILC's members are divided on whether State officials can still invoke functional immunity in proceedings for crimes under international law before the forum State. The idea of an exception to functional immunity in draft article 7 was adopted by vote, which indicates a lack of consensus on this issue.[336] Some delegations said in the Sixth Committee that draft article 7 did not reflect *lex lata* or a trend. It remains debatable whether this draft article is a codification or progressive development of international law.[337] Delegations also welcomed the conclusion that personal immunity remains fully applicable for committing international crimes.[338]

7.5.8 *Assessment and Conclusions*

This section shows that the *Arrest Warrant* case of the ICJ gave strength to personal immunity by openly stating it as a customary rule. Decisions of the ICC and the SCSL indicate a new trend of denying personal immunity before international tribunals. It is doubtful that a derogation from personal immunities can be grounded merely on the nature of the court. Other international jurisprudence, national cases and legislation, and the work of the ILC, however, send a different message. The examination also demonstrates that both States Parties and non-party States, such as Belgium, China, Malawi, Russia, South Africa, the Netherlands, the UK and the US, Arab States as well as some other African States, generally respect personal immunity of senior officials.[339] The scarcity of hard practice and a lack of supporting *opinio juris* indicate the absence of widespread recognition of the rule that personal immunity is no longer applicable in proceedings for international crimes under customary

---

335 UN Doc A/74/10 (2019), para 121; UN Doc A/CN.4/729 (2018), Annex I, 'Draft articles on immunity from foreign criminal jurisdiction of State officials provisionally adopted by the Commission', art 7.

336 UN Doc A/74/10 (2019), paras 74, 116-29: 21 voted in favour, 8 voted against and 1 abstention concerning art 7.

337 'Sixth and seventh reports on immunity of State officials from foreign criminal jurisdiction, by Special Rapporteur, Concepción Escobar Hernández', UN Doc A/CN.4/722 (2017), paras 9-20; UN Doc A/CN.4/729 (2018), paras 8, 12; UN Doc A/74/10 (2019), para 12.

338 UN Doc A/CN.4/722 (2017), para 14. See also Institut de Droit International (n 5), art III.

339 Committee on International Criminal Court, 'Third Report, by Professor Göran Sluiter, Co-rapporteur (Part I), Professor William A. Schabas, Co-rapporteur (Part II)' in International Law Association Report of the 73rd Conference (Rio de Janeiro 2008) (ILA, London 2008), 605-06.

law.[340] To date, no such customary international rule is emerging to create a rule of non-availability of personal immunity for international crimes in international and national proceedings. South African authorities still contend that personal immunity for international crimes continues under customary law.[341] Contrary to the view of its government, the decision of the South African Supreme Court might be the first departure at the national level. The reaction of the international community to its practice would be valuable evidence for further assessment of personal immunity under customary law for committing international crimes. At the present time, article 27(2) of the Rome Statute is not declaratory of a customary rule of non-availability of personal immunity for committing international crimes.

7.6 Concluding Remarks

Debates about personal immunity may arise when a head of a non-party State to the Rome Statute is involved in ICC proceedings. Identifying a customary rule is a good attempt to solve the jurisdictional and cooperation issues. This chapter shows that the rationale of personal immunity for sitting senior officials is not only a requisite of their function but also the status of the State in international relations. Article 27(2) of the Rome Statute with a denial of personal immunity departs from a pre-existing customary rule; besides, it also acknowledges the customary rule by providing an exception to the customary rule about personal immunity. Thus, article 27(2) confirms the existing customary law respecting personal immunity in international law at the time when the Rome Statute was adopted. In addition, an examination of evidence of the two elements of customary law shows that a modification of the pre-existing customary rule is not yet mature enough to provide an exception to absolute personal immunity for committing international crimes. To date, the customary law rule respecting personal immunity remains intact to a certain extent in international law, regardless of the nature of the crimes. In conclusion, article 27(2) was not declaratory of a modified customary international rule providing non-availability of personal immunity for international crimes when the Rome Statute was adopted in 1998. Moreover, article 27(2) is also not declaratory of such a customary rule at the present time.

340   Robinson (n 37) 540–65; Akande (n 37); UN Doc A/CN.4/701 (2016), paras 235-42. Cf. Kreß and Prost (n 2) 2139.
341   Singerman (n 17); Tunks (n 301).

CHAPTER 8

Conclusions

Treaty and custom are the two main sources of international (criminal) law. As has been noted at the beginning of this book the relationship between treaty and custom remains a controversial topic. After the adoption of the 1998 Rome Statute, customary law remains an essential source in the field of international criminal law and at the ICC.

This book analysed the nature of the Rome Statute as evidence of customary law. It examined whether a provision of the Rome Statute was or is declaratory of customary law. For this purpose, it first set out the method for the identification of customary law and clarified the term 'declaratory' that defines the relations between treaty and custom in chapter 2. Based on the methodology and the terms illustrated in chapter 2, its chapter 3–7 addressed key issues of war crimes, crimes against humanity, the crime of aggression, indirect co-perpetration and personal immunity. Chapter 3 analysed the relationship between article 8 of the Rome Statute and customary law concerning war crimes in non-international armed conflict. Chapter 4 examined article 7 of the Statute and customary law concerning crimes against humanity. Chapter 5 observed articles 8*bis* and 25 (3*bis*) of the Statute and customary law about the leadership element of the crime of aggression. Chapter 6 looked at article 25(3)(a) and customary law for indirect co-perpetration. Chapter 7 surveyed the interplay between article 27(2) and customary law about non-availability of personal immunity for committing international crimes.

Chapter 8 highlights the conclusions that can be drawn from this book. Section 8.1 briefly summarises the conclusions of this book with regard to the three sub-questions formulated in chapter 1. These sub-questions are:

1. whether a provision of the Rome Statute reflected a pre-existing customary rule at the adoption of the Rome Statute or crystallised itself into custom upon its inclusion in the Statute?
2. whether a provision of the Statute that was of a declaratory nature continues to be declaratory of a customary rule on the same subject matter?
3. whether a provision of the Statute that was not of a declaratory nature has subsequently become declaratory?

Finally, section 8.2 discusses the findings of this book.

8.1 Synthesis

There have been non-international armed conflicts since World War II,[1] and few prosecutions for war crimes committed in such armed conflicts. It has been said that

> As at 2015, there seem to have been only 17 reported cases over the previous 60 years where domestic courts or tribunals have exercised universal jurisdiction over perpetrators of war crimes. Interestingly, the vast majority of these cases arose in the last 20 years and concerned events which took place in non-international armed conflicts.[2]

The current armed conflicts around the world, for instance, conflicts in South Sudan and Syria, are conflicts not of an international character. At the international level, the ICTR, the SCSL and the ECCC were established for the prosecution of crimes during civil wars. Most Situations that are presented before the ICC for consideration today also occurred in non-international armed conflict, for example, Burundi, Central African Republic (CAR), Côte d'Ivoire, Democratic Republic of Congo (DRC), Darfur, Kenya, Libya, Mali and Uganda Situations.[3]

Chapter 3 examined the relationship between article 8 of the Rome Statute and customary law concerning war crimes in non-international armed conflict. Chapter 3 revisited the historical development of war crimes and analysed the negotiations of article 8 of the Rome Statute, and then moved on to examine the practice of prosecuting war crimes in non-international armed conflict after the adoption of the Rome Statute. The extensive research about debates, signing, ratification, amendments, national implementation

---

1 UCDP/PRIO Armed Conflict Dataset, <https://www.prio.org/Data/Armed-Conflict/UCDP-PRIO/> accessed 13 December 2020.
2 L. Cameron et al, 'Article 3' in ICRC (ed), *Commentary on the First Geneva Convention: Convention (I) for the Amelioration of the Condition of the Wounded and Sick in Armed Forces in the Field* (CUP 2016), para 880. ICRC, 'Table of National Case Law on International Crimes and Universal Jurisdiction' in *Report of the Third Universal Meeting of National Committees on International Humanitarian Law*, 'Preventing and Repressing International Crimes: Towards an "Integrated" Approach Based on Domestic Practice', Vol II, Annexes, prepared by AM. La Rosa (2014) 123–31.
3 Cameron et al, ibid, para 530; 'Report of the Independent International Commission of Inquiry on the Syrian Arab Republic' (13 August 2014), UN Doc A/HRC/27/60; *The Prosecutor v Bemba* (Judgment pursuant to Article 74 of the Statute, TC III) ICC-01/05-01/08-3343 (21 March 2016); *The Prosecutor v Al Mahdi* (Decision on the confirmation of charges against Ahmad Al Faqi Al Mahdi, PTC I) ICC-01/12-01/15 (24 March 2016).

legislation, international and national prosecutions as well as other specified tribunal instruments either echoed the view that article 8 is declaratory of custom with respect to war crimes in non-international armed conflict or indicated that this rule is recognised as a part of the corpus of customary law now. The main conclusion of chapter 3 is that war crimes for violations of Common Article 3 in non-international armed conflict were codified in article 8(2)(c) of the Rome Statute, whereas war crimes for other serious violations in non-international armed conflict were crystallised in article 8(2)(e) at the Rome Conference. Articles 8(2)(c) and (e) of the Rome Statute in general were and are declaratory of custom concerning war crimes in non-international armed conflict. This conclusion, however, does not extend to all underlying acts of war crimes in non-international armed conflict. As commentators mentioned, article 8(2)(e) is both a step back and a step forward with respect to customary law. Issues of sexual crimes, recruiting child soldiers and the use of chemical weapons were highly debated during the 1998 Rome Conference.[4] Further studies should keep an eye on developing customary rules about specific offences of war crimes in non-international armed conflict.

Chapter 4 focused on the relationship between article 7 of the Rome Statute and customary law concerning crimes against humanity. Crimes against humanity was a new type of international crime in the Nuremberg Charter. This crime had already been recognised as a crime under customary law before the adoption of the Rome Statute, which provides for crimes against humanity in article 7. There are several formulations of crimes against humanity in international instruments since World War II. However, these divergent formulations do not affect the customary status of crimes against humanity in general but indicate different understandings of elements of the crimes. Chapter 4 critically analysed two contextual requirements: the absence of a nexus with an armed conflict and the policy element. Research shows that the armed conflict nexus requirement was a substantive element for the notion of crimes against humanity in the Nuremberg Charter. Later on, the link with an armed conflict disassociated itself from the notion of crimes against humanity. It remains unclear when this nexus disappeared under customary law. By excluding the armed conflict nexus, article 7 codified or, at the very least, crystallised crimes against humanity under customary law. Chapter 4 concludes that article 7(1) was and is declaratory of custom on the absence of a nexus with an armed conflict.

---

4 UN Doc A/CONF.183/2/Add.1 and Corr.1.

In addition, 'policy' is considered as a legal requirement at the ICC in accordance with article 7(2)(a). The Appeals Chamber of the ICTY in *Kunarać et al* held that policy was deemed an evidentiary factor to establish an attack. *Kunarać et al*, however, is not persuasive. An analysis of case law and definitions of crimes against humanity indicated that policy was a required legal element. Article 7(2)(a) of the Rome Statute on the issue of policy is declaratory of the pre-existing customary rule. Alternatively, even if the *Kunarać et al* Appeals Chamber's view of no policy element for crimes against humanity is valid, this judgment is not conclusive evidence for the status of customary law on the policy issue now. Sufficient evidence suggests that policy is a requirement of crimes against humanity under customary law. In conclusion, article 7(2)(a) was and is declaratory of custom with regard to the policy element.

Chapter 5 analysed the relationship between articles 8*bis* and 25(3*bis*) of the Rome Statute and customary law about the leadership element of the crime of aggression. The 'control or direct' leadership clause in articles 8*bis* and 25(3*bis*) is a legal element of the crime of aggression at the ICC. The leadership element restricts the scope of potential perpetrators and participators prosecuted for the crime of aggression. However, a leadership element of crimes against peace was not evident in the Nuremberg and Tokyo precedents. The Tribunals established based on the Control Council Law No. 10 emphasised potential perpetrators' leadership role at the policymaking level, but they did not consistently adopt the 'shape or influence' leadership test. The work of the ILC further demonstrates that a precise leadership standard for the crime of aggression was not generally accepted. The drafting history of the crime of aggression, which leads to the 2010 Kampala Amendments, shows that the clause 'control or direct' was intentionally inserted to restrict the scope of potential persons. A consensus has been reached in the negotiation and drafting process that a leadership element was required for the crime of aggression. However, this conclusion does not apply to the 'control or direct' leadership clause. Further practice and national criminal provisions reaffirm that the 'control or direct' leadership element under articles 8*bis* and 25(3*bis*) has not attained customary law status. Chapter 5 concludes that articles 8*bis* and 25(3*bis*) neither were nor are declaratory of custom concerning the 'control or direct' leadership clause.

In contrast to other provisions or drafts of individual liability for international crimes,[5] article 25 of the Rome Statute provides many explicit rules of

---

5 Nuremberg Charter, art 6(2); Control Council Law No. 10, art 2(2); 1950 ILC Nuremberg Principles, Principles I, VI (a)(ii), and VII; 1948 Genocide Convention, art III; 1949 Geneva Conventions (GC: art 49 of GC I; art 50 of GC II; art 129 of GC III; and art 146 of GC IV); the 1977 Additional Protocol I, art 86; 1991 Draft Code of Crimes, arts 3(1)-(2); 1996 Draft Code of

individual criminal responsibility. International criminal tribunals also used different labels: the complicity liability for participation in a common plan/conspiracy, joint criminal enterprise and indirect co-perpetration. Chapter 6 delved into the relationship between article 25(3)(a) of the Rome Statute and customary law concerning indirect co-perpetration. Three forms of perpetration are embedded in article 25(3)(a). An examination of the text and the drafting history of article 25(3)(a) indicates that this provision does not contain indirect co-perpetration as the fourth form of perpetration or a form of co-perpetration. In this book, the analysis of the relationship between a treaty provision and custom requires a treaty rule covering a same subject. It seems that this precondition is not satisfied because indirect co-perpetration is not subsumed in the text of article 25(3)(a). However, it is valuable to examine the customary status of this liability to date, because subsequent jurisprudence of the ICC has subscribed to indirect co-perpetration and frequently endorsed the idea of indirect co-perpetration as a mode of liability embedded in article 25(3)(a). After analysing the post-World War II practice, the jurisprudence of other international criminal tribunals and the implementation legislation, chapter 6 concludes that evidence showing the acceptance of indirect co-perpetration liability is rare. Indirect co-perpetration serves a similar function to the ICTY's *Brđanin* JCE liability with respect to high-level leaders. Trial Chambers and the Appeals Chamber of the ICC, however, tend to assign liability to the accused under the label of indirect co-perpetration. Chapter 6 shows that indirect co-perpetration has not been sufficiently supported to qualify as a customary rule to date. Accordingly, based on the arguable presumption that article 25(3)(a) covers indirect co-perpetration, this chapter argues that article 25(3)(a) is not declaratory of a customary rule with respect to indirect co-perpetration.

Chapter 7 discussed the relationship between article 27(2) of the Rome Statute and customary law about an exception to personal immunity. Article 27(2) of the Rome Statute provides that international immunities and special procedural rules cannot bar the exercise of jurisdiction by the ICC. This book argued that article 27(2) with a derogation does not indicate the refusal to respect personal immunity of senior officials of non-party States in custom, but confirms the pre-existing customary law respecting personal immunity in international law at the time when the Rome Statute was adopted. An observation of the post-World War II instruments and case law has demonstrated that the personal immunity in traditional customary law also applies in prosecuting

Crimes, art 2(3); 1993 ICTY Statute, art 7(1); 1994 ICTR Statute, art 6(1); Statute of the SCSL, art 6(1); Law on the Establishment of the ECCC, art 29(1); and Protocol on Amendments to the Protocol on the Statute of the African Court of Justice and Human Rights, art 28N.

these international crimes. No rule existed with an exception to absolute personal immunity before the adoption of the Rome Statute. Finally, an examination of international jurisprudence, national cases and the attitude of the UN Security Council and the ILC shows whether an exception to absolute personal immunity for the commission of international crimes has been well recognised under customary law to date. This book concluded that there is no sufficient evidence to demonstrate a trend of an exception to personal immunity for the commission of international crimes. Thus, contemporary customary law still provides that incumbent senior officials are inviolable in international and national criminal proceedings. Chapter 7 concludes that article 27(2) neither was of a declaratory nature nor is declaratory of a customary rule respecting personal immunity.

8.2 Discussions and Concluding Remarks

Based on the methodological framework described in chapter 2, this study of the selected provisions of the Rome Statute as evidence of customary law found that provisions of the Statute were partly declaratory of custom when adopted in 1998, and that they are also partly declaratory of custom at the present time. Provisions concerning war crimes and crimes against humanity were reflections of custom, and they continue to be declaratory of custom. Meanwhile, provisions about the leadership clause for the crime of aggression, indirect co-perpetration liability and non-availability of personal immunity were not of a declaratory nature at the time when the Rome Statute or the Kampala Amendments was adopted, and they have not passed into customary law to date. This section discusses the findings and a combination of the findings of this book.

As shown above, provisions of the Rome Statute about substantive crimes were and are recognised as custom in general. The 'control or direct' leadership element of the crime of aggression and a mode of liability, indirect co-perpetration, were not and are not considered as customary law. In contrast to international crimes, it is difficult but not impossible for a mode of liability without sufficient roots in national laws to pass into customary law. The main reason may be that international crimes are mainly derived from international law, while many modes of liability and defences originate in national laws. This reason, however, does not apply to issues concerning *sui generis* liability and personal immunity. Traditional general international law still plays a vital role with respect to personal immunity. Whether a substantive customary rule exists at the relevant time is at the crossroads for the identification of customary law, the principle of legality and the principle of culpability. We should be cautious in applying customary law either as a source or as an interpretative aid to developing the scope of crimes, extending modes of liability, narrowing the scope of defences, and setting aside evidentiary problems.

At the Rome Conference, States were reluctant to recognise serious violations of laws and customs in non-international armed conflict as war crimes for several reasons.[6] Michael Bothe noted:

> The government side will claim that acts of repression performed during that conflict are nothing more than the maintenance of law and order as required by the legal system of that State. Thus, it will be argued, those acts were required under the law and consequently cannot be punished.[7]

Indeed, it is generally supposed that behaviour as a method of maintaining the law and order is required by the national system. Some acts of repression performed during non-international armed conflicts would be at the risk of prosecution if other violations in non-international armed conflicts were included as war crimes. For instance, the use of expanding bullets is lawful in law enforcement at the national level in order, for example, to avoid unnecessary harm to citizens surrounding the scene of a bank robbery or in the course of a hostage-taking.[8] However, the Rome Statute considered the use of expanding bullets as a war crime in non-international armed conflict.[9] In connection with the ambiguous definition of non-international armed conflict, States may object to criminalising some punishable acts as war crimes in non-international armed conflict because these acts are legitimate maintenance methods in national law.[10] At the Conference, diplomats as representative of States were not willing to restrain the enforcement powers or measures of their States. These considerations explain why the threshold of non-international

---

6 D. Momtaz, 'War Crimes in Non-International Armed Conflicts under the Statute of the International Criminal Court' (1999) 2 *YIHL* 177.
7 M. Bothe, 'War Crimes in Non-International Armed Conflicts' in Y. Dinstein and M. Tabory (eds), *War Crimes in International Law* (Martinus Nijhoff Publishers 1996) 295.
8 The Declaration of Czech Republic said: 'The prohibition to employ gases, and all analogous liquids, materials or devices, set out in article 8, paragraph 2(e)(xiv), is interpreted in line with the obligations arising from the Convention on the Prohibition of the Development, Production, stockpiling and Use of Chemical Weapons and on Their Destruction of 1993'.
9 1998 Rome Statute, art 8(2)(e)(xv) reads: '[e]mploying bullets which expand or flatten easily in the human body, such as bullets with a hard envelope which does not entirely cover the core or is pierced with incisions.'
10 Bothe (n 7) 295–96.

armed conflict was added, and why the list of punishable acts of war crimes in non-international armed conflict is somewhat shorter than that in international armed conflict under article 8.

The second reason is that the recognition of war crimes in non-international armed conflict does not seem to be in the interest of States. States were uneasy that their recognition would be deemed recognition of belligerents' status for anti-government forces, and would justify rebels' killings of their soldiers. Without a rule of war crimes in non-international armed conflict, the State can prosecute alleged individuals of an organised armed group for joining rebels or killing soldiers of government armed forces at the national level, regardless of whether perpetrators/rebels respected international humanitarian law applicable in non-international armed conflict. The existence of war crimes in non-international armed conflict indicates that it is less legitimate for States to prosecute individuals who behave in compliance with rules applicable in non-international armed conflict. A rule of criminalising serious violations in non-international armed conflict as war crimes leads to less control over the prosecution of rebels by national authorities. However, 'if the distinction is not made between behaviour in conformity with international humanitarian law and behaviour which is not, the value of criminal law in the repression of breaches of international humanitarian law is greatly reduced'.[11]

All these concerns show a struggle between State sovereignty and the aim to end impunity. This finding is also true for debates about the elements of crimes against humanity and the leadership element of the crime of aggression. As for the lack of substantial prosecution of the crime of aggression after World War II, Larry May observed that one reason might be the reluctance of theorists to simply rely on customary law alone to prosecute the crime of aggression. Another reason was the inability of States to reach a consensus on the precise definition of the crime of aggression in a multilateral treaty.[12] With the adoption of the Kampala Amendments and the ASP resolution activating the ICC's jurisdiction over the crime of aggression, the door is open for the ICC to establish precedents for the prosecution of the crime of aggression. It remains to be seen whether the 'control or direct' leadership test will be established in customary law.

Aside from the three crimes, selected provisions concerning participation in crimes and personal immunities were examined in this book. Government or

---

11 ibid 295.
12 L. May, *Aggression and Crimes Against Peace* (CUP 2008) 153, 159, 162. The reasons for the failure to arrive at an internationally agreed definition of the crime of aggression, see A. Cassese *et al* (eds), *Cassese's International Criminal Law* (3rd edn, OUP 2013) 138–39.

State leaders comprise most of the cases before international criminal tribunals, in which the attribution of liability is somewhat complicated. In addition, questions become controversial concerning the scope and the applicability of absolute personal immunity of senior State officials. If accountability and non-impunity mean prosecution of a person in the highest rank or on the top of the planning chain, then the introduction of indirect co-perpetration might be desirable, and personal immunity would seem to be a barrier to achieving that goal. Indirect co-perpetration has not been sufficiently supported to constitute a customary rule to date. Under current international law, it seems to be unjust to retain the personal immunity of senior officials, whereas it is also unjustified to invalidate it on the basis of custom because the evidence is not sufficient to form a new customary rule.

As examined at the beginning of the book, customary law is also valuable for modes of liability when the ICC's jurisdiction was triggered by Security Council referrals and State's acceptance. At the ICC, challenges 'to jurisdiction to prosecute under indirect co-perpetration liability' were required to be made before or at the commence of the trial. It is also acceptable to challenge the existence of that liability in the context of interpretation at later stages.[13] The different applications of liability, to solve the scenario like that in the ICC, indicate that the law is developing in this regard. If States tend to follow the ICC's approach in dealing with international crimes, a consensus on how to attribute liability to government or State leaders might be reached in international criminal tribunals, as a *sui generis* system of this regime. However, if States adopt different ways of attributing liability to the accused based on national laws, it would be difficult for States to reach a consensus on this unique mode of liability because of different criminal justice systems. The division of criminal law systems between common law and civil law would further enhance this difficulty. The question of whether the indirect co-perpetration liability might be a customary rule depends on the approach States will adopt, the ICC-oriented approach or the national-oriented one.[14]

The challenge to the regime of personal immunity also should not be exaggerated.[15] As the ICJ suggested, even if senior officials have committed international crimes, their personal immunities remain intact under customary law.

---

13   *The Prosecutor v Ongwen* (Decision on Defence Motions Alleging Defects in the Confirmation Decision, TC IX) ICC-02/04-01/15-1476 (7 March 2019), paras 31, 34-5.

14   C. Steer, *Translating Guilt: Identifying Leadership Liability for Mass Atrocity Crimes* (TMC Asser Press 2017).

15   W.A. Schabas, *The International Criminal Court: A Commentary on the Rome Statute* (2nd edn, OUP 2016) 594.

There are alternatives to prosecute sitting senior State officials in the future. A specific exception to the customary rule of personal immunity for international crimes through a treaty is acceptable.[16] When a person is deprived of personal immunity by a UN Security Council resolution, the person can no longer invoke personal immunity to challenge the jurisdiction of an UN-based tribunal.[17] State authorities concerned can waive personal immunity before national or international criminal tribunals. Another way to invalidate personal immunity is by pushing non-party States to join the Rome Statute, which requires a waiver of immunity before the ICC. It seems less necessary to retain it when all States are consistent in depriving personal immunity. International (criminal) law is facing the challenge 'to provide for stability in international relations and to guarantee respect for human rights by a means other than the impunity' of those allegedly most responsible for committing international crimes.[18]

It is also necessary to discuss the implication of the combination of the findings in this book. Firstly, a combination of the finding that a treaty rule 'was and is' declaratory indicates the existence of a customary rule on the same subject matter at the material time. Such a combination is found in chapters 3 and 4 on war crimes and crimes against humanity. In the two instances, the content of customary law in the past and at present is the same on the issues concerned. It should be noted that, as Mark Villiger wrote: 'customary law is dynamic and the customary rule underlying a treaty text may change; the treaty rule may generate new customary law and the treaty text may be influenced by different approaches of interpretation'.[19] Since customary law is not static and a parallel treaty rule is not frozen, such a combination of findings generally does not demonstrate what the content of a customary rule was and is.[20]

Secondly, a combination of the findings that a treaty rule 'was not' and 'is not' of a declaratory nature does not inherently imply that no customary rule exists on the same subject-matter in the past or at present. For instance, the

---

16   UN Doc A/63/10 (2008), para 310.
17   ibid.
18   *Arrest Warrant of 11 April 2000 (Democratic Republic of the Congo v Belgium)* (Joint Separate opinion of Judges Higgins, Kooijmans and Buergenthal), para 5; *The Prosecutor v Al Bashir* (Judgment in the Jordan Referral re Al-Bashir Appeal, A Ch) ICC-02/05-01/09-397-Anx1-Corr (17 May 2019) (Joint Concurring Opinion of Judges Eboe-Osuji, Morrison, Hofmański and Bossa), para 195.
19   M. Villiger, *Customary International Law and Treaties: A Study of Their Interactions and Interrelations, with Special Consideration of the 1969 Vienna Convention on the Law of Treaties* (Martinus Nijhoff Publishers 1985) 227, 238.
20   Vienna Convention on the Law of Treaties, art 31(3).

nature of article 27(2) of the Rome Statute as evidence of custom does not indicate that there was no customary rule on personal immunity in international law. Similarly, this combination of findings only implies the non-existence status of a rule 'underlying the treaty provision' at the critical time under customary law. The findings of articles 8*bis* and 25(3*bis*), article 25(3)(a) and article 27(2) as evidence of customary law reflect such a combination.

Thirdly, a combination of findings that a treaty rule 'was' but 'is not' declaratory of customary law indicates that a rule underlying the text was a pre-existing or emerging customary rule at the time when the treaty was adopted. This combination does not lead to conclusive findings on the status of customary law on the same subject matter at present. The treaty rule is not of a declaratory nature either for the reading of the treaty text has changed later on, or the content of the customary rule has been modified (extinguished) on the same subject at present, or both. Lastly, the combination of the findings that a treaty rule 'was not' but 'is' declaratory of customary law does not automatically demonstrate the status of a customary rule on the same subject-matter in the past. There may be several reasons for concluding that a treaty rule was not declaratory of custom. One of them may be that no pre-existing customary law existed. The other reason may be that the treaty rule was of a norm-making character or stipulated an exception to a pre-existing customary rule. A good example of the latter is article 27(2) concerning personal immunity at the ICC. If a rule of non-availability of personal immunity for committing international crimes is generally accepted in the future, the conclusion in chapter 7 would be that article 27(2) was not but 'is' at that moment declaratory of customary law. The latter two combinations of findings cannot be confirmed in this book with regard to the selected provisions under the present circumstances.

The 1998 Rome Statute exercises an essential impact on the content of customary law in the field of international criminal law. Customary law also continues to play a role in and outside the ICC framework. As Rosalyn Higgins wrote: 'international custom is the most flexible, the most fluid, and as such, is exceedingly responsive to the changing needs of the international community'.[21]

---

21   R. Higgins, *The Development of International Law Through the Political Organs of the United Nations* (OUP 1963) 1.

Bibliography

Books

Ambos, K., *Treatise on International Criminal Law, Vol I: Foundations and General Part* (OUP 2013).

Ambos, K., *Treatise on International Criminal Law, Vol II: The Crimes and Sentencing* (OUP 2014).

Arajärvi, N., *The Changing Nature of Customary International Law: Methods of Interpreting the Concept of Custom in International Criminal Tribunals* (Routledge 2014).

Barriga, S. and Kreß, C. (eds), *The Travaux Préparatoires of the Crime of Aggression* (CUP 2012).

Barriga, S. and Kreß, C., *The Crime of Aggression: A Commentary* (CUP 2017).

Bassiouni, M.C., *Crimes Against Humanity in International Criminal Law* (Martinus Nijhoff Publishers 1992).

Bassiouni, M.C., *Crimes Against Humanity* (CUP 2011).

Bassiouni, M.C., *Crimes Against Humanity: Historical Evolution and Contemporary Application* (CUP 2011).

Bassiouni, M.C., *Introduction to International Criminal Law* (2nd edn, Brill 2012).

Bassiouni, M.C. and Schabas, W.A. (eds), *The Legislative History of the International Criminal Court* (2nd Revised and expanded edn, Brill 2016).

Beham, M.P., *State Interest and the Sources of International Law: Doctrine, Morality, and Non-Treaty Law* (Routledge 2018).

Bellelli, R. (ed), *International Criminal Justice: Law and Practice from the Rome Statute to its Review* (Ashgate Publishing 2010).

Bergsmo, M. et al (eds), *Importing Core International Crimes into National Criminal Law* (2nd edn, TOAEP 2010).

Bevans, C.I. (ed), *United States Treaties and International Agreement, 1776–1949* (USGPO 1968–1976).

Blumenthal, D. and McCormack, T. (eds), *The Legacy of Nuremberg: Civilising Influence or Institutionalised Vengeance?* (Brill | Nijhoff 2007).

Boas, G. et al, *International Criminal Law Practitioner Library: Vol 1, Forms of Responsibility in International Criminal Law* (CUP 2007).

Boot, M., *Genocide, Crimes Against Humanity, War Crimes: Nullum Crimen Sine Lege and the Subject Matter Jurisdiction of the International Criminal Court* (Intersentia 2008).

Bradley, C. (ed), *Custom's Future: International Law in a Changing World* (CUP 2016).

Brody, R. and Ratner, M. (eds), *The Pinochet Papers: The Case of Augusto Pinochet Ugarte in Spain and Britain* (Kluwer Law International 2000).

Broomhall, B., *International Justice and the International Criminal Court: Between Sovereignty and the Rule of Law* (OUP 2004).
Byers, M., *Custom, Power and the Power of Rules: International Relations and Customary International Law* (CUP 1999).
Cassese, A. and Weiler, J. (eds), *Change and Stability in International Law-Making* (Walter de Gruyter 1988).
Cassese, A. et al (eds), *The Rome Statute of the International Criminal Court: A Commentary* (OUP 2002).
Cassese, A. et al (eds), *Cassese's International Criminal Law* (3rd edn, OUP 2013).
Crawford, J., *Brownlie's Principles of Public International Law* (9th edn, OUP 2019).
Cryer, R. et al, *An Introduction to International Criminal Law and Procedure* (3rd edn, CUP 2014).
D'Amato, A., *The Concept of Custom in International Law* (Cornell University Press 1971).
Darcy, S., *Judges, Law and War: The Judicial Development of International Humanitarian Law* (CUP 2014).
Dinstein, Y. and Tabory, M. (eds), *War Crimes in International Law* (Martinus Nijhoff Publishers 1996).
Dinstein, Y., *The Defence of 'Obedience of Superior Orders' in International Law* (OUP 2012).
Dinstein, Y., *War, Aggression and Self-Defence* (5th edn, CUP 2012).
Dubler, R. and Kalyk, M., *Crimes against Humanity in the 21st Century: Law, Practice, and Threats to International Peace and Security* (Brill | Nijhoff 2018).
Eser, A. et al (eds), *National Prosecution of International Crimes, Vols 1–7* (Ed. Iuscrim 2003–2006).
Ferdinandusse, W.N., *Direct Application of International Criminal Law in National Courts* (TMC Asser Press 2006).
Ferencz, B.B., *Defining International Aggression: The Search for World Peace (A Documentary History and Analysis)*, Vol 2 (Oceana Publications 1975).
Fitzpatrick, G. et al (eds), *Australia's War Crimes Trials 1945–51* (Brill | Nijhoff 2016).
Fletcher, G., *Basic Concepts of Criminal Law* (OUP 1998).
Gallant, K.S., *The Principle of Legality in International and Comparative Criminal Law* (CUP 2008).
Grover, L., *Interpreting Crimes in the Rome Statute of the International Criminal Court* (CUP 2014).
Heller, K.J., *The Nuremberg Military Tribunals and the Origins of International Criminal Law* (OUP 2011).
Henckaerts, JM. and Louise Doswald-beck, L. (eds), *Customary International Humanitarian Law*, Vols I and II (CUP 2005).
Hetherington, T. and Chalmers, W., *War Crimes: Report of the War Crimes Inquiry*, Command Paper 744 (HMSO 1989).

Higgins, R., *The Development of International Law Through the Political Organs of the United Nations* (OUP 1963).

Horder, J., *Ashworth's Principles of Criminal Law* (OUP 2016).

ICRC (ed), *Commentary on the First Geneva Convention: Convention (I) for the Amelioration of the Condition of the Wounded and Sick in Armed Forces in the Field* (CUP 2016).

Jennings, R. and Watts, A. (eds), *Oppenheim's International Law* (9th edn, Longmans 1996).

Kalshoven, F. and Zegveld, L., *Constraints on the Waging of War: An Introduction to International Humanitarian Law* (CUP 2011).

Kittichaisaree, K., *International Criminal Law* (OUP 2001).

Klamberg, M. (ed), *The Commentary on the Law of the International Criminal Court* (TAOEP 2017).

La Haye, E., *War Crimes in Internal Armed Conflicts* (CUP 2008).

Lee, R.S. (ed), *The International Criminal Court: The Making of the Rome Statute: Issues, Negotiations and Results* (Kluwer Law International 1999).

Lee, R.S., *The International Criminal Court, Elements of Crimes and Rule of Procedure and Evidence* (Transnational 2001).

Lepard, B., *Customary International Law: A New Theory with Practical Applications* (CUP 2010).

Lepard, B. (ed), *Reexamining Customary International Law* (CUP 2016).

Lijnzaad, L. (ed), *The Judge and International Custom* (Brill | Nijhoff 2016).

May, L., *Crimes Against Humanity: A Normative Account* (CUP 2005).

May, L., *Aggression and Crimes Against Peace* (CUP 2008).

McDougall, C., *The Crime of Aggression under the Rome Statute of the International Criminal Court* (CUP 2013).

Mendlllin Urquiaga, X., *Digest of Latin American Jurisprudence on International Crimes*, Vols I-II (Due Process of Law Foundation 2010, 2013).

Merkouris, P., *Article 31(3)(c) VCLT and the Principle of Systemic Integration: Normative Shadows in Plato's Cave* (Brill | Nijhoff 2015).

Mettraux, G., *International Crimes and the Ad hoc Tribunals* (OUP 2006).

Mettraux, G., *The Law of Command Responsibility* (OUP 2009).

Mettraux, G., *International Crimes and Practice Volume I: Genocide* (OUP 2019).

Meloni, C., *Command Responsibility in International Criminal Law* (TMC Asser Press 2010).

Meron, T., *Human Rights and Humanitarian Norms as Customary Law* (Clarendon Press 1989).

Olásolo, H., *Essays on International Criminal Justice* (Hart Publishing 2012).

Olásolo, H., *The Criminal Responsibility of Senior Political and Military Leaders as Principals to International Crimes* (Hart Publishing 2009).

Ormerod, D. and Laird, K., *Smith and Hogan's Criminal Law* (14th ed, OUP 2015).
Perna, L., *The Formation of the Treaty Law Applicable in Non-International Armed Conflicts* (Brill | Nijhoff 2006).
Perreau-Saussine, A. and Murphy, J. (eds), *The Nature of Customary Law* (CUP 2009).
Peters, A., *Beyond Human Rights: The Legal Status of the Individual in International Law* (OUP 2016).
Piccigallo, P.R., *The Japanese On Trial: Allied War Crimes Operations in the East, 1945–1951* (University of Texas Press 2013).
Pictet, J., *Commentary on the Geneva Conventions of 12 August 1949*, Vol I (ICRC 1952).
Pictet, J., *Commentary on the Geneva Conventions of 12 August 1949*, Vol II (ICRC 1960).
Pictet, J., *Commentary on the Geneva Conventions of 12 August 1949*, Vol III (ICRC 1952).
Pilloud, C. et al (eds), *Commentary on the Additional Protocols of 8 June 1977 to the Geneva Conventions of 12 August 1949* (Martinus Nijhoff Publishers 1987).
Pompe, C.A., *Aggressive War: An International Crime* (Springer 1953).
Raimondo, F., *General Principles of Law in the Decisions of International Criminal Courts and Tribunals* (Brill | Nijhoff 2008).
Rauter, T., *Judicial Practice, Customary International Criminal Law and Nullum Crimen Sine Lege* (Springer 2017).
Röling, B.V.A. and Cassese, A., *The Tokyo Trial and Beyond: Reflections of a Peacemonger* (Polity Press 1993).
Sadat, L.N. (ed), *Forging a Convention for Crimes against Humanity* (CUP 2011).
Sadat, L.N. (ed), *Seeking Accountability for the Unlawful Use of Force* (CUP 2018).
Schabas, W.A., *The UN International Criminal Tribunals: The Former Yugoslavia, Rwanda and Sierra Leone* (CUP 2006).
Schabas, W.A., *Genocide in International Law, The Crime of Crimes* (2nd edn, CUP 2009).
Schabas, W.A., *Unimaginable Atrocities: Justice, Politics, and Rights at the War Crimes Tribunals* (OUP 2012).
Schabas, W.A., (ed), *The Universal Declaration of Human Rights: The Travaux Préparatoires* (CUP 2013).
Schabas, W.A., *The European Convention on Human Rights: A Commentary* (OUP 2015).
Schabas, W.A., *The International Criminal Court: A Commentary on the Rome Statute* (2nd edn, OUP 2016).
Schabas, W.A., *An Introduction to the International Criminal Court* (6th edn, CUP 2020).
Schabas, W.A., *The Customary International Law of Human Rights* (forthcoming OUP 2021).
Scharf, M., *Customary International Law in Times of Fundamental Change: Recognizing Grotian Moments* (CUP 2013).
Schlütter, B., *Developments in Customary International Law: Theory and the Practice of the International Court of Justice and the International ad hoc Criminal Tribunals for Rwanda and Yugoslavia* (Brill | Nijhoff 2010).

Sellars, K.E., *'Crimes Against Peace' and International Law* (CUP 2013).
Shaw, M., *International Law* (8th edn, CUP 2017).
Shelton, D. (ed), *International Law and Domestic Legal Systems: Incorporation, Transformation, and Persuasion* (OUP 2011).
Simester, A. et al, *Simester and Sullivan's Criminal Law: Theory and Doctrine* (5th ed, Hart Publishing 2013).
Sivakumaran, S., *The Law of Non-International Armed Conflict* (OUP 2012).
Stahn, C. and El Zeidy, M.M. (eds), *The International Criminal Court and Complementarity: From Theory to Practice* (CUP 2011).
Stahn, C. (ed), *The Law and Practice of the International Criminal Court* (OUP 2015).
Stahn, C., *A Critical Introduction to International Criminal Law* (CUP 2018).
Staubach, P.G., *The Rule of Unwritten International Law: Customary Law, General Principles, and World Order* (Routledge 2018).
Steer, C., *Translating Guilt: Identifying Leadership Liability for Mass Atrocity Crimes* (TMC Asser Press 2017).
Taylor, T., *Final Report to the Secretary of the Army on the Nuremberg War Crimes Trials under Control Council Law No. 10* (USGPO 1949).
Thirlway, H., *The Sources of International Law* (2nd edn, OUP 2019).
Trahan, J., *Genocide, War Crimes, and Crimes Against Humanity: A Topical Digest of the Case Law of the International Criminal Tribunal for the Former Yugoslavia* (Human Rights Watch 2006).
Triffterer, O. and Ambos, K. (eds), *Commentary on the Rome Statute of the International Criminal Court: Observers' Notes, Article by Article* (3rd edn, Hart/Beck 2016).
United Nations War Crimes Commission (ed), *History of the United Nations War Crimes Commission and the Development of the Laws of War* (HMSO 1948).
United Nations War Crimes Commission (ed), *Transcripts of Proceedings and Documents of the International Military Tribunals for the Far East* (Tokyo Trials).
United Nations War Crimes Commission (ed), *Law Reports of Trial of War Criminals: Selected and Prepared by the United Nations War Crimes Commission* (HMSO 1947–1949).
Van Alebeek, R., *The Immunity of States and Their Officials in International Criminal Law and International Human Rights Law* (OUP 2008).
Van den Herik, L.J., *The Contribution of the Rwanda Tribunal to the Development of International Law* (Brill | Nijhoff 2005).
Van Sliedregt, E., *Individual Criminal Responsibility in International Law* (OUP 2012).
Van Sliedregt, E., *The Criminal Responsibility of Individuals for Violations of International Humanitarian Law* (CUP 2003).
Villiger, M., *Customary International Law and Treaties: A Study of Their Interactions and Interrelations, with Special Consideration of the 1969 Vienna Convention on the Law of Treaties* (Martinus Nijhoff Publishers 1985).

Villiger, M., *Customary International Law and Treaties: A Manual on the Theory and Practice of the International of Sources* (Fully revised 2nd edn, Kluwer Law International 1997).

Werle, G. and Jeßberger, F., *Principles of International Criminal Law* (3rd edn, OUP 2014).

Wilmshurst, E. and Breau, S. (eds), *Perspectives on the ICRC Study on Customary International Humanitarian Law* (CUP 2007).

Yang, X., *State Immunity in International Law* (CUP 2012).

Yanev, L.D., *Theories of Co-perpetration in International Criminal Law* (Brill | Nijhoff 2018).

Zahar, A. and Sluiter, G., *International Criminal Law: A Critical Introduction* (OUP 2008).

Contributions to Edited Books

Abi-Saab, G., 'The Concept of War Crimes' in Yee, S. and Wang, T. (eds), *International Law in the Post-Cold War World: Essays in Memory of Li Haopei* (Routledge 2001).

Akande, D., 'Sources of International Criminal Law' in Cassese, A. (ed), *Oxford Companion on International Criminal Justice* (OUP 2009).

Ambos, K., 'Article 25' in Triffterer, O. and Ambos, K. (eds), *Commentary on the Rome Statute of the International Criminal Court: Observers' Notes, Article by Article* (3rd edn, Hart/Beck 2016).

Andenas, M. and Bjorge, E., 'Introduction' in Andenas, M. and Bjorge, E. (eds), *A Farewell to Fragmentation: Reassertion and Convergence in International Law* (CUP 2015).

Anggadi, F. et al, 'Negotiating the Elements of the Crime of Aggression' in Barriga, S. and Kreß, C. (eds), *The Travaux Préparatoires of the Crime of Aggression* (CUP 2012).

Bassiouni, M.C., 'Revisiting the Architecture of Crimes Against Humanity' in Sadat, L.N. (ed), *Forging a Convention for Crimes against Humanity* (CUP 2011).

Bassiouni, M.C., 'The Status of Aggression in International Law from Versailles to Kampala – and What the Future Might Hold' in Sadat, L.N. (ed), *Seeking Accountability for the Unlawful Use of Force* (CUP 2018).

Barriga, S., 'Against the Odds: The Results of the Special Working Group on the Crime of Aggression' in Bellelli, R. (ed), *International Criminal Justice: Law and Practice from the Rome Statute to its Review* (Ashgate Publishing 2010).

Barriga, S., 'Negotiating on the Amendments on the crime of aggression' in Barriga, S. and Kreß, C. (eds), *The Travaux Préparatoires of the Crime of Aggression* (CUP 2012).

Bethlehem, D., 'The Methodological Framework of the Study' in Wilmshurst, E. and Breau, S. (eds), *Perspectives on the ICRC Study on Customary International Humanitarian Law* (CUP 2007).

Boas, G. and Lee, L., 'Command Responsibility and Other Grounds of Criminal Responsibility' in Fitzpatrick, G. et al (eds), *Australia's War Crimes Trials 1945–51* (Brill | Nijhoff 2016).

Bothe, M., 'War Crimes in Non-International Armed Conflicts' in Dinstein, Y. and Tabory, M. (eds), *War Crimes in International Law* (Martinus Nijhoff Publishers 1996).

Broomhall, B., 'Article 22' in Triffterer, O. (ed), *Commentary on the Rome Statute of the International Criminal Court –Observers' Notes, Article by Article* (2nd edn, Beck/Hart 2008).

Cameron, L. *et al*, 'Article 3' in International Committee of the Red Cross (ed), *Commentary on the First Geneva Convention: Convention (I) for the Amelioration of the Condition of the Wounded and Sick in Armed Forces in the Field* (CUP 2016).

Clark, R.S., 'Crimes against Humanity at Nuremberg' in Ginsburgs, G. and Kudriavtsev, V.N. (eds), *The Nuremberg Trial and International Law* (Martinus Nijhoff Publishers 1990).

Clark, R.S., 'History of Efforts to Codify Crimes Against Humanity' in Sadat, L.N. (ed), *Forging a Convention for Crimes against Humanity* (CUP 2011).

Clark, R.S., 'Negotiations on the Rome Statute, 1995–98' and 'General Principles of International Criminal Law' in Barriga, S. and Kreß, C. (eds), *The Crime of Aggression: A Commentary* (CUP 2017).

Cottier, M., 'Article 8' in Triffterer, O. and Ambos, K. (eds), *Commentary on the Rome Statute of the International Criminal Court: Observers' Notes, Article by Article* (3rd edn, Hart/Beck 2016).

Coracini, A.R., 'Evaluating Domestic Legislation on the Customary Crime of Aggression Under the Rome Statute's Complementarity Regime' in Stahn, C. and Sluiter, G. (eds), *The Emerging Practice of the International Criminal Court* (Brill | Nijhoff 2009).

Coracini, A.R., 'National Legislation on Individual Responsibility for Conduct Amounting to Aggression' in Bellelli, R. (ed), *International Criminal Justice: Law and Practice from the Rome Statute to its Review* (Ashgate Publishing 2010).

Coracini, A.R. and Wrange, P., 'Specificity of the Crime of Aggression' in Barriga, S. and Kreß, C. (eds), *The Crime of Aggression: A Commentary* (CUP 2017).

Cryer, R., 'The ICC and its Relationship to Non-States Parties' in Stahn, C. (ed), *The Law and Practice of the International Criminal Court* (OUP 2015).

Cryer, R., 'The Tokyo International Military Tribunal and Crimes Against Peace (Aggression): Is There Anything to Learn?' in Sadat, L.N. (ed), *Seeking Accountability for the Unlawful Use of Force* (CUP 2018).

Cullen, A., 'War Crimes' in Schabas, W.A. and Bernaz, N. (eds), *Routledge Handbook of International Criminal Law* (Routledge 2011).

D'Amato, A., 'Treaty-Based Rules of Custom' in D'Amato, A. (ed), *International Law Anthology* (Anderson Publishing Company 1994).

D'Aspremont, J., 'An Autonomous Regime of Identification of Customary International Humanitarian Law: Do Not Say What You Do or Do Not Do What You Say?' in Van Steenberghe, R. (eds), *Droit International Humanitaire: UN Régime Spécial De Droit International?* (Bruylant 2013).

DeGuzman, M.M., 'Article 21' in Triffterer O. and Ambos, K. (eds), *Commentary on the Rome Statute of the International Criminal Court: Observers' Notes, Article by Article* (3rd edn, Hart/Beck 2016).

DeGuzman, M.M., 'Crimes against Humanity' in Schabas, W.A. and Bernaz, N. (eds), *Routledge Handbook of International Criminal Law* (Routledge 2011).

Dinstein, Y., 'The Crime of Aggression under Customary International Law' in Sadat, L.N. (ed), *Seeking Accountability for the Unlawful Use of Force* (CUP 2018).

Eser, A., 'Individual Criminal Responsibility' in Cassese, A. *et al* (eds), *The Rome Statute of the International Criminal Court: A Commentary* (OUP 2002).

Fox, H., 'Article 31(3)(a) and (b) of the Vienna Convention and the *Kasikili/Sedudu Island* Case' in Fitzmaurice, M. *et al* (eds), *Treaty Interpretation and the Vienna Convention on the Law of Treaties: 30 Years on* (Martinus Nijhoff Publishers 2010).

Frulli, M., 'Piercing the Veil of Head-of-State Immunity: The Taylor Trial and Beyond' in Jalloh, C.C. (ed), *The Sierra Leone Special Court and its Legacy: The Impact for Africa and International Criminal Law* (CUP 2013).

Gaeta, P., 'Official Capacity and Immunities' in Cassese, A. *et al* (eds), *The Rome Statute of the International Criminal Court: A Commentary* (OUP 2002).

Gaeta, P. and Labuda, P.I., 'Trying Sitting Heads of State: The African Union versus the ICC in the *Al Bashir* and *Kenyatta* Cases' in Jalloh, C.C. and Bantekas, I. (eds), *The International Criminal Court and Africa* (OUP 2017).

Garraway, C., 'War Crimes' in Wilmshurst, E. and Breau, S. (eds), *Perspectives on the ICRC Study on Customary International Humanitarian Law* (CUP 2007).

Gatenacci, M., 'The Principle of Legality' in Lattanzi, F. and Schabas, W.A. (eds), *Essays on the Rome Statute of the International Criminal Court, Vol 2* (Editrice il Sirente 1999).

Glaser, S., 'The Charter of the Nuremberg Tribunal and New Principles of International Law' in Mattraux, G. (ed), *Perspectives on the Nuremberg Trial* (OUP 2008).

Glotova, S.V., 'Russia' in Barriga, S. and Kreß, C. (eds), *The Crime of Aggression: A Commentary* (CUP 2017).

Greenwood, C., 'Sovereignty: A View from the International Bench' in Rawlings, R. *et al* (eds), *Sovereignty and the Law: Domestic, European and International Perspectives* (OUP 2013).

Greppi, E., 'State Responsibility for Acts of Aggression Under the United Nations Charter: A Review of Cases' in Bellelli, R. (ed), *International Criminal Justice: Law and Practice from the Rome Statute to its Review* (Ashgate Publishing 2010).

Gut, T. and Wolpert, M., 'Canada' in Eser, A. *et al* (eds), *National Prosecution of International Crimes*, Vol 5 (Ed. Iuscrim 2005).

Hall, C. and Stahn, C., 'Article 7' in Triffterer, O. and Ambos, K. (eds), *Commentary on the Rome Statute of the International Criminal Court: Observers' Notes, Article by Article* (3rd edn, Hart/Beck 2016).

Henckaerts, JM. and Niebergall-Lackner, H., 'Introduction' in International Committee of the Red Cross (ed), *Commentary on the First Geneva Convention: Convention (I) for the Amelioration of the Condition of the Wounded and Sick in Armed Forces in the Field* (CUP 2016).

Heinsch, R., 'Commentary on Rule 84 "Individual Criminal Responsibility for War Crimes"' in Schmitt, M.N. (ed), *Tallinn Manual 2.0 on the International Law Applicable to Cyber Warfare* (2nd edn, CUP 2017).

Hoven, E., 'Germany' in Barriga, S. and Kreß, C. (eds), *The Crime of Aggression: A Commentary* (CUP 2017).

Jacobs, D., 'Commentary' in Klip, A. and Sluiter, G. (eds), *Annotated Leading Cases of the International Criminal Court: 2005–2007*, Vol 23 (Intersentia 2010).

Jacobs, D., 'The Frog That Wanted to Be an Ox: The ICC's Approach to Immunities and Cooperation' in Stahn, C. (ed), *The Law and Practice of the International Criminal Court* (OUP 2015).

Jørgensen, N., 'On Being "Concerned" in a Crime: Embryonic Joint Criminal Enterprise?' in Linton, S. (ed), *Hong Kong's War Crimes Trials* (OUP 2013).

Kemp, G., 'Implementing at national level the amendments to the Rome Statute of the International Criminal Court with respect to the crime of aggression: A South African perspective' in Ambos, K. and Maunganidze, O.A. (eds), *Power and Prosecution – Challenges and Opportunities for International Criminal Justice in Sub-Saharan Africa* (Göttingen University 2012).

Kerbrat, Y. and Marguerite, T., 'General Prosecutor v Gaddafi' in Nollkaemper, A. and Reinisch, A. (eds), *Oxford Reports on International Law in Domestic Courts*.

Kirsch, P. 'The Development of the Rome Statute' in Lee, R.S. (ed), *The International Criminal Court: The Making of the Rome Statute: Issues, Negotiations and Results* (Kluwer Law International 1999).

Kirsch, P. and Robinson, D., 'Reaching Agreement at the Rome Conference' in Cassese, A. et al (eds), *The Rome Statute of the International Criminal Court Commentary* (OUP 2002).

Kirsch, P. and Robinson, D., 'Foreword' in Dörmann, K. (ed), *Elements of War Crimes under the Rome Statute of the International Criminal Court: Sources and Commentary* (CUP 2003).

Kleffner, J.K., 'The Collective Accountability of Organized Armed Groups for System Crimes' in Nollkaemper, A. and Van der Wilt, H. (eds), *System Criminality in International Law* (CUP 2009).

Kreß, C., 'Decision on Immunity from Jurisdiction, Prosecutor v. Taylor, Case No. SCSL-2003-01-I, A. Ch., 31 May 2004: Commentary' in Klip, A. and Sluiter, G. (eds), *Annotated Leading Cases of International Criminal Tribunals: The Special Court for Sierra Leone 2003–2004*, Vol 9 (Intersentia 2010).

Kreß, C., 'The International Criminal Court and Immunities under International Law for States Not Party to the Court's Statute' in Bergsmo, M. and Ling, Y. (eds), *State Sovereignty and International Criminal Law* (TOAEP 2012).

Kreß, C. et al, 'Negotiating the Understandings on the Crime of Aggression' in Barriga, S. and Kreß, C. (eds), *The Travaux Préparatoires of the Crime of Aggression* (CUP 2012).

Kreß, C. and Prost, K., 'Article 98 – Cooperation with Respect to Waiver of Immunity and Consent to Surrender' in Triffterer, O. and Ambos, K. (eds), *Commentary on the Rome Statute of the International Criminal Court: Observers' Notes, Article by Article* (3rd edn, Hart/Beck 2016).

Kreß, C. and Prost, K., 'On the Activation of ICC Jurisdiction over the Crime of Aggression' in Šturma, P. (ed), *The Rome Statute of the ICC at Its Twentieth Anniversary: Achievements and Perspectives* (Brill | Nijhoff 2019).

La Haye, E., 'Article 49-Penal Sanctions' in International Committee of the Red Cross, *Commentary on the First Geneva Convention: Convention (I) for the Amelioration of the Condition of the Wounded and Sick in Armed Forces in the Field* (CUP 2016).

Lee, R.S., 'The Rome Conference and Its Contributions to International Law' in Lee, R.S. (ed), *The International Criminal Court: The Making of the Rome Statute: Issues, Negotiations and Results* (Kluwer Law International 1999).

Lind, C., 'Article 22' in Klamberg, M. (ed), *The Commentary on the Law of the International Criminal Court* (TAOEP 2017).

Liu, D., 'Has Non-Immunity for Heads of State Become a Rule of Customary International Law?' in Bergsmo, M. and Ling, Y. (eds), *State Sovereignty and International Criminal Law* (TAOEP 2012).

May, L., 'The Just War in Ancient Legal Thought' in Sadat, L.N. (ed), *Seeking Accountability for the Unlawful Use of Force* (CUP 2018).

McCormack, T., 'Crimes against Humanity' in McGoldrick, D. et al (eds), *The Permanent International Criminal Court: Legal and Policy Issues* (Hart Publishing 2004).

McCormack, T., 'From Sun Tzu to the Sixth Committee: The Evolution of an International Criminal Law Regime' in MacCormack, T. and Simpson, G.J. (eds), *The Law of War Crimes: National and International Approaches* (Kluwer Law International 1997).

McDougall, C., 'The Crimes Against Peace Precedent' in Barriga, S. and Kreß, C. (eds), *The Crime of Aggression: A Commentary* (CUP 2017).

Meron, T., 'Crimes under the Jurisdiction of the International Criminal Court' in Von Hebel, H. et al (eds), *Reflection on the International Criminal Court: Essays in Honour of Adriaan Bos* (TMC Asser Press 1999).

Meloni, C., 'Fragmentation of the Notion of Co-Perpetration in International Criminal Law' in Stahn, C. and Van den Herik, L.J. (eds), *The Diversification and Fragmentation of International Criminal Law* (Brill | Nijhoff 2012).

Mendelson, M.H., 'The International Court of Justice and the Sources of International Law' in Lowe, V. and Fitzmaurice, M. (eds), *Fifty Years of the International Court of Justice: Essays in Honour of Sir Robert Jennings* (CUP 2009).

Mettraux, G., 'The Definition of Crimes against Humanity and the Question of a "Policy" Element' in Sadat, L.N. (ed), *Forging a Convention for Crimes Against Humanity* (New York: CUP 2011).

Nerlich, V., 'The Status of ICTY and ICTR Precedent in Proceedings before the ICC' in Stahn, C. and Sluiter, G. (eds), *The Emerging Practice of the International Criminal Court* (Brill | Nijhoff 2009).

Ohlin, J.D., 'Co-Perpetration: German Dogmatik or German Invasion?' in Stahn, C. (ed), *The Law and Practice of the International Criminal Court* (OUP 2015).

O'Keefe, R., 'United Kingdom' in Barriga, S. and Kreß, C. (eds), *The Crime of Aggression: A Commentary* (CUP 2017).

Parmas, A., 'Estonia' in Barriga, S. and Kreß, C. (eds), *The Crime of Aggression: A Commentary* (CUP 2017).

Proelss, A., 'Article 38' in Dörr, O. and Schmalenbach, K. (eds), *Vienna Convention on the Law of Treaties: A Commentary* (2nd edn, Springer 2018).

Rastan, R., 'Jurisdiction' in Stahn, C. (ed), *The Law and Practice of the International Criminal Court* (OUP 2015).

Robinson, D., 'Immunities' in Cryer, R. et al (eds), *An Introduction to International Criminal Law and Procedure* (3rd edn, CUP 2014).

Röling, B.V.A., 'The Nuremberg and Tokyo Trials in Retrospect' in Mattraux, G. (ed), *Perspectives on the Nuremberg Trial* (OUP 2008).

Sadat, L.N. and Cohen, B., 'Impunity Through Immunity: The *Kenya* Situation and the International Criminal Court' in Ankumah, E.A. (ed), *The International Criminal Court and Africa: One Decade On* (Intersentia 2016).

Sands, P. and Commission, J., 'Treaty, Custom and Time: Interpretation/Application' Fitzmaurice, M. et al (eds), *Treaty Interpretation and the Vienna Convention on the Law of Treaties: 30 Years on* (Martinus Nijhoff Publishers 2010).

Schabas, W.A., 'Customary Law or Judge-Made Law: Judicial Creativity at the UN Criminal Tribunals' in Doria, J. et al (eds), *The Legal Regime of the International Criminal Court: Essays in Honour of Professor Igor Blishchenko (1930–2000)* (Brill | Nijhoff 2009).

Schabas, W.A., 'Kosovo, *Prosecutor v Milošević*, Decision on preliminary motions Case No IT-99-37-PT' in *Oxford Reports on International Law* (2010).

Schabas, W.A., 'Atrocity Crimes (Genocide, Crimes against Humanity and War Crimes)' in Schabas, W.A. (ed), *The Cambridge Companion to International Criminal Law* (CUP 2016).

Schabas, W.A., 'Strict Construction and the Rome statute' in Dewulf, S. (ed), *La (CVDW): Liber Amicorum Chris Van den Wyngaert* (Maklu 2018).

Schabas, W.A., 'Nuremberg and Aggressive War' in Sadat, L.N. (ed), *Seeking Accountability for the Unlawful Use of Force* (CUP 2018).

Schachter, O., 'Entangled Treaty and Custom' in Dinstein, Y. and Tabory, M. (eds), *International Law at a Time of Perplexity: Essays in Honour of Shabtai Rosenne* (Martinus Nijhoff Publishers 1989).

Scobbie, I., 'The Approach to Customary International Law in the Study' in Wilmshurst, E. and Breau, S. (eds), *Perspectives on the ICRC Study on Customary International Humanitarian Law* (CUP 2007).

Sellars, K.E., 'The First World War, Wilhelm II and Article 227: The Original of the Idea of "Aggression" in International Criminal Law' in Barriga, S. and Kreß, C. (eds), *The Crime of Aggression: A Commentary* (CUP 2017).

Sellars, K.E., 'Definitions of Aggression as Harbingers of International Change' in Sadat, L.N. (ed), *Seeking Accountability for the Unlawful Use of Force* (CUP 2018).

Shahabuddeen, M., 'Judicial Creativity and Joint Criminal Enterprise' in Darcy, S. and Powderly, J. (eds), *Judicial Creativity at the International Criminal Tribunals* (OUP 2010).

Sluiter, G., ' "Chapeau Elements" of Crimes Against Humanity in the Jurisprudence of the UN *ad hoc* Tribunals' in Sadat, L.N. (ed), *Forging a Convention for Crimes against Humanity* (CUP 2011).

Smeulers, A., 'A Criminological Approach to the ICC's Control Theory' in Heller, K.J. et al (eds), *The Oxford Handbook of International Criminal Law* (OUP 2020).

Trahan, J., 'The Crime of Aggression and the International Criminal Court' in Sadat, L.N. (ed), *Seeking Accountability for the Unlawful Use of Force* (CUP 2018).

Turković, K. and Vajda, M.M., 'Croatia' in Barriga, S. and Kreß, C. (eds), *The Crime of Aggression: A Commentary* (CUP 2017).

Van den Herik, L.J., 'The Decline of Customary International Law as a Source of International Criminal Law' in Bradley, C. (ed), *Custom's Future: International Law in a Changing World* (CUP 2016).

Van den Herik, L.J., 'Using Custom to Reconceptualize Crimes Against Humanity' in Darcy, S. and Powderly, J. (eds), *Judicial Creativity at the International Criminal Tribunals* (OUP 2010).

Van der Wilt, H., 'Immunities and the International Criminal Court' in Ruys, T. et al (eds), *The Cambridge Handbook of Immunities and International Law* (CUP 2019).

Von Hebel, H. and Robinson, D., 'Crimes within the Jurisdiction of the Court' in Lee, R.S. (ed), *The International Criminal Court: The Making of the Rome Statute: Issues, Negotiations and Results* (Kluwer Law International 1999).

Wickremasinghe, C., 'Immunities Enjoyed by Officials of States and International Organizations' in Evans, M. (ed), *International Law* (OUP 2010).

Wilmshurts, E., 'Jurisdiction of the Court' in Lee, R.S. (ed), *The International Criminal Court: The Making of the Rome Statute: Issues, Negotiations and Results* (Kluwer Law International 1999).

Wolfrum, R., 'Enforcement of International Humanitarian Law' in Fleck, D. (ed), *The Handbook of Humanitarian Law in Armed Conflicts* (OUP 1995).

Wouters, J. and Ryngaert, C., 'Impact on the Process of the Formation of Customary International Law' in Kamminga, M. and Scheinin, M. (eds), *The Impact of Human Rights Law on General International Law* (OUP 2009).

Wrange, P., 'The Crime of Aggression and Complementarity' in Bellelli, R. (ed), *International Criminal Justice: Law and Practice from the Rome Statute to its Review* (Ashgate Publishing 2010).

Wrange, P., 'The Crime of Aggression, Domestic Prosecutions and Complementarity' in Barriga, S. and Kreß, C. (eds), *The Crime of Aggression: A Commentary* (CUP 2017).

Yanev, L.D., 'The Theory of Joint Criminal Enterprise at the ECCC: A Difficult Relationship' in Meisenber, S. and Stegmiller, I. (eds), *The Extraordinary Chambers in the Courts of Cambodia* (TMC Asser Press 2016).

Zimmermann, A., 'Article 5' in Triffterer, O. and Ambos, K. (eds), *Commentary on the Rome Statute of the International Criminal Court: Observers' Notes, Article by Article* (3rd edn, Hart/Beck 2016).

Zimmermann, A., and Freiburg, E., 'Article 8bis' in Triffterer, O. and Ambos, K. (eds), *Commentary on the Rome Statute of the International Criminal Court: Observers' Notes, Article by Article* (3rd edn, Hart/Beck 2016).

Articles

Akande, D., 'International Law Immunities and the International Criminal Court' (2004) 98 *AJIL* 407.

Akande, D., 'The Effect of Security Council Resolutions and Domestic Proceedings on State Obligations to Cooperate with the ICC' (2012) 10 *JICJ* 299.

Akande, D. and Tzanakopoulos, A., 'Treaty Law and ICC Jurisdiction over the Crime of Aggression' (2018) 29 *EJIL* 939.

Akehurst, M., 'Custom as a Source of International Law' (1976) 47 *British Ybk Intl L* 1.

Alamuddin, A. and Webb, P., 'Expanding Jurisdiction over War Crimes under Article 8 of the ICC Statute' (2010) 8 *JICJ* 1219.

Aldrich, G., 'Jurisdiction of the International Criminal Tribunal for the Former Yugoslavia' (1996) 90 *AJIL* 64.

Ambos, K., 'General Principles of Criminal Law in the Rome Statute' (1999) 10 *CLF* 1.

Ambos, K., 'Is the Development of a Common Substantive Criminal Law for Europe Possible? Some Preliminary Reflections' (2005) 12 *MJECL* 173.

Ambos, K., 'Remarks on the General Part of International Law' (2006) 4 *JICJ* 660.

Ambos, K., 'Joint Criminal Enterprise and Command Responsibility' (2007) 5 *JICJ* 159.

Ambos, K., 'The *Fujimori* Judgment, A President's Responsibility for Crimes Against Humanity as Indirect Perpetrator by Virtue of an Organised Power Apparatus' (2011) 9 *JICJ* 137.

Arajärvi, N.J., 'The Requisite Rigour in the Identification of Customary International Law' (2017) 19 *I Community LR* 9.

Arajärvi, N.J., 'Looking Back from Nowhere: Is There a Future for Universal Jurisdiction over International Crimes?' (2011) 16 *Tilburg L Rev* 5.

Baker, R.B., 'Customary International Law in the 21st Century: Old Challenges and New Debates' (2010) 21 *EJIL* 173.
Bantekas, I., 'Reflections on Some Sources and Methods of International Criminal and Humanitarian Law' (2006) 6 *ICLR* 121.
Bassiouni, M.C., 'Searching for Justice in the World of Realpolitik' (2000) 12 *Pace Intl L Rev* 213.
Bassiouni, M.C., 'Justice and Peace: The Importance of Choosing Accountability Over Realpolitik' (2003) 35 *Case W Res J Intl L* 191.
Bassiouni, M.C., 'The Perennial Conflict Between International Criminal Justice and Realpolitik' (2006) 22 *GSU L Rev* 541.
Baxter, R.R., 'Multilateral Treaties as Evidence of Customary International Law' (1965) 41 *British Ybk Intl L* 275.
Baxter, R.R., 'Treaties and Custom' (1970) 129 *Recueil des cours* 27.
Bianchi, A., 'Immunity versus Human Rights: The Pinochet Case' (1999) 10 *EJIL* 237.
Blokker, N., 'International Organisations and Customary International Law' (2017) 14 *IOLR* 1.
Bogdan, A., 'Individual Criminal Responsibility in the Execution of a "Joint Criminal Enterprise" in the Jurisprudence of the *ad hoc* International Tribunal for the Former Yugoslavia' (2006) 6 *ICLR* 63.
Boister, N., 'The Application of Collective and Comprehensive Criminal Responsibility for Aggression at the Tokyo International Military Tribunal: The Measure of the Crime of Aggression?' (2010) 8 *JICJ* 425.
Broms, B., 'The Definition of Aggression' (1977) 154 *Recueil des cours* 299.
Brown, J., 'Australian Practice in International Law 1990 and 1991' (1990–1991) 13 *Australian Ybk Intl L* 195.
Bufalini, A., 'The Principle of Legality and the Role of Customary International Law in the Interpretation of the ICC Statute' (2015) 14 *LPICL* 233.
Butler, W., 'Custom, Treaty, State Practice and the 1982 Convention' (1988) 12 *Marine Policy* 182.
Buzzard, L., 'Holding an Arsonist's Feet to the Fire-The Legality and Enforceability of the ICC's Arrest Warrant for Sudanese President Omar Al-Bashir' (2008) 24 *Am U Intl L Rev* 897.
Carrillo-Santarelli, N., 'The Possibilities and Legitimacy of Non-State Participation in the Formation of Customary Law' (2017) 19 *Intl Community LR* 98.
Cassese, A., 'On the Current Trends towards Criminal Prosecution and Punishment of Breaches of International Humanitarian Law' (1998) 9 *EJIL* 2.
Cassese, A., 'The Martens Clause: Half a Loaf or simply Pie in the Sky?' (2000) 11 *EJIL* 187.
Cassese, A., 'When May Senior State Officials be Tried for International Crimes? Some Comments on the *Congo v Belgium* Case' (2002) 13 *EJIL* 853.

Cassese, A., 'The Proper Limits of Individual Responsibility under the Doctrine of Joint Criminal Enterprise' (2007) 5 *JICJ* 109.

Charney, J., 'The Persistent Objector Rule and the Development of Customary International Law' (1986) 56 *British Ybk Intl L* 1.

Chimni, B.S., 'Customary International Law: A Third World Perspective' (2018) 112 *AJIL* 1.

Chodosh, H.E., 'Neither Treaty nor Custom: The Emergence of Declarative International Law' (1991) 26 *Tex Intl LJ* 87.

Chodosh, H.E., 'An Interpretive Theory of International Law: The Distinction between Treaty and Customary Law' (1995) 28 *Vand J Transnatl L* 973.

Clarke, R.C., 'Together Again? Customary Law and Control over the Crime' (2015) 26 *CLF* 457.

Crook, J.R., 'Contemporary Practice of the United States Relating to International Law' (2006) 100 *AJIL* 219.

Cryer, R., 'Aggression at the Court of Appeal' (2005) 10 *Journal of Conflict & Security Law* 209.

D'Amato, A., 'Manifest Intent and the Generation by Treaty of Customary Rules of International Law' (1970) 64 *AJIL* 892.

Da Rocha Ferreira, A. *et al*, 'Formation and Evidence of Customary Law' (2013) 1 *UFRGSMUN* 182.

Dana, S., 'Beyond Retroactivity to Realizing Justice: A Theory on the Principle of Legality in International Criminal Law Sentencing' (2009) 99 *J Crim L & Criminology* 857.

Danilenko, G.M., 'The Statute of the International Criminal Court and Third States' (2000) 21 *Michigan J Intl L* 445.

Danner, A. and Martinez, J., 'Guilty Associations: Joint Criminal Enterprise, Command Responsibility, and the Development of International Criminal Law' (2005) 93 *Cali L Rev* 75.

Danner, A., 'When Courts Make Law: How the International Criminal Tribunals Recast the Laws of War' (2006) 59 *Vand L Rev* 1.

Danner, A., 'The Nuremberg Industrialist Prosecutions and Aggressive War' (2007) 46 *Virginia J Intl L* 651.

Davidson C., 'How to Read International Criminal Law: Strict Construction and the Rome Statute of the International Criminal Court' (2017) 91 *St. John's L Rev* 37.

Degan, V.-D., 'On the Sources of International Criminal Law' (2005) 4 *Chinese J Intl L* 45.

DeGuzman, M.M., 'Gravity and Legitimacy of the International Criminal Court' (2008) 32 *Fordham Intl LJ* 1400.

Dinstein, Y., 'Case Analysis: Crimes against Humanity after *Tadić*' (2000) 13 *LJIL* 373.

Dinstein, Y., 'The Interaction Between Customary Law and Treaty' (2006) 322 *Recueil des cours* 243.

Donaghue, S., 'Normative Habits, Genuine Beliefs and Evolving Law: Nicaragua and the Theory of Customary International Law' (1995) 16 *Australian Ybk Intl L* 327.

Dias, T.d.S., 'The Retroactive Application of the Rome Statute in Cases of Security Council Referrals and Ad hoc Declarations: An Appraisal of the Existing Solutions to an Under-discussed Problem' (2018) 16 *JICJ* 65.

Dörmann, K., 'War Crimes under the Rome Statute of the International Criminal Court, with a Special Focus on the Negotiations on the Elements of Crimes' (2003) 7 *MPUNYB* 341.

Droubi, S., 'The Role of the United Nations in the Formation of Customary International Law in the Field of Human Rights Law' (2017) 19 *Intl Community LR* 68.

Drumbl, M.A., 'The Push to Criminalize Aggression: Something Lost Amid the Gains' (2009) 41 *Case W Res J Intl L* 291.

Ehard, H., 'The Nuremberg Trial against the Major War Criminals and International Law' (1949) 43 *AJIL* 223.

Emanuelli, C., 'Comments on the ICRC Study on Customary International Humanitarian Law' (2007) 44 *Canadian Ybk Intl L* 437.

Farhang, C., 'Point of No Return: Joint Criminal Enterprise in *Brđanin*' (2010) 23 *LJIL* 137.

Fenrick, W.J., 'The Prosecution of War Criminals in Canada' (1989) 12 *Dalhousie LJ* 256.

Finch, G.A., 'The Peace Conference of Paris, 1919' (1919) 13 *AJIL* 159.

Fletcher, G. and Ohlin, J.D., 'Reclaiming Fundamental Principles of Criminal Law in the Darfur Case' (2005) 3 *JICJ* 539.

Fox, G. et al, 'The Contributions of United Nations Security Council Resolutions to the Law of Non-International Armed Conflict: New Evidence of Customary International Law' (2017) 67 *Am ULR* 649.

Gaeta, P., 'Does President Al Bashir Enjoy Immunity from Arrest?' (2009) 7 *JICJ* 315.

Gattini, A., 'War Crimes and State Immunity in the *Ferrini* Decision' (2005) *JICJ* 224.

Gattini, A., 'Pinochet Cases' in Wolfrum, R. (ed) (2007) *MPEPIL*.

Gil, A.G. and Maculan, E., 'Current Trends in the Definition of "Perpetrator" by the International Criminal Court: From the Decision on the Confirmation of Charges in the Lubanga Case to the Katanga Judgment' (2015) 28 *LJIL* 349.

Ginsburg, T., 'Bounded Discretion in International Judicial Lawmaking' (2004) 45 *Va J Intl L* 631.

Giustiniani, F.Z., 'Stretching the Boundaries of Commission Liability: The ICTR Appeal Judgment in *Seromba*' (2008) 6 *JICJ* 783.

Goy, B., 'Individual Criminal Responsibility before the International Criminal Court: A Comparison with the *Ad Hoc* Tribunals' (2012) 12 *ICLR* 1.

Graven, J., 'Les Crimes contre l'Humanité' (1950) 76 *Recueil des cours* 427.

Greenwood, C., 'International Humanitarian Law and the *Tadić* Case' (1996) 7 *EJIL* 265.

Gustafson, K., 'The Requirement of an "Express Agreement" for Joint Criminal Enterprise Liability: A Critique of Brđanin' (2007) 5 *JICJ* 134.

Hajdin, N., 'The Nature of Leadership in the Crime of Aggression: The ICC's New Concern?' (2017) 17 *ICLR* 54.

Halberstam, M., 'Belgium's Universal Jurisdiction Law: Vindication of International Justice or Pursuit of Politics Faculty Issue' (2003) 25 *Cardozo L Rev* 247.

Hathaway, O.A. et al, 'Aiding and Abetting in International Criminal Law' (2019) 104 *Cornell L Rev* 1593.

Heller, K.J., 'Specially-Affected States and the Formation of Custom' (2018) 112 *AIJL* 191.

Heinsch, R., 'The Crime of Aggression after Kampala: Success or Burden for the Future?' (2010) 2 *GoJIL* 713.

Huang, H., 'On Immunity of State Officials from Foreign Criminal Jurisdiction' (2014) 13 *Chinese J Intl L* 1.

Hunt, D., 'The International Criminal Court: High Hopes, "Creative Ambiguity" and an Unfortunate Mistrust in International Judges' (2004) 2 *JICJ* 56.

Jalloh, C.C., 'What Makes Crimes against Humanity Crimes against Humanity?' (2013) 28 *Am U Intl L Rev* 381.

Jia, B.B., 'The Crime of Aggression as Custom and the Mechanisms for Determining Acts of Aggression" (2015) 109 *AIJL* 569.

Kaul, H.-P. and Kreß, C., 'Jurisdiction and Cooperation in the Statute of the International Criminal Court: Principles and Compromises' (1999) 2 *YIHL* 143.

Kelly, J.P., 'The Twilight of Customary International Law' (2000) 40 *Va J Intl L* 449.

Kleffner, J.K., 'The Impact of Complementarity on National Implementation of Substantive International Criminal law' (2003) 1 *JICJ* 86.

Klip, A., 'Universal Jurisdiction: Regional Report for Europe' (2008) 79 *RIDP* 173.

Kirgis, F., 'Custom on a Sliding Scale' (1987) 81 *AIJL* 146.

Kirsch, P. and Holmes, J.T., 'The Rome Conference on an International Criminal Court: The Negotiating Process' (1999) 93 *AIJL* 2.

Kiyani, A.G., 'Al-Bashir & the ICC: The Problem of Head of State Immunity' (2013) 12 *Chinese J Intl L* 467.

Koessler, M., 'Borkum Island Tragedy and Trial' (1957) 47 *J Crim L & Criminology* 183.

Koh, H.H. & Buchwald, T.F., 'The Crime of Aggression: The United States Perspective' (2015) 109 *AIJL* 257.

Koskenniemi, M., 'The Normative Force of Habit: International Custom and Social Theory' (1990) 1 *Finnish Ybk Intl L* 77.

Kreß, C., 'War Crimes Committed in Non-International Armed Conflict and the Emerging System of International Criminal Justice' (2001) 30 *Israel Ybk HR* 103.

Kreß, C., 'The Iraqi Special Tribunal and the Crime of Aggression' (2004) 2 *JICJ* 347.

Kreß, C., 'The German Chief Federal Prosecutor's Decision Not to Investigate the Alleged Crime of Preparing Aggression against Iraq' (2004) 2 *JICJ* 245.

Kreß, C., 'Reflections on the *Iudicare* Limb of the Grave Breaches Regime' (2009) 7 *JICJ* 789.

Kreß, C., 'International Criminal Law' in Wolfrum, R. (ed) (2009) *MPEPIL*.

Kreß, C., 'Preliminary Observations on the ICC Appeals Chamber's Judgment of 6 May 2019 in the Jordan Referral re Al-Bashir Appeal' (2019) Occasional Paper Series No. 8.

Leich, M., 'Contemporary Practice of the United States Relating to International Law' (1983) 77 *AJIL* 298.

Linton, S., 'Rediscovering the War Crimes Trials in Hong Kong, 1946–48' (2012) 13 *Melbourne J Intl L* 284.

Manacorda, S. and Meloni, C., 'Indirect Perpetration versus Joint Criminal Enterprise Concurring Approaches in the Practice of International Criminal Law?' (2011) 9 *JICJ* 159.

McCormack, T. and Robertson, S., 'Jurisdictional Aspects of the Rome Statute for the New Industrial Criminal Court' (1999) 23 *Melbourne U L Rev* 635.

McDougall, C., 'Introductory Note to Report on the Facilitation on the Activation of the Jurisdiction of the International Criminal Court over the Crime of Aggression (Int'l Crim. Ct.) & Resolution ICC-ASP/16/RES. 5 on the Activation of the Jurisdiction of the Court over the Crime of Aggression' (2018) 57 *ILM* 513.

Mendelson, M.H., 'The Subjective Element in Customary International Law' (1995) 66 *British Ybk Intl L* 177.

Mendelson, M.H., 'The Formation of Customary International Law' (1998) 272 *Recueil des cours* 155.

Mendelson, M.H., 'The Effect of Customary International Law on Domestic Law: An Overview' (2004) 4 *Non-State Actors and International Law* 75.

Meron, T., 'The Case for War Crimes Trials in Yugoslavia' (1993) 72 *Foreign Affairs* 122.

Meron, T., 'War Crimes in Yugoslavia and the Development of International Law' (1994) 88 *AJIL* 78.

Meron, T., 'The Continuing Role of Custom in the Formation of International Humanitarian Law' (1996) 90 *AJIL* 31.

Meron, T., 'Is International Law Moving towards Criminalization?' (1998) 9 *EJIL* 18.

Meron, T., 'The Humanization of Humanitarian Law' (2000) 94 *AJIL* 239.

Meron, T., 'The Martens Clause, Principles of Humanity, and Dictates of Public Conscience' (2000) 94 *AJIL* 78.

Meron, T., 'Editorial Comment: Revival of Customary Humanitarian Law' (2005) 99 *AJIL* 817.

Meron, T., 'Reflections on the Prosecution of War Crimes by International Tribunals' (2006) 100 *AJIL* 551.

Merkouris, P., 'Interpreting the Customary Rules on Interpretation' (2017) 19 *Intl Community LR* 126.

Mettraux, G., 'Crimes against Humanity in the Jurisprudence of the International Criminal Tribunals for the Former Yugoslavia and for Rwanda' (2002) 43 *Harvard Intl LJ* 237.

Meyer, T., 'Codifying Custom' (2012) *U Pa L Rev* 160.

Milanović, M., 'Is the Rome Statute Binding on Individuals? (And Why We Should Care)' (2011) 9 *JICJ* 25.

Milanović, M., 'Aggression and Legality: Custom in Kampala' (2012) 10 *JICJ* 165.

Müllerson, R., 'On the Nature and Scope of Customary International Law' (1997) 2 *ARIEL* 341.

Muñoz-Conde, F. and Olásolo, H., 'The Application of the Notion of Indirect Perpetration through Organized Structures of Power in Latin America and Spain' (2011) 9 *JICJ* 113.

Nerlich, V., 'The Crime of Aggression and Modes of Lability – Is There Room Only for Principals?' (2017) 58 *Harvard Intl LJ* 44.

Nolte, G., 'How to Identify Customary International Law? – On the Outcome of the Work of the International Law Commission (2018)' (2019) 62 *Japanese Ybk Intl L* 251.

O'Brien, J.C., 'The International Tribunal for Violations of International Humanitarian Law in the Former Yugoslavia' (1993) 87 *AJIL* 639.

O'Neill, K.C., 'A New Customary Law of Head of State Immunity?: *Hirohito* and *Pinochet*' (2002) 38 *Stanford J Intl L* 291.

Odermatt, J., 'The Development of Customary International Law by International Organizations' (2017) 66 *ICLQ* 491.

Ohlin, J.D., 'Three Conceptual Problems with the Doctrine of Joint Criminal Enterprise' (2007) 5 *JICJ* 69.

Ohlin, J.D., 'Joint Intentions to Commit International Crimes' (2011) 11 *Chicago J Intl L* 693.

Ohlin, J.D., 'Second-Order Linking Principles: Combining Vertical and Horizontal Modes of Liability' (2012) 25 *LJIL* 771.

Osiel, M., 'Modes of Participation in Mass Atrocities' (2005) 38 *Cornell Intl LJ* 793.

Paust, J., 'Genocide in Rwanda, State Responsibility to Prosecute or Extradite, and Nonimmunity for Heads of State and Other Public Officials' (2011) 34 *Houston J Intl L* 57.

Pisillo-Mazzeschi, R., 'Treaty and Custom: Reflections on the Codification of International Law' (1997) 23 *CLB* 549.

Pocar, F., 'Transformation of Customary Law Through ICC Practice' (2018) 112 *AJIL Unbound* 182.

Posse, H.G.T.G., 'The Relationship between International Humanitarian Law and the International Criminal Tribunals' (2006) 88 *IRRC* 65.

Powles, S., 'Joint Criminal Enterprise: Criminal Liability by Prosecutorial Ingenuity and Judicial Creativity?' (2004) 2 *JICJ* 606.

Ramanathan, U., 'India and the ICC' (2005) 3 *JICJ* 627.

Roberts, A.E., 'Traditional and Modern Approaches to Customary International Law: A Reconciliation' (2001) 95 *AJIL* 757.

Robinson, D., 'Defining "Crimes Against Humanity" at the Rome Conference' (1999) 93 *AJIL* 43.

Rowe, P., 'Liability for War Crimes during a Non-International Armed Conflict' (1995) 34 *Mil L & L War Rev* 149.

Ryngaert, C. and Blommestijn, M., 'Exploring the Obligations for States to Act upon the ICC's Arrest Warrant for Omar Al-Bashir. A Legal Conflict between the Duty to Arrest and the Customary Status of Head of State Immunity' (2010) *ZIS* 428.

Sadat, L.N., 'Custom, Codification and Some Thoughts about the Relationship between the Two: Article 10 of the ICC Statute' (1999) 49 *DePaul L Rev* 909.

Sadat, L.N. and Carden, S.R., 'The New International Criminal Court: An Uneasy Revolution' (1999) 88 *Georgetown LJ* 381.

Sadat, L.N. and Jolly, J.M., 'Seven Canons of ICC Interpretation: Making Sense of Article 25's Rorschach Blot' (2014) 27 *LJIL* 755.

Sainz-Pardo, P.V., 'Is Child Recruitment as a War Crime Part of Customary International Law?' (2008) 12 *Intl J HR* 555.

Sayapin, S., 'The Compatibility of the Rome Statute's Draft Definition of the Crime of Aggression with National Criminal Justice Systems' (2010) 81 *RIDP* 165.

Sarkin, J. and Almeida, J., 'Understanding the Activation of the Crime of Aggression at the International Criminal Court: Progress and Pitfalls' (2018) 36 *Wis Intl LJ* 518.

Schabas, W.A., 'General Principles of Criminal Law in the International Criminal Court Statute (Part III)' (1998) 6 *EJCCLCJ* 400.

Schabas, W.A., 'State Policy as an Element of International Crimes' (2008) 98 *J Crim L & Criminology* 953.

Schabas, W.A., 'The Special Tribunal for Lebanon: Is a "Tribunal of an International Character" Equivalent to an "International Criminal Court"?' (2008) 21 *LJIL* 513.

Schabas, W.A., 'International War Crimes Tribunals and the United States' (2011) 35 *Diplomatic History* 769.

Schabas, W.A., 'Synergy or Fragmentation? International Criminal Law and the European Convention on Human Rights' (2011) 9 *JICJ* 609.

Schabas, W.A., 'The United Nations War Crimes Commission's Proposal for an International Criminal Court' (2014) 25 *CLF* 171.

Schachter, O., 'International Law in Theory and Practice: General Course in Public International Law' (1982) 178 *Recueil des cours* 32.

Scharf, M., 'Seizing the Grotian Moment: Accelerated Formation of Customary International Law in Times of Fundamental Change' (2010) 43 *Cornell Intl LJ* 439.

Scharf, M., 'Introductory Note to the Decision of the Appeals Chamber of the Special Tribunal for Lebanon on the Definition of Terrorism and Modes of Participation' (2011) 50 *ILM* 509.

Scharf, M., 'Universal Jurisdiction and the Crime of Aggression' (2012) 53 *Harvard Intl LJ* 358.

Schwelb, E., 'Crimes against Humanity' (1946) 23 *British Ybk Intl L* 178.

Scott, G. and Carr, C., 'Multilateral Treaties and the Formation of Customary International Law' (1996) 25 *Denver J Intl L& P* 71.

Scupin, HU., 'History of International Law, 1815 to World War I' in Wolfrum, R. (ed) (2011) *MPEPIL*.

Shahabuddeen, M., 'Does the Principle of Legality Stand in the Way of Progressive Development of Law?' (2004) 2 *JICJ* 1007.

Shihata, I.F.I., 'The Treaty as a Law-Declaring and Custom-Making Instrument' (1966) *Revue Egyptienne de Droit International* 51.

Simma, B. and Alston, P., 'The Sources of Human Rights Law: Custom, Jus Cogens, and General Principles' (1988–1989) 12 *Australian Ybk Intl L* 82.

Singerman, D. M., 'It's Still Good to Be the King: An Argument for Maintaining the *Status Quo* in Foreign Head of State Immunity' (2007) 21 *Emory Intl L Rev* 413.

Smith, J., 'Criminal Liability of Accessories: Law and Law Reform' (1997) 113 *LQR* 453.

Ssenyonjo, M., 'II. The International Criminal Court Arrest Warrant Decision for President Al Bashir of Sudan' (2010) 59 *ICLQ* 205.

Stahn, C. et al, 'The International Criminal Court's ad hoc Jurisdiction Revisited' (2005) 99 *AJIL* 421.

Stahn, C., 'Justice Delivered or Justice Denied? The Legacy of the *Katanga* Judgment' (2014) 12 *JICJ* 809.

Stoll, PT., 'State Immunity' in Wolfrum, R. (ed) (2011) *MPEPIL*.

Tabak, S., 'Article 124, War Crimes, and the Development of the Rome Statute' (2009) 40 *Georgetown J Intl L* 1069.

Talmon, S., 'Determining Customary International Law: The ICJ's Methodology between Induction, Deduction and Assertion' (2015) 26 *EJIL* 417.

Tams, C., 'Meta-Custom and the Court: A Study in Judicial Law-making' (2015) 14 *LPICT* 51.

Tan, Y., 'The Identification of Customary Rules in International Criminal Law' (2018) 34 *UJIEL* 92.

Taylor, T., 'The Nuremberg Trials' (1955) 55 *Columbia L Rev* 488.

Tladi, D., 'The ICC Decisions on Chad and Malawi: On Cooperation, Immunities and Article 98' (2013) 11 *JICJ* 199.

Tomka, P., 'Custom and the International Court of Justice' (2013) 12 *Law & Prac Intl Cts & Tribunals* 195.

Tomuschat, C., 'Obligations arising for States without or against their will' (1993) 241 *Recueil des cours* 195.

Tomuschat, C., 'International Law: Ensuring the Survival of Mankind on the Eve of a New Century' (1999) 281 *Recueil des cours* 9.

Tomuschat, C., 'The Legacy of Nuremberg' (2006) 4 *JICJ* 835.

Trahan, J., 'From Kampala to New York – The Final Negotiations to Activate the Jurisdiction of the International Criminal Court over the Crime of Aggression' (2018) 18 *ICLR* 197.

Treves, T., 'Customary International Law' in Wolfrum, R. (ed) (2006) *MPEPIL*.

Tunks, M., 'Diplomats or Defendants? Defining the Future of Head-of-State Immunity' (2002) 52 *Duke LJ* 651.

Van Alebeek, R., 'National Courts, International Crimes and the Functional Immunity of State Officials' (2015) 59 *Netherlands Intl L Rev* 5.

Van der Oije, S. and Freeland, S., 'Universal Jurisdiction in the Netherlands – the Right Approach but the Wrong case? Bouterse and the 'December Murders'' (2001) 7 *Australian J HR* 89.

Van der Wilt, H., 'Joint Criminal Enterprise: Possibilities and Limitations' (2007) 5 *JICJ* 91.

Van der Wilt, H., 'State Practice as Element of Customary International Law: A White Knight in International Criminal Law?' (2019) 20 *ICLR* 784.

Van Schaack, B., 'The Crime of Political Genocide: Repairing the Genocide Convention's Blind Spot' (1997) 106 *Yale L J* 2259.

Van Schaack, B., '*Crimen Sine Lege*: Judicial Lawmaking at the Intersection of Law and Morals' (2008) 97 *Georgetown LJ* 119.

Van Schaack, B., '*Par in Parem Imperium Non Habet* – Complementarity and the Crime of Aggression' (2012) 10 *JICJ* 133.

Van Sliedregt, E., 'Joint Criminal Enterprise as a Pathway to Convicting Individuals for Genocide' (2007) 5 *JICJ* 184.

Villarino Villa, C., 'The Crime of Aggression before the House of Lords: Chronicle of a Death Foretold' (2006) 4 *JICJ* 866.

Villiger, M., 'The 1969 Vienna Convention on the Law of Treaties: 40 Years After' (2009) 344 *Recueil des cours* 9.

Waldock, H., 'General Course on Public International Law' (1962) 106 *Recueil des cours* 41.

Wang, X., 'The Immunity of State Officials from Foreign Criminal Jurisdiction' (2010) 30 *Journal of Xi'an Jiaotong University (Social Sciences)* 67.

Watts, A., 'Heads of State' in Wolfrum, R. (ed) (2010) *MPEPIL*.

Weigend, T., 'Perpetration through an Organization: The Unexpected Career of a German Legal Concept' (2011) 9 *JICJ* 91.

Weisburd, A.M., 'Customary International Law: The Problem of Treaties' (1988) 21 *Vand J Transnatl L* 1.

Werle, G. and Burghardt, B., 'Claus Roxin on Crimes as Part of Organized Power Structures' (2011) 9 *JICJ* 191.

Werle, G. and Burghardt, B., 'Do Crimes Against Humanity Require the Participation of a State or a "State-like" Organization?' (2012) 10 *JICJ* 1151.

Willmott, D., 'Removing the Distinction Between International and Non-International Armed Conflict in the Rome Statute of the International Criminal Court' (2004) 5 *Melbourne J Intl L* 196.

Wise, E.M., 'General Rules of Criminal Law' (1996) 25 *Denver J Intl L& P* 313.

Wood, M., 'International Organizations and Customary International Law' (2015) 48 *Vand J Transnatl L* 609.

Wood, M., 'The present position within the ILC on the topic "Identification of customary international law": in partial response to Sienho Yee's Report on the ILC Project on "Identification of Customary International Law"' (2016) 15 *Chinese J Intl L* 3.

Yanev, L.D., 'A Janus-Faced Concept: Nuremberg's Law on Conspiracy *vis-à-vis* the Notion of Joint Criminal Enterprise' (2015) 26 *CLF* 419.

Yanev, L.D. and Kooijmans, T., 'Divided Minds in the Lubanga Trial Judgment: A Case Against the Joint Control Theory' (2013) 13 *ICLR* 789.

Yee, S., 'Report on the ILC Project on "Identification of Customary International Law"' (2015) 14 *Chinese J Intl L* 375.

Zappalà, S., 'Do Heads of State in Office Enjoy Immunity from Jurisdiction for International Crimes?' (2001) 12 *EJIL* 595.

Other Documents and Databases

American Law Institute, 'Restatement of the Law of Foreign Relations Law of the United States' (Third), 1986.

Amnesty International, 'Universal Jurisdiction: Belgian prosecutors can investigate crimes under international law committed abroad', 1 February 2003, IOR 53/001/2003.

'Commission on the Responsibility of the Authors of the War and on Enforcement of Penalties, Report Presented to the Preliminary Peace Conference' reprinted in (1920) 14 *AJIL* 95.

Cassese, A., 'Introductory Note to Affirmation of the Principles of International Law recognized by the Charter of the Nürnberg Tribunal General Assembly resolution 95 (I)' (June 2009), UN Audiovisual Library of International Law, Historical Archives <https://legal.un.org/avl/ha/ga_95-I/ga_95-I.html>.

Helfer, L.R. and Wuerth, I.B., 'Custom in the Age of Soft Law' (working paper) < https://www.iilj.org/wp-content/uploads/2016/07/WuerthIILJColloq2014.pdf >.

ICRC, 'Table of National Case Law on International Crimes and Universal Jurisdiction' in *Report of the Third Universal Meeting of National Committees on International Humanitarian Law*, 'Preventing and Repressing International Crimes: Towards an "Integrated" Approach Based on Domestic Practice', Vol II, Annexes, prepared by Anne-Marie La Rosa (2014).

ILA, Nationality and Naturalisation Committee, 'Draft Statute for the Permanent International Criminal Court, by Huge Bellot' in International Law Association Report of the 33rd Conference (Stockholm 1924) (ILA, London 1924).

ILA, Committee on Permanent International Criminal Court, 'Statute of the Court (as amended by the Conference)' in International Law Association Report of the 34th Conference (Vienna 1926) (ILA, London 1926).

ILA, Committee on Formation of Customary (General) International Law, 'Final Report, by Chairman Professor M.H. Mendelson, Rapporteur Professor Rein Müllerson' in International Law Association Report of the 65th Conference (London 2000) (ILA, London 2000).

Institut de Droit International, 'Obligations and rights *erga omnes* in international law', Resolution of the Fifth Commission (2005).

Institut de Droit International, 'Resolution on Immunity from Jurisdiction of the State and of Persons Who Act on Behalf of the State in case of International Crimes', Resolution of the Third Commission (2009).

MPICC, 'General Legal Principles of International Criminal Law on the Criminal Liability of Leaders of Criminal Groups and Networks', Project Coordination: Ulrich Sieber, Hans-Georg Koch and Jan Michael Simon <https://csl.mpg.de/en/research/projects/general-legal-principles-of-international-criminal-law-on-the-criminal-liability-of-leaders-of-criminal-groups-and-netwo/>.

Princeton Project on Universal Jurisdiction, 'The Princeton Principles on Universal Jurisdiction' (2001).

Reuters, 'Dutchman put on trial for Ethiopian war crimes in 1970s'<https://www.reuters.com/article/us-netherlands-ethiopia-war-crimes/dutchman-put-on-trial-for-ethiopian-war-crimes-in-1970s-idUSKBN1CT27U?il=0>.

Wilmshurst, E., 'Introductory Note to Definition of the Crime of Aggression: General Assembly resolution 3314 (XXIX)' (August 2008), UN Audiovisual Library of International Law, Historical Archives <https://legal.un.org/avl/ha/da/da.html>.

Asser Institute, International Crimes Database (ICD) <http://www.internationalcrimesdatabase.org/>.

ICC, National Implementing Legislation Database <https://iccdb.hrlc.net/data/>.

ICRC, Customary IHL Database <https://ihl-databases.icrc.org/customary-ihl/eng/docs/Home>.

ICRC, 'States Parties to the Following International Humanitarian Law and Other Related Treaties as of 15-Dec-2020' <https://ihl-databases.icrc.org/ihl>.

Legal Tools Database <https://www.legal-tools.org>.

UCDP/PRIO Armed Conflict Dataset, <https://www.prio.org/Data/Armed-Conflict/UCDP-PRIO/>.

United Nations Treaty Collection <https://treaties.un.org>.

World Courts, International Case Law Database <http://www.worldcourts.com/>.

Index

accessories   207, 209, 268, 302, 304
Ad Hoc Committee   31, 105–106, 108, 136, 150, 218, 259
ad hoc tribunals   37, 82, 130, 170, 173, 180, 184, 272–273, 294–295, 309–310, 348, 370, 373
Additional Protocol I   94–95, 100
Additional Protocol II   78–81, 84, 89, 94–95, 97–98, 100–102, 105–109, 111, 116, 120, 123
African Union   312, 366
African Union Protocol   130, 243, 366
aggression, act of (UN Charter)   192
aggression, crime of   16, 21–22, 32, 69, 99, 189–197, 199–200, 214, 216–223, 225, 227–228, 231–240, 242–246, 250, 378, 383, 385
    aggressive wars   194, 204–205, 207, 210, 212–214, 266, 340
    control or direct   21–22, 190–191, 196–200, 222, 228–230, 233, 237–239, 242–243, 246, 381, 383, 385
    industrialists   200, 220, 228–229, 232
    Kampala Amendments   42, 191, 195–196, 238–243, 246, 383, 385
    leaders   189, 199, 216, 219, 227
    leadership clause   21–22, 191, 194, 197, 202, 218, 222–224, 226, 228–230, 235–237, 242–243, 245, 383
    leadership element   21–22, 189–192, 196–198, 209–210, 212–213, 218–219, 221–222, 225–226, 229, 231–240, 246, 378, 381, 385
    leadership requirement. *see* leadership element
    leadership test. *see* leadership element
    leadership threshold. *see* leadership element
    Montreux Draft Elements of Crimes   231
    Montreux meeting   231–232
    participators   21, 215, 229, 236, 242–243, 246
    perpetrators   21, 215, 235–237, 241–243
    Princeton Process   225–229, 232
    prohibition of aggression   192
    shape or influence   199, 230, 235, 242
    Special Working Group   21, 200–201, 222, 225–226, 228–229, 231, 237
    statutory legislation   234
    Understandings   61, 64, 196, 200–201, 240
aiding and abetting   216, 251, 303–304, 307
Akehurst, Michael   40, 43, 55
Al-Dujail case   178, 307
Ambos, Kai   187-188, 255, 306
amicus curiae   86, 350, 366
amnesty   79–80, 117
arrest warrant   323, 330, 344–345, 348–351, 356, 358, 364, 367, 372
art 25 UN Charter   373
art 38 ICJ Statute   34
ASP. *see* Assembly of States Parties
Assembly of States Parties   42, 61, 131, 222, 239, 385
AU. *see* African Union
Australia *Regulations for the Trial of War Criminals*   271
Australia *War Crimes Act*   271

Bangladesh *International Crimes (Tribunals) Act*   146, 162
Barbie case   177
Barriga, Stefanie   223
Barnaba Yonga Tshopena case   306
Bassiouni, Cherif   83, 142, 147, 183
Baxter Paradox   56
Baxter, Richard   51–58, 60, 62–63
Bellot, Huge   142
Belsen case   175
Bemba case   167, 172
Blaškić case   180, 323
Bonn Text   109–110
Bothe, Michael   91, 384
Brđanin JCE   289–295, 297, 301, 304–306, 310–311, 382
British *Royal Warrant*   270
Broomhall, Bruce   6
Bureau Proposal   114, 120–121
Butler, William   64

Canada *Crimes against Humanity and War Crimes Act*   11, 125, 179

Cassese, Antonio   35, 92, 135, 163, 317–318, 372
Chad decision, 2011   356
Chechnya case   127
Chodosh, Hiram   58
civil law   3, 247, 254, 260, 266, 277–278, 306, 386
civil war. *see* non-international armed conflict
Clark, Roger   155–156, 220
Commission of Experts   83–84
Common Article 3   20, 66, 77–78, 81, 83–85, 87, 89–91, 94–95, 97, 99–100, 102, 104–109, 112–113, 123, 380
common design. *see* common plan
common law   36, 244, 247, 254, 260, 266, 277–278, 304, 386
common plan   204, 256, 262, 266–268, 273, 278, 286, 290–291, 294–295, 301, 307, 311
complementarity   106, 119, 238
complicity   176, 215–216, 266, 268–271, 304, 307, 309, 345, 382
  complicity through association   303
  complicity through organisation   266
conspiracy   204–206, 208, 214, 266–268, 301, 309
constitutive   54–56, 58
contextual elements   20, 26, 135, 149, 175–177, 188
Control Council Law No. 10   74, 146–147, 156, 158–159, 162, 206–209, 246, 267, 381
control over an organisation   255–256, 263
Convention on the Non-Applicability of Statutory Limitations   163
cooperation   326, 333, 352, 356–357, 359, 373–374, 377
co-perpetration   251, 253, 262–264, 279–280, 282–283, 298, 303
  legislation   297
co-perpetrators   253, 261, 273, 278–281, 283–284, 294–295
co-perpetratorship   278, 280–281, 283, 293, 310
Coracini, Astrid   234–235
Crawford, James   99
crimes against humanity   11, 15–16, 20, 26, 39, 69, 80, 84–85, 89–92, 99, 118, 134–136, 138–145, 147–151, 153–157, 159–162, 164–169, 171–172, 174–180, 183–185, 187–188, 259, 266–267, 295, 305–306, 316, 333, 346, 356, 360–361, 366, 368, 378, 380–381, 383, 385, 387
  legislation   185
  nexus with aggressive wars. *see* nexus with an armed conflict
  nexus with an armed conflict   20, 135, 147, 149–151, 153, 157–166, 187–188, 380
  policy element   21, 135, 147, 169, 173–175, 178–181, 183–188
  widespread or systematic   135–136, 169–170, 172, 174, 258–259
crimes against peace   144, 175, 193–194, 203, 205–206, 208, 211–212, 238, 267, 381
  industrialists   208–209, 212
  policy-influencing   212
  policy-making   211
  policy-shaping   211
  shape or influence   207, 210–211, 233
custom. *see* customary international law, customary law, customary rule
customary international law   1–8, 11, 13–16, 21–22, 25, 35, 38, 51, 57, 64, 66, 68, 84, 87–88, 99–100, 102–103, 108, 110, 116, 118, 121, 125, 134, 137, 148, 160, 164, 173, 177, 179, 181, 183, 187, 189–190, 194–195, 221, 224, 229, 233–234, 245, 248, 252, 257, 275, 281–282, 284, 287, 289, 299, 311–312, 314, 316, 320, 328, 346, 348, 355, 357–358, 361, 369, 388
  ascertainment   59–60, 352
  crystallisation   8, 13, 19–21, 52, 59, 67, 69, 111–112, 123–124, 133, 166, 180, 187–188, 239, 380
  declaratory   8, 13, 17–18, 21, 29, 33, 52, 55–59, 62, 64, 124, 132–133, 135, 146, 150, 153, 173, 184, 187–188, 191, 200, 202, 239, 246, 248, 264, 310, 378, 382–383, 388
  formation   15, 34–35, 75, 145, 184, 247
  identification   14, 18, 20, 26, 28, 33, 35–40, 44, 46, 50–51, 54, 56, 58, 65, 90, 173, 296, 378, 384
  modification   355, 377
  most engaged States   41–42
  opinio juris   18–19, 22, 34–43, 47–49, 51, 54–58, 64–65, 90, 112, 179, 186, 281, 284, 295, 342–343, 376

INDEX 415

practice of international
    organisations 45
specially affected States 41
State practice 19, 34, 38, 40–44, 51, 55–58, 90, 179
customary law. *see* customary international law, customary rule, custom
customary rule. *see* customary international Law

D'Amato, Anthony 43, 52–54, 56–57, 60
de facto 199–200, 329, 340
de jure 199
deductive method 36–37
differentiation system 302
Dinstein, Yoram 52–53
diplomatic immunity 332, 340
direct perpetration 253
Discussion Paper 113, 119, 152
Draft Code of Crimes 50, 67, 95, 97–98, 102, 107, 146–147, 173, 176–177, 185, 191, 195, 216–217, 219, 236, 246, 250, 265, 270, 317, 325, 327, 343, 353
Draft Code of Offences 94, 147, 161–163, 214–215
Draft Statute, 1994 10, 100–101, 107, 265
Draft Statute, 1998 111, 113, 119, 151, 260
Draft text, 1993 98–100
DRC decision, 2014 357
Drumble, Mark 213
Dubler, Robert and Kalyk, Matthew 15
Duch case 156, 160
Dutch *International Crimes Act* 127
Dutch *Wartime Offences Act* 103–104

ECCC Law 130, 146–147, 309
Einsatzgruppen case 158
Elements of Crimes 125, 168–169, 187, 195–197, 200, 225, 231, 237
erga omnes 68
essential contribution 268, 294
European Convention on Human Rights
    art 7 104, 163
Ezokola case 304

Farben case 207–209, 212–213
Finta case 178, 184

First Warrant of Arrest Decision 351–352
Flick case 158
Fujimori case 306
functional immunity 314, 318, 323

Gacumbitsi case 283
Gaddafi case 344–345
Gaeta, Paola 352
Gallant, Kenneth 3
general principles of international law 235
general principles of law 16, 24, 247, 287
genocide 16, 89–90, 139, 141, 156, 158, 178, 333
Genocide Convention 16, 156, 303, 341–343
German *Code of Crimes against International Law* 126, 242
Goy, Barbara 294
Graven, Jean 175–176
Grover, Leena 15, 17, 30, 68, 138

Heller, Kevin 191, 228, 230, 269
Higgins, Rosalyn 388
High Command case 207, 210, 212–213
House of Lords 195, 243–244, 344
ICJ *Arrest Warrant* case 345, 347–349, 354
ICRC 15, 50, 81, 92, 102, 109–110, 112, 117
ICRC *Study* 40, 48, 67, 79, 93, 129, 307
ICTR Statute
    art 3 146–147
    art 4 84, 86, 97, 103, 130
    art 6(1) 265
    art 6(2) 325, 342, 353
ICTY Statute
    art 2 82
    art 3 82, 86–87, 89, 107
    art 5 89, 146–148, 160
    art 7 303
    art 7(1) 265, 309
    art 7(2) 325, 342, 349, 351, 353
ILA. *see* International Law Association
ILC. *see* International Law Commission
immunity 245, 314, 316, 318, 325, 328, 330, 346, 348, 367, 375
impartiality 354
impunity 24, 30, 264, 317, 343, 347, 349, 385–386
IMT 72–73, 75–76, 139, 144, 154–155, 161, 174–175, 194, 203–204, 206, 236, 266–268, 270, 327, 338–340, 342

IMTFE 73, 194, 205–206, 236, 267, 339–340, 342
indirect co-perpetration 16, 22, 247–248, 251, 253, 256–259, 261–266, 268, 270, 278, 280–282, 284, 286, 288, 292–297, 301–311, 382
indirect perpetration 254, 256, 262–264, 282–283, 293, 299, 303, 307, 310
  legislation 298
indirect perpetration through an organisation. see indirect co-perpetration
individual criminal responsibility 85, 88–91, 105, 129, 176, 193, 206, 217, 252, 265–266, 307, 325, 328–329, 336, 342, 356, 382
internal armed conflict. see non-international armed conflict
international armed conflict 78, 86, 92, 94–95, 107, 109, 115, 131, 151–152, 165, 233
international community 5, 35, 68, 102, 132, 160, 234, 320, 322, 358–359, 372, 377, 388
international humanitarian law, violations of 66, 83, 85, 87, 89, 99, 102, 109, 112, 250
International Law Association 46, 71, 142
International Law Commission 10–11, 14, 18–19, 21, 31, 33, 35, 42, 67, 97–99, 134, 146, 158, 166, 176, 179, 186, 191, 198, 213–218, 236, 246, 250, 317, 327–328, 341, 375–376
international organisations 19, 44, 46, 50–51, 101
Iraqi High Criminal Court Law 130, 146, 233, 245, 307

Jackson, Robert 144, 154, 160, 174, 250
JCE 248, 272–273, 275, 277–278, 284–289, 293, 295, 303, 305, 310, 382
  agreement 286, 288–289, 296
  membership 286–288, 292
  size 285–286, 290
joint commission through an organisation. see indirect co-perpetration
joint criminal enterprise. see JCE
Jordan decision, 2017 357
Jordan decision, 2019 37, 321, 358, 374–375
Jørgensen, Nina 271
jus cogens 68–69, 137, 324, 370
jus puniendi 320
Justice case 139, 144, 158, 176–177, 269

Kalshoven, Frits 83
Katanga & Ngudjolo case 248, 257, 261–262, 278
Katanga case 262, 272
Kellogg–Briand Pact 192
Kemp, Gerhard 245
Kenyatta case, 2013 356
Kirgis, Frederic 38
Kirsch, Philippe 122–123
Kolk and Kislyiy v Estonia case 163
Korbely v Hungary case 163
Kreß, Claus 201
Krupp case 207, 213
Kunarać et al case 21, 180–184, 187–188, 381

Lauterpacht, Hersch 145
law-declaring. see declaratory
laws and customs of war 71, 76, 87, 103–104, 107, 140, 142, 337
laws of humanity 139–142, 337
leaders or organisers 216, 218, 220, 222, 236–237, 246
Lee, Roy 11
Lepard, Brian 40
Liberation Tigers of Tamil Elam case 127
London Conference 144, 154, 174, 250, 338
Lubanga case 263

Malawi decision 353, 355–356, 359
Martens Clause 140
material element 176, 190, 196, 261–262, 270, 274–275, 279, 294–295
  circumstance element 196–197
May, Larry 39, 385
McDougall, Carrie 199, 205, 209, 230
mental element 190, 196, 253, 262, 270, 275, 281–282, 284, 286, 289, 295, 305
Menten case 178
Meron, Theodor 12, 15, 35–36, 39, 84, 88–89, 91–92, 289
Military and Paramilitary Activities case 52
Milošević case 350, 354
Milutinović et al case 281–282
Ministries case 158, 177, 207, 211–212, 269
modes of liability 5, 42, 247, 249, 251, 264, 299, 338, 383–384, 386
Murphy, Sean 134

nexus with war. see nexus with an armed conflict

INDEX

Ngudjolo case   258, 262
Nicaragua case   1, 62
NMTs   74, 212–213, 224–225, 228, 230, 233, 236
non-international armed conflict   20, 42, 66–67, 69, 77–79, 83–88, 90–92, 95–104, 106–107, 109–113, 115–118, 120, 122–124, 127–132, 137, 152, 385
   threshold   113, 117, 119–121
non-party States   6–7, 24, 53, 56–57, 128, 132, 296, 331–333, 352, 356, 359–360, 368, 371, 376, 382, 387
norm-creating. *see* norm-making
norm-making   54–58, 63–65, 202, 239, 335, 388
North Sea Continental Shelf cases   2, 51–52, 54, 56, 62–63
Nuremberg Charter   73, 75, 138–139, 143–145, 149, 153–155, 157, 161, 173–175, 178, 193, 203, 265–266, 268, 327, 337, 339, 341, 353
Nuremberg Military Tribunals. *see* NMTs
Nuremberg Principles   76, 146–147, 158, 161–162, 214, 236, 325, 341, 353

O'Brien, James   91
O'Keefe, Roger   244
Ohlin, Jens   264, 293
Oppenheim, Lassa   44

personal immunity   16, 22, 24, 42, 312–315, 319, 321–325, 327–372, 374–378, 382–383, 386, 388
   horizontal   321–322, 330, 348, 355
   vertical   329
Peters case   304
physical perpetrators   148, 252, 254, 261, 267, 280–281, 285–288, 290–291, 293, 295, 308, 311
Pinochet (No 3) case   344, 350
Pocar, Fausto   35
Preparatory Commission   21, 124, 222–223, 225, 237
Preparatory Committee   9, 12, 32, 106–113, 137, 150, 169–170, 218–219, 221–222, 259–260, 325–326
preparatory works   18, 31, 52–54, 58, 69, 122, 136, 153, 165, 169, 173, 188, 246, 265, 313, 326–327, 333–334

Preuss Draft   72
principals   207, 209, 253, 268, 302, 304
principle of legality   3, 6, 18, 29–30, 33, 39, 41, 63
   analogy   29, 37
   certainty   3, 29, 39, 104
   foreseeable   3
   in dubio pro reo   39
   non-retroactivity   29
   retroactivity   144
   specificity   3, 29
principle of sovereignty and equality   314
principle of strict construction   18, 29, 150
procedural immunity   327, 329, 343, 351, 354

R v Jones et al   195, 233, 243
Relationship Agreement between the Court and the UN
   art 19   333
Report of the Commission on Responsibilities   70, 141, 335–337, 353
reservation   60–63
Review Conference   11, 21, 131, 189, 195, 201, 222, 231–232, 237–238
Roberts, Anthea   38
Robinson, Darryl   32, 171, 179
Roechling case   209–210, 213
Rome Conference   4, 9–10, 12–13, 20–21, 32, 42, 69, 113, 116, 121, 123–124, 136, 151, 165, 168, 170–171, 179, 189, 195, 221–222, 254, 260–261, 333, 380, 384
Rome Statute
   Preamble   67–68, 240
   art 5   68–69
   art 5(1)(d)   195
   art 6   16
   art 7   16, 20, 134, 136, 149, 166, 169, 172–173, 180, 188, 258, 380
   art 7(1)   136, 150, 185, 188
   art 7(2)   136
   art 7(2)(a)   136, 147, 166–168, 171, 184, 186–188, 381
   art 7(3)   136
   art 8   20, 67, 106, 131, 379
   art 8(2)(c)   111, 120, 124, 133
   art 8(2)(d)   120
   art 8(2)(e)   124, 133

Rome Statute (*cont.*)
  arts 8(2)(c) and (e) 16, 66, 68, 104, 111, 380
  art 8(2)(f) 122
  art 8(3) 122
  art 8*bis* 21, 189, 193, 195–197, 199, 222
  art 8*bis*(1) 196, 219
  art 8*bis*(2) 240
  arts 8*bis* and 25(3*bis*) 16, 21, 189, 191–192, 197, 200, 223, 233, 237–238, 246, 381
  art 10 13, 60–61, 63–64, 136, 202
  art 11(2) 6
  arts 11 and 24 62
  arts 12 and 13 62
  art 12(3) 6, 129
  art 13(b) 6
  arts 15*bis* and 15*ter* 195
  art 21(1) 5
  art 21(3) 17, 30
  art 22 29, 39, 150
  art 22(1) 5, 63
  art 22(2) 18, 29
  art 24(1) 6
  art 25 196, 251, 381
  art 25(2) 5
  art 25(3) 307
  art 25(3)(a) 16, 22, 247–248, 252–258, 260–261, 263–266, 272, 277, 281, 283, 303–305, 308, 310–311, 382
  art 25(3)(b) 251
  art 25(3)(d) 303–305
  art 25(3*bis*) 21, 189, 197, 229–230, 236, 239
  art 27 324–325, 327–329, 353, 363
  art 27(1) 325–327, 329, 337, 342, 349
  art 27(2) 16, 22, 312–313, 320, 323–327, 329–335, 342–343, 348, 352, 355, 357, 363, 372, 374, 377, 382, 388
  art 28 251
  art 30 196
  art 80 64
  art 87(7) 352
  art 98(1) 332–333
  art 120 61
  art 124 60–61, 63
  Preamble 67–68, 240
  withdrawal 128
Rowe, Peter 91
Ruto & Sang acquittal decision, 2016 357

SAH case 305
Samantar case 369
Sayapin, Sergey 234
Schabas, William 12, 15, 76, 162, 179, 293, 341, 354, 370
Schlütter, Birgit 35
Schwelb, Egon 155
SCSL Statute
  arts 3 and 4 130
  art 6(1) 146, 309
  art 6(2) 349
senior State officials 246, 313, 315–318, 322–324, 328, 330–331, 333, 339–342, 344, 347, 352, 354, 356, 361, 363, 366, 369–370, 376–377, 382, 386–387
Seromba case 283
Sharon et al case 364–365
Shawcross, Hartley 161
Simić et al case 283
Siracusa-Draft 219–220
Sivakumar case 270
Sivakumaran, Sandesh 78
Sixth Committee 44, 96, 98, 100, 110, 136, 215, 376
Sørensen, Max 38, 41
South Africa decision, 2017 357, 373
sovereignty 80, 85, 117, 121, 171, 229, 385
Stakić case 252, 278–281
State consent 6, 23, 322, 325, 327, 336, 339, 342, 359, 362, 364
State or organisational policy 135–136, 147, 167–168, 172
States Parties 24, 54–57, 63–64, 78–79, 81, 106, 123, 126, 234, 239–241, 296, 303, 325, 329–334, 342, 348, 351, 355, 359–360, 362, 364, 366–368, 374, 376
STL Statute 309
Subsequent Proceedings 21, 74, 76, 162, 212, 267, 269
substantive justice 90, 144

Tadić Interlocutory Appeal Decision 66, 86, 89–91, 93, 102, 104, 106, 111, 132, 159, 165
Tadić JCE 277–278, 290, 292, 295, 297, 305–306, 309–310
Taylor case 349–350, 372
Thiam, Doudou 94

INDEX

Tokyo Charter   73, 145, 155, 174, 193, 203, 265–266, 337, 353
Tomuschat, Christian   36
travaux préparatoires. *see* preparatory works
treaty   1, 7, 9–10, 13, 16–20, 23, 28, 31, 33, 44, 49–64, 68, 88, 91, 98, 100, 105, 162, 202, 235, 264, 316, 319, 324, 329, 334, 345, 348, 352, 366, 378, 382, 385, 387–388
Treaty of Lausanne   141
Treaty of Sèvres   141
Treaty of Versailles   70, 141, 336
Treves, Tullio   43, 46
two-element approach   18–19, 34–35, 37–38, 40, 51, 59, 65

UK *International Criminal Court Act*   244
UK joint enterprise   277–278, 304–305
UK *Manual of the Law of Armed Conflict*   125
UK *War Crimes Act*   145
UN *Historical Review of Developments relating to Aggression*   230
UN Resolution 1593   367, 370, 373–374
UN Resolution 3314 (XXIX)   192, 194
UN Resolution 827   370–373
UN Resolution 95(I)   214, 341
UN War Crimes Commission   26, 71–72, 142–143, 157–158, 176
unitary system   302
Universal Declaration of Human Rights

art 11   76
universal jurisdiction   24, 42, 48, 63, 128, 317, 322, 359–360, 364–365, 368
US *Foreign Sovereign Immunities Act*   369

Van Anraat case   103
Van den Herik, Larissa   90, 247
Van Sliedregt, Elies   272, 293
VCLT   17, 30, 33, 52–53, 61, 65
Verdross, Alfred   41
Villiger, Mark   13, 52, 55, 62, 387

waiver of immunity   322, 324, 327, 330, 332–334, 336, 347–348, 354–355, 357, 359, 362, 364–365, 369, 373, 387
war crimes   16, 20, 42, 67, 69–71, 73, 77–81, 85–86, 89–92, 95–104, 106–113, 115–124, 127–132, 136–137, 139, 143–145, 175, 267, 305, 307, 333, 385, 387
  enforced pregnancy   118–119
  enlisting child soldiers   12
  forced pregnancy   119
war crimes *stricto sensu*   142–143
Wood, Michael   35, 37

Yanev, Lachezar   293
Yee, Sienho   44

Zutphen meeting   111, 221

Printed in the United States
by Baker & Taylor Publisher Services